THE
TOP
10
OF
EVERYTHING

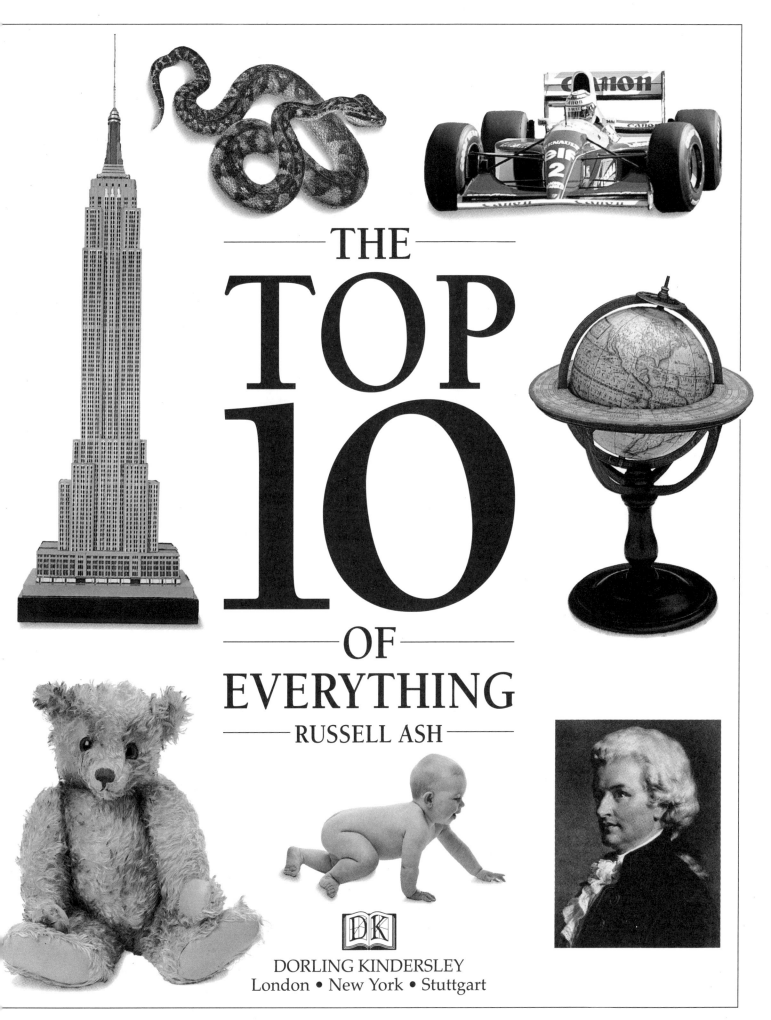

THE
TOP
10
OF
EVERYTHING

— RUSSELL ASH —

DORLING KINDERSLEY
London • New York • Stuttgart

A DORLING KINDERSLEY BOOK

Designed by **The Bridgewater Book Company**

Art Director Terry Jeavons

Designer James Lawrence

Editor Ian Whitelaw

Page make-up John Christopher

First published in Great Britain in 1994 by
Dorling Kindersley Limited,
9 Henrietta Street,
London WC2E 8PS

A CIP catalogue record for this book is
available from the British Library

ISBN 0 7513 0137 X

Reproduction by HBM Print Ltd, Singapore
Printed and bound in Belgium by Proost

CONTENTS

INTRODUCTION

You have opened the sixth annual edition of *The Top 10 of Everything*. Those of you who have seen previous editions will know that the lists represent a wide range of exclusively quantitative superlatives. They are not anyone's "10 Bests" (which are qualitative judgements), although there are some "10 Worsts", in the case of accidents and disasters, since these can be measured by numbers of victims. With the latter, it is not always possible to obtain definitive figures: disasters involving ferries, for example, are notable for their lack of passenger records, or they may be secret (no one knows precisely how many thousands were killed in the 1982 fire in the Salang Tunnel, as the Soviet Union occupied Afghanistan at the time). There are also some "Progressive" lists, such as that of the world land speed record or largest ocean liners, each of the entries representing a record-breaker that was in its day the fastest, the biggest, or whatever – until it was overtaken by the next one, and so on up to the present holder. There are some occasional ancillary lists, including those featuring the "10 First", or lists of the bestsellers of each year of a decade, which offer sidelights in the form of a time-shaft of the 10-year period, as well as additional information in the form of "Did You Know?" features.

THE PACE OF CHANGE

My principal challenge is to keep abreast of recent changes: ever taller skyscrapers are erected (increasingly, outside the US); art auction records are constantly overtaken (though less often than they used to be); the richest people get richer (and sometimes poorer); sporting records are broken (the "Fastest Men on Earth" list gained a new No. 1 while this book was in preparation); and films such as *Jurassic Park* and *Mrs Doubtfire* rapidly achieve "blockbuster" status, affecting various Top 10 lists. Even lists that one might expect to be "fixed", such as that of the world's tallest mountains, may be modified as measuring techniques are improved. The break-up of the former USSR and reunification of Germany call for statistics on the new countries that are not yet available, or sufficiently reliable, posing further problems. Countries appear and disappear, or change their names: Burma officially became Myanmar in

1989, but hardly anyone yet calls it by its new name. (Abbreviated names of country affiliations, incidentally – especially in sporting lists – follow customary practice, except for the use of "Aut" for Austria, to distinguish it from Australia, and "SA" for South Africa.) Figures for country and city populations are based on the latest available census, in most instances that of 1990, with estimates for increases where officially available – with sometimes surprising results: the census held in Nigeria showed that the country had 23,000,000 *fewer* inhabitants than had been estimated, and hence its population projection for the year 2000 has been down-rated by a staggering 40,000,000. In theory, with the passing of time and increasing availability of information, especially electronically, such figures should become more accurate and up-to-date. However, in many instances, especially with official or Government statistics, there is a delay in their being published, and certain figures may thus be as much as two years old.

FACT AND FICTION

By their nature, all reference book compilers enjoy facts and strive for 100% accuracy, and almost all fail to achieve it. In dealing with so much material, gathered from a vast range of international sources, I am perhaps more aware than most just how easy it is to make mistakes, and sometimes I do so myself. I gain some consolation (or *Schadenfreude*) in spotting the slips of others: my favourites this year are the respected book that describes the planet "Juniper", and another that puts the number of Roman Catholics in the UK at 75,600,000 – nearly 20,000,000 more than the entire population – while a reputable Sunday newspaper recently assured its readers that every British person annually consumes 7,000 kg of washing powder (more than the weight of an elephant) and Turkey's population 2,000 kg a head (a mere hippopotamus-weight). A clean story, but clearly fallacious.

As always, I would like to thank all those readers who have written to me about *The Top 10 of Everything*, often suggesting ideas for new lists. Your comments are always welcomed and help me to improve each new edition. I hope you will keep reading and continue to enjoy the book.

THE UNIVERSE & EARTH

TOP 10

THE 10 STARS NEAREST TO THE EARTH
(Excluding the Sun)

	Star	Light years*	km	miles
1	Proxima Centauri	4.22	39,923,310,000,000	24,792,500,000,000
2	Alpha Centauri	4.35	41,153,175,000,000	25,556,250,000,000
3	Barnard's Star	5.98	56,573,790,000,000	35,132,500,000,000
4	Wolf 359	7.75	73,318,875,000,000	45,531,250,000,000
5	Lalande 21185	8.22	77,765,310,000,000	48,292,500,000,000
6	Luyten 726-8	8.43	79,752,015,000,000	49,526,250,000,000
7	Sirius	8.65	81,833,325,000,000	50,818,750,000,000
8	Ross 154	9.45	89,401,725,000,000	55,518,750,000,000
9	Ross 248	10.40	98,389,200,000,000	61,100,000,000,000
10	Epsilon Eridani	10.80	102,173,400,000,000	63,450,000,000,000

* One light year = 9.4605 x 10^{12} km/5.875 x 10^{12} miles.

A spaceship travelling at 40,237 km/h/25,000 mph – which is faster than any human has yet reached in space – would take more than 113,200 years to reach the Earth's closest star, Proxima Centauri.

TOP 10

MOST FREQUENTLY SEEN COMETS

	Comet	Orbit period (years)
1	Encke	3.302
2	Grigg-Skjellerup	4.908
3	Honda-Mrkós-Pajdusáková	5.210
4	Tempel 2	5.259
5	Neujmin 2	5.437
6=	Brorsen	5.463
6=	Tuttle-Giacobini-Kresák	5.489
8	Tempel-L. Swift	5.681
9	Tempel 1	5.982
10	Pons-Winnecke	6.125

NATURAL PHENOMENON
This painting depicts the sighting of a comet in 1858.

THE 10 COMETS COMING CLOSEST TO THE EARTH

	Comet	Date*	Distance (AU)#
1	Lexell	1 Jul 1770	2.3
2	Tempel-Tuttle	26 Oct 1366	3.4
3	Halley	10 Apr 837	5.0
4	Biela	9 Dec 1805	5.5
5	Grischow	8 Feb 1743	5.8
6	Pons-Winnecke	26 Jun 1927	5.9
7	La Hire	20 Apr 1702	6.6
8	Schwassmann-Wachmann	31 May 1930	9.3
9	Cassini	8 Jan 1760	10.2
10	Schweizer	29 Apr 1853	12.6

* Of closest approach to the Earth.
# Astronomical units: 1AU = mean distance from the Earth to the Sun (149,598,200 km/92,955,900 miles).

MOST RECENT OBSERVATIONS OF HALLEY'S COMET

1 1986

Japanese, Soviet, and European probes were all sent to investigate the comet. All were heavily battered by dust particles, and it was concluded that Halley's comet is composed of dust bonded by water and carbon dioxide ice.

2 1910

Predictions of disaster were widely published, with many people convinced that the world would come to an end.

3 1835

Widely observed, but dimmer than in 1759.

4 1759

The comet's first return, as predicted by Halley, proving his calculations correct.

5 1682

Observed in Africa and China, and in Europe, where it was observed from 5 to 19 September by Edmund Halley, who successfully calculated its orbit and predicted its return.

6 1607

Seen extensively in China, Japan, Korea, and Europe, described by German astronomer Joannes Kepler and its position accurately measured by amateur Welsh astronomer Thomas Harriot.

7 1531

Observed in China, Japan, and Korea, and in Europe, where Peter Appian, German geographer and astronomer, noted that comets' tails point away from the Sun.

8 1456

Observed in China, Japan, Korea, and Europe. When Papal forces defeated the invading Turks, it was seen as a portent of their victory.

9 1378

Observed in China, Japan, Korea, and Europe.

10 1301

Seen in Iceland, parts of Europe, China, Japan, and Korea.

LARGEST REFLECTING TELESCOPES IN THE WORLD

	Telescope name	Location	Opened*	(m)
1	Keck Telescope	Mauna Kea Observatory, Hawaii, USA	1992	10.0
2	Bolshoi Teleskop Azimutal'ny	Special Astrophysical Observatory of the Russian Academy of Sciences, Mount Pastukhov, Russia	1976	6.0
3	Hale Telescope	Palomar Observatory, California, USA	1948	5.0
4	William Herschel Telescope	Observatorio del Roque de los Muchachos, La Palma, Canary Islands	1987	4.2
5=	Mayall Telescope#	Kitt Peak National Observatory, Arizona, USA	1973	4.0
5=	4-metre Telescope#	Cerro Tololo Inter-American Observatory, Chile	1976	4.0
7	Anglo-Australian Telescope	Siding Spring Observatory, New South Wales, Australia	1974	3.9
8=	ESO 3.6-metre Telescope	European Southern Observatory, La Silla, Chile	1975	3.6
8=	Canada-France-Hawaii Telescope	Mauna Kea Observatory, Hawaii, USA	1970	3.6
8=	United Kingdom Infrared Telescope	Mauna Kea Observatory, Hawaii, USA	1979	3.6

* Dedicated or regular use commenced.   # Northern/southern hemisphere "twin" telescopes.

COMPUTING COMETS
Astronomer Royal Edmund Halley (1656–1742) computed the orbits of no fewer than 24 comets. In 1759 the dramatic return of the comet he had observed in 1682 established the science of cometary observation.

If the Keck Telescope at No. 1 is discounted because its "mirror" is not in one piece, but comprises 36 hexagonal segments slotted together, then the 10th entry in the list becomes the 3.5-metre New Technology Telescope at the European Observatory, La Silla, Chile, which started operations in 1990. The Multiple Mirror Telescope at the Fred Lawrence Whipple Observatory, Arizona, USA, opened in 1979, has six linked 1.8-metre mirrors, together equivalent to a 4.5-metre telescope. These are being replaced by a single 6.5-metre mirror which is currently under construction.

THE PLANETS

TOP 10

LONGEST DAYS IN THE SOLAR SYSTEM

	Body	Length of day* days	hours	mins
1	Venus	244	0	0
2	Mercury	58	14	0
3	Sun	25#	0	0
4	Pluto	6	9	0
5	Mars		24	37
6	Earth		23	56
7	Uranus		17	14
8	Neptune		16	7
9	Saturn		10	39
10	Jupiter		9	55

* Period of rotation, based on Earth day.
\# Variable.

TOP 10

LONGEST YEARS IN THE SOLAR SYSTEM

	Body	Length of year* years	days
1	Pluto	247	256
2	Neptune	164	298
3	Uranus	84	4
4	Saturn	29	168
5	Jupiter	11	314
6	Mars	1	322
7	Earth		365
8	Venus		225
9	Mercury		88
10	Sun		0

* Period of orbit round the Sun, in Earth years/days.

INHOSPITABLE
The surface of Venus is extremely hot, with high atmospheric pressure and clouds of sulphuric acid.

TOP 10

BODIES FURTHEST FROM THE SUN
(In the Solar System, excluding satellites and asteroids)

	Body	Average distance from the Sun km	miles
1	Pluto	5,914,000,000	3,675,000,000
2	Neptune	4,497,000,000	2,794,000,000
3	Uranus	2,871,000,000	1,784,000,000
4	Chiron	2,800,000,000	1,740,000,000
5	Saturn	1,427,000,000	887,000,000
6	Jupiter	778,300,000	483,600,000
7	Mars	227,900,000	141,600,000
8	Earth	149,600,000	92,900,000
9	Venus	108,200,000	67,200,000
10	Mercury	57,900,000	36,000,000

GAS GIANT
Jupiter, seen here with two of its moons, is composed almost entirely of hydrogen and helium.

DID YOU KNOW

THE MYSTERY PLANETS

Chiron, named after the centaur who ascended to heaven after being accidentally slain by Hercules, is a "mystery object" that may be either a comet or an asteroid. It was discovered on 1 November 1977 by American astronomer Charles Kowal, and measures 200-300 km/125-190 miles in diameter and orbits between Saturn and Uranus. Another mystery, so-called "Planet X", is believed by some to orbit beyond Pluto. When Pluto was discovered, it was realized that such a small planet could not cause the irregularities noticed in the orbits of Uranus and Neptune. It was concluded that there must be another as yet undiscovered planet. However, the IRAS (Infra-Red Astronomical Satellite) failed to detect it, while data sent back by *Voyager 2* seemed to offer explanations for Neptune's orbit without the influence of a mysterious tenth planet. Its existence remains in doubt.

TOP 10

LARGEST BODIES IN THE SOLAR SYSTEM

Name	Maximum diameter km	miles
1 Sun	1,392,140	865,036
2 Jupiter	142,984	88,846
3 Saturn	120,536	74,898
4 Uranus	51,118	31,763
5 Neptune	49,532	30,778
6 Earth	12,756	7,926
7 Venus	12,103	7,520
8 Mars	6,794	4,222
9 Ganymede	5,268	3,273
10 Titan	5,150	3,200

Most of the planets are visible with the naked eye and have been observed since ancient times. The exceptions are Uranus, discovered on 13 March 1781 by the British astronomer Sir William Herschel; Neptune, found by German astronomer Johann Galle on 23 September 1846 (Galle was led to his discovery by the independent calculations of the French astronomer Urbain Leverrier and the British mathematician John Adams); and, outside the Top 10, Pluto, located using photographic techniques by American astronomer Clyde Tombaugh. The announcement of its discovery came on 13 March 1930; its diameter remains uncertain, but it is thought to be approximately 2,302 km/1,430 miles.

TOP 10

LARGEST PLANETARY MOONS

Moon	Planet	Diameter km	miles
1 Ganymede	Jupiter	5,268	3,273

Discovered by Galileo in 1609–10 and believed to be the largest moon in the Solar System, Ganymede – one of Jupiter's 16 satellites – is thought to have a surface of ice about 97 km/60 miles thick.

2 Titan	Saturn	5,150	3,200

Titan, the largest of Saturn's 18 confirmed moons, is actually larger than Mercury and Pluto. It was discovered by the Dutch astronomer Christian Huygens in 1655.

3 Callisto	Jupiter	4,820	2,995

Similar in composition to Ganymede, Callisto is heavily pitted with craters, perhaps more so than any other body in the Solar System.

4 Io	Jupiter	3,632	2,257

Most of what we know about Io was reported back by the 1979 Voyager probe, which revealed a crust of solid sulphur with massive volcanic eruptions in progress.

5 Moon	Earth	3,475	2,159

Our own satellite is a quarter of the size of the Earth, the 5th largest in the Solar System and, to date, the only one explored by humans.

6 Europa	Jupiter	3,126	1,942

Europa's fairly smooth icy surface is covered with mysterious black lines, some of them 64 km/40 miles wide and resembling canals.

7 Triton	Neptune	2,750	1,708

Discovered in 1846 by British brewer and amateur astronomer William Lassell, Triton is unique in revolving around its planet in the opposite direction to the planet's rotation.

8 Titania	Uranus	1,580	982

The largest of Uranus's 15 moons, Titania was discovered by William Herschel (who had discovered the planet six years earlier) in 1787 and has a snowball-like surface of ice.

9 Rhea	Saturn	1,530	951

Saturn's second largest moon was discovered by seventeenth-century Italian-born French astronomer Giovanni Cassini.

10 Oberon	Uranus	1,516	942

Oberon was discovered by Herschel and given the name of the fairy king husband of Queen Titania, both characters in Shakespeare's A Midsummer Night's Dream.

TOP 10

LARGEST ASTEROIDS

Name	Year discovered	Diameter km	miles
1 Ceres	1801	936	582
2 Pallas	1802	607	377
3 Vesta	1807	519	322
4 Hygeia	1849	450	279
5 Euphrosyne	1854	370	229
6 Interamnia	1910	349	217
7 Davida	1903	322	200
8 Cybele	1861	308	192
9 Europa	1858	288	179
10 Patienta	1899	275	171

Asteroids, sometimes known as "minor planets", are fragments of rock orbiting between Mars and Jupiter. There are perhaps 45,000 of them, but fewer than 10 per cent have been named. The first (and largest) to be discovered was Ceres, which was found by Giuseppe Piazzi (1746–1826), director of the Palermo observatory in Sicily, on New Year's Day, 1801. All have been numbered according to the order in which they were discovered. Some have only code numbers, but most also have names: women's names are especially popular and include Hilda (No. 153), Bertha (No. 154), Marilyn (No. 1,486), Sabrina (No. 2,264), and Samantha (No. 3,147). Among asteroids named after men are Mark Twain (No. 2,362) and Mr Spock from *Star Trek* (No. 2,309).

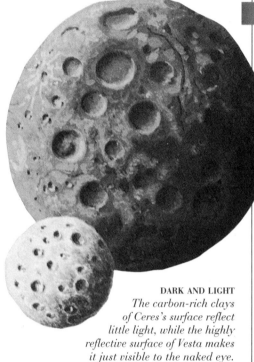

DARK AND LIGHT
The carbon-rich clays of Ceres's surface reflect little light, while the highly reflective surface of Vesta makes it just visible to the naked eye.

TOP 10

COLDEST BODIES IN THE SOLAR SYSTEM*

Planet	Lowest temperature (°C)
1 Pluto	–230
2 Uranus	–223
3 Neptune	–220
4 Mercury	–200
5 Saturn	–160
6 Jupiter	–145
7 Mars	–140
8 Earth	–89
9 Venus	+464
10 Sun	+5,500

* Excluding satellites.

Absolute zero, which has almost been attained on Earth under laboratory conditions, is –273.15°C, only 38.15°C below the surface temperature of Triton, a moon of Neptune. At the other extreme, it has been calculated theoretically that the core of Jupiter attains 30,000°C, more than five times the boiling point of tungsten, while the core of the Sun reaches 15,400,000°C.

SATURN'S LARGEST MOON
NASA and the European Space Agency plan to send a space probe to Titan in April 1996. It should reach Titan in October 2002.

REACHING FOR THE MOON

T O P 1 0

FIRST ANIMALS IN SPACE

	Animal	Country of origin	Date
1	Laika	USSR	3 Nov 1957

Name used by Western press – actually the name of the breed to which the dog named Kudryavka, a female Samoyed husky, belonged. Died in space.

2=	Laska and		
2=	Benjy (mice)	USA	13 Dec 1958

Re-entered the Earth's atmosphere, but not recovered.

4=	Able (female rhesus monkey) and		
4=	Baker (female squirrel monkey)	USA	28 May 1959

Successfully returned to Earth.

6=	Otvazhnaya (female Samoyed husky) and		
6=	An unnamed rabbit	USSR	2 Jul 1959

Recovered.

8	Sam (male rhesus monkey)	USA	4 Dec 1959

Recovered.

9=	Belka and		
9=	Strelka (female Samoyed huskies)	USSR	19 Aug 1960

First to orbit and return safely.

The first animal to be sent up in a rocket – but not into space – was Albert, a male rhesus monkey, in a US Air Force converted German V2 rocket in 1948. He died during the test, as did a monkey and 11 mice in a US *Aerobee* rocket in 1951. The earliest Soviet experiments with launching animals in rockets involved monkeys, dogs, rabbits, cats, and mice, most of whom died as a result. Laika, the first dog in space, went up with no hope of coming down alive. Able and Baker, launched in a *Jupiter* missile, were the first animals to be recovered (although Able died a few days later). Prior to the first US manned spaceflight, on 29 November 1961, Enos, a male chimpanzee, successfully completed two orbits and returned safely to the Earth.

T O P 1 0

LARGEST CRATERS ON THE MOON

(Near, or visible side only)

		Diameter	
	Crater	km	miles
1	Bailly	303	188
2	Deslandres	234	145
3	Schickard	227	141
4	Clavius	225	140
5	Grimaldi	222	138
6	Humboldt	207	129
7	Belkovich	198	123
8	Janssen	190	118
9	Schiller	179	111
10=	Gauss	177	110
10=	Petavius	177	110

The most characteristic features of the lunar landscape are its craters, many of which are named after famous astronomers and scientists. On the near side of the Moon there are some 300,000 craters with diameters greater than 1 km/0.6 mile, 234 of them larger than 100 km/62 miles. Those larger than about 60 km/37 miles are correctly known as "walled plains". The walled plains and smaller craters have been continually degraded by meteorite bombardment over millions of years and as a result, many contain numerous further craters within them. Bailly (named after Jean Sylvain Bailly, astronomer and Mayor of Paris, who was guillotined soon after the French revolution) is the largest crater on the visible side, with walls rising to 4,267 m/14,000 ft.

T O P 1 0

FIRST PEOPLE IN SPACE

	Name	Age	Orbits	Duration hr:min	Spacecraft/ country of origin	Date
1	Fl Major Yuri Alekseyivich Gagarin	27	1	1:48	*Vostok I* USSR	12 Apr 1961
2	Major Gherman Stepanovich Titov	25	17	25:18	*Vostok II* USSR	6–7 Aug 1961
3	Lt-Col John Herschel Glenn	40	3	4:56	*Friendship 7* USA	20 Feb 1962
4	Lt-Col Malcolm Scott Carpenter	37	3	4:56	*Aurora 7* USA	24 May 1962
5	Major Andrian Grigoryevich Nikolayev	32	64	94:22	*Vostok III* USSR	11–15 Aug 1962
6	Col Pavel Romanovich Popovich	31	48	70:57	*Vostok IV* USSR	12–15 Aug 1962
7	Cdr Walter Marty Schirra	39	6	9:13	*Sigma 7* USA	3 Oct 1962
8	Major Leroy Gordon Cooper	36	22	34:19	*Faith 7* USA	15–16 May 1963
9	Lt-Col Valeri Fyodorovich Bykovsky	28	81	119:60	*Vostok V* USSR	14–19 Jun 1963
10	Jr Lt Valentina Vladimirovna Tereshkova	26	48	70:50	*Vostok VI* USSR	16–19 Jun 1963

No. 10 was the first woman in space. Among early pioneering flights, neither Alan Shepard (5 May 1961: *Freedom 7*) nor Gus Grissom (21 July 1961: *Liberty Bell 7*) actually entered space, achieving altitudes of only 185 km/115 miles and 190 km/118 miles respectively, and neither flight lasted more than 15 minutes. Glenn was the first American to orbit the Earth.

COMMAND AND SERVICE MODULE

FIRST MOONWALKERS

	Astronaut	Birthdate	Spacecraft	Total EVA* hr:min	Mission dates
1	Neil A. Armstrong	5 Aug 1930	*Apollo 11*	2:32	16–24 Jul 1969
2	Edwin E. ("Buzz") Aldrin	20 Jan 1930	*Apollo 11*	2:15	16–24 Jul 1969
3	Charles Conrad Jr	2 Jun 1930	*Apollo 12*	7:45	14–24 Nov 1969
4	Alan L. Bean	15 Mar 1932	*Apollo 12*	7:45	14–24 Nov 1969
5	Alan B. Shepard	18 Nov 1923	*Apollo 14*	9:23	31 Jan–9 Feb 1971
6	Edgar D. Mitchell	17 Sep 1930	*Apollo 14*	9:23	31 Jan–9 Feb 1971
7	David R. Scott	6 Jun 1932	*Apollo 15*	19:08	26 Jul–7 Aug 1971
8	James B. Irwin	17 Mar 1930	*Apollo 15*	18:35	26 Jul–7 Aug 1971
9	John W. Young	24 Sep 1930	*Apollo 16*	20:14	16–27 Apr 1972
10	Charles M. Duke	3 Oct 1935	*Apollo 16*	20:14	16–27 Apr 1972

* Extra Vehicular Activity (i.e. time spent out of the lunar module on the Moon's surface).

Six US *Apollo* missions resulted in successful Moon landings (*Apollo 13*, 11–17 April 1970, was aborted after an oxygen tank exploded). During the last of these (*Apollo 17*, 7–19 December 1972), Eugene A. Cernan (b.14 March 1934) and Harrison H. Schmitt (b.3 July 1935) became the only other astronauts to date who have walked on the surface of the Moon, both spending a total of 22:04 in EVA. No further Moon landings are planned by the USA. Although Russian scientists recently proposed sending a series of unmanned probes to land on Mars, which, if successful, would have led to a follow-up manned mission between 2005 and 2010, the entire Russian space programme is suffering from such severe financial problems that its current missions appear to be in jeopardy.

SATURN V
This launch vehicle was built to send astronauts to the Moon.

THE FIRST 10 ARTIFICIAL SATELLITES

	Satellite	Country of origin	Launch date
1	*Sputnik 1*	USSR	4 Oct 1957
2	*Sputnik 2*	USSR	3 Nov 1957
3	*Explorer 1*	USA	1 Feb 1958
4	*Vanguard 1*	USA	17 Mar 1958
5	*Explorer 3*	USA	26 Mar 1958
6	*Sputnik 3*	USSR	15 May 1958
7	*Explorer 4*	USA	26 Jul 1958
8	*Score*	USA	18 Dec 1958
9	*Vanguard 2*	USA	17 Feb 1959
10	*Discoverer 1*	USA	28 Feb 1959

Artificial satellites for use as radio relay stations were first proposed by the British science-fiction writer Arthur C. Clarke in the October 1945 issue of *Wireless World*, but it was 12 years before his fantasy became reality with the launch of *Sputnik 1*, the first-ever artificial satellite to enter the Earth's orbit. A 83.6 kg/184 lb metal sphere, it transmitted signals back to the Earth for three weeks before its batteries failed, although it continued to be tracked until it fell back to the Earth and burned up on 4 January 1958. Its early successors were similarly short-lived, destroyed on re-entry (although *Vanguard 1* is destined to remain in orbit for the next 275 years and *Vanguard 2* for 125 years). *Sputnik 2* carried the first animal into space and *Explorer 1* first detected the radiation zone known as the Van Allen belts. *Explorer 2* failed to enter the Earth's orbit. *Score* (the Signal Communications Orbit Relay Experiment) transmitted a pre-recorded Christmas message from President Eisenhower. *Discoverer 1*, the first to be launched in a polar orbit, was a military satellite.

FIRST UNMANNED MOON LANDINGS

	Name	Country of origin	Date (launch/impact)
1	*Lunik 2*	USSR	12/14 Sep 1959
2	*Ranger 4**	USA	23/26 Apr 1962
3	*Ranger 6*	USA	30 Jan/2 Feb 1964
4	*Ranger 7*	USA	28/31 Jul 1964
5	*Ranger 8*	USA	17/20 Feb 1965
6	*Ranger 9*	USA	21/24 Mar 1965
7	*Luna 5**	USSR	9/12 May 1965
8	*Luna 7**	USSR	4/8 Oct 1965
9	*Luna 8**	USSR	3/7 Dec 1965
10	*Luna 9*	USSR	31 Jan/3 Feb 1966

In addition to these 10, debris left on the surface of the Moon includes the remains of several further *Luna* craft, including unmanned sample-collectors and *Lunakhod 1* and *2* (1966–71; all Soviet), seven *Surveyors* (1966–68), five *Lunar Orbiters* (1966–67), and the descent stages of six *Apollo* modules (all US) – to which one may add the world's most expensive used cars, the three Lunar Rovers used on *Apollo* missions Nos. 15 to 17 and worth $6,000,000 each.

* Crash-landing.

ASTRONAUTS

COUNTRIES WITH MOST SPACEFLIGHT EXPERIENCE

(To 1 January 1994)

	Country	Missions	Host country	Total duration of missions day	hr	min	sec
1	USSR	72	–	3,835	8	16	44
2	USA	89	–	738	3	57	25
3	Russia	4	–	710	6	23	5
4	France	5	1 USA/3 USSR/Russia*	74	4	43	36
5	Germany	5	3 USA/2 USSR	41	4	33	3
6	Canada	3	USA	26	3	34	31
7	Japan	2	1 USA/1 USSR	15	20	26	11
8	Bulgaria	2	USSR	11	19	11	6
9	Belgium	1	USA	8	22	9	25
10	Afghanistan	1	USSR	8	20	27	0

* *Russia became a separate independent state on 25 December 1991.*

FIRST MANNED ORBIT
On 12 April 1961 Soviet cosmonaut Yuri Gagarin became the first person in space when he completed one orbit of the Earth in his capsule, Vostok 1.

THE FIRST 10 SPACEWALKERS

	Astronaut	Spacecraft	EVA* hr:min	Launch date
1	Alexei Leonov	*Voskhod 2*	0:12	18 Mar 1965
2	Edward H. White	*Gemini 4*	0:23	3 Jun 1965
3	Eugene A. Cernan#	*Gemini 9*	2:08	3 Jun 1966
4	Michael Collins	*Gemini 10*	1:30	18 Jul 1966
5	Richard F. Gordon	*Gemini 11*	1:57	12 Sep 1966
6	Edwin E. ("Buzz") Aldrin**	*Gemini 12*	5:37	11 Nov 1966
7	Alexei Yeleseyev	*Soyuz 5*	‡	15 Jan 1969
8	Yevgeny Khrunov	*Soyuz 5*	‡	15 Jan 1969
9	David R. Scott##	*Apollo 9*	1:01	3 Mar 1969
10	Russell L. Schweickart	*Apollo 9*	1:07	3 Mar 1969

* *Extra Vehicular Activity.*
\# *7 December 1972 – first to walk in space four times.*
***16 July 1969 – first to walk in space twice.*
\#\#*26 July 1971 – first to walk in space three times.*
‡ *Short duration EVA transfer to Soyuz 4.*

FIRST 10 IN-FLIGHT SPACE FATALITIES

1 Vladimir M. Komarov   (b. 16 Mar 1927)

Launched on 24 April 1967, Soviet spaceship Soyuz 1 experienced various technical problems during its 18th orbit. After a successful re-entry, the capsule parachute was deployed at 7,010 m/23,000 ft, but its lines became tangled and it crash-landed near Orsk in the Urals, killing Komarov (the survivor of a previous one-day flight on 12 October 1964), who thus became the first-ever space fatality.

2= Georgi T. Dobrovolsky   (b. 1 Jun 1928)
2= Viktor I. Patsayev   (b. 19 Jun 1933)
2= Vladislav N. Volkov   (b. 23 Nov 1933)

After a then-record 23 days in space, and a link-up with the Salyut space station, the Soviet Soyuz 9 mission ended in disaster on 29 June 1971 when the capsule depressurized during re-entry. Although it landed intact, all three cosmonauts – who were not wearing spacesuits – were found to be dead. Their ashes were buried, along with those of Yuri Gagarin and Vladimir Komarov, at the Kremlin, Moscow. Spacesuits have been worn during re-entry on all subsequent missions.

5= Gregory B. Jarvis   (b. 24 Aug 1944)
5= Sharon C. McAuliffe   (b. 2 Sep 1948)
5= Ronald E. McNair   (b. 21 Oct 1950)
5= Ellison S. Onizuka   (b. 24 Jun 1946)
5= Judith A. Resnik   (b. 5 Apr 1949)
5= Francis R. Scobee   (b. 19 May 1939)
5= Michael J. Smith   (b. 30 Apr 1945)

Challenger STS-51-L, the 25th Space Shuttle mission, exploded on take-off from Cape Canaveral, Florida, on 28 January 1986. The cause was determined to have been leakage of seals in the joint between rocket sections. The disaster, watched by thousands on the ground and millions on television, halted the US space programme until a full review of engineering problems and safety methods had been undertaken, and it was not until 29 September 1988 that the next Space Shuttle, Discovery STS-26, was launched.

The 11 cosmonauts and astronauts in this list are, to date, the only in-flight space fatalities. They are not, however, the only other victims of accidents during the space programmes of the former USSR and the US. On 24 October 1960, five months before the first manned flight, Field Marshal Mitrofan Nedelin, the commander of the USSR's Strategic Rocket Forces, and an unknown number of other personnel (a total of 165 according to some authorities), were killed in the catastrophic launchpad explosion of an unmanned space rocket at the Baikonur cosmodrome, but the precise circumstances remain secret. Another explosion, during the refuelling of a *Vostok* rocket at the Plesetsk Space Centre on 18 March 1980, left some 50 dead. During a test countdown of *Apollo 1* on 27 January 1967, Roger B. Chaffee, Virgil I. "Gus" Grissom, veteran of the US's second and seventh space missions, and Edward H. White (who flew in the eighth US mission) were killed in a fire, probably caused by an electrical fault. This tragedy led to greatly improved capsule design and safety procedures.

A number of former astronauts and cosmonauts have also been killed in accidents during other activities: Yuri Gagarin, the first man in space, was killed on 27 March 1968 in an aeroplane crash. The same fate befell a number of US astronauts who trained for but were killed before their space missions: Charles A. Bassett, Theodore C. Freeman, Elliot M. See, and Clifton C. Williams all died during training in T-38 jet crashes in 1964–67. Stephen D. Thorne was killed in a 1986 aeroplane accident and Edward G. Givens in a 1967 car crash. John L. Swigert, who had survived the ill-fated *Apollo 13* mission in 1970, died of cancer on 27 December 1982, thus becoming the first American space explorer to die of natural causes. James B. Irwin, who died on 8 August 1991 as a result of a heart attack, became the first moonwalker to die.

T O P 1 0

MOST EXPERIENCED SPACEMEN
(*To 1 January 1994*)

	Name	Missions	Total duration of missions			
			days	hr	min	sec
1	Musa Manarov	2	541	0	31	18
2	Sergei Krikalyov	2	463	7	11	0
3	Yuri Romanenko	3	430	18	21	30
4	Alexander Volkov	3	391	11	54	0
5	Anatoli Solovyov	3	377	20	0	0
6	Leonid Kizim	3	374	17	57	42
7	Vladimir Titov	2	367	22	56	48
8	Vladimir Solovyov	2	361	22	50	0
9	Valeri Ryumin	3	361	21	31	57
10	Vladimir Lyakhov	3	333	7	48	37

All the missions listed were undertaken by the USSR (and, latterly, Russia). The durations of Soviet/Russian cosmonauts' space missions are far ahead of those of the US, whose closest rivals are the three *Skylab 4* astronauts Gerald P. Carr, Edward G. Gibson, and William R. Pogue. Each of them clocked up a total of 84 days 1 hr 15 min 31 sec in space (16 November 1973 to 8 February 1974) giving all three the equal US record for space experience. The four Space Shuttle missions of Daniel C. Brandenstein (*SST-8*, *STS-51-G*, *STS-32*, and *STS-49*) make him the most experienced Shuttle astronaut, with a total time in space of 32 days 21 hr 5 min 16 sec.

T O P 1 0

MOST EXPERIENCED SPACEWOMEN
(*To 1 January 1994*)

	Name*	Missions	Total duration of missions			
			days	hr	min	sec
1	Shannon W. Lucid	4	34	22	53	14
2	Bonnie J. Dunbar	3	31	17	15	33
3	Kathryn C. Thornton	3	23	41	15	30
4	Margaret Rhea Seddon	2	23	2	27	54
5	Kathryn D. Sullivan	3	22	4	48	39
6	Svetlana Savitskaya	2	19	17	7	0
7	Tamara E. Jernigan	2	18	23	10	33
8	Marsha S. Ivins	2	18	20	15	43
9	Ellen S. Baker	2	17	43	9	4
10	Sally K. Ride	2	14	7	47	43

* All US except 6 (USSR).

THE FACE OF THE EARTH

T O P 1 0

LARGEST METEORITE CRATERS IN THE WORLD

Crater	Diameter km	miles
1= Sudbury, Ontario, Canada	140	87
1= Vredefort, South Africa	140	87
3= Manicouagan, Québec, Canada	100	62
3= Popigai, Russia	100	62
5 Puchezh-Katunki, Russia	80	50
6 Kara, Russia	60	37
7 Siljan, Sweden	52	32
8 Charlevoix, Québec, Canada	46	29
9 Araguainha Dome, Brazil	40	25
10 Carswell, Saskatchewan, Canada	37	23

The jury is still out on the Earth's notable meteor craters: unlike those on the Solar System's other planets and moons, many astroblemes (collision sites) on the Earth have been weathered over time and obscured, and one of the ongoing debates in geology is thus whether or not certain crater-like structures are of meteoric origin or the remnants of long-extinct volcanoes. The Vredefort Ring, for example, long thought to be meteoric, was declared in 1963 to be volcanic, but has since been claimed as a definite meteor crater, as are all the giant meteorite craters in the Top 10, which are listed as such (along with 106 others) by the International Union of Geological Sciences Commission on Comparative Planetology. The relatively small Barringer Crater in Arizona (1.265 km/0.79 miles) is the largest that *all* scientists agree is definitely meteoric in origin.

T O P 1 0

LARGEST ISLANDS IN THE WORLD

	Island	Location	Approx. area* sq km	sq miles
1	Greenland (Kalaatdlit Nunaat)	Arctic Ocean	2,175,590	840,000
2	New Guinea	West Pacific	789,900	304,980
3	Borneo	Indian Ocean	751,000	289,961
4	Madagascar (Malagasy Republic)	Indian Ocean	587,041	226,657
5	Baffin Island, Canada	Arctic Ocean	507,451	195,926
6	Sumatra, Indonesia	Indian Ocean	422,200	163,011
7	Honshu, Japan	Northwest Pacific	230,092	88,839
8	Great Britain	North Atlantic	218,041	84,186
9	Victoria Island, Canada	Arctic Ocean	217,290	83,896
10	Ellesmere Island, Canada	Arctic Ocean	196,236	75,767

* *Mainlands, including areas of inland water, but excluding offshore islands.*

Australia is regarded as a continental land mass rather than an island; otherwise it would rank 1st, at 7,618,493 sq km/2,941,517 sq miles, or 35 times the size of Great Britain.

T O P 1 0

LARGEST DESERTS IN THE WORLD

	Desert	Location	Approx. area sq km	sq miles
1	Sahara	North Africa	9,000,000	3,500,000
2	Australian	Australia	3,800,000	1,470,000
3	Arabian	Southwest Asia	1,300,000	502,000
4	Gobi	Central Asia	1,040,000	401,500
5	Kalahari	Southern Africa	520,000	201,000
6	Turkestan	Central Asia	450,000	174,000
7	Takla Makan	China	327,000	125,000
8=	Sonoran	USA/Mexico	310,000	120,000
8=	Namib	Southwest Africa	310,000	120,000
10=	Thar	Northwest India/Pakistan	260,000	100,000
10=	Somali	Somalia	260,000	100,000

HOT AND BARREN
The Gobi Desert, in the dry heart of central Asia, occupies most of Mongolia and part of China. In recent years, exciting finds of fossil bones and dinosaur eggs have been unearthed there.

T O P   1 0

LARGEST ISLANDS IN EUROPE

	Island	Location	Approx area sq km	Approx area sq miles
1	Great Britain	North Atlantic	218,041	84,186
2	Iceland	North Atlantic	103,000	39,769
3	Ireland	North Atlantic	83,766	32,342
4	West Spitsbergen (Vestspitzbergen)	Arctic Ocean	39,368	15,200
5	Sicily	Mediterranean Sea	25,400	9,807
6	Sardinia	Mediterranean Sea	23,800	9,189
7	North East Land	Barents Sea	15,000	5,792
8	Cyprus	Mediterranean Sea	9,251	3,572
9	Corsica	Mediterranean Sea	8,720	3,367
10	Crete	Mediterranean Sea	8,260	3,189

D I D   Y O U   K N O W

ISLANDS LOST AND FOUND

• The South Atlantic Saxemberg Island and the Aurora Islands, allegedly discovered in 1762 by the crew of the *Aurora*, and once marked by marine charts, do not actually exist.

• Bouvet Island, also in the South Atlantic, was discovered in 1739 but then lost. It was sought by Captain Cook and other explorers and was rediscovered in 1808.

• One of the world's newest islands is the volcanic Surtsey, which emerged from the sea south-west of Iceland in November 1963.

T O P   1 0

LONGEST CAVES IN THE WORLD

	Cave	Location	Total Known Length m	Total Known Length ft
1	Mammoth cave system	Kentucky, USA	560,000	1,837,270
2	Optimisticeskaja	Ukraine	178,000	583,989
3	Hölloch	Switzerland	137,000	449,475
4	Jewel Cave	South Dakota, USA	127,000	416,667
5	Siebenhengsteholensystem	Switzerland	110,000	360,892
6	Ozernaya	Ukraine	107,300	352,034
7	Réseau de la Coume d'Hyouernede	France	90,500	296,916
8	Sistema de Ojo Guarena	Spain	89,100	292,323
9	Wind Cave	South Dakota, USA	88,500	290,354
10	Fisher Ridge cave system	Kentucky, USA	83,000	273,950
16	*Ease Gill cave system*	*West Yorkshire, UK*	*66,000*	*216,535*

T O P   1 0

DEEPEST DEPRESSIONS IN THE WORLD

	Depression	Maximum depth below sea level m	Maximum depth below sea level ft
1	Dead Sea, Israel/Jordan	400	1,312
2	Turfan Depression, China	154	505
3	Qattâra Depression, Egypt	133	436
4	Poluostrov Mangyshlak, Kazakhstan	132	433
5	Danakil Depression, Ethiopia	117	383
6	Death Valley, USA	86	282
7	Salton Sink, USA	72	235
8	Zapadny Chink Ustyurta, Kazakhstan	70	230
9	Prikaspiyskaya Nizmennost', Kazakhstan/Russia	67	220
10	Ozera Sarykamysh, Turkmenistan/Uzbekistan	45	148

The shore of the Dead Sea is the lowest exposed ground below sea level. However, the bed of the Sea, at 728 m/2,388 ft below sea level, is only half as deep as that of Lake Baikal, Russia, which is 1,485 m/4,872 ft below sea level. Much of Antarctica is also below sea level (some as low as 2,538 m/8,326 ft), but the land there is covered by an ice cap.

D I D   Y O U   K N O W

HOW LOW CAN YOU GO?

The greatest depth below ground level on land, that of the world's deepest mine, is far exceeded by the greatest chasm in the sea bed. The Marianas Trench in the Pacific Ocean plunges to a depth of 10,916 m/35,813 ft – 28.65 times the height of the Empire State Building. The bottom of the trench was reached on 23 January 1960 by Jacques Piccard and Donald Walls in the bathyscape *Trieste*.

ON TOP OF THE WORLD

T O P   1 0

HIGHEST MOUNTAINS IN THE WORLD

(Height of principal peak; lower peaks of the same mountain are excluded)

	Mountain	Country	m	ft
1	Everest	Nepal/Tibet	8,846	29,022
2	K2	Kashmir/China	8,611	28,250
3	Kanchenjunga	Nepal/Sikkim	8,598	28,208
4	Lhotse	Nepal/Tibet	8,501	27,890
5	Makalu I	Nepal/Tibet	8,470	27,790
6	Dhaulagiri I	Nepal	8,172	26,810
7	Manaslu I	Nepal	8,156	26,760
8	Cho Oyu	Nepal	8,153	26,750
9	Nanga Parbat	Kashmir	8,126	26,660
10	Annapurna I	Nepal	8,078	26,504

Many of the Top 10 mountains have alternative names: in Tibetan, Everest is known as Chomolungma ("Goddess Mother of the World"). K2 (so called because it was the second mountain in the Karakoram range counting from the Kashmir end) is also referred to by the local name Chogori, and sometimes as Godwin-Austen (after Lieutenant Henry Haversham Godwin-Austen (1834–1923), who first surveyed it in 1865). Manaslu is also known as Kutang I, and Nanga Parbat as Diamir.

T O P   1 0

HIGHEST MOUNTAINS IN THE UK

	Mountain	m	ft
1	Ben Nevis, Highland	1,344	4,408
2	Ben Macdhui, Grampian	1,309	4,296
3	Braeriach, Grampian/Highland	1,296	4,252
4	Cairn Toul, Grampian	1,293	4,241
5	Cairn Gorm, Grampian/Highland	1,245	4,084
6	Aonach Beag, Highland	1,236	4,054
7	Carn Mór Dearg, Highland	1,223	4,012
8	Aonach Mór, Highland	1,219	3,999
9	Ben Lawers, Tayside	1,214	3,984
10	Beinn a' Bhùird, Grampian	1,196	3,924

The ten tallest mountains in the UK are all in Scotland. The tallest outside Scotland is Snowdon, Gwynedd, Wales, at 1,085 m/3,560 ft. Slieve Donard, Co Down (852 m/2,796 ft) is the tallest in Northern Ireland. England's tallest is the 977-m/3,206-ft Scafell Pike, Cumbria – the county that also boasts the rest of England's Top 10 peaks.

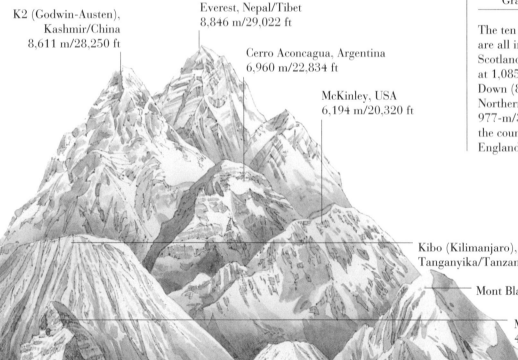

K2 (Godwin-Austen), Kashmir/China 8,611 m/28,250 ft

Everest, Nepal/Tibet 8,846 m/29,022 ft

Cerro Aconcagua, Argentina 6,960 m/22,834 ft

McKinley, USA 6,194 m/20,320 ft

Kibo (Kilimanjaro), Tanganyika/Tanzania 5,895 m/19,340 ft

Mont Blanc, France/Italy 4,807m/15,770 ft

Matterhorn, Italy/Switzerland 4,478m/14,691 ft

Fujiyama, Japan 3,776m/12,388 ft

T O P 1 0
HIGHEST MOUNTAINS IN AFRICA

	Mountain	Country	m	ft
1	Kibo (Kilimanjaro)	Tanganyika/Tanzania	5,895	19,340
2	Batian (Kenya)	Kenya	5,199	17,058
3	Ngaliema	Uganda/Zaïre	5,109	16,763
4	Duwoni	Uganda	4,896	16,062
5	Baker	Uganda	4,843	15,889
6	Emin	Zaïre	4,798	15,741
7	Gessi	Uganda	4,715	15,470
8	Sella	Uganda	4,627	15,179
9	Ras Dashen	Ethiopia	4,620	15,158
10	Wasuwameso	Zaïre	4,581	15,030

T O P 1 0
HIGHEST MOUNTAINS IN OCEANIA

	Mountain	m	ft
1	Jaya	5,030	16,500
2	Daam	4,920	16,150
3	Pilimsit	4,800	15,750
4	Trikora	4,750	15,580
5	Mandala	4,700	15,420
6	Wilhelm	4,690	15,400
7	Wisnumurti	4,590	15,080
8	Yamin	4,530	14,860
9	Kubor	4,360	14,300
10	Herbert	4,270	14,000

HOW HIGH?
The height of Everest was estimated in the 19th century as 8,840 m/29,002 ft. This was later revised to 8,848 m/ 29,029 ft, but on 20 April 1993, using the latest measuring techniques, the height was revised to the current "official" figure.

T O P 1 0
HIGHEST MOUNTAINS IN SOUTH AMERICA

	Mountain	Country	m	ft
1	Cerro Aconcagua	Argentina	6,960	22,834
2	Ojos del Salado	Argentina/Chile	6,885	22,588
3	Bonete	Argentina	6,873	22,550
4	Pissis	Argentina/Chile	6,780	22,244
5	Huascarán	Peru	6,768	22,205
6	Llullaillaco	Argentina/Chile	6,723	22,057
7	Libertador	Argentina	6,721	22,050
8	Mercadario	Argentina/Chile	6,670	21,884
9	Yerupajá	Peru	6,634	21,765
10	Tres Cruces	Argentina/Chile	6,620	21,720

T O P 1 0
HIGHEST MOUNTAINS IN NORTH AMERICA

	Mountain	Country	m	ft
1	McKinley	USA	6,194	20,320
2	Logan	Canada	6,050	19,850
3	Citlaltépetl (Orizaba)	Mexico	5,700	18,700
4	St Elias	USA/Canada	5,489	18,008
5	Popocatépetl	Mexico	5,452	17,887
6	Foraker	USA	5,304	17,400
7	Ixtaccihuatl	Mexico	5,286	17,343
8	Lucania	Canada	5,226	17,147
9	King	Canada	5,173	16,971
10	Steele	Canada	5,073	16,644

RIVERS AND WATERFALLS

TOP 10

LONGEST RIVERS IN EUROPE

(Excluding former USSR)

	River	Countries	km	miles
1	Danube	Germany/Austria/Slovakia/ Hungary/Yugoslavia (Serbia)/ Romania/Bulgaria	2,842	1,766
2	Rhine	Switzerland/Germany/ Holland	1,368	850
3	Elbe	Czechoslovakia/Germany	1,167	725
4	Loire	France	1,014	630
5	Tagus	Portugal	1,009	627
6	Meuse	France/Belgium/Holland	950	590
7	Ebro	Spain	933	580
8	Rhône	Switzerland/France	813	505
9	Guadiana	Spain/Portugal	805	500
10	Seine	France	776	482

TOP 10

LONGEST RIVERS IN THE WORLD

	River	Countries	km	miles
1	Nile	Tanzania/Uganda/ Sudan/Egypt	6,670	4,145
2	Amazon	Peru/Brazil	6,448	4,007
3	Yangtze–Kiang	China	6,300	3,915
4	Mississippi–Missouri– Red Rock	US	5,971	3,710
5	Yenisey–Angara–Selenga	Mongolia/Russia	5,540	3,442
6	Huang Ho (Yellow River)	China	5,464	3,395
7	Ob'–Irtysh	Mongolia/Kazakhstan/Russia	5,410	3,362
8	Zaïre (Congo)	Angola/Zaïre	4,700	2,920
9	Lena–Kirenga	Russia	4,400	2,734
10	Mekong	Tibet/China/Myanmar (Burma)/ Laos/Cambodia/Vietnam	4,350	2,703

TOP 10

LONGEST RIVERS IN NORTH AMERICA

	River	Country	km	miles
1	Mackenzie– Peace	Canada	4,241	2,635
2	Missouri– Red Rock	USA	4,088	2,540
3	Mississippi	USA	3,779	2,348
4	Missouri	USA	3,726	2,315
5	Yukon	USA	3,185	1,979
6	St Lawrence	Canada	3,130	1,945
7	Rio Grande	USA	2,832	1,760
8	Nelson	Canada	2,575	1,600
9	Arkansas	USA	2,348	1,459
10	Colorado	USA	2,334	1,450

The Mississippi, Missouri, and Red Rock rivers are often combined, thus becoming the 4th longest river in the world at 5,971 km/3,710 miles.

TOP 10

LONGEST RIVERS IN THE UK

	River	km	miles
1	Severn	354	220
2	Thames	346	215
3	Trent	298	185
4	Aire	259	161
5	Great Ouse	230	143
6	Wye	217	135
7	Tay	188	117
8	Nene	161	100
9	Clyde	159	98.5
10	Spey	158	98

During their courses, some of these rivers change their names; for example, the Trent becomes the Humber and the Thames becomes the Isis.

BRINGER OF LIFE
For thousands of years, since the time of the Ancient Egyptians, the Nile has attracted the peoples of north-east Africa to its fertile banks.

T O P 1 0

GREATEST WATERFALLS IN THE WORLD

(Based on volume of water)

	Waterfall	Country	Average flow (m³/sec)
1	Boyoma (Stanley)	Zaïre	17,000
2	Khône	Laos	11,610
3	Niagara (Horseshoe)	Canada/USA	5,830
4	Grande	Uruguay	4,500
5	Paulo Afonso	Brazil	2,890
6	Urubupungá	Brazil	2,750
7	Iguaçu	Argentina/ Brazil	1,700
8	Maribondo	Brazil	1,500
9	Churchill (Grand)	Canada	1,390
10	Kabalega (Murchison)	Uganda	1,200

DID YOU KNOW

THE CRYSTAL MOUNTAIN

In 1594 Sir Walter Raleigh journeyed up the Orinoco river in search of the legendary city of Eldorado. The climate, powerful currents, and dwindling supplies forced him to abandon his quest, but before turning back he saw at a distance a waterfall that resembled a "Mountain of Crystal... like a white church tower of an exceeding height". Raleigh had almost certainly discovered the world's highest waterfall, which subsequent Spanish explorers also reported seeing, but without naming it. The falls were named in honour of American adventurer James Angel, who was prospecting for gold in the Guiana Highlands. On 14 November 1933 he first spotted the falls from the air, later crash-landing his aeroplane on a nearby plateau. He survived and made his way back to civilization.

T O P 1 0

HIGHEST WATERFALLS IN THE UK

	Waterfall	Country	Drop m	ft
1	Eas Coul Aulin	Scotland	201	658
2	Falls of Glomach	Scotland	113	370
3	Pystyll y Llyn	Wales	91	300
4	Pistyll Rhaeadr	Wales	73	240
5	Falls of Foyers	Scotland	62.5	205
6	Falls of Clyde	Scotland	62.2	204
7=	Falls of the Bruar	Scotland	61	200
7=	Caldron Snout	England	61	200
7=	Grey Mare's Tail	Scotland	61	200
10	Falls of Measach	Scotland	46	150

T O P 1 0

HIGHEST WATERFALLS IN THE WORLD

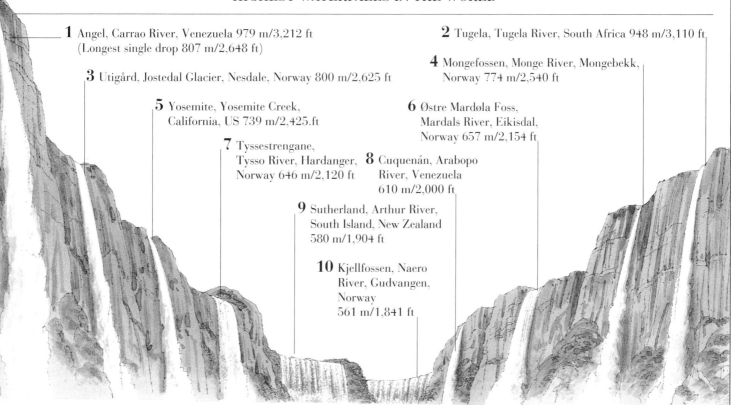

1 Angel, Carrao River, Venezuela 979 m/3,212 ft (Longest single drop 807 m/2,648 ft)

2 Tugela, Tugela River, South Africa 948 m/3,110 ft

3 Utigård, Jostedal Glacier, Nesdale, Norway 800 m/2,625 ft

4 Mongefossen, Monge River, Mongebekk, Norway 774 m/2,540 ft

5 Yosemite, Yosemite Creek, California, US 739 m/2,425.ft

6 Østre Mardøla Foss, Mardals River, Eikisdal, Norway 657 m/2,154 ft

7 Tyssestrengane, Tysso River, Hardanger, Norway 646 m/2,120 ft

8 Cuquenán, Arabopo River, Venezuela 610 m/2,000 ft

9 Sutherland, Arthur River, South Island, New Zealand 580 m/1,904 ft

10 Kjellfossen, Naero River, Gudvangen, Norway 561 m/1,841 ft

SEAS AND LAKES

TOP 10

LARGEST OCEANS AND SEAS IN THE WORLD

	Ocean/sea	Approx. area sq km	sq miles
1	Pacific Ocean	165,241,000	63,800,000
2	Atlantic Ocean	82,439,000	31,830,000
3	Indian Ocean	73,452,000	28,360,000
4	Arctic Ocean	13,986,000	5,400,000
5	Arabian Sea	3,864,000	1,492,000
6	South China Sea	3,447,000	1,331,000
7	Caribbean Sea	2,753,000	1,063,000
8	Mediterranean Sea	2,505,000	967,000
9	Bering Sea	2,269,000	876,000
10	Bay of Bengal	2,173,000	839,000

TOP 10

DEEPEST DEEP-SEA TRENCHES

	Name	Ocean	Deepest point m	ft
1	Mariana	Pacific	10,924	35,837
2	Tonga*	Pacific	10,800	35,430
3	Philippine	Pacific	10,497	34,436
4	Kermadec*	Pacific	10,047	32,960
5	Bonin	Pacific	9,994	32,786
6	New Britain	Pacific	9,940	32,609
7	Kuril	Pacific	9,750	31,985
8	Izu	Pacific	9,695	31,805
9	Puerto Rico	Atlantic	8,605	28,229
10	Yap	Pacific	8,527	27,973

Some authorities consider these parts of the same feature.

The eight deepest ocean trenches would be deep enough to submerge Mount Everest, which is 8,846 m/ 29,022 ft above sea level.

TOP 10

LAKES WITH THE GREATEST VOLUME OF WATER

	Lake	Location	Volume cubic km	cubic miles
1	Caspian Sea	Azerbaijan/Iran/Kazakhstan/ Russia/Turkmenistan	89,600	21,497
2	Baikal	Russia	22,995	5,517
3	Tanganyika	Burundi/Tanzania/Zaïre/Zambia	18,304	4,392
4	Superior	Canada/USA	12,174	2,921
5	Nyasa (Malawi)	Malawi/Mozambique/Tanzania	6,140	1,473
6	Michigan	USA	4,874	1,169
7	Huron	Canada/USA	3,575	858
8	Victoria	Kenya/Tanzania/Uganda	2,518	604
9	Great Bear	Canada	2,258	542
10	Great Slave	Canada	1,771	425

TOP 10

DEEPEST OCEANS AND SEAS IN THE WORLD

	Ocean/sea	Average depth m	ft		Ocean/sea	Average depth m	ft
1	Pacific Ocean	4,028	13,215	6	Bering Sea	1,547	5,075
2	Indian Ocean	3,963	13,002	7	Gulf of Mexico	1,486	4,874
3	Atlantic Ocean	3,926	12,880	8	Mediterranean Sea	1,429	4,688
4	Caribbean Sea	2,647	8,685	9	Japan Sea	1,350	4,429
5	South China Sea	1,652	5,419	10	Arctic Ocean	1,205	3,953

T O P 1 0

LARGEST LAKES IN THE WORLD

	Lake	Location	Approx. area sq km	sq miles
1	Caspian Sea	Azerbaijan/Iran/ Kazakhstan/Russia/ Turkmenistan	378,400	146,101
2	Superior	Canada/USA	82,100	31,699
3	Victoria	Kenya/Tanzania/Uganda	62,940	24,301
4	Huron	Canada/USA	59,580	23,004
5	Michigan	USA	57,700	22,278
6	Aral Sea	Kazakhstan/Uzbekistan	40,000	15,444
7	Tanganyika	Burundi/Tanzania/ Zaïre/Zambia	31,987	12,350
8	Baikal	Russia	31,494	12,160
9	Great Bear	Canada	31,153	12,028
10	Great Slave	Canada	28,570	11,031

Lake Superior is the world's largest freshwater lake. Lake Baikal (or Baykal) in Siberia, with a depth of as much as 1.63 km/1.02 miles in parts, is the world's deepest. It has been calculated that, as a result of two feeder rivers being diverted for irrigation, between 1973 and 1989 the area of the Aral Sea fell by so much that it dropped from 4th to 6th place and is in danger of becoming non-existent.

UNIQUELY RICH
Probably the world's oldest lake, Baikal is home to a remarkable range of plants and animals, including at least 1,300 species that are found nowhere else on the Earth. Lake Baikal contains approximately 20 per cent of the Earth's supply of fresh water.

T O P 1 0

LARGEST LAKES IN THE EC

	Lake	Location*	Area sq km	sq miles
1	Geneva	France (Switzerland)	582	225
2	Constance	Germany (Switzerland/Austria)	539	208
3	Neagh	Northern Ireland	382	147
4	Garda	Italy	366	141
5	Venice	Italy	280	108
6	Maggiore	Italy (Switzerland)	210	81
7	Corrib	Ireland	170	66
8	Como	Italy	146	56
9	Trasimeno	Italy	126	49
10	Muritz	Germany	120	46

* Non-EC countries in which portions of several lakes are also located appear in brackets.

If Venice is regarded as a saltwater lagoon rather than a lake, and hence discounted, No. 10 becomes Lower Lough Erne, Northern Ireland. If the Ijssel, Netherlands (1,210 sq km/ 470 sq miles), is considered a lake, it heads the list. Outside the EC, but in Europe, the largest lake is Ladoga, Russia (17,700 sq km/6,830 sq miles), and the largest outside Russia is Lake Vänern, Sweden (9,720 sq km/3,750 sq miles).

T O P 1 0

LARGEST LAKES IN THE UK

	Lake	Area sq km	sq miles
1	Lough Neagh, Northern Ireland	381.74	147.39
2	Lower Lough Erne, Northern Ireland	105.08	40.57
3	Loch Lomond, Scotland	71.22	27.50
4	Loch Ness, Scotland	56.64	21.87
5	Loch Awe, Scotland	38.72	14.95
6	Upper Lough Erne, Northern Ireland	31.73	12.25
7	Loch Maree, Scotland	28.49	11.00
8	Loch Morar, Scotland	26.68	10.30
9	Loch Tay, Scotland	26.39	10.19
10	Loch Shin, Scotland	22.53	8.70

The largest lake in England is Windermere, 14.74 sq km/5.69 sq miles.

NATURAL DISASTERS

SEARCHING FOR SURVIVORS
After Colombia's worst landslide, rescuers struggle to release victims from the mud and rubble.

T O P   1 0

WORST AVALANCHES AND LANDSLIDES OF THE 20TH CENTURY

(Excluding those where most deaths resulted from flooding caused by avalanches or landslides)

	Location	Incident	Date	Estimated no. killed
1	Yungay, Peru	Landslide	31 May 1970	17,500
2	Italian Alps	Avalanche	13 Dec 1916	10,000
3	Huarás, Peru	Avalanche	13 Dec 1941	5,000
4	Mount Huascaran, Peru	Avalanche	10 Jan 1962	3,500
5	Medellin, Colombia	Landslide	27 Sep 1987	683
6	Chungar, Peru	Avalanche	19 Mar 1971	600
7	Rio de Janeiro, Brazil	Landslide	11 Jan 1966	550
8=	Northern Assam, India	Landslide	15 Feb 1949	500
8=	Grand Rivière du Nord, Haiti	Landslide	13/14 Nov 1963	500
10	Blons, Austria	Avalanche	11 Jan 1954	411

The worst incident of all, the destruction of Yungay, Peru, in May 1970, was only part of a much larger cataclysm. The landslide, which wiped out the town and left just 2,500 survivors out of a population of 20,000, followed on the heels of an earthquake and widespread flooding that left a total of up to 70,000 dead.

T O P   1 0

WORST EARTHQUAKES IN THE WORLD

	Location	Date	Estimated no. killed
1	Near East/Mediterranean	20 May 1202	1,100,000
2	Shenshi, China	2 Feb 1556	820,000
3	Calcutta, India	11 Oct 1737	300,000
4	Antioch, Syria	20 May 526	250,000
5	Tang-shan, China	28 Jul 1976	242,419
6	Nan-shan, China	22 May 1927	200,000
7	Yeddo, Japan	1703 (exact date unknown)	190,000
8	Kansu, China	16 Dec 1920	180,000
9	Messina, Italy	28 Dec 1908	160,000
10	Tokyo/Yokohama, Japan	1 Sep 1923	142,807

There are some discrepancies between the "official" death tolls in many of the world's worst earthquakes and the estimates of other authorities: a figure of 750,000 is sometimes quoted for the the Tang-shan earthquake of 1976, for example, and totals ranging from 58,000 to 250,000 for the quake that devastated Messina in 1908. Several other earthquakes in China and Turkey resulted in deaths of 100,000 or more. In recent times, the Armenian earthquake of 7 December 1988 and that which struck northwest Iran on 21 June 1990 resulted in the deaths of more than 55,000 (official estimate 28,854) and 50,000 respectively. One of the most famous earthquakes, the one that destroyed San Francisco on 18 April 1906, killed between 500 and 1,000 people – mostly in the fires that resulted from broken gas pipes and electricity cables following the shock.

T O P   1 0

WORST TSUNAMIS ("TIDAL WAVES") IN THE WORLD

	Location	Year	Estimated no. killed
1	Atlantic coast (Morocco, western Europe, West Indies)	1775	60,000
2	Sumatra, Java	1883	36,000
3=	Japan	1707	30,000
3=	Italy	1783	30,000
5	Japan	1896	27,122
6	Chile, Hawaii	1868	25,000
7	Ryukyu Islands	1771	11,941
8	Japan	1792	9,745
9=	Japan	1498	5,000
9=	Japan	1611	5,000
9=	Peru	1756	5,000
9=	Chile, Hawaii, Japan	1960	5,000
9=	Philippines	1976	5,000

WORST VOLCANIC ERUPTIONS IN THE WORLD

	Location	Date	Estimated no. killed
1	Tambora, Indonesia	5–12 Apr 1815	92,000

The cataclysmic eruption of Tambora killed about 10,000 islanders immediately, with a further 82,000 dying subsequently from disease and famine resulting from crops being destroyed. An estimated 1,700,000 tonnes of ash were hurled into the atmosphere. This blocked out the sunlight and affected the weather over large areas of the globe during the following year. One effect of this was to produce brilliantly coloured sunsets, depicted strikingly in paintings from the period, especially in the works of J.M.W. Turner. It even had an influence on literary history: kept indoors by inclement weather at the Villa Diodati on Lake Geneva, Lord Byron and his companions amused themselves by writing horror stories, one of which was Mary Shelley's classic, Frankenstein.

	Location	Date	Estimated no. killed
2	Krakatoa, Sumatra/ Java	26–27 Aug 1883	36,380

After a series of eruptions over several days, the uninhabited island of Krakatoa exploded with what may have been the biggest bang ever heard by humans, recorded clearly 4,800 km/ 3,000 miles away. Some sources put the deaths as high as 200,000, most of them killed by subsequent tidal waves up to 30 m/100 ft high. The events were portrayed in the 1969 film Krakatoa, East of Java, but purists should note that Krakatoa is actually west of Java.

	Location	Date	Estimated no. killed
3	Miyi-Yama, Java	1793	53,000

Miyi-Yama, the volcano dominating the island of Kiousiou, erupted during 1793, engulfing all the local villages in mudslides and killing most of the rural population.

	Location	Date	Estimated no. killed
4	Mont Pelée, Martinique	8 May 1902	40,000

After lying dormant for centuries, Mont Pelée began to erupt in April 1902. Assured that there was no danger, the 30,000 residents of the main city, St. Pierre, stayed in their homes and were there when the volcano burst apart and showered the port with molten lava, ash, and gas, destroying all life and property. Some 50 people were killed by deadly fer-de-lance snakes, disturbed by the eruption.

	Location	Date	Estimated no. killed
5	Nevado del Ruiz, Colombia	13 Nov 1985	22,940

The Andean volcano gave warning signs of erupting, but by the time it was decided to evacuate the local inhabitants, it was too late. The hot steam, rocks, and ash ejected from mudslide engulfed the town of Armero.

	Location	Date	Estimated no. killed
6	Mount Etna, Italy	11 Mar 1669	more than 20,000

Europe's largest volcano (3,280 m/10,760 ft) has erupted frequently, but the worst instance occurred in 1669 when the lava flow engulfed the town of Catania, killing at least 20,000.

	Location	Date	Estimated no. killed
7	Laki, Iceland	Jan–Jun 1783	20,000

Iceland is one of the most volcanically active places on Earth but, being sparsely populated, eruptions seldom result in major loss of life. The worst exception took place at the Laki volcanic ridge, culminating on 11 June with the largest ever recorded lava flow. It engulfed many villages in a river of lava up to 80 km/ 50 miles long and 30 m/100 ft deep, releasing poisonous gases that killed those who managed to escape the lava.

	Location	Date	Estimated no. killed
8	Vesuvius, Italy	24 Aug 79	16–20,000

When the previously dormant Vesuvius erupted suddenly, the Roman city of Herculaneum was engulfed by a mudflow while Pompeii was buried under a vast layer of pumice and volcanic ash – which ironically preserved it in a near-perfect state that was not uncovered until excavations by archaeologists in the 19th and 20th centuries.

	Location	Date	Estimated no. killed
9	Vesuvius, Italy	16–17 Dec 1631	18,000

Although minor eruptions occurred at intervals after that of AD 79, the next major cataclysm was almost as disastrous, when lava and mudflows gushed down on to the surrounding towns, including Naples.

	Location	Date	Estimated no. killed
10	Mount Etna, Italy	1169	more than 15,000

Large numbers died in Catania cathedral where they believed they would be safe, and more were killed when a tidal wave hit the port of Messina.

CAST IN STONE
Victims in Pompeii left impressions in the deep ash that buried them, allowing plaster casts of their bodies to be made in the 19th century.

WEATHER EXTREMES

T O P 1 0

COLDEST AND HOTTEST INHABITED PLACES IN THE WORLD

#	Location		
1	Norilsk, Russia	-10.9°C	12.4°F
2	Yakutsk, Russia	-10.1°C	13.8°F
3	Yellowknife, Canada	-5.4°C	22.3°F
4	Ulan-Bator, Mongolia	-4.5°C	23.9°F
5	Fairbanks, Alaska, USA	-3.4°C	25.9°F
6	Surgut, Russia	-3.1°C	26.4°F
7	Chita, Russia	-2.7°C	27.1°F
8	Nizhnevartovsk, Russia	-2.6°C	27.3°F
9	Hailar, Mongolia	-2.4°C	27.7°F
10	Bratsk, Russia	-2.2°C	28.0°F

#	Location		
10=	Tiruchirapalli, India	28.8°C	83.8°F
10=	Thanjavur, India	28.8°C	83.8°F
10=	Ouagadougou, Burkina Faso	28.8°C	83.8°F
10=	Hudaydah, North Yemen	28.8°C	83.8°F
7=	Niamey, Niger	28.9°C	84.0°F
7=	Madurai, India	28.9°C	84.0°F
7=	Aden, South Yemen	28.9°C	84.0°F
5=	Santa Marta, Colombia	29.2°C	84.6°F
5=	Nellore, India	29.2°C	84.6°F
2=	Tuticorin, India	29.3°C	84.7°F
2=	Tirunelevi, India	29.3°C	84.7°F
2=	Timbuktu, Mali	29.3°C	84.7°F
1	Djibouti, Djibouti	30.0°C	86.0°F

T O P 1 0

WETTEST INHABITED PLACES IN THE WORLD

	Location	Average annual rainfall mm	in
1	Buenaventura, Colombia	6,743	265.47
2	Monrovia, Liberia	5,131	202.01
3	Pago Pago, American Samoa	4,990	196.46
4	Moulmein, Myanmar (Burma)	4,852	191.02
5	Lae, Papua New Guinea	4,465	182.87
6	Baguio, Luzon Island, Philippines	4,573	180.04
7	Sylhet, Bangladesh	4,457	175.47
8	Conakry, Guinea	4,341	170.91
9=	Padang, Sumatra Island, Indonesia	4,225	166.34
9=	Bogor, Java, Indonesia	4,225	166.34

The total annual rainfall of the Top 10 locations is equivalent to 26 1.83-m/6-ft adults standing on top of each other.

T O P 1 0

DRIEST INHABITED PLACES IN THE WORLD

	Location	Average annual rainfall mm	in
1	Aswan, Egypt	0.5	0.02
2	Luxor, Egypt	0.7	0.03
3	Arica, Chile	1.1	0.04
4	Ica, Peru	2.3	0.09
5	Antofagasta, Chile	4.9	0.19
6	Minya, Egypt	5.1	0.20
7	Asyut, Egypt	5.2	0.20
8	Callao, Peru	12.0	0.47
9	Trujilo, Peru	14.0	0.54
10	Fayyum, Egypt	19.0	0.75

The total annual rainfall of the Top 10 inhabited places is just 64.8 mm/2½ inches – the length of an adult little finger.

T O P 1 0

COLDEST PLACES IN BRITAIN

	Weather station	Average annual temperature* °C	°F
1	Dalwhinnie, Highland	6.0	42.8
2=	Leadhills, Strathclyde	6.3	43.3
2=	Braemar, Grampian	6.3	43.3
2=	Balmoral, Grampian	6.3	43.3
5	Tomatin, Highland	6.4	43.5
6	Granton-on-Spey, Highland	6.5	43.7
7	Lagganlia, Highland	6.6	43.9
8	Crawfordjohn, Strathclyde	6.7	44.1
9	Eskdalemuir, Dumfries & Galloway	6.8	44.2
10	Lerwick, Shetland	6.9	44.4

* Based on the Meteorological Office's averages for the period 1961–90.

T O P 1 0

HOTTEST YEARS IN BRITAIN

	Year	Average temperature °C	°F
1	1990	10.67	51.21
2	1949	10.64	51.15
3	1989	10.54	50.97
4	1959	10.52	50.94
5=	1834	10.51	50.92
5=	1921	10.51	50.92
7	1733	10.50	50.90
8	1779	10.41	50.74
9	1868	10.40	50.72
10	1736	10.33	50.59

* Since 1659.

These are mean averages for each year based on figures for meteorological stations in Central England, since comparable statistics for the whole UK are not available for early years.

T O P 1 0

SUNNIEST YEARS IN ENGLAND AND WALES*

	Year	Av. hours sunshine per day		Year	Av. hours sunshine per day
1	1989	4.83	6	1949	4.63
2	1990	4.71	7	1955	4.47
3	1959	4.67	8	1976	4.41
4	1911	4.65	9	1975	4.36
5	1921	4.64	10	1962	4.35

* Since 1909.

T O P 1 0

WETTEST PLACES IN BRITAIN

	Weather station	Average annual rainfall mm	in
1	Dalness, Strathclyde	3,306	130.2
2	Seathwaite, Cumbria	3,150	124.0
3	Glenfinnan, Highland	3,022	119.0
4	Inveraran, Central	2,701	106.3
5	Inveruglas, Central	2,662	104.8
6	Capel Curig, Gwynedd	2,555	100.6
7	Wythburn, Cumbria	2,535	99.8
8=	Tyndrum & Crianlarich, Central	2,500	98.4
8=	Chapel Stile, Cumbria	2,500	98.4
10	Lochgoilhead, Strathclyde	2,464	97.0

These figures are based on the Meteorological Office's 30-year averages for the period 1961–90, and are for the wettest inhabited places (villages and towns) in Great Britain.

T O P 1 0

WETTEST YEARS IN ENGLAND AND WALES

	Year	Total rainfall mm	inches
1	1872	1,288	50.70
2	1852	1,266	49.84
3	1768	1,192	46.92
4	1960	1,171	46.10
5	1903	1,147	45.15
6	1882	1,135	44.68
7	1877	1,134	44.64
8	1848	1,130	44.48
9	1841	1,120	44.09
10	1912	1,118	44.01

In 1866 the British meteorologist George Symons published a rainfall table for 1726–1865, listing 1852 as the wettest year. In 1872, this was beaten by an average annual rainfall that still holds the record. In modern times (1961–90), the annual average for England and Wales was 796 mm/31.33 in, and for Scotland 1,114 mm/43.86 in.

T O P 1 0

DRIEST PLACES IN BRITAIN

	Weather station	Average annual rainfall* mm	in
1	St Osyth, Essex	507	20.0
2	Shoeburyness & Southend-on-Sea, Essex	509	20.0
3	Burnham-on-Crouch, Essex	518	20.4
4=	Languard Point, Suffolk	524	20.6
4=	Peterborough, Cambridgeshire	524	20.6
6	Ely, Cambridgeshire	526	20.7
7=	Tilbury & Grays area, Essex	530	20.9
7=	Thamesmead, London	530	20.9
9	Huntingdon, Cambridgeshire	531	20.9
10	Walton-on-the-Naze, Essex	534	21.0

* Based on the Meteorological Office's averages for the period 1961–90.

LIFE ON EARTH

T O P 1 0

LARGEST DINOSAURS

1 *"Seismosaurus"*
Length: 30–36 m/98–119 ft
Estimated weight: 50–80 tonnes

A single skeleton of this colossal plant-eater was excavated in 1985 near Albuquerque, New Mexico, by US paleontologist David Gillette and given an unofficial name (i.e. one that is not yet an established scientific name) that means "earth-shaking lizard". It is currently being studied by the New Mexico Museum of Natural History.

2 *Supersaurus*
Length: 24–30 m/80–100 ft
Height: 16 m/54 ft
Estimated weight: 50 tonnes

The remains of Supersaurus *were found in Colorado in 1972 (like those of* Ultrasaurus, *by James A. Jensen). Some scientists have suggested a length of up to 42 m/138 ft and a weight of 75–100 tonnes.*

3 *Antarctosaurus*
Length: 18–30 m/60–98 ft
Estimated weight: 40–50 tonnes

Named Antarctosaurus *("southern lizard") by German paleontologist Friedrich von Huene in 1929, this creature's thigh bone alone measures 2.3 m/7 ft 6 in.*

4 *Barosaurus*
Length: 23–27.5 m/75–90 ft
Height and weight uncertain

Barosaurus *(meaning "heavy lizard", so named by US paleontologist Othniel C. Marsh in 1890) has been found in both North America and Africa, thus proving the existence of a land link in Jurassic times (205–140 million years ago).*

5 *Mamenchisaurus*
Length: 27 m/89 ft
Height and weight uncertain

An almost complete skeleton discovered in 1972 showed it had the longest neck of any known animal, comprising more than half its total body length – perhaps up to 15 m/49 ft. It was named by Chinese paleontologist Young Chung Chien after the place in China where it was found.

6 *Diplodocus*
Length: 23–27 m/75–89 ft
Estimated weight: 12 tonnes

As it was long and thin, Diplodocus *was a relative lightweight in the dinosaur world. It was also probably one of the most stupid dinosaurs, having the smallest brain in relation to its body size.* Diplodocus *was given its name (which means "double beam") in 1878 by Marsh. One skeleton was named* Diplodocus carnegii, *in honour of Scottish-American millionaire Andrew Carnegie, who financed the excavations that discovered it.*

7 *"Ultrasaurus"*
Length: Over 25 m/82 ft
Height: 16 m/52 ft
Estimated weight: 50 tonnes

Discovered by US paleontologist James A. Jensen in Colorado in 1979, it has not yet been fully studied. Some authorities put its weight at an unlikely 100–140 tonnes. Confusingly, although its informal name (which means "ultra lizard") was widely recognized, another, smaller dinosaur has been given the same official name.

8 *Brachiosaurus*
Length: 25 m/82 ft
Height: 16 m/52 ft
Estimated weight: 50 tonnes

Its name (given to it in 1903 by US paleontologist Elmer S. Riggs) means "arm lizard". Some have put the weight of Brachiosaurus *as high as 190 tonnes, but this seems improbable, in the light of theories of maximum weights of terrestrial animals.*

9 *Pelorosaurus*
Length: 24 m/80 ft
Weight
uncertain

The first fragments of Pelorosaurus ("monstrous lizard") were found in Sussex and named by British doctor and geologist Gideon Algernon Mantell as early as 1850.

10 *Apatosaurus*
Length: 20–21m/
66–70 ft

Estimated weight: 20–30 tonnes

Apatosaurus (its name, coined by Marsh, means "deceptive lizard") is better known by its former name of Brontosaurus ("thunder reptile"). The bones of the first one ever found, in Colorado in 1879, caused great confusion for many years because its discoverer attached a head from a different species to the rest of the skeleton.

The Top 10 is based on the most reliable recent evidence of their lengths and indicates the probable ranges, though these are undergoing constant revision. Lengths have often been estimated from only a few surviving fossilized bones, and there is much dispute even among experts about these and even more about the weights of most dinosaurs. Some, such as *Diplodocus* were long but not immensely heavy.

Everyone's favourite dinosaur, *Tyrannosaurus rex* ("tyrant lizard"), does not appear in the Top 10 list because although it was one of the fiercest flesh-eating dinosaurs, it was not as large as many of the herbivorous ones. However, measuring a probable 12 m/39 ft and weighing more than 6 tonnes, it certainly ranks as one of the largest flesh-eating animals yet discovered. Bones of an earlier dinosaur called *Epanterias* were found in Colorado in 1877 and 1934, but incorrectly identified until recently, when studies suggested that this creature was possibly larger than *Tyrannosaurus*.

To compare these sizes with living animals, note that the largest recorded crocodile measured 6.2 m/20 ft 4 in and the largest elephant 10.7 m/35 ft from trunk to tail and weighed about 12 tonnes. The largest living creature ever measured is the blue whale at 33.6 m/110 ft – slightly smaller than the size claimed for *Seismosaurus*.

T O P 1 0
FIRST DINOSAURS TO BE NAMED

	Name	Meaning	Named by	Year
1	*Megalosaurus*	Great lizard	William Buckland	1824
2	*Iguanodon*	Iguana tooth	Gideon Mantell	1825
3	*Hylaeosaurus*	Woodland lizard	Gideon Mantell	1832
4	*Macrodontophion*	Large tooth snake	A. Zborzewski	1834
5=	*Thecodontosaurus*	Socket-toothed lizard	Samuel Stutchbury and H. Riley	1836
5=	*Palaeosaurus*	Ancient lizard	Samuel Stutchbury and H. Riley	1836
7	*Plateosaurus*	Flat lizard	Hermann von Meyer	1837
8=	*Cladeiodon*	Branch tooth	Richard Owen	1841
8=	*Cetiosaurus*	Whale lizard	Richard Owen	1841
10	*Pelorosaurus*	Monstrous lizard	Gideon Mantell	1850

T O P 1 0
FINAL DATES WHEN 10 ANIMALS WERE LAST SEEN ALIVE

1 Aurochs 1627

This giant wild ox was last recorded in central Europe, after the advance of agriculture forced it to retreat from its former territory, which once stretched to the West as far as Britain.

2 *Aepyornis* 1649

Also known as the "Elephant bird", the 3 m/ 10 ft wingless bird was a native of Madagascar.

3 Dodo 1681

Discovered by European travellers in 1507, the last Dodo seen alive was on the island of Mauritius in 1681. Its name comes from the Portuguese for "stupid", and its lack of flight, tameness and taste made it extremely vulnerable to being caught and eaten.

4 Steller's sea cow 1768

A large marine mammal named after its 1741 discoverer, German naturalist Georg Wilhelm Steller, it was hunted to extinction. The Spectacled Cormorant, which Steller also found, became extinct at about the same time.

5 Great auk 1844

The last example of this flightless North Atlantic seabird breeding in Britain was in 1812, when one was nesting in the Orkneys, and the last seen in Britain in 1821 when one was killed for food on St Kilda. The last surviving pair in the world was killed on 4 June 1844 on Eldey island on behalf of a collector called Carl Siemsen. A stuffed example was sold at Sotheby's, London, in 1971.

6 Tarpan 1851

The European wild horse was last seen in the Ukraine. Another wild horse thought to be extinct, Przewalski's horse, has been rediscovered in Mongolia and new captive-bred stock has been re-introduced into its former range around the Gobi Desert.

7 Quagga 1883

This zebra-like creature found in South Africa, first recorded in 1685, was hunted by European settlers for food and leather to such an extent that by 1870 the last specimen in the wild had been killed. The last example, a female in Amsterdam Zoo, died on 12 August 1883.

8 Guadalupe Island Caracara 1900

On 1 December 1900, the last-ever example of this large brown hawk was sighted.

9 Passenger pigeon 1914

This is an example of a creature whose last moment can be stated precisely, when at 1.00 pm on 1 September 1914 at Cincinnati Zoo, a 29-year-old bird named Martha expired. Her stuffed body is displayed by the Smithsonian Institution, Washington, DC. Totals ran to a staggering five to nine billion in the 19th century, but they were remorselessly killed for food and to protect farm crops in the USA.

10 Carolina parakeet 1918

Like Martha the Passenger Pigeon, the last of this colourful species died at Cincinnati Zoo on 21 February 1918.

COMMON AND RARE

MOST ABUNDANT CLASSES OF ANIMAL

5 Molluscs

Includes snails, slugs, most shellfish, squids and octopus, and many tiny animals in the plankton horde.

6 Amphibians

Frogs, toads, newts, and the like: an estimated trillion (1,000,000,000,000) creatures.

7 Birds

Many birds share human habitats yet avoid conflict with us, so have the edge in numbers over most other larger wildlife outside the oceans. There are probably about 100,000,000,000 birds in the world and the commonest must include poultry species and specialist townies such as the sparrows.

8 Mammals (excluding humans)

Despite exploding human numbers and heavy pressures on many rare mammal species in the wild, other mammals probably still outnumber humans by at least four to one, boosted by the huge numbers of herd animals, pets, and "commensal" or scavenging animals such as rats and mice that share our habitat.

9 Humans

The baby that pushed the world's human population meter past the 5,000,000,000 mark was in all probability born in 1987.

10 Reptiles

Reptiles never recovered from the unknown cataclysm that finished off the dinosaurs, well before Homo sapiens arrived on the scene. Now largely through conflict and competition with humans, the world's snakes, lizards, turtles, crocodiles, and other scaly-skinned beasts are once more in decline and may number fewer than 2,000,000,000 individuals at present.

1 Insects and spiders

At least 5,000,000,000,000,000 individuals. Among the commonest insects are ants, fleas, flies, and the little-known springtails, which inhabit moist topsoil the world over. The latter alone probably outnumber the human race.

2 Crustaceans

Besides crabs, woodlice, and so on, this class also includes the krill and other tiny shrimp-like creatures that form a major ingredient in plankton, mainstay of life in the oceans.

3 Worms

Earthworms and other tube-like animals, including parasitic worms, can occur in great numbers in some habitats: more than 1,000,000 earthworms were counted in 0.4 hectare/1 acre of British farmland. But their distribution is variable compared with the teeming arthropods higher up the list.

4 Fish

Total fish population of the world's oceans has been estimated at around 760,000,000 tonnes – at least 100,000,000,000,000 individuals.

Microbes exist in staggering numbers: some nine trillion (9,000,000,000,000) of medium size could be packed into a box with sides 2.5 cm/1 inch long. But whether they are plants, animals, both, or neither is a matter of endless debate and we shall therefore disregard them.

Of animals that can be seen without a microscope, insects unquestionably top the numbers league: there are at least 1,000,000 insects for each of the Earth's 5,554,552,000 humans. Put together, they would weigh at least 12 times as much as the human race and at least three times more than the combined weight of all other living animals.

Estimates of the populations of other classes are at best "guesstimates", and this Top 10 should be viewed as a general picture of the relative numbers of each type of animal.

GROUPS WITH MOST KNOWN SPECIES

	Group	Approx. no. of known species
1	Insects	750–800,000
2	Higher plants	248,000
3	Non-insect arthropods (crustaceans, spiders, etc.)	123,000
4	Fungi	69,000
5	Molluscs	50,000
6	Algae	27,000
7=	Roundworms	12,000
7=	Flatworms	12,000
7=	Earthworms	12,000
10	Birds	9,000

The total number of known species is about 1,400,000. Approximately 27,000 species are being made extinct annually, principally in rainforests.

T O P   1 0

MOST ENDANGERED MAMMALS IN THE WORLD

Mammal	Number
1= Tasmanian wolf	?
1= Halcon fruit bat	?
1= Ghana fat mouse	?
4 Kouprey	10
5 Javan rhinoceros	50
6 Iriomote cat	60
7 Black lion tamarin	130
8 Pygmy hog	150
9 Tamaraw	200
10 Indus dolphin	400

The first three mammals on the list have not been seen for many years and may well be extinct, but zoologists are hopeful of the possibility of their survival: the Tasmanian wolf, for example, has been technically extinct since the last specimen died in a zoo in 1936, but occasional unconfirmed sightings suggest that there may still be animals in the wild, and a 648,000-hectare/1,601,240-acre nature reserve has been set aside for it in Tasmania in the expectation that it will be found again. The only Halcon fruit bat that has ever been seen is one that was discovered in the Philippines in 1937. (Another bat, the Tanzanian woolly bat, was discovered in the 1870s but has not been observed since, and is assumed to be extinct.)

All the species on this list, which is ranked in order of rarity, face global extinction – unlike many species which may be at serious risk in one area but flourishing elsewhere. Some species that would once have been on the "most endangered" list, such as the Arabian oryx, were "extinct" in the wild, but have been successfully bred in captivity and reintroduced into their natural habitats.

RAREST MARINE MAMMALS

Mammal	Estimated no.
1 Caribbean monk seal	200
2 Mediterranean monk seal	300–400
3 Juan Fernandez fur seal	750
4 West Indian manatee	1,000
5 Guadeloupe fur seal	1,600
6 New Zealand fur seal	2,000
7= Hooker's sea lion	4,000
7= Right whale	4,400
9 Fraser's dolphin	7,800
10 Amazon manatee	8,000

The hunting of seals for their fur and of whales for oil and other products, combined in many instances with the depletion of their natural food resources by the fishing industry, has resulted in a sharp decline in the population of many marine mammals. Populations of some species of seal formerly numbering millions have shrunk to a few thousands and it has been estimated that the world population of humpback whales has dwindled from 100,000 to 10,000.

COUNTRIES WITH THE MOST ELEPHANTS

Country	Elephants
1 Zaïre	195,000
2 Tanzania	100,000
3 Gabon	76,000
4 Congo	61,000
5 Botswana	51,000
6 Zimbabwe	43,000
7 Zambia	41,000
8 Sudan	40,000
9 Kenya	35,000
10 Cameroon	21,000

All the countries in the Top 10 are in Africa, which in 1987 was reckoned to have a total elephant population of 764,410. India's 20,000 Asian elephants just fail to enter the list and the entire surviving population of Asian elephants in the wild is only a fraction of that of Africa at between 30,000 and 55,000. In addition, about 16,000 tame elephants are found in Burma, India, Thailand, Vietnam, and Cambodia. Estimates of populations of Asian elephants are notoriously unreliable as this species is exclusively a forest animal and its numbers cannot be sampled using aerial survey techniques. The same is true of the forest variety of African elephant, distributed in heavily wooded countries such as Gabon or Zaïre, as distinct from the savannah elephant found in the wide-open spaces of scantily wooded countries including Tanzania and Zimbabwe, and this problem may account for widely varying estimates of elephant populations in such countries.

CREATURES GREAT AND SMALL

Diversity is one of the most impressive features of the animal kingdom, and even within a single species huge variations in size can be encountered. There are practical problems that make measurement difficult – it is virtually impossible to weigh an elephant in the wild, or to estimate the flight speed of a speeding bird, for example. The lists therefore represent "likely averages" based on the informed observations of specialist researchers, rather than one-off assessments or rare and extreme record-breaking cases.

T O P 1 0
HEAVIEST TERRESTRIAL MAMMALS

	Mammal	Length m	ft	Weight kg	lb
1	African elephant	7.2	23.6	5,000	11,023
2	Great Indian rhinoceros	4.2	13.8	4,000	8,818
3	Hippopotamus	4.9	16.1	2,000	4,409
4	Giraffe	5.8	19.0	1,200	2,646
5	American bison	3.9	12.8	1,000	2,205
6	Grizzly bear	3.0	9.8	780	1,720
7	Arabian camel (dromedary)	3.0	9.8	600	1,323
8	Moose	3.0	9.8	595	1,312
9	Tiger	2.8	9.2	300	661
10	Gorilla	2.0	6.6	220	485

The list excludes domesticated cattle and horses. It also avoids comparing close kin such as the African and Indian elephants, highlighting instead the sumo stars within distinctive large mammal groups such as the bears, deer, big cats, primates, and bovines (ox-like mammals). Sizes are not necessarily the top of the known range: records exist, for instance, of African elephant specimens weighing more than 6,000 kg/13,228 lb.

T O P 1 0
HEAVIEST PRIMATES

	Primate	Length* cm	in	Weight kg	lb
1	Gorilla	200	79	220	485
2	Man	177	70	77	170
3	Orangutan	137	54	75	165
4	Chimpanzee	92	36	50	110
5=	Baboon	100	39	45	99
5=	Mandrill	95	37	45	99
7	Gelada baboon	75	30	25	55
8	Proboscis monkey	76	30	24	53
9	Hanuman langur	107	42	20	44
10	Siamang gibbon	90	35	13	29

* Excluding tail.

The largest primates (including Man) and all the apes are rooted in the Old World (Africa, Asia, and Europe): only one member of a New World species of monkeys (the Guatemalan howler at 91 cm/36 in; 9 kg/20 lb) is a close contender for the Top 10. The difference between the prosimians (primitive primates), great apes, lesser apes, and monkeys is more to do with shape than size, though the great apes mostly top the table anyway. Lower down the list, the longer, skinnier, and lighter forms of the lemurs, langurs, gibbons, and monkeys, designed for serious monkeying around in trees, send the length column haywire.

T O P 1 0
LARGEST CARNIVORES

	Animal	Length m	ft	in	Weight kg	lb
1	Southern elephant seal	6.5	21	4	3,500	7,716
2	Walrus	3.8	12	6	1,200	2,646
3	Steller sea lion	3.0	9	8	1,100	2,425
4	Grizzly bear	3.0	9	8	780	1,720
5	Polar bear	2.5	8	2	700	1,543
6	Tiger	2.8	9	2	300	661
7	Lion	1.9	6	3	250	551
8	American black bear	1.8	6	0	227	500
9	Giant panda	1.5	5	0	160	353
10	Spectacled bear	1.8	6	0	140	309

Of the 273 species in the mammalian order Carnivora or meat-eaters, many (including its largest representatives on land, the bears) are in fact omnivorous and around 40 specialize in eating fish or insects. All, however, share a common ancestry indicated by the butchers-knife form of their canine teeth. As the Top 10 would otherwise consist exclusively of seals and related marine carnivores, only three representatives have been included in order to enable the terrestrial heavyweight division to make an appearance. The polar bear is probably the largest land carnivore if shoulder height (when the animal is on all fours) is taken into account: it tops an awesome 1.60 m/5 ft 3 in, compared with the 1.20 m/4 ft of its nearest rival, the grizzly. The common (or least) weasel is probably the smallest carnivore: small specimens are less than 17 cm/7 in long, not counting the tail, and can weigh as little as 80g (less than 3 oz).

T O P 1 0

LONGEST ANIMALS

	Animal	Length		
		m	ft	in
1	Blue whale	33.5	110	0
2	Royal python	10.7	35	0
3	Tapeworm	10.0	32	10
4	Whale shark	9.8	32	2
5	African elephant	7.2 *	23	6
6	Crocodile	5.9	19	5
7	Giraffe	5.8	19	0
8	Hippopotamus	4.9	16	1
9	Arabian camel (dromedary)	4.1	13	6
10=	Indian bison	3.4	11	2
10=	White rhinoceros	3.4	11	2

* Trunk to tail.

The "lion's mane" jellyfish, which lives in the Arctic Ocean, has tentacles as long as 40 m/131 ft trailing behind it, but its "body" is relatively small, and it has thus not been included. Only one fish (the whale shark is a fish, not a true whale) and one snake have been included.

T O P 1 0

SMALLEST MAMMALS

	Mammal	Weight		Length	
		gm	oz	cm	in
1	Kitti's hognosed bat	2.0	0.07	2.9	1.1
2	Pygmy shrew	1.5	0.05	3.6	1.4
3	Pipistrelle bat	3.0	0.11	4.0	1.6
4	Little brown bat	8.0	0.28	4.0	1.6
5	Masked shrew	2.4	0.08	4.5	1.8
6	Southern blossom bat	12.0	0.42	5.0	2.0
7	Harvest mouse	5.0	0.18	5.8	2.3
8	Pygmy glider	12.0	0.42	6.0	2.4
9	House mouse	12.0	0.42	6.4	2.5
10	Common shrew	5.0	0.18	6.5	2.5

The pygmy glider and another that does not quite make the Top 10, the pygmy possum, are marsupials, more closely related to kangaroos than to anything else in this list. Some classifications exclude marsupials from the mammal class. Among other contenders for the small world are the water shrew (12.0 gm/0.42 oz; 7.0 cm/2.8 in) and bank vole (15.0 gm/0.53 oz; 8.0 cm/3.2 in). The Kitti's hognosed bat is represented only by a few specimens in museum collections, so it may well have been short-changed.

T O P 1 0

LONGEST SNAKES

	Snake	Maximum length	
		m	ft
1	Royal python	10.7	35
2	Anaconda	8.5	28
3	Indian python	7.6	25
4	Diamond python	6.4	21
5	King cobra	5.8	19
6	Boa constrictor	4.9	16
7	Bushmaster	3.7	12
8	Giant brown snake	3.4	11
9	Diamondback rattlesnake	2.7	9
10	Indigo or gopher snake	2.4	8

Although the South American anaconda is sometimes claimed to be the longest snake, this has not been authenticated and it seems that the python remains entitled to claim pre-eminence.

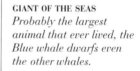

GIANT OF THE SEAS
Probably the largest animal that ever lived, the Blue whale dwarfs even the other whales.

T O P 1 0

HEAVIEST MARINE MAMMALS

	Mammal	Length		Weight			Mammal	Length		Weight
		m	ft	(tonnes)				m	ft	(tonnes)
1	Blue whale	33.5	110.0	130.0		9	Northern elephant seal	5.8	19.0	3.4
2	Fin whale	25.0	82.0	45.0		10	Pilot whale	6.4	21.0	2.9
3	Right whale	17.5	57.4	40.0						
4	Sperm whale	18.0	59.0	36.0						
5	Gray whale	14.0	46.0	32.7						
6	Humpback whale	15.0	49.2	26.5						
7	Baird's whale	5.5	18.0	11.0						
8	Southern elephant seal	6.5	21.3	3.6						

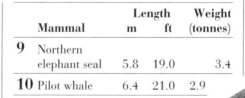

ANIMAL RECORD BREAKERS

DEADLIEST SNAKES IN THE WORLD

Most people fear snakes, but only a few dozen of the 3,000-odd snake species that exist can cause serious harm and many more are beneficial because they prey on vermin and on other snake species of worse repute. The strength of a snake's venom can be measured, but this does not indicate how dangerous it may be: the Australian smooth-scaled snake, for example, is believed to be the most venomous land snake, but no human victims have ever been recorded. The Top 10 takes account of the degree of threat posed by those snakes that have a record of causing fatalities. This is approximate, since such factors as the amount of venom injected and the victim's resistance can vary greatly.

	Species	Native region
1=	Taipan	Australia and New Guinea

Mortality is nearly 100 per cent unless antivenin is administered promptly.

	Species	Native region
1=	Black mamba	Southern and Central Africa

Mortality nearly 100 per cent without antivenin.

3	Tiger snake	Australia

Very high mortality without antivenin.

4	Common krait	South Asia

Up to 50 per cent mortality even with antivenin.

5	Death adder	Australia

Over 50 per cent mortality without antivenin.

	Species	Native region
6	Yellow or Cape cobra	Southern Africa

The most dangerous type of cobra, with high mortality.

7	King cobra	India and Southeast Asia

At 4.9 m/16 ft long, the king cobra is the largest poisonous snake in the world. It also injects the most venom into its victims.

8=	Bushmaster	Central and South America
8=	Green mamba	Africa
10	Coral snake	North, Central and South America

MAMMALS WITH THE LARGEST LITTERS

	Mammal	Average litter
1	Tailless tenrec	21
2	Golden hamster	11
3	Ermine	10
4	Coypu	8.5
5=	European hedgehog	7
5=	African hunting dog	7
7=	Meadow vole	6.5
7=	Wild boar	6.5
9=	Wolf	6
9=	Black-backed jackal	6

These are averages; extreme examples, for instance of pigs with litters of 30 or more, have been recorded. Although the tiny tenrec from Madagascar has similarly produced as many as 31 in a single litter, average mammalian litter sizes are minute when compared with those of other animals. Fish commonly lay more than 10,000 eggs at a time and many amphibians more than 1,000. The most staggeringly prolific creature of all is probably the Ocean sunfish, which lays as many as 300,000,000 eggs.

MAMMALS WITH THE LONGEST GESTATION PERIODS

	Mammal	Average gestation (days)
1	African elephant	660
2	Asiatic elephant	600
3	Baird's beaked whale	520
4	White rhinoceros	490
5	Walrus	480
6	Giraffe	460
7	Tapir	400
8	Arabian camel (dromedary)	390
9	Fin whale	370
10	Llama	360

The 480-day gestation of the walrus includes a delay of up to five months while the fertilized embryo is held as a blastocyst (a sphere of cells) but is not implanted until later in the wall of the uterus. This option enables offspring to be produced at the most favourable time of the year. Human gestation (ranging from 253 to 303 days) is exceeded not only by the Top 10 mammals but also by others including the porpoise, horse and water buffalo.

MAMMALS WITH THE SHORTEST GESTATION PERIODS

	Mammal	Average gestation (days)
1	Short-nosed bandicoot*	12
2	Opossum*	13
3	Shrew	14
4	Golden hamster	15
5=	Lemming	20
5=	Mouse	20
7	Rat	21
8	Gerbil	24
9=	Mole	28
9=	Rabbit	28

* These animals are marsupials. Their young are not fully developed when they are born and they are transferred into a "pouch" to continue their development.

TOP 10

FASTEST MAMMALS IN THE WORLD

	Mammal	Maximum recorded speed km/h	mph
1	Cheetah	105	65
2	Pronghorn antelope	89	55
3=	Mongolian gazelle	80	50
3=	Springbok	80	50
5=	Grant's gazelle	76	47
5=	Thomson's gazelle	76	47
7	Brown hare	72	45
8	Horse	69	43
9=	Greyhound	68	42
9=	Red deer	68	42

Although some authorities have alleged higher speeds, this list is based on data from reliable sources using accurate methods of measurement. In addition to these speeds, estimated over distances of up to 0.4 km/¼ mile, charging lions can achieve 80 km/h/50 mph over very short distances, while various members of the antelope family, wildebeests, elks, dogs, coyotes, foxes, hyenas, zebras and Mongolian wild asses, have all been credited with unsustained spurts of 64 km/h/40 mph or more. Just failing to make the list is the Sei whale, the fastest of the large sea mammals at 64 km/h/40.2 mph.

TOP 10

FASTEST FISH IN THE WORLD

	Fish	Maximum recorded speed km/h	mph
1	Sailfish	110	68
2	Marlin	80	50
3	Bluefin tuna	74	46
4	Yellowfin tuna	70	44
5	Blue shark	69	43
6	Wahoo	66	41
7=	Bonefish	64	40
7=	Swordfish	64	40
9	Tarpon	56	35
10	Tiger shark	53	33

TOP 10

LONGEST-LIVED ANIMALS

(*Excluding humans*)

	Animal	Maximum age (years)
1	Quahog (marine clam)	up to 200
2	Giant tortoise	150
3	Greek tortoise	110
4	Killer whale	90
5	European eel	88
6	Lake sturgeon	82
7	Sea anemone	80
8	Elephant	78
9	Freshwater mussel	75
10	Andean condor	70

The ages of animals in the wild are difficult to determine with accuracy as the precise birth and death dates of relatively few long-lived animals have ever been recorded. There are clues, such as annual growth of shells, teeth, and, in the case of whales, even ear wax. The Top 10 represents documented maximum ages of animals attained by more than one example – although there may well be extreme cases of animals exceeding these life spans. Although there are alleged instances of parrots living to ages of 80 years or more, few stand up to scrutiny.

TOP 10

LAZIEST ANIMALS IN THE WORLD

	Animal	Average hours of sleep
1	Koala	22
2	Sloth	20
3=	Armadillo	19
3=	Opossum	19
5	Lemur	16
6=	Hamster	14
6=	Squirrel	14
8=	Cat	13
8=	Pig	13
10	Spiny anteater	12

The list excludes periods of hibernation, which can last up to several months among creatures such as the ground squirrel, marmot and brown bear. At the other end of the scale comes the frantic shrew, which has to hunt and eat constantly or perish: it literally has no time for sleep. The incredible swift contrives to sleep on the wing, "turning off" alternate halves of its brain for shifts of two hours or more. Flight control is entrusted to whichever hemisphere is on duty at the time.

TOP 10

MOST INTELLIGENT MAMMALS

1	Man
2	Chimpanzee
3	Gorilla
4	Orang-utan
5	Baboon
6	Gibbon
7	Monkey
8	Smaller toothed whale
9	Dolphin
10	Elephant

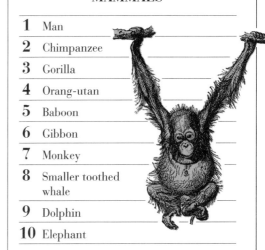

This list is based on research conducted by Edward O. Wilson, Professor of Zoology at Harvard University, who defined intelligence as speed and extent of learning performance over a wide range of tasks, also taking account of the ratio of the animal's brain size to its body bulk. It may come as a surprise that the dog does not make the Top 10, and that if Man is excluded, No. 10 becomes the pig.

BIRDS

FASTEST BIRDS IN THE WORLD

	Bird	Maximum recorded speed km/h	mph
1	Spine-tailed swift	171	106
2	Frigate bird	153	95
3	Spur-winged goose	142	88
4	Red-breasted merganser	129	80
5	White-rumped swift	124	77
6	Canvasback duck	116	72
7	Eider duck	113	70
8	Teal	109	68
9=	Mallard	105	65
9=	Pintail	105	65

Until aeroplane pilots cracked 306 km/h/ 190 mph in 1919, birds were the fastest animals on Earth: stooping (diving) peregrine falcons clock up speeds approaching 298 km/h/ 185 mph. However, most comparisons of air speed in birds rule out diving or wind-assisted flight: most small birds on migration can manage a ground speed of 97 km/h/60 mph to 113 km/h/70 mph if there is even a moderate following wind. This list therefore picks out star performers among the medium- to large-sized birds (mainly waterfowl) that do not need help from wind or gravity to hit their top speed.

RAREST BIRDS IN THE WORLD

	Bird	Pairs reported
1	Echo parakeet (Mauritius)	1
2	Mauritius kestrel	3
3	Mauritius parakeet	4
4	Cuban ivory-billed woodpecker	8
5	Madagascar sea eagle	10
6=	Pink pigeon (Mauritius)	12
6=	Magpie robin (Seychelles)	12
8	Imperial Amazon parrot	15
9	Siberian crane	25
10	Tomba bowerbird (Papua New Guinea)	30

Several rarer bird species are known from single sightings but are assumed to be extinct in the absence of records of breeding pairs. With nowhere to seek refuge, rare species come under pressure on islands such as Mauritius, where the Dodo met its fate in the 18th century. Petrels spend much of their lives far from land, so their numbers are virtually impossible to determine.

LARGEST FLIGHTED BIRDS

	Bird	Weight kg	lb	oz
1	Great bustard	20.9	46	1
2	Trumpeter swan	16.8	37	1
3	Mute swan	16.3	35	15
4=	Albatross	15.8	34	13
4=	Whooper swan	15.8	34	13
6	Manchurian crane	14.9	32	14
7	Kori bustard	13.6	30	0
8	Grey pelican	13.0	28	11
9	Black vulture	12.5	27	8
10	Griffon vulture	12.0	26	7

Wing size does not necessarily correspond to weight in flighted birds. The 4-m/13-ft wingspan of the marabou stork beats all the birds listed here, yet its body weight is usually no heavier than any of these. When laden with a meal of carrion, however, the marabou can double its weight and needs all the lift it can get to take off. It usually has to wait until dinner is digested.

UK GARDEN BIRDS

	Bird			Bird
1	Blue tit		6	House sparrow
2	Blackbird		7	Dunnock
3	Robin		8	Chaffinch
4	Starling		9	Greenfinch
5	Great tit		10	Collared dove

MOST ENDANGERED BIRDS IN THE UK*

	Bird			Bird
1	Roseate tern		6	Knot
2	Golden eagle		7	Dunlin
3	Red grouse		8	Bar-tailed godwit
4	Brent goose		9	Redshank
5	Pintail		10	Bittern

* *Based on data supplied by the Royal Society for the Protection of Birds.*

TOP 10

LARGEST FLIGHTLESS BIRDS

	Bird	Weight			Height	
		kg	lb	oz	cm	in
1	Ostrich	156.5	345	0	274.3	108.0
2	Emu	40.0	88	3	152.4	60.0
3	Cassowary	33.5	73	14	152.4	60.0
4	Rhea	25.0	55	2	137.1	54.0
5	Kiwi	29.0	63	15	114.3	45.0
6	Emperor penguin	29.4	64	13	114.0	44.9
7	King penguin	15.8	34	13	94.0	37.0
8	Southern gentoo	5.4	11	14	71.0	28.0
9=	Adelie penguin	4.9	10	13	71.0	28.0
9=	Magellanic penguin	4.9	10	13	71.0	28.0

There are 46 living and 16 recently extinct flightless birds on record. The largest bird in recorded history was the flightless "Elephant bird" (*Aepyornis*) of Madagascar. It weighed around 438 kg/966 lb and stood 3 m/10 ft tall. Its eggs were nearly 38 cm/15 in long and weighed over 18 kg/40 lb. The smallest known bird, the Bee hummingbird, weighs 1.7 gm/0.06 oz and measures 6.4 cm/2.5 in from beak to tail. Almost 100,000 bee hummingbirds would be needed to balance one ostrich on a pair of scales.

OSTRICH
An ostrich, when running, can reach a speed of 64 km/h/40 mph.

TOP 10

RAREST BREEDING BIRDS RECORDED IN THE UK

	Bird	Pairs
1=	Red-backed shrike	1 (0)
1=	Scarlet rosefinch	1 (0)
3	Crane	1 (1)
4=	Serin	2 (0)
4=	Parrot crossbill	2 (0)
6	Brambling	2 (1)
7=	Red-necked grebe	3 (3)
7=	Temminck's stint	3 (3)
9	Purple sandpiper	4 (1)
10	Whooper swan	5 (2)

The table shows maximum numbers of nesting pairs recorded in any breeding season during the survey period 1988–91, followed (in brackets) by the minimum. The snowy owl would have headed the list, with a single nest recorded in one survey year, but though the female owl in question laid eggs, no male was present and the eggs proved infertile.

TOP 10

COMMONEST BREEDING BIRDS RECORDED IN THE UK

	Bird	Pairs
1	Wren	7,100,000
2	Chaffinch	5,400,000
3	House sparrow	4,600,000
4	Blackbird	4,400,000
5	Robin	4,200,000
6	Blue tit	3,300,000
7	Woodpigeon	2,600,000
8	Willow warbler	2,300,000
9=	Dunnock	2,000,000
9=	Skylark	2,000,000

HOUSE SPARROW
This adaptable little bird is found worldwide, in urban as well as rural areas.

TOP 10

LARGEST BIRDS IN THE UK

	Bird	Length, beak to tail	
		cm	in
1	Mute swan	145–160	57–63
2	Bewick's swan	116–128	46–50
3	Canada goose	up to 110	up to 43
4	Grey heron	90–100	35–39
5	Cormorant	84–98	33–39
6	Gannet	86–96	34–38
7	Golden eagle	76–91	30–36
8	Capercaillie (male)	82–90	32–35
9	Greylag goose	71–89	28–35
10	Great black-backed gull	69–76	27–30

The Whooper swan once qualified for equal first position on this list, but as it no longer breeds in the British Isles it has been excluded, as has another former resident, the White-tailed sea eagle (69–91 cm/27–36 in). Pheasants sometimes measure 91 cm/36 in, but more than half the total is tail.

CATS, DOGS, AND OTHER PETS

TYPES OF PET IN THE UK

	Pet	% of households owning
1	Dog	26.9
2	Cat	21.5
3	Goldfish	9.1
4	Rabbit	4.5
5	Budgerigar	4.2
6	Tropical fish	2.9
7	Other caged bird(s)	2.8
8	Hamster	2.3
9	Guinea pig	1.5
10	Canary	1.2

This Top 10 is based on the results of a national poll where, if the miscellaneous category "Other caged bird(s)" is deleted, No. 10 becomes horse/pony/donkey (0.9 per cent). A similar survey conducted in 1993 by *Animal World*, the RSPCA's magazine for its junior members (57 per cent of whom are aged between 11 and 13), placed goldfish at the top by a long margin (33 per cent of respondents owned one or more), followed by cats (19 per cent), dogs (13 per cent), and rabbits (11 per cent) while 4 per cent owned a pet in a category described as "Exotic/unusual", which includes such creatures as stick insects, snails, and ferrets.

PETS' NAMES IN THE UK

(*Based on the RSPCA's 1993 Animal World magazine survey*)

1	Fluffy	**6**	Gizmo
2	Sooty	**7**	Charlie
3	Ben	**8**	Flopsy
4	Sammy	**9**	Max
5	Snowy	**10**	Sandy

DOGS' NAMES IN THE UK

	Female	Male
1	Sheba	Ben
2	Sam(antha)	Max
3	Bess	Sam
4	Gemma	Pip
5	Rosie	Duke
6	Megan	Prince
7	Lucky	Captain
8	Sandy	Tyson
9	Bonnie	Butch
10	Cindy	Oscar

DOG BREEDS IN THE UK

	Breed	No. registered by Kennel Club
1	Labrador	25,261
2	German Shepherd (Alsatian)	19,960
3	Golden Retriever	14,685
4	West Highland White Terrier	14,468
5	Cavalier King Charles Spaniel	13,705
6	Yorkshire Terrier	13,041
7	Cocker Spaniel	12,815
8	English Springer Spaniel	11,148
9	Boxer	8,139
10	Staffordshire Bull Terrier	5,729

As in the previous year, the 10 principal breeds of dogs registered by the Kennel Club in 1993 remained identical, but with some slight adjustments to the order, such as Yorkshire terriers dropping from 3rd to 6th place, replaced by Golden Retrievers, moving up from 5th position. Independent surveys of dog ownership present a similar picture, though with certain other popular breeds (among them Jack Russell, Border Collie, and Poodle) making a stronger showing than in the Kennel Club's list. Registrations of certain breeds have declined markedly. Rottweilers, in 6th place in 1988 with 9,088 registered, were 18th in 1993, with just 2,456.

DOGS' NAMES IN THE USA

1	Lady
2	King
3	Duke
4	Peppy
5	Prince
6	Pepper
7	Snoopy
8	Princess
9	Heidi
10=	Sam
10=	Coco

A recent study of male and female names appearing on dog licences in the USA produced a list that has only "Prince" and "Sam" in common with the British Top 10s. The same American list also revealed a number of bizarre dogs' names, including Beowulf, Bikini, Fag, Rembrandt, and Twit. Lassie, popularized by films from 1942 onwards, has declined to 82nd position, while Rover is in a humble 161st place.

DOG BREEDS IN THE USA

	Breed	No. registered by American Kennel Club
1	Cocker Spaniel	111,636
2	Labrador Retriever	91,107
3	Poodle	78,600
4	Golden Retriever	64,269
5	German Shepherd (Alsatian)	58,422
6	Rottweiler	51,291
7	Chow Chow	50,150
8	Dachshund	44,305
9	Beagle	43,314
10	Miniature Schnauzer	42,175

TOP 10

MOST INTELLIGENT DOG BREEDS

1 Border Collie

2 Poodle

3= German Shepherd (Alsatian)

3= Golden Retriever

5 Doberman Pinscher

6 Shetland Sheepdog

7 Labrador Retriever

8 Papillon

9 Rottweiler

10 Australian Cattle Dog

For his 1994 book *The Intelligence of Dogs*, American psychology professor and pet trainer Stanley Coren put 133 breeds of dog through a series of tests of obedience and work, ranking them accordingly. His canine IQ examinations produced some surprising – and to their devotees, controversial – results. The Bloodhound, the doggy Sherlock Holmes, was in 128th place, the bulldog, symbol of British might, in 131st place, and the Afghan Hound, the dizzy blonde of the canine world, bottom of the class.

TOP 10

BRANDS OF PETFOOD IN THE UK

1 Whiskas

2 Pedigree Chum

3 Felix

4 Arthur's

5 Pal

6 Choosy

7 Friskies

8 Prime

9 Kit-e-Kat

10 Cesar

Specific sales figures for the Top 10 brands are a trade secret, but it is estimated that in 1993 British owners of pets (almost entirely cats and dogs) spent a total of £557,200,000 on well over 1,000,000 tonnes of petfood.

TOP 10

PEDIGREE CAT BREEDS IN THE USA

	Breed	Total registered
1	Persian	52,837
2	Siamese	3,188
3	Maine Coon	2,844
4	Abyssinian	2,542
5	Exotic Short Hair	1,329
6	Oriental Short Hair	1,236
7	Scottish Fold	1,205
8	Burmese	1,065
9	American Short Hair	1,050
10	Birman	915

The Cat Fanciers' Association of the US is the world's largest pedigree cat registry. In 1991 it registered 75,525 cats of 35 different breeds, which represents a 10.86 per cent decline in total numbers from 84,729 in 1990. Although the Top 10 tends to include the same breeds from year to year, there are some changes in popularity – in 1991 Abyssinians were overtaken by Maine Coon cats, for example. Traditional, Pointed Pattern, and Colorpoint Carrier Persians were by far the most popular breed, with Oriental Longhairs the rarest.

TOP 10

CATS' NAMES IN THE USA

	Female	Male
1	Samantha	Tiger/Tigger
2	Misty	Smokey
3	Patches	Pepper
4	Cali/Calico	Max/Maxwell
5	Muffin	Simon
6	Angel/Angela	Snoopy
7	Ginger	Morris
8	Tiger/Tigger	Mickey
9	Princess	Rusty/Rusti
10	Punkin/Pumpkin	Boots/Bootsie

TOP 10

PEDIGREE CAT BREEDS IN THE UK

(Based on a total of 33,436 cats registered with the Governing Council of the Cat Fancy in 1993; 1992: 32,767)

	Breed	No. registered by Cat Fancy 1992	1993
1	Persian Long Hair	11,107	10,991
2	Siamese	5,618	5,471
3	Burmese	3,808	3,947
4	British Short Hair	3,588	3,727
5	Birman	2,046	2,152
6	Oriental Short Hair	1,275	1,360
7	Maine Coon	975	1,123
8	Exotic Short Hair	607	646
9	Abyssinian	662	603
10	Devon Rex	447	455

TOP 10

CATS' NAMES IN THE UK

(Based on an RSPCA survey conducted during National Pet Week, 1991)

1 Sooty

2 Tigger

3 Tiger

4 Smokey

5 Ginger

6 Tom

7 Fluffy

8 Lucy

9 Sam

10 Lucky

LIVESTOCK

TOP 10

TYPES OF LIVESTOCK IN THE WORLD

	Animal	World total
1	Chickens	11,279,000,000
2	Cattle	1,284,188,000
3	Sheep	1,138,363,000
4	Pigs	864,096,000
5	Ducks	580,000,000
6	Goats	574,181,000
7	Turkeys	259,000,000
8	Buffaloes	147,520,000
9	Horses	60,843,000
10	Donkeys	44,270,000

The world chicken population is more than double the human population, while the world's cattle population outnumbers the population of China. There are more pigs in the world than the entire population of India, enough turkeys for every US citizen to have one each for Thanksgiving, and sufficient horses for everyone in the UK to go riding.

TOP 10

CHICKEN COUNTRIES

	Country	Chickens
1	China	2,179,000,000
2	USA	1,437,000,000
3	Russia	628,000,000
4	Indonesia	600,000,000
5	Brazil	570,000,000
6	India	410,000,000
7	Japan	335,000,000
8	Mexico	282,000,000
9	Ukraine	233,000,000
10	France	208,000,000
	World total	*11,279,000,000*

The Top 10 countries have 61 per cent of the world's chicken population. In the UK the estimated chicken population of 124,000,000 outnumbers the human population more than twice over.

TOP 10

CATTLE COUNTRIES

	Country	Cattle
1	India	192,650,000
2	Brazil	153,000,000
3	USA	99,559,000
4	China	82,760,000
5	Russia	54,677,000
6	Argentina	50,020,000
7	Ethiopia	31,000,000
8	Mexico	30,157,000
9	Colombia	24,772,000
10=	Bangladesh	23,700,000
10=	Ukraine	23,700,000
	World total	*1,284,188,000*

The Top 10 – or in this instance 11 – countries own almost 60 per cent of the world's cattle. The UK's cattle population is 11,623,000, equivalent to more than one animal for every five people.

TOP 10

GOAT COUNTRIES

	Country	Goats
1	India	117,000,000
2	China	95,032,000
3	Pakistan	38,564,000
4	Nigeria	24,000,000
5	Iran	23,500,000
6	Sudan	18,700,000
7	Ethiopia	18,100,000
8	Bangladesh	18,000,000
9	Brazil	12,000,000
10	Indonesia	11,400,000
	World total	*574,181,000*

The goat is one of the most widely distributed of all domesticated animals. Its resilience to diseases such as the tuberculosis that affect cattle and its adaptability to harsh conditions make it ideally suited to less developed countries.

TOP 10

TURKEY COUNTRIES

	Country	Turkeys
1	USA	90,000,000
2	France	32,000,000
3	Russia	24,000,000
4	Italy	23,000,000
5=	Ukraine	10,000,000
5=	UK	10,000,000
7=	Brazil	6,000,000
7=	Mexico	6,000,000
7=	Portugal	6,000,000
10=	Argentina	5,000,000
10=	Canada	5,000,000
	World total	*259,000,000*

Some 88 per cent of the world's turkeys are found in the Top 10 countries – with the largest number, appropriately, in North America, their area of origin.

TOP 10

BUFFALO COUNTRIES

	Country	Buffaloes
1	India	78,550,000
2	China	21,983,000
3	Pakistan	18,273,000
4	Thailand	4,793,000
5	Indonesia	3,400,000
6	Nepal	3,058,000
7	Egypt	3,036,000
8	Vietnam	2,867,000
9	Philippines	2,569,000
10	Myanmar (Burma)	2,099,000
	World total	*147,520,000*

More than 95 per cent of the world's total buffalo population resides in the Top 10 countries. Only two European countries have significant herds: Romania with 180,000 and Italy (where buffalo milk is used to make mozzarella cheese) with 83,000.

TOP 10
SHEEP COUNTRIES

	Country	Sheep
1	Australia	146,820,000
2	China	111,143,000
3	New Zealand	53,500,000
4	Russia	52,535,000
5	Iran	45,000,000
6	India	44,407,000
7	Turkey	40,433,000
8	Kazakhstan	33,908,000
9	South Africa	32,100,000
10	UK	28,932,000
	World total	*1,138,363,000*

This is one of the few world lists in which the UK ranks considerably higher than the US, which has only 10,750,000 head of sheep. The Falkland Islands have 713,000 sheep to a human population of 2,121 (336 sheep per person), followed by New Zealand (16 sheep per person).

TOP 10
HORSE COUNTRIES

	Country	Horses
1	China	10,201,000
2	Brazil	6,200,000
3	Mexico	6,180,000
4	USA	5,450,000
5	Argentina	3,300,000
6	Ethiopia	2,750,000
7	Russia	2,610,000
8	Mongolia	2,300,000
9	Colombia	2,006,000
10	Kazakhstan	1,523,000
	World total	*60,843,000*

Mongolia makes an appearance in few Top 10 lists – but here it scores doubly as it is also the only country in the world where humans are outnumbered by horses. Throughout the world horse population has declined as they have been replaced by motor vehicles.

TOP 10
PIG COUNTRIES

	Country	Pigs
1	China	379,739,000
2	USA	57,684,000
3	Russia	35,384,000
4	Brazil	33,050,000
5	Germany	26,063,000
6	Poland	22,086,000
7	Ukraine	17,800,000
8	Spain	17,240,000
9	Mexico	16,502,000
10	Netherlands	13,727,000
	World total	*864,096,000*

The distribution of the world's pig population is determined by cultural, religious and dietary factors – few pigs are found in African and Islamic countries, for example – so there is a disproportionate concentration of pigs in those countries that do not have such prohibitions.

TOP 10
DONKEY COUNTRIES

	Country	Donkeys
1	China	11,200,000
2	Ethiopia	5,200,000
3	Pakistan	3,650,000
4	Mexico	3,189,000
5	Iran	1,935,000
6	Egypt	1,550,000
7	India	1,500,000
8	Brazil	1,350,000
9	Afghanistan	1,300,000
10	Nigeria	1,000,000
	World total	*44,270,000*

The donkey is used extensively throughout the world as a beast of burden, although its role in such countries as the UK (with an estimated donkey population of around 10,000) has been largely reduced to providing rides for children.

TOP 10
DUCK COUNTRIES

	Country	Ducks
1	China	381,000,000
2=	India	30,000,000
2=	Vietnam	30,000,000
4	France	18,000,000
5	Thailand	17,000,000
6	Bangladesh	12,000,000
7	Philippines	9,000,000
8	Egypt	8,000,000
9=	Mexico	7,000,000
9=	Poland	7,000,000
	World total	*580,000,000*

While it is extraordinary to consider that 66 per cent of the world's domestic ducks live in China, an examination of the menu of any Chinese restaurant reveals the duck's major role in oriental cuisine. In contrast, British ducks number barely 2,000,000.

DID YOU KNOW

"THE SHIP OF THE DESERT": CAMEL FACTS

The camel is outside the livestock Top 10, but has a respectable world population of over 17,000,000.

There are over 10,000,000 camels in the top five countries – Somalia, Sudan, India, Pakistan, and Ethiopia.

Camels were native to North America about 2,000,000 years ago and in the 19th century lived in the wild in the south-west and western US, descendants of a herd introduced by the government in 1856.

"The straw that broke the camel's back" is a graphic but untrue saying: camels can carry enormous loads but if they are over-laden will simply refuse to get up.

Camel-hair brushes are made not from camel hair but the hair from squirrels' tails.

The camel is a relative of the South American llama.

FRUIT SALAD

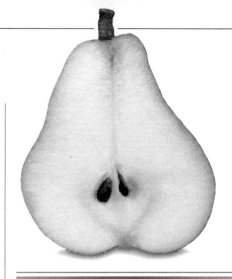

T O P 1 0

FRUIT CROPS IN THE WORLD

	Crop	Annual production (tonnes)
1	Grapes	60,655,000
2	Bananas	49,630,000
3	Apples	43,087,000
4	Coconuts	41,044,000
5	Plantains	26,797,000
6	Mangoes	16,987,000
7	Pears	10,692,000
8	Pineapples	10,490,000
9	Peaches & nectarines	10,076,000
10	Oranges	8,465,000

T O P 1 0

COCONUT-PRODUCING COUNTRIES

	Country	Annual production (tonnes)
1	Indonesia	13,015,000
2	Philippines	8,465,000
3	India	7,430,000
4	Sri Lanka	1,750,000
5	Thailand	1,353,000
6	Malaysia	1,087,000
7	Vietnam	1,050,000
8	Mexico	989,000
9	Brazil	878,000
10	Papua New Guinea	780,000
	World total	41,044,000

T O P 1 0

PEAR-PRODUCING COUNTRIES

	Country	Annual production (tonnes)
1	China	2,830,000
2	Italy	1,135,000
3	USA	862,000
4	Spain	602,000
5	Germany	537,000
6	Japan	452,000
7	Argentina	420,000
8	Turkey	415,000
9	France	394,000
10	Turkey	370,000
	World total	10,692,000

T O P 1 0

GRAPE-PRODUCING COUNTRIES

	Country	Annual production (tonnes)
1	Italy	10,178,000
2	France	8,514,000
3	Spain	5,676,000
4	USA	5,508,000
5	Turkey	3,460,000
6	Argentina	1,821,000
7	Iran	1,650,000
8=	Portugal	1,450,000
8=	South Africa	1,450,000
10	Greece	1,300,000
	World total	60,655,000

T O P 1 0

BANANA-PRODUCING COUNTRIES

	Country	Annual production (tonnes)
1	India	7,000,000
2	Brazil	5,650,000
3	Philippines	3,900,000
4	Ecuador	3,600,000
5	Indonesia	2,500,000
6	China	2,200,000
7	Colombia	1,900,000
8	Burundi	1,645,000
9	Costa Rica	1,633,000
10	Thailand	1,630,000
	World total	49,630,000

T O P 1 0

MANGO-PRODUCING COUNTRIES

	Country	Annual production (tonnes)
1	India	10,000,000
2	Mexico	1,120,000
3	Pakistan	800,000
4	Indonesia	700,000
5=	China	615,000
5=	Thailand	615,000
7	USA	597,000
8	Brazil	400,000
9	Philippines	290,000
10	Haiti	230,000
	World total	16,987,000

T O P   1 0

APPLE-PRODUCING COUNTRIES

	Country	Annual production (tonnes)
1	USA	4,876,000
2	China	4,817,000
3	Former USSR#	4,500,000
4	Germany	3,206,000
5	Italy	2,402,000
6	France	2,324,000
7	Turkey	2,000,000
8	Poland	1,570,000
9	Iran	1,520,000
10=	Argentina	1,110,000
10=	India	1,110,000
	World total	43,087,000

Figures for post-dissolution USSR not yet available.

Spain and Japan are the only other countries in the world with annual apple production of more than 1,000,000 tonnes. Having steadily declined during the 1980s in the face of cheap imports, the UK's commercial production of apples has recently increased again and in 1992 totalled 377,000 tonnes.

T O P   1 0

ORANGE-PRODUCING COUNTRIES

	Country	Annual production (tonnes)
1	Brazil	19,640,000
2	USA	8,038,000
3	China	5,090,000
4	Mexico	2,850,000
5	Spain	2,724,000
6	India	1,900,000
7	Italy	1,803,000
8	Egypt	1,690,000
9	Iran	1,300,000
10	Pakistan	1,150,000
	World total	57,048,000

During the 1980s, orange production progressively increased from a world total of less than 40,000,000 tonnes. China's production, in particular, rocketed up almost sevenfold during the decade, from under 800,000 tonnes to its present 3rd position in the world league table.

T O P   1 0

PINEAPPLE-PRODUCING COUNTRIES

	Country	Annual production (tonnes)
1	Thailand	1,900,000
2	Philippines	1,170,000
3	China	1,000,000
4	India	820,000
5	Brazil	800,000
6	Vietnam	500,000
7	USA	499,000
8	Indonesia	380,000
9	Colombia	347,000
10	Mexico	299,000
	World total	43,087,000

T O P   1 0

PEACH- AND NECTARINE-PRODUCING COUNTRIES

	Country	Annual production (tonnes)
1	Italy	1,886,000
2	USA	1,419,000
3	Greece	1,120,000
4	Spain	964,000
5	China	932,000
6	France	520,000
7	Former USSR	350,000
8	Turkey	270,000
9	Argentina	250,000
10	Chile	223,000
	World total	10,076,000

T O P   1 0

PLANTAIN-PRODUCING COUNTRIES

	Country	Annual production (tonnes)
1	Uganda	8,099,000
2	Rwanda	2,900,000
3	Colombia	2,745,000
4	Zaïre	1,830,000
5	Nigeria	1,350,000
6	Ghana	1,200,000
7	Côte d'Ivoire	1,170,000
8	Ecuador	930,000
9	Cameroon	860,000
10	Tanzania	794,000
	World total	26,797,000

TOP OF THE CROPS

TOP 10

FOOD CROPS IN THE WORLD

	Country	Annual production (tonnes)
1	Sugar cane	1,104,580,000
2	Wheat	563,649,000
3	Maize	526,410,000
4	Rice	525,475,000
5	Sugar beet	279,991,000
6	Potatoes	268,492,000
7	Barley	160,134,000
8	Cassava	152,218,000
9	Sweet potatoes	128,016,000
10	Soybeans	114,011,000

TOP 10

SUGAR CANE-GROWING COUNTRIES IN THE WORLD

	Country	Annual production (tonnes)
1	Brazil	270,672,000
2	India	249,300,000
3	China	77,548,000
4	Cuba	58,000,000
5	Thailand	46,805,000
6	Mexico	39,955,000
7	Pakistan	38,865,000
8	Australia	29,300,000
9	Colombia	28,930,000
10	Philippines	27,300,000
	World total	1,104,580,000

TOP 10

WHEAT-GROWING COUNTRIES IN THE WORLD

	Country	Annual production (tonnes)
1	China	101,003,000
2	USA	66,920,000
3	India	55,084,000
4	Russia	46,000,000
5	France	32,600,000
6	Canada	29,870,000
7	Ukraine	19,473,000
8	Turkey	19,318,000
9	Kazakhstan	18,500,000
10	Pakistan	15,684,000
	World total	563,649,000

TOP 10

MAIZE-GROWING COUNTRIES IN THE WORLD

	Country	Annual production (tonnes)
1	USA	240,774,000
2	China	95,340,000
3	Brazil	30,619,000
4	Mexico	14,997,000
5	France	14,613,000
6	Argentina	10,699,000
7	India	9,740,000
8	Indonesia	7,947,000
9	Italy	7,170,000
10	Romania	6,829,000
	World total	526,410,000

TOP 10

RICE-GROWING COUNTRIES IN THE WORLD

	Country	Annual production (tonnes)
1	China	188,150,000
2	India	109,511,000
3	Indonesia	47,770,000
4	Bangladesh	27,400,000
5	Vietnam	21,500,000
6	Thailand	18,500,000
7	Myanmar (Burma)	13,771,000
8	Japan	13,225,000
9	Brazil	9,961,000
10	Philippines	9,185,000
	World total	525,475,000

THE STAFF OF LIFE
Developed over millenia from wild grasses, wheat is the second largest food crop in the world. Bread wheat is ground up to make flour that has a high gluten content. This produces an elastic dough that makes light and airy bread. It is the most widely grown form of modern wheat.

T O P 1 0

SUGAR BEET-GROWING COUNTRIES IN THE WORLD

	Country	Annual production (tonnes)
1	France	31,334,000
2	Ukraine	28,546,000
3	Germany	27,150,000
4	USA	26,170,000
5	Russia	25,500,000
6	China	15,010,000
7	Turkey	14,800,000
8	Italy	14,300,000
9	Poland	11,052,000
10	UK	8,500,000
	World total	*279,991,000*

T O P 1 0

POTATO-GROWING COUNTRIES IN THE WORLD

	Country	Annual production (tonnes)
1	Russia	37,800,000
2	China	33,937,000
3	Poland	23,388,000
4	Ukraine	20,427,000
5	USA	18,671,000
6	India	15,500,000
7	Germany	10,975,000
8	Belarus	8,000,000
9	UK	7,882,000
10	Netherlands	7,595,000
	World total	*268,492,000*

T O P 1 0

BARLEY-GROWING COUNTRIES IN THE WORLD

	Country	Annual production (tonnes)
1	Russia	25,500,000
2	Germany	12,196,000
3	Canada	10,919,000
4	France	10,474,000
5	Ukraine	10,106,000
6	USA	9,936,000
7	Kazakhstan	8,000,000
8	UK	7,386,000
9	Turkey	6,900,000
10	Spain	5,995,000
	World total	*160,134,000*

T O P 1 0

CASSAVA-GROWING COUNTRIES IN THE WORLD

	Country	Annual production (tonnes)
1	Brazil	22,652,000
2	Thailand	21,130,000
3	Nigeria	20,000,000
4	Zaïre	18,300,000
5	Indonesia	16,318,000
6	Tanzania	7,111,000
7	India	5,200,000
8	Ghana	4,000,000
9	Uganda	3,780,000
10	China	3,358,000
	World total	*152,218,000*

T O P 1 0

SWEET POTATO-GROWING COUNTRIES IN THE WORLD

	Country	Annual production (tonnes)
1	China	109,200,000
2	Indonesia	2,172,000
3	Vietnam	2,110,000
4	Uganda	1,752,000
5	Japan	1,300,000
6	India	1,220,000
7	Rwanda	770,000
8	Brazil	705,000
9	Burundi	701,000
10	Philippines	670,000
	World total	*128,016,000*

T O P 1 0

SOYBEAN-GROWING COUNTRIES IN THE WORLD

	Country	Annual production (tonnes)
1	USA	59,780,000
2	Brazil	19,161,000
3	Argentina	11,315,000
4	China	9,707,000
5	India	2,950,000
6	Indonesia	1,881,000
7	Italy	1,434,000
8	Canada	1,387,000
9	Paraguay	1,315,000
10	Mexico	670,000
	World total	*114,011,000*

TREE TOPS

T O P   1 0

MOST FORESTED COUNTRIES IN THE WORLD

(By per cent forest cover)

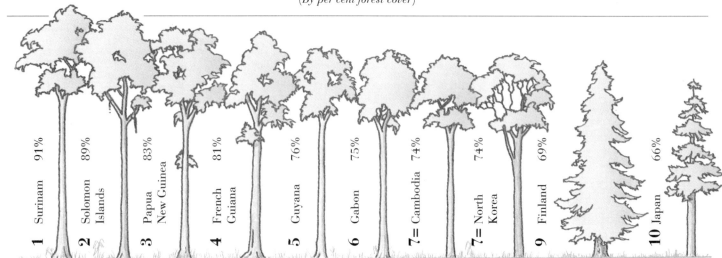

1 Surinam	91%	
2 Solomon Islands	89%	
3 Papua New Guinea	83%	
4 French Guiana	81%	
5 Guyana	76%	
6 Gabon	75%	
7= Cambodia	74%	
7= North Korea	74%	
9 Finland	69%	
10 Japan	66%	

T O P   1 0

TALLEST TREES IN THE UK

(The tallest known example of each of the 10 tallest species)

	Tree	Location	m	ft
1	Grand fir	Strone House, Argyll, Strathclyde	63.4	208
2	Douglas fir	The Hermitage, Dunkeld, Tayside	62.5	205
3	Sitka spruce	Private estate, Strath Earn, Tayside	61.6	202
4=	Giant sequoia	Castle Leod, Strathpeffer, Highland	53.0	174
4=	Low's fir	Diana's Grove, Blair Castle, Strathclyde	53.0	174
6	Norway spruce	Moniack Glenn, Highland	51.8	170
7=	Western hemlock	Benmore Younger Botanic Gardens, Argyll, Strathclyde	51.0	167
7=	Noble fir	Ardkinglas House, Argyll, Strathclyde	51.0	167
9	European silver fir	Armadale Castle, Skye, Highland	50.0	164
10	London plane	Bryanston School, Blandford, Dorset	48.0	157

Based on data supplied by *The Tree Register of the British Isles*.

T O P   1 0

TALLEST TREES IN THE US

(The tallest known example of each of the 10 tallest species)

	Tree	Location	m	ft
1	Coast redwood	Humboldt Redwoods State Park, California	110.6	363
2	Coast Douglas fir	Coos County, Oregon	100.27	329
3	General Sherman giant sequoia	Sequoia National Park, California	83.8	275
4	Noble fir	Mount St Helens National Monument, Washington	82.9	272
5	Sugar pine	Yosemite National Park, California	82.3	270
6	Western hemlock	Olympic National Park, Washington	73.5	241
7	Port-Orford cedar	Siskiyou National Forest, Oregon	66.8	219
8	Sitka spruce	Seaside, Oregon	62.8	206
9	Swamp chestnut (Basket) oak	Fayette County, Alabama	61.0	200
10	Pignut hickory	Robbinsville, North Carolina	57.9	190

The 110.6-m/363-ft champion Coast Redwood stands just 60 cm/24 in shorter than the cross on the dome on St Paul's Cathedral and more than twice the height of Nelson's Column. A close rival, known as the Dyerville Giant (from Dyerville, California), stood 110.3 m/362 ft high but fell in a storm on 27 March 1991. Several extinct Australian eucalyptus exceeded 122 m/400 ft.

TOP 10
BIGGEST TREES IN THE UK
(The biggest known example of each of the 10 biggest species)

	Tree	Location	cm	in
1	Sweet chestnut	Canford School, Dorset	426	167.7
2	Common English oak	Bowthorpe Park Farm, Lincolnshire	384	151.2
3	London plane	Mottisfont Abbey, Hampshire	367	144.5
4	Sequoiadendron (giant redwood)	Clunie Gardens, Tayside	345	135.8
5	Common yew	Defynnoc Church, Powys	342	134.6
6	Monterey cypress	Strete Raleigh, Devon	320	126.0
7	Sessile oak	Easthampton Farm, Shobdon, Hereford	318	125.2
8	Coast redwood	Woodstock, Co. Kilkenny	245	96.5
9	Lucombs oak	Phear Park, Exmouth, Devon	242	95.3
10	Small-leaved lime	Pitchford Hall, Shropshire	236	92.9

Diameter of trunk

Based on data supplied by *The Tree Register of the British Isles*.

TOP 10
BIGGEST TREES IN THE US
(The biggest known example of each of the 10 biggest species)

	Species	State	Points
1	General Sherman giant sequoia	Sequoia National Park, California	1,300
2	Coast redwood	Humboldt Redwoods State Park, California	1,017
3	Western red cedar	Forks, Washington	924
4	Sitka spruce	Olympic National Forest, Washington	922
5	Coast Douglas fir	Coos County, Oregon	762
6	Common bald cypress	Cat Island, Louisiana	748
7	Sycamore	Jeromesville, Ohio	737
8	Port-Orford cedar	Siskiyou National Forest, Oregon	680
9	Sugar pine	Yosemite National Park, California	635
10	Incense cedar	Marble Mountains Wilderness, California	626

The American Forestry Association operates a *National Register of Big Trees* which is constantly updated as new "champion trees" are nominated. Their method of measurement, which gives this Top 10 by species, is based not solely on height, but also takes account of the thickness of the trunk and spread of the upper branches and leaves, or crown. The formula adds the circumference in inches of the tree at 4½ feet above the ground to the total height of the tree in feet and to one-quarter of the average crown spread in feet. The General Sherman giant sequoia is 998 inches in circumference, 275 feet tall and with an average crown spread of 107 feet, hence 998 + 275 + 27 = 1,300 points. However it is measured, it comes out as the the largest living object on the planet.

TOP 10
LARGEST FORESTS IN THE UK

	Forest	hectares	acres
1	Dornoch	67,010	165,585
2	Kielder	61,250	151,352
3	Lochaber	50,952	125,905
4	Lorne	50,886	125,742
5	Newton Stewart	49,060	121,230
6	Ayrshire and Arran	44,351	109,594
7	Fort Augustus	40,350	99,707
8	Aberfoyle	38,512	95,165
9	Tay	36,081	89,158
10	Cowal	35,535	87,809

Area

The Kielder Forest is in Northumberland, but the other nine largest forests under the aegis of the Forestry Commission are all located in Scotland. The total area of woodland in the UK is 2,162,000 hectares/ 5,342,000 acres.

TOP 10
COMMONEST TREES IN THE UK

	Tree	% of total forest area
1	Sitka spruce	33
2	Scots pine	10
3	Oak	8
4=	Lodgepole pine	7
4=	Larch	7
6	Birch	6
7	Norway spruce	4
8=	Sycamore	3
8=	Beech	3
8=	Ash	3

THE HUMAN WORLD

T O P 1 0

LONGEST BONES IN THE HUMAN BODY

	Bone	Average length cm	in
1	Femur (thighbone – upper leg)	50.50	19.88
2	Tibia (shinbone – inner lower leg)	43.03	16.94
3	Fibula (outer lower leg)	40.50	15.94
4	Humerus (upper arm)	36.46	14.35
5	Ulna (inner lower arm)	28.20	11.10
6	Radius (outer lower arm)	26.42	10.40
7	Seventh rib	24.00	9.45
8	Eighth rib	23.00	9.06
9	Innominate bone (hipbone – half pelvis)	18.50	7.28
10	Sternum (breastbone)	17.00	6.69

These are average dimensions of the bones of an adult male measured from their extremities (ribs are curved, and the pelvis measurement is taken diagonally). The same bones in the female skeleton are usually 6 to 13 per cent smaller, with the exception of the sternum, which is virtually identical.

T O P 1 0

LARGEST HUMAN ORGANS

	Organ		Average weight g	oz
1	Liver		1,560	55.0
2	Brain	male	1,408	49.7
		female	1,263	44.6
3	Lungs	right	580	20.5
		left	510	18.0
		total	1,090	38.5
4	Heart	male	315	11.1
		female	265	9.3
5	Kidneys	left	150	5.3
		right	140	4.9
		total	290	10.2
6	Spleen		170	6.0
7	Pancreas		98	3.5
8	Thyroid		35	1.2
9	Prostate	male only	20	0.7
10	Adrenals	left	6	0.2
		right	6	0.2
		total	12	0.4

This list is based on average immediate post-mortem weights, as recorded by St Bartholomew's Hospital, London, and other sources during a 10-year period. Instances of organs far larger than the average have been recorded, including male brains of over 2,000 g/70.6 oz. According to some definitions, the skin may be considered an organ, and since it can comprise 16 per cent of a body's total weight (10,886 g/ 384 oz in a person weighing 68 kg/150 lb), it would head the Top 10.

THE BODY

TOP 10

COMMONEST BLOOD GROUPS IN THE UK

(Data provided by the National Blood Transfusion Service)

	Group	Percentage*		Group	Percentage*
1	O+	37.44	6	A1-	5.04
2	A1+	28.56	7	AB1+	2.72
3	B+	8.00	8	B-	2.00
4	A2+	7.14	9	A2-	1.26
5	O-	6.60	10	AB1-	0.48

In the UK the four ABO blood groups divide up as O (44 per cent), A (42 per cent), B (10 per cent), and AB (4 per cent). Of these approximately 15 per cent are Rhesus (Rh) negative. A and AB are further subdivided into A1 and A2 and AB1 and AB2 in ratios of approximately 80:20 in both cases.

* Total less than 100 per cent as a result of rounding-off and existence of rare sub-groups.

TOP 10

COMMONEST PHOBIAS

	Object of phobia	Medical term
1	Spiders	Arachnephobia or arachnophobia
2	People and social situations	Anthropophobia or sociophobia
3	Flying	Aerophobia or aviatophobia
4	Open spaces	Agoraphobia, cenophobia, or kenophobia
5	Confined spaces	Claustrophobia, cleisiophobia, cleithrophobia, or clithrophobia
6	Heights	Acrophobia, altophobia, hypsophobia, or hypsiphobia
7	Cancer	Carcinomaphobia, carcinophobia, carcinomatophobia, cancerphobia, or cancerophobia
8	Thunderstorms	Brontophobia or keraunophobia; related phobias are those associated with lightning (astraphobia), cyclones (anemophobia), and hurricanes and tornadoes (lilapsophobia)
9	Death	Necrophobia or thanatophobia
10	Heart disease	Cardiophobia

A phobia is a morbid fear that is out of all proportion to the object of the fear. Many people would admit to being uncomfortable about these principal phobias, as well as others, such as snakes (ophiophobia), injections (trypanophobia), or ghosts (phasmophobia), but most do not become obsessive about them nor allow such fears to rule their lives. True phobias often arise from some incident in childhood when a person has been afraid of some object and has developed an irrational fear that persists into adulthood. Nowadays, as well as the valuable work done by the Phobics Society and other organizations, phobias can be cured by taking special desensitization courses, for example, to conquer one's fear of flying.

TOP 10

COMMONEST ALLERGENS

(Substances that cause allergies)

Food		Environmental
Nuts	1	House dust mite (*Dermatophagoldes pteronyssinus*)
Shellfish/seafood	2	Grass pollens
Milk	3	Tree pollens
Wheat	4	Cats
Eggs	5	Dogs
Fresh fruit (apples, oranges, strawberries, etc)	6	Horses
Fresh vegetables (potatoes, cucumber, etc)	7	Moulds (*Aspergillus fumigatus, Alternaria Cladosporium*, etc)
Cheese	8	Birch pollen
Yeast	9	Weed pollen
Soya protein	10	Wasp/bee venom

An allergy has been defined as "an unpleasant reaction to foreign matter, specific to that substance, which is altered from the normal response and peculiar to the individual concerned". Allergens are commonly foods but may also be environmental agents, pollen as a cause of hay-fever being one of the best known. Reactions to them can result in symptoms ranging from severe mental or physical disability to minor irritations such as mild headache in the presence of fresh paint. "Elimination dieting" to pinpoint and avoid food allergens and the identification and avoidance of environmental allergens can result in complete cures from many allergies.

MATTERS OF LIFE AND DEATH

COUNTRIES WITH THE MOST HOSPITALS

	Country	Beds per 10,000	Hospitals
1	China	23	63,101
2	Brazil	37	28,972
3	India	8	25,452
4	Russia	135	12,711
5	Nigeria	9	11,588
6	Vietnam	25	10,768
7	Pakistan	6	10,673
8	Japan	136	10,096
9	North Korea	135	7,924
10	USA	47	6,738

COUNTRIES WITH THE MOST DOCTORS

	Country	Patients per doctor	Doctors
1	China	648	1,808,000
2	Russia	226	657,800
3	USA	416	614,000
4	India	2,337	365,000
5	Germany	313	251,877
6	Italy	228	249,704
7	Ukraine	226	228,900
8	Japan	583	211,797
9	Brazil	848	169,500
10	Spain	257	153,306

Comparing countries, their declared number of doctors, and hence the ratios of patients to doctors, is fraught with problems, especially since some countries, such as Russia and the Ukraine, include dentists with their doctors. China also includes practitioners of the traditional Chinese medicine.

COUNTRIES WITH THE HIGHEST MALE LIFE EXPECTANCY

	Country	Life expectancy at birth (years)
1	Japan	75.9
2=	Iceland	75.1
2=	Macau	75.1
4	Hong Kong	75.0
5	Israel	74.9
6	Sweden	74.6
7	Spain	74.4
8	Switzerland	74.1
9=	Andorra	74.0
9=	Netherlands	74.0
9=	Norway	74.0
	UK	72.7

The generally increasing life expectancy for males in the Top 10 countries contrasts sharply with that in many underdeveloped countries, particularly the majority of African countries, where it rarely exceeds 45 years, with Sierra Leone at the bottom of the league with 41.4 years.

COUNTRIES WITH THE HIGHEST FEMALE LIFE EXPECTANCY

	Country	Life expectancy at birth (years)
1	Japan	81.8
2=	France	81.0
2=	Andorra	81.0
4	Switzerland	80.9
5	Iceland	80.8
6=	Hong Kong	80.3
6=	Macau	80.3
8=	Sweden	80.2
8=	Netherlands	80.2
10	Norway	80.0
	UK	78.3

Female life expectancy in all the Top 10 countries exceeds 80 years. This represents the average: many women are now living beyond this age as die before attaining it. The comparative figure for such Third World countries as Sierra Leone, where it is 44.6 years for women, makes for less encouraging reading.

COMMONEST REASONS FOR VISITS TO THE DOCTOR

The Royal College of General Practitioners considers that these statistics represent the average number of consultations per condition that a doctor with a typical practice of 2,500 patients might expect to deal with in a year. These relatively common complaints contrast with others that are extremely rare, so that on average a doctor might expect to see a person with a dislocated hip only once every 20 years, or a patient with phenylketonuria (a metabolic disorder) just once in 200 years.

	Condition	Consulting rate per 2,500 patients
1	Upper respiratory tract infections	600
2	Non-specific "symptoms"	375
3	Skin disorders	350
4=	Psychoemotional problems	250
4=	High blood pressure	250
4=	Minor accidents	250
7	Gastro-intestinal conditions	200
8	Rheumatic aches and pains	150
9=	Chronic rheumatism	100
9=	Acute throat infections	100
9=	Acute bronchitis	100
9=	Lacerations	100
9=	Eczema/dermatitis	100

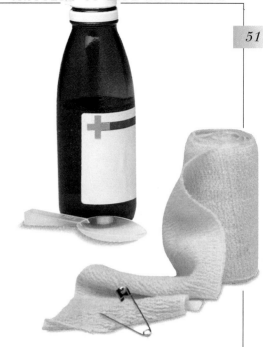

TOP 10

BESTSELLING PRESCRIPTION DRUGS IN THE WORLD

	Brand name	Manufacturer	Prescribed for	Annual revenue (US $)
1	Zantac	Glaxo	Ulcers	3,023,000,000
2	Vasotec	Merck & Co	High blood pressure, etc	1,745,000,000
3	Capoten	Bristol-Myers-Squibb	High blood pressure, etc	1,580,000,000
4	Voltaren	Ciba-Geigy	Arthritis	1,185,000,000
5	Tenormin	ICI	High blood pressure	1,180,000,000
6	Adalat	Bayer	Angina; high blood pressure	1,120,000,000
7	Tagamet	SmithKline Beecham	Ulcers	1,097,000,000
8	Mevacor	Merck & Co	High fat level in blood	1,090,000,000
9	Naproxen	Syntex	Arthritis	954,000,000
10	Ceclor	Eli Lilly	Infections	935,000,000

In 1991 the total revenue of the top 25 drug companies was $94,598,000,000. Fewer than 25 countries in the world have a gross domestic product (the total production of goods and services of the entire country) of more than this figure – which is approximately equivalent to the GDP of Norway. Of this total, the Top 10 drugs alone accounted for earnings of $13,909,000,000.

TOP 10

COMMONEST CAUSES OF DEATH IN THE UK

	Cause	England & Wales	Scotland	Northern Ireland	Total
1	Diseases of the circulatory system	254,683	28,766	7,112	290,571
2	Cancer and other neoplasms	145,963	15,132	3,621	164,716
3	Diseases of the respiratory system	60,388	6,999	2,423	69,810
4	Diseases of the digestive system	18,508	2,122	405	21,035
5	Injury and poisoning	16,681	2,535	581	19,797
6	Mental disorders	12,950	1,133	52	14,135
7	Diseases of the nervous system	11,577	947	181	12,705
8	Endocrine, nutritional and metabolic diseases, and immunity disorders	10,605	742	60	11,407
9	Diseases of the genito-urinary system	5,306	888	242	6,436
10	Diseases of the musculo-skeletal system	5,376	306	43	5,725
	Total deaths from all causes (including some that do not appear in the Top 10):	555,358	60,937	14,988	631,283

The 10 principal causes of death remain the same and in approximately the same order from year to year, with only slight fluctuations in total numbers (there were 14,898 – or 2.3 per cent – fewer deaths in the UK in 1992 than in the previous year). Deaths resulting from injury and poisoning overtook diseases of the digestive system in 1990 after several years in 5th place, but reverted to its former position in 1991 and 1992. Of deaths from accidents and violence, motor vehicle accidents accounted for most deaths, 4,774 in total, which is 434 fewer than in 1991 and represents the continuation of a downward trend.

TOP 10

MOST POPULAR NON-PRESCRIPTION MEDICINES IN THE UK

	Medicine	Sales (£)
1	Analgesics (painkillers such as aspirin)	195,600,000
2	Skin treatments	127,900,000
3	Food supplements	107,900,000
4	Cold remedies	96,400,000
5	Sore throat remedies	80,700,000
6	Vitamins and minerals	79,200,000
7	Indigestion remedies	64,800,000
8	Cough remedies	64,700,000
9	Smoking cessation	63,400,000
10	Oral hygiene products	50,100,000

In 1993 people in the UK spent an estimated £1,172,700,000 on non-prescription or "over-the-counter" home remedies, with the Top 10 product categories accounting for almost 80 per cent of the total. Such items appear to be largely "recession-proof": while the markets for many products were static or declined in 1993, sales of many of these increased. For example, sales of smoking cessation aids rose by a remarkable 78.6 per cent, as a result of which they entered the Top 10 for the first time. It should be borne in mind that some of these increases reflect price rises and the growing availability of remedies that were previously obtainable only from a pharmacist by doctor's prescription.

FOR BETTER OR FOR WORSE

Marriage rates for most Western countries have been steadily declining: there were 533,900 marriages in the UK's peak year of 1940, but only 349,739 in 1991. Although high divorce rates are a relatively modern phenomenon, national censuses taken around the turn of the century show that the US was already the world leader with 199,500 people (114,930 women and 84,570 men) recorded as divorced. The annual average for divorces in England and Wales – as in most other Western countries – has risen inexorably: in the period from 1871 to 1875 it numbered 357, by 1896–1900 it had reached 980, and by 1907 it stood at 1,288. The number of divorces more than doubled over the period from 1970 to 1991, reaching 158,745 in England and Wales, 12,399 in Scotland, and 2,344 in Northern Ireland.

TOP 10
COMMONEST CAUSES OF MARITAL DISCORD AND BREAKDOWN

1 Lack of communication

2 Continual arguments

3 Infidelity

4 Sexual problems

5 Physical or verbal abuse

6 Financial problems, recession, and redundancy fears

7 Work (usually one partner devoting excessive time to work)

8 Children (whether to have them; attitudes towards their upbringing)

9 Addiction (to drinking, gambling, spending, etc)

10 Step-parenting

TOP 10
COUNTRIES WITH THE HIGHEST DIVORCE RATE

	Country	Divorces per 1,000 p.a.
1	Maldives	25.5
2	Liechtenstein	7.3
3	Peru	6.0
4	USA	4.7
5	Puerto Rico	3.9
6	Ukraine	3.7
7	Cuba	3.6
8	Former USSR	3.4
9	Canada	3.1
10	Denmark	3.0
	UK	*2.9*

TOP 10
COUNTRIES WITH THE HIGHEST MARRIAGE RATE

	Country	Marriages per 1,000 p.a.*
1	Northern Mariana Islands	31.2
2	US Virgin Islands	18.0
3	Bermuda	15.2
4	Benin	12.8
5	Guam	12.0
6	Bangladesh	11.6
7	Mauritius	10.7
8	Azerbaijan	10.4
9=	Kazakhstan	10.0
9=	Cayman Islands	10.0
9=	Uzbekistan	10.0
	USA	*9.4*
	UK	*6.0*

* During latest period for which figures available.

The apparent world record marriage rate in the US territory of the Northern Mariana Islands, which has a total population of under 44,000, may be something of a statistical "blip" resulting from the recording of marriages by visitors, which has the effect of distorting the national pattern.

MARRIAGE IN THE MOVIES

The commercial success and critical acclaim of the British film *Four Weddings and a Funeral* (1994) places it in a long line of comedy films with weddings as their central theme. *Father of the Bride* (1991), itself a remake of a 1950 film with the same title, is one of the highest-earning, while *Lovers and Other Strangers* (1970), *A Wedding* (1978), and *Betsy's Wedding* (1990) have all been box-office hits. Weddings that are thwarted are another Hollywood staple, as in *The Philadelphia Story* (1940) and *The Graduate* (1967). Both of them, like the original *Father of the Bride*, were nominated for "Best Picture" Oscars – although all were jilted at the altar . . .

TOP 10
MONTHS FOR MARRIAGES IN ENGLAND AND WALES

	Month	Marriages
1	August	47,685
2	September	39,168
3	June	38,050
4	July	34,655
5	May	30,143
6	October	23,791
7	April	21,345
8	March	20,053
9	November	16,689
10	December	13,742

The figures are for 1991, when there were 306,756 marriages in England and Wales – a drop of almost 13 per cent on the 1981 figure of 351,973. The popularity of months is similar from year to year, but five Saturdays (the favoured day for weddings) in a month can boost the apparent popularity of the month; in 1991, March, June, August, and November each had five Saturdays. The least popular months were February (12,807) and January (8,628).

TOP 10

PROFESSIONS OF COMPUTER DATING MEMBERS

MEN	
Profession	**% of those registered**
1 Teachers	4.88
2 Civil servants	4.38
3 Engineers	4.18
4 Company directors	4.14
5 Accountants	3.57
6 Students	2.69
7 Self-employed	2.64
8 Computer programmers	2.43
9 Managers	1.61
10 Farmers	1.16

WOMEN	
Profession	**% of those registered**
1 Teachers	13.37
2 Secretaries	7.93
3 Nurses	7.37
4 Women at home	3.75
5 Civil servants	3.40
6 Clerks	3.15
7 Students	2.93
8 Social workers	1.46
9 Receptionists	1.44
10 Sales staff	1.18

Based on figures supplied by Dateline, the UK's largest and oldest-established computer dating agency.

THE FIRST 10 WEDDING ANNIVERSARY GIFTS

1	Cotton
2	Paper
3	Leather
4	Fruit and flowers
5	Wood
6	Sugar (or iron)
7	Wool or copper
8	Bronze (or electrical appliances)
9	Pottery (or willow)
10	Tin (or aluminium)

The custom of celebrating each wedding anniversary with a specific type of gift has a long tradition, but has changed much over the years – for example in the association of electrical appliances with the 8th anniversary. It varies considerably from country to country: in the UK and US many of the earlier themes are often disregarded in favour of the "milestone" anniversaries: the 25th (silver), 40th (ruby), 50th (gold), and 60th (diamond). Correctly, it is the 75th anniversary that is the "diamond", but few married couples live long enough to celebrate it, so it is usually commemorated as the 60th.

WHAT'S IN A NAME?

TOP 10
NAMES IN ENGLAND AND WALES

Daniel	1	Rebecca
Matthew	2	Charlotte
James	3	Laura
Christopher	4	Amy
Thomas	5	Emma
Joshua	6	Jessica
Adam	7	Lauren
Michael	8	Sarah
Luke	9	Rachel
Andrew	10	Catherine

TOP 10
COMMONEST UK SURNAMES

1 Smith
2 Jones
3 Williams
4 Brown
5 Taylor
6 Davies/Davis
7 Evans
8 Thomas
9 Roberts
10 Johnson

TOP 10
COMMONEST SURNAMES IN THE LONDON TELEPHONE DIRECTORY

1 Smith
2 Brown/Browne
3 Jones
4 Williams/Williamson
5 Clark/Clarke
6 Harris/Harrison
7 Taylor
8 Roberts/Robertson
9 Patel
10 James

TOP 10
BOYS' AND GIRLS' FIRST NAMES ANNOUNCED IN THE BIRTHS COLUMN OF THE *DAILY TELEGRAPH* (1993)

BOYS

1 Thomas
2 William
3 James
4 Alexander
5 George
6= Charles
6= Henry
8 Edward
9 Oliver
10 Jack

The survey of names announced in the births column of the *Daily Telegraph* shows a number of interesting similarities with that published by *The Times* – but also some divergences: Rebecca, for example, which now tops the national list of girls' first names, appears in the *Telegraph* list, but not *The Times*. Jack, the only new entry in the *Telegraph* chart, appears to be gaining in popularity (up from 12th place in 1992) – but fails to make a showing in The *Times* Top 10. *The Telegraph* survey also analyzed names outside the Top 10 and may provide pointers to some name fashions of future years: Georgia has risen to joint 18th place, with Amelia and Imogen at joint 20th. In joint 30th place (shared by six names), Holly and Lily appear – echoing the plant and flower names of past generations.

GIRLS

1 Charlotte
2 Sophie
3 Emily
4 Alice
5 Emma
6= Olivia
6= Eleanor
8 Lucy
9 Rebecca
10 Alexandra

TOP 10
BOYS' AND GIRLS' FIRST NAMES ANNOUNCED IN THE BIRTHS COLUMN OF *THE TIMES* (1993)

BOYS

1 Alexander
2 Thomas
3 James
4 William
5 Charles
6 George
7 Henry
8 Edward
9 Oliver
10 Nicholas

In 1947, when the names announced in *The Times* were first monitored, the most popular were Ann(e) and John – neither of which now makes an appearance in the first names Top 10s. In 1993 a total of 4,276 births were recorded – 2,029 girls and 2,247 boys. James had been the most popular boy's name consistently since 1964, but in 1992 was overtaken by Thomas, and has now slipped into third place. Both Olivia and George entered the first name list in 1989, and have risen steadily. All 10 boys' names remained the same as in 1992, but with slight changes of order (Alexander topped the list for the first time, with 128 nominations), whereas the girls' name list underwent more radical changes: Alexandra, Harriet, and Hannah departed, to be replaced by Eleanor, Emma, and Elizabeth.

GIRLS

1 Sophie
2 Olivia
3 Emily
4 Alice
5 Charlotte
6 Eleanor
7 Lucy
8 Emma
9 Elizabeth
10 Georgina

TOP 10

GREATEST DECLINES IN NAME POPULARITY THIS CENTURY

BOYS

	Name	1900	1990	Decline
1	William	897	136	761
2	John	726	82	644
3	George	609	48	561
4	Arthur	367	2	365
5	Frederick	376	16	360
6	Albert	333	2	331
7	Charles	390	76	314
8	Ernest	269	0	269
9	Alfred	260	4	256
10	Henry	261	36	225

The figures refer to the incidence per 10,000 registrations (as recorded in the Registrar General's Indexes of Births for England and Wales) of names registered in 1900 and 1990, so that in 1900, for example, 897 out of every 10,000 boys were given the name "William". While many of the most popular names of 1900 remain fashionable today – some, indeed, more so (380 Christophers and 400 Matthews in 1990, for instance, compared with seven and 22 respectively in 1900), a number of names have either declined so much in popularity that their frequency is noticeably reduced (names such as Elsie and Doris evoking a bygone era), or in some cases appear with an incidence of fewer than one per 10,000 and are therefore – at least statistically – considered to be virtually extinct.

GIRLS

	Name	1900	1990	Decline
1	Florence	394	0	394
2	Mary	391	10	381
3	Annie	357	2	355
4	Elsie	339	0	339
5	Edith	337	0	337
6	Alice	361	62	299
7	Erin	269	0	269
8	Doris	266	0	266
9	Ethel	246	0	246
10	Dorothy	246	3	243

TOP 10

BOYS' NAMES IN ENGLAND AND WALES 100 YEARS AGO

1	William		6	Frederick
2	John		7	Arthur
3	George		8	James
4	Thomas		9	Albert
5	Charles		10	Ernest

TOP 10

BOYS' NAMES IN ENGLAND AND WALES 200 YEARS AGO

1	William		6	Joseph
2	John		7	Richard
3	Thomas		8	Henry
4	James		9	Robert
5	George		10	Charles

TOP 10

BOYS' NAMES IN ENGLAND AND WALES 300 YEARS AGO

1	John		6	Robert
2	William		7	Joseph
3	Thomas		8	Edward
4	Richard		9	Henry
5	James		10	George

TOP 10

GIRLS' NAMES IN ENGLAND AND WALES 100 YEARS AGO

1	Florence		6	Edith
2	Mary		7	Elizabeth
3	Alice		8	Doris
4	Annie		9	Dorothy
5	Elsie		10	Ethel

TOP 10

GIRLS' NAMES IN ENGLAND AND WALES 200 YEARS AGO

1	Mary		6	Hannah
2	Ann		7	Susan
3	Elizabeth		8	Martha
4	Sarah		9	Margaret
5	Jane		10	Charlotte

TOP 10

GIRLS' NAMES IN ENGLAND AND WALES 300 YEARS AGO

1	Mary		6	Margaret
2	Elizabeth		7	Susan
3	Ann		8	Martha
4	Sarah		9	Hannah
5	Jane		10	Catherine

TOP 10

COMMONEST NAMES OF FILM CHARACTERS

	Name	Characters		Name	Characters
1	Jack	126	7=	Michael	59
2	John	104	7=	Tom	59
3	Frank	87	9	Mary	54
4	Harry	72	10	Paul	53
5	David	63			
6	George	62			

Based on Simon Rose's One FM Essential Film Guide *(1993) survey of feature films released in the period 1983–93.*

ORGANIZATIONS

T O P 1 0

MEMBERSHIP ORGANIZATIONS IN THE UK

	Organization	Membership
1	Trades Union Congress	7,646,832
2	Automobile Association	7,600,000
3	National Alliance of Women's Organizations	6,000,000
4	Royal Automobile Club	5,050,000
5	National Trust	2,173,875
6	UNISON *	1,486,984
7	Transport & General Workers Union	1,036,586
8	Amalgamated Engineering and Electrical Union	884,463
9	Royal Society for the Protection of Birds	870,000
10	GMB (formerly General, Municipal, Boilermakers and Allied Trades Union)	830,743

Formed 1 July 1993 by the merger of NALGO, NUPE, and COHSE.

T O P 1 0

ENVIRONMENTAL ORGANIZATIONS IN THE UK

	Organization	Membership
1	National Trust	2,173,875
2	Royal Society for the Protection of Birds*	870,000
3	Civic Trust	404,750
4	Greenpeace	400,000
5	English Heritage	307,825
6	National Trust for Scotland	235,000
7	Royal Society for Nature Conservation	229,880 #
8	World Wide Fund for Nature**	210,000
9	Woodland Trust	150,000
10	Friends of the Earth‡	116,000

* Includes the Young Ornithologists Club.
\# Excludes junior body, WATCH, with 22,000 individual and 900 school group members.
**Formerly the World Wildlife Fund.
‡ Excludes membership in Scotland.

T O P 1 0

LARGEST TRADE UNIONS IN THE UK

	Organization	Membership
1	UNISON	1,486,984
2	Transport & General Workers Union	1,036,586
3	Amalgamated Engineering and Electrical Union	884,463
4	GMB (formerly General, Municipal, Boilermakers and Allied Trades Union)	830,743
5	Manufacturing, Science & Finance Union (MSF)	552,000
6	Union of Shop, Distributive & Allied Workers (USDAW)	316,491
7	Royal College of Nursing (RCN)	304,000
8	Graphical Paper and Media Union (GPMU)	269,881
9	Union of Communications Workers (UCW)	175,266
10	National Union of Teachers (NUT)	162,192

There are about 300 trade unions in the UK, with a total membership of around 9,000,000, but the number of unions affiliated to the Trades Union Congress (TUC) has halved in the last 30 years.

TRANSPORT & GENERAL WORKERS UNION
This union, founded in 1922, was the largest trade union in the UK until 1993.

Until the 1960s there were still unions serving such bygone trades as glass bevelling and felt hat making, and even today some retain descriptive names evoking highly specialized industries, among them the Card Setting Machine Tenters' Society. Many of the smaller unions have been disbanded in recent years – the Spring Trapmakers' Society, for example, was dissolved in 1988 – although in marked contrast to the large unions in the Top 10 there are some tiny survivors, such as the Military and Orchestral Musical Instrument Makers' Trade Society (48 members) and the Sheffield Wool Shearers' Union (14).

T O P 1 0

WOMEN'S ORGANIZATIONS IN THE UK

	Organization	Membership		Organization	Membership
1	National Alliance of Women's Organizations	6,024,997	6	National Equal Rights Advisory Committee of GMB (formerly General, Municipal, Boilermakers and Allied Trades Union)	300,000
2	Trades Union Congress Women's Committee	3,000,000	7	The Mothers' Union	180,100
3=	Conservative Women's National Committee	500,000	8	Townswomen's Guilds	105,000
3=	Manufacturing, Science & Finance Union National Women's Sub-committee	500,000	9	Labour NEC Women's Committee	102,000
5	National Federation of Women's Institutes	320,000	10	Trefoil (Girl Guides Association)	20,841

TOP 10

YOUTH ORGANIZATIONS IN THE UK

	Organization	Membership*
1	Girl Guides	707,651
2	Youth Clubs	707,000#
3	Brownie Guides	345,460
4	Cub Scouts	220,974
5	National Association of Boys' Clubs	200,000
6	Boy Scouts	156,815
7	Beaver Scouts	129,757
8	Boys' Brigade	100,000
9	Combined Cadet Force	40,000
10	Girls' Brigade	38,195

* Fully paid-up members only – not those making occasional use of club facilities, etc.
# 700,000 individual; 7,000 clubs.

TOP 10

COUNTRIES WITH THE HIGHEST SCOUT MEMBERSHIP

	Country	Membership
1	USA	4,625,800
2	Philippines	2,350,710
3	India	2,272,700
4	Indonesia	2,134,368
5	UK	657,466
6	Bangladesh	368,063
7	Pakistan	326,753
8	South Korea	309,460
9	Thailand	274,123
10	Canada	269,425

Following an experimental camp held from 29 July to 9 August 1907 on Brownsea Island, Dorset, England, Sir Robert Baden-Powell (1857–1941) a former general in the British army, launched the Scouting Movement. There are now more than 25,000,000 Scouts in 211 countries and territories. There are believed to be just 13 countries in the world where Scouting either does not exist or is forbidden for political reasons, among which China is the largest.

TOP 10

COUNTRIES WITH THE HIGHEST GIRL GUIDE AND GIRL SCOUT MEMBERSHIP

	Country	Membership
1	USA	3,510,313
2	Philippines	1,250,928
3	India	758,575
4	UK	707,651
5	South Korea	184,993
6	Pakistan	101,634
7	Indonesia	98,656
8	Malaysia	92,539
9	Japan	88,331
10	Australia	87,331

The Girl Guide Movement was started in 1910 by Sir Robert Baden-Powell and his sister, Agnes (1858–1945). Today the World Association of Girl Guides and Girl Scouts has 128 national member organizations with a total membership of 8,500,000 around the world.

BOY SCOUTS
The Boy Scouts organization, founded in 1908, accepts boys between 11 and 15 years of age. It combines an emphasis on moral values with enjoyable and challenging physical activities.

TOP 10

LIVERY COMPANIES OF THE CITY OF LONDON

1	Mercers
2	Grocers
3	Drapers
4	Fishmongers
5	Goldsmiths
6=	Merchant Taylors
6=	Skinners
8	Haberdashers
9	Salters
10	Ironmongers

The "Great Twelve" also include the Vintners (11) and the Clothworkers (12). The Skinners and the Merchant Taylors switch their order in alternate years.

TOP 10

OLDEST ESTABLISHED CLUBS IN THE UK
(Other than golf clubs)

	Club/location	Established
1	White's Club, London	1693
2	Boodle's, London	1762
3	Brook's, London	1764
4	Norfolk Club, Norwich	1770
5	Royal Thames Yacht Club, London	1775
6	New Club, Edinburgh	1787
7	Marylebone Cricket Club, London	1787
8	The Athenaeum, Liverpool	1797
9	Royal Anglesey Yacht Club, Beaumaris	1802
10	City Club, Chester	1807

Although the New Club, Edinburgh, and the Marylebone Cricket Club (MCC) were both founded in 1787, the New Club was established on 1 February, whereas Marylebone is traditionally dated from its first cricket match, played on 1 June.

PEOPLE IN POWER

58

MRS INDIRA GANDHI
Unrelated to Mahatma Gandhi, but daughter of India's first Prime Minister Jawaharlal Nehru, Indira Gandhi died in office, shot by Sikh extremists. She was succeeded by her son Rajiv, who was later assassinated by Tamil Tigers.

TOP 10
FIRST COUNTRIES TO GIVE WOMEN THE VOTE

	Country	Year
1	New Zealand	1893
2	Australia (South Australia 1894; Western Australia 1898; Australia united 1901)	1902
3	Finland (then a Grand Duchy under the Russian Crown)	1906
4	Norway (restricted franchise; all women over 25 in 1913)	1907
5	Denmark and Iceland (a Danish dependency until 1918)	1915
6=	Netherlands	1917
6=	USSR	1917
8=	Austria	1918
8=	Canada	1918
8=	Germany	1918
8=	Great Britain and Ireland (Ireland was part of the UK until 1921. At first, vote was given only to women over 30 – voting age lowered to 21 in 1928)	1918
8=	Poland	1918

Although not a country, the Isle of Man was the first place to give women the vote, in 1880. Until 1920 the only other European countries to enfranchise women were Sweden in 1919 and Czechoslovakia in 1920. Certain states of the US gave women the vote at earlier dates (Wyoming in 1869, Colorado in 1894, Utah in 1895, and Idaho in 1896), but it was not granted nationally until 1920. A number of countries, such as France and Italy, did not give women the vote until 1945. Switzerland did not allow women to vote in elections to the Federal Council until 1971, and Liechtenstein was one of the last to relent, in 1984. In certain countries, such as Saudi Arabia, women are not allowed to vote at all – but neither are men.

TOP 10
EUROPEAN PARLIAMENTS WITH MOST WOMEN MEMBERS

	Country	Women MPs	Total MPs	% women
1	Sweden	133	349	38.1
2	Norway	60	165	36.4
3	Finland	63	200	31.5
4	Denmark	52	179	29.1
5	Netherlands	32	150	21.3
6	Iceland	13	63	20.6
7	West Germany	80	519	15.4
8	Luxembourg	9	60	15.0
9	Switzerland	33	246	13.4
10	Italy	81	630	12.9

Figures are based on the most recent general election results for all democratic European countries. With just 41 women MPs out of 650, the UK is in 16th place (only 6.4 per cent – although this is the highest ever proportion), beating Greece (4.3 per cent), and France (4.0 per cent).

TOP 10
WORLD'S FIRST FEMALE PRIME MINISTERS AND PRESIDENTS

	Name	Country	Period in office
1	Sirimavo Bandaranaike (PM)	Ceylon (Sri Lanka)	1960–64/1970–77
2	Indira Gandhi (PM)	India	1966–84
3	Golda Meir (PM)	Israel	1969–74
4	Maria Estela Perón (President)	Argentina	1974–75
5	Elisabeth Domitien (PM)	Central African Republic	1975
6	Margaret Thatcher (PM)	UK	May 1979–Nov 1990
7	Dr Maria Lurdes Pintasilgo (PM)	Portugal	Aug–Nov 1979
8	Vigdís Finnbogadóttir (President)	Iceland	Jun 1980–
9	Mary Eugenia Charles (PM)	Dominica	Jul 1980–
10	Gro Harlem Brundtland (PM)	Norway	Feb–Oct 1981/ May 1986–Oct 1989

The first ten have been followed by Corazón Aquino, who became President of the Philippines in 1986, Benazir Bhutto, Prime Minister of Pakistan (1988–90), Violeta Barrios de Chamorro, President of Nicaragua (1990–), Ertha Pascal-Trouillot, President of Haiti (1990–), and Mary Robinson, President of the Irish Republic (1990–). Since 1990, several further countries have appointed female Prime Ministers, including France (Edith Cresson), Canada (Kim Campbell), Burundi (Sylvie Kinigi), and Turkey (Tansu Çiller).

TOP 10

YOUNGEST BRITISH PRIME MINISTERS

	Prime Minister	Appointment* year	age
1	William Pitt (1759–1806)	1783	24
2	Duke of Grafton (1735–1811)	1768	33
3	Marquess of Rockingham (1730–82)	1765	35
4	Duke of Devonshire (1720–64)	1756	36
5	Lord North (1732–92)	1770	38
6	Earl of Liverpool (1770–1828)	1812	42
7	Henry Addington (1757–1844)	1801	43
8	Sir Robert Walpole (1676–1745)	1721	44
9	Viscount Goderich (1782–1859)	1827	44
10	Duke of Portland (1738–1809)	1783	44

* Where a prime minister served in more than one ministry, only the first is listed.

At 24 years 205 days, William Pitt was by a wide margin the youngest Prime Minister ever. He had entered Cambridge University at 14 and Parliament at 22, becoming Chancellor of the Exchequer at 23. Although the last three on this list all became Prime Minister at the age of 44, Sir Robert Walpole was Viscount Goderich's senior by less than three months, while there were just 50 days between the ages of Viscount Goderich and the Duke of Portland. The title "Prime Minister" was not officially used until 1878, so all those on this list technically held the office as "First Lord of the Treasury". The youngest Prime Minister to be so designated is John Major (47 years 244 days when he took office on 28 November 1990).

MRS (NOW LADY) THATCHER
In the course of more than 11 years as British Prime Minister, Margaret Thatcher succeeded in stamping her highly personal brand of philosophy on the nation's political and economic life.

TOP 10

OLDEST SERVING BRITISH PRIME MINISTERS

	Name/party	Born	Last year in office	Retirement age
1	William E. Gladstone (Lib)	1809	1894	84
2	Viscount Palmerston (Lib)	1784*	1865	80
3	Winston S. Churchill (Con)	1874	1955	80
4	Earl of Wilmington (W)	1663/64*	1743	79–80
5	Benjamin Disraeli (Con)	1804	1880	75
6	Earl Russell (Lib)	1792	1866	73
7	Marquess of Salisbury (Con)	1830	1902	72
8	Duke of Portland (Co)	1738	1809	71
9	Sir H. Campbell-Bannerman (Lib)	1836	1908	71
10	Neville Chamberlain (Co)	1869	1940	71

* Exact birthdate unknown.

Co = Coalition; Con = Conservative; Lib = Liberal; W = Whig.

Gladstone was aged 84 years and 64 days when he left office. Viscount Palmerston has the distinction of being the oldest prime minister to take office for the first time, at the age of 70 in 1855. A matter of months separates the last three prime ministers in the Top 10.

TOP 10

FIRST NATIONS TO RATIFY THE UN CHARTER

	Country	Date
1	Nicaragua	6 Jul 1945
2	USA	8 Aug 1945
3	France	31 Aug 1945
4	Dominican Republic	4 Sep 1945
5	New Zealand	19 Sep 1945
6	Brazil	21 Sep 1945
7	Argentina	24 Sep 1945
8	China	28 Sep 1945
9	Denmark	9 Oct 1945
10	Chile	11 Oct 1945

In New York on 26 June 1945, barely weeks after the end of the Second World War in Europe, 50 nations signed the World Security Charter. Each of the individual signatories ratified the Charter individually over the ensuing months, and the UN came into effect on 24 October.

ALL THE PRESIDENTS

TOP 10

THE FIRST 10 PRESIDENTS OF THE USA

	President (dates)	Period of office
1	George Washington (1732–99)	1789–97
2	John Adams (1735–1826)	1797–1801
3	Thomas Jefferson (1743–1826)	1801–09
4	James Madison (1751–1836)	1809–17
5	James Monroe (1758–1831)	1817–25
6	John Quincy Adams (1767–1848)	1825–29
7	Andrew Jackson (1767–1845)	1829–37
8	Martin Van Buren (1782–1862)	1837–41
9	William H. Harrison (1773–1841)	1841
10	John Tyler (1790–1862)	1841–45

ABRAHAM LINCOLN
Lincoln is most famous for having preserved the Union during the US Civil War and for the emancipation of the American slaves. He is perhaps less well known for being the tallest of the US Presidents!

TOP 10

TALLEST US PRESIDENTS

	President	Height		
		m	ft	in
1	Abraham Lincoln	1.93	6	4
2	Lyndon B. Johnson	1.91	6	3
3=	William Clinton	1.89	6	2½
3=	Thomas Jefferson	1.89	6	2½
5=	Chester A. Arthur	1.88	6	2
5=	George H.W. Bush	1.88	6	2
5=	Franklin D. Roosevelt	1.88	6	2
5=	George Washington	1.88	6	2
9=	Andrew Jackson	1.85	6	1
9=	Ronald W. Reagan	1.85	6	1

TOP 10

LONGEST-SERVING US PRESIDENTS

	President	Period in office	
		years	days
1	Franklin D. Roosevelt	12	39
2=	Grover Cleveland	8*	
2=	Dwight Eisenhower	8*	
2=	Ulysses S. Grant	8*	
2=	Andrew Jackson	8*	
2=	Thomas Jefferson	8*	
2=	James Madison	8*	
2=	James Monroe	8*	
2=	Ronald W. Reagan	8*	
2=	Woodrow Wilson	8*	

* Two four-year terms — now the maximum any US President may remain in office.

TOP 10

SHORTEST-SERVING US PRESIDENTS

	President	Period in office	
		years	days
1	William H. Harrison		32
2	James A. Garfield		199
3	Zachary Taylor	1	128
4	Gerald R. Ford	2	150
5	Warren G. Harding	2	151
6	Millard Fillmore	2	236
7	John F. Kennedy	2	306
8	Chester A. Arthur	3	166
9	Andrew Johnson	3	323
10	John Tyler	3	332

TOP 10

SHORTEST US PRESIDENTS

	President	Height		
		m	ft	in
1	James Madison	1.63	5	4
2=	Benjamin Harrison	1.68	5	6
2=	Martin Van Buren	1.68	5	6
4=	John Adams	1.70	5	7
4=	John Quincy Adams	1.70	5	7
4=	William McKinley	1.70	5	7
7=	William H. Harrison	1.73	5	8
7=	James K. Polk	1.73	5	8
7=	Zachary Taylor	1.73	5	8
10=	Ulysses S. Grant	1.74	5	8½
10=	Rutherford B. Hayes	1.74	5	8½

TOP 10

THE LAST 10 US PRESIDENTS AND VICE-PRESIDENTS TO DIE IN OFFICE

	Name/date	Office
1	John F. Kennedy* 22 November 1963	P
2	Franklin D. Roosevelt 12 April 1945	P
3	Warren G. Harding 2 August 1923	P
4	James S. Sherman 30 October 1912	V-P
5	William McKinley* 14 September 1901	P
6	Garret A. Hobart 21 November 1899	V-P
7	Thomas A. Hendricks 25 November 1885	V-P
8	James A. Garfield* 19 September 1881	P
9	Henry Wilson 10 November 1875	V-P
10	Abraham Lincoln* 15 April 1865	P

Assassinated.

TOP 10

LONGEST-LIVED US PRESIDENTS

	President	Age at death years	months
1	John Adams	90	8
2	Herbert Hoover	90	2
3	Harry S Truman	88	7
4	James Madison	85	3
5	Thomas Jefferson	83	2
6	Richard M. Nixon	81	3
7	John Quincy Adams	80	7
8	Martin Van Buren	79	7
9	Dwight D. Eisenhower	78	5
10	Andrew Jackson	78	2

TOP 10

YOUNGEST US PRESIDENTS

	President	Age at inauguration years	days
1	Theodore Roosevelt	42	322
2	John F. Kennedy	43	236
3	William Clinton	46	154
4	Ulysses S. Grant	46	236
5	Grover Cleveland	47	351
6	Franklin Pierce	48	101
7	James A. Garfield	49	105
8	James K. Polk	49	122
9	Millard Fillmore	50	184
10	John Tyler	51	8

TOP 10

OLDEST US PRESIDENTS

	President	Age at inauguration years	days
1	Ronald W. Reagan	69	349
2	William H. Harrison	68	23
3	James Buchanan	65	315
4	George H.W. Bush	64	223
5	Zachary Taylor	64	100
6	Dwight D. Eisenhower	62	98
7	Andrew Jackson	61	354
8	John Adams	61	125
9	Gerald R. Ford	61	26
10	Harry S Truman	60	339

DID YOU KNOW

THE WEIGHT OF OFFICE

While James Madison, the shortest US President, weighed just 45 kg/ 100 lb, Howard Taft (in office 1909–13) is believed to have been the heaviest at 150 kg/332 lb. He was so large that a special bath tub had to be installed in the White House for him. Bill Clinton has attained 107 kilos/235 lbs, making him probably the third heaviest President after Grover Cleveland.

JOHN F. KENNEDY
As well as being the second youngest man ever to be elected President, Kennedy was also the first Roman Catholic ever to hold this office.

ROYAL HIGHNESSES

TOP 10

FIRST ROMAN EMPERORS

	Caesar	Born	Acceded	Died	Fate
1	Julius Caesar	12 Jul 100 BC	48 BC	15 Mar 44 BC	Assassinated
2	Augustus	23 Sep 63 BC	27 BC	19 Aug AD 14	Died
3	Tiberius	16 Nov 42 BC	14 BC	16 Mar AD 37	Died
4	Caligula	31 Aug AD 12	AD 37	24 Jan AD 41	Assassinated
5	Claudius	1 Aug AD 10	AD 41	13 Oct AD 54	Assassinated
6	Nero	15 Dec AD 37	AD 54	9 Jun AD 68	Suicide
7	Galba	24 Dec AD 3	AD 68	15 Jan AD 69	Assassinated
8	Otho	28 Apr AD 32	AD 69	16 Apr AD 69	Suicide
9	Vitellius	24 Sep AD 15	AD 69	22 Dec AD 69	Assassinated
10	Vespasian	18 Nov AD 9	AD 69	23 Jun AD 79	Died

TOP 10

SHORTEST-REIGNING BRITISH MONARCHS

	Monarch	Reign	Duration
1	Jane	1553	14 days
2	Edward V	1483	75 days
3	Edward VIII	1936	325 days
4	Richard III	1483–85	2 years
5	James II	1685–88	3 years
6	Mary I	1553–58	5 years
7	Mary II	1689–94	5 years
8	Edward VI	1547–53	6 years
9	William IV	1830–37	7 years
10	Edward VII	1901–10	9 years

TOP 10

WORLD'S LONGEST-REIGNING MONARCHS

	Monarch	Country	Reign	Age at accession	Reign years
1	Louis XIV	France	1643–1715	5	72
2	John II	Liechtenstein	1858–1929	18	71
3	Franz-Josef	Austria–Hungary	1848–1916	18	67
4	Victoria	UK	1837–1901	18	63
5	Hirohito	Japan	1926–89	25	62
6	George III	UK	1760–1820	22	59
7	Louis XV	France	1715–74	5	59
8	Pedro II	Brazil	1831–89	6	58
9	Wilhelmina	Netherlands	1890–1948	10	58
10	Henry III	England	1216–72	9	56

TOP 10

LONGEST-REIGNING QUEENS IN THE WORLD*

	Queen	Country	Reign	Reign years
1	Victoria	UK	1837–1901	63
2	Wilhelmina	Netherlands	1890–1948	58
3	Wu Chao	China	655–705	50
4	Salote Tubou	Tonga	1918–65	47
5	Elizabeth I	England	1558–1603	44
6	Elizabeth II	UK	1952–	42
7	Maria Theresa	Hungary	1740–80	40
8	Maria I	Portugal	1777–1816	39
9	Joanna I	Italy	1343–81	38
10=	Suiko Tenno	Japan	593–628	35
10=	Isabella II	Spain	1833–68	35

Some authorities have claimed a 73-year reign for Alfonso I of Portugal, but his father, Henry of Burgundy, who conquered Portugal, ruled as Count, and it was this title that Alfonso inherited on 30 April 1112, at the age of two. His mother, Theresa of Castile, ruled until he took power in 1128, but he did not assume the title of king until 25 July 1139, during the Battle of Ourique at which he vanquished the Moors. He thus ruled as king for 46 years until his death on 6 December 1185. More extravagant claims are sometimes made for long-reigning monarchs in the ancient world. One example is the alleged 94 years of Phiops II, a Sixth Dynasty Egyptian pharaoh, but since his dates of birth and death are uncertain, he has not been included.

Queens and empresses who ruled in their own right, not as consorts of kings or emperors.

As well as being the longest-reigning queen, Victoria is among the longest-reigning monarchs in the world. She also holds first place as the British monarch who occupied the throne for the longest time, beating her nearest rival, George III, by some four years.

LE ROI SOLEIL
Nicknamed the "Sun King" because of the splendour of his court, Louis XIV began his reign at five years of age, but he was not crowned until he was 16 years old.

T O P 1 0

YOUNGEST BRITISH MONARCHS

(Since the Norman Conquest)

	Monarch	Reign	Age at accession years	months
1	Henry VI	1422–61	0	8
2	Henry III	1216–72	9	1
3	Edward VI	1547–53	9	3
4	Richard II	1377–99	10	5
5	Edward V	1483	12	5
6	Edward III	1327–77	14	2
7	Jane	1553	15	8
8	Henry VIII	1509–47	17	10
9	Victoria	1837–1901	18	1
10	Charles II	1660–85	18	8

Henry VI was born on 6 December 1421 and became King of England on 1 September 1422, the day after the death of his father, Henry V. At the age of 10 months (following the death of his grandfather, Charles VI, on 21 October 1422), he also became King of France. Before the Norman Conquest, Edward the Martyr became king in 975 when aged about 12 and Ethelred II ("the Unready") in 978 at the age of about 10.

T O P 1 0

LONGEST-REIGNING BRITISH MONARCHS

	Monarch	Reign	Age at accession	Age at death	Reign years
1	Victoria	1837–1901	18	81	63
2	George III	1760–1820	22	81	59
3	Henry III	1216–72	9	64	56
4	Edward III	1327–77	14	64	50
5	Elizabeth I	1558–1603	25	69	44
6	Elizabeth II	1952–	25	–	42
7	Henry VI	1422–61 (deposed, d.1471)	8 months	49	38
8	Henry VIII	1509–47	17	55	37
9	Charles II	1660–85	19	54	36
10	Henry I	1100–35	31–32*	66–67*	35

* Henry I's birthdate is unknown, so his age at accession and death are uncertain.

This list excludes the reigns of monarchs before 1066, so omits such rulers as Ethelred II who reigned for 37 years. Queen Elizabeth II overtook Henry VI's reign (38 years and 185 days) in August 1990 and is on target to pass that of her namesake Queen Elizabeth I in June 1996. If she is still on the throne on 11 September 2015, she will have beaten Queen Victoria's record by one day. She will then be 89 years old, and will be the UK's oldest ruler.

QUEEN VICTORIA
After her father's brothers, George IV and William IV, died, Princess Alexandria Victoria became Queen of Great Britain and Ireland, and Empress of India.

T O P 1 0

OLDEST MONARCHS TO ASCEND THE BRITISH THRONE

	Monarch	Reign	Age at accession
1	William IV	1830–37	64
2	Edward VII	1901–10	59
3	George IV	1820–30	57
4	George I	1714–27	54
5	James II	1685–88	51
6	George V	1910–36	44
7	George II	1727–60	43
8	Edward VIII	1936	41
9	George VI	1936–52	40
10	William I	1066–87	39

T O P 1 0

LONGEST-REIGNING LIVING MONARCHS IN THE WORLD

(Including hereditary rulers of principalities, dukedoms, etc.)

	Monarch	Country	Date of birth	Accession
1	Bhumibol Adulyadej	Thailand	5 Dec 1927	9 Jun 1946
2	Rainier III	Monaco	31 May 1923	9 May 1949
3	Elizabeth II	UK	21 Apr 1926	6 Feb 1952
4	Hussein	Jordan	14 Nov 1935	11 Aug 1952
5	Hassan II	Morocco	9 Jul 1929	26 Feb 1961
6	Isa bin Sulman al-Khalifa	Bahrain	3 Jul 1933	2 Nov 1961
7	Malietoa Tanumafili II	Western Samoa	4 Jan 1913	1 Jan 1962
8	Jean	Luxembourg	5 Jan 1921	12 Nov 1964
9	Taufa'ahau Tupou IV	Tonga	4 Jul 1918	16 Dec 1965
10	Qaboos bin Said	Oman	18 Nov 1942	23 Jul 1970

There are 25 countries that have emperors, kings, queens, princes, dukes, sultans, or other hereditary rulers as their heads of state. Malaysia, uniquely, has an elected monarchy.

64 EXPLORATION AND ENDEAVOUR

TOP 10

FIRST EXPLORERS TO LAND IN THE AMERICAS

	Explorer	Nationality	Discovery/ exploration	Year
1	Christopher Columbus	Italian	West Indies	1492
2	John Cabot	Italian/ English	Nova Scotia/ Newfoundland	1497
3	Alonso de Hojeda	Spanish	Brazil	1499
4	Vicente Yañez Pinzón	Spanish	Amazon	1500
5	Pedro Alvarez Cabral	Portuguese	Brazil	1500
6	Gaspar Corte Real	Portuguese	Labrador	1500
7	Rodrigo de Bastidas	Spanish	Central America	1501
8	Vasco Nuñez de Balboa	Spanish	Panama	1513
9	Juan Ponce de León	Spanish	Florida	1513
10	Juan Díaz de Solís	Spanish	Río de la Plata	1515

After his pioneering voyage of 1492, Columbus made three subsequent journeys to the West Indies and South America. Following him, several expeditions landed on the same islands of the West Indies (these have not been included as new explorations). Although Hojeda (or Ojeda) was the leader of the 1499 expedition, Amerigo Vespucci, after whom America is named, was also on the voyage. Of the three voyages that arrived in 1500, that of Pinzón (who had also been with Columbus on his 1492 voyage) takes precedence as he landed on 26 January. Cabral followed in April, while Corte Real, who is thought to have landed late in 1500, disappeared on the voyage.

TOP 10

FIRST MOUNTAINEERS TO CLIMB EVEREST

	Mountaineer	Nationality	Date
1	Edmund Hillary	New Zealander	29 May 1953
2	Tenzing Norgay	Nepalese	29 May 1953
3	Jürg Marmet	Swiss	23 May 1956
4	Ernst Schmied	Swiss	23 May 1956
5	Hans-Rudolf von Gunten	Swiss	24 May 1956
6	Adolf Reist	Swiss	24 May 1956
7	Wang Fu-chou	Chinese	25 May 1960
8	Chu Ying-hua	Chinese	25 May 1960
9	Konbu	Tibetan	25 May 1960
10=	Nawang Gombu	Indian	1 May 1963
10=	James Whittaker	American	1 May 1963

Nawang Gombu and James Whittaker are 10th equal because, neither man wishing to deny the other the privilege of being the first to reach the summit, they ascended the last few metres together, side by side.

CAPTAIN WEBB AND THE FIRST CROSS-CHANNEL SWIM

Captain Matthew Webb (1848–83) was one of the most celebrated men in Victorian England. The son of a Shropshire doctor and one of 12 children, he went to sea at the age of 12 and soon became renowned for his strength and stamina in the water, saving the lives of swimmers – including one of his brothers – and winning medals for bravery. Yet his fame derived largely from a single exploit, when in 1875 he became the first person to swim the English Channel.

During the next 36 years no fewer than 71 people, 22 of them women, tried to emulate Webb's cross-Channel swim, but it was not until 1911 that 37-year-old Thomas William Burgess of Rotherham, Yorkshire, finally succeeded in becoming the second man to swim the Channel. It was to be a further 16 years before the tally reached 10, three of them women.

TOP 10

FIRST CROSS-CHANNEL SWIMMERS

	Swimmer	Nationality	Time hr:min	Date
1	Matthew Webb	British	21:45	24–25 Aug 1875
2	Thomas Burgess	British	22:35	5–6 Sep 1911
3	Henry Sullivan	American	26:50	5–6 Aug 1923
4	Enrico Tiraboschi	Italian	16:33	12 Aug 1923
5	Charles Toth	American	16:58	8–9 Sep 1923
6	Gertrude Ederle	American	14:39	6 Aug 1926
7	Millie Corson	American	15:29	27–28 Aug 1926
8	Arnst Wierkotter	German	12:40	30 Aug 1926
9	Edward Temme	British	14:29	5 Aug 1927
10	Mercedes Gleitze	British	15:15	7 Oct 1927

The first three crossings were from England to France, the rest from France to England. Gertrude Ederle was the first woman to swim the Channel, and on 11 September 1951 American Florence Chadwick became the first woman to swim from England to France. In 1934 Edward Temme also swam from England to France, becoming the first person successfully to cross in both directions. The Channel has been swum underwater (by Fred Baldasare in 1962), and by an 11-year-old girl. The record for the fastest crossing was held at one time by a 16-year-old American girl, Lynne Cox. It is now held by another American, Penny Dean, who crossed in 7 hr 40 min on 29 July 1978.

TOP 10

FASTEST CROSS-CHANNEL SWIMMERS

	Swimmer	Nationality	Year	Time hr: min
1	Penny Lee Dean	American	1978	7:40
2	Philip Rush	New Zealander	1987	7:55
3	Richard Davey	British	1988	8:05
4	Irene van der Laan	Dutch	1982	8:06
5	Paul Asmuth	American	1985	8:12
6	Anita Sood	Indian	1987	8:15
7	Monique Wildschutt	Dutch	1984	8:19
8	Eric Johnson	American	1985	8:20
9	Susie Maroney	Australian	1990	8:29
10	Lyndon Dunsbee	British	1984	8:34

TOP 10

FIRST PEOPLE TO REACH THE SOUTH POLE

	Name	Nationality	Date
1=	Roald Amundsen*	Norwegian	14 Dec 1911
1=	Olav Olavsen Bjaaland	Norwegian	14 Dec 1911
1=	Helmer Julius Hanssen	Norwegian	14 Dec 1911
1=	Helge Sverre Hassel	Norwegian	14 Dec 1911
1=	Oscar Wisting	Norwegian	14 Dec 1911
6=	Robert Falcon Scott*	British	17 Jan 1912
6=	Henry Robertson Bowers	British	17 Jan 1912
6=	Edgar Evans	British	17 Jan 1912
6=	Lawrence Edward Grace Oates	British	17 Jan 1912
6=	Edward Adrian Wilson	British	17 Jan 1912

* Expedition leader.

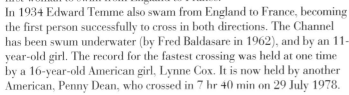

SCOTT'S TELESCOPE

Just 33 days separated the first two expeditions to reach the South Pole. Although several voyages had sailed close to Antarctica, no one had set foot on the mainland until the 19th century. Robert Falcon Scott, a young naval lieutenant, first landed in the Antarctic in 1902 and examined the feasibility of reaching the South Pole. In 1909 Ernest Shackleton marched to within 182 km/113 miles of the Pole, and a multi-nation race for its conquest began. A British Antarctic Expedition, led by Scott, was organized in 1910 with the goal "to reach the South Pole and to secure for the British Empire the honour of this achievement", but on his arrival in Australia, Scott learned that the Norwegian Roald Amundsen had also embarked on an expedition to the Pole. After reaching the Antarctic, Scott undertook scientific research and acclimatized his team to local conditions. His party, leaving later than Amundsen's, suffered severe weather and, after problems with motor sleds, ponies, and dogs, relied entirely on man-hauled sleds. Amundsen, in contrast, depended exclusively on dogs, and even used them as part of his team's food supply, viewing them as a "mobile larder" (which the British expedition considered barbaric). When Scott finally reached the Pole, his party found that the Norwegians had beaten them. Plagued by illness, hunger, bad weather, and exhaustion, they began the journey back to their base during which Evans died after injuring himself. Realizing that they had insufficient rations, Oates stepped out into a blizzard in a famous act of self-sacrifice. At precisely the time that Amundsen's achievement was being reported to the world, the remaining three died in their tent.

CROSS-COUNTRY SKIS
These heavy wooden cross-country skis were used by Scott on his first Antarctic expedition.

NOBEL PRIZES

T O P   1 0

NOBEL PRIZE WINNING COUNTRIES

	Country	Phy	Che	Ph/Med	Lit	Pce	Eco	Total
1	USA	57	38	70	10	17	21	213
2	UK	20	23	23	8	10	6	90
3	Germany	19	27	14	6	4	–	70
4	France	11	7	7	12	9	1	47
5	Sweden	4	4	7	7	5	2	29
6	Switzerland	2	5	5	2	3	–	17
7	USSR	7	1	2	3	2	1	16
8	Stateless institutions	–	–	–	–	14	–	14
9	Italy	3	1	3	5	1	–	13
10=	Denmark	3	–	5	3	1	–	12
10=	Netherlands	6	2	2	–	1	1	12

Phy – Physics; Che – Chemistry; Ph/Med – Physiology or Medicine; Lit – Literature; Pce – Peace; Eco – Economic Sciences.

A century ago, on 27 November 1895, the Swedish scientist Alfred Nobel signed his will in which he left the major part of his fortune of 31,600,000 Swedish kroner, amassed through his invention of dynamite, to establish a trust fund, which is now estimated to be worth over £150,000,000. Nobel died the following year, but interest earned from this money has enabled annual prizes to be awarded since 1901 to those who have achieved the greatest common good in the fields of Physics, Chemistry, Physiology or Medicine, Literature, Peace, and, since 1969, Economic Sciences. All the award ceremonies take place in Stockholm, Sweden, with the exception of the Peace Prize, which is awarded in Oslo, Norway.

T O P   1 0

FIRST BRITISH WINNERS OF THE NOBEL PRIZE FOR MEDICINE

	Winner	Prize year
1	Sir Ronald Ross (1857–1932)	1902
2	Sir Archibald Hill* (1886–1977)	1922
3	Sir Frederick Hopkins (1861–1947)	1929
4=	Lord Edgar Adrian (1889–1977)	1932
4=	Sir Charles Sherrington (1857–1952)	1932
6	Sir Henry Dale* (1875–1968)	1936
7=	Sir Ernest Boris Chain (1906–79)	1945
7=	Sir Alexander Fleming (1881–1955)	1945
7=	Lord Howard Florey (1898–1968)	1945
10	Sir Hans Krebs*# (1900–81)	1953

* Prize shared with other nationalities.
 # German-born.

T O P   1 0

FIRST BRITISH WINNERS OF THE NOBEL PEACE PRIZE

	Winner	Prize year
1	Sir William Cremer (1838–1908)	1903
2	Sir Joseph Austen Chamberlain (1863–1937)	1925
3	Sir Norman Angell (1872–1967)	1933
4	Arthur Henderson (1863–1935)	1934
5	Lord Robert Cecil (1864–1958)	1937
6	The Friends' Service Council*	1947
7	Lord John Boyd Orr (1880–1971)	1949
8	Lord Philip Noel-Baker (1889–1982)	1959
9=	Mairead Corrigan (b.1944)	1976
9=	Betty Williams (b.1943)	1976

* Shared with the American Friends' Service Committee.

T O P   1 0

FIRST BRITISH WINNERS OF THE NOBEL PRIZE FOR PHYSICS

	Winner	Prize year
1	John Strutt (Lord Rayleigh) (1842–1919)	1904
2	Sir Joseph Thomson (1856–1940)	1906
3=	Sir William Henry Bragg* (1862–1942)	1915
3=	Sir William L. Bragg (1890–1971)	1915
5	Charles Barkla (1877–1944)	1917
6	Charles Wilson# (1869–1959)	1927
7	Sir Owen Richardson (1879–1959)	1928
8	Paul Dirac# (1902–84)	1933
9	Sir James Chadwick (1891–1974)	1935
10	Sir George Thomson (1892–1975)	1937

* The youngest-ever winner at 25.
 # Prize shared with other nationalities.

TOP 10

FIRST WOMEN TO WIN A NOBEL PRIZE

	Winner	Nationality	Prize	Year
1	Marie Curie* (1867–1934)	Polish	Physics	1903
2	Bertha von Suttner (1843–1914)	Austrian	Peace	1905
3	Selma Lagerlöf (1858–1940)	Swedish	Literature	1909
4	Marie Curie (1867–1934)	Polish	Chemistry	1911
5	Grazia Deledda (1875–1936)	Italian	Literature	1926#
6	Sigrid Undset (1882–1949)	Norwegian	Literature	1928
7	Jane Addams** (1860–1935)	American	Peace	1931
8	Irène Joliot-Curie‡ (1897–1956)	French	Chemistry	1935
9	Pearl Buck (1892–1973)	American	Literature	1938
10	Gabriela Mistral (1899–1957)	Chilean	Literature	1945

The first British woman to win a Nobel Prize was Dorothy Crowfoot Hodgkin (b.1910, Cairo), whose 1964 Nobel Chemistry Prize was awarded for her work on the structure of penicillin and vitamin B12. Belfast-born Betty Williams and Mairead Corrigan were awarded the 1976 Peace Prize.

* *Shared half with husband Pierre Curie; other half to Henri Becquerel.*
\# *Awarded 1927.*
***Shared with Nicholas Murray Butler.*
‡ *Shared with husband Frédéric Joliot-Curie.*

TOP 10

FIRST BRITISH WINNERS OF THE NOBEL PRIZE FOR CHEMISTRY

	Winner	Prize year
1	Sir William Ramsay (1852–1916)	1904
2	Lord Ernest Rutherford (1871–1937)	1908
3	Frederick Soddy (1877–1956)	1921
4	Francis Aston (1877–1945)	1922
5	Sir Arthur Harden* (1865–1940)	1929
6	Sir Walter Haworth* (1883–1950)	1937
7	Sir Robert Robinson (1886–1975)	1947
8=	Archer Martin (b.1910)	1952
8=	Richard Synge (b.1914)	1952
10	Sir Cyril Hinshelwood* (1897–1967)	1956

* *Prize shared with other nationalities.*

Britons have won the Nobel Prize for Chemistry a total of 23 times since it was first awarded in 1901.

TOP 10

THE FIRST BRITISH WINNERS OF THE NOBEL PRIZE FOR LITERATURE

	Winner	Prize year
1	Rudyard Kipling (1865–1936)	1907
2	George Bernard Shaw (1856–1950)	1925
3	John Galsworthy (1867–1933)	1932
4	Thomas Stearns Eliot* (1888–1965)	1948
5	Bertrand Russell (1872–1970)	1950
6	Winston Churchill (1874–1965)	1953
7	Elias Canetti# (b.1905)	1981
8	William Golding (1911–93)	1983

* *US-born.*
\# *Bulgarian-born.*

France, with 12 winners, and the US with 10, are the only nations to have won the Nobel Prize for Literature more often than the UK. Sweden has had seven winners.

TOP 10

FIRST US WINNERS OF THE NOBEL PRIZE FOR LITERATURE

	Winner	Prize year
1	Sinclair Lewis (1885–1951)	1930
2	Eugene O'Neill (1888–1953)	1936
3	Pearl Buck (1892–1973)	1938
4	William Faulkner (1897–1962)	1949
5	Ernest Hemingway (1899–1961)	1954
6	John Steinbeck (1902–68)	1962
7	Saul Bellow (b.1915)	1976
8	Isaac Bashevis Singer (1904–91)	1978
9	Czeslaw Milosz* (b.1911)	1980
10	Joseph Brodsky# (b.1940)	1987

* *Polish-born.*   \# *Russian-born.*

The most recent US recipient of the Nobel Prize for Literaure is Toni Morrison (b.1931), awarded the prize in 1993.

THE GOOD & THE BAD

TOP 10

ORGANIZED RELIGIONS IN THE WORLD

	Religion	Followers
1	Christianity	1,869,751,000
2	Islam	1,014,372,000
3	Hinduism	751,360,000
4	Buddhism	334,002,000
5	Sikhism	19,853,000
6	Judaism	18,153,000
7	Confucianism	6,230,000
8	Baha'ism	5,742,000
9	Jainism	3,927,000
10	Shintoism	3,336,800

This list excludes the followers of various tribal and folk religions, new religions, and shamanism. Since reforms in the former USSR, many who practised Christianity in secret while following the Communist anti-religion line in public have now declared their faith openly. The list is based on the work of David B. Barrett, who has been monitoring world religions for many years.

TOP 10

LARGEST HINDU POPULATIONS IN THE WORLD

	Country	Total Hindu population
1	India	700,900,000
2	Nepal	17,240,000
3	Bangladesh	13,960,000
4	Sri Lanka	2,730,000
5	Pakistan	1,930,000
6	Malaysia	1,340,000
7	Mauritius	580,000
8	South Africa	430,000
9	UK	410,000
10	USA	340,000

TOP 10

LARGEST BUDDHIST POPULATIONS IN THE WORLD

	Country	Total Buddhist population
1	Japan	97,090,000 *
2	China	71,000,000
3	Thailand	54,570,000
4	Vietnam	47,260,000
5	Myanmar (Burma)	39,900,000
6	South Korea	15,990,000
7	Sri Lanka	12,210,000
8	Taiwan	9,000,000
9	Cambodia	8,210,000
10	Hong Kong#	4,380,000

* Including many who also practise Shintoism.
 # Buddhist and Taoist.

T O P 1 0

LARGEST MUSLIM POPULATIONS IN THE WORLD

	Country	Total Muslim population
1	Indonesia	164,140,000
2	Pakistan	123,870,000
3	Bangladesh	99,710,000
4	India	99,000,000
5	Turkey	59,390,000
6	Iran	55,000,000
7	Egypt	51,400,000
8	Nigeria	41,200,000
9	China	28,000,000
10	Algeria	26,890,000

T O P 1 0

LARGEST JEWISH POPULATIONS IN THE WORLD

	Country	Total Jewish population
1	USA	5,981,000
2	Israel	4,240,000
3	Former USSR	2,236,000
4	France	640,000
5	Canada	350,000
6	UK	315,000
7	Argentina	220,000
8	Brazil	183,000
9	South Africa	120,000
10	Australia	80,000

The Diaspora or scattering of Jewish people has been in progress for nearly 2,000 years, and as a result Jewish communities are found in virtually every country in the world. In 1939 it was estimated that the total world Jewish population was 17,000,000. Some 6,000,000 fell victim to Nazi persecution, reducing the figure to about 11,000,000, but by 1993 it was estimated to have grown again and now exceeds 18,000,000.

T O P 1 0

RELIGIOUS AFFILIATIONS IN THE USA

	Religion/organization	Membership
1	Roman Catholic Church	58,267,424
2	Southern Baptist Convention	15,232,347
3	United Methodist Church	8,785,135
4=	Muslim	8,000,000 *
4=	National Baptist Convention, USA, Inc	8,000,000 *
6	Jews	5,981,000 #
7	Church of God in Christ	5,499,875
8	Evangelical Lutheran Church in America	5,245,177
9	Church of Jesus Christ of Latter-day Saints (Mormons)	4,336,000
10	Presbyterian Church	3,788,358

* Estimated.
 # Combined membership of several groups.

It is claimed that out of the total US population of 248,709,873 (1990 Census), 156,336,384, or 62.86 per cent, are active members of a religious organization. Those represented in the Top 10 are the principal sects of often larger groups.

T O P 1 0

CHRISTIAN DENOMINATIONS IN THE WORLD

	Denomination	Adherents
1	Roman Catholic	872,104,646
2	Slavonic Orthodox	92,523,987
3	United (including Lutheran/Reformed)	65,402,685
4	Pentecostal	58,999,862
5	Anglican	52,499,051
6	Baptist	50,321,923
7	Lutheran (excluding United)	44,899,837
8	Reformed (Presbyterian)	43,445,520
9	Methodist	31,718,508
10	Disciples (Restorationists)	8,783,192

T O P 1 0

LARGEST CHRISTIAN POPULATIONS IN THE WORLD

	Country	Total Christian population
1	USA	223,240,000
2	Brazil	136,100,000
3	Former USSR	105,469,000
4	Mexico	85,080,000
5	Germany	61,340,000
6	Philippines	56,900,000
7	UK	50,470,000
8	Italy	47,560,000
9	Nigeria	44,860,000
10	France	44,080,000

Although Christian communities are found in almost every country in the world, it is difficult to put a precise figure on nominal membership rather than active participation, and these figures therefore represent only approximations.

The Top 10 is based on mid-1980s estimates supplied by MARC Europe, a Christian research and information organization. A subsequent estimate by the Vatican increased the figure for Roman Catholics to 911,000,000 while retaining the 52,000,000 figure for Anglicans – which indicates something of the problem of arriving even at "guesstimates" when it comes to global memberships. More recent estimates are not yet available.

THE CHRISTIAN FAITH

THE 10
COMMANDMENTS

1 Thou shalt have no other gods before Me.

2 Thou shalt not make unto thee any graven image.

3 Thou shalt not take the name of the Lord thy God in vain.

4 Remember the sabbath day, to keep it holy.

5 Honour thy father and thy mother.

6 Thou shalt not kill.

7 Thou shalt not commit adultery.

8 Thou shalt not steal.

9 Thou shalt not bear false witness against thy neighbour.

10 Thou shalt not covet thy neighbour's house, thou shalt not covet thy neighbour's wife, nor his manservant, nor his maidservant, nor his ox, nor his ass, nor any thing that is thy neighbour's.

Exodus 20:3.

CONFIRMED CHRISTIAN
A young girl in traditional white kneels to receive Holy Communion for the first time.

TOP 10
ANIMALS MOST MENTIONED IN THE BIBLE

	Animal	OT*	NT*	Total
1	Sheep	155	45	200
2	Lamb	153	35	188
3	Lion	167	9	176
4	Ox	156	10	166
5	Ram	165	0	165
6	Horse	137	27	164
7	Bullock	152	0	152
8	Ass	142	8	150
9	Goat	131	7	138
10	Camel	56	6	62

*Occurrences in verses in the King James Bible (Old and New Testaments), including plurals.

The sheep are sorted from the goats (itself a biblical expression – "a shepherd divideth his sheep from the goats", in Matthew 25:32) in this Top 10, in a list of the animals regarded as most significant in biblical times, either economically or symbolically. A number of generic terms are also found: beast (337 references), cattle (153), fowl (90), fish (56), and bird (41). Some creatures are mentioned only once, in Leviticus 11, which contains a list of animals that are considered "unclean" (such as the weasel, chameleon, and tortoise). There are 40 references to the dog, but the cat is not mentioned anywhere in the bible.

TOP 10
NAMES MOST MENTIONED IN THE BIBLE

	Name	OT*	NT*	Total
1	Jesus (984) Christ (576)	0	1,560	1,560
2	David	1,005	59	1,064
3	Moses	767	80	847
4	Jacob	350	27	377
5	Aaron	347	5	352
6	Solomon	293	12	305
7=	Joseph	215	35	250
7=	Abraham	176	74	250
9	Ephraim	182	1	183
10	Benjamin	162	2	164

* Occurrences in verses in the King James Bible (Old and New Testaments), including possessive uses, such as "John's".

The name Judah also appears 816 times, but the total includes references to the land as well as the man with that name. At the other end of the scale there are many names that appear only once or twice, among them Berodach-baladan and Tiglath-pileser. "God" is mentioned 4,105 times (2,749 Old Testament, 1,356 New Testament). The most mentioned place names produce few surprises: Israel (2,600 references) heads the list, followed by Jerusalem (814), Egypt (736), Babylon (298), and Assyria (141).

TOP 10
WORDS MOST MENTIONED IN THE BIBLE

	Word	OT*	NT*	Total
1	The	52,948	10,976	63,924
2	And	40,975	10,721	51,696
3	Of	28,518	6,099	34,617
4	To	10,207	3,355	13,562
5	That	9,152	3,761	12,913
6	In	9,767	2,900	12,667
7	He	7,348	3,072	10,420
8	For	6,690	2,281	8,971
9	I	6,669	2,185	8,854
10	His	7,036	1,437	8,473

A century before computers were invented, Thomas Hartwell Horne (1780–1862), a dogged Biblical researcher, undertook a manual search of the King James Bible to work out the frequency of occurrence of particular words. He concluded that the word "and" appeared a total of 35,543 times in the Old Testament and 10,684 times in the New Testament. He was fairly close on the latter – but he clearly missed quite a few instances in the Old Testament, as a recent computer search of the King James Bible indicates.

* Occurrences in verses in the King James Bible (Old and New Testaments).

T O P 1 0

THE FIRST 10 POPES

1	Saint Peter
2	Saint Linus
3	Saint Anacletus
4	Saint Clement I
5	Saint Evaristus
6	Saint Alexander I
7	Saint Sixtus I
8	Saint Telesphorus
9	Saint Hyginus
10	Saint Pius I

The first 10 popes all lived during the first 150 years of the Christian Church. As well as all being revered as martyrs, they have one other feature in common: virtually nothing is known about any of them.

UNENVIABLE RECORD
Pope Urban VII died of malaria before his coronation, 12 days after being elected.

T O P 1 0

NATIONALITIES OF POPES

	Nationality	No.
1	Roman/Italian	208–209 *
2	French	15–17 #
3	Greek	15–16 **
4	Syrian	6
5	German	4–6 #
6	Spanish	5
7	African	2–3
8	Galilean	2
9=	Dutch	1
9=	English	1
9=	Polish	1
9=	Portuguese	1

* *Gelasius I was Roman, but of African descent; it is unknown whether Miltiades was African or Roman.*

\# *The Franco-German frontier was variable at the births of two popes, hence their nationalities are uncertain.*

***Theodore I was of Greek descent, but born in Jerusalem.*

Before John Paul II (the only Polish pope to date) took office, the last non-Italian pope was Hadrian VI, a Dutchman, who reigned for less than two years from 1522 to 1523. Nicholas Breakspear, who took the name Hadrian IV in 1154, was the only English pope to date.

T O P 1 0

LONGEST-SERVING POPES

	Pope	Period in office	Years
1	Pius IX	16 Jun 1846–7 Feb 1878	31
2	Leo XIII	20 Feb 1878–20 Jul 1903	25
3	Peter	c.42–67	c.25
4	Pius VI	15 Feb 1775–29 Aug 1799	24
5	Adrian I	1 Feb 772–25 Dec 795	23
6	Pius VII	14 Mar 1800–20 Aug 1823	23
7	Alexander III	7 Sep 1159–30 Aug 1181	21
8	Sylvester	31 Jan 314–31 Dec 335	21
9	Leo I	29 Sep 440–10 Nov 461	21
10	Urban VIII	6 Aug 1623–29 Jul 1644	20

If he is still in office, the present pope, John Paul II, will enter the Top 10 in 1999 and could top it in 2010, when he will be 90 years old.

T O P 1 0

SHORTEST-SERVING POPES

	Pope	Year in office	Duration (days)
1	Urban VII	1590	12
2	Valentine	827	c.14
3	Boniface VI	896	15
4	Celestine IV	1241	16
5	Sisinnius	708	20
6	Sylvester III	1045	21
7	Theodore II	897	c.21
8	Marcellus II	1555	22
9	Damasus II	1048	23
10=	Pius III	1503	26
10=	Leo XI	1605	26

Many of those in this list were already elderly and in poor health when they were elected. Boniface VI and Sylvester III were deposed, and Damasus II possibly poisoned. Pope Johns have been particularly unlucky: John XXI lasted nine months but was killed in 1277 when a ceiling collapsed on him, while John XII was beaten to death by the husband of a woman with whom he was having an affair. In modern times, John Paul I was pontiff for just 33 days in 1978.

T O P 1 0

COMMONEST NAMES OF POPES

	Name	No.
1	John	23
2	Gregory	16
3	Benedict	15
4	Clement	14
5=	Innocent	13
5=	Leo	13
7	Pius	12
8	Boniface	9
9=	Alexander	8
9=	Urban	8

CRIME

T O P 1 0
COUNTRIES WITH THE HIGHEST CRIME RATES

Country	Reported crime rate per 100,000 population
1 Dominica	22,432
2 Suriname	17,819
3 St Kitts and Nevis	15,468
4 Sweden	14,188
5 New Zealand	13,247
6 Canada	11,443
7 Greenland	10,339
8 Denmark	10,270
9 Gibraltar	10,039
10 Guam	9,229
England and Wales	*8,986*
USA	*5,820*

These figures are based on reported crimes: the reporting of crimes is not solely a response to lawlessness, but also relates to the public confidence in the ability of the police. There are many countries in which crime is so commonplace and law enforcement so inefficient or corrupt that many incidents go unreported, since victims know that doing so would achieve no result.

T O P 1 0
COUNTRIES WITH MOST BURGLARIES

Country	Annual burglaries per 100,000 population
1 Netherlands	2,621.8
2 Bahamas	2,580.4
3 Israel	2,483.0
4 New Zealand	2,447.6
5 Denmark	2,382.9
6 Bermuda	2,092.3
7 England and Wales	1,991.2
8 Australia	1,962.8
9 Malta	1,907.1
10 Sweden	1,801.8
USA	*1,235.9*

T O P 1 0
COUNTRIES WITH THE LOWEST CRIME RATES

Country	Reported crime rate per 100,000 population
1 Togo	11.0
2 Bangladesh	16.8
3 Nepal	29.1
4= Congo	32.0
4= Niger	32.0
6 Guinea	32.4
7 Mali	33.0
8 Burkina Faso	41.0
9 Syria	73.0
10 Burundi	87.0

T O P 1 0
COMMONEST CRIMES 100 YEARS AGO

Offence	No. reported
1 Larcenies	63,740
2 Burglary and housebreaking	7,495
3 Frauds	2,628
4 Crimes of violence (other than murder)	1,975
5 Attempted suicide	1,861
6 Crimes against morals	1,736
7 Receiving	908
8 Robbery and extortion	375
9 Forgery	343
10 Arson	328

These are the annual averages of indictable crimes reported to the police in England and Wales during the period 1893–97. Falling just outside are the now virtually defunct crime of "coining" – the forgery of coins (230 cases) – and murder (143 cases). In the same period, various non-indictable offences also resulted in large numbers of trials – most notably for incidents of drunkenness (179,496), assault (73,048), and vagrancy (25,228).

T O P 1 0
COUNTRIES WITH MOST CAR THEFTS

Country	Annual thefts per 100,000 population
1 Switzerland	1,504.6*
2 New Zealand	1,026.4
3 England and Wales	977.4
4 Sweden	879.0
5 Australia	770.6
6 USA	657.8
7 Norway	608.7
8 Denmark	575.9
9 Italy	546.0
10 France	519.6

* Including motor cycles and bicycles.

T O P 1 0
UK DIPLOMATIC MISSIONS WITH THE MOST UNPAID PARKING FINES

Mission	Total unpaid fines 1992	1993
1 Nigeria	167	91
2 India	66	71
3 Saudi Arabia	127	60
4 Bangladesh	41	59
5 Pakistan	57	54
6= Germany	60	51
6= United Arab Emirates	128	51
8= Jordan	38	50
8= Hungary	60	50
10 Spain	60	48

For many years diplomats have used their immunity from prosecution to avoid paying parking fines. Since 1985, however, this practice has been challenged and pressure brought to bear on the offending embassies and international organizations to make their staffs behave responsibly. The total in 1993 was 1,941, a 53.4 per cent reduction on the 1992 figure of 4,166.

T O P   1 0

COMMONEST MOTORING OFFENCES IN THE UK

	Offence	% of motoring offences
1	Driving while uninsured	13.53
2	Speeding	10.78
3	Failing to pay road tax	9.38
4	Drink-driving	6.41
5	Careless driving	5.38
6	Driving without a licence	3.58
7	Defective tyres	3.42
8	Driving without L-plates	3.26
9	Unaccompanied L-driver	2.52
10	Driving while disqualified	2.22

T O P   1 0

COMMONEST REPORTED CRIMINAL OFFENCES IN ENGLAND AND WALES

		Offences		Increase %
		1982	1992	
1	Burglary	805,400	1,355,300	68
2	Theft from a motor vehicle	449,000	961,300	114
3	Criminal damage	417,800	892,600	113
4	Other theft*	515,800	702,600	36
5	Theft of a motor vehicle	351,200	587,900	67
6	Theft from a shop	242,300	288,700	19
7	Theft of a pedal cycle	125,000	222,200	78
8	Violence against the person	108,700	201,800	86
9	Fraud and forgery	123,100	168,600	37
10	Robbery	22,800	52,900	132
	Total (including those not in list)	*3,262,400*	*5,591,700*	*71*

* *Category not specified elsewhere.*

T O P   1 0

WORST AREAS FOR CAR CRIME IN ENGLAND AND WALES

	Police force	Total car crimes*	Risk factor
1	Avon & Somerset	62,238	43.5
2	Greater Manchester	110,357	43.1
3	West Yorkshire	87,091	42.2
4	Cleveland	22,435	40.2
5	South Wales	51,189	38.9
6	Humberside	33,606	38.4
7	Bedfordshire	20,281	38.0
8	Nottinghamshire	38,219	37.6
9	Northumbria	53,130	37.0
10	South Yorkshire	47,487	36.7

* *Includes both thefts of vehicles and thefts from vehicles.*

This league table for 1993 calculates the risk factor as crimes per 1,000 of the population in each police area. The safest area is shown to be Dyfed-Powys with 4,214 crimes – just 9.0 per 1,000, while Cleveland heads the table for thefts of (rather than from) cars with a risk factor of 23.7 per 1,000.

T O P   1 0

COMMONEST OFFENCES IN ENGLAND AND WALES IN 1992

	Offence	Offenders found guilty
1	Motoring offences	733,800
2	Theft and handling stolen goods	127,900
3	Burglary	44,300
4	Violence against the person	43,600
5	Other offences	36,000
6	Drug offences	22,700
7	Fraud and forgery	20,000
8	Criminal damage	9,800
9	Robbery	5,100
10	Sexual offences	5,000
	Total	*1,519,700*

This list includes both indictable offences (those normally calling for a trial before a jury), of which there were 324,900, and summary offences (usually tried before a magistrates' court), of which there were 1,194,800. In the latter category, motoring offences comprise the largest proportion, but other offences are less precisely itemized.

T O P   1 0

POLICE FORCE AREAS IN ENGLAND AND WALES HANDLING THE MOST CRIMES

	Police force	Offences reported
1	Metropolitan Police	942,000
2	Greater Manchester	390,862
3	West Midlands	335,663
4	West Yorkshire	305,679
5	Northumbria	221,792
6	Thames Valley	199,725
7	Avon & Somerset	183,994
8	South Wales	170,821
9	Nottinghamshire	165,863
10	Kent	163,229

In the year ending June 1993, a total of 5,676,734 offences were reported to the 43 police forces of England and Wales, a 3.8 per cent increase on the previous year and equivalent to one every five and a half seconds. The force that handled the smallest number was the City of London, with 6,182.

MURDER FACTS

COUNTRIES WITH THE HIGHEST MURDER RATES

	Country	Murders p.a. per 100,000 population
1	Swaziland	87.8
2	Bahamas	52.6
3	Lesotho	51.1
4	Colombia	40.5
5	Aruba	37.5
6	Sudan	30.5
7	Philippines	30.1
8	Guernsey	27.4
9	Nauru	25.0
10	Greenland	23.5
	USA	*9.1*
	England	*1.3*

WORST CITIES FOR MURDER IN THE US

	City	Murders
1	New York	1,995
2	Los Angeles	1,094
3	Chicago	939
4	Detroit	595
5	Houston	465
6	Washington DC	443
7	Philadelphia	425
8	Dallas	387
9	Baltimore	335
10	New Orleans	279

The identity of America's 10 murder capitals remains fairly consistent from year to year, with only some slight adjustment to the order. The figures here are for 1992, when the Top 10 accounted for 6,957, or 31 per cent of the total 22,540 murders committed in the US.

THE POINT OF THE MATTER
Contrary to press reports, killings involving guns in England and Wales have actually declined from a 1987 peak of 78, while homicides caused by sharp instruments have become more widespread.

COMMONEST MURDER WEAPONS/METHODS IN ENGLAND AND WALES

	Weapon/method	Victims
1	Sharp instrument	226
2	Hitting and kicking	140
3	Strangulation and asphyxiation	80
4	Shooting	52
5	Blunt instrument	51
6	Burning	24
7	Drowning	15
8	Poison and drugs	14
9	Motor vehicle	9
10	Explosives	4

According to Home Office statistics, there were 622 homicides in 1992 in England and Wales (382 male and 240 female victims). In addition to those in the list, the apparent method in five incidents is described as "other" and two of unknown cause. This represents a fall on the previous year, but the general trend has been one of increase – although it should be noted that some offences first recorded as homicides were later reclassified. The number of victims first exceeded the 400 mark in 1952, 500 in 1974, and 600 in 1979. Based on the 1992 statistic, however, England and Wales are still relatively safe countries: the odds of being murdered in England and Wales are one in 79,090. One is more than six times as likely to be killed in the US.

WORST YEARS FOR GUN MURDERS IN THE US

	Year	Victims
1	1992	15,377
2	1991	14,265
3	1980	13,650
4	1990	12,847
5	1981	12,523
6	1974	12,474
7	1975	12,061
8	1989	11,832
9	1982	11,721
10	1986	11,381

DID YOU KNOW

US CRIME CLOCK

The murder rate in the US (1992 statistics) is equivalent to one murder every 23 minutes. More common crimes produce equally alarming statistics: there is a robbery every 47 seconds, a motor vehicle theft every 20 seconds, and a burglary every 11 seconds.

TOP 10

WORST YEARS FOR MURDER IN THE US

	Year	Victims
1	1992	22,540
2	1980	21,860
3	1991	21,505
4	1981	20,053
5	1990	20,045
6	1982	19,485
7	1986	19,257
8	1989	18,954
9	1983	18,673
10	1975	18,642

TOP 10

COMMONEST MURDER WEAPONS/METHODS IN THE US

	Weapon/method	Victims
1	Handguns	12,489
2	Knives or cutting instruments	3,265
3	"Personal weapons" (hands, feet, fists, etc)	1,114
4	Shotguns	1,104
5	Firearms (type not stated)	1,086
6	Blunt objects (hammers, clubs, etc)	1,029
7	Rifles	698
8	Strangulation	313
9	Fire	203
10	Asphyxiation	114

Less common methods included drowning (27 cases), explosives (19) and poison (13). The total number of murders for the year amounted to 22,540 – or one person in every 11,034. The order of the weapons has not changed much in recent years, but the numbers have increased dramatically: in 1965, for example, there were 8,773 murder victims in the US, with firearms used in 5,015 cases. By 1992 the figure had risen by 257 per cent, with 15,377, or 68 per cent, committed using firearms.

DID YOU KNOW

ENGLAND AND WALES CRIME CLOCK

Based on 1992 crime figures for England and Wales, a murder is committed, on average, every 14 hours, a robbery every 10 minutes, a violent crime every three minutes, a motor vehicle theft every 53 seconds, and a burglary every 23 seconds. If comparing with the US crime clock (see facing page), it should be borne in mind that the population of the US is almost exactly five times that of England and Wales.

TOP 10

RELATIONSHIPS OF HOMICIDE VICTIMS TO PRINCIPAL SUSPECTS IN ENGLAND AND WALES

	Relationship	Victims
1	Male friend or acquaintance	131
2	Male stranger	97
3	Wife, ex-wife, or female cohabitant	91
4	Female friend or acquaintance	39
5	Son	31
6	Daughter	28
7	Female stranger	22
8	Husband, ex-husband, or male cohabitant	20
9	Female lover, ex-lover, or lover's spouse	18
10	Father	8

In 1992 five mothers were killed by their sons or daughters, and 13 homicide victims were unspecified male and 10 female family members.

GUN MURDERS
Handguns are the number one murder weapon in the US while shooting ranks only fourth as a method of killing in the UK.

TOP 10

WORST STATES FOR MURDER IN THE US

	State	Firearms used	Total murders
1	California	2,851	3,921
2	New York	1,760	2,370
3	Texas	1,627	2,239
4	Illinois	832	1,217
5	Florida	712	1,176
6	Michigan	655	934
7	North Carolina	450	708
8	Pennsylvania	450	684
9	Georgia	443	671
10	Louisiana	507	659

Of the 14,579 murders committed in the Top 10 states in 1992, firearms were used in 10,287, or 70.6 per cent. In that year, there were more murders in Pennsylvania, ranked 8th in the list, and with an estimated 1992 resident population of 12,009,000, than in the whole of England and Wales, with more than four times as many inhabitants. The top three states all had murder rates of close to 13.0 per 100,000 of the population, while of those appearing in the Top 10, the highest murder rate (15.4 per 100,000) occurred in Louisiana and the lowest (5.7 per 100,000) in Pennsylvania.

MURDER MOST FOUL

MOST PROLIFIC SERIAL KILLERS OF THE 20TH CENTURY

Serial killers are mass murderers who kill repeatedly, often over long periods, in contrast to the so-called "spree killers" who have been responsible for massacres on single occasions, usually with guns, and other perpetrators of single outrages, often by means of bombs, resulting in multiple deaths. Because of the secrecy surrounding their horrific crimes, and the time-spans involved, it is almost impossible to calculate the precise numbers of serial killers' victims. The numbers of murders attributed to these criminals should be taken as "best estimates" based on the most reliable evidence available. Such is the magnitude of the crimes of some of them, however, that some of the figures may be under-estimates.

1   Pedro Alonzo (or Armando) López

Up to his 1980 capture, López, known as the "Monster of the Andes", led police to 53 graves, but probably murdered a total of more than 300 young girls in Colombia, Ecuador, and Peru. He was sentenced to life imprisonment.

2   Henry Lee Lucas

The subject of the film, Henry, Portrait of a Serial Killer, *Lucas (b.1937) may have*

committed up to 200 murders. In 1983 he admitted to 360 and was convicted of 11, and is currently on Death Row in Huntsville, Texas. His full catalogue of victims will probably never be known.*

3   Bruno Lüdke

Lüdke (b.1909) was a German who confessed to murdering 86 women between 1928 and 29 January 1943. Declared insane, he was incarcerated in a Vienna hospital where he was subjected to medical experiments, apparently dying on 8 April 1944 after a lethal injection.

4   Delfina and Maria de Jesús Gonzales

After abducting girls to work in their Mexican brothel, Rancho El Angel, the Gonzales sisters murdered as many as 80 of them, and an unknown number of their customers, and buried them in the grounds. In 1964 the two were sentenced to 40 years' imprisonment.

5   Daniel Camargo Barbosa

Coincidentally, eight years after the arrest of Lopez in Ecuador, Barbosa was captured following a similar series of horrific murders of children – with a probable total of 71 victims. He was sentenced to just 16 years in prison.

6   Kampatimar Shankariya

Caught after a two-year spree during which he killed as many as 70 times, Shankariya was hanged in Jaipur, India, on 16 May 1979.

ANDREI CHIKATILO
Chikatilo successfully led a double life as a married father and schoolteacher and Communist party member for the 12 years he preyed on the citizens of Rostov-on-Don.

MOST PROLIFIC MURDERERS IN THE UK

1   Mary Ann Cotton

Cotton (b.1832), a former nurse, is generally held to be the UK's worst mass murderer. Over a 20-year period, it seems probable that she disposed of 14–20 victims, including her husband, children, and stepchildren, by arsenic poisoning. She was hanged at Durham on 24 March 1873.

2   Michael Ryan

On 19 August 1987 in Hungerford, Berkshire, Ryan (b.1960), who had no previous convictions, armed himself with an AK47 Kalashnikov assault rifle, an M1 carbine, and a 9-mm Beretta pistol and went on a rampage, shooting 14 dead – including his mother – and wounding 16 others (two of whom died later) before shooting himself.

3= William Burke and William Hare

Two Irishmen living in Edinburgh, Burke and Hare murdered at least 15 people in order to sell their bodies (for £8 to £14 each) to anatomists in the period before human

dissection was legal. Burke was hanged on 28 January 1829 while Hare, having turned king's evidence , was released a week later and allegedly died a blind beggar in London in the 1860s.*

3= Bruce Lee

In 1981 Lee was convicted of arson that resulted in the deaths of 26 residents of an old people's home. He was later cleared by the Court of Appeal of 11 of the deaths. He is currently in a mental hospital.

3= Dennis Andrew Nilsen

Nilsen (b.1948) admitted to murdering 15 men between 1978 and 1983. On 4 November 1983 he was sentenced to life imprisonment on six charges of murder and two charges of attempted murder.

6   Dr William Palmer

Dubbed the "Rugeley Poisoner" after the Staffordshire town where he lived, Palmer (b.1824) may have killed at least 13, probably

14, and perhaps as many as 16. These included his wife, brother, and children, killed in order to claim insurance, and various men whom he robbed to pay off his gambling debts. He was hanged at Stafford on 14 June 1856. The true number of his victims remains uncertain.*

7   Peter Sutcliffe

Known as the "Yorkshire Ripper", Sutcliffe (b.1946) was caught on 2 January 1981. On 22 May 1981 he was found guilty of murdering 13 women and of seven attempted murders between 1975 and 1980. He was sentenced to life imprisonment on each charge and is currently in Parkhurst Prison.

8   Peter Thomas Anthony Manuel

Found guilty of murdering seven people, and hanged at Barlinnie Prison on 11 July 1958, Manuel may have killed as many as 12.

9   John George Haigh

Haigh, the so-called "Acid Bath Murderer", certainly killed six and may have disposed of

7 Randolph Kraft

From 1972 until his arrest on 14 May 1983, Kraft is thought to have murdered 67 men. On 29 November 1989 he was found guilty on 16 counts and was sentenced to death in the San Quentin gas chamber.

8 Dr Marcel André Henri Felix Petiot

Dr Marcel Petiot (b.1897), once mayor of Villeneuve, is known to have killed at least 27 but admitted to 63 murders at his Paris house during the Second World War. He claimed that they were Nazi collaborators, but it is probable that they were wealthy Jews whom he robbed and killed after pretending to help them escape from occupied France. Petiot was guillotined on 26 May 1946.

9 Donald Harvey

Working as an orderly in hospitals in Kentucky and Ohio, Harvey is believed to have murdered some 58 patients up to the time of his arrest in March 1987. He pleaded guilty to 24 murders for which he received multiple life sentences, later confessing to further charges and receiving additional sentences.

10 Andrei Chikatilo

Russia's worst serial killer was convicted in Rostov-on-Don in 1992 of killing 52 women and children between 1978 and 1990. He was executed by a firing squad at Novocherkassk prison on 14 February 1994.

---

up to nine victims. He was hanged at Wandsworth Prison on 10 August 1949.

10 "Jack the Ripper"

In 1888 in Whitechapel, London, "Jack the Ripper" killed and mutilated five or six women. Despite more than a century of speculation and a list of possible candidates now running into dozens, his true identity and dates remain unknown.

Other multiple murderers in British history include John Reginald Halliday Christie, who may have killed as many as six women at 10 Rillington Place, London, and was hanged at Pentonville Prison on 15 July 1953. On 7 May 1981 John Thompson was found guilty on one specimen charge of murder by arson during an incident in which a total of 37 died at the Spanish Club, Denmark Street, London.

T O P   1 0

WORST GUN MASSACRES OF ALL TIME

(By individuals, excluding terrorist and military actions; totals exclude perpetrator)

Perpetrator/location/date circumstances	Killed
1 Woo Bum Kong Sang-Namdo, South Korea, 28 April 1982	57

Off-duty policeman Woo Bum Kong (or Wou Bom-Kon), 27, went on a drunken rampage with rifles and hand grenades, killing 57 and injuring 38 before blowing himself up.

Perpetrator/location/date circumstances	Killed
2 Baruch Goldstein Hebron, Occupied West Bank, Israel, 25 February 1994	29

Goldstein, a 42-year-old US immigrant doctor, carried out a gun massacre of Palestinians at prayer at the Tomb of the Patriarchs before being beaten to death by the crowd.

Perpetrator/location/date circumstances	Killed
3= James Oliver Huberty San Ysidro, California, USA, 18 July 1984	22

Huberty, aged 41, opened fire in a McDonald's restaurant, killing 21 before being shot dead by a SWAT marksman. A further 19 were wounded, one of whom died the following day.

Perpetrator/location/date circumstances	Killed
3= George Hennard Killeen, Texas, USA, 16 October 1991	22

Hennard drove his pick-up truck through the window of Luby's Cafeteria and, in 11 minutes, killed 22 with semi-automatic pistols before shooting himself.

Perpetrator/location/date circumstances	Killed
5= Charles Joseph Whitman, Austin, Texas, USA, 31 July–1 August 1966	16

25-year-old ex-Marine marksman Whitman killed his mother and wife and the following day took the lift to the 27th floor of the campus tower and ascended to the observation deck at the University of Texas at Austin, from where he shot 14 and wounded 34 before being shot dead by police officer Romero Martinez.

Perpetrator/location/date circumstances	Killed
5= Michael Ryan, Hungerford, Berkshire, UK, 19 August 1987	16

Ryan, 26, shot 14 dead and wounded 16 others (two of whom died later) before shooting himself.

Perpetrator/location/date circumstances	Killed
5= Ronald Gene Simmons Russellville, Arkansas, USA, 28 December 1987	16

47-year-old Simmons killed 16, including 14 members of his own family, by shooting or strangling. He was caught and on 10 February 1989 was sentenced to death.

Perpetrator/location/date circumstances	Killed
8= Wagner von Degerloch Muehlhausen, Germany, 3–4 September 1913	14

Wagner von Degerloch, a 39-year-old school-teacher, murdered his wife and four children before embarking on a random shooting spree as a result of which nine more were killed and 12 injured. Regarded as one of the first "spree killers", von Degerloch was committed to a mental asylum where he died in 1938.

Perpetrator/location/date circumstances	Killed
8= Patrick Henry Sherrill Edmond, Oklahoma, USA, 20 August 1986	14

Sherrill, aged 44, shot 14 dead and wounded six others at the post office where he worked before killing himself.

Perpetrator/location/date circumstances	Killed
8= Christian Dornier Luxiol, Doubs, France, 12 July 1989	14

Dornier, a 31-year-old farmer, went on a rampage leaving 14 dead and nine injured, including several children, before being wounded and caught by police.

Perpetrator/location/date circumstances	Killed
8= Marc Lépine Montreal University, Canada, 6 December 1989	14

In Canada's worst gun massacre, Lépine, a 25-year-old student, went on an armed rampage, firing only at women, then shot himself.

GEORGE HENNARD
Police found over 100 spent cartridges in the carnage that spree killer Hennard left behind.

POLICE AND PRISONS

TOP 10

COUNTRIES WITH MOST POLICE OFFICERS

	Country	Population per police officer
1	Angola	14*
2	Kuwait	80
3	Nicaragua	90*
4	Brunei	100
5=	Nauru	110
5=	Cape Verde	110
7=	Antigua and Barbuda	120
7=	Mongolia	120
7=	Seychelles	120
10=	Iraq	140
10=	United Arab Emirates	140
	USA	345
	UK	420

* Including civilian militia.

DID YOU KNOW

A MAN OF MANY PARTS

The original model for Sherlock Holmes, the most famous of all fictional detectives, is claimed to have been Dr Joseph Bell (1837–1911), an Edinburgh surgeon whose methods of deducing details of his patients' lives from their appearance was observed first-hand by Arthur Conan Doyle when he was a medical student. Others have also been credited with providing elements of Holmes's character, among them another Scottish doctor, Professor Sir Robert Christison, called as an expert witness in the Burke and Hare body-snatching trial, and Wendel Scherer, a real-life "consulting detective". His first name may come from the cricketer Mordecai Sherlock, and Holmes is perhaps a tribute to the American author and physician Oliver Wendell Holmes. Features such as Holmes's famous deerstalker hat were invented by the illustrators and actors who first portrayed him.

TOP 10

COUNTRIES WITH FEWEST POLICE OFFICERS

	Country	Population per police officer
1	Maldives	35,710
2	Canada	8,640
3	Rwanda	4,650
4	Ivory Coast	4,640
5	Gambia	3,310
6	Benin	3,250
7	Madagascar	2,900
8	Central African Republic	2,740
9	Bangladesh	2,560
10	Niger	2,350*

* Including paramilitary forces.

TOP 10

COMMONEST REASONS FOR ARREST IN THE US

	Offence	Arrests
1	Driving under the influence	1,624,500
2	Larceny-theft	1,504,500
3	Drug abuse violations	1,066,400
4	Drunkenness	832,300
5	Disorderly conduct	753,100
6	Aggravated assault	507,210
7	Fraud	424,200
8	Burglary	424,000
9	Vandalism	323,100
10	Weapons*	239,300

* Carrying, possessing, etc.

The total number of arrests in the US in 1992, including those for offences not appearing in the Top 10, was 14,075,100 – equivalent to 5.5 per cent of the population. Of these, 81 per cent were males – although larceny-theft was the crime for which most females were arrested, and accounted for the greatest number of arrests for both sexes among those under the age of 18.

TOP 10

US CITIES WITH THE LARGEST POLICE FORCES

	City	State	No. of police officers
1	New York	New York	28,249
2	Chicago	Illinois	12,238
3	Los Angeles	California	7,800
4	Philadelphia	Pennsylvania	6,233
5	Washington	D.C.	4,224
6	Houston	Texas	4,201
7	Detroit	Michigan	3,845
8	Dallas	Texas	2,882
9	Baltimore	Maryland	2,844
10	Milwaukee	Wisconsin	2,002

In 1992 there were 544,309 law enforcement officers (plus 204,521 civilians) serving the US, a national average of 2.2 per 1,000 of the population. Of these, 91 per cent were male and 9 per cent female. A bill announced in August 1993 provided funds for a further 50,000 officers as the first step towards an additional 100,000. In the period from 1980 to 1992 an average of 146 officers a year were killed in the line of duty, either feloniously or as a result of accidents.

TOP 10

COMMONEST REASONS FOR HIRING PRIVATE DETECTIVES

1	Tracing debtors
2	Serving writs
3	Locating assets
4	Assessing accident cases
5	Tracing missing persons
6	Insurance claims
7	Matrimonial
8	Countering industrial espionage
9	Criminal cases
10	Vetting personnel

T O P   1 0

LARGEST PRISONS IN ENGLAND AND WALES

	Prison	Inmates
1	Walton, Liverpool	1,253
2	Armley, Leeds	896
3	Wandsworth, London	800
4	Winson Green, Birmingham	798
5	Feltham, London	718
6	Glen Parva, Leicester	688
7	Belmarsh, London	678
8	Wormwood Scrubs, London	669
9	Wakefield, North Yorkshire	642
10	Pentonville, London	631

Figures are for average prison populations in 1993. Strangeways, Manchester, formerly England's largest prison, was wrecked during a prisoners' riot in April 1990 and had not been fully re-opened.

T O P   1 0

LARGEST PRISONS IN SCOTLAND

	Prison	Inmates
1	Barlinnie, Glasgow	930
2	Edinburgh	555
3	Shotts, Lanarkshire	468
4	Perth	420
5	Glenochil, near Alloa	375
6	Low Moss, near Glasgow	346
7	Peterhead, near Aberdeen	207
8	Greenock	182
9	Longriggend, near Airdrie	157
10	Cornton Vale	128

The figures are as at 24 December 1993, when a number of prisoners would have been released on parole for Christmas, and are hence not representative of peak populations in these prisons.

DID YOU KNOW

INSIDE STORIES

Perhaps the most productive of prison industries, at least in terms of literature, has been authorship, for many famous books have been penned by prisoners. While in prison in Spain, Miguel de Cervantes wrote *Don Quixote* (1605); Sir Walter Raleigh's *History of the World* (1614) was written during his stay in the Tower of London; and John Bunyan's *The Pilgrim's Progress* was written after he was thrown into Bedford gaol in 1660 for preaching without a licence.

T O P   1 0

PRISON INDUSTRIES IN ENGLAND AND WALES

	Industry	Workshop places
1	Textiles	2,426
2	Tailoring/shirts	2,257
3	Contract services	1,779
4	Laundries	1,082
5	Engineering	780
6	Woodwork	758
7	Weaving	334
8	Printing and binding	286
9	Footwear/leatherwork	266
10	Others*	210

* Including concrete and plastic moulding, brushmaking, computer aided drafting, etc.

Sewing mailbags is perhaps the best known of prison industries, but has been replaced by ever more sophisticated activities which are increasingly encouraged – "purposeful activity" (including vocational and other courses) of 24.9 hours a week per prisoner is the official 1994 target. The value of goods and services currently produced is £55,000,000 per annum, from which prisoners earn on average £6.00 a week, while those involved in specialized contract work for external companies (such as making mozzarella cheese at East Sutton Park, a women's open prison near Maidstone, in Kent) can earn £3.00 an hour.

CAPITAL PUNISHMENT

TOP 10

FIRST COUNTRIES TO ABOLISH CAPITAL PUNISHMENT

	Country	Abolished
1	Russia	1826
2	Venezuela	1863
3	Portugal	1867
4=	Brazil	1882
4=	Costa Rica	1882
6	Ecuador	1897
7	Panama	1903
8	Norway	1905
9	Uruguay	1907
10	Colombia	1910

Some countries abolished capital punishment in peacetime only, or for all crimes except treason, generally extending it totally at a more recent date. Some countries retained capital punishment on their statute books, but effectively abolished it: the last execution in Liechtenstein, for example, took place in 1795, in Mexico in 1946, and in Belgium in 1950.

THE HOT SEAT
This form of capital punishment was first adopted by the State of New York, and the first person to be executed in this way was William Kemmler, on 6 August 1890, in Auburn Prison.

THE TEN

LAST MEN HANGED FOR MURDER IN THE UK

1 Samuel McLaughlin   25 Jul 1961
Crumlin Road Gaol, Belfast, for the murder of his wife Nellie.

2 Hendryk Niemasz   8 Sep 1961
Wandsworth Prison, London, for the shotgun murder of Hubert Buxton and his wife Alice.

3 James Hanratty   4 Apr 1962
Bedford Jail, for the gun murder of Michael Gregsten at Deadman's Hill – the so-called "A6 murder".

4 Oswald Grey   20 Nov 1962
Hanged at Winson Green prison, Birmingham, for the murder by shooting of newsagent Thomas Bates.

5 James Smith   28 Nov 1962
Strangeways Prison, Manchester, for the murder of shopkeeper Isabella Cross.

6 Henry Burnett   5 Aug 1963
Hanged at Aberdeen Prison for the shotgun murder of merchant seaman Thomas Guyan – the first hanging in Aberdeen for 106 years.

7 Russell Pascoe   17 Dec 1963
Bristol Prison, for the murder by bludgeoning and stabbing of wealthy Cornish recluse William Rowe.

8 Dennis Whitty   17 Dec 1963
Winchester Prison, for the same crime as Russell Pascoe.

9 Peter Anthony Allen   13 Aug 1964
Walton Jail, for the robbery, and the murder by battering and stabbing, of John Alan West.

10 John Robson Welby   13 Aug 1964
      (aka Gwynne Owen Evans)
Strangeways Prison, Manchester, for the same crime as Peter Allen.

THE TEN

LAST EXECUTED AT THE TOWER OF LONDON

1 Wilhelm Johannes Roos   30 Jul 1915
A Dutchman who had posed as a cigar salesman, sending coded messages to a firm in Holland detailing ship movements in British ports, Roos was the third spy of the First World War to be shot at the Tower of London.

2 Haike Marinus
     Petrus Janssen   30 Jul 1915
An accomplice of Roos who used the same methods. They were tried together, with Janssen shot 10 minutes after Roos, at 6.10 in the morning.

3 Ernst Waldemar Melin   10 Sep 1915
A German spy, shot after General Court Martial.

4 Agusto Alfredo Roggen   17 Sep 1915
A German who attempted to escape the death penalty by claiming to be Uruguayan, he was found guilty of spying on tests of a new torpedo at Loch Lomond, then sending information in invisible ink.

5 Fernando Buschman   19 Oct 1915
Posing as a Dutch violinist, he spied while offering entertainment at Royal Navy bases.

6 Georg T. Breeckow   26 Oct 1915
Posing as an American, Reginald Rowland, with a forged passport, he was caught when he sent a parcel containing secret messages, but addressed in German style, with country and town name preceding that of the street.

7 Irving Guy Ries   27 Oct 1915
A German commercial traveller sentenced to death on spying charges.

8 Albert Meyer   2 Dec 1915
Like Ries, a German spy posing as a commercial traveller.

9 Y. L. Zender-Hurwitz   11 Apr 1916
A spy of Peruvian descent charged with sending information to Germany about British troop movements, for which he received a salary of £30 a month.

10 Josef Jakobs   15 Aug 1941
A German army sergeant caught when he parachuted into England wearing civilian clothes and with an identity card in the name of James Rymer. Following General Court Martial, he was shot at 7.15 am – the only spy executed at the Tower in the Second World War.

TOP 10

NAZI WAR CRIMINALS HANGED AT NUREMBERG

(Following the International Military Tribunal trials, 20 November 1945 to 31 August 1946)

1 Joachim Von Ribbentrop, 53, former Ambassador to Great Britain and Hitler's last Foreign Minister (the first to be hanged, at 1.02 am)

2 Field Marshal Wilhelm Von Keitel, 64, who had ordered the killing of 50 Allied air force officers after the Great Escape

3 General Ernst Kaltenbrunner, 44, SS and Gestapo leader

4 Reichminister Alfred Rosenburg, 53, ex-Minister for Occupied Eastern territories

5 Reichminister Hans Frank, 46, ex-Governor of Poland

6 Reichminister Wilhelm Frick, 69, former Minister of the Interior

7 Gauleiter Julius Streicher, 61, editor of anti-Semitic magazine *Die Stürmer*

8 Reichminister Fritz Sauckel, 52, ex-General Plenipotentiary for the Utilization of Labour (the slave-labour programme)

9 Colonel-General Alfred Jodl, 56, former Chief of the General Staff

10 Gauleiter Artur Von Seyss-Inquart, Governor of Austria and later Commissioner for Occupied Holland (the last to be hanged)

TOP 10

CAPITAL PUNISHMENT STATES IN THE USA

	State	Death penalty now in force	Executed 1930–87
1	Georgia	Electrocution	378
2	New York	None	329
3	Texas	Lethal injection	323
4	California	Lethal gas	292
5	North Carolina	Lethal gas or injection	266
6	Florida	Electrocution	187
7	Ohio	Electrocution	172
8	South Carolina	Electrocution	164
9	Mississippi	Lethal injection	157
10	Pennsylvania	Electrocution	152

PRISON TOWER
Construction of the Tower of London fortress, on the north bank of the River Thames, was begun in 1078 by William the Conqueror. The Beauchamp Tower, built in the 12th century, has housed many illustrious prisoners, including Lady Jane Grey and Sir Walter Raleigh.

CRIME OF PASSION?
At her trial, Ruth Ellis was asked what her intentions had been when, on 10 April 1955, she emptied a Smith and Wesson revolver into her ex-lover, David Blakely, outside a London pub. She replied, "I intended to kill him". The jury took 14 minutes to reach a verdict of guilty, and on 13 July 1955 she became the last woman to be hanged for murder in the UK.

THE TEN

LAST WOMEN HANGED FOR MURDER IN THE UK

1 Edith Thompson   9 Jan 1923

Hanged at Holloway Prison, London, on the same day that her accomplice Frederick Bywaters was hanged at Pentonville Prison, London, for stabbing to death Edith's husband Percy.

2 Susan Newell   10 Oct 1923

Duke Street Prison, Glasgow, for strangling 13-year-old paperboy John Johnston.

3 Louie Calvert (aka Louise Jackson/Gomersal)   26 Jun 1926

Strangeways Prison, Manchester, for battering and strangling landlady Lily Waterhouse.

4 Ethel Major   19 Dec 1934

Hull Prison, for murdering her husband Arthur with strychnine-laced corned beef.

5 Dorothea Waddingham   16 Apr 1936

Winson Green Prison, Birmingham. Waddingham, a nurse, killed her patient Ada Baguley, and probably Ada's mother.

6 Charlotte Bryant   15 Jul 1936

Exeter Gaol, for the arsenic poisoning of her husband Frederick.

7 Margaret Allen   12 Jan 1949

Strangeways Prison, Manchester, for battering Nancy Chadwick to death with a coal hammer.

8 Louisa May Merrifield   18 Sep 1953

Strangeways Prison, Manchester, for poisoning her employer Sarah Ann Ricketts in order to inherit her property.

9 Styllou Christofi   13 Dec 1954

Holloway Prison, London, for strangling and burning the body of her daughter-in-law Hella Christofi.

10 Ruth Ellis   13 Jul 1955

Holloway Prison, London, for shooting racing driver David Blakely.

THE WORLD AT WAR

ALLIES
World War I badge showing the united flags of France, Britain, and Belgium.

T O P 1 0

LARGEST ARMED FORCES OF WORLD WAR I

	Country	Personnel*
1	Russia	12,000,000
2	Germany	11,000,000
3	British Empire	8,904,467
4	France	8,410,000
5	Austria-Hungary	7,800,000
6	Italy	5,615,000
7	USA	4,355,000
8	Turkey	2,850,000
9	Bulgaria	1,200,000
10	Japan	800,000

* *Total at peak strength.*

T O P 1 0

COUNTRIES SUFFERING THE GREATEST MILITARY LOSSES IN WORLD WAR I

	Country	Killed
1	Germany	1,773,700
2	Russia	1,700,000
3	France	1,357,800
4	Austria-Hungary	1,200,000
5	British Empire*	908,371
6	Italy	650,000
7	Romania	335,706
8	Turkey	325,000
9	USA	116,516
10	Bulgaria	87,500

The number of battle fatalities and deaths from other causes among military personnel varied enormously from country to country: Romania's death rate was highest at 45 per cent of its total mobilized forces; Germany's was 16 per cent, Austria-Hungary's and Russia's 15 per cent, and the British Empire's 10 per cent, with the USA's 2 per cent and Japan's 0.04 per cent among the lowest.

* *Including Australia, Canada, India, New Zealand, South Africa, etc.*

AFTERMATH
A forest strewn with dead Russian soldiers after a First World War battle.

BELGIAN ARMS AND FLAG

DID YOU KNOW

THE WORST WARS OF THE 20TH CENTURY

While the military fatalities of the First and Second World Wars were the worst of the 20th century, several other wars of the past 60 years have resulted in horrifically high levels of casualties. The Korean War of 1950–53 produced an estimated 1,893,100 military deaths, while the Sino-Japanese War (1937–41) and the Biafra-Nigeria Civil War (1967–70) are each believed to have caused 1,000,000 losses, and the Spanish Civil War (1936–39) an estimated 611,000. The Vietnam War (1961–73) produced 546,000, and some 200,000 were sustained in each of three further campaigns: the India-Pakistan War (1947), the USSR's invasion of Afghanistan (1979–89), and the Iran-Iraq War (1980–88).

T O P 1 0

COUNTRIES WITH THE MOST PRISONERS OF WAR, 1914–18

	Country	Captured		Country	Captured
1	Russia	2,500,000	6	Turkey	250,000
2	Austria-Hungary	2,200,000	7	British Empire	191,652
3	Germany	1,152,800	8	Serbia	152,958
4	Italy	600,000	9	Romania	80,000
5	France	537,000	10	Belgium	34,659

TOP 10

SMALLEST ARMED FORCES OF WORLD WAR II

	Country	Personnel*
1	Costa Rica	400
2	Liberia	1,000
3=	El Salvador	3,000
3=	Honduras	3,000
3=	Nicaragua	3,000
6	Haiti	3,500
7	Dominican Republic	4,000
8	Guatemala	5,000
9=	Bolivia	8,000
9=	Paraguay	8,000
9=	Uruguay	8,000

* Total at peak strength.

Several of the South American countries entered the Second World War at a very late stage: Argentina, for example, did not declare war on Germany and Japan until 27 March 1945. The smallest European armed force was that of Denmark, with a maximum strength of 15,000. Just 13 of the Danish soldiers were killed during the one-day German invasion of 9 April 1940, when Denmark became the second country after Poland to be occupied.

TOP 10

LARGEST ARMED FORCES OF WORLD WAR II

	Country	Personnel*
1	USSR	12,500,000
2	USA	12,364,000
3	Germany	10,000,000
4	Japan	6,095,000
5	France	5,700,000
6	UK	4,683,000
7	Italy	4,500,000
8	China	3,800,000
9	India	2,150,000
10	Poland	1,000,000

* Total at peak strength.

TOP 10

TANKS OF WORLD WAR II

	Tank/country/(introduced)	Weight (tonnes)	No. produced
1	Sherman, USA (1942)	31.0	41,530
2	T34 Model 42, USSR (1940)	28.5	35,120
3	T34/85, USSR (1944)	32.0	29,430
4	M3 General Stuart, USA (1941)	12.2	14,000
5	Valentine II, UK (1941)	17.5	8,280
6	M3A1 Lee/Grant, USA (1941)	26.8	7,400
7	Churchill VII, UK (1942)	40.0	5,640
8=	Panzer IVD, Germany (pre-war)	20,0	5,500
8=	Panzer VG, Germany (1943)	44.8	5,500
10	Crusader I, UK (1941)	19.0	4,750

TOP 10

COUNTRIES SUFFERING THE GREATEST MILITARY LOSSES IN WORLD WAR II

	Country	Killed
1	USSR	13,600,000
2	Germany	3,300,000
3	China	1,324,516
4	Japan	1,140,429
5	British Empire* (of which UK	357,116 264,000)
6	Romania	350,000
7	Poland	320,000
8	Yugoslavia	305,000
9	USA	292,131
10	Italy	279,800

* Including Australia, Canada, India, New Zealand, etc.

The actual numbers killed in the Second World War have been the subject of intense argument for nearly 50 years. The immense level of the military casualty rate of the USSR in particular is hard to comprehend. It is included here at its likely lowest level, but most authorities now reckon that of the 30,000,000 Soviets who bore arms, as many as 8,500,000 died in action and up to 2,500,000 of wounds received in battle and disease. Some 5,800,000 were taken prisoner, of which perhaps 3,300,000 may have died in captivity. It should also be borne in mind that these were military losses: to these should be added many untold millions of civilian war deaths.

MOUNTAIN GUN
The WWII 3.7-in howitzer was ideal for use in hilly terrain, as the barrel could be raised high enough to fire over peaks. This "pack howitzer" could be broken down into eight pieces for transporting by mules.

ACES HIGH

T he term "ace" was first used during the First World War for a pilot who had brought down at least five enemy aircraft; the British regarded the tally for an "ace" as varying from three to ten aircraft. The first reference in print to an air "ace" appeared in an article in *The Times* (14 September 1917). The names of French pilots who achieved this feat were recorded in official communiqués, but while US and other pilots followed the same system, the British definition of an "ace" was never officially approved, remaining an informal concept during both world wars. The German equivalent of the air "ace" was *Oberkanone*, which means "top gun".

LVG CVI, 1917
This German aircraft, fitted with guns and able to carry bombs, was one of the most versatile of the World War I aeroplanes.

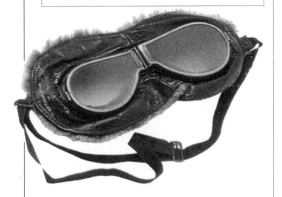

T O P 1 0

BRITISH AND COMMONWEALTH AIR ACES OF WORLD WAR I

	Pilot	Nationality	Kills claimed
1	Edward Mannock	British	73
2	William Avery Bishop	Canadian	72
3	Raymond Collishaw	Canadian	60
4	James Thomas Byford McCudden	British	57
5=	Anthony Wetherby Beauchamp-Proctor	British	54
5=	Donald Roderick MacLaren	British	54
7	William George Barker	Canadian	53
8	Robert Alexander Little	Australian	47
9=	Philip Fletcher Fullard	British	46
9=	George Edward Henry McElroy	Irish	46

This Top 10 takes account of British Empire pilots belonging to the Royal Flying Corps, the Royal Naval Air Service, and (after 1 April 1918) the Royal Air Force. The total of Edward "Mick" Mannock (1887–1918) may actually be greater than those definitely credited to him. Similarly, British pilot Albert Ball is generally credited with 44 kills (and hence not in the Top 10), but with the qualification that his total may have been greater. If this list were extended to include French pilots it would have (at No. 1) René Paul Fonck (1894–1953) with 75 kills and Georges-Marie Ludovic Jules Guynemer (1894–1917) with 54.

T O P 1 0

GERMAN AIR ACES OF WORLD WAR I

	Pilot	Kills claimed
1	Manfred von Richthofen*	80
2	Ernst Udet	62
3	Erich Loewenhardt	53
4	Werner Voss	48
5	Fritz Rumey	45
6	Rudolph Berthold	44
7	Paul Bäumer	43
8=	Josef Jacobs	41
8=	Bruno Loerzer	41
10=	Oswald Boelcke	40
10=	Franz Büchner	40
10=	Lothar Freiherr von Richthofen*	40

* Brothers.

Top World War I "ace" Rittmeister Manfred, Baron von Richthofen's claim of 80 kills has been disputed, since only 60 of them have been completely confirmed. Richthofen, known as the "Red Baron" and leader of the so-called "Flying Circus" (because the aircraft of his squadron were painted in distinctive bright colours), shot down 21 Allied fighters in the single month of April 1917. His own end a year later, on 21 April 1918, has been the subject of controversy ever since, and it remains uncertain whether his Fokker triplane was shot down in aerial combat with British pilot Captain A. Roy Brown (who was credited with the kill) or by shots from Australian machine gunners on the ground.

THE "RED BARON"
Baron von Richthofen has passed into legend as the greatest air ace of the First World War.

BRITISH AND COMMONWEALTH AIR ACES OF WORLD WAR II

	Pilot	Nationality	Kills claimed
1	Marmaduke Thomas St John Pattle	South African	41
2	James Edgar "Johnny" Johnson	British	38
3	Adolf Gysbert "Sailor" Malan	South African	35
4	Brendan "Paddy" Finucane	Irish	32
5	George Frederick Beurling	Canadian	31⅓
6=	John Robert Daniel Braham	British	29
6=	Robert Roland Stanford Tuck	British	29
8	Neville Frederick Duke	British	28⅝
9	Clive Robert Caldwell	Australian	28½
10	Frank Reginald Carey	British	28⅓

Kills that are expressed as fractions refer to those that were shared with others, the number of fighters involved and the extent of each pilot's participation determining the proportion allocated to him. As a result of this precise reckoning, British pilot James Harry "Ginger" Lacey, with 28 kills, misses sharing 10th place with Carey by ⅓ of a kill.

US AIR ACES OF WORLD WAR I

	Pilot	Kills claimed
1	Edward Vernon Rickenbacker	26
2	Frank Luke Jr	21
3	Gervais Raoul Lufbery	17
4	George Augustus Vaughn Jr	13
5=	Field E. Kindley	12
5=	David Endicott Putnam	12
5=	Elliot White Springs	12
8=	Reed Gresham Landis	10
8=	Jacques Michael Swaab	10
10=	Lloyd Andrews Hamilton	9
10=	Chester Ellis Wright	9

Edward ("Eddie") Rickenbacker (1890–1973) first achieved fame in the USA as a champion motor-racing driver. A visit to England in 1917 encouraged his interest in flying and when the USA entered the First World War (6 April 1917) he enlisted, serving initially as chauffeur to General Pershing before transferring to active service as a pilot. On 19 March 1918 Rickenbacker took part in the first-ever US patrol over enemy lines and on 29 April shot down his first aeroplane. A month later, with five kills to his credit, he became an acknowledged "ace", eventually achieving a total of 26 kills (22 aircraft and four balloons) and winning the US Congressional Medal of Honor, the country's highest award. Rickenbacker also served in the Second World War and later became chairman of Eastern Airlines. He died in 1973. As well as the 151 kills credited to the pilots in the Top 10, a further 76 US pilots each shot down between five and nine enemy aircraft. Frank Leaman Baylies had 12 kills, but served solely with the French air force and is hence not included in the US list.

LUFTWAFFE ACES OF WORLD WAR II

	Pilot	Kills claimed
1	Eric Hartmann	352
2	Gerhard Barkhorn	301
3	Günther Rall	275
4	Otto Kittel	267
5	Walther Nowotny	255
6	Wilhelm Batz	237
7	Erich Rudorffer	222
8	Heinrich Baer	220
9	Herman Graf	212
10	Heinrich Ehrler	209

Although these apparently high claims have been dismissed by some military historians as inflated for propaganda purposes, it is worth noting that many of them relate to kills on the Eastern Front, where the Luftwaffe was undoubtedly superior to its Soviet opponents. Few have questioned the so-called "Blond Knight" Eric Hartmann's achievement, however, and his victories over Soviet aircraft so outraged the USSR that after the war he was arrested and sentenced to 25 years in a Russian labour camp. He was released in 1955, returned to serve in the West German air force, and died on 20 September 1993.

MISSING
Most of "Pat" Pattle's kills were made flying an ancient Gladiator biplane. On 22 April 1941, after three kills, he was himself shot down over the Aegean and was never seen again.

US AIR ACES OF WORLD WAR II

	Pilot	Kills claimed
1	Richard I. Bong	40
2	Thomas B. McGuire	38
3	David McCampbell	34
4	Frances S. Gabreski	31
5=	Gregory Boynington	28
5=	Robert S. Johnson	28
7	Charles H. MacDonald	27
8=	George E. Preddy	26
8=	Joseph J. Foss	26
10	Robert M. Hanson	25

AIR WARFARE

Seldom has a weapon had as many different names as the V1. Originally called the Fi-103 (From Fiesler, its main manufacturer) or *Flakzeitlgerät 76* ("anti-aircraft aiming device 76") or FZG 76, it was developed under the code name *Kirschkern*, "cherry stone". The weapon eventually became known to the Germans as the V1 (from *Vergeltungswaffe Eins* – "vengeance weapon 1"), and to its British victims as the "flying bomb", "buzz bomb", or "doodlebug". These pilotless jet-propelled aircraft, measuring 7.7 m/25 ft 4½ in, were made of sheet steel and plywood and carried 850 kg/1,874 lb of high explosive. Using 1,591 litres/150 gallons of petrol oxidized by compressed air, they achieved an average speed of 563 km/h/350 mph and a range of about 209 km/130 miles, which they reached in 20–25 minutes. Their engines then cut out, and eyewitnesses tell of the "ominous silence" before the explosion some 12 seconds later.

The first ten V1 rockets were launched against England on 13 June 1944. Of these, five crash-landed near their launch site in Watten, France, one vanished (probably falling into the Channel), and four reached England. Only one reached its London target and caused casualties – six killed in Grove Road, Bethnal Green.

The second wave, on the night of 15/16 June, was more successful: 244 missiles were launched, of which 73 reached their goal of London, where 11 were shot down. In subsequent months more than 8,000 were launched. Many were erratic and strayed off course or crashed, and of those that continued toward London, a large proportion were brought down by barrage balloons, anti-aircraft fire, and particularly by fighter pilots either shooting them down or flying alongside and "tipping their wings" to send them away from their targets. Nonetheless, they managed to cause over 23,000 casualties.

The V1 was the precursor of the far deadlier V2. Masterminded by Werner von Braun (1912–77), later leader of the US space programme, the 14 m/46 ft V2 rocket (known to its German developers as the "A4") was more accurate and far more powerful than the V1. It produced a thrust of 25,400 kg/56,000 lb capable of carrying 1 tonne of explosive up to 362 km/225 miles, while its speed of 5,794 km/h/3,600 mph made it virtually impossible to combat with anti-aircraft fire or to intercept with fighter aircraft. V2 technology was used by the US to develop missiles suitable for carrying nuclear bombs.

T O P 1 0

LONDON BOROUGHS RECEIVING THE MOST V2 HITS

	Borough	V2s
1	Woolwich	33
2	West Ham	27
3	Greenwich	22
4	Barking	21
5	Dagenham	19
6=	Erith	17
6=	Chislehurst	17
8	Waltham	15
9=	East Ham	14
9=	Wanstead	14

The first two V2 rockets were launched from Holland against Paris on 6 September 1944. On 8 September two fell on London, followed by more than 1,000 over the next seven months, resulting in a total of 2,855 deaths. (Even more were directed at Belgium, killing 4,483). On 25 November 1944 a V2 hit Woolworth's in Deptford, killing at least 160 shoppers, and on 8 March 1945 one hit Smithfield Market, with 110 killed. On 27 March one of the last V2s hit a block of flats in Stepney, killing 131.

T O P 1 0

LONDON BOROUGHS RECEIVING THE MOST V1 HITS

	Borough	V1s
1	Croydon	141
2	Wandsworth	122
3	Lewisham	114
4	Camberwell	80
5	Woolwich	77
6	Lambeth	71
7	Beckenham	70
8	Orpington	63
9	West Ham	58
10	Coulsdon	54

During 1944, V1 flying bombs destroyed approximately 24,000 houses in London and damaged a further 800,000, chiefly in the southern suburbs, which were the nearest to the V1 launch sites on the Channel coast of France. Casualty figures were also very high: in one incident, on Sunday 18 June, 121 members of the congregation – 63 servicemen and 58 civilians – were killed when a V1 hit the Guards Chapel at the Wellington Barracks during a service, while on the same day V1s that fell in Putney and Battersea killed, respectively, 28 and 19 people. The V1 was notoriously inaccurate, however: although most were targeted on London, many fell short or overshot, some dropping, with often devastating effect, on the counties in their flightpath (1,444 in Kent and 880 in Sussex, for example), while others came down as far away as Northampton. One particularly errant example even landed near Hitler's headquarters at Soissons, France.

TOP 10

LUFTWAFFE AIRCRAFT OF WORLD WAR II

	Model	Type	No. produced
1	Messerschmitt Me 109	Fighter	30,480
2	Focke-Wulf Fw 190	Fighter	20,000
3	Junkers Ju 88	Bomber	15,000
4	Messerschmitt Me 110	Fighter-bomber	5,762
5	Heinkel He 111	Bomber	5,656
6	Junkers Ju 87	Dive bomber	4,881
7	Junkers Ju 52	Transport	2,804
8	Fiesler Fi 156	Communications	2,549
9	Dornier Do 217	Bomber	1,730
10	Heinkel He 177	Bomber	1,446

Over 60 years after its first flight, the Junkers Ju 52 is still in service as a transport aeroplane in South America.

V2 ROCKET
German V1s and V2s were the only long-range missiles successfully employed in the Second World War. The V2 was more precise than the notoriously inaccurate V1 – there was no effective defence against it.

TOP 10

FASTEST FIGHTER AIRCRAFT OF WORLD WAR II

	Aircraft	Country	Maximum speed mph	km/h
1	Messerschmitt Me 163	Germany	596	959
2	Messerschmitt Me 262	Germany	560	901
3	Heinkel He 162A	Germany	553	890
4	P-51-H Mustang	USA	487	784
5	Lavochkin La11	USSR	460	740
6	Spitfire XIV	UK	448	721
7	Yakovlev Yak-3	USSR	447	719
8	P-51-D Mustang	USA	440	708
9	Tempest VI	UK	438	705
10	Focke-Wulf FW190D	Germany	435	700

Also known as the *Komet*, the Messerschmitt Me 163 was a short-range rocket-powered interceptor brought into service in 1944–45. During this time, the aircraft scored a number of victories over its slower Allied rivals. The Messerschmitt Me 262 was the first jet in operational service.

TOP 10

MOST HEAVILY BLITZED CITIES IN THE UK

	City	Major raids	Tonnage of high explosive dropped
1	London	85	23,949
2	Liverpool/ Birkenhead	8	1,957
3	Birmingham	8	1,852
4	Glasgow/Clydeside	5	1,329
5	Plymouth/ Devonport	8	1,228
6	Bristol/ Avonmouth	6	919
7	Coventry	2	818
8	Portsmouth	3	687
9	Southampton	4	647
10	Hull	3	593

The list, which is derived from official German sources, is based on total tonnage of high explosives dropped in major night attacks during the "Blitz" period, from 7 September 1940 to 16 May 1941.

TOP 10

CITIES MOST BOMBED BY THE RAF AND USAAF, 1939–45

	City	Estimated civilian deaths
1	Dresden	100,000+
2	Hamburg	55,000
3	Berlin	49,000
4	Cologne	20,000
5	Magdeburg	15,000
6	Kassel	13,000
7	Darmstadt	12,300
8=	Heilbronn	7,500
8=	Essen	7,500
10=	Dortmund	6,000
10=	Wuppertal	6,000

The high level of casualties in Dresden resulted principally from the saturation bombing and the firestorm that ensued after Allied raids on the lightly defended city. The scale of the raids was massive: 775 British bombers took part in the first night's raid, on 13 February 1945, followed the next day by 450 US bombers, with a final attack by 200 US bombers on 15 February.

TOP 10

AREAS OF EUROPE MOST BOMBED BY ALLIED AIRCRAFT*, 1939–45

	Area	Bombs dropped (tonnes)
1	Germany	1,350,321
2	France	583,318
3	Italy	366,524
4	Austria, Hungary, and the Balkans	180,828
5	Belgium and Netherlands	88,739
6	Southern Europe and Mediterranean	76,505
7	Czechoslovakia and Poland	21,419
8	Norway and Denmark	5,297
9	Sea targets	564
10	British Channel Islands	93

* *British and US.*

Between August 1942 and May 1945 alone, Allied air forces (Bomber Command plus 8 and 15 US Air Forces) flew 731,969 night sorties (and Bomber Command a further 67,598 day sorties), dropping a total of 1,850,919 tons of bombs.

WAR AT SEA

TOP 10

LARGEST BATTLESHIPS OF WORLD WAR II

	Name	Country	Status	Length m/ft	Tonnage
1=	*Musashi*	Japan	Sunk 25 Oct 1944	263/862	72,809
1=	*Yamato*	Japan	Sunk 7 Apr 1945	263/862	72,809
3=	*Iowa*	USA	Still in service with US Navy	270/887	55,710
3=	*Missouri*	USA	Still in service with US Navy	270/887	55,710
3=	*New Jersey*	USA	Still in service with US Navy	270/887	55,710
3=	*Wisconsin*	USA	Still in service with US Navy	270/887	55,710
7=	*Bismarck*	Germany	Sunk 27 May 1941	251/823	50,153
7=	*Tirpitz*	Germany	Sunk 12 Nov 1944	251/823	50,153
9=	*Jean Bart*	France	Survived WWII, later scrapped	247/812	47,500
9=	*Richelieu*	France	Survived WWII, later scrapped	247/812	47,500

TOP 10

COUNTRIES SUFFERING THE GREATEST MERCHANT SHIPPING LOSSES IN WORLD WAR I

	Country	Vessels sunk Number	Tonnage
1	UK	2,038	6,797,802
2	Italy	228	720,064
3	France	213	651,583
4	USA	93	372,892
5	Germany	188	319,552
6	Greece	115	304,992
7	Denmark	126	205,002
8	Netherlands	74	194,483
9	Sweden	124	192,807
10	Spain	70	160,383

TOP 10

COUNTRES SUFFERING THE GREATEST MERCHANT SHIPPING LOSSES IN WORLD WAR II

	Country	Vessels sunk Number	Tonnage
1	UK	4,786	21,194,000
2	Japan	2,346	8,618,109
3	Germany	1,595	7,064,600
4	USA	578	3,524,983
5	Norway	427	1,728,531
6	Netherlands	286	1,195,204
7	Italy	467	1,155,080
8	Greece	262	883,200
9	Panama	107	542,772
10	Sweden	204	481,864

During 1939–45, Allied losses in the Atlantic alone totalled 3,843 ships (16,899,147 tonnes). June 1942 was the worst period of the war, with 131 vessels (652,487 tonnes) lost in the Atlantic and a further 42 (181,709 tonnes) lost elsewhere.

BRAZILIAN BATTLESHIP
In the early 20th century, Dreadnought-type vessels incorporating the latest advances in steam propulsion, gunnery, and armour plating revolutionized sea warfare.

UP PERISCOPE
As submarines are enhanced with nuclear power and the ability to fire long-range missiles underwater, tacticians increasingly consider them the most important of all strategic weapons.

TOP 10

U-BOAT COMMANDERS OF WORLD WAR II

	Commander	U-boats commanded	Ships sunk
1	Otto Kretschmer	U-23, U-99	45
2	Wolfgang Luth	U-9, U-138, U-43, U-181	44
3	Joachim Schepke	U-3, U-19, U-100	39
4	Erich Topp	U-57, U-552	35
5	Victor Schutze	U-25, U-103	34
6	Heinrich Leibe	U-38	30
7	Karl F. Merten	U-68	29 *
8	Günther Prien	U-47	29 *
9	Johann Mohr	U-124	29 *
10	Georg Lassen	U-160	28

* Gross tonnage used to determine ranking order.

Günther Prien (born 16 January 1908, killed in action 7 March 1941) performed the remarkable feat of penetrating the British naval base at Scapa Flow on 14 October 1939 and sinking the Royal Navy battleship *Royal Oak* at anchor. For this exploit he was awarded the Knight's Cross, the first of 318 to be won by members of the German navy during the Second World War. Prien was killed when U-47 was sunk.

DID YOU KNOW

OLD WAR-HORSE

One ship that survived the Japanese attack on the US fleet at Pearl Harbor (7 December 1941) was the USS *Phoenix*. After serving throughout the rest of the war, she was sold to Argentina in 1951 and renamed the *General Belgrano*. On 2 May 1982, during the Falklands War, she was sunk by a British submarine, with the loss of 368 lives.

TOP 10

NAVIES 100 YEARS AGO

	Country	Guns	Men	Ships*		Country	Guns	Men	Ships*
1	UK	3,631	94,600	659	**6**	Austria	309	9,000	168
2	France	1,735	70,600	457	**7**	Netherlands	256	10,000	140
3	Russia	710	31,000	358	**8**	Spain	305	16,700	136
4	Italy	611	23,000	267	**9**	Turkey	382	23,000	124
5	Germany	608	16,500	217	**10**	USA	284	10,000	95

* Battleships, cruisers, gun-boats, and torpedo-boats.

TOP 10

US NAVY SUBMARINE COMMANDERS OF WORLD WAR II

	Commander	Submarines commanded	Ships sunk
1	Richard H. O'Kane	*Tang*	31
2	Eugene B. Fluckley	*Barb*	25
3	Slade D. Cutter	*Seahorse*	21
4	Samuel D. Dealey	*Harder*	20½
5	William S. Post Jr	*Gudgeon* and *Spot*	19
6	Reuben T. Whitaker	*S-44* and *Flasher*	18½
7	Walter T. Grifith	*Bowfin* and *Bullhead*	17 *
8	Dudley W. Morton	*R-5* and *Wahoo*	17 *
9	John E. Lee	*S-12*, *Grayling* and *Croaker*	16
10	William B. Sieglaff	*Tautog* and *Tench*	15

* Gross tonnage used to determine ranking order.
½ refers to shared "kills".

TOP 10

SUBMARINE FLEETS OF WORLD WAR II

	Country	Submarines
1	Japan*	163
2	USA*	112
3	France	77
4	USSR	75
5	Germany	57
6	UK	38
7	Netherlands	21
8	Italy	15
9	Denmark	12
10	Greece	6

* Strength at December 1941.

The list shows submarine strengths at the outbreak of the war. During hostilities, the belligerent nations increased their production prodigiously: from 1939 to 1945, the Axis powers (Germany, Italy, and Japan) commissioned a further 1,337 submarines (1,141 by Germany alone), and the Allies 422.

MODERN MILITARY

T O P 1 0

FIRST VCs TO BE AWARDED

	Name	Rank	Action	Date
1	Charles Davis Lucas	Mate (later Rear-Admiral)	HMS *Hecla*, the Baltic	21 Jun 1854
2	John Bythesea	Lt (later Rear-Admiral)	HMS *Arrogant*, the Baltic	9–12 Aug 1854
3	William Johnstone	Stoker	HMS *Arrogant*, the Baltic	9–12 Aug 1854
4	James McKechnie	Sgt, Scots Guards	Crimea	20 Sep 1854
5	John Grieve	Sgt-Maj (later Lt and Adjt)	Crimea*	25 Oct 1854
6	Samuel Parkes	Private, Light Dragoons	Crimea*	25 Oct 1854
7	Alexander Roberts Dunn	Lt (later Col), Scots Guards	Crimea*	25 Oct 1854
8	Gerald Littlehales Goodlake	Major (later Lt Gen), Coldstream Guards	Crimea	28 Oct 1854
9	James Owens	Cpl (later Sgt), 1st Battalion, 49th Regiment	Crimea	30 Oct 1854
10	William Hewett	Lt (later Vice-Admiral)	Crimea	26 Oct/5 Nov 1854

* *Charge of the Light Brigade.*

T O P 1 0

CAMPAIGNS IN WHICH THE MOST VICTORIA CROSSES HAVE BEEN WON

	Campaign	VCs
1	First World War (1914–18)	634
2=	Indian Mutiny (1857–58)	182
2=	Second World War (1939–45)	182
4	Crimean War (1854–56)	111
5	Second Boer War (1899–1902)	78
6	Zulu War (1879)	23
7	Second Afghan War (1878–80)	16
8	Waikato-Hauhau Maori War (1863–66)	13
9	Third China War (1860)	7
10=	Basuto War (1879–82)	6
10=	First Boer War (1880–81)	6

The Top 10 accounts for all but 92 of the 1,350 VCs ever awarded up to the 1982 Falklands conflict, in which two VCs were awarded, posthumously, to Lt-Col "H" Jones and Sgt Ian McKay, both of the Parachute Regiment. Prior to that the last had been given to Warrant Officer Keith Payne of Australia for an action in the Vietnam war. The youngest ever recipient of a VC was Andrew Fitzgibbon, for an action in China in 1860, when he was 15 years 3 months old.

T O P 1 0

LARGEST ARMED FORCES IN THE WORLD

	Country	Estimated active forces			Total
		Army	Navy	Air	
1	China	2,300,000	260,000	470,000	3,030,000
2	Russia	1,400,000	320,000	300,000	2,720,000 *
3	USA	586,200	693,600#	449,900	1,729,700
4	India	1,100,000	55,000	110,000	1,265,000
5	North Korea	1,000,000	45,000	82,000	1,127,000
6	Vietnam	700,000	42,000	115,000	857,000
7	South Korea	520,000	60,000	53,000	633,000
8	Pakistan	510,000	22,000	45,000	577,000
9	Turkey	370,000	50,000	80,900	500,900
10	Taiwan	312,000	59,300	70,000	442,000
	UK	*133,058*	*58,513*	*79,341*	*270,912*

* *Balance of total comprises Strategic Deterrent Forces, Paramilitary, National Guard, etc.*
# *Navy 546,650, Marines 193,000.*

In addition to the active forces listed here, many of the world's foremost military powers have considerable reserves on standby, South Korea's estimated at some 4,500,000, Vietnam's 3–4,000,000, Russia's 3,000,000, the US's 1,784,050, China's 1,200,000, and Turkey's 1,107,000.

RANKS OF THE ROYAL NAVY, ARMY, AND ROYAL AIR FORCE

	Navy	Army	Royal Air Force
1	Admiral of the Fleet	Field Marshal	Marshal of the Royal Air Force
2	Admiral	General	Air Chief Marshal
3	Vice-Admiral	Lieutenant-General	Air Marshal
4	Rear-Admiral	Major-General	Air Vice-Marshal
5	Commodore	Brigadier	Air Commodore
6	Captain	Colonel	Group Captain
7	Commander	Lieutenant-Colonel	Wing Commander
8	Lieutenant Commander	Major	Squadron Leader
9	Lieutenant	Captain	Flight Lieutenant
10	Sub-Lieutenant	Lieutenant	Flying Officer

20TH-CENTURY WARS WITH MOST MILITARY FATALITIES

	War	Years	Military fatalities
1	Second World War	1939–45	15,843,000
2	First World War	1914–18	8,545,800
3	Korean War	1950–53	1,893,100
4=	Sino-Japanese War	1937–41	1,000,000
4=	Biafra-Nigeria Civil War	1967–70	1,000,000
6	Spanish Civil War	1936–39	611,000
7	Vietnam War	1961–73	546,000
8=	India-Pakistan War	1947	200,000
8=	USSR invasion of Afghanistan	1979–89	200,000
8=	Iran-Iraq War	1980–88	200,000

COUNTRIES WITH THE LARGEST DEFENCE BUDGETS

	Country	Budget (US $)		Country	Budget (US $)
1	USA	323,500,000,000	6	France	33,100,000,000
2	Russia	52,500,000,000	7	Italy	22,700,000,000
3	UK	42,000,000,000	8	China	15,000,000,000
4	Germany	39,500,000,000	9	Saudi Arabia	14,500,000,000
5	Japan	36,700,000,000	10	South Korea	12,600,000,000

Based on World Military and Social Expenditures, 1987–88 *(1984 figures) – updated 1992; 1994 update CIA.*

SMALLEST ARMED FORCES IN THE WORLD*

	Country	Estimated total active forces
1	Belize	660
2	Luxembourg	800
3	The Bahamas	850
4	The Gambia	900
5	Equatorial Guinea	1,100
6=	Cape Verde	1,300
6=	The Seychelles	1,300
8	Malta	1,650
9	Suriname	2,200
10	Trinidad and Tobago	2,650

* *Excluding those countries not declaring a defence budget.*

COLONELS-IN-CHIEF

	Colonel-in-Chief	Positions held*
1	Queen Elizabeth II	38
2	Prince Philip	15
3	The Queen Mother	13
4	The Prince of Wales	12
5	The Princess Royal	11
6	Princess Margaret	7 #
7	Princess Alice, Duchess of Gloucester	5 #
8=	Princess Alexandra	4 **
8=	The Duchess of Gloucester	4
10=	The Princess of Wales	3
10=	The Duchess of Kent	3
10=	The Duke of Kent	3

* *Ranks held in British and Commonwealth army regiments and corps.*
# *Also Deputy Colonel-in-Chief of the Royal Anglian Regiment.*
** *Also Deputy Colonel-in-Chief of the Light Infantry.*

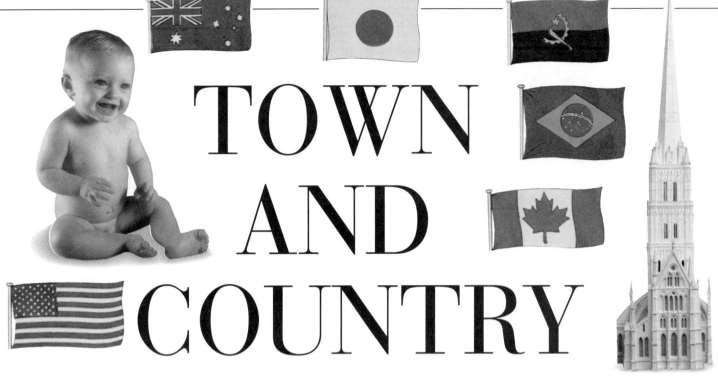

TOWN AND COUNTRY

TOP 10

SMALLEST COUNTRIES IN THE WORLD

	Country	Area sq km	sq miles
1	Vatican City	0.44	0.17
2	Monaco	1.81	0.7
3	Gibraltar	6.47	2.5
4	Macao	16.06	6.2
5	Nauru	21.23	8.2
6	Tuvalu	25.90	10.0
7	Bermuda	53.35	20.6
8	San Marino	59.57	23.0
9	Liechtenstein	157.99	61.0
10	Antigua	279.72	108.0

The "country" status of several of these micro-states is questionable, since their government, defence, currency, and other features are often intricately linked with those of larger countries – the Vatican City with Italy, Monaco with France, for example, while Gibraltar and Bermuda are dependent territories of the UK.

TOP 10

LARGEST COUNTRIES IN THE WORLD

	Country	Area sq km	sq miles
1	Russia	17,070,289	6,590,876
2	Canada	9,970,537	3,849,646
3	China	9,596,961	3,705,408
4	USA	9,372,614	3,618,787
5	Brazil	8,511,965	3,286,488
6	Australia	7,686,848	2,967,909
7	India	3,287,590	1,269,346
8	Argentina	2,766,889	1,068,302
9	Kazakhstan	2,716,626	1,048,895
10	Sudan	2,505,813	967,500
	UK	244,046	94,227
	World total	*136,597,770*	*52,740,700*

The break-up of the former USSR has effectively introduced two new countries, with Russia taking pre-eminent position while Kazakhstan, which enters in 9th position, ousts Algeria from the bottom of the list.

TOP 10

LONGEST FRONTIERS IN THE WORLD

	Country	km	miles
1	China	22,143	13,759
2	Russia	20,139	12,514
3	Brazil	14,691	9,129
4	India	14,103	8,763
5	USA	12,248	7,611
6	Zaïre	10,271	6,382
7	Argentina	9,665	6,006
8	Canada	8,893	5,526
9	Mongolia	8,114	5,042
10	Sudan	7,697	4,783

The 12,248 km/7,611 miles of the US's frontiers include those shared with Canada (6,416 km/3,987 miles of which comprise the longest continuous frontier in the world), the 2,477-km/1,539-mile boundary between Canada and Alaska, that with Mexico (3,326 km/2,067 miles), and between the US naval base at Guantánamo and Cuba (29 km/18 miles).

COUNTRIES WITH MOST NEIGHBOURS

	Country/neighbours	No. of neighbours
1	China	*16*

Afghanistan, Bhutan, Hong Kong, India, Kazakhstan, Kyrgyzstan, Laos, Macao, Mongolia, Myanmar (Burma), Nepal, North Korea, Pakistan, Russia, Tajikistan, Vietnam

2	Russia	*14*

Azerbaijan, Belarus, China, Estonia, Finland, Georgia, Kazakhstan, Latvia, Lithuania, Mongolia, North Korea, Norway, Poland, Ukraine

3	Brazil	*10*

Argentina, Bolivia, Colombia, French Guiana, Guyana, Paraguay, Peru, Suriname, Uruguay, Venezuela

4=	Germany	*9*

Austria, Belgium, Czech Republic, Denmark, France, Luxembourg, Netherlands, Poland, Switzerland

4=	Sudan	*9*

Central African Republic, Chad, Egypt, Eritrea, Ethiopia, Kenya, Libya, Uganda, Zaïre

4=	Zaïre	*9*

Angola, Burundi, Central African Republic, Congo, Rwanda, Sudan, Tanzania, Uganda, Zambia

7=	Austria	*8*

Czech Republic, Germany, Hungary, Italy, Liechtenstein, Slovakia, Slovenia, Switzerland

7=	France	*8*

Andorra, Belgium, Germany, Italy, Luxembourg, Monaco, Spain, Switzerland

7=	Saudi Arabia	*8*

Iraq, Jordan, Kuwait, Oman, People's Democratic Republic of Yemen, Qatar, United Arab Emirates, Yemen Arab Republic

7=	Tanzania	*8*

Burundi, Kenya, Malawi, Mozambique, Rwanda, Uganda, Zaïre, Zambia

7=	Turkey	*8*

Armenia, Azerbaijan, Bulgaria, Georgia, Greece, Iran, Iraq, Syria

COUNTRIES WITH THE LONGEST COASTLINES

	Country	km	miles
1	Canada	243,791	151,485
2	Indonesia	54,716	33,999
3	Greenland	44,087	27,394
4	Russia	37,653	23,396
5	Philippines	36,289	22,559
6	Australia	25,760	16,007
7	Norway	21,925	13,624
8	USA	19,924	12,380
9	New Zealand	15,134	9,404
10	China	14,500	9,010

LARGEST COUNTRIES IN ASIA

	Country	Area sq km	sq miles
1	China	9,596,961	3,705,408
2	India	3,287,590	1,269,346
3	Kazakhstan	2,716,626	1,049,155
4	Saudi Arabia	2,149,640	830,000
5	Indonesia	1,904,569	735,358
6	Iran	1,648,000	636,296
7	Mongolia	1,565,000	604,250
8	Pakistan	803,950	310,407
9	Turkey (in Asia)	790,200	305,098
10	Myanmar (Burma)	676,552	261,218

LARGEST COUNTRIES IN EUROPE

	Country	Area sq km	sq miles
1	Russia (in Europe)	4,710,227	1,818,629
2	Ukraine	603,700	233,090
3	France	547,026	211,208
4	Spain	504,781	194,897
5	Sweden	449,964	173,732
6	Germany	356,999	137,838
7	Finland	337,007	130,119
8	Norway	324,220	125,182
9	Poland	312,676	120,725
10	Italy	301,226	116,304

LARGEST COUNTRIES IN AFRICA

	Country	Area sq km	sq miles
1	Sudan	2,505,813	967,500
2	Algeria	2,381,741	919,595
3	Zaïre	2,345,409	905,567
4	Libya	1,759,540	679,362
5	Chad	1,284,000	495,755
6	Niger	1,267,080	489,191
7	Angola	1,246,700	481,354
8	Mali	1,240,000	478,791
9	Ethiopia	1,221,900	471,778
10	South Africa	1,221,031	471,445

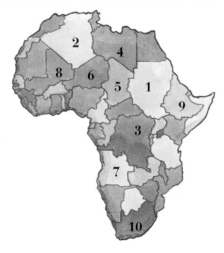

WORLD POPULATIONS

TOP 10

WORLD POPULATION

Year	Estimated total
1000	254,000,000
1500	460,000,000
1600	579,000,000
1700	679,000,000
1800	954,000,000
1850	1,094,000,000
1900	1,633,000,000
1950	2,515,312,000
1960	3,019,376,000
1970	3,697,918,000
1980	4,450,210,000
1985	4,853,848,000
1993	5,554,552,000

World population is believed to have exceeded 5,000,000 before 8000 BC, and surpassed 5,000,000,000 in 1987. The United Nations has estimated the future growth of world population within three ranges – "low", "medium", and "high", depending on the extent of birth control measures and other factors during the coming decades. The high scenario, which assumes that few additional checks are placed on population expansion, implies a 78 per cent global increase by the year 2025. Estimates suggest that by the turn of the century more than 60 per cent of the world's population will be in Asia.

Year	Low	Medium	High
1995	5,679,685,000	5,765,861,000	5,854,986,000
2000	6,088.506,000	6,251,055,000	6,410,707,000
2005	6,463,211,000	6,728,574,000	6,978,754,000
2010	6,805,064,000	7,190,762,000	7,561,301,000
2015	7,109,736,000	7,639,547,000	8,167,357,000
2020	7,368,995,000	8,062,274,000	8,791,432,000
2025	7,589,731,000	8,466,516,000	9,422,749,000

TOP 10

MOST HIGHLY POPULATED COUNTRIES 100 YEARS AGO

	Country	Population
1	China	360,250,000
2	India	286,696,960
3	Russia	108,843,192
4	USA	62,981,000
5	Germany	49,421,803
6	Austria	41,345,329
7	Japan	40,072,020
8	France	38,343,192
9	UK	37,888,153
10	Turkey	32,978,100

In the 1890s many national boundaries were quite different from their present form: for example, India encompassed what are now Pakistan and Bangladesh, Poland was part of Russia, and Austria and Turkey were extensive empires that included all their territories in their censuses. The 1891 census of the UK indicated that the population of England and Wales was 29,001,018. The estimated total population of the entire British Empire at this time was 340,220,000, making it second only to China's.

TOP 10

MOST HIGHLY POPULATED COUNTRIES IN THE WORLD

	Country	Population* 1983	Population* 1993
1	China	1,008,175,288	1,177,585,000
2	India	683,880,051	903,159,000
3	USA	226,545,805	258,104,000
4	Indonesia	153,000,000	197,232,000
5	Brazil	119,098,922	156,664,000
6	USSR/Russia	271,203,000	149,300,000
7	Pakistan	83,780,000	125,314,000
8	Japan	118,390,000	124,712,000
9	Bangladesh	94,700,000	122,255,000
10	Nigeria	85,000,000	95,060,000
	UK	55,776,422	57,970,000

* Based on closest census or most recent estimate.

In the 1980s world population increased from 4,450,000,000 at the beginning of the decade to 5,292,000,000 at the end – a growth of almost 19 per cent. The figures for the past 10 years show that the population of China is now more than 20 times that of the UK and represents over 21 per cent of the total population of the world in 1993 (now estimated to be more than 5,554,552,000). Although differential rates of population increase result in changes in the order, the members of the Top 10 remain largely the same from year to year: the population of Pakistan, for example, only recently overtook that of Japan. Despite the anomaly that the USSR no longer exists, Russia, its largest former component state, maintains an independent place in the ranking.

COUNTRIES WITH THE HIGHEST ESTIMATED POPULATION IN THE YEAR 2000

	Country	Population
1	China	1,260,154,000
2	India	1,018,105,000
3	USA	275,327,000
4	Indonesia	219,496,000
5	Brazil	169,543,000
6	Russia	151,460,000
7	Pakistan	148,540,000
8	Bangladesh	143,548,000
9	Japan	127,554,000
10	Nigeria	118,620,000
	UK	58,951,000

Asia contains many of the countries with the highest estimated populations in the year 2000. The part of the territory of the former USSR in Asia previously placed the USSR as one of the most populated countries in Asia. Following the break-up of the Soviet Union, no one of its individual states has such a high population. The largest country at present, Uzbekistan, has a population of 22,128,000.

LEAST POPULATED COUNTRIES IN THE WORLD

	Country	Population
1	Vatican City	738
2	Falkland Islands	1,916
3	Nauru	8,100
4	Tuvalu	8,229
5	Wallis and Fortuna	14,800
6	Cook Islands	17,185
7	San Marino	22,361
8	Monaco	28,000
9	Liechtenstein	28,181
10	Gibraltar	28,848

MOST DENSELY-POPULATED COUNTRIES AND COLONIES IN THE WORLD

	Country/colony	Area sq km	sq miles	Population	Population per sq km
1	Macau	16.06	6.2	479,000	29,826
2	Monaco	1.81	0.7	28,000	15,470
3	Hong Kong	1,037.29	400.5	5,900,000	5,688
4	Singapore	619.01	39.0	2,826,000	4,565
5	Gibraltar	6.47	2.5	28,848	4,459
6	Vatican City	0.44	0.17	738	1,677
7	Malta	313.39	121.0	362,950	1,158
8	Bermuda	53.35	20.6	58,460	1,096
9	Bangladesh	143,998.15	55,598.0	122,255,000	849
10	Bahrain	675.99	261.0	568,000	840
	UK	244,046.79	94,227.0	57,970,000	238
	USA	9,372,614.90	3,618,787.0	258,104,000	28
	World total	135,597,770.00	52,509,600.0	5,554,552,000	average 41

COUNTRIES WITH THE HIGHEST BIRTH RATE

	Country	Birth rate*
1	Rwanda	58.0
2	Malawi	54.3
3	Yemen	53.6
4	Uganda	51.9
5	Ethiopia	50.4
6	Niger	50.2
7	Mali	50.1
8	Burundi	50.0
9	Afghanistan	49.0
10	Tanzania	47.7

* Live births per annum per 1,000 population.

The 10 countries with the highest birth rate during the 1990s to date correspond very closely with those countries that have the highest fertility rate (the average number of children born to each woman in that country). In the case of Rwanda, the fertility rate is 8.29.

COUNTRIES WITH THE LOWEST BIRTH RATE

	Country	Birth rate*
1	Italy	10.0
2=	Greece	10.7
2=	Japan	10.7
4	Spain	11.4
5	Austria	11.5
6	Germany	11.7
7=	Hong Kong	12.1
7=	Hungary	12.1
9=	Denmark	12.4
9=	Portugal	12.4

* Live births per annum per 1,000 population.

As with the highest birth rate, there is a close correlation between the countries that have the lowest birth rate and those with the lowest fertility rate. Fertility rates of less than 2.0 effectively imply that the woman and her partner are not replacing themselves, which means that the population is declining.

WORLD CITIES

Calculating the populations of the world's cities is fraught with difficulties, not least that of determining whether the city is defined by its administrative boundaries or by its continuously expanding built-up areas or conurbations. Since different countries adopt different schemes, and some have populations concentrated in city centres while others are spread out in suburbs sprawling over hundreds of square miles, it has been impossible to compare them meaningfully. In order to resolve this problem, the US Bureau of the Census has adopted the method of defining cities as population clusters or "urban agglomerations" with densities of more than 5,000 inhabitants per square mile (equivalent to 1,931 per sq km). Totals based on this system will differ considerably from those of other methods: according to this system, for example, the hugely spread-out city of Shanghai has a population of 6,936,000, compared with the total of 12,670,000 estimated for its metropolitan area. On this basis, the city in the Top 10 with the greatest area is New York (3,300 sq km/1,274 sq miles) and the smallest Bombay (246 sq km/95 sq miles) – which also means that Bombay has the greatest population density, 49,191 inhabitants per sq km/127,379 per sq mile – more than 12 times that of London.

One recent change to note in the Top 10 is the inexorable rise in the population of Brazil's second-largest city, Rio de Janeiro, the total of which has now overtaken that of Buenos Aires. These two remain the most populous cities in the southern hemisphere, with Jakarta, Indonesia, the runner-up (9,882,000 in 1991, using this method of calculation).

TOP 10
MOST HIGHLY POPULATED CITIES IN THE WORLD

	City/Country	Population
1	Tokyo/Yokohama, Japan	27,245,000
2	Mexico City, Mexico	20,899,000
3	São Paulo, Brazil	18,701,000
4	Seoul, South Korea	16,792,000
5	New York, USA	14,625,000
6	Osaka-Kobe-Kyoto, Japan	13,872,000
7	Bombay, India	12,101,000
8	Calcutta, India	11,898,000
9	Rio de Janeiro, Brazil	11,688,000
10	Buenos Aires, Argentina	11,657,000

TOP 10
FIRST CITIES IN THE WORLD WITH POPULATIONS OF MORE THAN ONE MILLION

	City	Country
1	Rome	Italy
2	Angkor	Cambodia
3	Hangchow	China
4	London	UK
5	Paris	France
6	Peking	China
7	Canton	China
8	Berlin	Prussia
9	New York	USA
10	Vienna	Austria

Rome's population was reckoned to have exceeded 1,000,000 some time in the second century BC, and both Angkor and Hangchow had reached this figure by about AD 900 and 1200 respectively, although all three subsequently declined (Angkor was completely abandoned in the 15th century). No other city attained 1,000,000 until London in the early years of the 19th century. The next cities to pass the million mark did so between about 1850 and the late 1870s. Now at least 130 cities have populations of 1,000,000 or more.

TOP 10
MOST HIGHLY POPULATED CITIES IN THE WORLD 100 YEARS AGO

	City	Population
1	London	4,231,431
2	Paris	2,423,946
3	Peking	1,648,814
4	Canton (Kwangchow)	1,600,000
5	Berlin	1,579,244
6	Tokyo	1,552,457
7	New York	1,515,301
8	Vienna	1,364,548
9	Chicago	1,099,850
10	Philadelphia	1,046,964

In 1890 Nanking in China was the only other city in the world with a population of more than 1,000,000, with another Chinese city, Tientsin (now Tianjin), close behind. Several other cities, including Constantinople, St Petersburg, and Moscow, all had populations in excess of 750,000. It is remarkable that in 1890, Brooklyn, with a population 806,343, was marginally larger than Bombay (804,470 in 1891), whereas Bombay's present population of 12,571,720 is more than five times that of the whole of Brooklyn county.

TOP 10
MOST HIGHLY POPULATED CITIES IN NORTH AMERICA

	City	Country	Population
1	Mexico City	Mexico	20,899,000
2	New York	USA	14,625,000
3	Los Angeles	USA	10,130,000
4	Chicago	USA	6,529,000
5	Philadelphia	USA	4,003,000
6	San Francisco	USA	3,987,000
7	Miami	USA	3,471,000
8	Guadalajara	Mexico	3,370,000
9	Toronto	Canada	3,145,000
10	Detroit/ Windsor	USA/ Canada	2,969,000

The method used by the US Bureau of the Census for calculating city populations (see introduction, above) takes account of often widely spread "urban agglomerations" – in the instance of Detroit and Windsor giving rise to the anomaly of a "city" that straddles two countries.

T O P 1 0

MOST HIGHLY POPULATED CITIES IN EUROPE

	City	Country	Population
1	Moscow*	Russia	10,446,000
2	London*	UK	9,115,000
3	Paris*	France	8,720,000
4	Essen	Germany	7,452,000
5	Istanbul#	Turkey	6,678,000
6	Milan	Italy	4,749,000
7	St Petersburg	Russia	4,672,000
8	Madrid*	Spain	4,513,000
9	Barcelona	Spain	4,227,000
10	Manchester	UK	4,030,000

* Capital city.
# Located in Turkey in Europe.

The problem of defining a city's boundaries means that population figures generally relate to "urban agglomerations", which often include suburbs sprawling over very large areas. The US Bureau of the Census method of identifying city populations (see introduction) produces this list – although one based on cities minus their suburbs would present a very different picture.

GROWING ALL THE TIME
Tokyo's bustling streets will be busier than ever if, as predicted, the city's population increases by over two and a half million before the year 2000.

T O P 1 0

LARGEST CITIES IN THE WORLD IN THE YEAR 2000

	City/Country	Estimated population 2000*
1	Tokyo-Yokohama, Japan	29,971,000
2	Mexico City, Mexico	27,872,000
3	São Paulo, Brazil	25,354,000
4	Seoul, South Korea	21,976,000
5	Bombay, India	15,357,000
6	New York, USA	14,648,000
7	Osaka-Kobe-Kyoto, Japan	14,287,000
8	Tehran, Iran	14,251,000
9	Rio de Janeiro, Brazil	14,169,000
10	Calcutta, India	14,088,000

* Based on US Bureau of the Census method of calculating city populations; this gives a list that differs from that calculated by other methods, such as those used by the United Nations.

T O P 1 0

MOST DENSELY POPULATED CITIES IN THE WORLD

	City	Country	Population per sq mile
1	Hong Kong	Hong Kong	247,501
2	Lagos	Nigeria	142,821
3	Jakarta	Indonesia	130,026
4	Bombay	India	127,379
5	Ho Chi Minh City	Vietnam	120,168
6	Ahmadabad	India	115,893
7	Shenyang	China	109,974
8	Tianjin	China	98,990
9	Cairo	Egypt	97,106
10	Bangalore	India	96,041

T O P 1 0

LARGEST NON-CAPITAL CITIES IN THE WORLD

	City	Country	Capital/population	Population
1	Shanghai	China	Beijing 10,860,000	12,670,000
2	Bombay	India	Delhi 8,375,188	12,571,000
3	Calcutta	India	Delhi 8,375,188	10,916,272
4	São Paulo	Brazil	Brasília 1,803,478	10,063,110
5	New York	USA	Washington, DC 604,000	7,322,564
6	Rio de Janeiro*	Brazil	Brasília 1,803,478	6,603,388
7	Karachi*	Pakistan	Islamabad 350,000	6,500,000
8	Tianjin	China	Beijing 10,860,000	5,700,000
9	St Petersburg*	Russia	Moscow 8,967,000	5,020,000
10	Alexandria	Egypt	Cairo 14,000,000	5,000,000

* Former capital.

Based on comparison of population within administrative boundaries – hence not comparable with the list of The 10 Largest Cities in the World.

THE COUNTIES OF BRITAIN

COUNTIES WITH THE LONGEST COASTLINES

(England and Wales only)

	County	Total coastline km	miles
1	Cornwall	1,104.89	686.27
2	Dyfed	1,043.04	647.85
3	Devon	857.34	532.51
4	Essex	839.44	521.39
5	Gwynedd	835.20	518.76
6	Norfolk	797.26	495.19
7	Cumbria	682.15	423.70
8	Kent	589.20	365.96
9	Humberside	485.32	301.44
10	Lancashire	476.50	295.96

COUNTIES WITH THE SHORTEST COASTLINES

(England and Wales only)

	County	Total coastline km	miles
1	Powys	5.30	3.29
2	Durham	23.33	14.49
3	Mid Glamorgan	29.55	18.36
4	South Yorkshire	36.19	22.48
5	Nottinghamshire	59.48	36.94
6	South Glamorgan	101.13	62.81
7	Cambridgeshire	107.96	67.05
8	Isles of Scilly	109.89	68.25
9	Avon	126.34	78.48
10	Cheshire	126.56	78.61

It may be a surprise to see the landlocked counties of South Yorkshire, Nottinghamshire, and Cambridgeshire included here, but the Ordnance Survey, from whose database this list and the Longest Coastlines list were compiled, uses a method of measurement that follows the high water level of rivers from their mouths up to their NTLs (Normal Tidal Limits), and then continues down the opposite bank.

LARGEST BRITISH COUNTIES

	County	Area sq km	sq miles		County	Area sq km	sq miles
1	Highland Region	24,100	9,305	6	Cumbria	7,150	2,761
2	Strathclyde Region	10,633	4,105	7	Devon	6,819	2,633
3	Grampian Region	8,757	3,381	8	Dumfries and Galloway Region	6,457	2,493
4	North Yorkshire	8,312	3,209	9	Lincolnshire	6,083	2,349
5	Tayside Region	7,624	2,944	10	Dyfed	5,854	2,260

SMALLEST BRITISH COUNTIES

	County	Area sq km	sq miles		County	Area sq km	sq miles
1	Isle of Wight	394	152	6	Merseyside	823	318
2	South Glamorgan	433	167	7	West Glamorgan	871	336
3	Tyne and Wear	550	212	8	West Midlands	896	346
4	Cleveland	614	237	9	Mid Glamorgan	1,019	393
5	Gwynedd	746	288	10	Bedfordshire	1,232	476

Before the reorganization of British counties 20 years ago, the county of Rutland was the smallest at 394 sq km/152 sq miles – which is precisely the same area as the current smallest, the Isle of Wight. Loyalty to the old counties remains an emotive issue, but if recent proposals are adopted, there is every possibility that certain of them are likely to experience a comeback.

LARGEST PARISHES IN GREAT BRITAIN

	Parish	County	Area sq km	sq miles
1	Stanhope	Kent	255.5	98.7
2	Holyhead	Gwynedd	214.6	82.9
3	Dartmoor Forest	Devon	204.8	79.1
4	Rochester	Northumberland	179.1	69.2
5	Alwinton	Northumberland	155.0	59.9
6	Alston Moor	Cumbria	149.4	57.7
7	Kielder	Northumberland	143.8	55.5
8	Bradfield	South Yorkshire	142.1	54.9
9	Holbeach	Lincolnshire	139.8	54.0
10	Rhayader	Powys	139.4	53.8

T O P 1 0

BRITISH COUNTIES WITH THE LONGEST PERIMETERS

	County	Total perimeter km	miles
1	Highland Region	2,417	1,052
2	Strathclyde Region	1,661	1,032
3	North Yorkshire	729	453
4	Dyfed	728	453
5	Dumfries and Galloway Region	709	441

	County	Total perimeter km	miles
6	Cornwall	672	417
7	Devon	665	413
8	Essex	592	368
9	Lincolnshire	572	355
10	Powys	569	354

T O P 1 0

BRITISH COUNTIES WITH THE SHORTEST PERIMETERS

	County	Total perimeter km	miles
1	South Glamorgan	115	71
2	Isle of Wight	122	76
3	Tyne and Wear	170	106
4	Cleveland	178	111
5	Mid Glamorgan	202	126

	County	Total perimeter km	miles
6	West Glamorgan	219	136
7	Bedfordshire	242	150
8	South Yorkshire	246	153
9	West Midlands	249	155
10	Greater Manchester	251	156

The Ordnance Survey's method of measuring perimeters encompasses both county boundaries and coastlines at low water mark (which is the legal extent of the realm). One of the many effects of re-drawing the county map of Britain in the mid-1970s was to split Glamorgan into three parts: West Glamorgan, Mid-Glamorgan, and South Glamorgan.

T O P 1 0

SMALLEST PARISHES IN GREAT BRITAIN

	Parish	County	Area sq km	sq miles
1	Chester Castle	Cheshire	0.043	0.016
2	St Michael's Mount	Cornwall	0.24	0.09
3	Manningtree	Essex	0.27	0.10
4	Downswood	Kent	0.37	0.14
5	Bache	Cheshire	0.38	0.15
6	Prior's Heys	Cheshire	0.43	0.17
7	Edgerley	Cheshire	0.49	0.19
8	Cotcliffe	North Yorkshire	0.535	0.206
9	Churton Heath	Cheshire	0.536	0.207
10	Stanhope	Durham	0.57	0.22

T O P 1 0

BRITISH COUNTIES WITH MOST PARISHES

	County	Parishes
1	North Yorkshire	762
2	Norfolk	539
3	Lincolnshire	513
4	Suffolk	471
5	Devon	422
6	Hereford and Worcester	347
7	Cheshire	328
8	Somerset	327
9	Oxfordshire	320
10	Essex	286

T O P 1 0

BRITISH COUNTIES WITH FEWEST PARISHES

	County	Parishes
1	Greater London	0
2	Tyne and Wear	10
3	Greater Manchester	13
4	West Midlands	14
5	Merseyside	22
6	Isle of Wight	26
7	Cleveland	32
8	South Glamorgan	54
9=	Surrey	78
9=	West Yorkshire	78

Civil parishes (not to be confused with ecclesiastical parishes) are the smallest units of local government in rural areas: there are few in urban or built-up areas, and many in predominantly rural areas. By law, parish councils must be established in parishes with more than 200 electors. There are more than 7,000 parish councils in England, and 734 in Wales (where they are correctly termed community councils).

PLACE NAMES

TOP 10

LONGEST PLACE NAMES IN THE WORLD

(Including single-word, hyphenated, and multiple names)

Name	Letters
1 Krung thep mahanakhon bovorn ratanakosin mahintharayutthaya mahadilok pop noparatratchathani burirom udomratchanivetma hasathan amornpiman avatarnsa thit sakkathattiyavisnukarmprasit	167

When the poetic name of Bangkok, capital of Thailand, is used, it is usually abbreviated to "Krung Thep" (City of Angels).

Name	Letters
2 Taumatawhakatangihangakoauau-otamateaturipukakapikimaunga-horonukupokaiwhenuakitanatahu	85

This is the longer version (the other has a mere 83 letters) of the Maori name of a hill in New Zealand. It translates as "The place where Tamatea, the man with the big knees, who slid, climbed, and swallowed mountains, known as land-eater, played on the flute to his loved one".

Name	Letters
3 Gorsafawddacha'idraigodanhed-dogleddollônpenrhynareur-draethceredigion	67

A name contrived by the Fairbourne Steam Railway, Gwynedd, North Wales, for publicity purposes and in order to outdo its rival, No. 4. It means "The Mawddach station and its dragon teeth at the Northern Penrhyn Road on the golden beach of Cardigan Bay".

Name	Letters
4 Llanfairpwllgwyngyllgogerychwyrn-drobwllllantysiliogogogoch	58

This is the place in Gwynedd famed especially for the length of its railway tickets. It means "St Mary's Church in the hollow of the white hazel near to the rapid whirlpool of Llantysilio of the Red Cave". Its authenticity is suspect, since its official name comprises only the first 20 letters, and the full name appears to have been invented as a hoax in the 19th century by local inhabitant John Evans.

Name	Letters
5 El Pueblo de Nuestra Señora la Reina de los Angeles de la Porciuncula	57

The site of a Franciscan mission and the full Spanish name of Los Angeles; it means "the town of Our Lady the Queen of the Angels of the Little Portion". Now it is customarily known by its initial letters "LA", making it also one of the shortest-named cities in the world.

Name	Letters
6 Chargoggagoggmanchauggagogg-chaubunagungamaugg	45

America's longest place name, a lake near Webster, Massachusetts. Its Indian name, loosely translated, means "You fish on your side, I'll fish on mine, and no one fishes in the middle". It is pronounced "Char-gogg-a-gogg (pause) man-chaugg-a-gogg (pause) chau-bun-a-gung-a-maugg".

Name	Letters
7= Lower North Branch Little Southwest Miramichi	40

Canada's longest place name – a short river in New Brunswick.

Name	Letters
7= Villa Real de la Santa Fe de San Francisco de Asis	40

The full Spanish name of Santa Fe, New Mexico, translates as "Royal city of the holy faith of St Francis of Assisi".

Name	Letters
9 Te Whakatakanga-o-te-ngarehu-o-te-ahi-a-Tamatea	38

The Maori name of Hammer Springs, New Zealand; like the second name in this list, it refers to a legend of Tamatea, explaining how the springs were warmed by "the falling of the cinders of the fire of Tamatea".

Name	Letters
10 Meallan Liath Coire Mhic Dhubhghaill	32

The longest multiple name in Scotland, a place near Aultanrynie, Highland, alternatively spelled Meallan Liath Coire Mhic Dhughaill

TOP 10

LONGEST PLACE NAMES IN THE UK

(Single and hyphenated only)

Name	Letters
1 Gorsafawddacha'idraigodanhed-dogleddollônpenrhynareur-draethceredigion (*see* The 10 Longest Place Names in the World)	67
2 Llanfairpwllgwyngyllgogerych-wyrndrobwllllantysiliogogogoch (*see* The 10 Longest Place Names in the World)	58
3 Sutton-under-Whitestonecliffe, North Yorkshire	27
4 Llanfihangel-yng-Ngwynfa, Powys	22
5= Llanfihangel-y-Creuddyn, Dyfed	21
5= Llanfihangel-y-traethau, Gwynedd	21
7 Cottonshopeburnfoot, Northumberland	19
8= Blakehopeburnhaugh, Northumberland	18
8= Coignafeuinternich, Inverness-shire	18
10= Claddach-baleshare, North Uist, Outer Hebrides	17
10= Claddach-knockline, North Uist, Outer Hebrides	17

Runners-up include Combeinteignhead, Doddiscombsleigh, Moretonhampstead, Stokeinteignhead, and Woolfardisworthy (pronounced "Woolsery"), all of which are in Devon and have 16 letters. The longest multiple name in England is North Leverton with Habblesthorpe, Nottinghamshire (30 letters), followed by Sulhampstead Bannister Upper End, Berkshire (29). In Wales the longest are Lower Llanfihangel-y-Creuddyn, Dyfed (26) followed by Llansantffraid Cwmdeuddwr, Powys (24), and in Scotland Meallan Liath Coire Mhic Dhughaill, Highland, (32), a loch on the island of Lewis called Loch Airidh Mhic Fhionnlaidh Dhuibh (31), and Huntingtower and Ruthvenfield (27). If the parameters are extended to include Ireland, Castletownconyersmaceniery (26), Co. Limerick, Muikeenachidirdhashaile (24), and Muckanaghederdauhalia (21), both in Co. Galway, are scooped into the net. The shortest place name in the UK is Ae in Dumfries and Galloway, Scotland.

T O P 1 0

COUNTRIES WITH THE LONGEST OFFICIAL NAMES

	Official name*	English name	Common Letters
1	al-Jamāhīrīyah al-ᶜArabīya al-Lībīyah ash-Shaᶜbīyah al-Ishtirākīyah	Libya	56
2	al-Jumhūrīyah al-Jazāʾirīyah ad-Dīmuqrāṭīyah ash-Shaᶜbīyah	Algeria	49
3	United Kingdom of Great Britain and Northern Ireland	United Kingdom	45
4	Sri Lankā Prajathanthrika Samajavadi Janarajaya	Sri Lanka	43
5	Jumhūrīyat al-Qumur al-Ittihādīyah al-Islāmīyah	The Comores	41
6=	al-Jumhūrīyah al-Islāmīyah al-Mūrītānīyah	Mauritania	36
6=	The Federation of St Christopher and Nevis	St Christopher	36
8	Jamhuuriyadda Dimuqraadiga Soomaaliya	Somalia	35
9	al-Mamlakah al-Urdunnīyah al-Hāshimīyah	Jordan	34
10	Repoblika Demokratika nʾi Madagaskar	Madagascar	32

* *Some official names have been transliterated from languages that do not use the Roman alphabet; their length may vary according to the method used.*

There is clearly no connection between the length of names and the longevity of the nation states that bear them, for since this list was last published in 1991, three countries have ceased to exist: Socijalistička Federativna Republika Jugoslavija (Yugoslavia, 45 letters), Soyuz Sovetskikh Sotsialisticheskikh Respublik (USSR, 43), and Československá Socialistická Republika (Czechoslovakia, 36).

LONGEST ENGLISH CIVIL PARISH NAMES

	Civil parish	County	Letters
1	St Mary, South Elmham otherwise Homersfield	Suffolk	37
2	Lindrick with Studley Royal and Fountains	North Yorkshire	36
3	Macclesfield Forest and Wildboarclough	Cheshire	35
4=	All Saints and St Nicholas South Elmham	Suffolk	33
4=	Bradfield Combust with Stanningfield	Suffolk	33
4=	Castle Bolton with East and West Bolton	North Yorkshire	33
7	Aubourn Haddington and South Hykeham	Lincolnshire	32
8	Temple Bruer with Temple High Grange	Lincolnshire	31
9	Horsham St Faith and Newton St Faith	Norfolk	30
10	St Cosmus and St Damien in the Blean	Kent	29

COMMONEST PLACE NAMES IN THE UK

	Name	No. of occurrences
1	Newton	150
2	Blackhill/Black Hill	141
3	Mountpleasant/Mount Pleasant	130
4	Castlehill/Castle Hill	127
5	Woodside/Wood Side	116
6	Newtown/New Town	111
7	Greenhill/Green Hill	108
8	Woodend/Wood End	106
9	Burnside	105
10	Beacon Hill	94

Research undertaken specially for *The Top 10 of Everything* by Adrian Room (the author of *A Concise Dictionary of Modern Place-names in Great Britain and Ireland*) reveals the place names most frequently encountered in the UK. These include the names of towns and villages, as well as woods, hills, and other named locations, but exclude combinations of these names with others (Newton Abbot and Newton-le-Willows, for example, are not counted with the Newtons). A further study of the 250,000 names appearing on the Ordnance Survey 1:50,000 scale "Landranger" maps shows that certain names of farms and houses appear even more frequently than the general names in this list:

	Name	No. of occurrences
1	Manor Farm	590
2	Park Farm	357
3	Hill Farm	355
4	Home Farm	341
5	Manor House	288
6=	Grange Farm	265
6=	Lodge Farm	265
8	The Grange	202
9	Hall Farm	182
10	Glebe Farm	171

THE STREETS OF LONDON

FLEET STREET
*Nostalgia for Fleet Street's former place at the hub of the British newspaper
industry may have helped to make this the most prized name at an auction
of enamelled City street signs.*

TOP 10

COMMONEST STREET NAMES IN GREATER LONDON

	Name/most frequent combination	Occurrences
1	Church (Road)	380
2	Park (Road)	323
3	Station (Road)	248
4	High (Street)	236
5	Manor (Road)	202
6	Orchard (Road)	173
7	Green (Lane)	150
8=	Grove (Road)	138
8=	West (Road)	138
10	Queen's (Road)	127

A survey of more than 75,000 street names
in Greater London and a number of
surrounding towns reveals Top 10 names
and the generic term (road, street, etc.)
with which it is most frequently combined.
Based on frequency of name plus generic
term, in the specific area of Greater London
(excluding adjacent towns), Station Road
wins with 125 uses compared with 110
for Church Road.

TOP 10

MOST VALUABLE CITY OF LONDON STREET NAMES*

	Street/no. of signs in lot	Price (£)
1	Fleet Street, EC4 (6)	17,600
2	Threadneedle Street, EC2 (6)	13,200
3	Old Bailey, EC4 (1)	6,050
4	Middlesex Street, E1 (5)	3,300
5=	Little Britain, EC1 (4)	2,420
5=	Pudding Lane, EC3 (2)	2,420
7	Paternoster Square, EC4 (3)	2,227
8	Lombard Street, EC3 (3)	1,760
9	Cornhill, EC3 (4)	1,650
10	Bishopsgate, EC2 (6)	1,430

* *Based on auction sales of disused signs held
at Bonhams of Knightsbridge on 25 June
and 9 July 1991.*

TOP 10

"BLUE PLAQUE" LONDON BOROUGHS

	Borough	No. of plaques
1	Westminster	277
2	Kensington and Chelsea	114
3	Camden	106
4	Tower Hamlets	23
5	Wandsworth	21
6=	Lambeth	20
6=	Hammersmith and Fulham	20
8	Greenwich	13
9	Islington	11
10	Lewisham	10

The commemoration of the homes of notable people in London by erecting a blue plaque on the wall of their former residences was started in 1867 by the Royal Society of Arts. It was later taken over by the London County Council and its successor, the Greater London Council. Since the GLC was disbanded on 1 April 1986 (one of its last acts was to put up a plaque to itself at the entrance to County Hall), the erection of blue plaques has been the responsibility of English Heritage. Not all of the earlier plaques were actually the familiar blue ceramic with white lettering, but this has been the standard for nearly 60 years. To qualify for a blue plaque, a person has to have been born more than 100 years ago or dead for over 20, should have made some worthwhile contribution to human welfare and happiness, and must be known to the well-informed passer-by. A few commemorate not individuals but organizations (the Labour Party), ships (*The Great Eastern*), events (the first flying bomb to hit London), and the buildings themselves (Collins Music Hall). By May 1993 a total of 628 had been installed – as well as a number of "unofficial" ones, such as that in South Street W1, to Catherine "Skittles" Walters (1839-1920), mistress of Edward, Prince of Wales, who is described on it as "The Last Victorian Courtesan". There are also occasional mistakes: that to another of the Prince's mistresses, Lily Langtry on the Cadogan Hotel in Pont Street SW1, for example, gives the wrong date of her birth (1852 instead of 1853), while some are believed to have been sited on the wrong houses. Westminster is by far the leading blue plaque borough, largely because of the number of politicians who have lived in proximity to government offices and the Houses of Parliament. As well as the Top 10 boroughs, several have only one plaque, while the boroughs of Barking, Enfield, Havering, Hillingdon, and Kingston have none at all.

TOP 10

GREATER LONDON STREET NAMES (PEOPLE AND CITIES)

	Name	Occurrences
1	Victoria	114
2	York	92
3	Tudor	88
4	Albert	87
5	Alexandra	84
6	Cambridge	82
7	Grosvenor	81
8	Warwick	77
9	Stanley	75
10	Gordon	71

There are more streets in Greater London (the London postal area and outlying towns) named after Queen Victoria than after any other individual, although other royal family names (including her husband, Prince Albert, and daughter-in-law Princess Alexandra) make a strong showing. Some streets may equally have been called after dukes and earls (such as York and Warwick) or the places from which they derived their names. Runners-up include writers and assorted British heroes such as Byron and Nelson. Names of saints and of trees are the other two most fertile sources for London street names.

TOP 10

COMMONEST "THE" STREET NAMES IN GREATER LONDON

	Name	Occurrences
1	The Drive	74
2	The Avenue	70
3	The Green	51
4	The Crescent	46
5	The Grove	42
6	The Close	41
7	The Chase	34
8	The Ridgeway	27
9	The Broadway	25
10=	The Rise	20
10=	The Spinney	20

TOP 10

SAINTS IN LONDON STREET NAMES

	Name	Occurrences
1	St John	97
2	St Mary	86
3	St George	66
4	St Peter	51
5	St Andrew	50
6=	St Paul	39
6=	St Alban	39
8=	St James	35
8=	St Margaret	35
10	St Stephen	31

TOP 10

TREES IN LONDON STREET NAMES

	Name	Occurrences
1	Elm	126
2=	Beech	97
2=	Chestnut	97
4	Willow	95
5	Cedar	90
6	Oak	80
7	Maple	61
8	Linden	60
9	Ash	59
10	Birch	53

NATIONAL PARKS

TOP 10

LARGEST NATURE RESERVES IN SCOTLAND

	Nature Reserve	Area hectares	acres
1	Cairngorms, Grampian and Highland Regions	25,949	64,121
2	Inverpolly, Highland Region	10,857	26,828
3	Rùm, Highland Region	10,684	26,401
4	Caerlaverock, Dumfries and Galloway Region	7,706	19,042
5	Ben Wyvis, Highland Region	5,673	14,026
6	Beinn Eighe, Highland Region	4,758	11,757
7	Glen Tanar, Grampian Region	4,185	10,341
8	Ben Lawers, Tayside and Central Regions	4,060	10,032
9	Creag Meagaidh, Highland Region	3,948	9,756
10	Caenlochan, Tayside Region	3,714	9,177

TOP 10

LARGEST NATIONAL PARKS IN ENGLAND AND WALES

	National Park	Established	Area sq km	sq miles
1	Lake District	9 May 1951	2,292	885
2	Snowdonia	18 Oct 1951	2,142	827
3	Yorkshire Dales	13 Oct 1954	1,769	683
4	Peak District	17 Apr 1951	1,438	555
5	North York Moors	28 Nov 1952	1,436	554
6	Brecon Beacons	17 Apr 1957	1,351	522
7	Northumberland	6 Apr 1956	1,049	405
8	Dartmoor	30 Oct 1951	954	368
9	Exmoor	19 Oct 1954	693	268
10	Pembrokeshire Coast	29 Feb 1952	584	225

Following the National Parks and Access to the Countryside Act of 1949, the National Parks were established in the 1950s to conserve and protect some of the most picturesque landscapes of England and Wales from unsuitable development, at the same time allowing the public free access to them. The total area is 14,011 sq km/5,410 sq miles (about nine per cent of the total area of the country), of which 9,934 sq km/3,836 sq miles is in England and 4,077 sq km/1,574 sq miles in Wales. In addition to the 10 National Parks, the Norfolk and Suffolk Broads (303 sq km/ 117 sq miles) became a National Park in all but name on 1 April 1989. There are also plans for the New Forest and parts of Scotland to be designated National Parks.

TOP 10

LARGEST NATURE RESERVES IN WALES

	Nature Reserve	Area hectares	acres
1	Dyfi, Dyfed	2,095	5,177
2	Y Wyddfa, Gwynedd	1,677	4,144
3	Newborough Warren, Gwynedd	1,301	3,216
4	Morfa Harlech, Gwynedd	884	2,185
5	Cors Caron, Dyfed	792	1,957
6	Whiteford, West Glamorgan	782	1,932
7	Rhinog, Gwynedd	598	1,478
8	Kenfig Pool and Dunes, Mid Glamorgan	518	1,281
9	Cadair Idris, Gwynedd	430	1,063
10	Ogof Ffynnon Ddu, Powys	413	1,021

TOP 10

LARGEST NATURE RESERVES IN ENGLAND

	Nature Reserve	Area hectares	acres
1	The Wash, Lincolnshire	9,899	24,461
2	Ribble Marshes, Lancashire/Merseyside	4,112	10,161
3	Holkham, Norfolk	3,925	9,699
4	Moor House, Cumbria	3,894	9,622
5	Lindisfarne, Northumberland	3,541	8,750
6	Upper Teesdale, North Yorkshire	3,493	8,631
7	Bridgwater Bay, Somerset	2,559	6,323
8	Dengie, Essex	2,293	5,666
9	Lizard, Cornwall	1,375	3,398
10	Blackwater Estuary, Essex	1,031	2,548

National Nature Reserves are sites designated under the National Parks and Access to the Countryside Act of 1949 for the study and preservation of flora and fauna or geological and physiological features. They are either owned or controlled by English Nature or approved bodies such as Wildlife Trusts. In 1992 there were 140 such sites in England, a total of 47,327 hectares/116,947 acres. A further 290 sites (1992 total: 13,000 hectares/32,124 acres) are maintained by local authorities as Local Nature Reserves.

MAJESTIC BEAUTY
The Lake District in Cumbria, the UK's largest National Park, has been a favourite subject for poets such as William Wordsworth and Samuel Taylor Coleridge. The area, which encompasses 16 lakes, is unrivalled in England for its beauty and varied scenery.

T O P   1 0

LONGEST NATIONAL TRAILS IN THE UK*

	National trail	Opened	km	miles
1	South West Coast Path	May 1973/Sep 1974/ May 1978	962	598
2	Pennine Way	Apr 1965	412	256
3	Thames Path	#	343	213
4	Southern Upland Way	Apr 1984	340	212
5	Pembrokeshire Coast Path	May 1970	292	181
6	Offa's Dyke Path	Jul 1971	285	177
7	North Downs Way	Sep 1978	246	153
8	Cleveland Way	May 1969	175	109
9	West Highland Way	Oct 1980	152	95
10	Peddars Way and Norfolk Coast Path	Jul 1986	150	93

* *The Scottish equivalent of National Trails*
is Long-Distance Footpaths.
\# *Not yet officially opened.*

LONGEST HERITAGE COASTS IN THE UK

	Heritage Coast	Defined	km	miles
1	North Northumberland	Feb 1973	96	60
2	Lleyn	Mar 1974	90	56
3	St David's Peninsula	Jul 1974	83	52
4	South Devon	Dec 1986	75	47
5=	Isles of Scilly	Dec 1974	64	40
5=	North Norfolk	Apr 1975	64	40
7	South Pembrokeshire	Jul 1974	62	39
8	Gower	Jun 1973	59	37
9=	Suffolk	Sep 1979	57	35
9=	North Yorkshire and Cleveland	May 1981	57	35

The total length of Heritage Coasts in England and Wales is 1,448 km/900 miles. Scotland does not have any Heritage Coasts.

LARGEST AREAS OF OUTSTANDING NATURAL BEAUTY IN ENGLAND AND WALES

	Area	Established	sq km	sq miles
1	Cotswolds	Aug 1966/ Dec 1990	2,038	787
2	North Pennines	Jun 1988	1,983	766
3	North Wessex Downs	Dec 1972	1,730	668
4	High Weald	Oct 1983	1,460	564
5	Dorset	Jul 1959	1,129	436
6=	Sussex Downs	Apr 1966	983	380
6=	West Wiltshire Downs	Oct 1983	983	380
8	Cornwall/Camel Estuary	Nov 1959/ Oct 1983	958	370
9	Kent Downs	Jul 1968	878	339
10	Chilterns	Dec 1965/ Mar 1990	833	322

England and Wales have 39 Areas of Outstanding Natural Beauty, amounting to 20,052 sq km/7,742 sq miles (19,208 sq km/7,416 sq miles in England and 844 sq km/326 sq miles in Wales), which represents some 13 per cent of the total area of the two countries. There are also nine Areas of Outstanding Natural Beauty in Northern Ireland, and 40 National Scenic Areas designated in Scotland occupying some 1,001,800 hectares/2,475,448 acres.

WORLD'S TALLEST BUILDINGS

T O P 1 0

TALLEST BUILDINGS ERECTED MORE THAN 100 YEARS AGO

	Building	Location	Year completed	Height m	ft
1	Eiffel Tower	Paris, France	1889	300	984
2	Washington Memorial	Washington DC, USA	1885	169	555
3	Ulm Cathedral	Ulm, Germany	1890	161	528
4	Lincoln Cathedral	Lincoln, England	c.1307 (destroyed 1548)	160	525
5	Cologne Cathedral	Cologne, Germany	1880	156.4	513
6	Notre-Dame	Rouen, France	1530	156	512
7	St Pierre Church	Beauvais, France	1568 (collapsed 1573)	153	502
8	St Paul's Cathedral	London, England	1315 (destroyed 1561)	149	489
9	Rouen Cathedral	Rouen, France	1876	148	485
10	Great Pyramid	Giza, Egypt	c.2580 BC	146.5	481

T O P 1 0

TALLEST HABITABLE BUILDINGS IN THE WORLD

	Building	Location	Year completed	Storeys	Height m	ft
1	Sears Tower with spires	Chicago, USA	1974	110	443 *520*	1,454 *1,707*
2	World Trade Center*	New York City, USA	1973	110	417	1,368
3	Empire State Building with spire	New York City, USA	1931	102	381 *449*	1,250 *1,472*
4	Amoco Building	Chicago, USA	1973	80	346	1,136
5	John Hancock Center with spire	Chicago, USA	1968	100	343 *450*	1,127 *1,476*
6	Yu Kyong Hotel	Pyongyang, North Korea	1992	105	320	1,050
7	Central Plaza with spire	Hong Kong	1992	78	309 *374*	1,015 *1,228*
8	First Interstate World Center	Los Angeles, USA	1990	73	310	1,017
9	Texas Commerce Tower	Houston, USA	1981	75	305	1,002
10	Bank of China Tower with spires	Hong Kong	1989	70	305 *368*	1,001 *1,209*

* *Twin towers; the second tower, completed in 1973, has the same number of storeys but is slightly smaller at 415 m/1,362 ft – although its spire takes it up to 521 m/1,710 ft.*

Heights do not include TV and radio antennae and uninhabited extensions. This list is scheduled to change in 1995, when two new skyscrapers are completed: the 95-storey Petronas Tower, Kuala Lumpur (450 m/1,476 ft) will be "world's tallest", while the Tour Sans Fin (426 m/1,398 ft) in Paris will become the third tallest.

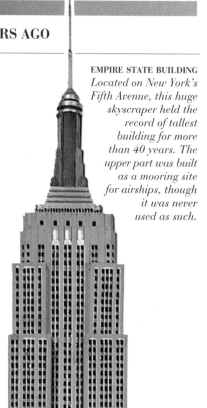

EMPIRE STATE BUILDING
Located on New York's Fifth Avenue, this huge skyscraper held the record of tallest building for more than 40 years. The upper part was built as a mooring site for airships, though it was never used as such.

TOP 10

TALLEST CHIMNEYS IN THE WORLD

	Chimney/location	Height m	ft
1	Ekibastuz Power Station, Kazakhstan	420	1,377
2	International Nickel Company, Sudbury, Ontario, Canada	381	1,250
3	Pennsylvania Electric Company, Homer City, Pennsylvania, USA	371	1,216
4	Kennecott Copper Corporation, Magna, Utah, USA	370	1,215
5	Ohio Power Company, Cresap, West Virginia, USA	368	1,206
6	Zasavje Power Station, Trboulje, Yugoslavia	360	1,181
7	Empresa Nacional de Electricidad SA, Puentes de Garcia Rodriguez, Spain	356	1,169
8	Appalachian Power Company, New Haven, West Virginia, USA	336	1,103
9	Indiana & Michigan Electric Company, Rockport, Indiana, USA	316	1,037
10	West Penn Power Company, Reesedale, Pennsylvania, USA	308	1,012

Nos. 2 to 5 and 7 to 10 were all built by Pullman Power Products Corporation (formerly a division of M.W. Kellogg), an American engineering company that has been in business since 1902 and has built many of the world's tallest chimneys. The largest internal volume is No. 7 – 6,700,000 cubic feet. The diameter of No. 1, completed in 1991, tapers from 44 m/144 ft at the base to 14 m/47 ft at the top; the outside diameter of No. 4, built in 1974 and formerly the world's largest, is 38 m/124 ft at the base, tapering to 12 m/40 ft.

TOP 10

TALLEST TELECOMMUNICATIONS TOWERS IN THE WORLD

	Tower/location	Year completed	Height m	ft
1	CN Tower, Toronto, Canada	1975	553	1,815
2	Ostankino Tower, Moscow, Russia	1967	537	1,762
3	Alma-Ata Tower, Kazakhstan	1983	370	1,214
4	TV Tower, Berlin, Germany	1969	365	1,198
5	TV Tower, Tashkent, Uzbekistan	1983	357	1,171
6	Tokyo Tower, Tokyo, Japan	1959	333	1,093
7	TV Tower, Frankfurt, Germany	1977	331	1,086
8	National Transcommunications Transmitter, Emley Moor, West Yorkshire, UK	1971	329	1,080
9	Eiffel Tower, Paris, France	1889	321	1,053
10	Sydney Tower, Sydney, Australia	1981	305	1,001

All the towers listed are self-supporting, rather than masts braced with guy wires, and all have observation facilities, the highest being that in the CN Tower, Toronto (the world's tallest self-supporting structure of any kind) at 447 m/1,467 ft. Towers new to the Top 10, both currently under construction and due for completion in 1995, will be the KL Tower, Kuala Lumpur, Malaysia (420 m/1,378 ft) and the Sky Tower, Auckland, New Zealand (328 m/1,076 ft). As a result, the Eiffel Tower will drop out of the Top 10 and the Vegas World Tower, Las Vegas, USA (309 m/1,012 ft), also scheduled for completion in 1995, will not achieve Top 10 status.

TOP 10

TALLEST STRUCTURES THAT ARE NO LONGER STANDING

	Structure	Location	Completed	Destroyed	Height m	ft
1	Warszawa Radio Mast	Konstantynow, Poland	1974	1991	646	2,120
2	KSWS TV Mast	Roswell, New Mexico, USA	1956	1960	491	1,610
3	IBA Mast	Emley Moor, UK	1965	1969	385	1,265
4	No. 6 Flue (chimney), Matla Power Station	Kriel, South Africa	1980	1981	275	902
5	Singer Building	New York, USA	1908	1970	200	656
6	New Brighton Tower	Merseyside, UK	1900	1919	171	562
7	Lincoln Cathedral	Lincoln, England	c.1307	1548	160	525
8	St Pierre Church	Beauvais, France	1568	1573	153	502
9	St Peter's	Louvain, Flanders	1497	1606	152	500
10	Lin-He Pagoda	Hang Zhou, China	970	1121	150	492

The Matla Power Station chimney was never fully operational and following an accident that resulted in two fatalities was demolished. If excluded for this reason, the 10th entry is the 125-m/410-ft Legal & General Building, Sydney, Australia, built in 1977 and dismantled floor by floor in nine months during 1991.

BIGGEST BUILDINGS – UK

TALLEST LIGHTHOUSES IN THE UK

Lighthouse/location	Height	
	m	ft
1= Bishop Rock, Scilly Isles	49	161
1= Eddystone, English Channel	49	161
3 Skerryvore, Hebrides	48	157
4 Chicken Rock, Calf of Man	44	144
5= Beachy Head, East Sussex	43	141
5= Dungeness, Kent	43	141
7 North Ronaldsay, Orkney	42	138
8= The Smalls, Dyfed	41	135
8= Tarbat Ness, Ross and Cromarty	41	135
8= Portland, Dorset	41	135
8= Wolf Rock, Cornwall	41	135

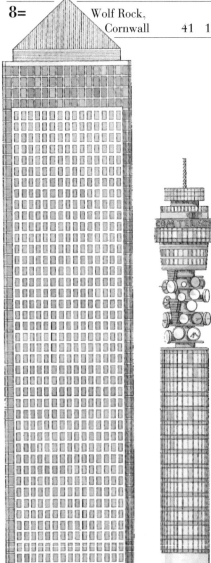

TALLEST HABITABLE BUILDINGS IN THE UK

Building	Year completed	Height	
		m	ft
1 Canary Wharf Tower, London E14	1991	244	800
2 National Westminster Tower, London EC2	1979	183	600
3 British Telecom Tower, London W1	1966	177	580
4 Blackpool Tower	1894	158	519
5 Barbican, London EC2:			
Shakespeare Tower	1971	128	419
Cromwell Tower	1973	128	419
Lauderdale Tower	1974	128	419
6 Euston Centre, Euston Road, London NW1	1969	124	408
7 Cooperative Insurance Society Building, Miller Street, Manchester	1962	122	399
8 Centre Point, New Oxford Street, London WC1	1966	121	398
9 Britannic House, Moor Lane, London EC2	1967	120	395
10= Millbank Tower, Millbank, London SW1	1963	118	387
10= Commercial Union, Undershaft, London EC3	1969	118	387

The 244-m/800-ft Canary Wharf Tower, in London's Docklands, is now not only the tallest habitable building in the UK, but also the second tallest in Europe, after the Frankfurt Messeturm (256 m/841 ft). On a global scale, however, it would appear only in 47th position, and is just 2.4 m/8 ft taller than one of the world's first skyscrapers, the Woolworth Building in New York, which was built in 1913. The Barbican towers are the tallest blocks of flats in the UK.

THEN AND NOW
Built a quarter of a century apart, both the British Telecom Tower (formerly the Post Office Tower) and Canary Wharf have held the record as the UK's tallest building.

TALLEST MASTS IN THE UK

Mast	Height	
	m	ft
1 Belmont, Lincolnshire	385	1,265
2 Emley Moor, West Yorkshire	330	1,082
3 Durris, Grampian	320	1,049
4 Strabane, Northern Ireland	315	1,034
5 Caldbeck, Cumbria	314.3	1,031
6 Waltham on the Wolds, Leicestershire	314.0	1,030
7 Arfon, Gwynedd	313.9	1,029
8 Bilsdale West Moor, North Yorkshire	312	1,022
9 Winter Hill, Lancashire	307.7	1,009
10 Lichfield, Staffordshire	307.0	1,007

All are TV transmitting masts. The 210-tonne Belmont mast, built in 1965, is the tallest structure of any kind in the UK. Meteorological equipment added in 1967 raises its total height to 387 m/1,272 ft.

T O P 1 0
LARGEST HOTELS IN THE UK

	Hotel	Rooms*
1	Regent Palace, London	946
2	Forum, London#	910
3	Cumberland, London	890
4	Copthorne Tara, London	825
5	Excelsior, Heathrow	823
6	Tower Thistle, London	808
7	Metropole, Birmingham	802
8	Strand Palace, London	777
9	London Kensington Hilton	603
10	The White House, London	575

* Excluding suites.
# The UK's tallest hotel: 27 storeys, 132 m/380 ft.

T O P 1 0
HOTEL GROUPS IN THE UK WITH MOST BEDROOMS

	Hotel group	Hotels	Bedrooms
1	Trusthouse Forte	323	29,363
2	Thistle Hotels	105	14,000
3	Queens Moat Houses	102	10,411
4	Hilton International	35	7,137
5	Holiday Inns	33	5,913
6	Rank and Mecca	26	4,331
7	Swallow Hotels	32	4,070
8	Stakis Hotels	30	3,800
9	Jarvis Hotels	41	3,150
10	De Vere Hotels	25	2,771

SALISBURY CATHEDRAL
The 123-m/404-ft spire rests on foundations just 2 m/6 ft deep in swampy ground.

T O P 1 0
TALLEST CATHEDRALS IN ENGLAND

		Height	
	Cathedral	m	ft
1	Salisbury (spire)	123	404
2	London (now St Paul's) (dome)	111	364
3	Liverpool (Anglican) (tower)	101	331
4	Norwich (spire)	96	320
5	Coventry (spire)	91	300
6	Chichester (spire)	84	277
7	Westminster (Roman Catholic) (tower)	83	273
8	Lincoln (towers)	83	271
9	Lichfield (spire)	79	258
10	Truro (central tower)	76	250

T O P 1 0
TALLEST CHURCHES IN ENGLAND

		Height	
	Church	m	ft
1	St Botolph, Boston, Lincolnshire (tower)	83	272
2	St Wulfram, Grantham, Lincolnshire	82	270
3	St Augustine, Kilburn, London	77	254
4	St Mary Magdalen, Newark	73	240
5	Christ Church, Spitalfields, London	71	234
6	Westminster Abbey (towers)	69	225
7	St Mary-le-Bow, London	66	217
8	St Patrick, Patrington	58	189
9	St Martin-in-the-Fields, London	56	185
10	St Mary, Higham Ferrers	52	170

All of these churches, apart from Nos. 1 and 6, have spires.

DID YOU KNOW

LONGEST CATHEDRALS – UK

The longest British cathedral is the Anglican Cathedral in Liverpool, which measures 194 m/636 ft. Commenced in 1904 and completed in 1978, it overtook Winchester (169 m/554 ft), which had held the record for more than 500 years. Its closest rivals are St Albans (164 m/537 ft), with York, Lincoln, St Paul's, Durham, and Norwich runners up in the Top 10.

BRIDGES AND TUNNELS

T O P 1 0

LONGEST SUSPENSION BRIDGES IN THE WORLD

	Bridge	Completed	Length of main span m	ft
1	Messina Strait Bridge, Sicily to Calabria, Italy	(?)*	3,319.9	10,892
2	Akashi-Kaikyo, Japan	(1998)*	1,990.0	6,529
3	Great Belt East Bridge, Denmark	(1997)*	1,624.0	5,328
4	Humber Estuary, UK	1980	1,410.0	4,626
5	Verrazano Narrows, New York, USA	1964	1,298.5	4,260
6	Golden Gate, San Francisco, USA	1937	1,280.2	4,200
7	Mackinac Straits, Michigan, USA	1957	1,158.2	3,800
8	Bosphorus, Istanbul, Turkey	1973	1,074.1	3,524
9	George Washington, New York, USA	1931	1,066.8	3,500
10	Ponte 25 Abril (Ponte Salazar), Lisbon, Portugal	1966	1,012.9	3,323

* *Under construction.*

The Messina Bridge remains a speculative project, but if constructed according to plan it will have by far the longest centre span of any bridge (although at 3,910 m/12,828 ft the Akashi-Kaikyo bridge will be the world's longest overall). If only completed bridges are included, the Humber Estuary Bridge heads the list. Nos. 8 and 9 are two further British structures: the Forth Road Bridge (completed 1964; 1,005.8 m/3,300 ft), and the Severn Bridge (1966; 987.6 m/3,240 ft). No. 10 then becomes the Tacoma Narrows II, Washington (1950; 853.4 m/2,800 ft).

T O P 1 0

LONGEST CANTILEVER BRIDGES IN THE WORLD

	Bridge	Completed	Longest span m	ft
1	Pont de Québec, Canada	1917	548.6	1,800
2	Firth of Forth, Scotland	1890	521.2	1,710
3	Minato, Osaka, Japan	1974	509.9	1,673
4	Commodore John Barry, New Jersey/Pennsylvania, USA	1974	494.4	1,622
5	Greater New Orleans, Louisiana, USA	1958	480.1	1,575
6	Howrah, Calcutta, India	1943	457.2	1,500
7	Transbay, San Francisco, USA	1936	426.7	1,400
8	Baton Rouge, Louisiana, USA	1969	376.4	1,235
9	Tappan Zee, Tarrytown, New York, USA	1955	369.4	1,212
10	Longview, Oregon/Washington, USA	1930	365.8	1,200

T O P 1 0

LONGEST STEEL ARCH BRIDGES IN THE WORLD

	Bridge	Completed	Longest span m	ft
1	New River Gorge, Fayetteville, West Virginia, USA	1977	518.2	1,700
2	Bayonne, New Jersey/Staten Island, New York, USA	1931	503.5	1,652
3	Sydney Harbour, Australia	1932	502.9	1,650
4	Fremont, Portland, Oregon, USA	1973	373.4	1,225
5	Zdákov, Czech Republic	1967	370.0	1,214
6	Port Mann, Vancouver, Canada	1964	365.8	1,200
7	Thatcher Ferry, Panama Canal	1962	343.8	1,128
8	Laviolette, Québec, Canada	1967	335.3	1,100
9	Runcorn-Widnes, UK	1961	329.8	1,082
10	Birchenough, Fort Victoria, Zimbabwe	1935	329.2	1,080

T O P 1 0

LONGEST BRIDGES IN THE UK

	Bridge	Year completed	Length of main span m	ft
1	Humber Estuary	1980	1,410.0	4,626
2	Forth Road Bridge	1964	1,005.8	3,300
3	Severn Bridge	1966	987.6	3,240
4	Firth of Forth	1890	521.2	1,710
5	Tamar, Saltash	1961	335.3	1,100
6	Runcorn–Widnes	1961	329.8	1,082
7	Clifton Suspension	1864	214.0	702
8	Menai Straits	1834	176.5	579
9	Tyne Bridge, Newcastle	1930	161.9	531
10=	Medway (M2 Motorway)	1963	152.4	500
10=	George Street, Newport	1964	152.4	500

GOLDEN GATE BRIDGE
This magnificent suspension bridge spans the Golden Gate waterway that links San Francisco Bay with the Pacific Ocean.

T O P 1 0

LONGEST TUNNELS IN THE UK

	Tunnel	Length km	miles
1	Severn, Avon/Gwent (rail)	7.02	4.36
2	Totley, South Yorkshire (rail)	5.70	3.54
3	Standedge, Manchester/West Yorkshire (canal)	5.10	3.17
4	Standedge, Manchester/West Yorkshire (rail)	4.89	3.04
5	Sodbury, Avon (rail)	4.07	2.53
6	Disley, Cheshire (rail)	3.54	2.20
7	Ffestiniog, Gwynedd (rail)	3.52	2.19
8	Bramhope, West Yorkshire (rail)	3.44	2.14
9	Mersey, Merseyside (road)	3.43	2.13
10	Cowburn, Derbyshire (rail)	3.38	2.10

T O P 1 0

LONGEST RAIL TUNNELS IN THE WORLD

	Tunnel/country	Year completed	Length km	miles
1	Seikan, Japan	1988	53.90	33.49
2	Channel Tunnel, France/England	1994	49.94	31.03
3	Moscow Metro (Medvedkovo/Belyaevo section), Russia	1979	30.70	19.07
4	London Underground (East Finchley/Morden Northern Line), UK	1939	27.84	17.30
5	Dai-Shimizu, Japan	1982	22.17	13.78
6	Simplon II, Italy/Switzerland	1922	19.82	12.31
7	Simplon I, Italy/Switzerland	1906	19.80	12.30
8	Shin-Kanmon, Japan	1975	18.68	11.61
9	Apennine, Italy	1934	18.49	11.49
10	Rokko, Japan	1972	16.25	10.10

The first purpose-built passenger rail tunnel was the 766-m/2,514-ft Tyler Hill Tunnel, Kent, opened on 4 May 1830. The longest rail tunnel built in the 19th century is the 15-km/9.32-mile St Gotthard Tunnel, Switzerland, opened on 20 May 1882.

T O P 1 0

LONGEST ROAD TUNNELS IN THE WORLD

	Tunnel/country	Year completed	Length km	miles
1	St Gotthard, Switzerland	1980	16.32	10.14
2	Arlberg, Austria	1978	13.98	8.69
3	Fréjus, France/Italy	1980	12.90	8.02
4	Mont-Blanc, France/Italy	1965	11.60	7.21
5	Gudvangen, Norway	1992	11.40	7.08
6	Leirfjord, Norway	*	11.11	6.90
7	Kan-Etsu, Japan	1991	11.01	6.84
8	Kan-Etsu, Japan	1985	10.93	6.79
9	Gran Sasso, Italy	1984	10.17	6.32
10	Plabutsch, Austria	1987	9.76	6.06

* Under construction.

All the road tunnels in the Top 10 were built during the past 30 years. Previously, the record for "world's longest" had been held by the 5.04-km/3.13-mile Viella Tunnel, Cataluña, Spain, which was opened in 1941. This tunnel itself overtook the 3.43-km/2.13-mile Mersey Tunnel connecting Liverpool and Birkenhead, built in 1925–34.

OTHER STRUCTURES

T O P 1 0

LARGEST MAN-MADE LAKES IN THE WORLD

(Includes only those formed as a result of dam construction)

	Dam/lake	Location	Year completed	Volume (m³)
1	Owen Falls	Uganda	1954	204,800,000,000
2	Kariba	Zimbabwe	1959	181,592,000,000
3	Bratsk	Russian Federation	1964	169,270,000,000
4	High Aswan	Egypt	1970	168,000,000,000
5	Akosombo	Ghana	1965	148,000,000,000
6	Daniel Johnson	Canada	1968	141,852,000,000
7	Guri (Raul Leoni)	Venezuela	1986	136,000,000,000
8	Krasnoyarsk	Russian Fed.	1967	73,300,000,000
9	Bennett	Canada	1967	70,309,000,000
10	Zeya	Russian Fed.	1978	68,400,000,000

SEASIDE FAVOURITE
Southend's pier, the longest in the country, is a key seafront attraction. Southport moved up to second position in 1978, when storms robbed the 1,154-m (3,787-ft) pier at Herne Bay, Kent, of three-quarters of its length.

T O P 1 0

LONGEST SEASIDE PIERS IN THE UK

	Pier	m	ft
1	Southend, Essex	2,158.0	7,080
2	Southport, Merseyside	1,107.3	3,633
3	Walton-on-the-Naze, Essex	1,097.3	3,600
4	Ryde, Isle of Wight	804.7	2,640
5	Llandudno, Gwynedd	699.5	2,295
6	Ramsay, Isle of Man	691.9	2,270
7=	Clacton, Essex	640.1	2,100
7=	Hythe, Hampshire	640.1	2,100
9	Brighton (Palace Pier), East Sussex	536.5	1,760
10	Bangor (Garth Pier), Gwynedd	472.4	1,550

T O P 1 0

LARGEST VOLUME* DAMS IN THE WORLD

*(*Material used in construction – earth, rocks, concrete, etc.)*

	Dam	Location	Completed	Volume (m³)
1	Syncrude Tailings	Alberta, Canada	1992	540,000,000
2	Pati	Paraná, Argentina	1990	230,180,000
3	New Cornelia Tailings	Ten Mile Wash, Arizona, USA	1973	209,500,000
4	Tarbela	Indus, Pakistan	1976	105,922,000
5	Fort Peck	Missouri, Montana, USA	1937	96,050,000
6	Lower Usuma	Usuma, Nigeria	1990	93,000,000
7	Atatürk	Euphrates, Turkey	1990	84,500,000
8	Yacyreta-Apipe	Paraná, Paraguay/ Argentina	1991	81,000,000
9	Guri (Raul Leoni)	Caroni, Venezuela	1986	77,971,000
10	Rogun	Vakhsh, Tajikstan	1987	75,500,000

T O P 1 0

OLDEST CATHEDRALS IN THE UK

	Cathedral	Founded
1	Canterbury	1071
2	Lincoln	1073
3	Rochester	1077
4=	Hereford	1079
4=	Winchester	1079
6	York	1080
7	Worcester	1084
8	London (now St Paul's)	1087
9	Durham	1093
10	Exeter	1114

Despite the recent cancellation of several dams on environmental grounds, such as two in the Cantabrian Mountains, Spain, numerous major projects are in development for completion by the end of the century, when this Top 10 will contain some notable new entries. Among several in Argentina is the Chapeton dam under construction on the Paraná, and scheduled for completion in 1998; it will have a volume of 296,200,000 m³ and will thus become the second largest dam in the world. The Pati, also on the Paraná, will be 238,180,000 m³. The Cipasang dam under construction on the Cimanuk, Indonesia, will have a volume of 90,000,000 m³.

T O P 1 0

LARGEST RESERVOIRS IN THE UK

	Reservoir	County	Capacity litres	Capacity gallons
1	Kielder Water	Northumberland	200,027,870,000	44,000,000,000
2	Loch Awe	Strathclyde	159,722,201,000	35,133,948,000
3	Rutland Water	Leicestershire	122,744,370,000	27,000,000,000
4	Elan Valley	Dyfed	100,013,930,000	22,000,000,000
5	Loch Lomond	Central/Strathclyde Regions	86,249,436,000	18,972,232,000
6	Loch Doon	Strathclyde	81,957,360,000	18,028,107,000
7	Haweswater	Cumbria	81,829,584,000	18,000,000,000
8	Loch Katrine	Central Region	64,553,649,000	14,199,824,000
9	Megget	Borders Region	63,722,515,000	14,017,000,000
10	Lake Vyrnwy	Powys	63,645,232,000	14,000,000,000

T O P 1 0

LARGEST BELLS IN THE WESTERN WORLD

	Bell/location	Year cast	Weight (tonnes)
1	*Tsar Kolokol*, Kremlin, Moscow, Russia	1735	201.90
2	*Voskresenskiy (Resurrection)*, Ivan the Great Bell Tower, Kremlin, Moscow, Russia	1746	65.50
3	*Petersglocke*, Cologne Cathedral, Germany	1923	25.40
4	Lisbon Cathedral, Portugal	post-1344	24.40
5	St Stephen's Cathedral, Vienna, Austria	1957	21.39
6	Bourdon, Strasbourg Cathedral, France	1521	20.00
7	*Savoyarde*, Sacre-Coeur Basilica, Paris, France	1891	18.85
8	Bourdon, Riverside Church, New York, USA	1931	18.54
9	Olmütz, Czechoslovakia	1931	18.19
10	*Campagna gorda*, Toledo Cathedral, Spain	1753	17.27

The largest bell in the world is the *Tsar Kolokol*, cast in Moscow for the Kremlin, which is 6.14 m/20 ft 2 in high and 6.6 m/21ft 8in in diameter. It cracked before it had been installed and has remained there, unrung, ever since. New York's Riverside Church bell (the largest ever cast in England) is the bourdon (that sounding the lowest note) of the Laura Spelman Rockefeller Memorial carillon. This bell, with a diameter of 3.10 m/10 ft 2 in, is one of the 74-bell carillon, the world's largest, the total weight of which is 103.64 tonnes.

T O P 1 0

LARGEST CEMETERIES IN LONDON

	Cemetery/founded	Area (acres)
1	St Pancras and Islington, N2 (1854)	182
2	City of London, E12 (1856)	130*
3	Kensal Green, NW19 (1832)	77
4=	Battersea New, Morden (1891)	70
4=	Streatham Park, SW16 (1909)	70
6	Lee, SE6 (1873)	65
7	Camberwell New, SE23 (1927)	61
8	Great Northern, N11 (1861)	60
9	Merton and Sutton, Morden (1947)	57.5#
10	Tottenham, N17 (1856)	56

* *Plus 46 in reserve.*
\# *22 in use.*

Despite the appalling overcrowding of inner-city church graveyards, public cemeteries such as Père-Lachaise, Paris, which opened in 1804, took much longer to become established in England. In 1832 Kensal Green became the first to open in London. It was gradually followed by some 100 more serving London's needs. Today, though many are neglected and overgrown, they are worth visiting for their often remarkable last resting places of both the famous and unknown – some, such as Highgate Cemetery, even organize guided tours. Among the interesting tombs in the 10 largest are those of Henry Croft, the original "Pearly King", and Ford Madox-Brown, the Pre-Raphaelite painter, both at St Pancras and Islington; Winston Churchill's nanny, Elizabeth Everest, at the City of London; the comedian Will Hay and numerous other variety artists at Streatham Park. Kensal Green, perhaps the finest of all London cemeteries, contains the tombs of numerous eminent Victorians, including the engineer Isambard Kingdom Brunel, Blondin the tightrope walker, novelists Wilkie Collins, William Thackeray, and Anthony Trollope (who also invented the pillarbox), and Major Walter Wingfield, the inventor of lawn tennis.

THE BELL THAT NEVER RANG
An 11.5-tonne fragment broke off the Tsar Kolokol bell when water was thrown onto it during a fire in 1737.

CULTURE & LEARNING

TOP 10

LARGEST UNIVERSITIES IN THE WORLD

	University	Students
1	State University of New York, USA	369,318
2	University of Calcutta, India	300,000
3	University of Mexico, Mexico	271,358
4	University of Paris, France	263,680
5	University of Buenos Aires, Argentina	248,453
6	University of Bombay, India	222,713
7	University of Guadalajara, Mexico	214,986
8	University of Rajasthan, India	192,039
9	University of Rome, Italy	180,000
10	University of California, USA	157,331

Several other universities in the US, India, Egypt, and Italy have more than 100,000 students. Where universities are divided into numerous separate centres, figures are for the totals of all centres.

TOP 10

LARGEST UNIVERSITIES IN THE UK

(Excluding Open University)

	University	Full-time students*
1	London	59,633
2	Manchester Metropolitan	19,434
3	Edinburgh	15,643
4	Leeds	15,618
5	Manchester	15,325
6	Sheffield Hallam	14,706
7	Glasgow	14,688
8	Oxford	14,594
9	Cambridge	14,580
10	Liverpool John Moores	13,080

* Undergraduates and post-graduates.

One effect of the elevation of polytechnics to university status has been the arrival of three "new" large universities in the Top 10: Manchester Metropolitan, Sheffield Hallam, and Liverpool John Moores.

TOP 10

COUNTRIES WITH MOST UNIVERSITIES

	Country	Universities
1	India	7,301
2	USA	3,559
3	Mexico	1,832
4	Argentina	1,540
5	Japan	1,114
6	China	1,075
7	France	1,062
8	Bangladesh	997
9	Brazil	918
10	Indonesia	900
	UK	*86*

As a result of the 1992 Further and Higher Education Acts, the UK increased its tally of universities from 48 to 86 by re-classifying former polytechnics and colleges of further education. Of the total, 70 are in England, 12 in Scotland, two in Wales, and two in Northern Ireland.

TOP 10

OLDEST UNIVERSITIES IN THE UK

	University	Year founded
1	Oxford	1249
2	Cambridge	1284
3	St Andrew's	1411
4	Glasgow	1451
5	Aberdeen	1495
6	Edinburgh	1583
7	Durham	1832
8	London	1836
9	Manchester	1851
10	Newcastle	1852

Although Newcastle was founded in 1852, it was a college of Durham University until 1963. If only universities that were established as such are included, No. 10 becomes the University of Wales (1893). No other British universities date from before 1900, but several teaching establishments founded during the 19th century have since acquired university status.

TOP 10

OLDEST SCHOOLS IN THE UK

	School	Year founded
1	King's School, Canterbury	c.600
2	King's School, Rochester	604
3	St Peter's School, York	627
4	Warwick School	914
5	King's School, Ely	970
6	Wells Cathedral School	1180
7	Dundee High School	1239
8	Norwich School	1250
9	Abingdon School	1256
10	Winchester College	1382

All these are boys' schools. The oldest girls' school in England is Christ's Hospital, Hertford, founded in 1552. The oldest girl's school in Scotland is Mary Erskine School, Edinburgh (1694).

TOP 10

OLDEST CAMBRIDGE COLLEGES

	College	Year founded
1	Peterhouse	1284
2	Clare	1326
3	Pembroke	1347
4	Gonville & Caius	1348
5	Trinity Hall	1350
6	Corpus Christi	1352
7	King's	1441
8	Queens'	1448
9	St Catharine's	1473
10	Jesus	1496

Although there were students at Cambridge earlier in the 13th century, Peterhouse was founded by Hugo de Balsham, Bishop of Ely, to provide a hall of residence.

TOP 10

MOST EXPENSIVE PUBLIC SCHOOLS IN THE UK*

	School	Boarding fees per annum (£)
1	Millfield, Somerset	12,930
2	Harrow School, Middlesex	12,360
3	Winchester College, Hampshire	12,270
4	Bryanston School, Dorset	12,255
5	Oundle School, Northamptonshire	12,021
6	Stowe School, Buckinghamshire	12,000
7	Roedean School, East Sussex	11,985
8	Eton College, Berkshire	11,934
9	Charterhouse, Surrey	11,910
10	Bedales School, Hampshire	11,901

Excluding specialist schools for the disabled, music schools, and religious schools, some of which are more expensive than these.

TOP 10

OLDEST OXFORD COLLEGES

	College	Year founded
1	University	1249
2	Balliol	1263
3	Merton	1264
4	St Edmund Hall	1278
5	Exeter	1314
6	Oriel	1326
7	Queen's	1340
8	New	1379
9	Lincoln	1427
10	All Souls	1438

Oxford pre-dates Cambridge, with records of teaching as early as 1115. The first college, "The Great Hall of the University", was founded by a bequest from William of Durham.

TOP 10

OPEN UNIVERSITY COURSES

1 Culture and Belief in Europe
2 The Enlightenment
3 Fundamentals of Computing
4 Introduction to Psychology
5 Social Problems and Social Welfare
6 Personality, Development and Learning
7 Microprocessor-based Computers
8 Health and Disease
9 Science Matters
10 Running the Country

The Open University was established in 1969 and has grown to become the UK's largest single teaching institution. At any one time there are some 200,000 students.

LIBRARIES

LARGEST LIBRARIES IN THE WORLD

	Library	Location	Founded	Books
1	Library of Congress	Washington DC, USA	1800	28,000,000
2	British Library	London, UK	1753*	18,000,000
3	Harvard University Library	Cambridge, MA, USA	1638	12,394,894
4	Russian State Library #	Moscow, Russia	1862	11,750,000
5	New York Public Library	New York, NY, USA	1848	11,300,000**
6	Yale University Library	New Haven, CT, USA	1701	9,937,751
7	Biblioteca Academiei Romane	Bucharest, Romania	1867	9,397,260
8	Bibliothèque Nationale	Paris, France	1480	9,000,000
9	University of Illinois	Urbana, IL, USA	1867	8,096,040
10	National Library of Russia ‡	St Petersburg, Russia	1795	8,000,000

LIBRARY OF CONGRESS
Originally founded in 1800, to make books available to Members of Congress, the Library of Congress in Washington DC is in effect the national library of the US. The world's largest collection of books and pamphlets, manuscripts, photographs, maps, and music has been amassed through purchase, exchanges, gifts, and copyright deposits.

* *Founded as part of the British Museum 1753; became an independent body 1973.*
\# *Founded as Rumyantsev Library; formerly State V.I. Lenin Library.*
** *Reference holdings only, excluding books in lending library branches.*
‡ *Formerly M.E. Saltykov-Shchedrin State Public Library.*

T O P 1 0

LARGEST UNIVERSITY LIBRARIES IN THE US

	Library	Location	Founded	Books
1	Harvard University	Cambridge, MA	1638	12,394,894
2	Yale University	New Haven, CT	1701	9,173,981
3	University of Illinois	Urbana, IL	1867	8,096,040
4	University of California	Berkeley, CA	1868	7,854,630
5	University of Texas	Austin, TX	1883	6,680,406
6	University of Michigan	Ann Arbor, MI	1817	6,598,574
7	Columbia University	New York, NY	1754	6,262,162
8	University of California	Los Angeles, CA	1868	6,247,320
9	Stanford University	Stanford, CA	1885	6,127,388
10	Cornell University	Ithaca, NY	1865	5,468,870

T O P 1 0

LARGEST LIBRARIES IN THE UK

	Library	Founded	Books
1	British Library, London	1753	18,000,000
2=	Bodleian Library, Oxford	1602	6,000,000
2=	National Library of Scotland, Edinburgh	1682	6,000,000
4	University of Cambridge Library	c.1400	5,204,000
5	National Library of Wales, Aberystwyth	1907	5,000,000
6	Hertfordshire Library, Hertford	1925	3,800,000
7=	Hampshire County Library, Winchester	1974	3,500,000
7=	John Rylands University Library of Manchester*	1851	3,500,000
9	Lancashire County Library, Preston	1924	3,312,863
10	Kent County Library, Maidstone	1921	3,300,000

T O P 1 0

LARGEST UNIVERSITY LIBRARIES IN THE UK

	Library	Founded	Books
1	Bodleian Library, Oxford	1602	6,000,000
2	University of Cambridge	c.1400	5,204,000
3	John Rylands University Library of Manchester	1851	3,500,000
4	University of Leeds	1874	2,300,000
5=	University of Edinburgh	1580	2,000,000
5=	University of Birmingham	1880	2,000,000
7	University of Glasgow	c.1400	1,600,000
8	University of London	1838	1,400,000
9	University of Liverpool	1881	1,300,000
10	University College, London	1828	1,250,000

In 1972 the John Rylands Library (founded 1900) was amalgamated with Manchester University Library (1851).

In addition to the books held by these libraries, many have substantial holdings of manuscripts, periodicals, and other printed material: the Bodleian Library, for example, has almost 1,000,000 maps.

BRITISH LIBRARY
Started with the book collection of Sir Hans Sloane, and greatly enlarged by the acquisition of King George III's library in 1823, this is now the second largest library in the world. Use of the library is restricted to people involved in research, and the books may not be removed from the premises.

WORDS AND LANGUAGE

T O P 1 0

LONGEST WORDS IN THE ENGLISH LANGUAGE

1 Acetylseryltyrosylserylisoleucylthreonylserylprolylserylglutaminylphenylalanylvalylphenylalanylleucylserylserylvalyltryptophylalanylaspartylprolylisoleucylglutamylleucyclleucyllasparaginylvalylcysteinylthreonylserylserylleucylglycllasparaginylglutaminylphenylalanylglutaminylthreonylglutaminylglutaminylalanylarginylthreonylthreonylglutaminylvalylglutaminylglutaminylphenylalanylserylglutaminylvalyltryptophyllysylprolylphenylalanylprolylglutaminylserylthreonylvalylarginylphenylalanylprolylglycylaspartylvalyltyrosyllsyslvalyltyrosylarginyltyrosylasparaginylalanylvalylleucylaspartylprolylleucylisoleucylthreonylalanylleucylleucylglycylthreonylphenylalanylaspartylthreonylarginylasparaginylarginylisoleucylisoleucylglutamylvalylglutamylasparaginylglutaminylglutaminylserylprolylthreonylthreonylalanylglutamylthreonylleucylaspartylalanylthreonylarginylarginylvalylaspartylaspartylalanylthreonylvalylalanylisoleucylarginylserylalanylasparaginylisoleucylasparaginylleucylvallasparaginylglutamylleucylvalylarginylglycylthreonylglycylleucyltyrosylasparaginylglutaminylasparaginylthreonylphenylalanylglutamylserylmethionylserylglycylleucylvalyltryptophylthreonylserylalanylprolylalanylserine (1,185 letters)

The word for the Tobacco Mosaic Virus, Dahlemense Strain, qualifies as the longest word in English because it has actually been used in print (in the American Chemical Society's Chemical Abstracts *– and in the first edition of* The Top 10 of Everything *(1989), where a typesetting error robbed it of a single "l", which surprisingly went unnoticed by its readers), whereas certain even longer words for chemical compounds, which have been cited in such sources as the* Guinness Book of Records, *are bogus in the sense that they have never been used by scientists or appeared in full in print. Long words for chemical compounds may be regarded by purists as cheating, since such words as trinitrophenyl-methylnitramine (29 letters) – a type of explosive – can be created by linking together the scientific names of their components. Other words that are also discounted are those that have been invented with the sole intention of being long words, such as a 100-letter word used by James Joyce in* Finnegans Wake.

2 Aopadotenachoselachogaleokranioleipsanodrimhipotrimmatosilphioparaomelitokatakechymenokichlepikossyphophattoperisteralektryonoptekephalliokigklopeleiolagoiosiraiobaphetraganopterygon (182 letters)

The English transliteration of a 170-letter Greek word that appears in The Ecclesiazusae *(a comedy on government by women) by the Greek playwright Aristophanes (c.448–380 BC) as a description of a 17-ingredient dish.*

3 Aequeosalinocalcalinosetaceoaluminosocupreovitriolic (52 letters)

Invented by a medical writer, Dr Edward Strother (1675–1737), to describe the spa waters at Bath.

4 Asseocarnisanguineoviscericartilaginonervomedullary (51 letters)

Coined by writer and East India Company official Thomas Love Peacock (1785–1866), and used in his satire Headlong Hall *(1816) to describe the structure of the human body.*

5 Pneumonoultramicroscopicsilicovolcanoconiosis (45 letters)

It first appeared in print (though ending in "-koniosis") in F. Scully's Bedside Manna [sic] *(1936), then found its way into* Webster's Dictionary *and is now in the* Oxford English Dictionary *– but with the note that it occurs "... chiefly as an instance of a very long word". It is said to mean a lung disease caused by breathing very fine dust.*

6 Hepaticocholangiocholecystenterostomies (39 letters)

Surgical operations to create channels of communication between gall bladders and hepatic ducts or intestines.

7= Pseudoantidisestablishmentarianism (34 letters)

A word meaning "false opposition to the withdrawal of state support from a Church", derived from that perennial favourite long word, antidisestablishmentarianism (a mere 28 letters). Another composite made from it (though usually hyphenated) is ultra-antidisestablishmentarianism, which means "extreme opposition to the withdrawal of state support from a Church" (33 letters).

7= Supercalifragilisticexpialidocious (34 letters)

Although an invented word, perhaps it is now eligible since it has appeared in the Oxford English Dictionary. It was popularized by the song of this title in the film Mary Poppins *(1964) where it is used to mean "wonderful", but it was originally written in 1949 in an unpublished song by Parker and Young who spelt it "supercalafajalistickespialadojus" (32 letters). In 1965–66, Parker and Young unsuccessfully sued the makers of* Mary Poppins, *claiming infringement of copyright. In summarizing the case, the US Court decided against repeating this mouthful, stating that "All variants of this tongue-twister will hereinafter be referred to collectively as 'the word'".*

9= Encephalomyeloradiculoneuritis (30 letters)

A syndrome caused by a virus associated with encephalitis.

9= Hippopotomonstrosesquipedalian (30 letters)

Appropriately, the word that means "pertaining to an extremely long word".

9= Pseudopseudohypoparathyroidism (30 letters)

First used (hyphenated) in the US in 1952 and (unhyphenated) in the UK in The Lancet *in 1962 to describe a medical case in which a patient appeared to have symptoms of pseudohypoparathyroidism, but with "no manifestations suggesting hypoparathyroidism". If the rules are changed and No. 1 is disqualified as a compound chemical name, and No. 2 because it is a transliteration from Greek, the next longest word is Floccinaucinihilipilification (29 letters). Alternatively spelt "Flocci-nauci-nihilipilification" or, by Sir Walter Scott, in his* Journal *(18 March 1829), "Flocci-paucinihilipilification", it means the action of estimating as worthless. Until supercalifragilisticexpialidocious, floccinaucinihilipilification was the longest word in the* Oxford English Dictionary. *Honorificabilitudinitatibus, a 27-letter monster word, is used by Shakespeare in* Love's Labour's Lost *(Act V, Scene i) to mean honourably.*

T O P 1 0

MOST WIDELY SPOKEN LANGUAGES IN THE WORLD

	Country	Approx. no. of speakers
1	Chinese (Mandarin)	901,000,000
2	English	451,000,000
3	Hindustani	377,000,000
4	Spanish	360,000,000
5	Russian	291,000,000
6	Arabic	207,000,000
7	Bengali	190,000,000
8	Portuguese	178,000,000
9	Malay-Indonesian	148,000,000
10	Japanese	126,000,000

According to 1992 estimates by Sidney S. Culbert of the University of Washington, there are only two other languages that are spoken by more than 100,000,000 individuals: French (122,000,000) and German (118,000,000). A further 10 languages are spoken by between 50,000,000 and 100,000,000 people: Urdu (98,000,000), Punjabi (89,000,000), Korean (73,000,000), Telugu (70,000,000), Tamil (68,000,000), Marathi (67,000,000), Italian (63,000,000), Javanese (61,000,000), Vietnamese (60,000,000), and Turkish (57,000,000).

T O P 1 0

MOST WIDELY SPOKEN LANGUAGES IN THE EC

	Language	Approx. no. of speakers
1	German	75,667,000
2	English	59,595,000
3	French	56,943,000
4	Italian	55,370,000
5	Spanish	28,672,000
6	Dutch	20,463,000
7	Portuguese	10,431,000
8	Greek	10,120,000
9	Catalan	6,370,000
10	Danish	5,005,000

T O P 1 0

COMMONEST WORDS IN ENGLISH, FRENCH, AND GERMAN

	Spoken English	Written English*	Written French	Written German
1	the	the	de	der
2	and	of	le	die
3	I	to	la	und
4	to	in	et	in
5	of	and	les	des
6	a	a	des	den
7	you	for	est	zu
8	that	was	un	das
9	in	is	une	von
10	it	that	du	für

* *Based on a survey of newspaper usages.*

T O P 1 0

MOST USED LETTERS IN WRITTEN ENGLISH

	i	ii
1	e	e
2	t	t
3	a	a
4	o	i
5	i	n
6	n	o
7	s	s
8	r	h
9	h	r
10	l	d

Column **i** is the order as indicated by a survey across approximately 1,000,000 words appearing in a wide variety of printed texts, ranging from newspapers to novels. Column **ii** is the order estimated by Samuel Morse, the inventor in the 1830s of Morse Code, based on his calculations of the respective quantities of type used by a printer. The number of letters in the printer's type trays ranged from 12,000 for "e" to 4,400 for "d", with only 200 for "z".

T O P 1 0

COUNTRIES WITH THE MOST FRENCH LANGUAGE SPEAKERS

	Country	%	Approx. no. of speakers
1	France	98.0	55,000,000
2	Algeria	30.0	7,470,000
3	Canada	25.0	6,580,000
4	Morocco	18.0	4,610,000
5	Belgium	45.5	4,500,000
6	Ivory Coast	30.0	3,630,000
7	Tunisia	30.0	2,370,000
8	Cameroon	18.0	1,940,000
9	Zaïre	5.0	1,740,000
10	Switzerland	18.5	1,220,000

T O P 1 0

COUNTRIES WITH THE MOST ENGLISH LANGUAGE SPEAKERS

	Country	Approx. no. of speakers
1	USA	215,000,000
2	UK	56,000,000
3	Canada	17,000,000
4	Australia	14,000,000
5	Ireland	3,300,000
6	New Zealand	3,000,000
7	Jamaica	2,300,000
8	South Africa	2,000,000
9	Trinidad and Tobago	1,200,000
10	Guyana	900,000

The Top 10 represents the countries with the greatest numbers of inhabitants who speak English as their mother tongue. After the 10th entry, the figures dive to around 250,000 in the case of both Barbados and the Bahamas, while Zimbabwe occupies 13th place with some 200,000 English speakers. In addition to these and others that make up a world total probably in excess of 451,000,000, there are perhaps as many as 1,000,000,000 who speak English as a second language.

THE OXFORD ENGLISH DICTIONARY

Although conceived earlier, work on the *Oxford English Dictionary* started in earnest in 1879 with James Murray as editor. He and his colleagues scoured thousands of English texts for quotations representing the changing usages of English words, frequently chopping up copies of rare books, pasting extracts onto slips of paper, and filing them. The first part covering A–Ant was published in 1884 and other sections followed at intervals. Murray died in 1915, but work continued until 1928 when the first edition was complete. Its 12 volumes defined 414,825 words and phrases, with about 2,000,000 quotations providing information on the first recorded use, continuing usage, and later variations in the use of each word. Supplements were added over the ensuing years until it was decided to computerize all the material, work on which commenced in 1984. The original *Dictionary*, *Supplements*, and new entries were incorporated into a gigantic, 540 megabyte database. Over 120 keyboard operators keyed in more than 350,000,000 characters, their work checked by over 50 proof-readers. The complete second edition, costing about £10,000,000 to produce, was published in 1989. Its 20 volumes, currently priced at £1,650, contain 21,728 pages with about 60,000,000 words of text defining some 557,889 words (over 34 per cent more than the first edition), together with 2,435,671 quotations. The entire dictionary is now available on CD-ROM (a single compact disc) for £495.

T O P   1 0

EARLIEST DATED WORDS IN THE *OXFORD ENGLISH DICTIONARY*

	Word	Source	Date
1=	town	Laws of Ethelbert	601–4
1=	priest	Laws of Ethelbert	601–4
3	earl	Laws of Ethelbert	616
4	this	Bewcastle Column	*c.*670
5	streale	Ruthwell Cross	*c.*680
6	ward	Cædmon, Hymn	680
7	thing	Laws of Hlothær and Eadric	685–6
8	theft	Laws of Ine	688–95
9	worth	Laws of Ine	695
10	then	Laws of King Wihtræd	695–6

The 10 earliest citations in the *OED* come from 7th-century Anglo-Saxon documents and stone inscriptions. All have survived as commonly used English words, with the exception of "streale", which is another name for an arrow. A few other English words can be definitely dated to before 700, among them "church" which, like "then", appears in a law of King Wihtræd.

A WORD IN EDGEWAYS
This is a complete set of the Oxford English Dictionary, *the ultimate lexicon of the English language.*

T O P   1 0

LONGEST WORDS IN THE *OXFORD ENGLISH DICTIONARY*

	Word	Letters
1	pneumonoultramicroscopicsilicovolcanoconiosis	45
2	supercalifragilisticexpialidocious	34
3	pseudopseudohypoparathyroidism	30
4=	floccinaucinihilipilification	29
4=	triethylsulphonemethylmethane	29
6=	antidisestablishmentarianism	28
6=	octamethylcyclotetrasiloxane	28
6=	tetrachlorodibenzoparadioxin	28
9	hepaticocholangiogastronomy	27
10=	radioimmunoelectrophoresis	26
10=	radioimmunoelectrophoretic	26

Words that are hyphenated, including such compound words as "transformational-generative" and "tristhio-dimethyl-benzaldehyde", have not been included. Only one unhyphenated word did not make it into the Top 10, the 25-letter "psychophysicotherapeutics". After this, there is a surprisingly large number of words containing 20–24 letters (radioimmunoprecipitation, spectrophotofluorometric, thyroparathyroidectomize, hypergammaglobulinaemia, roentgenkymographically and immunosympathectomized, for example) – few of which are ever used by anyone except scientists and crossword compilers.

T O P 1 0
WORDS WITH MOST MEANINGS IN THE *OXFORD ENGLISH DICTIONARY*

	Word	Meanings
1	set	464
2	run	396
3	go	368
4	take	343
5	stand	334
6	get	289
7	turn	288
8	put	268
9	fall	264
10	strike	250

T O P 1 0
LETTERS OF THE ALPHABET WITH MOST ENTRIES IN THE *OXFORD ENGLISH DICTIONARY*

	Letter	Entries
1	S	34,556
2	C	26,239
3	P	24,980
4	M	17,495
5	A	15,880
6	T	15,497
7	R	15,483
8	B	14,633
9	D	14,519
10	U	12,943

This list of the 10 commonest first letters does not correspond with the list of the 10 most frequently used letters in written English, which is generally held to be ETAINOSHRD. If the alphabet were restricted to just these letters, among the useful phrases that could be created – without repeating any letters – are "the inroads", "note radish", "date rhinos", and "hot sardine".

T O P 1 0
MOST-QUOTED AUTHORS IN THE *OXFORD ENGLISH DICTIONARY*

	Author	Approx. no. of references
1	William Shakespeare (1564–1616)	33,303
2	Sir Walter Scott (1771–1832)	16,659
3	John Milton (1608–74)	12,465
4	John Wyclif (*c.*1330–84)	11,972
5	Geoffrey Chaucer (*c.*1343–1400)	11,902
6	William Caxton (*c.*1422–91)	10,324
7	John Dryden (1631–1700)	9,139
8	Charles Dickens (1812–70)	8,557
9	Philemon Holland (1552–1637)	8,419
10	Alfred, Lord Tennyson (1809–92)	6,972

The figures given here may not be exact because of variations in the way in which sources are quoted, or in instances where more than one example is included from the same author. All those in the Top 10 are prolific "classic" British authors whose works were widely read in the late 19th century.

T O P 1 0
MOST-QUOTED SOURCES IN THE *OXFORD ENGLISH DICTIONARY*

	Source	Approx. no. of references*
1	*The Times*	19,098
2	*Cursor Mundi*#	11,035
3	*Encyclopaedia Britannica*	10,102
4	*Daily News*	9,650
5	*Nature*	9,150
6	*Transactions of the Philological Society*	8,972
7	*Chronicle*	8,550
8	*Westminster Gazette*	7,478
9	*History of England*	7,180
10	*Listener*	7,139

* *These figures may not be absolutely precise because of variations in the way in which source books and journals are quoted, where there is more than one example from the same source, etc.*

\# *Cursor Mundi is a long 14th-century Northumbrian poem which is extensively cited for early uses of English words.*

References to *Daily News*, Chronicle, *and* History of England *may include several different works with similar titles.*

T O P 1 0
LETTERS OF THE ALPHABET WITH FEWEST ENTRIES IN THE *OXFORD ENGLISH DICTIONARY*

	Letter	Entries
1	X	152
2	Z	733
3	Q	1,824
4	Y	2,298
5	J	2,326
6	K	3,491
7	V	5,430
8	N	5,933
9	O	7,737
10	W	8,804

The number of entries beginning with "x" has increased in the past 100 years, with the introduction of such terms as "x-ray" in 1896, "X-certificate" or "X-rated" films (1950), "xerography" (the photocopying process, invented by Chester F. Carlson in 1948), and "Xerox", the proprietary name derived from it in 1952.

BOOKS AND READERS

T O P 1 0

THE FIRST PUBLICATIONS PRINTED IN ENGLAND

1 *Propositio ad Carolum ducem Burgundiae*

2 Cato, *Disticha de Morbidus*

3 Geoffrey Chaucer, *The Canterbury Tales*

4 *Ordinale seu Pica ad usem Sarum* ("*Sarum Pie*")

5 John Lydgate, *The Temple of Glass*

6 John Lydgate, *Stans puer mensam*

7 John Lydgate, *The Horse, the Sheep and the Goose*

8 John Lydgate, *The Churl and the Bird*

9 *Infanta Salvatoris*

10 William Caxton, advertisement for "*Sarum Pie*"

All of the first ten known publications in England were printed at Westminster by William Caxton (*c.*1422–*c.*1491). He had previously printed books in Bruges, where in about 1474 he printed the first book in English, *Recuyell of the Historyes of Troye*, followed by *The Game* and *Playe of the Chesse*. He then moved to England where *Propositio ad Carolum ducem Burgundiae* was printed some time before September 1476; the others were all printed at unknown dates in either 1476 or 1477. It is probable that Chaucer's *Canterbury Tales* was the first book in English to be printed in England.

POPULAR PRESS
The advent of printing brought books such as the Canterbury Tales *within the reach of many.*

T O P 1 0

MOST BORROWED AUTHORS IN THE UK IN 1993

1 Catherine Cookson

2 Danielle Steel

3 Dick Francis

4 Agatha Christie

5 Ruth Rendell

6 Enid Blyton

7 Roald Dahl

8 Wilbur Smith

9 Ellis Peters

10 Jack Higgins

According to figures produced by the Public Lending Right office (the organization that pays registered authors fees according to the number of times their books are borrowed from public libraries), books by a total of 22 authors – including all those in the Top 10 – were borrowed more than 1,000,000 times.

T O P 1 0

MOST BORROWED CLASSIC AUTHORS IN THE UK IN 1993

1 Daphne Du Maurier

2 Beatrix Potter

3 Thomas Hardy

4 J. R. R. Tolkien

5 Charles Dickens

6 Anthony Trollope

7 Jane Austen

8 A. A. Milne

9 William Shakespeare

10 D. H. Lawrence

Public Lending Right figures indicate that each of the authors featured in this list was borrowed between 200,000 and 500,000 times.

T O P 1 0

THE FIRST PENGUIN PAPERBACKS

COLLECTORS' ITEMS
The first Penguin titles brought quality to the paperback market.

1 André Maurois, *Ariel*

2 Ernest Hemingway, *A Farewell to Arms*

3 Eric Linklater, *Poet's Pub*

4 Susan Ertz, *Madame Claire*

5 Dorothy L. Sayers, *The Unpleasantness at the Bellona Club*

6 Agatha Christie, *The Mysterious Affair at Styles*

7 Beverley Nichols, *Twenty-five*

8 E. H. Young, *William*

9 Mary Webb, *Gone to Earth*

10 Compton Mackenzie, *Carnival*

The British publisher Allen Lane (1902–70; knighted 1952) remarked "I would be the first to admit that there is no fortune in this series for anyone concerned", as he launched his first "Penguin" titles in the UK on 30 July 1935. Originally, Penguins were paperback reprints of books previously published as hardbacks; their quality, range of subjects, and low price established them as pioneers in the "paperback revolution". Pocket Books, first published in 1939, was the American counterpart to Penguin, and in 1946 was responsible for publishing what is probably the all-time bestselling paperback, Dr Benjamin Spock's *The Common Sense Book of Baby and Child Care*.

TOP 10

MOST EXPENSIVE BOOKS AND MANUSCRIPTS EVER SOLD AT AUCTION

	Book/manuscript/sale	Price (£)*
1	*The Gospels of Henry the Lion*, c.1173–75 Sotheby's, London, 6 December 1983	7,400,000

The most expensive manuscript, book, or work of art other than a painting ever sold.

2	*The Gutenberg Bible*, 1455 Christie's, New York, 22 October 1987 ($5,390,000)	2,934,131

One of the first books ever printed, by Johann Gutenberg and Johann Fust in 1455, it holds the record for the most expensive printed book.

3	*The Northumberland Bestiary*, c.1250–60 Sotheby's, London, 29 November 1990	2,700,000

The highest price ever paid for an English manuscript.

4	Autographed manuscript of nine symphonies by Wolfgang Amadeus Mozart, c.1773–74 Sotheby's, London, 22 May 1987	2,350,000

The record for a music manuscript and for any post-medieval manuscript.

5	John James Audubon's *The Birds of America*, 1827–38 Sotheby's, New York, 6 June 1989 ($3,600,000)	2,292,993

The record for any natural history book. Further copies of the same book, a collection of more than 400 large, hand-coloured engravings, have also fetched high prices: Sotheby's, London, 21 June 1990 (£1,600,000); Christie's, New York, 24 April 1992 ($2,120,000/£1,187,000); Christie's, New York, 29 October 1993 ($2,700,000/£1,898,000). A facsimile reprint of Audubon's The Birds of America *published in 1985 by Abbeville Press, New York, is listed at $30,000/£15,000, making it the most expensive book ever published.*

6	The Bible in Hebrew Sotheby's, London, 5 December 1989	1,850,000

A manuscript written in Iraq, Syria, or Babylon in the ninth or tenth century, it holds the record for any Hebrew manuscript.

7	*The Monypenny Breviary*, illuminated manuscript, c.1490–95 Sotheby's, London, 19 June 1989	1,700,000

The record for any French manuscript.

8	*The Hours and Psalter of Elizabeth de Bohun, Countess of Northampton*, c.1340–45 Sotheby's, London, 21 June 1988	1,400,000

9	*Biblia Pauperum* Christie's, New York, 22 October 1987 ($2,200,000)	1,320,000

A block-book bible printed in the Netherlands in c.1460 (the pages of block-books, with text and illustrations, were printed from single carved woodblocks rather than moveable type).

10	*The Gospels of St. Hubert*, c.860–80 Sotheby's, London, 26 November 1985	1,300,000

* *Excluding premiums.*

TOP 10

MOST PUBLISHED AUTHORS OF ALL TIME

	Author	Nationality
1	William Shakespeare (1564–1616)	British
2	Charles Dickens (1812–70)	British
3	Sir Walter Scott (1771–1832)	British
4	Johann Goethe (1749–1832)	German
5	Aristotle (384–322 BC)	Greek
6	Alexandre Dumas (*père*) (1802–70)	French
7	Robert Louis Stevenson (1850–94)	British
8	Mark Twain (1835–1910)	American
9	Marcus Cicero (106–43 BC)	Roman
10	Honoré de Balzac (1799–1850)	French

This Top 10 is based on a search of a major US library computer database. Citations, which include both books by and about the author, total more than 15,000 for Shakespeare.

TOP 10

BOOKS CHOSEN BY CASTAWAYS ON DESERT ISLAND DISCS

1	*Encyclopaedia Britannica*
2	Unspecified encyclopaedia
3	Leo Tolstoy, *War and Peace*
4	Marcel Proust, *Remembrance of Things Past*
5	*The Oxford Book of English Verse*
6	Edward Gibbon, *The Decline and Fall of the Roman Empire*
7	*The Oxford English Dictionary*
8	J. R. R. Tolkien, *The Lord of the Rings*
9	Lewis Carroll, *Alice in Wonderland*
10	Charles Dickens, complete novels

"Castaways" on BBC Radio's long-running programme automatically receive the Bible and complete works of Shakespeare, whether they want them, or, like Alan Whicker, not.

WORLD BESTSELLERS

T O P 1 0

BESTSELLING BOOKS OF ALL TIME

1 The Bible   6,000,000,000

No one really knows how many copies of the Bible have been printed, sold, or distributed. The Bible Society's attempt to calculate the number printed between 1816 and 1975 produced the figure of 2,458,000,000. A more recent survey up to 1992 put it closer to 6,000,000,000 in more than 2,000 languages and dialects. Whatever the precise figure, it is by far the bestselling book of all time.

2 Quotations from the Works of Mao Tse-tung   800,000,000

Chairman Mao's "Little Red Book" could scarcely fail to become a bestseller: between the years 1966 and 1971 it was compulsory for every Chinese adult to own a copy. It was both sold and distributed to the people of China – though what proportion voluntarily bought it must remain open to question. Some 100,000,000 copies of his Poems *were also disseminated.*

3 American Spelling Book *by Noah Webster*   100,000,000

First published in 1783, this reference book by American man of letters Noah Webster (1758–1843) – of Webster's Dictionary *fame – remained a bestseller in the USA throughout the 19th century.*

4 The Guinness Book of Records   74,000,000+

First published in 1955, The Guinness Book of Records *stands out as the greatest contemporary publishing achievement. In the UK there have now been 37 editions (it was not published annually until 1964), as well as numerous foreign language editions.*

5 The McGuffey Readers *by William Holmes McGuffey*   60,000,000

Published in numerous editions from 1853, some authorities have put the total sales of these educational textbooks, originally compiled by American anthologist William Holmes McGuffey (1800–73), as high as 122,000,000. It has also been claimed that 60,000,000 copies of the 1879 edition were printed, but as this is some 10,000,000 more than the entire population of the USA at the time, the publishers must have been extremely optimistic about its success.

6 A Message to Garcia *by Elbert Hubbard*   40–50,000,000

Now forgotten, Hubbard's polemic on the subject of labour relations was published in 1899 and within a few years had achieved these phenomenal sales, largely because many American employers purchased bulk supplies to distribute to their employees. The literary career of Elbert Hubbard (1856–1915) was cut short in 1915 when he went down with the Lusitania, *but even in death he was a record-breaker: his posthumous* My Philosophy *(1916) was published in one of the largest-ever "limited editions", of 9,983 copies – all of them signed.*

7 The Common Sense Book of Baby and Child Care *by Benjamin Spock*   39,200,000+

Dr Spock's 1946 manual became the bible of infant care for subsequent generations of parents. Most of the sales have been of the paperback edition of the book.

8 World Almanac   36,000,000+

Having been published annually since 1868 (with a break from 1876 to 1886), this wide-ranging reference book has remained a bestseller ever since.

9 Valley of the Dolls *by Jacqueline Susann*   28,712,000+

This racy tale of sex, violence, and drugs by Jacqueline Susann (1921–74), first published in 1966, is perhaps surprisingly the world's bestselling novel. Susann's closest rival for bestselling work of fiction is Margaret Mitchell, whose Gone With the Wind *has achieved sales approaching 28,000,000.*

10 In His Steps: "What Would Jesus Do?" *by Rev. Charles Monroe Sheldon*   28,500,000

Though virtually unknown today, Charles Sheldon (1857–1946) achieved fame and fortune with this 1896 religious treatise.

It is extremely difficult to establish precise sales even of contemporary books, and virtually impossible to do so with books published long ago. How many copies of the complete works of Shakespeare or Conan Doyle's Sherlock Holmes books have been sold in countless editions? The publication of variant editions, translations, and pirated copies all affect the global picture, and few publishers or authors are willing to expose their royalty statements to public scrutiny. As a result, this Top 10 list offers no more than the "best guess" at the great bestsellers of the past, and it may well be that there are other books with a valid claim to a place in it.

There are problems of definition: what, for example, is the status of a book that is revised and reissued annually, and what precisely is a "book"? A UNESCO conference in 1950 decided it was "a non-periodical literary publication containing 49 or more pages, not counting the covers" (which is baffling in itself, since all publications have to contain an even number of pages, while, according to this criterion, a 32-page children's book would not be regarded as a book at all). If *Old Moore's Almanac* is classed as a book rather than a periodical or a pamphlet, it would appear high on the list. Having been published annually since 1697, its total sales to date are believed to be over 112,000,000. More than 107,000,000 copies of the Jehovah's Witness tract, *The Truth That Leads to Eternal Life,* first published in 1968, are believed to have been distributed in 117 languages, usually in return for a donation to the sect, but as they were not sold it does not rank as a "bestseller".

WORLD'S BESTSELLING FICTION

As with the bestselling books of all time, it is virtually impossible to arrive at a definitive list of fiction bestsellers that encompasses all permutations including hardback and paperback editions, book club sales, and translations, and takes account of the innumerable editions of earlier classics such as *Robinson Crusoe* or the works of Jane Austen, Charles Dickens, or popular foreign authors such as Jules Verne. Although only Jacqueline Susann's *Valley of the Dolls* appears in the all-time list, and publishers' precise sales data remains tantalizingly elusive (it has been said that the most published fiction is publishers' own sales figures), there are many other novels that must be close contenders for the Top 10. It seems certain that all the following have sold in excess of 10,000,000 copies in hardback and paperback worldwide:

Richard Bach	*Jonathan Livingstone Seagull*
William Blatty	*The Exorcist*
Peter Benchley	*Jaws*
Erskine Caldwell	*God's Little Acre*
Joseph Heller	*Catch-22*
D.H. Lawrence	*Lady Chatterley's Lover*
Harper Lee	*To Kill a Mockingbird*
Colleen McCullough	*The Thorn Birds*
Grace Metalious	*Peyton Place*
Margaret Mitchell	*Gone With the Wind*
George Orwell	*Animal Farm*
George Orwell	*1984*
Mario Puzo	*The Godfather*
Harold Robbins	*The Carpetbaggers*
J.D. Salinger	*Catcher in the Rye*
Erich Segal	*Love Story*

There are also several prolific popular novelists whose books have achieved combined international sales of colossal proportions. The field is led by detective story authoress *extraordinaire* Agatha Christie, with total sales of more than 2,000,000,000 since 1920, followed by romantic novelist Barbara Cartland (650,000,000), Belgian detective novelist Georges Simenon (600,000,000), and American crime-writer Erle Stanley

Gardner (320,000,000). If this list were extended to embrace other prolific bestselling novelists during the post-war period, it would probably include such writers as Jeffrey Archer, Catherine Cookson, Ian Fleming, Robert Ludlum, Alistair MacLean, and Mickey Spillane.

In the area of children's books, the sales of Beatrix Potter's *The Tale of Peter Rabbit*, originally published privately in 1901 and by Frederick Warne since 1902, exceed 10,000,000, making it possibly the bestselling children's book of all time – although the innumerable editions of other long-established children's "classics", such as Robert Louis Stevenson's *Treasure Island* and various works of Hans Christian Andersen, the Brothers Grimm, Mark Twain, Lewis Carroll, and Edward Lear must collectively have achieved global totals approaching this figure. Among modern children's books are those of the American author Dr Seuss (Theodor Seuss Giesel), the French author René Goscinny (Asterix books), and the Belgian author-artist Hergé (Tintin books): the last two have sold totals of more than 220,000,000 and 150,000,000 respectively. The only English-language author to rival them is Enid Blyton: her Noddy books alone have sold more than 60,000,000 copies, and they represent only a fraction of her output of more than 700 titles.

THE LONG AND THE SHORT OF IT

The longest single word in a book title appears in M.C.A. Kinneby's *Le "Boschmannschucrutund-kakafresserdeutschkolossal-kulturdestruktokathedralibu-sundkinden"*, published in Paris in 1915. Its longest English rival is Miles Peter Andrews's *The Baron Kinkvervankotsdorspra-kingatchdern* (1781). At the other extreme, Sir Walter Newman Flower was the author of a book published in 1925 with the title *?*.

BOOKS WITH MOST APPEARANCES AT NO. 1 IN THE UK

	Author/title	Appearances at No. 1
1	Edith Holden, *The Country Diary of an Edwardian Lady* (1977)	66
2	Rosemary Conley, *The Complete Hip and Thigh Diet* (1989)	55 *
3	Peter Mayle, *A Year in Provence* (1990)	52 *
4	Stephen Hawking, *A Brief History of Time* (1988)	51
5	David Attenborough, *Life on Earth* (1979)	40 #
6	Sue Townsend, *The Growing Pains of Adrian Mole* (1984)	39 **
7	Jung Chang, *Wild Swans* (1993)	37 *‡
8	Derrik Mercer (ed.), *Chronicle of the 20th Century* (1988)	32
9	Richard Adams, *Watership Down* (1974)	30 *
10=	J. R. R. Tolkien, *The Silmarillion* (1977)	26
10=	Sue Townsend, *The Secret Diary of Adrian Mole, Aged 13¾* (1983)	26 *

* *Paperback edition.*
\# *Collins edition; the Reader's Digest version also had two appearances at No. 1.*
** *Hardback edition.*
‡ *Includes two weeks of hardback No. 1.*

This list is based on the total number of appearances at No. 1 since the *Sunday Times* bestseller lists were first published on 14 April 1974. The achievement of *The Country Diary of an Edwardian Lady* is especially remarkable given that it was published 57 years after the death of its previously unknown author-illustrator. The *Diary*, which contained Edith Holden's watercolours of plants and animals, became an international bestseller and gave rise to a number of products in a nostalgic "Country Diary" style.

UK BESTSELLERS

T O P 1 0

LONGEST-RUNNING BESTSELLERS IN THE UK

	Author/title/publication*	Appearances#
1	Stephen Hawking, *A Brief History of Time* (H; 1988)	234
2	Edith Holden, *The Country Diary of an Edwardian Lady* (H; 1977)	183
3=	Peter Mayle, *A Year in Provence* (P; 1990)	165**
3=	Rosemary Conley, *The Complete Hip and Thigh Diet* (P; 1989)	159
5	David Attenborough, *Life on Earth* (H; 1979)	139
6	Delia Smith, *Delia Smith's Complete Illustrated Cookery Course* (H; 1989)	131
7	Sue Townsend, *The Secret Diary of Adrian Mole, Aged 13¾* (P; 1983)	119
8	Jacob Bronowski, *The Ascent of Man* (H; 1974)	114
9	Delia Smith, *Delia Smith's Complete Cookery Course* (H; 1986)	113
10	Christopher Brickell (ed.), *RHS Gardeners' Encyclopedia of Plants and Flowers* (H; 1989)	109

* H = Hardback, P = Paperback.
# As at 20 March 1994, based on number of appearances in Sunday Times bestseller lists 14 April 1974 to 20 March 1994.
**Includes appearances in TV tie-in paperback edition.

T O P 1 0

BESTSELLING BOOKS OF EACH YEAR OF THE 1980s IN THE UK

Year	Bestselling hardback	Bestselling paperback
1980	Frederick Forsyth, *The Devil's Alternative*	Delia Smith, *Delia Smith's Cookery Course, Part Two*
1981	James Clavell, *Noble House*	Douglas Adams, *The Hitchhiker's Guide to the Galaxy*
1982	Jeffrey Archer, *The Prodigal Daughter*	Audrey Eyton, *The F-Plan Diet*
1983	John Le Carré, *The Little Drummer Girl*	Audrey Eyton, *The F-Plan Diet*
1984	David Attenborough, *The Living Planet*	Sue Townsend, *The Secret Diary of Adrian Mole, Aged 13¾*
1985	Sue Townsend, *The Growing Pains of Adrian Mole*	Sue Townsend, *The Secret Diary of Adrian Mole, Aged 13¾*
1986	John Le Carré, *A Perfect Spy*	Barbara Taylor Bradford, *Hold the Dream*
1987	Anthony Jay and Jonathan Lynn, *Yes Prime Minister, Vol. 1*	Jeffrey Archer, *A Matter of Honour*
1988	Michael Jackson, *Moonwalk*	Catherine Cookson, *The Parson's Daughter*
1989	Michael Palin, *Around the World in 80 Days*	Jilly Cooper, *Rivals*

BESTSELLING PROFESSOR
Writing on one of the topics least likely to top the charts, Stephen Hawking has brought theoretical physics to the widest possible audience.

T O P 1 0

BESTSELLING BOOKER PRIZE WINNER IN THE UK

	Author/title/prize year	Estimated sales*
1	Roddy Doyle, *Paddy Clarke Ha Ha Ha* (1993)	110,000
2	Thomas Keneally, *Schindler's Ark* (1982)	90,000
3	Kingsley Amis, *The Old Devils* (1986)	80,000
4	Peter Carey, *Oscar and Lucinda* (1988)	70,000
5	Kazuo Ishiguro, *The Remains of the Day* (1989)	65,000
6	Anita Brookner, *Hotel du Lac* (1984)	62,000
7	William Golding, *Rites of Passage* (1980)	60,000
8	Penelope Lively, *Moon Tiger* (1987)	59,000
9	A. S. Byatt, *Possession* (1990)	50,000
10	J. M. Coetzee, *The Life and Times of Michael K* (1983)	45,000

* Hardback only, excluding book club sales, to 20 March 1994.

TOP 10
AUTHORS WITH MOST BOOKS GOING STRAIGHT TO NO. 1*

	Author	Instant No. 1s
1	Dick Francis	9
2	John Le Carré	7
3	Wilbur Smith	5
4=	Jeffrey Archer	4
4=	Catherine Cookson	4
4=	Frederick Forsyth	4
4=	Jack Higgins	4
8=	William Golding	3
8=	Graham Greene	3
8=	Garrison Keillor	3
8=	Robert Ludlum	3

* In the Sunday Times Hardback Fiction bestseller list, 14 April 1974 to 20 March 1994.

Twelve other authors have achieved the feat twice. Sally Beauman in 1987, Robert Harris in 1992, and Edwina Currie in 1994 are the only authors whose first novels have gone straight to No. 1. HRH The Prince of Wales's children's book *The Old Man of Lochnagar* went straight to No. 1 in 1980.

TOP 10
FASTEST SELLING BOOKS IN THE UK*

	Author/title	Sale#
1	*The Highway Code* (new edition) (1993)	217,520
2	Ben Elton, *Stark* (1989)	126,000
3	Margaret Thatcher, *The Downing Street Years*** (1993)	98,790
4	Barry Lynch, *The BBC Diet* (1989)	97,984
5	Barbara Taylor Bradford, *To Be the Best* (1989)	93,983
6	Jilly Cooper, *Polo* (1992)	90,788
7	Jilly Cooper, *Rivals* (1989)	81,990
8	Terry Pratchett, *Reaper Man* (1992)	77,310
9	James Herbert, *Haunted* (1989)	75,218
10	Dick Francis, *The Edge* (1989)	73,710

* During the past five years.
# Estimated, during the first two weeks from publication.
**Hardback; all others are paperback.

TOP 10
BESTSELLING CHILDREN'S BOOKS OF 1993 IN THE UK*

1	Terry Pratchett, *Only You Can Save Mankind*
2	Nick Butterworth, *After the Storm*
3	Eric Carle, *The Very Hungry Caterpillar*
4	Carol Ellis, *The Window*
5	Colin Dann, *The Animals of Farthing Wood*
6	Piers Morgan, *Take That: Our Story*
7	Martin Handford, *Where's Wally?* (mini edition)
8	*Jungle Book*
9	Stephen Biesty, *Incredible Cross Sections*
10	*Jurassic Park: The Junior Novelization*

* UK book trade only, excluding book club sales and exports.

SUE TOWNSEND
With a total of 119 weeks in the Sunday Times bestseller lists, The Secret Diary of Adrian Mole, Aged 13 3/4 will be hard to beat.

TOP 10
LONGEST-RUNNING PAPERBACK FICTION BESTSELLERS IN THE UK

	Author/title	Weeks at No. 1	Total*
1	Sue Townsend, *The Secret Diary of Adrian Mole, Aged 13¾* (1983)	26	119
2	Richard Adams, *Watership Down* (1974)	30	93
3	Joanna Trollope, *The Rector's Wife* (1992)	5	55
4	Thomas Harris, *The Silence of the Lambs* (1991)	14	53
5	Colleen McCullough, *The Thorn Birds* (1978)	8	50
6	Douglas Adams, *The Hitchhiker's Guide to the Galaxy* (1979)	7	48
7	Peter Benchley, *Jaws* (1975)	13	46
8	Jack Higgins, *The Eagle Has Landed* (1975)	4	42
9	Jeffrey Archer, *Kane and Abel* (1981)	3	39
10	Rosamunde Pilcher, *The Shell Seekers* (1988)	–	38 #

* Appearances in Sunday Times bestseller lists, 14 April 1974 to 20 March 1994.
# Includes one week as large-format paperback.

READ ALL ABOUT IT

TOP 10

DAILY NEWSPAPERS IN THE WORLD
(Excluding the UK)

	Newspaper	Country	Average daily circulation
1	Yomiuri Shimbun	Japan	8,700,000
2	Asahi Shimbun	Japan	7,400,000
3	People's Daily	China	6,000,000
4	Bild Zeitung	Germany	5,900,000
5	Wall Street Journal	USA	1,857,131*
6	USA Today	USA	1,632,345
8	New York Times	USA	1,230,461 #
7	Los Angeles Times	USA	1,138,353 **
9	Washington Post	USA	855,171 ‡
10	New York Daily News	USA	769,801 ##

* National edition; Eastern edition average 798,515.
\# Daily; Sunday 1,521,197.
** Daily; Sunday 1,812,458.
‡ Daily; Sunday 977,599.
\## Daily; Sunday 1,170,150.

The official Soviet newspaper *Pravda*, which is no longer published, formerly topped this list with alleged daily sales peaking in May 1990 at 21,975,000 copies. If true, it would hold the world record for a daily newspaper.

TOP 10

OLDEST NEWSPAPERS IN THE UK

Newspaper	First published
1 The London Gazette	16 Nov 1665

Originally published in Oxford as The Oxford Gazette, *while the royal court resided there during an outbreak of the plague. After 23 issues it moved to London with the court and changed its name.*

Newspaper	First published
2 Berrow's Worcester Journal	c.1709

Britain's oldest surviving provincial newspaper (the Norwich Post *was founded in 1701, but is defunct), it first appeared as the* Worcester Post-Man *and changed its name to* Berrow's Worcester Journal *in 1808. Its claim to have started as early as 1690 has never been substantiated.*

Newspaper	First published
3 Lincoln, Rutland and Stamford Mercury	c.1710

Originally published as the Stamford Mercury *c.1710 (allegedly 1695, and possibly in 1712), it later became the* Lincoln, Rutland and Stamford Mercury.

Newspaper	First published
4 Lloyds List	1726

Providing shipping news, originally weekly, but since 1734 Britain's oldest daily.

Newspaper	First published
5 News Letter (Belfast)	6 March 1738

Published daily since 1855.

Newspaper	First published
6 Hampshire Chronicle	1772

Published in Winchester, it subsequently amalgamated with the Hampshire Observer.

Newspaper	First published
7 The Times	1 January 1785

First published as the Daily Universal Register, *it changed its name to* The Times *on 1 March 1788.*

Newspaper	First published
8 Observer	4 December 1791

The first Sunday newspaper in the UK was Johnson's British Gazette and Sunday Monitor, *which was first published on 2 March 1780. It survived only until 1829, making the* Observer *the longest-running Sunday newspaper.*

Newspaper	First published
9 The Licensee	8 February 1794

Britain's oldest trade newspaper (a daily established by the Licensed Victuallers Association to earn income for its charity), and the first national paper on Fleet Street, the Morning Advertiser *changed its name to* The Licensee *and became a twice-weekly news magazine in 1994, at the time of its 200th anniversary.*

Newspaper	First published
10 Sunday Times	February 1821

Issued as the New Observer *until March 1821 and the* Independent Observer *from April 1821 until 21 October 1822, when it changed its name to the* Sunday Times. *On 4 February 1962 it became the first British newspaper to issue a colour supplement.*

The *Guardian*, a weekly from 1821 until 1855 (and called the *Manchester Guardian* until 1959), misses a place in the Top 10 by just three months.

TOP 10

UK REGIONAL NEWSPAPERS

	Newspaper	Average sales per issue*
1	*Evening Standard* (London)	482,780
2	*Manchester Evening News*	225,041
3	*West Midlands Express & Star*	218,336
4	*Birmingham Evening Mail*	207,213
5	*Liverpool Echo*	176,887
6	*Birmingham Sunday Mercury*	152,013
7	*Glasgow Evening Times*	150,398
8	*Belfast Telegraph*	130,987
9	*Newcastle Evening Chronicle*	126,576
10	*Leicester Mercury*	122,170

* *Monday to Friday editions; Saturday sales generally lower.*

TOP 10

BRITISH NATIONAL SUNDAY NEWSPAPERS

	Newspaper	Average sales per issue (1993/94)
1	*News of the World*	4,713,860
2	*Sunday Mirror*	2,569,889
3	*The People*	1,987,247
4	*Mail on Sunday*	1,935,970
5	*Sunday Express*	1,624,771
6	*Sunday Times*	1,247,059
7	*Sunday Telegraph*	613,831
8	*Observer*	496,952
9	*Independent on Sunday*	356,480
10	*Sunday Sport*	241,775

TOP 10

COUNTRIES WITH MOST DAILY NEWSPAPERS

	Country	No. of daily newspapers
1	Russia	4,808
2	India	2,281
3	USA	1,611
4	Kazakhstan	456
5	Turkey	399
6	Brazil	356
7	Germany	354
8	Mexico	285
9	Uzbekistan	279
10	Pakistan	237
	UK	*104*

	Country	Sales per 1,000 inhabitants
1	Latvia	1,637
2	Estonia	1,620
3	Romania	1,119
4	Lithuania	712
5	Georgia	671
6	Hong Kong	632
7	Norway	614
8	Japan	587
9	Iceland	572
10	Moldova	561
	USA	*250*

Certain countries have large numbers of newspapers each serving relatively small areas and hence with restricted circulations: the US is the most notable example, with 1,611 daily newspapers, but only five of them with average daily sales of more than 1,000,000, while the UK, with fewer individual newspapers, also has five with circulations of over 1,000,000. If the table is arranged by total sales of daily newspapers per 1,000 inhabitants, the result is somewhat different (see following list):

"Official" figures from former Soviet Bloc countries should always be regarded with some degree of circumspection.

One curious anomaly is that of the Vatican City's one newspaper, *L'Osservatore Romano*, an average of 70,000 of which are printed. Since the population of the Vatican is only about 738, it implies a daily sale of 94,850 per 1,000, or 95 copies per head. In fact, of course, most of them are sent outside the Holy See.

TOP 10

BRITISH NATIONAL DAILY NEWSPAPERS

	Newspaper	Average daily sale (1993/94)
1	*The Sun*	3,851,929
2	*Daily Mirror*	2,523,944
3	*Daily Mail*	1,716,070
4	*Daily Express*	1,397,852
5	*Daily Telegraph*	1,017,326
6	*Daily Star*	751,448
7	*Today*	564,169
8	*The Times*	448,962
9	*The Guardian*	401,705
10	*The Independent*	311,046

The 11th bestselling daily newspaper in the UK is the *Financial Times*, with total average worldwide daily sales during this period of 291,119 copies (including editions published in Frankfurt and New York). The combined sales of all the "quality" daily newspapers (*Daily Telegraph*, *Guardian*, *The Times*, *Independent*, and *Financial Times*) are fewer than those of the *Daily Mirror*.

MAGAZINES AND COMICS

T O P 1 0

D.C. THOMSON CHILDREN'S COMICS AND MAGAZINES

	Comic	First issue
1	*Beano*	30 Jul 1938
2	*Shout* (fortnightly)	5 Mar 1993
3	*Dandy*	4 Dec 1937
4	*Bunty*	14 Jan 1958
5	*Twinkle*	27 Jan 1968
6	*Beano Superstars* (monthly)	31 Jan 1992
7	*Mandy* and *Judy*	21 Jan 1967/ 8 Jan 1960*
8	*Beano Comic Libraries* (monthly)	Apr 1982
9	*Dandy Comic Libraries* (monthly)	Apr 1983
10	*Dandy Cartoon Libraries* (monthly)	Jul 1987

* Amalgamated 18 May 1991.

D.C. Thomson & Co of Dundee began publishing comics in the 1920s. Their boys' adventure papers, *Rover* (1922–61), *Wizard* (1922–63), and *Hotspur* (1933–59), presented footballers and other working-class heroes with whom their audiences could identify more readily than the public school chaps featured in rival publications such as *The Boy's Own Paper* (1879–1967) and *Magnet* (1908–40), but by the early 1960s changing fashions and the rise of popular culture based on television and pop music ousted this style of publication. D.C. Thomson's old-established humour favourites are still going strong, however, and their two pre-war comics remain prominent among their bestsellers: *Dandy*, first published in 1937 and featuring Desperate Dan and Korky the Cat, and *Beano*, dating from 1938, which introduced its best-known character, Dennis the Menace, in 1951.

T O P 1 0

BESTSELLING BRITISH CHILDREN'S COMICS AND MAGAZINES

1	*Beano*
2	*Shout*
3	*Dandy*
4	*Fast Forward*
5	*Thunderbirds*
6	*Look In*
7	*Playdays*
8	*Thomas the Tank Engine & Friends*
9	*Rupert Bear & Friends*
10	*It's Fun to Learn with Thomas the Tank Engine & Friends*

Beano and *Dandy*, which have maintained their pre-eminence for more than 50 years, have been recently joined by a newcomer, another D.C. Thomson publication, the fortnightly *Shout*, first published on 5 March 1993. The children's comic market is highly volatile and increasingly influenced by fads, currently popular television programmes, and films (a former bestseller, *Teenage Mutant Hero Turtles*, for example, is no longer published). It is therefore highly likely that by the time you read this, certain short-term blockbusters will have been eclipsed by other new kids on the block.

T O P 1 0

BESTSELLING BRITISH COMICS OF ALL TIME

1	*Beano* (1938–)
2	*Comic Cuts* (1890–1953)
3	*Dandy* (1937–)
4	*Eagle* (1950–69; revived 1982)
5	*Film Fun* (1920–62)
6	*Illustrated Chips* (1890–1953)
7	*Mickey Mouse Weekly* (1936–57)
8	*Radio Fun* (1938–61)
9	*Rainbow* (1914–56)
10	*School Friend* (1950–65)

Accurate circulation figures for British comics are hard to come by, but information supplied by the Association of Comics Enthusiasts indicates that all 10 comics listed (in alphabetical order) achieved very high circulation figures – *Eagle*, *Film Fun*, *Rainbow*, and *School Friend* all hitting 1,000,000 at their peak.

T O P 1 0

LONGEST-RUNNING CHILDREN'S COMICS AND MAGAZINES IN THE UK

	Publication	First issue
1	*Scouting* (name changed from *The Scouter*, 1971)	1 Jan 1923
2	*Dandy*	4 Dec 1937
3	*Beano*	30 Jul 1938
4	*Beezer* and *Topper*	21 Jan 1956/ 7 Feb 1953
5	*Bunty*	14 Jan 1958*
6	*Mandy* and *Judy*	21 Jan 1967/ 16 Jan 1960
7	*Buster* (incorporating *Whizzer & Chips***)	28 May 1960#
8	*Victor*	25 Feb 1961
9	*The Brownie* (monthly)	Jan 1962
10	*Plus* (monthly)	Jan 1966

* Amalgamated 22 September 1990.
 # Amalgamated 18 May 1991.
**First published 18 October 1969; amalgamated 3 November 1990.

T O P 1 0

WOMEN'S MAGAZINES IN THE UK

	Magazine	Average sales per issue
1	*Bella*	1,202,229
2	*Take a Break*	1,137,283
3	*Woman's Weekly*	826,922
4	*Woman*	716,837
5	*Woman's Own*	700,178
6	*Prima*	682,191
7	*Best*	572,098
8	*Hello*	487,704
9	*Cosmopolitan*	472,770
10	*Chat*	450,038

MAGAZINES IN THE UK

	Magazine	Average sales per issue
1	Radio Times	1,592,741
2	Reader's Digest	1,521,437
3	What's on TV	1,431,398
4	Bella	1,202,229
5	Take a Break	1,137,283
6	TV Times	1,113,997
7	Viz	875,408
8	Woman's Weekly	826,922
9	Woman	716,837
10	Woman's Own	700,178

Billed as "The Official Organ of the BBC", the Radio Times, the UK's bestselling magazine, was first published on 28 September 1923 priced twopence.

Sales of Radio Times have been overtaken on occasions by its close rival, Reader's Digest, which had its origins during the First World War. In 1916, American bank clerk DeWitt Wallace published a booklet called Getting the Most Out of Farming, which consisted of extracts from various US Government agricultural publications. While recovering after being wounded in France during the war, he contemplated applying the same principle to a general interest magazine and in 1920 produced a sample copy of Reader's Digest. He and his new wife, Lila Acheson, solicited sales by subscription and published 5,000 copies of the first issue in February 1922. It was an enormous success, rapidly becoming the bestselling monthly magazine in the US. The British office opened in 1938, followed by further branches throughout the world, and today 41 editions are published in 17 languages.

OLDEST PERIODICALS IN PRINT IN THE UK

	Periodical*	Founded
1	Philosophical Transactions of the Royal Society	1665
2	The Scots Magazine	1739
3	Archaeologia (Journal of the Society of Antiquaries)	1770
4	Curtis's Botanical Magazine	1787
5	The Lancet #	1823
6	The Spectator	1828
7=	Nautical Magazine	1832
7=	Royal Society of Edinburgh Proceedings	1832
9	Gospel Standard	1835
10	Justice of the Peace	1837

* Includes only those continuously published under their original titles.
# The oldest British weekly.

The Philosophical Transactions of the Royal Society was first published on 6 March 1665. The magazine Tatler, which appeared on 12 April 1709, ceased publication in 1711; the present-day magazine of that name was founded at a later date, and is thus ineligible for this list. Other British periodicals dating back more than 100 years include such specialist publications as the Numismatic Chronicle (1839), the British Medical Journal (1840), the Pharmaceutical Journal (1841) and the Archaeological Journal (1844). Several religious magazines have a similarly long history, among them The Tablet (1840) and The Friend (1843). Punch, first published on 17 July 1841, was once Britain's foremost humour magazine, selling about 170,000 copies a week in the 1940s, but ceased publication on 8 April 1992. Notes & Queries, founded in 1849 as a monthly journal (it is now published quarterly), contains letters raising questions on almost any topic posed by readers which are answered, often in great detail, by other readers – a style that The Guardian and other newspapers have copied successfully. The Bookseller, "The Organ of the Book Trade", was first published in 1858. Exchange & Mart, the first publication to consist entirely of advertisements, was launched in 1868.

SPECIALIST MAGAZINES IN THE UK

	Magazine	Average sales per issue
1	National Trust Magazine	1,163,887
2	Expression! (American Express)	595,513
3	Saga Magazine	540,006
4	Birds (RSPB)	504,611
5	Puzzler Collection	413,432
6	Auto Trader (combined, all editions)	363,927
7	Puzzler	305,500
8	En Route (The Caravan Club)	290,841
9	What Car?	138,274
10	BBC Wildlife	132,217

MAGAZINES IN THE US

	Magazine	Average sales per issue
1	Reader's Digest	16,258,476
2	TV Guide	14,498,341
3	National Geographic Magazine	9,708,254
4	Better Homes and Gardens	8,002,585
5	Family Circle	5,283,660
6	Good Housekeeping	5,139,355
7	Ladies Home Journal	5,041,143
8	Woman's Day	4,810,445
9	McCall's	4,704,772
10	Time	4,203,991

In the US, Reader's Digest has remained the consistent No. 1 for many years. The syndicated colour weekly Parade, which is distributed with more than 350 Sunday newspapers across the United States, had a circulation of 36,730,000.

ART AT AUCTION

T O P 1 0

MOST EXPENSIVE PAINTINGS EVER SOLD

Artist/work/sale	Price (£)
1 Vincent van Gogh, *Portrait of Dr Gachet* Christie's, New York, 15 May 1990	44,378,696

Sold to Ryoei Saito, head of Japanese Daishowa Paper Manufacturing.

2 Pierre-Auguste Renoir, *Au Moulin de la Galette* Sotheby's, New York, 17 May 1990	42,011,832

Also purchased by Ryoei Saito – two days later.

3 Pablo Picasso, *Les Noces de Pierrette Binoche et Godeau* Paris, 30 November 1989	33,123,028

Sold by Swedish financier Fredrik Roos and bought by Tomonori Tsurumaki, a property developer, bidding from Tokyo by phone.

4 Vincent van Gogh, *Irises* Sotheby's, New York, 11 November 1987	28,000,000

After much speculation, its mystery purchaser was eventually confirmed as Australian businessman Alan Bond. However, as he was unable to pay for it in full, its former status as the world's most expensive work of art has been disputed. In 1990 it was sold to the J. Paul Getty Museum, Malibu, for an undisclosed sum, with speculation ranging from $60,000,000 to as little as $35,000,000.

5 Pablo Picasso, Self Portrait: *Yo Picasso* Sotheby's, New York, 9 May 1989	26,687,116

The anonymous purchaser may have been Greek shipping magnate Stavros Niarchos.

6 Pablo Picasso, *Au Lapin Agile* Sotheby's, New York, 15 November 1989	23,870,968

The painting depicts Picasso as a harlequin at the bar of the café Lapin Agile. The owner of the café acquired the picture in exchange for food and drink at a time when Picasso was hard up. In 1989 it was bought by the Walter Annenberg Foundation.

7 Vincent van Gogh, *Sunflowers* Christie's, London, 30 March 1987	22,500,000

At the time, the most expensive picture ever sold (and still the most expensive sold in the UK), it was bought by the Yasuda Fire and Marine Insurance Company of Tokyo.

8 Jacopo da Carucci (Pontormo), *Portrait of Duke Cosimo I de Medici* Christie's, New York, 31 May 1989	20,253,164

The world record price for an Old Master – and the only one in the Top 10 – it was bought by the J. Paul Getty Museum, Malibu.

9 Pablo Picasso, *Acrobate et Jeune Arlequin* Christie's, London, 28 November 1988	19,000,000

Until the sale of Yo Picasso, *this held the world record for a 20th-century painting. It was bought by Mitsukoshi, a Japanese department store. (In Japan, many major stores have important art galleries.)*

10 Paul Cézanne, *Nature Morte – Les Grosses Pommes* Sotheby's, New York, 11 May 1993	16,993,464

Sold by one Greek shipowner, George Embiricos, and bought by another, Stavros Niarchos.

T O P 1 0

ARTISTS WITH MOST PAINTINGS SOLD FOR MORE THAN £1,000,000

DR GACHET BY VINCENT VAN GOGH

	Artist	No. sold for £1M+
1	Pablo Picasso	96
2	Claude Monet	95
3	Auguste Renoir	79
4	Edgar Degas	34
5	Paul Cézanne	27
6	Camille Pissarro	26
7	Henri Matisse	25
8	Amedeo Modigliani	24
9	Vincent van Gogh	22
10	Marc Chagall	21

T O P 1 0

MOST EXPENSIVE PRE-RAPHAELITE PAINTINGS

Artist/work/sale	Price (£)
1 Dante Gabriel Rossetti (1828–82), *Proserpine* Christie's, London, 27 November 1987	1,300,000
2 John Brett (1830–1902), *Val d'Aosta* Sotheby's, London, 20 June 1989	1,200,000
3 Sir John Everett Millais (1829–96), *The Proscribed Royalist* Christie's, London, 25 November 1983	780,000
4 Sir Edward Burne-Jones (1833–98), *Nativity* Sotheby's, London, 21 November 1989	700,000
5 Sir Edward Burne-Jones, *The King and the Shepherd* Sotheby's, London, 21 November 1989	620,000
6 Sir Edward Burne-Jones, *Pygmalion Series: The Heart Desires; The Hand Refrains; The Godhead Fires; The Soul Attains* (group of four paintings) Sotheby's, London, 8 June 1993	600,000
7 Sir Edward Burne-Jones, *Portrait of Amy Gaskell* Sotheby's, London, 8 June 1993	450,000
8 Dante Gabriel Rossetti, *La Ghirlandata* Sotheby's, London, 8 June 1993	420,000
9 Sir Edward Burne-Jones, *The Sleeping Princess* Christie's, London, 25 November 1988	400,000
10 John William Waterhouse (1849–1917), *Ophelia* Christie's, London, 11 June 1993	380,000

TOP 10

MOST EXPENSIVE OLD MASTER PAINTINGS

	Artist/work/sale	Price (£)
1	Jacopo da Carucci (Pontormo), *Portrait of Duke Cosimo I de Medici* Christie's, New York, 31 May 1989	20,253,164
2	Canaletto, *The Old Horse Guards, London, from St James's Park* Christie's, London, 15 April 1992	9,200,000
3	Francesco Guardi, *View of the Giudecca and the Zattere, Venice* Sotheby's, Monaco, 1 December 1989	8,937,960
4	Andrea Mantegna, *Adoration of the Magi* Christie's, London, 18 April 1985	7,500,000
5	Titian, *Venus and Adonis* Christie's, London, 13 December 1991	6,800,000
6	Rembrandt, *Portrait of a Girl Wearing a Gold-trimmed Cloak* Sotheby's, London, 10 December 1986	6,600,000
7	Canaletto, *View of Molo from Bacino di San Marco, Venice*, and *View of the Grand Canal Facing East from Campo di Santi, Venice* (pair) Sotheby's, New York, 1 June 1990	5,988,024
8	Bartolomeo di Giovanni, *Argonauts in Colchis* Sotheby's, London, 6 December 1989	4,600,000
9	Francisco José de Goya y Lucientes, *Bullfight – Suerte de Varas* Sotheby's, London, 9 December 1992	4,500,000
10	Lucas Cranach the Elder, *Portraits of Kurfurst Herzog Johann von Sachsen and his son Johann Friedrich* (pair) Christie's, London, 6 July 1990	4,400,000

TOP 10

MOST EXPENSIVE PAINTINGS BY AMERICAN ARTISTS

	Artist/work/sale	Price (£)
1	Willem de Kooning (b.1904), *Interchange* Sotheby's, New York, 8 November 1989	11,898,735
2	Jasper Johns (b.1930), *False Start* Sotheby's, New York, 10 November 1988	8,611,112
3	Jasper Johns, *Two Flags* Sotheby's, New York, 8 November 1989	6,962,025
4	Jackson Pollock (1912–56), *Number 8, 1950* Sotheby's, New York, 2 May 1989	6,325,302
5	Frederic Edwin Church (1826–1900), *Home by the Lake, Scene in the Catskill Mountains*, Sotheby's, New York, 24 May 1989	4,746,836
6	Willem de Kooning, *July*, Christie's, New York, 7 November 1990	4,081,633
7	Robert Rauschenberg (b.1925), *Rebus* Sotheby's, New York, 30 April 1991	3,905,325
8	Willem de Kooning, *Palisade*, Sotheby's, New York, 8 May 1990	3,869,048
9	Jasper Johns, *White Flag*, Christie's, New York, 9 November 1988	3,555,556
10	Roy Lichtenstein (b.1923), *Kiss II* Christie's, New York, 7 May 1990	3,273,810

TOP 10

MOST EXPENSIVE PAINTINGS BY PABLO PICASSO

	Work/sale	Price (£)
1	*Les Noces de Pierrette* Binoche et Godeau, Paris, 30 November 1989	33,123,028
2	*Self Portrait: Yo Picasso* Sotheby's, New York, 9 May 1989	26,687,116
3	*Au Lapin Agile* Sotheby's, New York, 15 November 1989	23,870,968
4	*Acrobate et Jeune Arlequin* Christie's, London, 28 November 1988	19,000,000
5	*Le Miroir* Sotheby's, New York, 15 November 1989	15,483,872
6	*Les Tuileries* Christie's, London, 25 June 1990	12,500,000
7	*Maternité* Christie's, New York, 14 June 1988	12,362,638
8	*Mère et Enfant* Sotheby's, New York, 15 November 1989	10,967,743
9	*Famille de l'Arlequin* Christie's, New York, 14 November 1989	9,032,259
10	*La Cage d'Oiseaux* Sotheby's, New York, 10 November 1988	7,777,778

DID YOU KNOW

TOP 10 WOMEN ARTISTS

Seven of the ten most expensive paintings by women are by the American Impressionist Mary Cassatt (1845–1926). In first place is *The Conversation*, sold in 1988 for $4,100,000. *Black Hollyhocks with Blue Larkspur* by American Georgia O'Keeffe (1887–1986), fetched $1,800,000 in 1987. Finnish artist Helene Schjerfbeck (1862–1946) is the other woman in this list; her *Balskorna – Dancing Shoe* sold in 1990 for £1,000,000.

THE IMPRESSIONISTS

MOST EXPENSIVE PAINTINGS BY VINCENT VAN GOGH

Painting/sale	Price (£)
1 *Portrait du Dr Gachet* Christie's, New York, 15 May 1990	44,378,696
2 *Irises* Sotheby's, New York, 11 November 1987	28,000,000
3 *Sunflowers* Christie's, London, 30 March 1987	22,500,000
4 *Autoportrait* Christie's, New York, 15 May 1990	14,201,184
5 *Le Vieil If* Christie's, New York, 14 November 1989	11,935,485
6 *Le Pont de Trinquetaille* Christie's, London, 29 June 1987	11,500,000
7 *Paysage au Soleil Levant* Sotheby's, New York, 24 April 1985	7,200,000
8 *Carrière Près de Saint-Remy* Sotheby's, New York, 15 November 1989	6,774,194
9 *Adeline Ravoux* Christie's, New York, 11 May 1988	6,648,936
10 *Romans Parisiens, les Livres Jaunes* Christie's, London, 27 June 1988	6,500,000

MOST EXPENSIVE PAINTINGS BY PAUL CEZANNE

Painting/sale	Price (£)
1 *Nature Morte – les Grosses Pommes* Sotheby's, New York, 11 May 1993	16,993,464
2 *Pommes et Serviette* Christie's, London, 27 November 1989	10,000,000
3 *Pichet et Fruits sur une Table* Sotheby's, New York, 9 May 1989	6,441,718
4 *La Côté du Galet, à Pontoise* Sotheby's, New York, 10 May 1988	4,468,085
5 *Arlequin* Sotheby's, London, 29 November 1988	4,000,000
6 *Carrière de Bibemus* Sotheby's, New York, 15 November 1989	3,870,968
7 *Le Jas de Bouffan* Sotheby's, New York, 12 November 1990	3,299,492
8 *Saint-Henri et la Baie de l'Estaque* Sotheby's, New York, 10 May 1988	3,297,872
9 *L'Homme à la Pipe* Christie's, London, 30 November 1992	3,200,000
10 *Les Reflets dans l'Eau* Sotheby's, New York, 18 October 1989	2,893,082

MOST EXPENSIVE PAINTINGS BY PAUL GAUGUIN

Painting/sale	Price (£)
1 *Mata Mua – in Olden Times* Sotheby's, New York, 9 May 1989	13,496,934
2 *Entre les Lys* Sotheby's, New York, 15 November 1989	6,451,613
3 *Te Fare Hyménée, La Maison des Chants*, Sotheby's, London, 4 April 1989	6,000,000
4 *Petit Breton a l'Oie* Sotheby's, London, 28 November 1989	4,000,000
5 *Ferme en Bretagne II* Christie's, New York, 10 May 1989	3,803,681
6 *L'Allée des Alyscamps, Arles* Christie's, London, 28 November 1988	3,500,000
7 *Mata Mua – in Olden Times* Sotheby's, New York, 15 May 1984	2,536,232
8 *Vaches au Bord de la Mer* Sotheby's, New York, 18 October 1989	2,264,151
9 *Les Trois Huttes, Tahiti* Christie's, London, 30 November 1987	2,200,000
10 *Fruits Exotiques et Fleurs Rouges* Sotheby's, London, 27 June 1989	2,100,000

DID YOU KNOW

THE IMPRESSIONIST BOOM

After having their brand of art mocked and derided during their lifetimes, several of the pioneer Impressionists lived just long enough to see the public come to appreciate their work. However, since most of them had experienced years of poverty while they produced these masterpieces they would have been amazed by the escalation in the prices of their paintings. At the beginning of the 20th century, it was still possible to buy a painting by Vincent van Gogh for about £40, a Cézanne for £200, a Manet for £400, a Monet for less than £1,000, and a Renoir for £2,000. Prices rose slowly but appreciably throughout the century; in 1958 van Gogh's *Public Garden in Arles* achieved a new record of £132,000 and by 1970 paintings by Impressionists including van Gogh, Monet, and Renoir had all achieved prices of more than £500,000. This upward trend continued apace: in 1980 van Gogh's *Le Jardin de Poète, Arles* was sold for £2,270,000, and in 1985 his *Paysage au Soleil Levant* made £7,200,000. A colossal price surge followed in the late 1980s, with van Gogh paintings consistently leading the way. In 1987 the sale of his *Sunflowers* trebled the previous record price for a van Gogh, and subsequently this figure was itself overtaken by *Irises* (sold later that year) and by *Portrait du Dr Gachet* (sold in 1990). The latter is currently the most expensive painting in the world.

T O P 1 0

MOST EXPENSIVE PAINTINGS
BY EDOUARD MANET

	Painting/sale	Price (£)
1	*La rue Mosnier aux Drapeaux* Christie's, New York, 14 November 1989	15,483,872
2	*Le Banc, le Jardin de Versailles* Christie's, New York, 15 May 1990	8,875,740
3	*La Promenade* Sotheby's, New York, 15 November 1989	8,709,679
4	*La rue Mosnier au Paveurs* Christie's, London, 1 December 1986	7,000,000
5	*La Promenade* Christie's, New York, 15 November 1983	2,416,107
6	*Bouquet de Pivoines* Sotheby's, New York, 13 November 1990	2,030,457
7	*Fleurs dans un Vase de Cristal* Christie's, New York, 14 November 1990	1,725,888
8	*Portrait de Madame Brunet* Christie's, New York, 16 May 1984	1,438,849
9	*Femme Assise au Jardin, ou Le Tricot* Christie's, London, 27 June 1988	1,100,000
10	*Les Travailleurs de la Mer* Christie's, New York, 12 May 1992	983,607

T O P 1 0

MOST EXPENSIVE PAINTINGS
BY CLAUDE MONET

	Painting/sale	Price (£)
1	*Dans la Prairie* Sotheby's, London, 28 June 1988	13,000,000
2	*Le Parlement, Coucher de Soleil* Christie's, New York, 10 May 1989	7,975,460
3	*Le Bassin aux Nymphéas* Christie's, New York, 11 November 1992	7,284,770
4=	*Le Grand Canal* Sotheby's, New York, 15 November 1989	6,774,194
4=	*Nymphéas* Christie's, New York, 14 November 1989	6,774,194
6	*Le Pont du Chemin de Fer à Argenteuil* Christie's, London, 28 November 1988	6,200,000
7	*Garden House on the Banks of the Zaan* Sotheby's, New York, 9 May 1989	6,134,970
8	*Santa Maria della Salute et le Grand Canal, Venise* Sotheby's, London, 4 April 1989	6,100,000
9	*Le Parlement, Soleil Couchant* Christie's, New York, 14 November 1989	5,806,452
10	*La Jetée du Havre* Christie's, New York, 12 May 1993	5,751,634

T O P 1 0

MOST EXPENSIVE PAINTINGS
BY PIERRE AUGUSTE RENOIR

	Painting/sale	Price (£)
1	*Au Moulin de la Galette* Sotheby's, New York, 17 May 1990	42,011,832
2	*Jeune Fille au Chat* Sotheby's, New York, 17 May 1990	9,763,314
3	*La Promenade* Sotheby's, London, 4 April 1989	9,400,000
4	*La Liseuse* Christie's, New York, 14 November 1989	8,387,097
5	*La Tasse de Chocolat* Sotheby's, New York, 12 November 1990	8,375,635
6	*Jeune Fille au Chapeau Garni de Fleurs des Champs* Sotheby's, New York, 9 May 1989	7,668,712
7	*La Loge* Christie's, New York, 10 May 1989	6,748,467
8	*Jeune Fille Portant une Corbeille de Fleurs* Christie's, London, 21 June 1993	5,200,000
9	*Gabrielle à sa Coiffure* Christie's, New York, 14 November 1989	5,161,291
10	*Baigneuse, Femme en Jupe Rouges Essuyant les Pieds* Sotheby's, New York, 11 November 1988	4,532,164

ART ON SHOW

BEST-ATTENDED EXHIBITIONS AT THE BRITISH MUSEUM

	Exhibition	Total attendance
1	Treasures of Tutankhamen* 1972	1,694,117
2	The Vikings*, 1980	465,000
3	The Ancient Olympic Games 1980	334,354
4	Treasures of the Nation* 1988–89	294,837
5	Buddhism, Art and Faith 1984–85	223,370
6	The Drawings of Rembrandt 1992	220,000
7	Archaeology in Britain* 1986–87	181,921
8	Ceramic Art of the Italian Renaissance, 1987	150,000
9	Money: From Cowrie Shells to Credit Cards 1986	127,026
10	Masterpieces of the British Museum, 1984	125,858

* *Admission charged, all others free.*

MUMMY MASK
Tutankhamen's mask was the highlight of the British Museum's exhibition of his tomb treasures. Made of solid gold and inlaid with glass and stones, it weighs over 10.2 kg (22.5 lb).

BEST-ATTENDED EXHIBITIONS AT THE TATE GALLERY, LONDON

	Exhibition	Year	Total attendance
1	John Constable	1976	313,659
2	Salvador Dali – A Retrospective	1980	236,615
3	The Pre-Raphaelites	1984	219,292
4	David Hockney – A Retrospective	1988–89	173,162
5	Constable	1991	169,412
6	Late Picasso, 1953–1972	1988	139,349
7	The Essential Cubism	1983	122,246
8	Thomas Gainsborough	1980–81	112,517
9	Francis Bacon	1985	109,732
10	William Blake	1978	106,229

Although the Top 10 exhibitions are ranked according to total attendance, the figures are affected by the duration of a show, which may be open for a period from as little as a month to as long as over three months. Dali comes out on top of the highest attendance per day chart, with an average of 3,879 over the 61 days the exhibition was open.

BEST-ATTENDED EXHIBITIONS AT THE HAYWARD GALLERY, LONDON

	Exhibition	Total attendance
1	Renoir, 1985	364,430
2	Toulouse-Lautrec, 1991	266,367
3	Leonardo da Vinci, 1989	262,221
4	Picasso's Picasso, 1981	215,801
5	Van Gogh, 1968	198,453
6	Dada and Surrealism, 1978	188,655
7	Sacred Circles, 1976	176,980
8	Rodin/Boyle Family, 1986	174,130
9	Rodin, 1970	160,926
10	The Thirties, 1979	160,441

BEST-ATTENDED EXHIBITIONS AT THE VICTORIA AND ALBERT MUSEUM, LONDON

	Exhibition	Total attendance
1	Britain Can Make It, 1946	1,500,000
2	Spanish Art Treasures, 1881	1,022,000
3	Scientific Apparatus, 1876	275,813
4	Wedding Presents (Prince & Princess of Wales), 1863	229,425
5	Six Wives of Henry VIII (BBC drama costumes), 1970	182,825
6	Visions of Japan, 1991	177,669
7	Sovereign, 1992	174,078
8	Meyrick Armour, 1879	172,708
9	Fabergé, 1977	152,645
10	Ferragamo, 1988	125,920

The Victoria and Albert Museum is unusual in having records of exhibitions held dating as far back as 1863.

BEST-ATTENDED EXHIBITIONS AT THE ROYAL ACADEMY, LONDON

(During the past 25 years, the only period for which detailed comparative figures exist)

	Exhibition	Total attendance
1	The Genius of China, 1974	771,466
2	Monet: The Series Paintings, 1990	658,289
3	Pompeii AD79, 1977	633,347
4	Post-Impressionism, 1980	558,573
5	The Great Japan Exhibition, 1982	523,005
6	The Genius of Venice, 1983	452,885
7	J.M.W. Turner, 1975	424,629
8	The Great Age of Chivalry, 1987–88	349,750
9	The Gold of El Dorado, 1979	319,006
10	Chagall, 1985	282,851

SYMBOL OF
FREEDOM
*Standing on a
massive pedestal,
Liberty bears a
book of law and
a burning torch
that reaches
93 m (305 ft)
above sea level.*

T O P 1 0

MOST EXPENSIVE PHOTOGRAPHS EVER SOLD AT AUCTION

	Photographer/photograph/sale	Price ($)
1	Edward S. Curtis (American, 1868–1952), *The North American Indian**, 1907–30, Sotheby's, New York, 7 October 1993	662,500
2	Alfred Stieglitz (American, 1864–1946), *Georgia O'Keeffe: A Portrait – Hands with Thimble*, 1930, Christie's, New York, 8 October 1993	398,500
3=	Alfred Stieglitz, *Equivalents (21)**, 1920s Christie's, New York, 30 October 1989	396,000
3=	Edward S. Curtis, *The North American Indian**, 1907–30 Christie's, New York, 13 October 1992	396,000
5	Man Ray (American, 1890–1976), *Noir et Blanche**, 1926 Christie's, New York, 21 April 1994	354,500
6	Man Ray, *Hier, Demain, Aujourd'hui* (triptych), 1930–32 Christie's, New York, 8 October 1993	222,500
7	Man Ray, *Glass Tears*, c.1930 Sotheby's, London, 7 May 1993 (£122,500)	195,000
8	Tina Modotti (Mexican, 1896–1942), *Two Callas*, 1925 Christie's, New York, 8 October 1993	189,500
9	Alexander Rodchenko (Russian, 1891–1956), *Girl with Leica*, 1934 Christie's, London, 29 October 1992 (£115,500)	181,450
10	Tina Modotti, *Roses, Mexico*, 1925 Sotheby's, New York, 17 April 1991	165,000

* *Collections; all others are single prints.*

T O P 1 0

TALLEST FREE-STANDING STATUES IN THE WORLD

	Statue	Height m	ft
1	*Chief Crazy Horse*, Thunderhead Mountain, South Dakota, USA	172	563

Started in 1948 by Polish-American sculptor Korczak Ziolkowski and continued after his death in 1982 by his widow and eight of his children, this gigantic equestrian statue is even longer than it is high (195 m/641 ft). It is not expected to be completed until the next century.

	Statue	Height m	ft
2	*Buddha*, Tokyo, Japan	120	394

This Japan-Taiwanese project, unveiled in 1993, took seven years to complete and weighs 100 tonnes.

	Statue	Height m	ft
3	*The Indian Rope Trick*, Riddersberg Säteri, Jönköping, Sweden	103	337

Sculptor Calle Örnemark's 144-tonne wooden sculpture depicts a long strand of "rope" held by a fakir, while another figure ascends.

	Statue	Height m	ft
4	*Motherland, 1967*, Volgograd, Russia	82	270

Unveiled in 1967, this concrete statue of a woman with raised sword commemorates the Soviet victory at the Battle of Stalingrad (1942–43).

	Statue	Height m	ft
5	*Buddha*, Bamian, Afghanistan	53	173

Near this 3rd–4th century AD statue lie the remains of the even taller Sakya Buddha, said to have measured 305 m/1,000 ft.

	Statue	Height m	ft
6	*Kannon*, Otsubo-yama, near Tokyo, Japan	52	170

The immense statue of the goddess of mercy was unveiled in 1961 in honour of the dead of the Second World War.

	Statue	Height m	ft
7	*Statue of Liberty*, New York, USA	46	151

Designed by Auguste Bartholdi and presented to the USA by the people of France, the statue was shipped in sections to Liberty (formerly Bedloes) Island where it was assembled. It was unveiled on 28 October 1886, and restored and reinaugurated on 4 July 1986. It consists of sheets of copper on an iron frame, and weighs 229 tonnes in total.

	Statue	Height m	ft
8	*Christ*, Rio de Janeiro, Brazil	38	125

The work of sculptor Paul Landowski and engineer Heitor da Silva Costa, the figure of Christ weighs 1,163 tonnes. It was unveiled in 1931 and has recently been restored.

	Statue	Height m	ft
9	*Tian Tan (Temple of Heaven) Buddha* Po Lin Monastery, Lantau Island, Hong Kong	34	112

Completed after 20 years work and unveiled on 29 December 1993, the bronze statue weighs 250 tonnes and cost £6,000,000.

	Statue	Height m	ft
10	*Colossi of Memnon*, Karnak, Egypt	21	70

Two seated sandstone figures of Pharaoh Amenhotep III.

MUSIC

TOP 10

SINGLES OF ALL TIME WORLDWIDE

	Artist/title	Sales exceed
1	Bing Crosby, *White Christmas*	30,000,000
2	Bill Haley & His Comets, *Rock Around The Clock*	17,000,000
3	Beatles, *I Want To Hold Your Hand*	12,000,000
4=	Elvis Presley, *It's Now Or Never*	10,000,000
4=	Whitney Houston, *I Will Always Love You*	10,000,000
6=	Elvis Presley, *Hound Dog/ Don't Be Cruel*	9,000,000
6=	Paul Anka, *Diana*	9,000,000
8=	Beatles, *Hey Jude*	8,000,000
8=	Monkees, *I'm A Believer*	8,000,000
10=	Beatles, *Can't Buy Me Love*	7,000,000
10=	Band Aid, *Do They Know It's Christmas?*	7,000,000
10=	USA For Africa, *We Are The World*	7,000,000

TOP 10

SINGLES OF ALL TIME IN THE UK

	Artist/title	Approx. sales
1	Band Aid, *Do They Know It's Christmas?* (1984)	3,510,000
2	Queen, *Bohemian Rhapsody* (1975/91)	2,130,000
3	Wings, *Mull Of Kintyre* (1977)	2,050,000
4	Boney M, *Rivers Of Babylon/ Brown Girl In The Ring* (1978)	1,995,000
5	Frankie Goes To Hollywood, *Relax* (1984)	1,910,000
6	Beatles, *She Loves You* (1963)	1,890,000
7	John Travolta and Olivia Newton-John, *You're The One That I Want* (1978)	1,870,000
8	Boney M, *Mary's Boy Child/ Oh My Lord* (1978)	1,790,000
9	Stevie Wonder, *I Just Called To Say I Love You* (1984)	1,775,000
10	Beatles, *I Want To Hold Your Hand* (1963)	1,640,000

A total of 46 singles have sold over 1,000,000 copies apiece in the UK during the last 40 years, and these are the cream of that crop. The Band Aid single had a host of special circumstances surrounding it, and it is difficult to imagine, even if a similarly special case arose in the future, such sales ever being approached again by a single in this country. Two years, 1978 and 1984, were the all-time strongest for million-selling singles, and this chart fittingly has three representatives from each. Prior to the huge sales of Queen's *Bohemian Rhapsody* in the wake of Freddie Mercury's death in 1991, it stood at number 23 in this list, its elevation to the Top 10 ousting Ken Dodd's *Tears* (1965).

SINGLES – WORLD/UK

TOP 10

SINGLES WITH MOST WEEKS AT NO. 1 IN THE UK

	Artist/title	Weeks at No. 1
1	Frankie Laine, *I Believe*	18
2	Bryan Adams, *(Everything I Do) I Do It For You*	16
3	Queen, *Bohemian Rhapsody*	14
4	Slim Whitman, *Rose Marie*	11
5=	David Whitfield, *Cara Mia*	10
5=	Whitney Houston, *I Will Always Love You*	10
7=	Paul Anka, *Diana*	9
7=	Al Martino, *Here In My Heart*	9
7=	Wings, *Mull Of Kintyre*	9
7=	Eddie Calvert, *Oh Mein Papa*	9
7=	Doris Day, *Secret Love*	9
7=	Frankie Goes To Hollywood, *Two Tribes*	9
7=	John Travolta and Olivia Newton-John, *You're The One That I Want*	9

The totals for *I Believe* and *Bohemian Rhapsody* are cumulative of more than one run at the top, in the former case because the single dropped to No. 2 for two weeks in what otherwise would have been a 20-week spell at No. 1, and in the latter case through a return to the top for a second lengthy run 16 years after its first. All other totals are for consecutive chart-topping weeks, which means Bryan Adams is the champion in terms of an unbroken No. 1 run.

TOP 10

YOUNGEST SINGERS TO HAVE A NO. 1 SINGLE IN THE UK
(To 31 March 1994)

	Artist	Title	Age yrs	mths
1	Little Jimmy Osmond	*Long Haired Lover From Liverpool*	9	8
2	Donny Osmond	*Puppy Love*	14	6
3	Helen Shapiro	*You Don't Know*	14	10
4	Paul Anka	*Diana*	16	0
5	Tiffany	*I Think We're Alone Now*	16	3
6	Nicole	*A Little Peace*	17	0
7	Glenn Medeiros	*Nothing's Gonna Change My Love*	18	0
8	Mary Hopkin	*Those Were The Days*	18	4
9	Cliff Richard	*Living Doll*	18	8
10	Adam Faith	*What Do You Want?*	19	5

The ages are those of the artists in the week in which they first topped the UK chart. Kylie Minogue just missed this list, having been 19 years 8 months old when she first hit No. 1 in 1988 with *I Should Be So Lucky.*

TOP 10

OLDEST SINGERS TO HAVE A NO. 1 SINGLE IN THE UK
(To 31 March 1994)

	Artist	Title	Age yrs	mths
1	Louis Armstrong	*What A Wonderful World*	67	10
2	Frank Sinatra	*Somethin' Stupid*	51	4
3	Telly Savalas	*If*	51	1
4	Cliff Richard	*Saviour's Day*	50	2
5	Righteous Brothers	*Unchained Melody*	50 50	2 1
6	Charles Aznavour	*She*	50	1
7	Clive Dunn	*Grandad*	49	0
8	Ben E. King	*Stand By Me*	48	5
9	Gene Pitney	*Something's Gotten Hold Of My Heart*	48	0
10	Mantovani	*Theme From "Moulin Rouge"*	47	9

The ages listed are those of the artists during the final week of their last (to date) No. 1 hit. Gene Pitney was just a day over 48 as his 1989 duet success with Marc Almond finished its chart-topping run. Seven of the 10 are still alive, so there is room for further improvement.

SINGLES – UK DECADES

TOP 10

SINGLES OF EACH YEAR OF THE 1960s IN THE UK

1960	Elvis Presley, *It's Now Or Never*
1961	Elvis Presley, *Are You Lonesome Tonight?*
1962	Frank Ifield, *I Remember You*
1963	Beatles, *She Loves You*
1964	Beatles, *Can't Buy Me Love*
1965	Ken Dodd, *Tears*
1966	Tom Jones, *Green, Green Grass Of Home*
1967	Engelbert Humperdinck, *Release Me*
1968	Beatles, *Hey Jude*
1969	Archies, *Sugar Sugar*

TOP 10

SINGLES OF EACH YEAR OF THE 1970s IN THE UK

1970	Elvis Presley, *The Wonder Of You*
1971	George Harrison, *My Sweet Lord*
1972	New Seekers, *I'd Like To Teach The World To Sing*
1973	Gary Glitter, *I Love You Love Me Love*
1974	New Seekers, *You Won't Find Another Fool Like Me*
1975	Queen, *Bohemian Rhapsody*
1976	Brotherhood of Man, *Save Your Kisses For Me*
1977	Wings, *Mull Of Kintyre*
1978	Boney M, *Rivers Of Babylon/ Brown Girl In The Ring*
1979	Village People, *Y.M.C.A.*

TOP 10

SINGLES OF EACH YEAR OF THE 1980s IN THE UK

1980	Police, *Don't Stand So Close To Me*
1981	Human League, *Don't You Want Me?*
1982	Dexy's Midnight Runners, *Come On Eileen*
1983	Culture Club, *Karma Chameleon*
1984	Band Aid, *Do They Know It's Christmas?*
1985	Jennifer Rush, *The Power Of Love*
1986	Nick Berry, *Every Loser Wins*
1987	Rick Astley, *Never Gonna Give You Up*
1988	Cliff Richard, *Mistletoe And Wine*
1989	Black Box, *Ride On Time*

TOP 10

SINGLES OF THE 1950s IN THE UK

	Title	Artist	Year
1	*Rock Around The Clock*	Bill Haley & His Comets	1955
2	*Diana*	Paul Anka	1957
3	*Mary's Boy Child*	Harry Belafonte	1957
4	*The Harry Lime Theme (The Third Man)*	Anton Karas	1950
5	*Living Doll*	Cliff Richard	1959
6	*Jailhouse Rock*	Elvis Presley	1958
7	*What Do You Want To Make Those Eyes At Me For?*	Emile Ford	1959
8	*All I Have To Do Is Dream/ Claudette*	Everly Brothers	1958
9	*What Do You Want?*	Adam Faith	1959
10	*All Shook Up*	Elvis Presley	1957

Record sales boomed in the 1950s with the advent of rock 'n' roll in 1955–56, and thus most of this Top 10 are from the latter half of the decade, with the top three representing the first three singles (and the only ones of the 1950s) to sell over 1,000,000 copies apiece in the UK. Anton Karas's zither instrumental theme from the film *The Third Man* pre-dates the first UK charts, but sold 900,000 copies between 1950 and 1954 – virtually all of which were on 78-rpm singles.

TOP 10

SINGLES OF THE 1960s IN THE UK

	Title	Artist	Year
1	*She Loves You*	Beatles	1963
2	*I Want To Hold Your Hand*	Beatles	1963
3	*Tears*	Ken Dodd	1965
4	*Can't Buy Me Love*	Beatles	1964
5	*I Feel Fine*	Beatles	1964
6	*We Can Work It Out/ Day Tripper*	Beatles	1965
7	*The Carnival Is Over*	Seekers	1965
8	*Release Me*	Engelbert Humperdinck	1967
9	*It's Now Or Never*	Elvis Presley	1960
10	*Green, Green Grass Of Home*	Tom Jones	1966

The Beatles' domination of the 1960s is clear, with five of the decade's top six singles being by the group. Intriguingly, all the other five in this Top 10 are ballads of varying degrees of what, in those days, would have been termed squareness. This was an era when the great silent majority of occasional record buyers purchased singles, not albums, and Messrs Dodd, Humperdinck, *et al* were the lucky recipients of their custom.

SINGLES OF THE 1970s IN THE UK

	Title	Artist	Year
1	*Mull Of Kintyre*	Wings	1977
2	*Rivers Of Babylon/ Brown Girl In The Ring*	Boney M	1978
3	*You're The One That I Want*	John Travolta and Olivia Newton-John	1978
4	*Mary's Boy Child/Oh My Lord*	Boney M	1978
5	*Summer Nights*	John Travolta and Olivia Newton-John	1978
6	*Y.M.C.A*	Village People	1979
7	*Bohemian Rhapsody*	Queen	1975
8	*Heart Of Glass*	Blondie	1979
9	*Merry Xmas Everybody*	Slade	1973
10	*Don't Give Up On Us*	David Soul	1977

Most of the biggest sellers of the 1970s in the UK occurred in an 18-month period between December 1977 and May 1979. The single that started this golden (or, rather, platinum) era, *Mull Of Kintyre*, was the first-ever in the UK to top 2,000,000 copies, and it inherited the "All-time Biggest Seller" title from the Beatles' *She Loves You*, which had held it for 14 years. *Bohemian Rhapsody* came almost to double its sales in 1991, following Freddie Mercury's death, allowing it just to overtake *Mull* on an all-time basis.

LIVE APPEAL
Led by Bob Geldof, Band Aid's all-star line-up included George Michael, Paul Young, and Freddie Mercury.

SINGLES OF THE 1980s IN THE UK

	Title	Artist	Year
1	*Do They Know It's Christmas?*	Band Aid	1984
2	*Relax*	Frankie Goes To Hollywood	1984
3	*I Just Called To Say I Love You*	Stevie Wonder	1984
4	*Two Tribes*	Frankie Goes To Hollywood	1984
5	*Don't You Want Me?*	Human League	1981
6	*Last Christmas*	Wham!	1984
7	*Karma Chameleon*	Culture Club	1983
8	*Careless Whisper*	George Michael	1984
9	*The Power Of Love*	Jennifer Rush	1985
10	*Come On Eileen*	Dexy's Midnight Runners	1982

Singles from the boom year of 1984 dominate the UK 1980s Top 10, two of them by newcomers Frankie Goes To Hollywood, and two by Wham!/George Michael (who also sang one of the Band Aid leads – as did Boy George from Culture Club). Stevie Wonder and Jennifer Rush are the sole US entrants; in fact, they were the only two Americans to have UK million-sellers during this decade.

CLASSIC ROCK AND POP

T O P 1 0

ABBA SINGLES IN THE UK

1	*Dancing Queen*	1976
2	*Knowing Me, Knowing You*	1977
3	*Fernando*	1976
4	*Super Trouper*	1980
5	*The Name Of The Game*	1977
6	*Take A Chance On Me*	1978
7	*Mamma Mia*	1975
8	*Money Money Money*	1976
9	*The Winner Takes It All*	1980
10	*Waterloo*	1974

Abba are one of the biggest singles-selling groups ever in the UK. Nine of these 10 records reached No. 1, and the top eight all sold in excess of 500,000 copies each, which represents amazing consistency at a very high level. Their last year together (1982) showed a notable sales decline, at which point they split to pursue solo careers (Agnetha Fälskog and Anni-Frid "Frida" Lyngstad) or wider musical projects such as the stage show *Chess* (Björn Ulvaeus and Benny Andersson).

T O P 1 0

BEACH BOYS SINGLES IN THE UK

1	*Good Vibrations*	1966
2	*Sloop John B*	1966
3	*God Only Knows*	1966
4	*Do It Again*	1968
5	*Cottonfields*	1970
6	*I Get Around*	1964
7	*Then I Kissed Her*	1967
8	*Barbara Ann*	1966
9	*Break Away*	1969
10	*Lady Lynda*	1979

Good Vibrations was also a Top 20 hit when reissued a decade after its initial success, cementing its status as the Beach Boys' biggest UK seller by far. In addition, the group were co-vocalists on the Fat Boys' revival of *Wipe Out* in 1987; this single would appear at No. 8 if included.

T O P 1 0

ROLLING STONES SINGLES IN THE UK

1	*The Last Time*	1965
2	*(I Can't Get No) Satisfaction*	1965
3	*Honky Tonk Women*	1969
4	*It's All Over Now*	1964
5	*Get Off Of My Cloud*	1965
6	*Paint It Black*	1966
7	*Jumpin' Jack Flash*	1968
8	*Little Red Rooster*	1964
9	*Miss You*	1978
10	*Brown Sugar*	1971

The mid-1960s were the Rolling Stones' singles-selling heyday, when the first eight of these titles reached No. 1 in the UK. Though arguably the next most popular group to the Beatles for most of that decade, the Stones' record sales rarely approached those of the Fab Four: their *The Last Time* only just outsold *A Hard Day's Night*, the Beatles' eighth most successful single.

STILL GOING STRONG
Mick Jagger continues to be as energetic as ever on the Rolling Stones' world tours.

T O P 1 0

ELVIS PRESLEY SINGLES IN THE UK

1	*It's Now Or Never*	1960
2	*Jailhouse Rock*	1958
3	*Are You Lonesome Tonight*	1961
4	*Wooden Heart*	1961
5	*Return To Sender*	1962
6	*Can't Help Falling In Love*	1962
7	*The Wonder Of You*	1970
8	*Surrender*	1961
9	*Way Down*	1977
10	*All Shook Up*	1957

Elvis was at his sales peak in the UK not in his 1950s heyday, but shortly after he left the army on 5 March 1960. *It's Now Or Never* was his only million-seller on UK sales alone, though all the records in this list registered sales in excess of 600,000, and these 10 singles accounted for a total of 46 weeks at the top of the UK chart between them.

THE KING
The staying power of Elvis Presley's appeal is clear from the 20-year span of his Top 10 bestselling singles.

T O P 1 0

BEATLES SINGLES IN THE UK

1	*She Loves You*	1963
2	*I Want To Hold Your Hand*	1963
3	*Can't Buy Me Love*	1964
4	*I Feel Fine*	1964
5	*We Can Work It Out/ Day Tripper*	1965
6	*Help!*	1965
7	*Hey Jude*	1968
8	*A Hard Day's Night*	1964
9	*From Me To You*	1963
10	*Hello Goodbye*	1967

The Beatles' two bestselling UK singles, both from the late 1963 "Beatlemania" period, are still among the UK's all-time Top 10 singles. Their sales later in the 1960s were generally lower, although *Hey Jude* proved a match for the earlier mega-hits. Nos. 1 to 5 were all million-plus UK sellers; no other act had ever had more than two million-selling UK singles.

T O P 1 0

DIRE STRAITS SINGLES IN THE UK

1	*Private Investigations*	1982
2	*Walk Of Life*	1986
3	*Money For Nothing*	1985
4	*Sultans Of Swing*	1979
5	*Romeo And Juliet*	1981
6	*Twisting By The Pool*	1983
7	*Brothers In Arms*	1985
8	*So Far Away*	1985
9	*Your Latest Trick*	1986
10	*Calling Elvis*	1991

A band whose albums have always considerably outsold their singles, Dire Straits have only amassed these 10 Top 30 hits in a career spanning almost 15 years. It is worth noting that half the songs here (Nos 2, 3, 7, 8, and 9) are taken from the album *Brothers In Arms*, which has sold 3,000,000 copies in the UK.

T O P 1 0

DAVID BOWIE SINGLES IN THE UK

1	*Space Oddity*	1969/1975
2	*Let's Dance*	1983
3	*Dancing In The Street* with Mick Jagger	1985
4	*Ashes To Ashes*	1981
5	*Under Pressure* with Queen	1981
6	*The Jean Genie*	1972
7	*Life On Mars*	1973
8	*Sorrow*	1973
9	*China Girl*	1983
10	*The Laughing Gnome*	1973

Bowie's *Space Oddity* was a Top 5 success when first released, then reached No. 1 on its reissue in 1975. *The Laughing Gnome*, a rather foolish novelty song, was a 1960s recording; it became a major hit after an astute reissue by Bowie's earlier record label, much to the artist's embarrassment.

RECORD BREAKERS

TOP 10

SINGLES BY FEMALE SINGERS IN THE UK

1 Whitney Houston, *I Will Always Love You* (1992)

2 Jennifer Rush, *The Power Of Love* (1985)

3 Julie Covington, *Don't Cry For Me Argentina* (1977)

4 Irene Cara, *Fame* (1982)

5 Cilla Black, *Anyone Who Had A Heart* (1964)

6 Kelly Marie, *Feels Like I'm In Love* (1980)

7 Barbra Streisand, *Woman In Love* (1980)

8 Sinead O'Connor, *Nothing Compares 2 U* (1990)

9 Diana Ross, *Chain Reaction* (1986)

10 Madonna, *Like A Virgin* (1984)

The most significant aspect of this list is how comparatively recent most of its entries are. Only two were released before 1980, and only Cilla Black's 1964 chart-topper is of real vintage. Statistically, therefore, a female artist stands a better chance of chart success today than in any of pop music's past golden ages – indeed, Madonna (who has clearly helped this state of affairs) was the bestselling act of the 1980s.

TOP 10

CHRISTMAS SINGLES OF ALL TIME IN THE UK

1 Band Aid, *Do They Know It's Christmas?* (1984)

2 Boney M, *Mary's Boy Child/Oh My Lord* (1978)

3 Wham!, *Last Christmas* (1984)

4 Slade, *Merry Christmas Everybody* (1973)

5 Harry Belafonte, *Mary's Boy Child* (1957)

6 Bing Crosby, *White Christmas* (1977)*

7 Cliff Richard, *Mistletoe And Wine* (1988)

8 Johnny Mathis, *When A Child Is Born* (1976)

9 John Lennon, *Happy Xmas (War Is Over)* (1980)*

10 Mud, *Lonely This Christmas* (1974)

* *Year of highest chart position.*

Band Aid's *Do They Know It's Christmas?* has now sold over 3,500,000 copies in the UK alone. Slade's *Merry Christmas Everybody* has charted on eight seasonal occasions. Bing Crosby's *White Christmas*, despite having sold over 30,000,000 copies worldwide since 1942, charted for the first time in the UK as late as 1977, a few weeks after the singer's death.

TOP 10

FOREIGN-LANGUAGE SINGLES IN THE UK

	Artist/title	Language
1	Jane Birkin and Serge Gainsbourg, *Je T'aime…Moi Non Plus*	French
2	Falco, *Rock Me Amadeus*	German
3	Julio Iglesias, *Begin The Beguine*	Spanish
4	Manhattan Transfer, *Chanson D'Amour*	French
5	Los Lobos, *La Bamba*	Spanish
6	Marino Marini, *Come Prima/Volare*	Italian
7	Luciano Pavarotti, *Nessun Dorma*	Italian
8	Vanessa Paradis, *Joe Le Taxi*	French
9	Kaoma, *Lambada*	Portuguese
10	Singing Nun, *Dominique*	French

Although foreign-language hits are extremely rare in the UK, the top five of this list all reached UK No. 1, while the remainder all made the Top 10.

HEAVY METAL SINGLES OF ALL TIME IN THE UK

1 Meat Loaf, *I'd Do Anything For Love (But I Won't Do That)*
2 Survivor, *Eye Of The Tiger*
3 Europe, *The Final Countdown*
4 Foreigner, *I Want To Know What Love Is*
5 Free, *All Right Now*
6 Black Sabbath, *Paranoid*
7 Alice Cooper, *School's Out*
8 Status Quo, *Down Down*
9 Deep Purple, *Black Night*
10 Jimi Hendrix Experience, *Voodoo Chile*

Meat Loaf's comeback single was the biggest seller (from the biggest album) of 1993 and sold over 800,000 copies in the UK. Survivor's *Eye Of The Tiger* benefited greatly from its exposure in the *Rocky III* movie. *All Right Now* has charted on four further occasions since originally hitting UK No. 2 in 1970, twice on the *Free* EP in 1978 and 1982, re-charting in its own right in 1983 and yet again in 1991 – thanks to its exposure in a Wrigley chewing gum commercial – reaching UK No. 8. In addition to hitting UK No. 1 in 1970, Jimi Hendrix Experience's *Voodoo Chile* also sold as one of three tracks on the 1990 No. 52 *All Along The Watchtower* EP.

KYU SAKAMOTO

Pop singer Kyu Sakamoto was among the passengers killed in the worst ever aviation disaster involving a single aircraft, the crash in Japan on 12 August 1985 of a Boeing 747 in which 520 died. In 1963 he had attained a place in the UK Top 10 with *Sukiyaki*, a single that sold a million copies both in his native Japan and in the US.

COUNTRY SINGLES OF ALL TIME IN THE UK

1 Jim Reeves, *I Love You Because*
2 Jim Reeves, *I Won't Forget You*
3 Kenny Rogers, *Ruby (Don't Take Your Love To Town)*
4 Roger Miller, *King Of The Road*
5 Kenny Rogers, *Lucille*
6 Tammy Wynette, *Stand By Your Man*
7 Kenny Rogers, *Coward Of The County*
8 Jim Reeves, *Distant Drums*
9 Slim Whitman, *Rose Marie*
10 Tennessee Ernie Ford, *Give Me Your Word*

Even though *I Love You Because* only made UK No. 5, it is still the bestselling country single ever in Britain, shifting over 750,000 copies in 1964 alone. Reeves has been by far the most popular country artist in the UK, amassing 29 chart entries between 1960 and 1972 – although *Distant Drums* was his only chart-topper.

INSTRUMENTAL SINGLES OF ALL TIME IN THE UK

1 Mr Acker Bilk, *Stranger On The Shore*
2 Simon Park Orchestra, *Eye Level*
3 Tornados, *Telstar*
4 Anton Karas, *The Harry Lime Theme (The Third Man)*
5 Royal Scots Dragoon Guards Band, *Amazing Grace*
6 Ennio Morricone, *Chi Mai*
7 Shadows, *Wonderful Land*
8 Shadows, *Apache*
9 Fleetwood Mac, *Albatross*
10 Lieutenant Pigeon, *Mouldy Old Dough*

If this Top 10 reveals anything, it is that non-vocal hits are more likely to be found in the "middle-of-the-road" sector than in rock 'n' roll. Most of these pieces are the equivalent of ballads, with only *Apache*, possibly *Telstar*, and just possibly *Mouldy Old Dough* – which is really a novelty instrumental – qualifying as rock music.

POSTHUMOUS SINGLES IN THE UK

	Artist/title	Died	Hit year
1	John Lennon, *Imagine*	1980	1981
2	Jackie Wilson, *Reet Petite*	1984	1986
3	Buddy Holly, *It Doesn't Matter Anymore*	1959	1959
4	John Lennon, *Woman*	1980	1981
5	Elvis Presley, *Way Down*	1977	1977
6	Jim Reeves, *I Won't Forget You*	1964	1964
7	Jim Reeves, *Distant Drums*	1964	1966
8	Eddie Cochran, *Three Steps To Heaven*	1960	1960
9	Jimi Hendrix, *Voodoo Chile*	1970	1970
10	Laurel & Hardy, *The Trail Of The Lonesome Pine*	1965/1957	1975

Jackie Wilson's *Reet Petite* had originally been a chart hit early in his career during the 1950s, but it was the posthumous 1986 UK reissue that saw by far the greater success. The same applied to *Imagine*, which had been a more moderate hit for John Lennon when released in 1975. Excluded from this list is the 1991 reissue of Queen's *Bohemian Rhapsody*, which would be at the top if it were included: since Queen continued to exist as a group after the death of singer Freddie Mercury, the release was not strictly posthumous.

IS THIS A RECORD?

T O P 1 0

SINGLES OF ALL TIME IN THE UK BANNED BY THE BBC

1 Frankie Goes To Hollywood, *Relax*

2 Jane Birkin and Serge Gainsbourg, *Je T'Aime . . . Moi Non Plus*

3 Ricky Valance, *Tell Laura I Love Her*

4 Sex Pistols, *God Save The Queen*

5 George Michael, *I Want Your Sex*

6 Jasper Carrott, *Magic Roundabout*

7 Wings, *Hi Hi Hi*

8 Max Romeo, *Wet Dream*

9 Judge Dread, *Big Seven*

10 Judge Dread, *Big Six*

Until recent years, BBC radio was prone to keep records off the airwaves if (a) their melody was a desecration of a classical piece (though, oddly, *Nut Rocker* never succumbed), (b) their lyrics were deemed offensive because of a concern with sex, drugs, death, or politics, or (c) they mentioned commercial trade names, which was reckoned to be against the BBC's charter. Most of those on the list were adjudged to be in category (b) – and yet they all became Top 10 hits regardless. (A sign of the changing times: George Michael's disc was banned only from daytime play, but permitted after the 9 pm "watershed".) Numerous potentially offensive records remained unbanned since no one in authority understood their lyrics . . . .

T O P 1 0

JUKEBOX SINGLES OF ALL TIME IN THE USA

1 Patsy Cline, *Crazy* (1962)

2 Bob Seger, *Old Time Rock 'n' Roll* (1979)

3 Elvis Presley, *Hound Dog/Don't Be Cruel* (1956)

4 Marvin Gaye, *I Heard It Through The Grapevine* (1968)

5 Bobby Darin, *Mack The Knife* (1959)

6 Bill Haley & His Comets, *Rock Around The Clock* (1955)

7 Doors, *Light My Fire* (1967)

8 Otis Redding, *(Sittin' On) The Dock Of The Bay* (1968)

9 Temptations, *My Girl* (1965)

10 Frank Sinatra, *New York, New York* (1980)

This list was compiled in 1992 by the Amusement and Music Operators Association, whose members service and operate over 250,000 jukeboxes in the USA, and is based on the estimated popularity of jukebox singles from 1950 to the present day. The list is updated every three years: 1989's chart-topper was the double A-side *Hound Dog/Don't Be Cruel*, while the Righteous Brothers' *Unchained Melody* was the highest new entry into the Top 40 in 1992 (at No. 12), due, not least, to its rebirth as the featured song in the hit movie *Ghost*.

T O P 1 0

THE FIRST 10 "OLDIES" USED ON LEVI'S TV COMMERCIALS IN THE UK

1 Marvin Gaye, *I Heard It Through The Grapevine*

2 Sam Cooke, *Wonderful World*

3 Ben E. King, *Stand By Me*

4 Percy Sledge, *When A Man Loves A Woman*

5 Eddie Cochran, *C'Mon Everybody*

6 Muddy Waters, *Mannish Boy*

7 Ronettes, *Be My Baby*

8 B.B. King, *Ain't Nobody Home*

9 Bad Company, *Can't Get Enough*

10 Steve Miller Band, *The Joker*

In 1986, Levi's jeans began to use hit records from the past as the soundtracks to their UK TV commercials. This proved beneficial not only to Levi's sales, but to the fortunes of the singles that were reissued to capitalize on this exposure. Ben E. King and Steve Miller reached No. 1 (as did the 11th track used, the Clash's *Should I Stay Or Should I Go?*), and only the Ronettes' single failed completely, through not being reissued. Sadly, this latter-day success came too late for several of the featured artists, as the re-releases of the songs by Marvin Gaye, Sam Cooke, Eddy Cochran, and Muddy Waters were all posthumous.

T O P 1 0

KARAOKE TUNES

1 *You've Lost That Lovin' Feelin'*

2 *I Will Survive*

3 *Like a Virgin*

4 *Summer Nights*

5 *Love Shack*

6 *New York, New York*

7 *Pretty Woman*

8 *Should I Stay Or Should I Go?*

9 *It's Not Unusual*

10 *My Way*

T O P 1 0

ONE-HIT WONDERS IN THE UK

1 Simon Park Orchestra, *Eye Level* (1973)

2 Archies, *Sugar Sugar* (1969)

3 Clive Dunn, *Grandad* (1971)

4 Joe Dolce, *Shaddap You Face* (1981)

5 St Winifred's School Choir, *There's No One Quite Like Grandma* (1980)

6 Lena Martell, *One Day At A Time* (1979)

7 Phyllis Nelson, *Move Closer* (1985)

8 Lee Marvin, *Wand'rin' Star* (1970)

9 Norman Greenbaum, *Spirit In The Sky* (1970)

10 Robin Beck, *First Time* (1988)

These are all singles that were No. 1 hits in the UK, but which the artist then failed to follow with a record in the charts at any position. It is actually quite difficult to have a hit which, as in the case of this entire Top 10, sells more than 500,000 copies, and then fail to interest even a few thousand people in something with theoretically similar appeal, but clearly it can be done.

TOP 10

MOST FREQUENTLY RECORDED SONGS IN THE US, 1900–50

	Title	Year first recorded
1	*St Louis Blues*	1914
2	*Tea For Two*	1924
3	*Body And Soul*	1930
4	*After You've Gone*	1918
5	*How High The Moon*	1940
6	*Blue Skies*	1927
7	*Dinah*	1925
8	*Ain't Misbehavin'*	1929
9	*Honeysuckle Rose*	1929
10	*Stardust*	1929

TOP 10

WORST RECORDS OF ALL TIME?

1	Jimmy Cross, *I Want My Baby Back*
2	Zara Leander, *Wunderbar*
3	Legendary Stardust Cowboy, *Paralysed*
4	Pat Campbell, *The Deal*
5	Nervous Norvus, *Transfusion*
6	Jess Conrad, *This Pullover*
7	Mel & Dave, *Spinning Wheel*
8	Dickey Lee, *Laurie*
9	Mrs Miller, *A Lover's Concerto*
10	Tania Day, *I Get So Lonely*

In 1978, London Capital Radio DJ Kenny Everett polled his listeners on their least favourite songs from the discs he regularly played in a "ghastly records" spot. From 6,000 replies, these were the Top (or Bottom) 10, which went on to headline a special "All-Time Worst" show. Mostly obscure before Everett dragged them up, several of these have since become bywords of bad taste on vinyl, particularly Jimmy Cross's 1965 tale of necrophiliac love which proudly tops this grisly list.

TOP 10

FIRST WORDS OF POPULAR SONGS

	Word	Incidence		Word	Incidence
1	I	226	9	Oh	48
2	My	115	10=	If	46
3	I'm	94	10=	I'll	46
4	When	93			
5	You	72			
6=	It's	58			
6=	Little	58			
8	In	55			

This Top 10 is based on a survey of about 6,500 popular songs published or released as records in the period 1900–75. If all the variants of "I" (I, I'd, I'll, I'm, and I've) are combined, the total goes up to 405.

TOP 10

UK CHART SINGLES WITH THE LONGEST TITLES

	Title	Artist	Highest position	Year	No. of letters
1	*I'm In Love With The Girl On A Certain Manchester Megastore Checkout Desk*	Freshies	54	1981	60
2	*If I Said You Had A Beautiful Body Would You Hold It Against Me?*	Bellamy Brothers	3	1979	50
3	*Gilly Gilly Ossenfeffer Katzenallen Bogen By The Sea*	Max Bygraves	7	1954	45
4=	*There's A Guy Works Down The Chipshop Swears He's Elvis*	Kirsty MacColl	14	1981	44
4=	*Have You Seen Your Mother Baby, Standing In The Shadow?*	Rolling Stones	5	1966	44
6	*When The Girl In Your Arms Is The Girl In Your Heart*	Cliff Richard	3	1961	41
7	*I'm Gonna Sit Right Down And Write Myself A Letter*	Billy Williams / Barry Manilow	22 / 36	1957 / 1982	40 / 40
8=	*Loving You's A Dirty Job But Someone's Got To Do It*	Bonnie Tyler	73	1985	39
8=	*Itsy Bitsy Teeny Weeny Yellow Polka Dot Bikini*	Bryan Hyland	8	1960	39
8=	*You Don't Have To Be In The Army To Fight In The War*	Mungo Jerry	13	1971	39
8=	*Two Pints Of Lager And A Packet Of Crisps Please*	Splodgenessabounds	7	1980	39

This list includes only titles that do not contain words or phrases in brackets. It also includes only chart hits, and thus does not contain such memorable gems as *How Could You Believe Me When I Said "I Love You", When You Know I've Been A Liar All My Life* (69 letters), *There's Something Nice About Everyone, But Everything's Nice About You* (57), and *Where Did Robinson Crusoe Go With Friday On Saturday Night?* (49) – and not forgetting Fairport Convention's 172-letter album track, *Sir B. MacKenzie's Daughter's Lament For The 77th Mounted Lancers' Retreat From The Straits Of Loch Knombe In The Year Of Our Lord 1717, On The Occasion Of The Announcement Of Her Marriage To The Laird Of Kinleakie*.

LONG PLAYERS

T O P   1 0

ALBUMS OF ALL TIME IN THE USA

1	Michael Jackson, *Thriller*
2	Fleetwood Mac, *Rumours*
3	Soundtrack, *Saturday Night Fever*
4	Pink Floyd, *Dark Side of The Moon*
5	Bruce Springsteen, *Born in the USA*
6	Soundtrack, *The Bodyguard*
7	Prince, *Purple Rain*
8	Lionel Richie, *Can't Slow Down*
9	MC Hammer, *Please Hammer, Don't Hurt 'Em*
10	Soundtrack, *Dirty Dancing*

Thriller's US sales are over 20,000,000, so it will take a mighty album indeed ever to catch it up. The rest of this field, all of which have sold in excess of 10,000,000 copies apiece, are well behind by comparison, with second-placed *Rumours* having sold between 13,000,000 and 14,000,000 copies, and *Saturday Night Fever*, in third place, between 11,000,000 and 12,000,000. A lot of these albums were originally released before the CD age, so have benefited from "second copy" buying, as people replace favourite old vinyl copies with compact discs.

BEATLES AND FRIENDS
Originally released in 1967, Sgt Pepper's Lonely Hearts Club Band has clocked up sales of around 25 million copies.

DID YOU KNOW

40 YEARS OF THE LP

Although there were several earlier attempts to introduce long-playing records, the first successful product was the 12-inch 33⅓-rpm vinyl album, with 23 minutes of recorded sound on each side, publicly launched in June 1948. LPs were first sold in the UK in August 1950. The death-knell of the vinyl album was sounded on 1 March 1983, however, when the first compact disc players went on sale in Europe. By 1988 compact disc sales in the UK had overtaken those of vinyl, and by 1990 CDs were selling more than 60,000,000 a year.

T O P   1 0

ALBUMS OF ALL TIME WORLDWIDE

1	Michael Jackson, *Thriller*
2	Soundtrack, *The Bodyguard*
3	Soundtrack, *Saturday Night Fever*
4	Beatles, *Sgt Pepper's Lonely Hearts Club Band*
5	Soundtrack, *Grease*
6	Simon and Garfunkel, *Bridge Over Troubled Water*
7	Bruce Springsteen, *Born in the USA*
8	Soundtrack, *The Sound of Music*
9	Fleetwood Mac, *Rumours*
10	Dire Straits, *Brothers in Arms*

Total worldwide sales of albums have traditionally been notoriously hard to gauge, but even with the huge expansion of the album market during the 1980s, and multiple million sales of many major releases, this Top 10 is still élite territory, the sales of the entries being between 20,000,000 and 25,000,000 globally, with *The Bodyguard* near 26,000,000, and the apparently uncatchable *Thriller* on 40,000,000.

T O P   1 0

CDs OF ALL TIME IN THE UK

1 Simply Red, *Stars*

2 Michael Jackson, *Bad*

3 Dire Straits, *Brothers in Arms*

4 Queen, *Greatest Hits*

5 Michael Jackson, *Thriller*

6 Phil Collins, *. . . But Seriously*

7 Madonna, *The Immaculate Collection*

8 Whitney Houston, *Whitney*

9 Fleetwood Mac, *Tango in the Night*

10 Whitney Houston,
Soundtrack, *The Bodyguard*

After two years as the UK best-selling album, most of those sales being on the CD format, Simply Red's *Stars* became, by the end of 1992, the top UK CD seller to date. Meanwhile, new to the Top 10 is a second Whitney Houston entry, in the shape of the soundtrack to her film with Kevin Costner, *The Bodyguard*.

T O P   1 0

ACTS WITH THE MOST CHART ALBUMS IN THE UK

(To 31 March 1994)

	Artist	Albums
1	Elvis Presley	95
2	James Last	57
3	Frank Sinatra	51
4	Cliff Richard	49
5	Rolling Stones	38
6	Bob Dylan	36
7=	Elton John	32
7=	Diana Ross	32
9	Shirley Bassey	30
10	David Bowie	29

T O P   1 0

ALBUMS OF ALL TIME IN THE UK

1 Beatles,
Sgt Pepper's Lonely Hearts Club Band

2 Michael Jackson, *Bad*

3 Dire Straits, *Brothers in Arms*

4 Queen, *Greatest Hits*

5 Simply Red, *Stars*

6 Michael Jackson, *Thriller*

7 Phil Collins, *. . . But Seriously*

8 Simon and Garfunkel,
Bridge Over Troubled Water

9 Simon and Garfunkel, *Greatest Hits*

10 Fleetwood Mac, *Rumours*

On the occasion of the album's 25th anniversary in 1992, EMI Records conducted new research into the sales of *Sgt Pepper* and concluded that it had sold over 4,250,000 copies in the UK, substantially more than *Brothers in Arms*, which was previously thought to have bettered it. Michael Jackson's *Bad* has now also overtaken *Brothers*, with UK sales of a fraction over 4,000,000 to Dire Straits' 3,600,000. Queen, Simply Red, and Michael Jackson (*Thriller*) albums have each sold over 3,000,000 copies, while all the others in this list have achieved UK sales in excess of 2,500,000.

DID YOU KNOW

SLOWEST TO REACH NO. 1 IN UK ALBUM CHARTS

The Tyrannosaurus Rex album *My People Were Fair and Had Sky in Their Hair, But Now They're Content to Wear Stars on Their Brows* is not only the album with the longest title ever to chart in the UK, but is also the slowest album ever to rise to No. 1 in the UK. Originally charting in July 1968, it had to wait until the heyday of T. Rex (as they had then become) in May 1972 to re-chart as one half of a double album re-package with *Prophets, Seers and Sages, The Angels of the Ages*. It finally hit No. 1 199 weeks (nearly four years) after its first chart appearance. Only three other albums have taken longer than a year to hit pole position after they first appeared on the UK charts: Elvis Presley's *40 Greatest Hits* (114 weeks), *Fame: The Original Soundtrack* (98 weeks), and Mike Oldfield's *Tubular Bells* (65 weeks). The latter is also the most successful pop instrumental album of all time. Two further slow climbers to No. 1 in the UK, Fleetwood Mac's *Rumours* (49 weeks) and Bruce Springsteen's *Born in the USA* (36 weeks), also appear in the Top 10 Albums Of All Time Worldwide.

T O P   1 0

ALBUMS THAT STAYED LONGEST IN THE UK CHARTS

(To 31 March 1994)

	Artist/title	First year in chart
1	Fleetwood Mac, *Rumours*	1977
2	Meat Loaf, *Bat Out of Hell*	1978
3	Original Cast, *The Sound of Music*	1965
4	Queen, *Greatest Hits*	1981
5	Simon and Garfunkel, *Bridge Over Troubled Water*	1970
6	Pink Floyd, *Dark Side of the Moon*	1973
7	Original Cast, *South Pacific*	1958
8	Simon and Garfunkel, *Greatest Hits*	1972
9	Phil Collins, *Face Value*	1981
10	Mike Oldfield, *Tubular Bells*	1973

The 10 longest-staying records virtually took up residence in the album charts (the Top 50, 75, or 100, depending on the years during which the charts were compiled), remaining there for periods ranging from over five years for *Tubular Bells* to the astonishing nine-year occupation by Meat Loaf's *Bat Out of Hell*.

ALBUMS OF THE DECADES

TOP 10

ALBUMS OF EACH YEAR OF THE 1960s IN THE UK

1960	Soundtrack, *South Pacific*
1961	Elvis Presley, *G.I. Blues*
1962	Soundtrack, *West Side Story*
1963	Beatles, *With The Beatles*
1964	Beatles, *Beatles For Sale*
1965	Soundtrack, *The Sound Of Music*
1966	Soundtrack, *The Sound Of Music*
1967	Beatles, *Sgt Pepper's Lonely Hearts Club Band*
1968	Soundtrack, *The Sound Of Music*
1969	Beatles, *Abbey Road*

TOP 10

ALBUMS OF EACH YEAR OF THE 1970s IN THE UK

1970	Simon and Garfunkel, *Bridge Over Troubled Water*
1971	Simon and Garfunkel, *Bridge Over Troubled Water*
1972	Various Artists, *20 Dynamic Hits*
1973	Elton John, *Don't Shoot Me, I'm Only The Piano Player*
1974	Carpenters, *The Singles, 1969–1973*
1975	Stylistics, *The Best Of The Stylistics*
1976	Abba, *Greatest Hits*
1977	Abba, *Arrival*
1978	Soundtrack, *Saturday Night Fever*
1979	Supertramp, *Breakfast In America*

DID YOU KNOW

ALBUM HITS OF THE 1950s

The LP boom began in 1948. Album charts were not published in the UK in the 1950s, but those from the US were dominated by Original Cast and Soundtrack recordings, led by *South Pacific* (1958), and *My Fair Lady* (1956). Elvis Presley had the seventh bestselling album of the decade – *Elvis Presley* (1956).

TOP 10

ALBUMS OF EACH YEAR OF THE 1980s IN THE UK

1980	Abba, *Super Trouper*	1985	Dire Straits, *Brothers In Arms*
1981	Adam & The Ants, *Kings Of The Wild Frontier*	1986	Madonna, *True Blue*
1982	Barbra Streisand, *Love Songs*	1987	Michael Jackson, *Bad*
1983	Michael Jackson, *Thriller*	1988	Kylie Minogue, *Kylie*
1984	Lionel Richie, *Can't Slow Down*	1989	Jason Donovan, *Ten Good Reasons*

DID YOU KNOW

LISTENER'S CHOICE

The recent introduction of the compact disc-playing jukebox has opened a new chapter in the century-old story. This began with a hand-operated Edison phonograph with a coinbox and four listening tubes that was unveiled at the Palais Royal Saloon, San Francisco on 23 November 1889. The word "jukebox" first appeared in print in *Time* magazine of 27 November 1939, in a feature on bandleader Glenn Miller. Wurlitzer, the best-known manufacturer of jukeboxes, dominated the market in the post-war period. In the 1950s the introduction of the 45-rpm single revolutionized the design of the jukebox, and models from this period are now highly prized by collectors for their decorative appearance and nostalgic associations.

TOP 10

ALBUMS OF THE 1960s IN THE UK

1 Beatles, *Sgt Pepper's Lonely Hearts Club Band* (1967)

2 Various, *The Sound Of Music (Original Soundtrack)* (1965)

3 Beatles, *With The Beatles* (1963)

4 Beatles, *Abbey Road* (1969)

5 Various, *South Pacific (Original Soundtrack)* (1958)

6 Beatles, *Beatles For Sale* (1964)

7 Beatles, *A Hard Day's Night* (1964)

8 Beatles, *Rubber Soul* (1965)

9 Beatles, *The Beatles ("White Album")* (1968)

10 Various, *West Side Story* (1962)

Not only did the Beatles dominate the Top 10, but three further albums of theirs, *Revolver, Please Please Me*, and *Help!*, were also the 11th, 12th, and 13th bestselling albums of a decade that belonged to the most successful group in pop history. Meanwhile, the success of *South Pacific* continued: released before the 1960s began, but with 262 weeks on the chart, 31 of them at No. 1, it clocked up sufficient sales to warrant its place as fifth bestselling album of the decade.

TOP 10

ALBUMS OF THE 1970s IN THE UK

1 Simon and Garfunkel, *Bridge Over Troubled Water* (1970)

2 Simon and Garfunkel, *Simon And Garfunkel's Greatest Hits* (1972)

3 Fleetwood Mac, *Rumours* (1977)

4 Pink Floyd, *Dark Side Of The Moon* (1973)

5 Mike Oldfield, *Tubular Bells* (1973)

6 Abba, *Greatest Hits* (1976)

7 Meat Loaf, *Bat Out Of Hell* (1978)

8 Various, *Saturday Night Fever (Original Soundtrack)* (1978)

9 Perry Como, *And I Love You So* (1973)

10 Carpenters, *The Singles 1969–1973* (1974)

Each of the top five albums of the 1970s clocked up over 250 weeks on the British chart, with Fleetwood Mac's *Rumours* outdistancing them all with an astonishing 443 weeks on the survey. The success of *Tubular Bells*, recorded by Mike Oldfield for a pittance, boosted the fortunes of the Virgin record company, and so formed the foundation of the business empire run by Virgin label boss Richard Branson.

TOP 10

ALBUMS OF THE 1980s IN THE UK

1 Dire Straits, *Brothers In Arms* (1985)

2 Michael Jackson, *Bad* (1987)

3 Michael Jackson, *Thriller* (1982)

4 Queen, *Greatest Hits* (1981)

5 Kylie Minogue, *Kylie* (1988)

6 Whitney Houston, *Whitney* (1987)

7 Fleetwood Mac, *Tango In The Night* (1987)

8 Phil Collins, *No Jacket Required* (1985)

9 Madonna, *True Blue* (1986)

10 U2, *The Joshua Tree* (1987)

While Michael Jackson's *Thriller* was his bestselling album in most countries around the world (and, of course, the bestselling global album of all time), British buyers eventually preferred *Bad*. Fleetwood Mac is the only group to feature on the bestseller lists in two decades, their achievement with *Rumours* in the 1970s being followed by success with *Tango in the Night*. As the 1990s commenced, for the first time ever, classical albums began to sell in sufficient numbers to enable violinist Nigel Kennedy and tenors José Carreras, Placido Domingo, and Luciano Pavarotti to rub shoulders with pop stars.

ALBUM GREATS

TOP 10

"GREATEST HITS" ALBUMS OF ALL TIME IN THE UK

1 Queen, *Greatest Hits*

2 Simon and Garfunkel, *Simon And Garfunkel's Greatest Hits*

3 Abba, *Abba's Greatest Hits*

4 Dire Straits, *Money For Nothing*

5 Queen, *Greatest Hits II*

6 Madonna, *The Immaculate Collection*

7 Carpenters, *The Singles, 1969–1973*

8 Beach Boys, *20 Golden Greats*

9 Bob Marley & The Wailers, *Legend*

10 Cliff Richard, *Private Collection, 1977–1988*

Some of the biggest of these hits compilations have achieved truly immense sales in the UK – far more, in many cases, than the hit singles they anthologize. All the albums here have sold at least 1,500,000 copies, while Queen's *Greatest Hits* (its sales boosted by Freddie Mercury's death) has topped 3,000,000, and Simon and Garfunkel's compilation is on 2,500,000.

TOP 10

POP INSTRUMENTAL ALBUMS OF ALL TIME IN THE UK

1 Mike Oldfield, *Tubular Bells*

2 Shadows, *20 Golden Greats*

3 Jean Michel Jarre, *Oxygène*

4 Shadows, *String Of Hits*

5 Sky, *Sky 2*

6 Vangelis, *Chariots Of Fire*

7 Mike Oldfield, *Tubular Bells II*

8 Sky, *Sky*

9 Mike Oldfield, *Hergest Ridge*

10 Shadows, *Moonlight Shadows*

A handful of names have dominated the purely instrumental field for many years, the longest-established being the Shadows, who had their first No. 1 album as long ago as 1961. Mike Oldfield's *Tubular Bells*, with sales of more than 2,000,000, looks unlikely ever to be seriously challenged by another non-vocal recording – his own later *Tubular Bells II* has mustered no more than a quarter of the sales of the original.

TOP 10

ORIGINAL SOUNDTRACK ALBUMS OF ALL TIME IN THE UK

1	*The Sound of Music*	1965
2	*Saturday Night Fever*	1978
3	*Grease*	1978
4	*Dirty Dancing*	1987
5	*South Pacific*	1958
6	*West Side Story*	1962
7	*The Bodyguard*	1992
8	*Top Gun*	1986
9	*A Star is Born*	1977
10	*Fame*	1980

The Beatles' *A Hard Day's Night* and *Help!* albums have been excluded from this list because only one side of each contained the film's soundtrack songs, the remainder in each case being made up of new non-movie material. If included, they would stand at Nos. 6 and 10, and *A Star is Born* and *Fame* would disappear.

WE ARE THE CHAMPIONS
Queen's Greatest Hits *album topped the UK chart in November 1981 and stayed there for 312 weeks, returning within weeks of lead singer Freddy Mercury's death ten years later.*

GREASE IS THE WORD
John Travolta starred in both Saturday Night Fever *and* Grease. *From the latter, two duets with Olivia Newton-John,* You're The One That I Want *and* Summer Nights, *were No. 1 singles in the UK.*

T O P 1 0

HEAVY METAL ALBUMS OF ALL TIME IN THE UK

1	Meat Loaf, *Bat Out of Hell*
2	Meat Loaf, *Bat Out of Hell II – Back to Hell*
3	Led Zeppelin, *Led Zeppelin II*
4	Def Leppard, *Hysteria*
5	Led Zeppelin, *Led Zeppelin IV*
6	Bryan Adams, *So Far So Good*
7	ZZ Top, *Eliminator*
8	Guns N' Roses, *Appetite For Destruction*
9	Bon Jovi, *Slippery When Wet*
10	AC/DC, *Back In Black*

Unlike its 1993 sequel, which made No.1 in the UK, *Bat Out Of Hell* only ever peaked at UK No. 9, but logged an impressive 470 weeks on the chart, an achievement split over three decades. Between 1969 and 1979, Led Zeppelin hit UK No. 1 with each of their eight albums from *Led Zeppelin II* right up to *In Through The Out Door.*

REPEAT PERFORMANCE
Meat Loaf had a huge success with Bat Out Of Hell. *Released in the UK in 1978, it was still in the album charts when its sequel,* Bat Out Of Hell II, *came out in 1993.*

T O P 1 0

COUNTRY ALBUMS OF ALL TIME IN THE UK

1	Johnny Cash, *Johnny Cash At San Quentin*
2	Glen Campbell, *20 Golden Greats*
3	John Denver, *The Best Of John Denver*
4	Jim Reeves, *40 Golden Greats*
5	Don Williams, *Images*
6	Glen Campbell, *Greatest Hits*
7	Slim Whitman, *The Very Best Of Slim Whitman*
8	Tammy Wynette, *The Best Of Tammy Wynette*
9	John Denver, *Live In London*
10	Johnny Cash, *Johnny Cash Live At Folsom Prison*

Of Johnny Cash's two celebrated live albums recorded at two of America's most severe penal institutions, the San Quentin release holds the record for the longest-charting Country album in UK chart history with 114 weeks notched up between 1969 and 1971. Country music sales in the UK and elsewhere have never matched those in its native United States, and usually benefit only in a "greatest hits" package: Garth Brooks, for example, the top-selling Country artist in the US, has sold more than 20,000,000 albums there in the past four years, compared with a few hundred thousand across the whole of Europe.

THE MAN IN BLACK
Johnny Cash (b. 1932) is one of the most consistently successful Country stars. His live album Johnny Cash at San Quentin *first charted in the UK in 1969 and remained there for 114 weeks.*

MUSIC ON RADIO AND TV

T O P 1 0

SINGLES REVIEWED BY THE BEATLES ON *JUKE BOX JURY*

Single	Hit/miss	Highest chart position
1 Chants, *I Could Write a Book*	Hit (4–0)	–
2 Elvis Presley, *Kiss Me Quick*	Hit (4–0)	14
3 Swinging Blue Jeans, *Hippy Hippy Shake*	Hit (4–0)	2
4 Paul Anka, *Did You Have a Happy Birthday?*	Miss (0–4)	–
5 Shirley Ellis, *The Nitty Gritty*	Miss (0–4)	–
6 Steve Lawrence and Eydie Gorme, *I Can't Stop Talking About You*	Hit (3–1)*	–
7 Billy Fury, *Do You Really Love Me Too?*	Hit (4–0)	13
8 Bobby Vinton, *There, I've Said It Again*	Miss (0–4)	34
9 Orchids, *Love Hit Me*	Miss (1–3)	–
10 Merseybeats, *I Think of You*	Hit (4–0)	5

* Dissenting vote from John who said, "They're getting on a bit – I don't like it."

The four Beatles appeared on BBC television's *Juke Box Jury* on 7 December 1963, the first time a group had constituted the entire panel. They discussed and voted upon the likely hit potential of 10 singles introduced by DJ David Jacobs, and were accurate in their predictions on seven of the records.

T O P 1 0

WORKS ON CLASSIC FM, 1993

Work	Plays
1 Henryk Górecki, *Symphony of Sorrowful Songs*, 2nd movement	78
2= Georg Friedrich Handel, *Music for the Royal Fireworks*, Minuet and Trio	52
2= Richard Wagner, *Lohengrin*, Prelude to Act II	52
4= Antonio Vivaldi, Flute Concerto, 1st movement	47
4= Jacques Offenbach, *La Vie Parisienne*	47
4= Carl Ziehrer, *The Dancing Temptress*, Op. 4	47
4= Franz Lehár, *The Merry Widow*, Overture	47
8= Jeremiah Clarke, *The King's March*	42
8= Antonio Vivaldi, *Piccolo Concerto*	42
8= Aram Khachaturian, *Masquerade Suite – Galop*	42

T O P 1 0

OF *YOUR HUNDRED BEST TUNES*

1 Georges Bizet, *In the Depths of the Temple* from *The Pearl Fishers*

2 Max Bruch, Adagio from Violin Concerto No. 1 in G Minor

3 Giuseppe Verdi, *Chorus of the Hebrew Slaves* from *Nabucco*

4 Sir Edward Elgar, *Nimrod*, from *Enigma Variations*

5 Ludwig van Beethoven, Final movement from Symphony No. 6 ("Pastoral")

6 Jean Sibelius, *Finlandia*

7 Wolfgang Amadeus Mozart, Andante from Piano Concerto No. 21

8 Pietro Mascagni, Intermezzo from *Cavaleria Rusticana*

9 Sergei Rachmaninov, Piano Concerto No. 2 in C Minor

10 Georg Friedrich Handel, Hallelujah Chorus from *Messiah*

The Top 10 comes from the BBC Radio 2 programme's 1993 listeners' poll of all-time favourites.

T O P 1 0

COMPOSERS ON CLASSIC FM, 1993

Composer	Approx. total plays
1 Wolfgang Amadeus Mozart	1,930
2 Johann Sebastian Bach	1,700
3 Ludwig van Beethoven	1,670
4 Joseph Haydn	1,470
5 Peter Ilyich Tchaikovsky	1,420
6 Georg Friedrich Handel	1,360
7 Giuseppe Verdi	1,100
8 Franz Schubert	1,090
9 Felix Mendelssohn	1,050
10 Johannes Brahms	1,010

T O P 1 0

MOST REQUESTED RECORDS ON *DESERT ISLAND DISCS*

1 Ludwig van Beethoven, *O Freunds, nicht diese Tone* (chorus) from Symphony No. 9

2 Claude Debussy, *Claire de Lune*

3 Edward Elgar, *Pomp and Circumstance*, March No. 1

4 Richard Wagner, Liebestod from *Tristan und Isolde*

5 George Gershwin, *Rhapsody in Blue*

6 Johann Christian Bach/Charles François Gounod, *Ave Maria*

7 Felix Mendelssohn, Nocturne from *A Midsummer Night's Dream*

8 Ludwig van Beethoven, Symphony No. 5

9 Georg Friedrich Handel, Hallelujah Chorus from *Messiah*

10 Giuseppe Verdi, Dies Irae from *Requiem*

The Beethoven at No. 1 has been requested by more than 60 of the eminent "castaways" in the programme's 52-year history. No pop music title appears in the Top 20, although the Beatles are showing signs of catching up their classical counterparts.

POPULAR AS EVER
Wolfgang Amadeus Mozart was Classic FM's most played composer in 1993, with almost 2,000 broadcasts of works by him in the course of the year.

T O P 1 0

BBC RADIO 1 LISTENERS' FAVOURITE ALBUMS OF ALL TIME

1	Simply Red, *Stars*	1991
2	Beatles, *Sgt Pepper's Lonely Hearts Club Band*	1967
3	U2, *The Joshua Tree*	1987
4	Meat Loaf, *Bat out of Hell*	1978
5	Pink Floyd, *Dark Side of the Moon*	1973
6	R.E.M., *Out of Time*	1991
7	Michael Jackson, *Thriller*	1982
8	Dire Straits, *Brothers in Arms*	1985
9	R.E.M., *Automatic for the People*	1992
10	Nirvana, *Nevermind*	1991

The Top 10 comes from an "All-time Top 100" chart compiled in 1993 by Radio 1 and the *Daily Mail* from some 35,000 votes cast. There is a mixture of classic and relative newcomers – some surprising omissions from the Top 100 are Whitney Houston, the Rolling Stones, Stevie Wonder, and Tina Turner.

T O P 1 0

SINGLES OF TV THEME TUNES IN THE UK

	Artist/title	Programme
1	Mr Acker Bilk, *Stranger on the Shore*	*Stranger On The Shore*
2	Simon Park Orchestra, *Eye Level*	*Van Der Valk*
3	Wombles, *The Wombling Song*	*The Wombles*
4	TV Cast, *The Army Game*	*The Army Game*
5	Cilla Black, *Something Tells Me*	*The Cilla Black Show*
6	Dennis Waterman, *I Could Be So Good for You*	*Minder*
7	Elmer Bernstein, *Staccato's Theme*	*Johnny Staccato*
8	Clannad, *Theme From Harry's Game*	*Harry's Game*
9	Gheorghe Zamfir, *Doina De Jale*	*Light Of Experience*
10	Jan Hammer, *Miami Vice Theme*	*Miami Vice*

These themes, equally divided between instrumentals and vocal, cover more than 30 years of British TV shows. All those listed here were Top 5 hits following exposure on the programme concerned, and the top two not only both reached No. 1 on the chart, but also each sold over 1,000,000 in the UK. One or two of the records have also decidedly outgrown their parent shows – who today still recalls the 1961 children's drama series *Stranger on the Shore*?

MUSIC IN THE SALEROOM

John Lennon's 30-year-old jacket fetched £24,200 at auction.

TOP 10

MOST EXPENSIVE ITEMS OF POP MEMORABILIA EVER SOLD AT AUCTION

(Excluding rock stars' clothing – see previous list)

	Item/sale	Price (£)*
1	John Lennon's 1965 Rolls-Royce Phantom V touring limousine, finished in psychedelic paintwork Sotheby's, New York, 29 June 1985 ($2,299,000)	1,768,462
2	Acoustic guitar owned by David Bowie, Paul McCartney, and George Michael Christie's, London, 18 May 1994	220,000
3	Jimi Hendrix's Fender *Stratocaster* electric guitar Sotheby's, London, 25 April 1990	198,000
4	Buddy Holly's Gibson acoustic guitar, *c.*1945, in a tooled leather case made by Holly Sotheby's, New York, 23 June 1990 ($242,000)	139,658
5	John Lennon's 1970 Mercedes-Benz 600 Pullman four-door limousine Christie's, London, 27 April 1989	137,500
6	Elvis Presley's 1963 Rolls-Royce Phantom V touring limousine Sotheby's, London, 28 August 1986	110,000
7	Elvis Presley's 1942 Martin D-18 guitar (used to record his first singles, 1954–56) Red Baron Antiques, Atlanta, Georgia, 3 October 1991 ($180,000). The same guitar was resold by Christie's, London, 14 May 1993 for £99,000.	106,825
8	Buddy Holly's Fender *Stratocaster* electric guitar, 1958 Sotheby's, New York, 23 June 1990 ($110,000)	63,481
9	John Lennon's handwritten lyrics for *A Day In The Life* Sotheby's, London, 27 August 1992	48,400
10	Elton John's 1977 Panther de Ville Coupé Sotheby's, London, 22 August 1991	46,200

* *Including 10 per cent buyer's premium, where appropriate.*

Pioneered particularly by Sotheby's in London, pop memorabilia has become big business – especially if it involves personal association with mega-stars such as the Beatles and, latterly, Buddy Holly (whose spectacles were sold by Sotheby's, New York, 23 June 1990 for $45,100/£30,000). In addition to the Top 10, high prices have also been paid for other musical instruments once owned by notable rock stars, such as a guitar belonging to John Entwistle of the Who and pianos formerly owned by Paul McCartney and John Lennon.

TOP 10

MOST EXPENSIVE ITEMS OF ROCK STARS' CLOTHING SOLD AT AUCTION IN THE UK

	Item/sale	Price (£)*
1	Elvis Presley's one-piece "Shooting Star" stage outfit, *c.*1972 Phillips, London, 24 August 1988	28,600
2	John Lennon's black leather jacket, *c.*1960–62 Christie's, London, 7 May 1992	24,200
3	Four "super hero"-style costumes worn by glam rock group Kiss in the film *Kiss Meets the Phantom* (1978) Christie's, London, 14 May 1993	20,900
4	Michael Jackson's white rhinestone glove Christie's, London, 19 December 1991	16,500
5	Elvis Presley's blue stage costume, *c.*1972 Phillips, London, 24 August 1988	15,400
6	Jimi Hendrix's black felt hat Sotheby's, London, 22 August 1991	14,300
7	Elvis Presley's one-piece stage costume, as worn on the cover of his *Burning Love* album Phillips, London, 25 August 1992	13,200
8	Elton John's giant Dr Marten boots from the film *Tommy* Sotheby's, London, 6 September 1988	12,100
9=	Michael Jackson's black sequinned jacket Sotheby's, London, 22 August 1991	11,000
9=	Prince's *Purple Rain* stage costume, 1984 Christie's, London, 19 December 1991	11,000

* *Including 10 per cent buyer's premium.*

TOP 10

MOST EXPENSIVE MUSIC MANUSCRIPTS EVER SOLD AT AUCTION

	Manuscript/sale	Price (£)*
1	Nine symphonies by Wolfgang Amadeus Mozart Sotheby's, London, 22 May 1987	2,350,000
2	Ludwig van Beethoven's Piano Sonata in E Minor, Opus 90 Sotheby's, London, 6 December 1991	1,000,000
3=	Robert Schumann's Piano Concerto in A Minor, Opus 54 Sotheby's, London, 22 November 1989	800,000
3=	Wolfgang Amadeus Mozart's Fantasia in C Minor and Sonata in C Minor Sotheby's, London, 21 November 1990	800,000
5	Ludwig van Beethoven's first movement of the Sonata for Violoncello and Piano in A Major, Opus 69 Sotheby's, London, 17 May 1990	480,000
6	Johann Sebastian Bach's cantata *Auf Christi Himmelfahrt allein* Sotheby's, London, 22 November 1989	390,000
7	Igor Stravinsky's *Rite of Spring* Sotheby's, London, 11 November 1982	300,000
8	Henry Purcell, 21 pieces for the harpsichord (the highest price for a British manuscript) Sotheby's, London, 26 May 1994	276,500
9	Franz Schubert's Quartet in B flat Major (No. 8) D.112, Opus 168 Christie's, London, 24 June 1992	270,000
10	Johann Sebastian Bach's cantata *O Ewigkeit, Du Donnerwort* Sotheby's, London, 11 November 1982	190,000

* "Hammer prices", excluding premiums.

The collection of nine symphonies by Mozart not only holds the record for the highest price ever paid for a music manuscript, but also for any post-medieval manuscript.

TOP 10

MOST EXPENSIVE MUSICAL INSTRUMENTS EVER SOLD AT AUCTION

	Instrument/sale	Price (£)*
1	"Mendelssohn" Stradivarius violin Christie's, London, 21 November 1990	902,000
2	"Cholmondley" Stradivarius violoncello Sotheby's, London, 22 June 1988	682,000
3	Acoustic guitar owned by David Bowie, Paul McCartney, and George Michael Christie's, London, 18 May 1994	220,000
4	Jimi Hendrix's Fender *Stratocaster* electric guitar Sotheby's, London, 25 April 1990	198,000
5	Steinway grand piano, decorated by Lawrence Alma-Tadema and Edward Poynter for Henry Marquand, 1884–87 Sotheby Parke Bernet, New York, 26 March 1980 ($390,000)	163,500
6	Verne Powell platinum flute Christie's, New York, 18 October 1986 ($187,000)	126,200
7	Flemish single-manual harpsichord made by Johan Daniel Dulken of Antwerp, 1755 Sotheby's, London, 27 March 1990	82,280
8	Kirkman double-manual harpsichord Christie's, London, 26 June 1987	77,000
9	Columnar alto recorder made by Hans van Schratt, mid-16th century Christie's, London, 16 March 1988	44,000
10	"Portable Grand Piano" made by John Isaac Hawkins, c.1805 (a very early example of an upright piano, considerably pre-dating the modern type, and one of only three examples known) Sotheby's, London, 4 July 1985	14,300

* *Including 10 per cent buyer's premium, where appropriate.*

This list shows the most expensive example of each type of instrument. The two harpsichords and two pianos are of different types but from the same family, so perhaps numbers 7 and 9 should be disqualified. In that case, 9 and 10 would be a pair of German kettle drums, c.1700, sold at Sotheby's, London, on 21 November 1974 for £3,900, and a Swiss sachbut made by J. Steimer of Zofinger in the early 18th century (Sotheby's, London, 6 May 1976, £3,080).

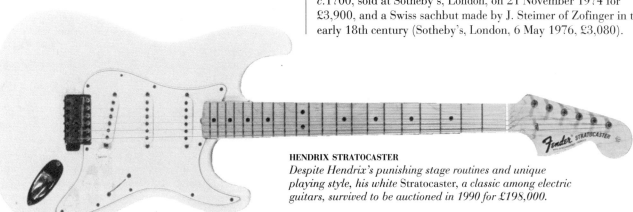

HENDRIX STRATOCASTER
Despite Hendrix's punishing stage routines and unique playing style, his white Stratocaster, a classic among electric guitars, survived to be auctioned in 1990 for £198,000.

CLASSICAL AND OPERA

OPERAS MOST FREQUENTLY PERFORMED AT THE ROYAL OPERA HOUSE, COVENT GARDEN, 1833–1993

	Opera	Composer	First performance	Total
1	La Bohème	Giacomo Puccini	2 Oct 1897	493
2	Carmen	Georges Bizet	27 May 1882	478
3	Aïda	Giuseppe Verdi	22 Jun 1876	446
4	Faust	Charles Gounod	18 Jul 1863	428
5	Rigoletto	Giuseppe Verdi	14 May 1853	423
6	Don Giovanni	Wolfgang Amadeus Mozart	17 Apr 1834	373
7	Tosca	Giacomo Puccini	12 Jul 1900	363
8	Norma	Vincenzo Bellini	12 Jul 1833	353
9	Madama Butterfly	Giacomo Puccini	10 Jul 1905	342
10	La Traviata	Giuseppe Verdi	25 May 1858	339

The total number of performances is up to 31 December 1993. The records are complete back to 1847, but for the two operas premiered earlier, the figure is based on the best available evidence.

CLASSICAL COMPOSERS IN PERFORMANCE, 1993

	Composer	Performances
1	Ludwig van Beethoven	44
2	Wolfgang Amadeus Mozart	36
3	Gustav Mahler	21*
4	Dmitri Shostakovich	21
5=	Joseph Haydn	20
5=	Peter Tchaikovsky	20
7	Antonin Dvorák	18
8	Franz Schubert	16
9	Johannes Brahms	12
9=	Jean Sibelius	12

* Plus two movements.

Based on the survey conducted annually by David Chesterman, who since 1952 has written to *The Times* reporting on the 10 composers whose works have been most performed at the Royal Albert, Royal Festival, Barbican, and Queen Elizabeth Halls and at St John's, Smith Square, London.

OPERAS MOST FREQUENTLY PERFORMED AT THE ROYAL OPERA HOUSE, COVENT GARDEN, 1946–93*

	Opera	Composer	First post-war performance	Total
1	La Bohème	Giacomo Puccini	15 Oct 1948	285
2	Carmen	Georges Bizet	14 Jan 1947	269
3	Aïda	Giuseppe Verdi	29 Sep 1948	253
4	Tosca	Giacomo Puccini	18 Nov 1950	228
5	Die Zauberflöte	Wolfgang Amadeus Mozart	20 Mar 1947	203
6=	Rigoletto	Giuseppe Verdi	31 Oct 1947	194
6=	Le Nozze di Figaro	Wolfgang Amadeus Mozart	22 Jan 1949	194
8	Madama Butterfly	Giacomo Puccini	17 Jan 1950	181
9	La Traviata	Giuseppe Verdi	6 Apr 1948	173
10	Der Rosenkavalier	Richard Strauss	22 Apr 1947	161

* Royal Opera at Royal Opera House only, excluding performances on tour and performances by visiting companies.

Contrasting with the Royal Opera House's "all-time" list, this Top 10 gives a view of modern taste. Although the first three operas are identical in both lists, *Le Nozze di Figaro*, *Die Zauberflöte*, and *Der Rosenkavalier* do not appear at all in the all-time list while *Faust*, *Don Giovanni*, and *Norma* do not feature in the post-war Top 20.

CLASSICAL ALBUMS OF ALL TIME IN THE UK

1	Luciano Pavarotti	The Essential Pavarotti
2	Carreras, Domingo, Pavarotti	The Three Tenors Concert
3	Nigel Kennedy/ECO	Vivaldi: The Four Seasons
4	Various	The Essential Mozart
5	Various	Essential Opera
6	Nigel Kennedy/ECO	Mendelssohn/Bruch: Violin Concertos
7	Nigel Kennedy/LPO	Brahms: Violin Concerto
8	London Sinfonia/David Zinman	Gorecki: Symphony No 3
9	Luciano Pavarotti	The Essential Pavarotti, 2
10	Various	Essential Ballet

Sales of classical music boomed to unprecedented heights at the end of the 1980s and into the 1990s, the rider to this being that it was the records by a select band of superstars – tenors José Carreras, Placido Domingo, and Luciano Pavarotti (particularly the latter, who even had a top three single with *Nessun Dorma*), and young-gun violinist Nigel Kennedy – that soared way ahead of the field as a whole.

TOP 10

LARGEST OPERA HOUSES IN THE WORLD

	Opera house	Location	seating	Capacity standing	total
1	The Metropolitan Opera	New York, USA	3,800	265	4,065
2	Cincinnati Opera	Cincinnati, USA	3,630	–	3,630
3	Lyric Opera of Chicago	Chicago, USA	3,563	–	3,563
4	San Francisco Opera	San Francisco, USA	3,176	300	3,476
5	The Dallas Opera	Dallas, USA	3,420	–	3,420
6	Canadian Opera Company	Toronto, Canada	3,167	–	3,167
7	Los Angeles Music Center Opera	Los Angeles, USA	3,098	–	3,098
8	San Diego Opera	San Diego, USA	2,992	84	3,076
9	Seattle Opera	Seattle, USA	3,017	–	3,017
10	L'Opéra de Montréal	Montreal, Canada	2,874	–	2,874

THE PLACE TO BE SEEN
New York's Metropolitan Opera House was built in 1883 as a showcase for the world's best singers – and for the city's opera-going high society.

TOP 10

LARGEST OPERA HOUSES IN EUROPE

	Opera house	Location	seating	Capacity standing	total
1	Opéra Bastille	Paris, France	2,716	–	2,716
2	Gran Teatre del Liceu	Barcelona, Spain	2,700	–	2,700
3	English National Opera	London, UK	2,356	75	2,431
4	Staatsoper	Vienna, Austria	1,709	567	2,276
5	Teatro alla Scala	Milan, Italy	2,015	150	2,165
6	Bolshoi Theatre	Moscow, Russia	2,153	*	2,153
7	The Royal Opera	London, UK	2,067	42	2,109
8	Bayerische Staatsoper	Munich, Germany	1,773	328	2,101
9	Bayreuth Festspielhaus	Bayreuth, Germany	1,925	–	1,925
10	Teatro Comunale	Florence, Italy	1,890	–	1,890

* *Standing capacity unspecified.*

OPERA'S LONDON HOME
Built in 1858, on a site occupied by a succession of theatres since 1732, the Royal Opera House is home to the Royal Opera and Royal Ballet Companies.

TOP 10

LONGEST OPERAS PERFORMED AT THE ROYAL OPERA HOUSE, COVENT GARDEN

	Opera/composer	hr:min*
1	Götterdämmerung Richard Wagner	6:00
2	Die Meistersinger von Nürnberg Richard Wagner	5:40
3	Siegfried Richard Wagner	5:25
4	Tristan und Isolde Richard Wagner	5:19
5	Die Walküre Richard Wagner	5:15
6	Parsifal Richard Wagner	5:09
7	Donnerstag aus Licht Karlheinz Stockhausen	4:42
8	Lohengrin Richard Wagner	4:26
9	Der Rosenkavalier Richard Strauss	4:25
10	Don Carlo Giuseppe Verdi	4:19

* *Including intervals.*

STAGE & SCREEN

T O P   1 0

LONGEST-RUNNING SHOWS OF ALL TIME IN THE UK

	Show	Performances
1	*The Mousetrap*	17,215*
2	*No Sex, Please – We're British*	6,761
3	*Cats*	5,390*
4	*Starlight Express*	4,163*
5	*Oliver!*	4,125
6	*Oh! Calcutta!*	3,918
7	*Les Misérables*	3,449*
8	*Jesus Christ, Superstar*	3,357
9	*The Phantom of the Opera*	3,190*
10	*Evita*	2,900

* *Still running; total at 31 March 1994.*

All the longest-running shows in the UK have been London productions. *The Mousetrap* opened on 25 November 1952 at the Ambassadors Theatre. After 8,862 performances it transferred to St Martin's Theatre, re-opening on 25 March 1974.

T O P   1 0

LONGEST-RUNNING COMEDIES OF ALL TIME IN THE UK

	Show	Performances
1	*No Sex, Please – We're British*	6,761
2	*Run for Your Wife*	2,638
3	*There's a Girl in My Soup*	2,547
4	*Pyjama Tops*	2,498
5	*Boeing Boeing*	2,035
6	*Blithe Spirit*	1,997
7	*Worm's Eye View*	1,745
8	*Dirty Linen*	1,667
9	*Reluctant Heroes*	1,610
10	*Seagulls Over Sorrento*	1,551

T O P   1 0

LONGEST-RUNNING NON-MUSICALS OF ALL TIME IN THE UK

	Show	Performances
1	*The Mousetrap*	17,215*
2	*No Sex, Please – We're British*	6,761
3	*Oh! Calcutta!*#	3,918
4	*Run for Your Wife*	2,638
5	*There's a Girl in My Soup*	2,547
6	*Pyjama Tops*	2,498
7	*Sleuth*	2,359
8	*Boeing Boeing*	2,035
9	*Blithe Spirit*	1,997
10	*Worm's Eye View*	1,745

* *Still running; total at 31 March 1994*
\# Oh! Calcutta! *is included here as it is regarded as a revue with music, rather than a musical.*

IN THE LONG RUN

NINE LIVES
Cats *has been a huge success both in the UK and worldwide.*

LONGEST-RUNNING MUSICALS OF ALL TIME IN THE UK

	Show	Performances
1	Cats	5,390*
2	Starlight Express	4,163*
3	Les Misérables	3,449*
4	Jesus Christ, Superstar	3,357
5	Phantom of the Opera	3,190*
6	Evita	2,900
7	The Sound of Music	2,386
8	Salad Days	2,283
9	My Fair Lady	2,281
10	Miss Saigon	1,981*

* Still running; total at 31 March 1994.

LONGEST-RUNNING CAMERON MACKINTOSH PRODUCTIONS

	Production	Performances
1	Cats (London)	5,390
2	Cats (New York)	4,790
3	Les Misérables (London)	3,449
4	The Phantom of the Opera (London)	3,190
5	Les Misérables (New York)	2,943
6	The Phantom of the Opera (New York)	2,576
7	Miss Saigon (London)	1,981
8	Five Guys Named Moe (London)	1,330
9	Miss Saigon (New York)	1,272
10	Oliver! (London)	1,139

All still on except No. 10; total, 31 March 1994.

LONGEST-RUNNING SHOWS OF ALL TIME ON BROADWAY

	Show	Performances
1	A Chorus Line (1975–90)	6,137
2	Oh! Calcutta! (1976–89)	5,959
3	Cats (1982–)	4,790*
4	42nd Street (1980–89)	3,486
5	Grease (1972–80)	3,388
6	Fiddler on the Roof (1964–72)	3,242
7	Life with Father (1939–47)	3,224
8	Tobacco Road (1933–41)	3,182
9	Les Misérables (1987–)	2,943*
10	Hello Dolly! (1964–71)	2,844

* Still running; total at 31 March 1994.

LONGEST-RUNNING MUSICALS OF ALL TIME ON BROADWAY

	Show	Performances
1	A Chorus Line (1979–90)	6,137
2	Cats (1982–)	4,790*
3	42nd Street (1980–89)	3,486
4	Grease (1972–80)	3,388
5	Fiddler on the Roof (1964–72)	3,242
6	Les Misérables (1987–)	2,943*
7	Hello Dolly! (1964–71)	2,844
8	My Fair Lady (1956–62)	2,717
9	The Phantom of the Opera (1988–)	2,576*
10	Annie (1977–83)	2,377

* Still running; total at 31 March 1994.

Off Broadway, the musical show *The Fantasticks* by Tom Jones and Harvey Schmidt has been performed continuously at the Sullivan Street Playhouse, New York, since 3 May 1960 – a total of more than 13,500 performances.

VIVE LA REVOLUTION
With almost 6,500 performances so far in New York and London, Les Misérables *is proving to be another smash hit for Cameron Mackintosh.*

LONGEST-RUNNING NON-MUSICALS OF ALL TIME ON BROADWAY

	Show	Performances
1	Oh! Calcutta! (1976–89)	5,959
2	Life with Father (1939–47)	3,224
3	Tobacco Road (1933–41)	3,182
4	Abie's Irish Rose (1922–27)	2,327
5	Deathtrap (1978–82)	1,792
6	Gemini (1977–81)	1,788
7	Harvey (1944–49)	1,775
8	Born Yesterday (1946–49)	1,642
9	Mary, Mary (1961–65)	1,572
10	Voice of the Turtle (1943–47)	1,557

More than half the longest-running non-musical shows on Broadway began their runs before the Second World War; the others all date from the period up to the 1970s, before the long-running musical completely dominated the Broadway stage. Off Broadway, these records have all been broken by *The Drunkard*, which was performed at the Mart Theatre, Los Angeles, from 6 July 1933 to 6 September 1953, and then re-opened with a musical adapation and continued its run from 7 September 1953 until 17 October 1959 – a grand total of 9,477 performances seen by some 3,000,000 people.

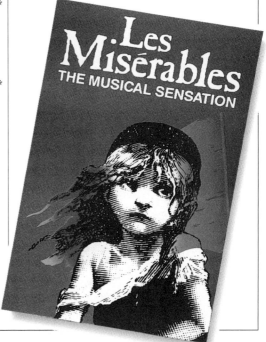

ALL THE WORLD'S A STAGE

T O P 1 0	
OLDEST LONDON THEATRES	
Theatre	Date opened
1 Theatre Royal, Drury Lane	7 May 1663
2 Sadler's Wells, Rosebery Avenue	3 June 1683
3 The Haymarket (Theatre Royal), Haymarket	29 December 1720
4 Royal Opera House, Covent Garden	7 December 1732
5 The Adelphi (originally Sans Pareil), Strand	27 November 1806
6 The Old Vic (originally Royal Coburg), Waterloo Road	11 May 1818
7 The Vaudeville, Strand	16 April 1870
8 The Criterion, Piccadilly Circus	21 March 1874
9 The Savoy, Strand	10 October 1881
10 The Comedy, Panton Street	15 October 1881

These are London's 10 oldest theatres still operating on their original sites – although most of them have been rebuilt, some several times. The Lyceum, built in 1771 as "a place of entertainment", was not originally licensed as a theatre and in its early years was used for such events as circuses and exhibitions, with only occasional theatrical performances. The Savoy was gutted by fire in 1990, but has undergone extensive rebuilding.

T O P 1 0	
LARGEST THEATRES IN LONDON	
Theatre	Seats
1 Apollo Victoria	2,572 *
2 London Coliseum	2,358
3 London Palladium	2,298
4 Theatre Royal, Drury Lane	2,237
5 Royal Opera House	2,099
6 Dominion	2,007
7 Prince Edward Theatre	1,666
8 Victoria Palace	1,565
9 Adelphi Theatre	1,500
10 Sadler's Wells	1,499

* Official capacity; reduced to 1,524 for current production of Starlight Express.

The Hammersmith Odeon has 3,483 seats, but is used for rock concerts and other non-theatrical events. Among London's newest theatres, neither the Olivier at the National Theatre (1,160 seats) nor the Barbican (1,166 seats) rank in the Top 10. London also boasts several large concert halls, including the Royal Festival Hall (3,111 seats), Barbican Hall (2,047 seats), and the Royal Albert Hall, which can accommodate up to 7,000 depending on the nature of the performance. The recently-opened London Arena is the largest, seating 12,500. The largest theatre – and the largest stage – in the UK is the Blackpool Opera House with a capacity of 2,975.

WITHOUT EQUAL
London's Adelphi Theatre, originally called the Sans Pareil, was opened in 1806 by wealthy tradesman John Scott in order to launch his daughter's stage career.

T O P   1 0

FIRST PLAYS STAGED AT THE NATIONAL THEATRE

(At the South Bank)

	Play	Author	Director	Opening date
1	*Hamlet*	William Shakespeare	Peter Hall	16 Mar 1976
2	*John Gabriel Borkman*	Henrik Ibsen	Peter Hall	17 Mar 1976
3	*Plunder*	Ben Travers	Michael Blakemore	19 Mar 1976
4	*Watch It Come Down*	John Osborne	Bill Bryden	20 Mar 1976 *
5	*Happy Days*	Samuel Beckett	Peter Hall	20 Mar 1976 #
6	*No Man's Land*	Harold Pinter	Peter Hall	12 Apr 1976
7	*The Playboy of the Western World*	John Millington Synge	Bill Bryden	3 Jun 1976
8	*Blithe Spirit*	Noël Coward	Harold Pinter	24 Jun 1976
9	*Weapons of Happiness*	Howard Brenton	David Hare	14 Jul 1976
10	*Jumpers*	Tom Stoppard	Peter Wood	21 Sep 1976

* Matinee performance. # Evening performance.

A British National Theatre was first proposed in 1848, but it was not until the National Theatre Bill was passed more than 100 years later that the project received serious attention. Under this act of 1949, a grant of £1,000,000 was made available and a committee set up under Sir Laurence Olivier and Norman Marshall. The National Theatre thus came into existence, but had no permanent home, and Denys Lasdun was appointed to design one. The Old Vic was used as temporary home from 1963 onwards.

Although the Queen Mother (then Queen Elizabeth) laid a foundation stone on the South Bank in 1951, subsequent development proceeded slowly. Building started in earnest in 1969. It was plagued by a series of industrial disputes and construction costs rose finally to exceed £16,000,000. The Lyttelton Theatre (named after Oliver Lyttelton, Lord Chandos, chairman of the National Theatre Board from 1963–71), the first of the three stages in the building to be completed, was inaugurated on 15 March 1976. All the first 10 National Theatre productions took place at the Lyttelton and the theatre was formally opened by The Queen on 25 October 1976. The first production at the Olivier was Christopher Marlowe's *Tamburlaine the Great*, directed by Peter Hall, which opened on 4 October 1976, and the first at the Cottesloe was Ken Campbell and Christopher Langham's *Illuminatus!*, directed by Ken Campbell, which opened on 4 March 1977. The National Theatre was awarded the prefix "Royal" in 1988.

T O P   1 0

WORST DISASTERS AT THEATRE AND ENTERTAINMENT VENUES

(19th and 20th centuries, excluding sports stadiums and racetracks)

	Location	Date	No. killed
1	Canton, China (theatre)	25 May 1845	1,670
2	Shanghai, China (theatre)	June 1871	900
3	Lehmann Circus, St Petersburg, Russia	14 February 1836	800
4	Antoung, China (cinema)	13 February 1937	658
5	Ring Theatre, Vienna	8 December 1881	620
6	Iroquois Theatre, Chicago	30 December 1903	591
7	Coconut Grove Night Club, Boston	28 November 1942	491
8	Abadan, Iran (theatre)	20 August 1978	422
9	Niteroi, Brazil (circus)	17 December 1961	323
10	Brooklyn Theatre, New York	5 December 1876	295

All the worst theatre disasters have been caused by fire. The figure for the Ring Theatre fire also varies greatly according to source, some claiming it to be as high as 850. The UK's worst theatre fire left 188 dead at the Theatre Royal, Exeter, on 4 September 1887. The US's worst circus fire (which caused a stampede) was at Ringling Brothers' Circus, Hartford, Connecticut, on 6 July 1944 when 168 lives were lost and 480 injured.

T O P   1 0

THEATRE-GOING COUNTRIES IN THE WORLD

	Country	Annual theatre attendance per 1,000 population
1	Cuba	2,559
2	Mongolia	1,700
3	Vietnam	1,000
4	UK	720
5	Iceland	658
6	Bulgaria	650
7	Luxembourg	613
8	Albania	590
9	Romania	578
10	Netherlands	575
	USA	*170*

In countries such as Egypt, theatre visits are only 9 per 1,000, and in Pakistan and the Philippines they amount to just 0.6.

THE IMMORTAL BARD

SHAKESPEARE'S MOST PRODUCED PLAYS

	Play	Productions
1	*As You Like It*	64
2=	*Hamlet*	58
2=	*The Merchant of Venice*	58
2=	*Twelfth Night*	58
5=	*Much Ado About Nothing*	56
5=	*The Taming of the Shrew*	56
7	*A Midsummer Night's Dream*	49
8=	*Macbeth*	47
8=	*The Merry Wives of Windsor*	47
8=	*Romeo and Juliet*	47

This list, which is based on an analysis of Shakespearean productions from 31 December 1878 to 1 January 1994 at Stratford-on-Avon, and by the Royal Shakespeare Company in London, provides a reasonable picture of his most popular plays. Records do not, however, indicate the total number of individual performances during each production.

SHAKESPEARE'S LONGEST PLAYS

	Play	Lines
1	*Hamlet*	3,901
2	*Richard III*	3,886
3	*Coriolanus*	3,820
4	*Cymbeline*	3,813
5	*Othello*	3,672
6	*Antony and Cleopatra*	3,630
7	*Troilus and Cressida*	3,576
8	*Henry VIII*	3,450
9	*Henry V*	3,368
10	*The Winter's Tale*	3,354

WILLIAM SHAKESPEARE (1564–1616)
England's best-known poet, actor, and playwright was born in Stratford-on-Avon, Warwickshire, the town to which he returned at the end of a life spent in the theatrical world of London.

SHAKESPEARE'S FIRST PLAYS

	Play	Approx. year written
1	*Titus Andronicus*	1588–90
2	*Love's Labour's Lost*	1590
3	*Henry VI, Parts I–III*	1590–91
4=	*The Comedy of Errors*	1591
4=	*Richard III*	1591
4=	*Romeo and Juliet*	1591
7	*The Two Gentlemen of Verona*	1592–93
8	*A Midsummer Night's Dream*	1593–94
9	*Richard II*	1594
10	*King John*	1595

Few authorities agree on the precise dating of Shakespeare's plays. There are only scant contemporary records of their early performances, and only half of them appeared in print in his lifetime – and even those that were published before his death in 1616 were generally much altered from his originals. It was not until after 1623, with the publication of the so-called "Folios", that Shakespeare's complete works were progressively published. There is much argument over the dating of *Romeo and Juliet* in particular, which may have been written as early as 1591 or as late as 1596–97; if the latter, it would be pre-dated by Nos. 7–10 on the list and by *The Merchant of Venice* (c. 1596).

SHAKESPEARE ON FILM

Kenneth Branagh's 1993 version of *Much Ado About Nothing* continues a tradition of adapting Shakespeare's plays as films, which began in the silent era. There are more than 50 versions of *Hamlet*; the 1990 remake, starring Mel Gibson, is the highest-earning. Franco Zeffirelli's *Romeo and Juliet* (1968) remains the most commercially successful adaptation of a Shakespeare play.

TOP 10

POLONIUS'S PRECEPTS FOR LAERTES

1 *Give thy thoughts no tongue, Nor any unproportioned thought his act.*

2 *Be thou familiar, but by no means vulgar.*

3 *Those friends thou hast, and their adoption tried, Grapple them to thy soul with hoops of steel;*

4 *But do not dull thy palm with entertainment Of each new-hatch'd, unfledged comrade.*

5 *Beware of entrance to a quarrel, but being in, Bear't that the opposed may beware of thee.*

6 *Give every man thy ear, but few thy voice;*

7 *Take each man's censure, but reserve thy judgment.*

8 *Costly thy habit as thy purse can buy, But not express'd in fancy; rich, not gaudy; For the apparel oft proclaims the man, And they in France of the best rank and station Are of a most select and generous chief in that.*

9 *Neither a borrower nor a lender be; For loan oft loses both itself and friend, And borrowing dulls the edge of husbandry.*

10 *This above all: to thine ownself be true, And it must follow, as the night the day, Thou canst not then be false to any man.*

In Act I, Scene iii of *Hamlet*, Polonius, the Lord Chamberlain and father of Hamlet's friend Laertes, gives his son these 10 pieces of advice before Laertes sets sail for France.

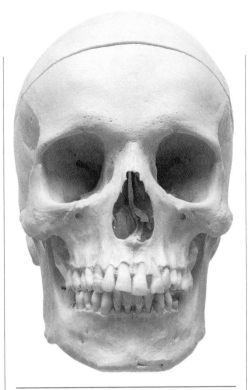

TOP 10

SHAKESPEARE'S MOST DEMANDING ROLES

	Role	Play	Lines
1	Hamlet	*Hamlet*	1,422
2	Falstaff	*Henry IV, Parts I and II*	1,178
3	Richard III	*Richard III*	1,124
4	Iago	*Othello*	1,097
5	Henry V	*Henry V*	1,025
6	Othello	*Othello*	860
7	Vincentio	*Measure for Measure*	820
8	Coriolanus	*Coriolanus*	809
9	Timon	*Timon of Athens*	795
10	Antony	*Antony and Cleopatra*	766

Hamlet's role comprises 11,610 words — over 36 per cent of the total number of lines spoken in the play, but if multiple plays are considered, he is beaten by Falstaff who, as well as appearing in *Henry IV, Parts I and II*, also appears in *The Merry Wives of Windsor* where he has 436 lines. His total of 1,614 lines thus makes him the most talkative of all Shakespeare's characters. By the same criterion, Henry V appears (as Prince Hal) in *Henry IV Part I*, where he speaks 117 lines, making his total 1,142.

TOP 10

WORDS MOST USED BY SHAKESPEARE

	Word	Frequency
1	The	27,457
2	And	26,285
3	I	21,206
4	To	19,938
5	Of	17,079
6	A	14,675
7	You	14,326
8	My	13,075
9	That	11,725
10	In	11,511

In his complete works, William Shakespeare wrote a total of 884,647 words – 118,406 lines comprising 31,959 separate speeches. He used a total vocabulary of 29,066 different words, some – such as "America" – appearing only once (*The Comedy of Errors*, III.ii), while at the other end of the scale the Top 10 accounts for all those words that he used on more than 10,000 occasions. Perhaps surprisingly, their relative frequency is not dissimilar to what we might encounter in modern usage: supposedly "Shakespearean" words such as "prithee" and "zounds!" actually make a poor showing in the frequency table. A further 18 words appear more than 5,000 times, in descending order: is, not, me, for, it, with, be, his, this, your, he, but, have, as, thou, so, him, and will. It should be noted that these statistics are derived from a computer analysis of Shakespeare's works conducted in the late 1960s – which, although comprehensive, was rather ahead of its time, since the software for such a monumental task was much less sophisticated than it would be today – and it is possible that the odd instance of a word's use may have slipped through the net. Reports of missing examples will be gratefully received.

100 YEARS OF CINEMA

Firsts in 1895 include:

22 March: First film screened: *Workers Leaving the Lumière Factory*, shown to an engineering society in Paris (earlier films were viewed individually, in "peep-show" machines).

30 March: First film of a public sporting event: the Oxford and Cambridge boat race, London, by British pioneer Birt Acres (1854–1918).

21 April: First movie shown in the US: at Woodville Latham's Pantoptikon, New York.

20 May: First film screened publicly: a boxing match ("Young Griffo" *v* "Battling (Charles) Barnett"), filmed at Madison Square Garden on 5 May and shown at 153 Broadway, New York.

20 June: First news film: Birt Acres' "newsreel" of the opening of the Kiel Canal, Hamburg, by Kaiser Wilhelm II. This, and other films by Acres, were first shown in London on 14 January 1896.

28 December: First film in Europe shown to a paying audience: by Louis and Auguste Lumière, at the Grand Café, Paris.

T O P 1 0

CINEMA REMAKES

	Original film	Remake
1	*Father of the Bride* (1950)	1991
2	*The Ten Commandments* (1923)	1956
3	*A Star Is Born* (1954)	1976
4	*Ben Hur* (1926)	1959
5	*King Kong* (1933)	1976
6	*Dragnet* (1954)	1987
7	*The Three Musketeers* (1948)	1974
8	*Hamlet* (1964)	1990
9	*The Postman Always Rings Twice* (1946)	1981
10	*King Solomon's Mines* (1950)	1985

This Top 10 includes only remakes with the identical title, and hence such retitled remakes as *Anna and the King of Siam* (1946)/*The King and I* (1956) and *Dracula* (1979)/*Bram Stoker's Dracula* (1992) are ineligible. The "original" film is the last significant Hollywood version of a film, but many subjects have been remade on more than one occasion – *The Three Musketeers* and *Hamlet* being notable examples.

T O P 1 0

MOST EXPENSIVE ITEMS OF FILM MEMORABILIA SOLD AT AUCTION

	Item/sale	Price £*
1	James Bond's Aston Martin DB5 from *Goldfinger* Sotheby's, New York, 28 June 1986	179,793
2	Herman J. Mankiewicz's scripts for *Citizen Kane* and *The American* Christie's, New York, 21 June 1989	139,157
3	Judy Garland's ruby slippers from *The Wizard of Oz* Christie's, New York, 21 June 1988	104,430
4	Piano from the Paris scene in *Casablanca* Sotheby's, New York, 16 December 1988	97,469
5	Charlie Chaplin's hat and cane Christie's, London, 11 December 1987 (resold at Christie's, London, 17 December 1993)	82,500 55,000
6	Clark Gable's script from *Gone With the Wind* Sotheby's, New York, 16 December 1988	48,734
7	Charlie Chaplin's boots Christie's, London, 11 December 1987	38,500
8	A special effects painting of the Emerald City from *The Wizard of Oz* Camden House, Los Angeles, 1 April 1991	29,944
9	A 1932 Universal poster for *The Old Dark House*, starring Boris Karloff Christie's, New York, 9 December 1991	26,600
10	16mm film of the only meeting between Danny Kaye and George Bernard Shaw Christie's, London, 27 April 1989	20,900

* $/£ conversion at rate then prevailing.

This list excludes animated film celluloids or "cels" – the individually painted scenes that are shot in sequence to make up cartoon films – which are now attaining colossal prices: just one of the 150,000 colour cels from *Snow White* (1937) was sold in 1991 for $209,000/£115,000, and in 1989 $286,000/£171,250 was reached for a black-and-white cel depicting Donald Duck in *Orphan's Benefit* (1934). If memorabilia relating to film stars is included, Orson Welles' annotated script from the radio production of *The War of the Worlds* ($143,000/ £90,500 in 1988) would qualify for the Top 10, while near-misses are the witch's hat from *The Wizard of Oz* ($33,000/ £20,886 in 1988) and Marilyn Monroe's "shimmy" dress from *Some Like it Hot* (£19,800 in 1988).

TOP 10
FILMS OF THE SILENT ERA

1	*The Birth of a Nation*	1915
2	*The Big Parade*	1925
3	*Ben Hur*	1926
4	*The Ten Commandments*	1923
5=	*What Price Glory?*	1926
5=	*The Covered Wagon*	1923
7=	*Way Down East*	1921
7=	*Hearts of the World*	1918
9=	*Wings*	1927
9=	*The Four Horsemen of the Apocalypse*	1921

The Birth of a Nation is not only at the top of the list, but, having earned almost twice as much as *The Big Parade*, is ranked as the most successful film made before 1937, when *Snow White and the Seven Dwarfs* took the crown. All the films in this list were black and white, with the exception of *Ben Hur*, which, despite its early date, contains a colour sequence.

TOP 10
BLACK-AND-WHITE FILMS

1	*Young Frankenstein*	1974
2	*Schindler's List*	1993
3	*Black Rain*	1990
4	*Paper Moon*	1973
5	*Manhattan*	1979
6	*Mom and Dad*	1944
7	*Who's Afraid of Virginia Woolf?*	1966
8	*Easy Money*	1983
9	*The Last Picture Show*	1971
10	*From Here to Eternity*	1953

Perhaps surprisingly, all the most successful black-and-white films date from the modern era, when the choice of filming in colour or monochrome was available and the decision to use the latter was thus deliberate.

YOUNG FRANKENSTEIN
Marty Feldman brings a comic slant to the classic tale of Frankenstein's monster.

TOP 10
FEES EARNED BY ACTORS IN *CASABLANCA*

	Actor	Part	Fee ($)
1	Humphrey Bogart	Rick Blaine	36,667
2=	Ingrid Bergman	Ilse Lund	25,000
2=	Paul Henreid	Victor Laszlo	25,000
2=	Conrad Veidt	Major Strasser	25,000
5	Claude Rains	Captain Louis Renault	22,000
6	Sydney Greenstreet	Ferrari	7,500
7	Dooley Wilson	Sam	3,500
8	S.Z. Sakall	Carl	2,600
9	Peter Lorre	Ugarte	2,333
10	Leonid Kinskey	Sascha	2,267

YOU MUST REMEMBER THIS
Humphrey Bogart and Ingrid Bergman feature in a scene in Rick's Bar, in Casablanca.

These are the budgeted fees that formed a major component of the total cost of the 1942 film. It was budgeted at $878,000, but actually cost $950,000 to make. After being nominated for eight Academy Awards and winning three ("Best Film", "Best Director", and "Best Screenplay"), *Casablanca* went on to achieve both commercial success and critical acclaim, many considering it the greatest Hollywood movie of all time.

TOP 10
YEARS FOR FILM RELEASES IN THE US

	Year	US produced	Imported	Total released
1	1928	641	193	884
2	1921	854	0	854
3	1918	841	0	841
4	1920	796	0	796
5	1937	538	240	778
6	1938	455	314	769
7	1935	525	241	766
8	1939	483	278	761
9	1922	748	0	748
10	1927	678	65	743

As this list indicates, the pre-war years were Hollywood's most prolific period – although from the late 1920s onwards, the proportion of home-grown to imported films gradually declined (imports actually overtook home-produced films for the first time in 1958, and it was not until 1975 that the trend was reversed). The total number of films released into the US marketplace reached an all-time low of 354 in 1978.

TOP 10
YEARS FOR FILM PRODUCTION IN THE UK

	Year	Films produced
1	1936	192
2	1937	176
3	1935	165
4	1920	155
5	1934	145
6	1921	137
7	1938	134
8	1962	126
9	1919	122
10	1933	115

The peak year for the British movie industry was almost 60 years ago, and apart from a curious "blip" in 1962, it has never recovered the eminence it once attained in this "golden age". British film production declined steadily, hitting triple figures for the last time in 1970 (when 103 films were produced in the UK), and dipping to an all-time low of 27 in 1988, with 42 (including co-productions) in 1992.

FILM HITS AND MISSES

Films that appear in the lists of "10 Most Successful" for various categories and Top 10s of films in which various stars have appeared are ranked according to the total rental fees paid to distributors by cinemas in North America (US and Canada). This is regarded by the film industry as a reliable guide to what a film has earned in those markets, while as a rough rule of thumb – also used by the industry itself – doubling the North American rental receipts gives a very approximate world total.

Rental income is not the same as "box office gross", another commonly used way of comparing the success of films. While the latter method is certainly valid over a short period – for example, to compare films released in the same year – it indicates what the cinemas rather than the films themselves earned and it varies according to ticket price.

Inflation is a key factor in any calculation of "success". As cinema ticket prices go up, so do box office income and the rental fees charged by distributors. This means that the biggest earners tend to be among the most recent releases. If inflation is taken into account, the most successful film ever is *Gone With the Wind*; while it has earned actual rental fees of almost $80,000,000 (ranking it only 40th in the all-time list), inflation since the film's release in 1939 makes this worth over $500,000,000 in today's money.

T O P 1 0

HIGHEST-GROSSING FILMS OF ALL TIME IN THE UK

	Film	Year	Approx. gross (£)
1	*Jurassic Park*	1993	32,000,000
2	*Ghost*	1990	23,300,000
3	*E.T. The Extra-Terrestrial*	1983	21,700,000
4	*Crocodile Dundee*	1987	21,500,000
5	*Robin Hood: Prince of Thieves*	1991	20,500,000
6	*Terminator 2: Judgment Day*	1991	18,400,000
7	*The Silence of the Lambs*	1991	17,100,000
8	*The Bodyguard*	1993	16,800,000
9	*Indiana Jones and the Last Crusade*	1989	15,900,000
10	*Who Framed Roger Rabbit?*	1989	15,600,000

Inevitably, bearing inflation in mind, the top-grossing films of all time are releases from the 1980s and 1990s, though it is also true that UK cinema admissions have risen sharply through these decades too. From the nadir of the late 1960s and 1970s, today's films are more widely viewed (even excluding video) than those of 15 to 25 years ago, as well as grossing considerably more at the box office.

T O P 1 0

FILMS OF 1993 IN THE UK

1	*Jurassic Park*
2	*The Bodyguard*
3	*The Fugitive*
4	*Home Alone 2: Lost in New York*
5	*Indecent Proposal*
6	*Cliffhanger*
7	*Sleepless in Seattle*
8	*A Few Good Men*
9	*Sister Act*
10	*The Jungle Book*

T O P 1 0

BRITISH FILMS OF ALL TIME
(*Excluding James Bond films*)

1	*Chariots of Fire**	1981
2	*2001: A Space Odyssey*	1968
3	*Revenge of the Pink Panther*	1978
4	*Gandhi**	1982
5	*Greystoke: The Legend of Tarzan*	1984
6	*Time Bandits*	1981
7	*Lawrence of Arabia**	1962
8	*Return of the Pink Panther*	1975
9	*The Pink Panther Strikes Again*	1976
10	*Murder on the Orient Express*	1974

**Academy Award for "Best Picture".*

A list of the 10 most successful British films of all time would contain no fewer than seven James Bond films, while a list of the Top 20 would contain 11. The list is therefore of British films other than Bonds. While many British-made films appear in the list of all-time successes, very few date from recent years – a sad indictment of the decline of the British film industry.

T O P 1 0

FILM RENTAL BLOCKBUSTERS OF ALL TIME

1	*E.T. The Extra-Terrestrial*	1982
2	*Jurassic Park*	1993
3	*Star Wars*	1977
4	*Return of the Jedi*	1983
5	*Batman*	1989
6	*The Empire Strikes Back*	1980
7	*Home Alone*	1990
8	*Ghostbusters*	1984
9	*Jaws*	1975
10	*Raiders of the Lost Ark*	1981

The first two films in this list have each earned more than $200,000,000 in North American rentals alone, while the rest of this elite group have all earned in excess of $100,000,000. Only seven other films have ever earned more than $100,000,000: *Indiana Jones and the Last Crusade* (1989), *Terminator 2* (1991), *Indiana Jones and the Temple of Doom* (1984), *Beverly Hills Cop* (1984), *Back to the Future* (1985), *Home Alone 2: Lost in New York* (1993), and *Batman Returns* (1992).

FILM SEQUELS OF ALL TIME

1	*Star Wars/The Empire Strikes Back/ Return of the Jedi*
2	*Raiders of the Lost Ark/ Indiana Jones and the Temple of Doom/ Indiana Jones and the Last Crusade*
3	*Rocky I–VI*
4	*Star Trek I–VI*
5	*Batman /Batman Returns*
6	*Home Alone 1–2*
7	*Back to the Future I–III*
8	*Jaws I–IV*
9	*Ghostbusters I–II*
10	*Superman I–IV*

Based on total earnings of the original film and all its sequels up to the end of 1993, the *Star Wars* trilogy stands head and shoulders above the rest, having made more than $500,000,000 in the North American market alone. All the other films in the Top 10 have achieved total earnings of around $200,000,000 or more, with *Lethal Weapon 1–3* and *Beverly Hills Cop I–II* lagging just outside the Top 10. A successful film does not guarantee a successful sequel, however: although their total earns them a place in the Top 10, each of the four *Superman* films actually earned less than the previous one, with *Superman IV* earning just one-tenth of the original. *Smokey and the Bandit Part III* earned just one-seventeenth of the original, and while the 1973 film *The Sting* was a box-office blockbuster, its 1983 sequel earned less than one-fifteenth as much, and *Grease 2* less than one-tenth of the original *Grease*. On the other hand, *Terminator 2* has already earned six times as much as its "prequel".

The James Bond films are not presented as sequels, but if they were taken into account, their total earnings would place them in 2nd position in this list.

BIGGEST FILM FLOPS OF ALL TIME

	Film	Year	Loss ($)
1	*The Adventures of Baron Münchhausen*	1988	48,100,000
2	*Ishtar*	1987	47,300,000
3	*Hudson Hawk*	1991	47,000,000
4	*Inchon*	1981	44,100,000
5	*The Cotton Club*	1984	38,100,000
6	*Santa Claus – The Movie*	1985	37,000,000
7	*Heaven's Gate*	1980	34,200,000
8	*Billy Bathgate*	1991	33,000,000
9	*Pirates*	1986	30,300,000
10	*Rambo III*	1988	30,000,000

Since the figures shown here are based upon North American rental earnings balanced against the films' original production cost, some in the list may eventually recoup a proportion of their losses via overseas earnings, video, and TV revenue, while for others, such as *Inchon* and *Pirates*, time has run out. The recent entry of *Hudson Hawk* and *Billy Bathgate*, two newcomers to the "flops" league table, means that the British-produced *Raise the Titanic* (1980), reputed to have lost $29,200,000, has finally sunk from the Top 10.

FILM SEQUELS THAT EARNED THE GREATEST AMOUNT MORE THAN THE ORIGINAL

	Original	Outearned by
1	*Alien*	*Aliens*
2	*Die Hard*	*Die Hard 2*
3	*First Blood*	*Rambo: First Blood Part II/Rambo III*
4	*48 Hours*	*Another 48 Hours*
5	*Lethal Weapon*	*Lethal Weapon 2 / Lethal Weapon 3*
6	*A Nightmare on Elm Street*	*A Nightmare on Elm Street 2, 3, 4, 5*
7	*The Pink Panther*	*Return of the Pink Panther/ The Pink Panther Strikes Again/ Revenge of the Pink Panther/*
8	*Rocky*	*Rocky III/Rocky IV*
9	*Star Trek*	*Star Trek IV: The Voyage Home*
10	*Terminator*	*Terminator 2: Judgment Day*

AVENGING ANGEL
Arnold Schwarzenegger starred in both the original Terminator *film and the even more successful* Terminator 2: Judgment Day.

FILMS OF THE DECADE

TOP 10

FILMS OF THE 1930s

	Film	Year
1	Gone With the Wind*	1939
2	Snow White and the Seven Dwarfs	1937
3	The Wizard of Oz	1939
4	King Kong	1933
5	San Francisco	1936
6=	Mr Smith Goes to Washington	1939
6=	Lost Horizon	1937
6=	Hell's Angels	1930
9	Maytime	1937
10	City Lights	1931

* Winner of "Best Picture" Academy Award.

Both Gone With the Wind and Snow White and the Seven Dwarfs have generated considerably more income than any other pre-war films, appearing respectively within the Top 40 and the Top 60 films of all time – although if the income of Gone With the Wind is adjusted to allow for inflation in the period since its release, it could with some justification be regarded as the most successful film ever. Gone With the Wind and The Wizard of Oz both celebrated their 50th anniversaries in 1989, the extra publicity generated by these events further enhancing their rental income. The Academy Award-winning Cavalcade (1932) is a potential contender for a place in this Top 10, but its earnings have been disputed.

TOP 10

FILMS OF THE 1940s

	Film	Year
1	Bambi	1942
2	Fantasia	1940
3	Cinderella	1949
4	Pinocchio	1940
5	Song of the South	1946
6	Mom and Dad	1944
7	Samson and Delilah	1949
8=	The Best Years of Our Lives*	1946
8=	Duel in the Sun	1946
10	This Is the Army	1943

* Winner of "Best Picture" Academy Award.

With the top four films of the decade classic Disney cartoons (and Song of the South part animated/part live action), the 1940s may truly be regarded as the "golden age" of the animated film. The genre was especially appealing in this era as colourful escapism during and after the drabness and grim realities of the war years. The songs from two of these films – "When You Wish Upon a Star" from Pinocchio and "Zip-A-Dee-Doo-Dah" from Song of the South – won "Best Song" Academy Awards. The cumulative income of certain of the Disney cartoons has increased as a result of their systematic re-release in the cinema and as bestselling videos. Samson and Delilah heralded the epic movies of the 1950s.

TOP 10

FILMS OF THE 1950s

	Film	Year
1	The Ten Commandments	1956
2	Lady and the Tramp	1955
3	Peter Pan	1953
4	Ben Hur*	1959
5	Around the World in 80 Days*	1956
6	Sleeping Beauty	1959
7=	South Pacific	1958
7=	The Robe	1953
9	Bridge on the River Kwai*	1957
10	This Is Cinerama	1952

* Winner of "Best Picture" Academy Award.

While the popularity of animated films continued with Lady and the Tramp, Peter Pan, and Sleeping Beauty, the 1950s were outstanding as the decade of the "big" picture. Many of the most successful films were enormous in terms of cast (Around the World in 80 Days boasted no fewer than 44 stars, most in cameo performances) and scale (Ben Hur, with its vast sets, broke all records by costing then a staggering $4,000,000 to make, while The Robe was the first picture to offer the wide screen of Cinemascope). They were also enormous in the magnitude of the subjects they tackled. Three of these were major biblical epics. Bridge on the River Kwai was unusual in that it was a British-made and mostly British-starring success.

WIND-FALL!
Vivien Leigh and Clark Gable are shown in a scene from Gone With the Wind. In cash terms, the film has earned almost 20 times the then record $4,230,000 it cost to make – but indexing its earnings over the 55 years since its release would establish it as Hollywood's all-time money earner.

T O P   1 0

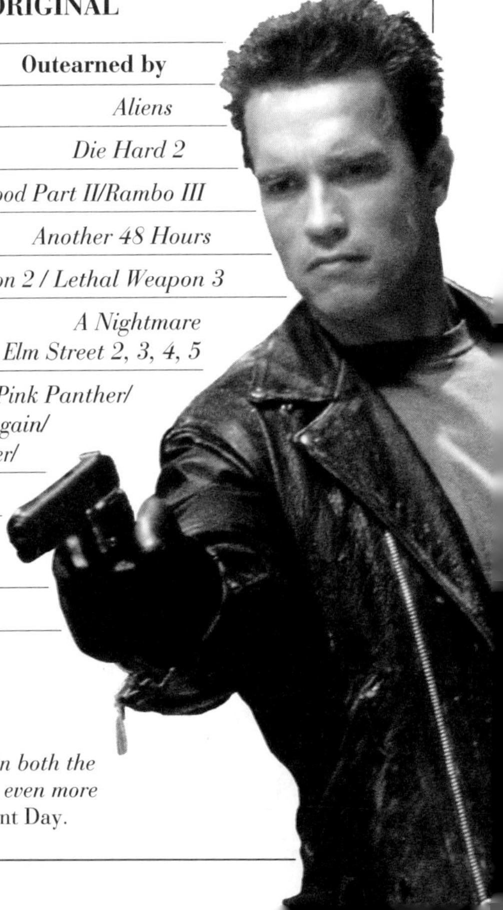

TOP 10

FILMS OF THE 1960s

	Film	Year
1	The Sound of Music*	1965
2	101 Dalmatians	1961
3	The Jungle Book	1967
4	Doctor Zhivago	1965
5	Butch Cassidy and the Sundance Kid	1969
6	Mary Poppins	1964
7	The Graduate	1968
8	My Fair Lady*	1964
9	Thunderball	1965
10	Funny Girl	1968

During the 1960s the growth in popularity of soundtrack record albums and featured singles often matched the commercial success of the films from which they were derived: four of the Top 10 films of the decade were avowed musicals, while all had a high musical content, every one of them generating either an album or a hit single or two. *The Sound of Music*, the highest-earning film of the decade, produced the fastest-selling album ever, with over half a million sold in two weeks – as well as the first million-selling tape cassette. *Mary Poppins* was a No. 1 album, as were albums of *The Jungle Book* and *Doctor Zhivago*.

* Winner of "Best Picture" Academy Award

TOP 10

FILMS OF THE 1970s

	Film	Year
1	Star Wars	1977
2	Jaws	1975
3	Grease	1978
4	The Exorcist	1973
5	The Godfather*	1972
6	Superman	1978
7	Close Encounters of the Third Kind	1977/80
8	The Sting*	1973
9	Saturday Night Fever	1977
10	National Lampoon's Animal House	1978

* Winner of "Best Picture" Academy Award.

In the 1970s the arrival of the two prodigies, Steven Spielberg and George Lucas, set the scene for the high adventure blockbusters whose domination has continued ever since. Lucas directed his first science-fiction film, *THX 1138*, in 1970 and went on to write and direct *Star Wars* (and wrote the two sequels, *The Empire Strikes Back* and *Return of the Jedi*). Spielberg directed *Jaws* and wrote and directed *Close Encounters* (which derives its success from the original release and the 1980 "Special Edition").

TOP 10

FILMS OF THE 1980s

	Film	Year
1	E.T. The Extra-Terrestrial	1982
2	Return of the Jedi	1983
3	Batman	1989
4	The Empire Strikes Back	1980
5	Ghostbusters	1984
6	Raiders of the Lost Ark	1981
7	Indiana Jones and the Last Crusade	1989
8	Indiana Jones and the Temple of Doom	1984
9	Beverly Hills Cop	1984
10	Back to the Future	1985

The 1980s were clearly the decade of the adventure film, with George Lucas and Steven Spielberg continuing to assert their control of Hollywood, carving up the Top 10 between them, with Lucas as producer of 2 and 4 and Spielberg director of 1, 6, 7, 8 and 10. Paradoxically, despite their colossal box office success, they consistently failed to match this with a "Best Picture" Academy Award. *E.T.* and *Raiders of the Lost Ark* were both nominated, but neither they nor any of the other high-earning films of the 1980s won this Oscar. By way of compensation, each made more than $100,000,000 in North American rentals.

TOP 10

FILMS OF THE 1990s

	Film	Year
1	Jurassic Park	1993
2	Home Alone	1990
3	Terminator 2	1991
4	Home Alone 2: Lost in New York	1992
5	Batman Returns	1992
6	Mrs Doubtfire	1993
7	Ghost	1990
8	The Fugitive	1993
9	Robin Hood: Prince of Thieves	1991
10	Aladdin	1992

HOME ALONE
This film, starring the young Macaulay Culkin, is not only one of the highest-earning films of the early 1990s but is ranked among the 10 most successful ever. So far, it has earned over $100,000,000 in North American rentals alone.

Just four years into the decade, all 10 of these films have amassed rental income from the North American market alone in excess of $80,000,000, an achievement matched by only 15 films in the whole of the 1980s and just seven in the 1970s. *Home Alone* has been so successful that it now ranks as one of the Top 10 films of all time. The sequel, *Home Alone 2: Lost in New York*, which was made in 1992, is now ranked 16th in the list of all-time top films. A further 22 films released since 1990, including several released as recently as 1993, have each earned more than $50,000,000.

MOVIE MAGIC

T O P 1 0

ANIMATED FILMS

1	*Aladdin*	1992
2	*Who Framed Roger Rabbit?**	1988
3	*Beauty and the Beast*	1991
4	*One Hundred and One Dalmatians*	1961
5	*Snow White and the Seven Dwarfs*	1937
6	*Jungle Book*	1967
7	*Bambi*	1942
8	*Fantasia*	1940
9	*Cinderella*	1949
10	*Pinocchio*	1940

* *Part-animated, part-live action.*

For more than 50 years the popularity of animated films has been so great that they stand out among the most successful films of each decade: *Snow White* was the second highest-earning film of the 1930s (after *Gone With the Wind*); *Bambi, Fantasia,* and *Cinderella* – and, through the success of its recent re-release, *Pinocchio* – were the four most successful films of the 1940s. *Lady and the Tramp*, though just outside the Top 10, was the second most successful of the 1950s (after *The Ten Commandments*). *One Hundred and One Dalmatians* and *Jungle Book* were the second and third most successful films of the 1960s (after *The Sound of Music*).

Runners-up include, in descending order: *Lady and the Tramp* (1955); *The Little Mermaid* (1989); *Peter Pan* (1953); *The Rescuers* (1977); *The Fox and the Hound* (1981); the part-animated *Song of the South* (1946); and *The Aristocats* (1970); *Oliver and Company* (1988); *The Land Before Time* (1988); *An American Tail* (1986); and *Sleeping Beauty* (1989).

T O P 1 0

SCIENCE-FICTION AND FANTASY FILMS

1	*E.T. The Extra-Terrestrial*	1982
2	*Star Wars*	1977
3	*Return of the Jedi*	1983
4	*Batman*	1989
5	*The Empire Strikes Back*	1980
6	*Ghostbusters*	1984
7	*Terminator 2*	1991
8	*Back to the Future*	1985
9	*Batman Returns*	1992
10	*Ghost*	1990

Reflecting our taste for escapist fantasy adventures, the first six in this list also appear in the all-time Top 10, and all 10 are among the 17 most successful films ever, having earned more than $80,000,000 each from North American rentals alone. Eight further contenders just outside the Top 10 also achieved rental income in excess of $60,000,000: *Close Encounters of the Third Kind*; *Gremlins*; *Honey, I Shrunk the Kids*; *Back to the Future, Part II*; *Teenage Mutant Ninja Turtles*; *Superman II*; *Total Recall*; and *Ghostbusters II*.

T O P 1 0

COMEDY FILMS

1	*Home Alone*	1990
2	*Mrs Doubtfire*	1993
3	*Beverly Hills Cop*	1984
4	*Ghost*	1990
5	*Home Alone 2: Lost in New York*	1992
6	*Tootsie*	1982
7	*Pretty Woman*	1990
8	*Three Men and a Baby*	1987
9	*Beverly Hills Cop II*	1987
10	*The Sting*	1973

The two *Beverly Hills Cop* films are regarded by certain purists as "action thrillers" rather than comedies. If they are excluded, Nos. 9 and 10 become National Lampoon's *Animal House* (1978) and *Crocodile Dundee* (1986). If *Ghost* and *Pretty Woman*, which are arguably either comedies or romances with comedy elements, are also excluded, the next two on this list are *Look Who's Talking* (1989) and *Coming to America* (1988). Other high-earning comedy films include *Sister Act* (1992), *City Slickers* (1991), *Nine to Five* (1980), *Smokey and the Bandit* (1977), *Stir Crazy* (1980), *Crocodile Dundee II* (1988), and *The Addams Family* (1991).

WHO FRAMED ROGER RABBIT?
Bob Hoskins faces his co-star in this part-animated, part-live action film.

TOP 10

CHILDREN'S FILMS
(Excluding animated films)

1	*Honey, I Shrunk the Kids*	1989
2	*Hook*	1991
3	*Teenage Mutant Ninja Turtles*	1990
4	*The Karate Kid Part II*	1986
5	*Mary Poppins*	1964
6	*The Karate Kid*	1984
7	*Teenage Mutant Ninja Turtles II*	1991
8	*War Games*	1983
9	*The Muppet Movie*	1979
10	*The Goonies*	1985

Some of the most successful films of all time, such as *E.T.*, *Star Wars* and its two sequels, the two *Ghostbusters* films, *Home Alone* and *Home Alone 2: Lost in New York*, have been those that are unrestricted by classification, appeal to the broadest possible base of the "family audience", and consequently attract the greatest revenue. This list, however, is of films that are aimed primarily at a young audience – though some are undoubtedly also appreciated by accompanying adults.

TOP 10

MUSICAL FILMS

1	*Grease*	1978
2	*The Sound of Music*	1965
3	*Saturday Night Fever*	1977
4	*American Graffiti*	1973
5	*The Best Little Whorehouse in Texas*	1982
6	*Mary Poppins*	1964
7	*Fiddler on the Roof*	1971
8	*Annie*	1982
9	*A Star Is Born*	1976
10	*Flashdance*	1983

Traditional musicals (films in which the cast actually sing) and films in which a musical soundtrack are a major component of the film are included. Several other musical films have also each earned in excess of $30,000,000 in North American rentals; among them *Coalminer's Daughter* (1980), *The Rocky Horror Picture Show* (1975), *Footloose* (1984), *The Blues Brothers* (1980), and *Purple Rain* (1984), but it would appear that the era of the blockbuster musical film is over.

TOP 10

DISASTER FILMS

1	*Die Hard 2*	1990
2	*The Towering Inferno*	1975
3	*Airport*	1970
4	*The Poseidon Adventure*	1972
5	*Die Hard*	1988
6	*Earthquake*	1974
7	*Airport 1975*	1974
8	*Airport '77*	1977
9	*The Hindenburg*	1975
10	*Black Sunday*	1977

Disasters involving blazing buildings, natural disasters such as volcanoes, earthquakes and tidal waves, train and air crashes, sinking ships, and terrorist attacks have long been a staple of Hollywood films, of which these are the most successful. Firemen fighting fires are also part of the theme of *Backdraft* (1991), which, if included, would enter at No. 5. *The China Syndrome* (1979) would appear in seventh place, except that the threatened nuclear diasaster that provides the story line is actually averted.

TOP 10

BIBLICAL FILMS

1	*The Ten Commandments*	1956
2	*Ben Hur*	1959
3	*The Robe*	1953
4	*Jesus Christ Superstar*	1973
5	*Quo Vadis*	1951
6	*Samson and Delilah*	1949
7	*Spartacus*	1960
8	*Jesus*	1979
9	*The Greatest Story Ever Told*	1965
10	*King of Kings*	1961

Biblical subjects have been standard Hollywood fare since the pioneer days, but are now less fashionable – Martin Scorsese's controversial *The Last Temptation of Christ* (1988) actually earned less than silent versions of *Ben Hur* (1926) and *The Ten Commandments* (1923).

TOP 10

HORROR FILMS

1	*Jurassic Park*	1993
2	*Jaws*	1975
3	*The Exorcist*	1973
4	*Jaws II*	1978
5	*Bram Stoker's Dracula*	1992
6	*Aliens*	1986
7	*Alien*	1979
8	*Poltergeist*	1982
9	*King Kong*	1976
10	*The Amityville Horror*	1979

This list encompasses supernatural and science-fiction horror and monsters (including dinosaurs, gorillas, and oversized sharks), but omits science-fiction films that do not have a major horrific component.

TOP 10

FILMS FEATURING DINOSAURS

1	*Jurassic Park*	1993
2	*Fantasia*	1940
3	*The Land Before Time**	1988
4	*Baby . . . Secret of the Lost Legend*	1985
5	*One of Our Dinosaurs is Missing*	1975
6	*Journey to the Centre of the Earth*	1959
7	*King Kong*	1933
8	*At the Earth's Core*	1976
9	*One Million Years BC*	1966
10	*When Dinosaurs Ruled the Earth*	1970

* Animated.

TOUGH GUYS

TOP 10

JAMES BOND FILMS

	Film	Year	Bond actor
1	Octopussy	1983	Roger Moore
2	Moonraker	1979	Roger Moore
3	Thunderball	1965	Sean Connery
4	Never Say Never Again	1983	Sean Connery
5	The Living Daylights	1987	Timothy Dalton
6	For Your Eyes Only	1981	Roger Moore
7	A View to a Kill	1985	Roger Moore
8	The Spy Who Loved Me	1977	Roger Moore
9	Goldfinger	1964	Sean Connery
10	Diamonds Are Forever	1967	Sean Connery

Ian Fleming's 12 James Bond novels have miraculously become the basis of 18 films. After his death in 1964, *For Your Eyes Only*, *Octopussy*, and *The Living Daylights* were developed by other writers from his short stories; *Never Say Never Again* was effectively a remake of *Thunderball*, while *A View to a Kill* and *Licence to Kill* (1989, in 11th place) were written without reference to Fleming's writings. *Casino Royale*, the 13th highest-earning Bond film, featuring 56-year-old David Niven as the retired spy Sir James Bond, is an oddity in that it was presented as an avowed comedy, rather than an adventure with comic elements. Outside the Top 10, George Lazenby played Bond in a single film, *On Her Majesty's Secret Service*, which ranks next to bottom in the earnings league; the very first Bond film, *Dr No* (1963), has earned the least – less, in fact, than *Chitty Chitty Bang Bang*, the film based on Ian Fleming's children's book of this title.

TOP 10

PRISON AND PRISON ESCAPE FILMS*

1	Stir Crazy	1980
2	Papillon	1973
3	Escape from Alcatraz	1979
4	Ernest Goes to Jail	1990
5	Breakout	1975
6	Cool Hand Luke	1967
7	We're No Angels	1989
8	Chained Heat	1983
9	Penitentiary	1980
10	Jailhouse Rock	1957

* Excluding war films with prison scenes (such as The Dirty Dozen) or prisoner-of-war movies (The Great Escape, Stalag 17, etc.).

AL PACINO
Although best known for his roles in Scarface *and the* Godfather *films, Al Pacino did not receive an Oscar for any of them. His first "Best Actor" award was for* Scent of a Woman *(1992).*

TOP 10

COP FILMS

1	Beverly Hills Cop	1984
2	Beverly Hills Cop II	1987
3	Lethal Weapon 3	1993
4	Lethal Weapon 2	1989
5	Die Hard 2	1990
6	Dick Tracy	1990
7	Basic Instinct	1992
8	Naked Gun 2½: The Smell of Fear	1991
9	Another 48 Hrs	1990
10	Police Academy	1984

This list includes only films in which policemen or detectives are the central characters. *The Silence of the Lambs* (1991) and *The Untouchables* (1987) earned enough to qualify, but the main characters in both are with the FBI rather than police officers. A close runner-up is *Turner & Hooch* (1989), where it is arguable whether the cop or the dog is the star. *Lethal Weapon 2* and *3* feature prominently in this list, along with *Another 48 Hrs*, but what happened to the original films? Like *The Terminator /Terminator 2*, they are classic examples of originals out-earned by their sequels – in the instance of *Lethal Weapon*, each of the successors made more than twice as much as the prototype. Each of the five *Police Academy* sequels, on the other hand, earned progressively less than its predecessor.

TOP 10

MAFIA FILMS

1	The Godfather	1972
2	The Firm	1993
3	The Godfather, Part III	1990
4	The Untouchables	1987
5	The Godfather, Part II	1974
6	Scarface	1983
7	Goodfellas	1990
8	Prizzi's Honor	1985
9	The Cotton Club	1984
10	Married to the Mob	1988

TOP 10
WESTERNS

1	*Dances with Wolves*	1990
2	*Butch Cassidy and the Sundance Kid*	1969
3	*Unforgiven*	1992
4	*Jeremiah Johnson*	1972
5	*How the West Was Won*	1962
6	*Pale Rider*	1985
7	*Young Guns*	1988
8	*Young Guns II*	1990
9	*Bronco Billy*	1980
10	*Little Big Man*	1970

TOP 10
WAR FILMS

1	*Platoon*	1986
2	*Good Morning, Vietnam*	1987
3	*Apocalypse Now*	1979
4	*M*A*S*H*	1970
5	*Patton*	1970
6	*The Deer Hunter*	1978
7	*Full Metal Jacket*	1987
8	*Midway*	1976
9	*The Dirty Dozen*	1967
10	*A Bridge Too Far*	1977

Surprisingly few war films have appeared in the high-earning bracket in recent years, which suggests that the days of big-budget films in this genre may be over. This list, however, excludes successful films that are not technically "war" films but that have military themes, such as *A Few Good Men* (1992), *The Hunt for Red October* (1990), and *An Officer and a Gentleman* (1982), which would otherwise be placed in the top five. Another such film is *Top Gun* (1986), which would actually head the list, just beating *Rambo: First Blood 2* (1985), a post-Vietnam war action film that is also disqualified.

Clint Eastwood is in the unusual position of directing and starring in a film that has forced another of his own films out of the Top 10, since the recent success of *Unforgiven* has ejected *The Outlaw Josey Wales* (1976). Although it has a Western setting, *Back to the Future, Part III* (1990) is essentially a science-fiction film (if it were a true Western, it would rate in 2nd place). According to some criteria, *The Last of the Mohicans* (1992) qualifies as a Western; if included, it would be in 4th position.

SETTING THE STAGE
Films are either shot on location or on a studio set. Hollywood westerns inevitably included a dusty frontier town, and usually featured a confrontation scene in the saloon.

OSCAR WINNERS – FILMS

FILMS NOMINATED FOR THE MOST OSCARS

(Oscar® is a registered trade mark)

	Film	Year	Awards	Nominations
1	*All About Eve*	1950	6	14
2=	*Gone With the Wind*	1939	8*	13
2=	*From Here to Eternity*	1953	8	13
2=	*Mary Poppins*	1964	5	13
2=	*Who's Afraid of Virginia Woolf?*	1966	5	13
6=	*Mrs Miniver*	1942	6	12
6=	*The Song of Bernadette*	1943	4	12
6=	*Johnny Belinda*	1948	1	12
6=	*A Streetcar Named Desire*	1951	4	12
6=	*On the Waterfront*	1954	8	12
6=	*Ben Hur*	1959	11	12
6=	*Becket*	1964	1	12
6=	*My Fair Lady*	1964	8	12
6=	*Reds*	1981	3	12
6=	*Dances with Wolves*	1990	7	12
6=	*Schindler's List*	1993	7	12

* *Plus two special awards.*

The Turning Point (1977) and *The Color Purple* (1985) suffered the ignominy of receiving 11 nominations without a single win.

FILMS TO WIN MOST OSCARS

	Film	Year	Awards
1	*Ben Hur*	1959	11
2	*West Side Story*	1961	10
3=	*Gigi*	1958	9
3=	*The Last Emperor*	1987	9
5=	*Gone With the Wind*	1939	8
5=	*From Here to Eternity*	1953	8
5=	*On the Waterfront*	1954	8
5=	*My Fair Lady*	1964	8
5=	*Cabaret*	1972	8
5=	*Gandhi*	1982	8
5=	*Amadeus*	1984	8

Going My Way (1944), *The Best Years of Our Lives* (1946), *The Bridge on the River Kwai* (1957), *Lawrence of Arabia* (1962), *Patton* (1970), *The Sting* (1973), *Out of Africa* (1985), *Dances with Wolves* (1990), and *Schindler's List* (1993) all won seven Oscars each.

"BEST PICTURE" OSCAR WINNERS AT THE BOX OFFICE

1	*Rain Man*	1988
2	*The Godfather*	1972
3	*Dances with Wolves*	1990
4	*The Sound of Music*	1965
5	*Gone With the Wind*	1939
6	*The Sting*	1973
7	*Platoon*	1986
8	*Kramer vs Kramer*	1979
9	*One Flew Over the Cuckoo's Nest*	1975
10	*The Silence of the Lambs*	1991

Winning the Academy Award for "Best Picture" is no guarantee of box-office success: the award is given for a picture released the previous year, and by the time the Oscar ceremony takes place, the filmgoing public has already effectively decided on the winning picture's fate. Receiving the Oscar may enhance a successful picture's continuing earnings, but it is generally too late to revive a film that may already have been judged mediocre.

"BEST PICTURE" OSCAR WINNERS OF THE 1960s

Year	Film
1960	*The Apartment*
1961	*West Side Story*
1962	*Lawrence of Arabia*
1963	*Tom Jones*
1964	*My Fair Lady*
1965	*The Sound of Music*
1966	*A Man for All Seasons*
1967	*In the Heat of the Night*
1968	*Oliver!*
1969	*Midnight Cowboy*

The 1960 winner, *The Apartment*, was the last black-and-white film to receive a "Best Picture" Oscar until Steven Spielberg's *Schindler's List* in 1993.

TOP 10

"BEST PICTURE" OSCAR WINNERS OF THE 1930s

Year	Film
1930	All Quiet on the Western Front
1931	Cimarron
1932	Grand Hotel
1933	Cavalcade
1934	It Happened One Night*
1935	Mutiny on the Bounty
1936	The Great Ziegfeld
1937	The Life of Emile Zola
1938	You Can't Take it With You
1939	Gone With the Wind

* Winner of Oscars for "Best Director", "Best Actor", "Best Actress", and "Best Screenplay".

The first Academy Awards, popularly known as Oscars, were presented at a ceremony at the Hollywood Roosevelt Hotel on 16 May 1929, and were for films released in the period 1927–28. A second ceremony held at the Ambassador Hotel on 31 October of the same year was for films released in 1928–29.

TOP 10

"BEST PICTURE" OSCAR WINNERS OF THE 1970s

Year	Film
1970	Patton
1971	The French Connection
1972	The Godfather
1973	The Sting
1974	The Godfather, Part II
1975	One Flew Over the Cuckoo's Nest*
1976	Rocky
1977	Annie Hall
1978	The Deer Hunter
1979	Kramer vs Kramer

* Winner of Oscars for "Best Director", "Best Actor", "Best Actress", and "Best Screenplay".

TOP 10

"BEST PICTURE" OSCAR WINNERS OF THE 1940s

Year	Film
1940	Rebecca
1941	How Green Was My Valley
1942	Mrs Miniver
1943	Casablanca
1944	Going My Way
1945	The Lost Weekend
1946	The Best Years of Our Lives
1947	Gentleman's Agreement
1948	Hamlet
1949	All the King's Men

TOP 10

"BEST PICTURE" OSCAR WINNERS OF THE 1980s

Year	Film
1980	Ordinary People
1981	Chariots of Fire
1982	Gandhi
1983	Terms of Endearment
1984	Amadeus
1985	Out of Africa
1986	Platoon
1987	The Last Emperor
1988	Rain Man
1989	Driving Miss Daisy

The winners of "Best Picture" Oscars during the 1990s are: 1990 Dances With Wolves; 1991 The Silence of the Lambs – which also won Oscars for "Best Director", "Best Actor", "Best Actress", and "Best Screenplay"; 1992 Unforgiven; and 1993 Schindler's List – which also won six other awards. These were for "Best Director", "Best Adapted Screenplay", "Best Film Editing", "Best Art Direction", "Best Cinematography", and "Best Original Score".

TOP 10

"BEST PICTURE" OSCAR WINNERS OF THE 1950s

Year	Film
1950	All About Eve
1951	An American in Paris
1952	The Greatest Show on Earth
1953	From Here to Eternity
1954	On the Waterfront
1955	Marty
1956	Around the World in 80 Days
1957	The Bridge on the River Kwai
1958	Gigi
1959	Ben Hur

GOLDEN IDOL
Standing 30 cm (13.5 in) high, gold-plated "Oscar" was reputedly named for his resemblance to a film librarian's Uncle Oscar.

DID YOU KNOW

LANDMARKS
Wings (1927), the first film to receive a "Best Picture" award, was silent. The first talkie, and the first musical, to win an Oscar was Broadway Melody (1928). The film was a novelty in that it contained sequences shot in a primitive, two-colour form of Technicolor (using only red and green). Gone With the Wind was the first all-colour winner of the "Best Picture" award.

OSCAR WINNERS – STARS & DIRECTORS

TOP 10

ACTORS AND ACTRESSES WITH MOST OSCAR NOMINATIONS

	Actor/actress/nomination years	Nominations
1	Katharine Hepburn 1932–33*; 1935; 1940; 1942; 1951; 1955; 1956; 1959; 1962; 1967*; 1968*(shared); 1981*	12
2=	Bette Davis 1935*; 1938*; 1939; 1940; 1941; 1942; 1944; 1950; 1952; 1962	10
2=	Jack Nicholson 1969#; 1970; 1973; 1974; 1975*; 1981#; 1983#; 1985; 1987; 1992#	10
2=	Laurence Olivier 1939; 1940; 1946; 1948*; 1956; 1960; 1965; 1972; 1976#; 1978	10
5	Spencer Tracy 1936; 1937*; 1938*; 1950; 1955; 1958; 1960; 1961; 1967	9
6=	Marlon Brando 1951; 1952; 1953; 1954*; 1957; 1972*; 1973; 1989#	8
6=	Jack Lemmon 1955#; 1959; 1960; 1962; 1973*; 1979; 1980; 1982	8
6=	Al Pacino 1972#; 1973; 1974; 1975; 1979; 1990#; 1992*; 1992#	8
6=	Geraldine Page 1953#; 1961; 1962; 1966; 1972; 1978; 1984; 1985*	8
10=	Ingrid Bergman 1943; 1944*; 1945; 1948; 1956*; 1974#; 1978	7
10=	Richard Burton 1952#; 1953; 1964; 1965; 1966; 1969; 1977	7
10=	Jane Fonda 1969; 1971*; 1977; 1978; 1979; 1986; 1981#	7
10=	Greer Garson 1939; 1941; 1942*; 1943; 1944; 1945; 1960	7
10=	Paul Newman** 1958; 1961; 1963; 1967; 1981; 1982; 1986*	7
10=	Peter O'Toole 1962; 1964; 1968; 1969; 1972; 1980; 1982	7

* Won Academy Award.
# Nomination for
   "Best Supporting Actor"
   or "Best Supporting Actress".
**Also won an honorary Oscar in 1985.

JACK NICHOLSON
*Although in equal second place
on this list, with 10 nominations,
he has only won two Oscars.*

As the Top 10 shows, a number of actors and actresses have received numerous nominations without actually winning many (or, in Richard Burton's and Peter O'Toole's cases, any) Oscars. Two actresses and two actors tie in first place with totals of eight unsuccessful nominations for "Best Actor", "Best Actress", "Best Supporting Actor", or "Best Supporting Actress": Bette Davis, Katharine Hepburn, Jack Nicholson, and Laurence Olivier. Deborah Kerr was nominated as "Best Actress" and Thelma Ritter six times as "Best Supporting Actress", but neither ever won (although Deborah Kerr won an Honorary Award in 1993). It is clearly worth persevering, however: up to 1992, Al Pacino had been nominated four times as "Best Actor" and twice as "Best Supporting Actor" without winning, but in that year he found himself nominated in both categories and broke his losing streak by winning the "Best Actor" Oscar for *Scent of a Woman*.

TOP 10

"BEST ACTOR" OSCAR WINNERS OF THE 1970s

Actor	Film	Year
George C. Scott	*Patton**	1970
Gene Hackman	*The French Connection**	1971
Marlon Brando	*The Godfather**	1972
Jack Lemmon	*Save the Tiger*	1973
Art Carney	*Harry and Tonto*	1974
Jack Nicholson	*One Flew Over the Cuckoo's Nest**#	1975
Peter Finch	*Network***	1976
Richard Dreyfuss	*The Goodbye Girl*	1977
John Voight	*Coming Home***	1978
Dustin Hoffman	*Kramer vs Kramer**	1979

* Winner of "Best Picture" Oscar.
# Winner of "Best Director", "Best Actress",
   and "Best Screenplay" Oscars.
**Winner of "Best Actress" Oscar.

Peter Finch was the first (and so far only) "Best Actor" to be honoured posthumously: he died on 14 January 1977 and the award was announced at the 1976 ceremony held on 28 March 1977. He was not the first posthumous winner of any Academy Award, however: that distinction went to Sidney Howard for his screenplay for *Gone With the Wind*. Howard died on 23 August 1939, and on 29 February 1940 the Nobel Prize-winning novelist Sinclair Lewis received the Oscar on his behalf.

The oldest "Best Actor" Oscar winner (and nominee) is Henry Fonda, who was 76 at the time of his 1981 win for *On Golden Pond*. The oldest "Best Actress" Oscar-winner (and also oldest nominee) is Jessica Tandy (for *Driving Miss Daisy*, 1989 Awards), who was in her 80th year at the time of the ceremony. The oldest "Best Supporting Actor" is George Burns, aged 80 (*The Sunshine Boys*, 1975). Ralph Richardson was 82 when he was nominated as "Best Supporting Actor" for his role in *Greystoke: The Legend of Tarzan* (1984), as was Eva Le Gallienne, nominated as "Best Supporting Actress" for her part in *Resurrection* (1980), but the oldest winner in the latter category is Peggy Ashcroft, aged 77, for *A Passage to India* (1984).

T O P 1 0

"BEST ACTRESS" OSCAR WINNERS OF THE 1970s

Actress	Film	Year
Glenda Jackson	Women in Love	1970
Jane Fonda	Klute	1971
Liza Minelli	Cabaret	1972
Glenda Jackson	A Touch of Class	1973
Ellen Burstyn	Alice Doesn't Live Here Any More	1974
Louise Fletcher	One Flew Over the Cuckoo's Nest* **	1975
Faye Dunaway	Network#	1976
Diane Keaton	Annie Hall*	1977
Jane Fonda	Coming Home#	1978
Sally Field	Norma Rae	1979

* Winner of "Best Picture" Oscar. # Winner of "Best Actor" Oscar.
**Winner of "Best Director", "Best Actor", and "Best Screenplay" Oscars.

DIANE KEATON
Her "Best Actress" award was for her starring role in Woody Allen's film Annie Hall.

T O P 1 0

"BEST DIRECTOR" OSCAR WINNERS OF THE 1970s

Director	Film	Year
Franklin J. Schaffner	Patton*	1970
William Friedkin	The French Connection*	1971
Bob Fosse	Cabaret	1972
George Roy Hill	The Sting*	1973
Francis Ford Coppola	The Godfather Part II*	1974
Milos Forman	One Flew Over the Cuckoo's Nest*	1975
John G. Avildsen	Rocky*	1976
Woody Allen	Annie Hall*	1977
Michael Cimino	The Deer Hunter*	1978
Robert Benton	Kramer vs Kramer*	1979

* Winner of "Best Picture" Oscar.

T O P 1 0

"BEST ACTOR" OSCAR WINNERS OF THE 1980s

Actor	Film	Year
Robert De Niro	Raging Bull	1980
Henry Fonda	On Golden Pond#	1981
Ben Kingsley	Gandhi*	1982
Robert Duvall	Tender Mercies	1983
F. Murray Abraham	Amadeus*	1984
William Hurt	Kiss of the Spider Woman	1985
Paul Newman	The Color of Money	1986
Michael Douglas	Wall Street	1987
Dustin Hoffman	Rain Man*	1988
Daniel Day-Lewis	My Left Foot	1989

* Winner of "Best Picture" Oscar.
 # Winner of "Best Actress" Oscar.

The "Best Actor" Oscar-winners of the 1990s to date are – 1990: Jeremy Irons for *Reversal of Fortune*; 1991: Anthony Hopkins for *The Silence of the Lambs* (which also won "Best Picture" and "Best Actress" Oscars); 1992: Al Pacino for *Scent of a Woman*; 1993: Tom Hanks for *Philadelphia*.

T O P 1 0

"BEST ACTRESS" OSCAR WINNERS OF THE 1980s

Actress	Film	Year
Sissy Spacek	The Coal Miner's Daughter	1980
Katharine Hepburn	On Golden Pond#	1981
Meryl Streep	Sophie's Choice	1982
Shirley MacLaine	Terms of Endearment*	1983
Sally Field	Places in the Heart	1984
Geraldine Page	The Trip to Bountiful	1985
Marlee Matlin	Children of a Lesser God	1986
Cher	Moonstruck	1987
Jodie Foster	The Accused	1988
Jessica Tandy	Driving Miss Daisy*	1989

* Winner of "Best Picture" Oscar.
 # Winner of "Best Actor" Oscar.

The winners of "Best Actress" Oscars during the 1990s are – 1990: Kathy Bates for *Misery*; 1991: Jodie Foster for *The Silence of the Lambs*; 1992: Emma Thompson for *Howard's End*; 1993: Holly Hunter for *The Piano*.

T O P 1 0

"BEST DIRECTOR" OSCAR WINNERS OF THE 1980s

Director	Film	Year
Robert Redford	Ordinary People*	1980
Warren Beatty	Reds	1981
Richard Attenborough	Gandhi*	1982
James L. Brooks	Terms of Endearment*	1983
Milos Forman	Amadeus*	1984
Sydney Pollack	Out of Africa*	1985
Oliver Stone	Platoon*	1986
Bernardo Bertolucci	The Last Emperor*	1987
Barry Levinson	Rain Man*	1988
Oliver Stone	Born on the Fourth of July	1989

* Winner of "Best Picture" Oscar.

The winners of "Best Director" Oscars in the 1990s are – 1990: Kevin Costner for *Dances with Wolves*; 1991: Jonathan Demme for *The Silence of the Lambs*; 1992: Clint Eastwood for *Unforgiven*; 1993: Steven Spielberg for *Schindler's List*.

FILM STARS – ACTORS

T O P 1 0

TOM CRUISE FILMS

1	*Rain Man*	1988
2	*Top Gun*	1986
3	*The Firm*	1993
4	*A Few Good Men*	1992
5	*Days of Thunder*	1990
6	*Born on the Fourth of July*	1989
7	*Cocktail*	1988
8	*Risky Business*	1983
9	*Far and Away*	1992
10	*The Color of Money*	1986

T O P 1 0

MICHAEL DOUGLAS FILMS

1	*Fatal Attraction*	1987
2	*Basic Instinct*	1992
3	*The War of the Roses*	1989
4	*The Jewel of the Nile*	1985
5	*Romancing the Stone*	1984
6	*The China Syndrome*	1979
7	*Black Rain*	1989
8	*Wall Street*	1987
9	*Falling Down*	1993
10	*Coma*	1978

T O P 1 0

ANTHONY HOPKINS FILMS

1	*The Silence of the Lambs*	1991
2	*Bram Stoker's Dracula*	1992
3	*A Bridge Too Far*	1977
4	*Magic*	1978
5	*Howard's End*	1992
6	*The Elephant Man*	1980
7	*Shadowlands*	1993
8	*The Remains of the Day*	1993
9	*The Lion in Winter*	1968
10	*Freejack*	1992

T O P 1 0

HARRISON FORD FILMS

1	*Star Wars*	1977
2	*Return of the Jedi*	1983
3	*The Empire Strikes Back*	1980
4	*Raiders of the Lost Ark*	1981
5	*Indiana Jones and the Last Crusade*	1989
6	*Indiana Jones and the Temple of Doom*	1984
7	*The Fugitive*	1993
8	*American Graffiti*	1973
9	*Presumed Innocent*	1990
10	*Apocalypse Now*	1979

Harrison Ford is in the fortunate position of having appeared in so many successful films that even if, for example, *Apocalypse Now* were deleted from the Top 10 (since his role in it amounted to little more than a cameo), several similarly profitable films in which he starred could easily replace it, among them *Patriot Games* (1992), *Working Girl* (1988), *Witness* (1985), *Regarding Henry* (1991), and *Blade Runner* (1982). One film organization has recently voted Ford "Box Office Star of the Century".

T O P 1 0

SEAN CONNERY FILMS

1	*Indiana Jones and the Last Crusade*	1989
2	*The Hunt for Red October*	1990
3	*The Untouchables*	1987
4	*Rising Sun*	1993
5	*Thunderball*	1965
6	*Never Say Never Again*	1983
7	*Goldfinger*	1964
8	*Medicine Man*	1992
9	*Time Bandits*	1981
10	*A Bridge Too Far*	1977

If Sean Connery's fleeting cameo entry in the final two minutes of *Robin Hood: Prince of Thieves* (1991) is taken into account, it would be placed 2nd in the list.

T O P 1 0

SYLVESTER STALLONE FILMS

1	*Rambo: First Blood 2*	1985
2	*Rocky IV*	1985
3	*Rocky III*	1982
4	*Rocky*	1976
5	*Cliffhanger*	1993
6	*Rocky II*	1979
7	*Tango and Cash*	1989
8	*Cobra*	1986
9	*Demolition Man*	1993
10	*First Blood*	1982

T O P 1 0

AL PACINO FILMS

1	*The Godfather*	1972
2	*Dick Tracy*	1990
3	*The Godfather Part III*	1990
4	*The Godfather Part II*	1974
5	*Sea of Love*	1989
6	*Scent of a Woman*	1992
7	*Scarface*	1983
8	*Dog Day Afternoon*	1975
9	*Carlito's Way*	1993
10	*Serpico*	1973

T O P 1 0

JACK NICHOLSON FILMS

1	*Batman*	1989
2	*A Few Good Men*	1992
3	*One Flew Over the Cuckoo's Nest*	1975
4	*Terms of Endearment*	1983
5	*The Witches of Eastwick*	1987
6	*The Shining*	1980
7	*Broadcast News*	1987
8	*Reds*	1981
9	*Easy Rider*	1969
10	*Carnal Knowledge*	1971

TOP 10

CLINT EASTWOOD'S FIRST 10 FILMS

1	*Revenge of The Creature*	1955
2	*Lady Godiva*	1955
3	*Tarantula*	1955
4	*Never Say Goodbye*	1956
5	*The First Traveling Saleslady*	1956
6	*Star in the Dust*	1956
7	*Escapade in Japan*	1957
8	*Ambush at Cimarron Pass*	1958
9	*Lafayette Escadrille*	1958
10	*A Fistful of Dollars*	1964

Eastwood's first roles were as a laboratory technician in the 1955 sequel to *The Creature from the Black Lagoon*, *Revenge of the Creature*, as "First Saxon" in *Lady Godiva*, as the squadron leader of the force that attacks the giant spiders in *Tarantula*, and back to his role as a lab assistant in *Never Say Goodbye*. *The First Traveling Saleslady*, a bizarre Western about a corset-seller, was his first film in the genre that he was to make his own: after a brief excursion as a soldier called Dumbo in *Escapade in Japan*, and his appearance in *Lafayette Escadrille*, a film about First World War flying aces, all the rest of his early films were Westerns – and it was with the "spaghetti Western" that he finally broke through to superstardom.

TOP 10

ARNOLD SCHWARZENEGGER FILMS

1	*Terminator 2: Judgment Day*	1991
2	*Total Recall*	1990
3	*Twins*	1988
4	*Kindergarten Cop*	1990
5	*Predator*	1987
6	*Last Action Hero*	1993
7	*Conan the Barbarian*	1981
8	*Commando*	1985
9	*The Terminator*	1984
10	*The Running Man*	1987

TOP 10

CLINT EASTWOOD FILMS

1	*Every Which Way But Loose*	1978
2	*In The Line of Fire*	1993
3	*Unforgiven*	1992
4	*Any Which Way You Can*	1980
5	*Sudden Impact*	1983
6	*Firefox*	1982
7	*The Enforcer*	1976
8	*Tightrope*	1984
9	*Heartbreak Ridge*	1986
10	*Escape from Alcatraz*	1979

Unforgiven, Eastwood's 1992 multi-Oscar-winning film ("Best Picture", "Director", "Editing", "Supporting Actor"), rapidly made an impact and by the end of the following year had become his third highest-earning film ever, though just overtaken by *In The Line of Fire*.

TOP 10

KEVIN COSTNER FILMS

1	*Robin Hood: Prince of Thieves*	1991
2	*Dances With Wolves*	1990
3	*The Bodyguard*	1992
4	*The Untouchables*	1987
5	*JFK*	1991
6	*Field of Dreams*	1989
7	*The Big Chill*	1983
8	*Bull Durham*	1988
9	*Silverado*	1985
10	*No Way Out*	1987

Costner's acting role in *The Big Chill* was cut, and we see only parts of his body as it is being prepared for a funeral. If this entry is ignored, his 10th most successful film is *Night Shift* (1982). Ten years after his first film, Costner (born 18 January 1955, Lynwood, California) received huge acclaim (and seven Oscars) for *Dances With Wolves*, which was the first film he directed. He followed it with the smash commercial success *Robin Hood: Prince of Thieves*, and is now ranked by *Premiere* magazine as the most powerful actor in Hollywood.

TOP 10

CLINT EASTWOOD DIRECTED FILMS

1	*Unforgiven*	1992
2	*Sudden Impact*	1983
3	*Firefox*	1982
4	*Heartbreak Ridge*	1986
5	*Pale Rider*	1985
6	*The Gauntlet*	1977
7	*Bronco Billy*	1980
8	*A Perfect World*	1993
9	*The Outlaw Josey Wales*	1976
10	*The Rookie*	1990

His directorial debut was of a single scene in *Dirty Harry* (1971). If this were included, it would appear in 6th place.

TOP 10

BRUCE WILLIS FILMS

1	*Look Who's Talking**	1989
2	*Die Hard 2*	1990
3	*Die Hard*	1988
4	*Death Becomes Her*	1992
5	*The Last Boy Scout*	1991
6	*Blind Date*	1987
7	*National Lampoon's Loaded Weapon 1#*	1993
8	*The Bonfire of the Vanities*	1990
9	*Hudson Hawk*	1991
10	*Mortal Thoughts*	1991

* *Voice only.*
\# *Uncredited cameo performance.*

It is somewhat ironic to consider that the most successful film role of an actor whose screen persona is of a tough-guy should be that of a baby in *Look Who's Talking* – and that consisting only of Willis's dubbed voice. If discounted, either of two other films, *Sunset* (1988) and *In Country* (1989) could be considered as contenders for 10th place, although neither can be regarded as in any sense high-earning films. Willis has also had cameo roles – as himself – in *The Player* (1992) and *National Lampoon's Loaded Weapon 1* (1993).

FILM STARS – ACTRESSES

T O P 1 0

DEMI MOORE FILMS

1	Ghost	1990
2	A Few Good Men	1992
3	Indecent Proposal	1993
4	St Elmo's Fire	1985
5	About Last Night	1986
6	Young Doctors in Love	1982
7	Blame it on Rio	1984
8	Mortal Thoughts	1991
9	The Seventh Sign	1988
10	One Crazy Summer	1986

DEMI MOORE
Former star of TV soap General Hospital, *Demi Moore (real name Demi Guynes) has appeared in hit films for more than a decade. She has been married to actor Bruce Willis since 1987.*

T O P 1 0

SIGOURNEY WEAVER FILMS

1	Ghostbusters	1984
2	Ghostbusters II	1989
3	Aliens	1986
4	Alien	1979
5	Alien^3	1992
6	Dave	1993
7	Working Girl	1988
8	Gorillas in the Mist	1988
9	The Deal of the Century	1983
10	The Year of Living Dangerously	1982

Sigourney Weaver also had a fleeting minor part in *Annie Hall* (1977). If included, this would appear in 7th position.

T O P 1 0

SHARON STONE FILMS

1	Total Recall	1990
2	Basic Instinct	1992
3	Last Action Hero	1993
4	Sliver	1993
5	Police Academy 4: Citizens on Patrol	1987
6	Action Jackson	1988
7	Above The Law/Nico	1988
8	Irreconcilable Differences	1984
9	King Solomon's Mines	1985
10	He Said, She Said	1991

MICHELLE PFEIFFER
In 1994 Premiere *magazine ranked her in 97th place among the 100 most powerful people in Hollywood.*

T O P 1 0

MICHELLE PFEIFFER FILMS

1	Batman Returns	1992
2	The Witches of Eastwick	1987
3	Scarface	1983
4	Tequila Sunrise	1988
5	Dangerous Liaisons	1988
6	The Age of Innocence	1993
7	Frankie and Johnny	1991
8	The Russia House	1990
9	The Fabulous Baker Boys	1989
10	Married to the Mob	1988

T O P 1 0

KATHLEEN TURNER FILMS

1	Who Framed Roger Rabbit?*	1988	7	Prizzi's Honor	1985
2	The War of the Roses	1989	8	Body Heat	1981
3	The Jewel of the Nile	1985	9	V.I. Warshawski	1991
4	Romancing the Stone	1984	10	The Man with Two Brains	1983
5	Peggy Sue Got Married	1986			
6	The Accidental Tourist	1988			

* *Speaking voice of Jessica Rabbit; if excluded, the 10th film in which she acted is* Switching Channels *(1988).*

T O P 1 0

KIM BASINGER FILMS

1	Batman	1989
2	9½ Weeks	1986
3	Never Say Never Again	1983
4	Wayne's World 2	1993
5	The Natural	1984
6	Blind Date	1987
7	Final Analysis	1992
8	No Mercy	1986
9	The Marrying Man	1991
10	My Stepmother is an Alien	1988

T O P 1 0

DIANE KEATON FILMS

1	The Godfather	1972
2	The Godfather, Part II	1974
3	Father of the Bride	1991
4	The Godfather, Part III	1990
5	Reds	1981
6	Annie Hall	1977
7	Manhattan	1979
8	Looking for Mr Goodbar	1977
9	Baby Boom	1987
10	Crimes of the Heart	1986

T O P 1 0

MEG RYAN FILMS

1	Top Gun	1986
2	Sleepless in Seattle	1993
3	When Harry Met Sally	1989
4	Joe Versus the Volcano	1990
5	The Doors	1991
6	Innerspace	1987
7	The Presido	1988
8	Rich and Famous	1981
9	D.O.A	1988
10	Amityville 3-D	1983

T O P 1 0

CARRIE FISHER FILMS

1	Star Wars	1977
2	Return of the Jedi	1983
3	The Empire Strikes Back	1980
4	When Harry Met Sally	1989
5	The Blues Brothers	1980
6	Shampoo	1975
7	Hannah and Her Sisters	1986
8	The 'Burbs	1989
9	Soapdish	1991
10	Sibling Rivalry	1990

Along with Mark Hamill and Harrison Ford, Carrie Fisher has had the remarkable good fortune to appear in three of the Top 6 highest-earning films of all time. If she had managed to negotiate a 10 per cent stake in just the North American rental income of these three, she would have received more than $50,000,000. Her part in *Shampoo* was very minor; if excluded, her 10th entry would be *Under the Rainbow* (1981).

T O P 1 0

JODIE FOSTER FILMS

1	The Silence of the Lambs	1990
2	Sommersby	1993
3	The Accused	1988
4	Taxi Driver	1976
5	Freaky Friday	1976
6	Little Man Tate*	1991
7	Alice Doesn't Live Here Any More	1975
8	Candleshoe	1977
9	Tom Sawyer	1973
10	The Hotel New Hampshire	1984

* Also directed.

SILENCE IS GOLDEN
Jodie Foster wins her second "Best Actress" Oscar, for The Silence of the Lambs. *She had previously won for her role in* The Accused.

T O P 1 0

MELANIE GRIFFITH FILMS

1	Working Girl	1988
2	Pacific Heights	1990
3	One-on-One	1977
4	Shining Through	1992
5	Paradise	1991
6	The Bonfire of the Vanities	1990
7	The Milagro Beanfield War	1988
8	Body Double	1984
9	Something Wild	1986
10	The Harrad Experiment*	1973

* Appeared as extra only.

FILM STARS – COMEDY

TOP 10

DAN AYKROYD FILMS

1	Ghostbusters	1984
2	Indiana Jones and the Temple of Doom	1984
3	Ghostbusters II	1989
4	Driving Miss Daisy	1989
5	Trading Places	1983
6	The Blues Brothers	1980
7	Spies Like Us	1985
8	Dragnet	1987
9	My Girl	1991
10	Sneakers	1992

TOP 10

DANNY DEVITO FILMS

1	Batman Returns	1992
2	One Flew Over the Cuckoo's Nest	1975
3	Twins	1988
4	Terms of Endearment	1983
5	The War of the Roses*	1989
6	The Jewel of the Nile	1985
7	Romancing the Stone	1984
8	Ruthless People	1986
9	Throw Momma from the Train*	1987
10	Hoffa*	1992

* Also director.

DANNY DEVITO
The comedy star has had success as a director as well as in his film roles.

Danny DeVito had a relatively minor role in *One Flew Over the Cuckoo's Nest*. If this is discounted from the reckoning, his 10th most successful film becomes *Other People's Money* (1991).

HORROR STORY
Rick Moranis was an unlikely hero in Little Shop of Horrors.

TOP 10

RICK MORANIS FILMS

1	Ghostbusters	1984
2	Honey, I Shrunk the Kids	1989
3	Ghostbusters II	1989
4	Parenthood	1989
5	Honey, I Blew Up the Kid	1992
6	Brewster's Millions	1985
7	Little Shop of Horrors	1986
8	Spaceballs	1987
9	My Blue Heaven	1990
10	Club Paradise	1986

TOP 10

MEL BROOKS FILMS

1	Blazing Saddles*#	1974
2	Young Frankenstein#	1975
3	The Muppet Movie*	1979
4	Look Who's Talking Too* **	1990
5	Silent Movie*	1976
6	High Anxiety*#	1977
7	Spaceballs*#	1987
8=	Robin Hood: Men in Tights	1993
8=	History of the World – Part I*#	1981
10	To Be or Not to Be*	1983

** Appeared in. # Directed or co-directed.
**Voice only.*

TOP 10

ROBIN WILLIAMS FILMS

1	Mrs Doubtfire	1993
2	Hook	1991
3	Good Morning, Vietnam	1987
4	Dead Poets Society	1989
5	Popeye	1980
6	Awakenings	1990
7	The Fisher King	1991
8	Dead Again	1991
9	The World According to Garp	1982
10	Cadillac Man	1990

Robin Williams's voice appears as that of the genie in the 1992 animated blockbuster *Aladdin*. If this were included, its earnings would place it second in the list. If his minor cameo role in *Dead Again* is excluded, his 10th most successful film would be *Toys* (1992).

CLEANING UP
Robin Williams has had an amazing success with his role as the housekeeper Mrs Doubtfire.

TOP 10
BILL MURRAY FILMS

1	*Ghostbusters*	1984
2	*Tootsie*	1982
3	*Ghostbusters II*	1989
4	*Stripes*	1981
5	*Groundhog Day*	1993
6	*Scrooged*	1988
7	*What About Bob?*	1991
8	*Meatballs*	1979
9	*Caddyshack*	1980
10	*Little Shop of Horrors*	1986

TOP 10
WOODY ALLEN FILMS

1	*Annie Hall* (A, S, D)	1977
2	*Hannah and Her Sisters* (A, S, D)	1986
3	*Manhattan* (A, S, D)	1979
4	*Casino Royale* (A)	1967
5	*Everything You Always Wanted to Know about Sex (But Were Afraid to Ask)* (A, S, D)	1972
6	*What's New, Pussycat?* (A, S)	1965
7	*Sleeper* (A, S, D)	1973
8	*Crimes and Misdemeanors* (A, S, D)	1989
9	*Love and Death* (A, S, D)	1975
10	*Zelig* (A, S, D)	1983

A – actor S – scriptwriter
D – director

This list includes films which Woody Allen has either written, starred in, or directed. If it were restricted only to films he has directed, *Casino Royale* and *What's New, Pussycat?* would be dropped from the list, and the new 9th and 10th entries would be *Radio Days* (1987) and *Broadway Danny Rose* (1984). *Annie Hall* was the first occasion since 1941 that one individual has been nominated for "Best Picture", "Best Actor", "Best Director", and "Best Screenplay" (the previous nominee was Orson Welles for *Citizen Kane*; he won only for "Best Screenplay", jointly with Herman J. Manciewicz). The film won Allen "Best Picture" and "Best Screenplay" Oscars – which, characteristically, he did not bother to collect.

TOP 10
TOM HANKS FILMS

1	*Sleepless in Seattle*	1993
2	*A League of Their Own*	1992
3	*Big*	1988
4	*Turner & Hooch*	1989
5	*Splash!*	1984
6	*Philadelphia*	1993
7	*Dragnet*	1987
8	*Bachelor Party*	1984
9	*Joe Versus the Volcano*	1990
10	*The 'Burbs*	1989

TOP 10
EDDIE MURPHY FILMS

1	*Beverly Hills Cop*	1984
2	*Beverly Hills Cop 2*	1987
3	*Coming to America*	1988
4	*Trading Places*	1983
5	*Another 48 Hrs*	1990
6	*The Golden Child*	1986
7	*Boomerang*	1992
8	*Harlem Nights**	1989
9	*48 Hours*	1982
10	*The Distinguished Gentleman*	1992

* Also director.

Eddie Murphy Raw (1987), which features Murphy live on stage, is one of an elite group of documentary or "non-fiction" films that rank alongside major feature films in terms of their earnings, both from screenings and video sales and rental.

TOP 10
WHOOPI GOLDBERG FILMS

1	*Ghost*	1990
2	*Sister Act*	1992
3	*The Color Purple*	1985
4	*Sister Act 2: Back in the Habit*	1993
5	*Made in America*	1993
6	*Soapdish*	1991
7	*National Lampoon's Loaded Weapon 1*	1993
8	*Jumpin' Jack Flash*	1986
9	*Burglar*	1987
10	*Fatal Beauty*	1987

TOP 10
STEVE MARTIN FILMS

1	*Parenthood*	1989
2	*The Jerk**	1979
3	*Father of the Bride*	1991
4	*Housesitter*	1992
5	*Planes, Trains and Automobiles*	1987
6	*¡Three Amigos!**	1986
7	*Little Shop of Horrors*	1986
8	*Dirty Rotten Scoundrels*	1988
9	*Roxanne*	1987
10	*Grand Canyon*	1991

* Also co-writer.

Steve Martin was also one of the many "guest stars" in *The Muppet Movie* (1979). If included, it would appear in 5th place.

BEING A PARENT
Steve Martin appeared as the troubled father in Parenthood.

DIRECTORS

T O P 1 0

FILMS DIRECTED BY ACTOR-DIRECTORS

	Film	Year	Director
1	*Pretty Woman*	1990	Gary Marshall
2	*Dances With Wolves*	1990	Kevin Costner
3	*Three Men and a Baby*	1987	Leonard Nimoy
4	*Rocky IV*	1985	Sylvester Stallone
5	*A Few Good Men*	1992	Rob Reiner
6	*Rocky III*	1982	Sylvester Stallone
7	*On Golden Pond*	1981	Mark Rydell
8	*Dick Tracy*	1990	Warren Beatty
9	*Stir Crazy*	1980	Sidney Poitier
10	*Star Trek IV: The Voyage Home*	1986	Leonard Nimoy

Heading this list, *Pretty Woman* director Garry Marshall is the brother of actress-director Penny Marshall, who only just fails to achive a place in this Top 10, but makes three appearances in the *Top 10 Films Directed by Women*. (Keeping it in the family, she was also once married to Top 10 actor-director Rob Reiner.) Among other actors who have also directed may be numbered Marlon Brando (*One-Eyed Jacks*, 1961), Mel Brooks (*Blazing Saddles*, 1974, *Young Frankenstein*, 1975), Robert de Niro (*A Bronx Tale*, 1993), Danny DeVito (*The War of the Roses*, 1989, *Throw Momma From the Train*, 1987), Clint Eastwood (*Sudden Impact*, 1983, *Unforgiven*, 1992), Mel Gibson (*The Man Without a Face*, 1993), former child-star Ron Howard (*Splash!*, 1984, *Parenthood*, 1989), Eddie Murphy (*Harlem Nights*, 1989), Paul Newman (*Rachel, Rachel*, 1968, *The Effect of Gamma Rays on Man-in-the-Moon Marigolds*, 1972), Jack Nicholson (*Drive, He Said*, 1971, *The Two Jakes*, 1990), Robert Redford (*Ordinary People*, 1980, *A River Runs Through It*, 1992), Burt Reynolds (*The End*, 1978, *Sharky's Machine*, 1981), William Shatner (*Star Trek V: The Final Frontier*, 1989), Orson Welles (*Citizen Kane*, 1941), and Gene Wilder (*The World's Greatest Lover*, 1977, *The Woman in Red*, 1984). British actor-directors include Richard Attenborough (*A Bridge Too Far*, 1977, *Gandhi*, 1982), Kenneth Branagh (*Henry V*, 1989, *Dead Again*, 1991), Terry Jones (*Monty Python's Life of Brian*, 1979, *Monty Python's The Meaning of Life*, 1983), and Laurence Olivier (*Henry V*, 1944, *The Prince and the Showgirl*, 1957). Notable actress-directors are Barbra Streisand (*The Prince of Tides*, 1991, *Yentl*, 1983) and Jodie Foster (*Little Man Tate*, 1991).

T O P 1 0

FILMS DIRECTED OR PRODUCED BY GEORGE LUCAS

1	*Star Wars* (D)	1977
2	*Return of the Jedi* (P)	1983
3	*The Empire Strikes Back* (P)	1980
4	*Raiders of the Lost Ark* (P)	1981
5	*Indiana Jones and the Last Crusade* (P)	1989
6	*Indiana Jones and the Temple of Doom* (P)	1984
7	*American Graffiti* (D)	1973
8	*Willow* (P)	1988
9	*The Land Before Time* (P)	1988
10	*Howard the Duck* (P)	1986

D – director P – producer

George Lucas made the move from directing to producing after the phenomenal success of *Star Wars*, but he clearly has a Midas touch in both fields, the first six films on this list ranking among the 14 highest-earning of all time. *Howard the Duck* can be mercifully relegated from the list if his uncredited role as executive producer of *Body Heat* (1981) replaces it in 10th position.

T O P 1 0

FILMS DIRECTED BY JOHN LANDIS

1	*National Lampoon's Animal House*	1978
2	*Coming to America*	1988
3	*Trading Places*	1983
4	*The Blues Brothers*	1980
5	*Spies Like Us*	1985
6	*Three Amigos*	1986
7	*Twilight Zone – The Movie**	1983
8	*An American Werewolf in London*	1981
9	*Oscar*	1991
10	*The Kentucky Fried Movie*	1977

* *Part only; other segments directed by Joe Dante, George Miller, and Steven Spielberg.*

TOP 10

FILMS DIRECTED BY WOMEN

	Film	Year	Director
1	*Look Who's Talking*	1989	Amy Heckerling
2	*Sleepless in Seattle*	1993	Nora Ephron
3	*Wayne's World*	1992	Penelope Spheeris
4	*Big*	1988	Penny Marshall
5	*A League of Their Own*	1992	Penny Marshall
6	*The Prince of Tides*	1991	Barbra Streisand
7	*Pet Sematary*	1989	Mary Lambert
8	*National Lampoon's European Vacation*	1985	Amy Heckerling
9	*Awakenings*	1990	Penny Marshall
10	*Look Who's Talking Too*	1990	Amy Heckerling

TOP 10

FILMS DIRECTED BY BRITISH-BORN DIRECTORS

	Film	Year	Director	Birthdate/place
1	*Return of the Jedi*	1983	Richard Marquand	1938, Cardiff; d.1987
2	*Beverly Hills Cop II*	1987	Tony Scott	1944, Newcastle
3	*Top Gun*	1986	Tony Scott	1944, Newcastle
4	*Saturday Night Fever*	1977	John Badham	1939, Luton
5	*Fatal Attraction*	1997	Adrian Lyne	1941, Peterborough
6	*The Bodyguard*	1992	Mick Jackson	Undisclosed
7	*Indecent Proposal*	1972	Adrian Lyne	1941, Peterborough
8	*The Towering Inferno**	1974	John Guillermin	1923, London
9	*Doctor Zhivago*	1965	David Lean	1908, Croydon; d.1991
10	*Mary Poppins*	1964	Robert Stevenson	1905, London; d.1986

* Co-directed with US-born Irwin Allen.

TOP 10

FILMS DIRECTED BY STEVEN SPIELBERG

1	*E.T. The Extra-Terrestrial*	1982
2	*Jurassic Park*	1993
3	*Jaws*	1975
4	*Raiders of the Lost Ark*	1981
5	*Indiana Jones and the Last Crusade*	1989
6	*Indiana Jones and the Temple of Doom*	1984
7	*Close Encounters of the Third Kind*	1977/80
8	*Hook*	1991
9	*The Color Purple*	1985
10	*Schindler's List*	1993

TOP 10

FILMS DIRECTED BY ALFRED HITCHCOCK

1	*Psycho*	1960		6	*Frenzy*	1972
2	*Rear Window*	1954		7	*Vertigo*	1958
3	*North by Northwest*	1959		8	*The Man Who Knew Too Much*	1956
4	*Family Plot*	1976		9	*The Birds*	1963
5	*Torn Curtain*	1966		10	*Spellbound*	1945

PSYCHO
Anthony Perkins starred as the deranged killer Norman Bates in Psycho *(1960).*

STUDIOS

COLUMBIA
Dominated for many years by Harry Cohn, who founded it in 1924, Columbia was taken over by Coca-Cola and briefly (1986–88) run by British film producer David Puttnam.

TOP 10
ORION FILMS OF ALL TIME

1	Dances With Wolves	1990
2	Platoon	1986
3	The Silence of the Lambs	1991
4	Arthur	1981
5	Back to School	1986
6	10	1979
7	Throw Momma from the Train	1987
8	Robocop	1987
9	Amadeus	1984
10	First Blood	1982

20TH CENTURY-FOX
This studio was formed in 1935 by the merging of William Fox's film production company and studio, which made feature films and Movietone newsreels, and 20th Century Pictures. It was recently acquired by Rupert Murdoch.

TOP 10
COLUMBIA FILMS OF ALL TIME

1	Ghostbusters	1984
2	Tootsie	1982
3	Close Encounters of the Third Kind	1977/80
4	A Few Good Men	1992
5	City Slickers	1991
6	Ghostbusters II	1989
7	Kramer vs Kramer	1979
8	Stir Crazy	1980
9	The Karate Kid Part II	1986
10	A League of Their Own	1992

MGM
Metro-Goldwyn-Mayer was established in 1924 and became the leading Hollywood studio during the 1930s. Leo the Lion, MGM's familiar logo, was devised by advertising executive Howard Dietz, who based it on the lion featured in the Columbia college magazine. White Shadows of the South (1928) was the first film in which Leo was heard roaring.

TOP 10
20TH CENTURY-FOX FILMS OF ALL TIME

1	Star Wars	1977
2	Return of the Jedi	1983
3	The Empire Strikes Back	1980
4	Home Alone	1990
5	Mrs Doubtfire	1993
6	Home Alone 2	1992
7	The Sound of Music	1965
8	Die Hard 2	1990
9	9 to 5	1980
10	Porky's	1982

TOP 10
MGM FILMS OF ALL TIME

1	Rain Man	1988
2	Gone With the Wind	1939
3	Rocky IV	1985
4	Rocky III	1982
5	Doctor Zhivago	1965
6	The Goodbye Girl	1977
7	War Games	1983
8	Poltergeist	1982
9	Ben Hur	1959
10	Moonstruck	1987

TOP 10
TRI-STAR FILMS OF ALL TIMES

1	Terminator 2	1991
2	Rambo: First Blood 2	1985
3	Look Who's Talking	1989
4	Hook	1991
5	Sleepless in Seattle	1993
6	Total Recall	1990
7	Basic Instinct	1992
8	Cliffhanger	1993
9	Steel Magnolias	1989
10	Rambo 3	1988

TOP 10

WARNER BROTHERS FILMS OF ALL TIME

1	*Batman*	1989
2	*Batman Returns*	1992
3	*The Fugitive*	1993
4	*The Exorcist*	1973
5	*Robin Hood: Prince of Thieves*	1991
6	*Superman*	1978
7	*Lethal Weapon 3*	1993
8	*Gremlins*	1984
9	*Lethal Weapon 2*	1989
10	*Superman II*	1981

PARAMOUNT
After several changes of name, Paramount Pictures appeared in 1933. Following various setbacks, it was rescued from the commercial doldrums in 1972 by its film The Godfather.

TOP 10

PARAMOUNT FILMS OF ALL TIME

1	*Raiders of the Lost Ark*	1981
2	*Indiana Jones and the Last Crusade*	1989
3	*Indiana Jones and the Temple of Doom*	1984
4	*Beverly Hills Cop*	1984
5	*Ghost*	1990
6	*Grease*	1978
7	*The Godfather*	1972
8	*Beverly Hills Cop II*	1987
9	*Top Gun*	1986
10	*The Firm*	1993

TOP 10

BUENA VISTA/WALT DISNEY FILMS OF ALL TIME

1	*Aladdin*	1992
2	*Pretty Woman*	1990
3	*Three Men and a Baby*	1987
4	*Who Framed Roger Rabbit?*	1988
5	*Honey, I Shrunk the Kids*	1989
6	*Beauty and the Beast*	1991
7	*101 Dalmatians*	1961
8	*Sister Act*	1992
9	*Snow White and the Seven Dwarfs**	1937
10	*The Jungle Book*	1967

* *Originally released by RKO.*

TOP 10

UNITED ARTISTS FILMS OF ALL TIME

1	*One Flew Over the Cuckoo's Nest*	1975
2	*Rocky*	1976
3	*Rocky II*	1979
4	*Fiddler on the Roof*	1971
5	*Apocalypse Now*	1979
6	*Moonraker*	1979
7	*Thunderball*	1965
8	*Revenge of the Pink Panther*	1978
9	*The Spy Who Loved Me*	1977
10	*Around the World in 80 Days*	1956

United Artists was formed in 1919 by actors including Charlie Chaplin and Douglas Fairbanks, together with director D.W. Griffith, to provide an independent means of producing and distributing their films. It never actually owned a studio, but rented production facilities. After many vicissitudes, and a successful run in the 1970s with the consistently successful James Bond films, it was merged with MGM in 1981.

TOP 10

UNIVERSAL FILMS OF ALL TIME

1	*E.T. The Extra-Terrestrial*	1982
2	*Jurassic Park*	1993
3	*Jaws*	1975
4	*Back to the Future*	1985
5	*The Sting*	1973
6	*Back to the Future, Part II*	1989
7	*National Lampoon's Animal House*	1978
8	*On Golden Pond*	1981
9	*Smokey and the Bandit*	1977
10	*Twins*	1988

RADIO, TV, & VIDEO

T O P 1 0

LONGEST-RUNNING PROGRAMMES ON BBC RADIO

	Programme	First broadcast
1	*The Week's Good Cause*	24 January 1926
2	*Choral Evensong*	7 October 1926
3	*Daily Service*	2 January 1928*
4	*The Week in Westminster*	6 November 1929
5	*Sunday Half Hour*	14 July 1940
6	*Desert Island Discs*	29 January 1942
7	*Saturday Night Theatre*	3 April 1943
8	*Composer of the Week#*	2 August 1943
9	*Letter From America (originally American Letter)*	24 March 1946
10	*From Our Own Correspondent*	4 October 1946

1968-695

B.B.C.
TELEVISION O.B.s
(LONDON)

In addition to these 10 long-running programmes, a further six that started in the 1940s are still on the air: *Woman's Hour* (first broadcast 7 October 1946 – although the BBC's London station 2LO had previously first broadcast a programme with this name on 2 May 1923), *Down Your Way* (29 December 1946), *Round Britain Quiz* (2 November 1947), *Any Questions?* (12 October 1948), *Book at Bedtime* (6 August 1949), and *Morning Story* (17 October 1949). *Gardeners' Question Time* was first broadcast on 9 April 1947 as *How Does Your Garden Grow?* Its name was changed in 1950. A pilot for *The Archers* was broadcast in the Midland region for a one-week trial beginning on 29 May 1950, but the serial began its national run on 1 January 1951.

* *Experimental broadcast; national transmission began December 1929.*
\# *Formerly* This Week's Composer.

RADIO STATIONS IN THE UK IN 1993

	Station	Listener hours*
1	BBC Radio 1	145,832,000
2	BBC Radio 2	109,773,000
3	BBC Radio 4	93,739,000
4	Capital Radio#	47,357,000
5	Metro Tyne Tees#	29,501,000
6	Metro Yorkshire#	25,127,000
7	Classic FM	24,782,000

	Station	Listener hours*
8	Atlantic 252	24,712,000
9	Virgin 1215	18,331,000
10	LBC#	17,267,000

* *Total number of hours spent by
all adults (over 15) listening to the
station in an average week.*
\# *Split frequency stations; listener
hours are totals for all frequencies.*

LUXURIES MOST CHOSEN BY CASTAWAYS
ON DESERT ISLAND DISCS

1	Piano
2	Writing materials
3	Bed
4	Guitar
5	Typewriter
6	Radio receiver
7	Golf club and balls
8	Painting materials
9	Wine
10	Perfume

"An inanimate object, purely for the senses, which is not going to help you live", was how the programme's creator Roy Plomley described what is now known more simply as the "luxury object" that "castaways" are permitted to take to their mythical desert island. As well as those in the Top 10, less frequently requested objects have included the Taj Mahal, the Albert Memorial, Nelson's Column, the *Mona Lisa* (requested by miners' leader Arthur Scargill), and a fish-and-chip shop.

NATION SHALL SPEAK UNTO NATION
Broadcasting House is the headquarters of the BBC's national radio services. Built in 1931, in provided a suitably modern setting for the brand new medium of broadcasting.

RADIO-OWNING COUNTRIES

	Country	Radio sets per 1,000 population
1	USA	2,091
2	Bermuda	1,710
3	UK	1,240
4	Australia	1,144
5	Finland	984
6	New Zealand	902
7	Virgin Islands (USA)	884
8	France	866
9	Sweden	842
10	Canada	828

MOST POPULAR PROGRAMMES ON BBC RADIO 4

	Programme/day/time	Average audience
1	*News* (Mon–Fri, 8:00 am)	2,310,000
2	*News* (Mon–Fri, 7:00 am)	1,880,000
3	*Today* (excluding *News*, Mon–Fri, 6:30 am)	1,820,000
4	*News* (Sat, 8:00 am)	1,760,000
5	*Readings* (Mon–Fri, 8:45 am)	1,620,000
6	*Today* (excluding *News*, Sat, 7:00 am)	1,430,000

	Programme/day/time	Average audience
7	*The Archers* (Sun, 10:15 am)	1,410,000
8	*News* (Sun, 8:00 am)	1,370,000
9	*News* (Sun, 9:00 am)	1,350,000
10	*Letter from America* (Sun, 9:15 am)	1,320,000

Based on a survey conducted by RAJAR (Radio Joint Audience Research) during the period 21 December 1992 to 21 March 1993.

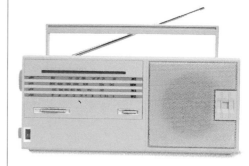

TV FIRSTS

TOP 10

FIRST COUNTRIES TO HAVE TELEVISION*

	Country	Year
1	UK	1936
2	USA	1939
3	USSR	1939
4	France	1948
5	Brazil	1950
6	Cuba	1950
7	Mexico	1950
8	Argentina	1951
9	Denmark	1951
10	Netherlands	1951

* *High-definition regular public broadcasting service.*

TOP 10

FIRST PROGRAMMES ON BBC TELEVISION

	Time	Programme
		Monday 2 November 1936
1	15:02	Opening ceremony by Postmaster General G. C. Tryon
2	15:15	British Movietone News No. 387 (repeated several times during the next few days)
3	15:23	*Variety* – Adele Dixon (singer), Buck and Bubbles (comic dancers), and the Television Orchestra
		(15.31 close; 15.32 Television Orchestra continues in sound only with music.)
4	21:05	Film: *Television Comes to London*
5	21:23	*Picture Page* (magazine programme featuring interviews with transatlantic flyer Jim Mollison, tennis champion Kay Stammers, King's Bargemaster Bossy Phelps and others, ghost stories from Algernon Blackwood and various musical interludes)
6	22:11	Speech by Lord Selsdon, followed by close
		Tuesday 3 November 1936
7	15:04	Exhibits from the Metropolitan and Essex Canine Society's Show – "Animals described by A. Croxton Smith, OBE"
8	15:28	*The Golden Hind* – "a model of Drake's famous ship, made by L. A. Stock, a bus driver"
9	15:46	*Starlight* with comedians Bebe Daniels and Ben Lyon (followed by repeat of items 7 and 8)
10	21:48	*Starlight* with Manuela Del Rio

Although there were earlier low-definition experimental broadcasts, BBC television's high-definition public broadcasting service – the first in the world – was inaugurated on a daily basis on 2 November 1936. During the first three months, two parallel operating systems were in use: the opening programmes were thus broadcast twice, first on the Baird system, and repeated slightly later on the Marconi-EMI system.

TOP 10

FIRST PROGRAMMES BROADCAST ON BBC 2

The programmes for the official opening night on Monday 20 April 1964 were postponed after much of central London was blacked out by a power cut, and only a handful of announcements and news items were actually transmitted. Originally broadcast only in the London area, BBC 2 was the first British station to broadcast exclusively on the 625-line system for sharper definition, but a survey published on 9 June 1964 indicated that only 7.6 per cent of homes in the area had a television set capable of receiving such transmissions. By 6 December 1964 viewers in the Birmingham area were able to tune in to BBC 2, and the service was steadily extended to the rest of the country.

	Time	Programme
		Tuesday 21 April 1964
1	11:00	*Play School*
2	19:15	*Zero Minus Five* (introductory programme)
3	19:20	*Line-Up* (arts programme)
4	19:30	*The Alberts' Channel Too* (variety show)
5	20:00	*Kiss Me Kate* (musical starring Howard Keel and Millicent Martin)
6	21:35	Arkady Raikin (Soviet comedian)
7	22:20	*Off With a Bang* (fireworks from Southend pier)
8	22:35	*Newsroom*
9	23:02	*Jazz 625* (Duke Ellington in concert)
		Wednesday 22 April 1964
10	11:00	*Play School*

FIRST PROGRAMMES BROADCAST ON CHANNEL 4

	Time	Audience	Programme
1	16:45	3,681,000	*Countdown* (quiz game introduced by Richard Whiteley)
2	17:15	2,724,000	*Preview* (review of forthcoming programmes)
3	17:30	2,124,000	*The Body Show* (keep-fit programme)
4	18:00	1,508,000	*People's Court* (Californian court cases re-enacted)
5	18:30	984,000	*Book on Four* (book review programme featuring Len Deighton, William Boyd, and Fay Weldon)
6	19:00	1,239,000	*Channel 4 News* (presented by Trevor McDonald, Peter Sissons, etc)
7	20:00	2,779,000	*Brookside* (first episode of the long-running soap)
8	20:30	3,598,000	*The Paul Hogan Show* (Australian comedy series)
9	21:00	3,737,000	*Walter* (feature film commissioned by Channel 4, starring Ian McKellen)
10	22:15	3,360,000	*The Comic Strip Presents: Five Go Mad in Dorset*

Channel 4 first went on the air on Tuesday 2 November 1982. Of the four terrestrial British TV stations, it is unique in having detailed audience figures for its first programmes. The final programme broadcast on the first night was The Raving Beauties' *In the Pink* (an all-female cabaret), from 22.45 to 23.45, which attracted an audience of 1,031,000.

FIRST PROGRAMMES ON ITV

	Time	Programme
		Thursday 22 September 1955
1	19:15	*The Ceremony at the Guildhall* (The Hallé Orchestra conducted by Sir John Barbirolli playing *Cockaigne* by Sir Edward Elgar and inaugural speeches by the Lord Mayor of London, Sir Seymour Howard, the Postmaster General, Dr Charles Hill, and Chairman of the Independent Television Authority, Sir Kenneth Clark)
2	20:00	*Channel Nine* variety show from ABC's television theatre, featuring Shirley Abicair (Australian zither-player), Reg Dixon (organist), Hughie Green, Harry Secombe, and other stars
3	20:40	Drama: Robert Morley introduces extracts from Oscar Wilde's *The Importance of Being Earnest* (starring Dame Edith Evans and Sir John Gielgud), Saki's *Baker's Dozen* and Noël Coward's *Private Lives*
4	21:10	Professional boxing from Shoreditch, Terence Murphy *v* Lew Lazar
5	22:00	*News and Newsreel*
6	22:15	*Gala Night at the Mayfair* (fashion show from the Mayfair Hotel, London)
7	22:30	*Star Cabaret* with Billy Ternant and his Orchestra
8	22:50	Preview of future Independent Television programmes
9	23:00	*Epilogue* (followed by National Anthem and close)
		Friday 23 September 1955
10	10:45	*Sixpenny Corner* (the first episode of a daily "soap" set in a rural garage)

The first-ever TV commercial broadcast in the UK was an advertisement for Gibbs SR Toothpaste shown in the first break in the *Channel Nine* programme, at 20.12.

TOP TV

ELECTRICITY SURGES OF ALL TIME IN THE UK

	TV programme	Channel	Date	Pick-up time	Mega-watts
1	World Cup Semi-final:	BBC1	4 Jul 1990	21.38	
	West Germany *v* England	ITV	4 Jul 1990	21.48	2,800
2	*The Thorn Birds*	BBC1	22 Jan 1984	21.07	2,600
3=	*The Thorn Birds*	BBC1	16 Jan 1984	21.30	2,200
3=	*Dallas*	BBC1	8 May 1985	20.56	
	This is Your Life	ITV	8 May 1985	21.00	2,200
3=	*The Darling Buds of May*	ITV	28 Apr 1991	20.40	2,200
6=	*Dallas*	BBC1	1 May 1985	20.56	
	This is Your Life	ITV	1 May 1985	21.00	2,100
6=	*The Colbys*	BBC1	19 Feb 1986	21.00	2,100
8=	*Coronation Street*	ITV	2 Apr 1984	19.57	
	Blue Thunder	BBC1	2 Apr 1984	20.00	2,000
8=	*Dallas*	BBC1	15 May 1984	20.50	2,000
8=	*EastEnders*	BBC1	1 Apr 1986	20.00	2,000
8=	*Coronation Street*	ITV	2 Apr 1986	19.57	
	A Song for Europe	BBC1	2 Apr 1986	20.00	2,000
8=	*Dallas*	BBC1	30 Apr 1986	20.57	
	Minder	ITV	30 Apr 1986	21.00	2,000
8=	*EastEnders*	BBC1	4 Sep 1986	20.00	2,000
8=	World Cup Semi-final:	BBC1	3 Jul 1990	21.51	
	Italy *v* Argentina	ITV	3 Jul 1990	21.57	2,000
8=	*The Darling Buds of May*	ITV	12 May 1991	20.45	2,000

Demand for electricity in the UK varies during the day: as it gets dark, progressively more lights are switched on, or, during the winter, heating comes on at varying times during the early morning, and the National Grid responds to such increases by steadily increasing the supply. The effect of television programmes is far more dramatic, however. It is not the programmes themselves but when they end that causes surges in demand (known as "TV pick-ups"), as millions of viewers get up and switch on electric kettles and other appliances (even the action of flushing lavatories has an effect, as demand for electricity from water pumping stations increases). Because barely a few minutes separates the ends of certain programmes on BBC1 and ITV, it is not possible to differentiate between them, but all those listed contributed to national TV pick-ups of 2,000 megawatts or more. The end of *Elizabeth R* (at 21.50 on BBC1 on 6 February 1992) resulted in a 1,200-megawatt surge that was widely reported in the Press the following day, but was in fact unremarkable when compared with those in the Top 10. With the increasing spread of viewing across BBC, ITV, satellite, and cable channels, and the use of video recorders, however, such notable TV pick-ups will probably be less evident in the future.

LONGEST-RUNNING PROGRAMMES ON BRITISH TELEVISION

	Programme	First shown
1	*Come Dancing*	29 Sep 1950
2	*Panorama*	11 Nov 1953
3	*What the Papers Say*	5 Nov 1956
4	*The Sky at Night*	24 Apr 1957
5	*Grandstand*	11 Oct 1958
6	*Blue Peter*	16 Oct 1958
7	*Coronation Street*	9 Dec 1960
8	*Songs of Praise*	1 Oct 1961
9	*Dr Who*	23 Nov 1963
10	*Top of the Pops*	1 Jan 1964

Only programmes appearing every year since their first screenings are listed, and all are BBC programmes except *Coronation Street*. Several other BBC programmes, such as *The Good Old Days* (1953–83) ran for many years but are now defunct. *The Sky at Night* has the additional distinction of having had the same presenter, Patrick Moore, since its first programme. Although *The Sooty Show* has been screened intermittently, Sooty is the longest-serving TV personality.

THE MELODY LINGERS ON
With a run of well over 40 years, Come Dancing *holds the record as the UK's longest-running television programme. Despite the ebb and flow of fashion, this window on the world of ballroom dancing remains a firm favourite.*

FAIRYTALE WEDDING
Joined by many millions more around the world, 39,000,000 viewers in the UK shared the splendour and the pageantry of Prince Charles' marriage to Lady Diana Spencer. After the wedding in St Paul's Cathedral, the couple greeted crowds from the balcony of Buckingham Palace.

TOP 10

TV AUDIENCES OF ALL TIME IN THE UK

	Programme	Date	Audience
1	Royal Wedding of HRH Prince Charles to Lady Diana Spencer	29 Jul 1981	39,000,000
2	Brazil *v* England 1970 World Cup	10 Jun 1970	32,500,000
3=	England *v* West Germany 1966 World Cup Final	30 Jul 1966	32,000,000
3=	Chelsea *v* Leeds Cup Final Replay	28 Apr 1970	32,000,000
5	*EastEnders* Christmas episode	26 Dec 1987	30,000,000
6	*Morecambe and Wise Christmas Show*	25 Dec 1977	28,000,000
7=	World Heavyweight Boxing Championship: Joe Frazier *v* Cassius Clay	8 Mar 1971	27,000,000
7=	*Dallas* (episode revealing who shot J.R. Ewing)	22 Nov 1980	27,000,000
9	*To The Manor Born* (last episode)	11 Nov 1979	24,000,000
10	*Live And Let Die* (James Bond film)	20 Jan 1980	23,500,000

TOP 10

CHANNEL 4 AUDIENCES, 1993

	Programme	Day	Date	Audience
1	Film: *Nuns on the Run*	Sun	18 Apr	9,201,000
2	*Brookside*	Sun	7 Nov	8,267,000 *
3	Film: *Bill and Ted's Excellent Adventure*	Sun	11 Apr	7,293,000
4	Film: *The Abyss*	Sun	24 Jan	7,014,000
5	Cutting Edge: *Navy Blues*	Sun	12 Dec	6,926,000 *
6	Film: *Good Morning, Vietnam*	Sun	25 Apr	6,747,000
7	Film: *Dirty Dancing*	Sat	13 Feb	5,632,000
8	Film: *The Krays*	Sun	14 Mar	5,582,000
9	*Lipstick on Your Collar*	Sun	21 Feb	5,572,000
10	*Desmond's*	Mon	25 Jan	5,452,000

* Aggregates two screenings of the same programme, with date of week ending.

TOP 10

TV-OWNING COUNTRIES IN THE WORLD

	Country	Homes with TV
1	China	103,009,000
2	Former USSR	100,900,000
3	USA	94,857,000
4	Brazil	45,567,000
5	Japan	40,667,000
6	Germany	35,379,000
7	UK	22,538,000
8	Indonesia	22,365,000
9	Italy	21,793,000
10	France	20,807,000

Taking population into account, China disappears from the list and the US comes top with 790 sets per 1,000 people.

TOP 10

BESTSELLING BBC TV PROGRAMMES

	Programme	Countries
1	*The Living Planet*	77
2	*Flight of the Condor*	74
3=	*Animal Olympians*	66
3=	*The Onedin Line*	66
3=	*The Six Wives of Henry VIII*	66
6=	*The Impossible Bird*	63
6=	*Supersense*	63
8=	*Ascent of Man*	62
8=	*Tender is the Night*	62
10	*Fawlty Towers*	60

BBC Enterprises is responsible for selling BBC TV programmes to TV stations around the world. Drama, comedy, documentary, and educational programmes all feature strongly among their bestsellers – *Dr Who* has been sold in 57 countries and both *Elizabeth R* (a documentary about Queen Elizabeth II) and *Miss Marple* in 54 countries – but, as the Top 10 suggests, the international appeal of high-quality natural history programmes makes them particularly saleable overseas.

VIDEO

T O P 1 0
COUNTRIES WITH MOST VCRs

		1980		1993	
	Country	As % of homes with TV	VCRs	As % of homes with TV	VCRs
1	USA	2.5	1,950,000	70.2	66,560,000
2	Japan	6.1	1,975,000	74.0	30,095,000
3	Germany	3.2	775,000	61.5	21,770,000
4	Brazil	0.7	100,000	45.4	20,669,000
5	UK	3.1	580,000	72.6	16,354,000
6	France	0.8	144,000	64.5	13,417,000
7	Italy	0.2	30,000	40.6	8,851,000
8	Canada	1.3	100,000	64.1	6,955,000
9	Spain	0.5	48,000	51.7	5,866,000
10	Former USSR	–	–	5.6	5,648,000
	World total	*1.7*	*7,687,000*	*36.9*	*275,055,000*

The 1980s have rightly been described as the "Video Decade": according to estimates published by *Screen Digest*, the period from 1980 to 1990 saw an increase in the number of video recorders in use in the world of more than 27 times, from 7,687,000 to 210,159,000, while the estimated 1993 total for the UK alone is more than double the entire world total for 1980. Since 1992, more than one-third of all world homes with TV have also had video.

T O P 1 0
FIRST VIDEOS TO TOP THE UK RENTAL CHART

1	*Jaws*
2	*Star Trek: The Motion Picture*
3	*Scanners*
4	*The Exterminator*
5	*Superman: The Movie*
6	*The Jazz Singer*
7	*Monty Python's Life Of Brian*
8	*Watership Down*
9	*Chariots Of Fire*
10	*Star Wars*

A varied mix of titles headed the rental chart during 1981 and 1982, the early years of the UK video rental industry. *Scanners* and *The Exterminator* were both 18-certificate shockers, while *Watership Down* was an animated family film and *The Jazz Singer* was a musical.

T O P 1 0
MOST-RENTED VIDEO CATEGORIES IN THE UK

	Category	Percentage of total rentals
1	Comedy	32
2	Adventure	19
3	Thriller	12
4	Drama	10
5	Children's	7
6	Horror	5
7	Science-fiction	3
8	War	2
9=	Sport	1
9=	Adult	1
9=	Film musical	1
9=	Educational	1

The percentage figures are each category's share of total video rentals.

T O P 1 0
MOST-PURCHASED VIDEO CATEGORIES IN THE UK

	Category	Percentage of total sales
1	Children's	24
2	Comedy	17
3	Pop/rock music	12
4=	Adventure	7
4=	Sport	7
6=	Educational	6
6=	Thriller	6
8	Drama	5
9	Film musical	4
10	Non-pop music	3

These figures – and those for the most rented categories – were polled for the first quarter of 1991 by the British Videogram Association from a survey of a sample of regular video viewers.

T O P 1 0
BESTSELLING VIDEOS IN THE UK, 1993

1	*The Jungle Book*
2	*Beauty And The Beast*
3	*Peter Pan*
4	*The Muppet Christmas Carol*
5	*Home Alone 2 - Lost In New York*
6	*The Bodyguard*
7	*Lethal Weapon 3*
8	*Sister Act*
9	*Take That – Take That And Party*
10	*Cherfitness – Bodyfitness*

Inevitably, the big Walt Disney releases, selling in millions, dominate the year's big sellers, leaving room for four other major films, one musical, and one keep fit title.

TOP 10

VIDEO CONSUMERS IN THE WORLD

	Country	Spending per video household (US $)		
		Rental	Purchase	Total
1	Netherlands	147.28	116.28	263.56
2	Japan	88.31	110.21	198.52
3	Australia	174.58	13.13	187.71
4	Canada	139.80	35.24	175.04
5	USA	116.21	47.85	164.06
6	Ireland	118.06	32.95	151.01
7	Norway	133.20	8.35	141.55
8	New Zealand	89.55	13.43	102.99
9	UK	56.09	37.76	93.85
10	Italy	27.10	62.93	90.03

Based on figures prepared by *Screen Digest* for 1991 (except Australia and Canada, which are for 1990). Total spending per head of population, rather than per household with video, produces a somewhat different picture, with Japan at the top of the list, followed closely by the US, Canada, and Australia. Norway moves up to 5th place and the UK to 6th. Ireland, New Zealand, Germany, and Sweden make up the rest of the list.

TOP 10

VIDEOS THAT SPENT LONGEST AT No.1 IN THE RENTAL CHART

	Title	Weeks at No.1
1	*Jaws* (1981)	17
2	*Raiders Of The Lost Ark* (1983)	15
3=	*The Jazz Singer* (1982)	13
3=	*Airplane* (1982)	13
3=	*Police Academy* (1985)	13
6	*First Blood* (1983)	12
7=	*Star Trek: The Motion Picture* (1981)	9
7=	*An Officer And A Gentleman* (1984)	9
7=	*Tightrope* (1985)	9
7=	*Pretty Woman* (1990)	9

Long chart-topping residencies were easier to achieve in the less crowded and less competitive video rental market of the early 1980s. Over a decade on, a movie that can hold No.1 for a full month is special indeed, such is the urgency with which box office successes now transfer to the home market.

TOP 10

BESTSELLING VIDEOS OF ALL TIME IN THE UK

(To 31 March 1994)

1	*The Jungle Book*
2	*Fantasia*
3	*Beauty And The Beast*
4	*Cinderella*
5	*The Little Mermaid*
6	*Bambi*
7	*Lady And The Tramp*
8	*Peter Pan*
9	*Dirty Dancing*
10	*The Three Tenors Concert*

Disney titles now dominate the bestselling video list, with enormous sales for the limited-period releases in 1992–94 of Disney classics such as *The Jungle Book* (over 4,500,000 sold), *Fantasia* (3,200,000), *Beauty And The Beast* (2,000,000), and *Cinderella* (1,750,000).

TOP 10

MOST RENTED VIDEOS OF ALL TIME IN THE UK

(To 31 December 1993)

1	*Dirty Dancing*
2	*Crocodile Dundee*
3	*Basic Instinct*
4	*Home Alone*
5	*Sister Act*
6	*Ghost*
7	*Pretty Woman*
8	*The Silence of the Lambs*
9	*Robocop*
10	*A Fish Called Wanda*

Of these 10 titles, *Sister Act* and *Basic Instinct* were still renting buoyantly in video libraries (the latter 18 months after its original release) in the spring of 1994, and both have the potential to rise higher still in the all-time stakes.

VIDEO BESTSELLERS

TOP 10

BESTSELLING AEROBICS AND KEEP-FIT VIDEOS OF ALL TIME IN THE UK

1 *Callanetics*
2 *Jane Fonda's New Workout*
3 *Beginning Callanetics*
4 *Lizzie Webb's Body Programme*
5 *Seven Pounds in Seven Days*
6 *The Y Plan*
7 *Super Callanetics*
8 *3 Stages to Fitness with Lizzie Webb*
9 *Jane Fonda's Low Impact Workout*
10 *Rosemary Conley's Whole Body Programme*

Keep fit is now a major area in the video market, most programmes being aimed at women. *Callanetics*, said to have worked for the Duchess of York, is the fourth bestselling video of all time in the UK and its sequels clearly benefited from its exceptional success.

TOP 10

BESTSELLING BLACK-AND-WHITE FILMS ON VIDEO IN THE UK

1 *A Hard Day's Night*
2 *Jailhouse Rock*
3 *Flying Down to Rio*
4 *King Creole*
5 *The Elephant Man*
6 *The Longest Day*
7 *It's a Wonderful Life*
8 *Love Me Tender*
9 *Psycho*
10 *Stagecoach*

Black and white is generally considered the kiss of death for video; any monochrome movies that have sold well generally have strong star associations (the most successful in this list feature the Beatles, Elvis Presley, and Fred Astaire and Ginger Rogers), or possess historical or cult collectability.

TOP 10

BESTSELLING CHILDREN'S VIDEOS IN THE UK*

1 *The Jungle Book*
2 *Beauty and the Beast*
3 *Cinderella*
4 *The Little Mermaid*
5 *Bambi*
6 *Lady and the Tramp*
7 *Peter Pan*
8 *Watch With Mother*
9 *Sleeping Beauty*
10 *Pinocchio*

* *To March 1994.*

With the exception of the BBC's *Watch With Mother* compilation, all of these are Disney titles, which have reached new sales heights (over 4,500,000 copies of *The Jungle Book*) during 1993–94.

TOP 10

MOST RENTED COMEDY VIDEOS OF ALL TIME IN THE UK

1 *Crocodile Dundee*
2 *Home Alone*
3 *Sister Act*
4 *Pretty Woman*
5 *A Fish Called Wanda*
6 *Police Academy*
7 *Beverly Hills Cop*
8 *Three Men and a Baby*
9 *Twins*
10 *The Naked Gun*

Should those who have problems with genre boundaries consider that *Beverly Hills Cop* (a comedy action thriller), the romance-with-comedy-elements *Pretty Woman*, and *Three Men and a Baby* are interlopers in this Top 10, the next three most popular titles would be *Porky's*, *Look Who's Talking*, and *Naked Gun 2½*.

TOP 10

BESTSELLING SPORTS VIDEOS OF ALL TIME IN THE UK

	Video	Sport
1	*Arsenal: Official Review of Division One Game by Game, 1988-89*	Football
2	*Liverpool FC: The Mighty Reds*	Football
3	*Botham's Ashes*	Cricket
4	*Italia '90: Gascoigne's Glory*	Football
5	*Genius: The George Best Story*	Football
6	*Gazza: The Real Me*	Football
7	*Liverpool: Team of the Decade*	Football
8	*Play Better Golf with Peter Alliss*	Golf
9	*Manchester United: Champions 1993/94*	Football
10	*Mike Tyson's Greatest Hits*	Boxing

For years, football has taken the largest slice of sports video sales, with such normally TV-friendly sports as snooker faring surprisingly poorly on cassette. In addition, the early 1990s have seen a surge of enthusiasm for professional wrestling tapes, of which *Wrestlemania 3*, just outside the Top 10, is the biggest seller so far.

TOP 10

MOST-RENTED HORROR VIDEOS OF ALL TIME IN THE UK

1 *The Evil Dead*
2 *Poltergeist*
3 *A Nightmare on Elm Street*
4 *The Fly*
5 *A Nightmare on Elm Street 2: Freddy's Revenge*
6 *Poltergeist 2*
7 *The Entity*
8 *The Thing*
9 *Christine*
10 *An American Werewolf in London*

TOP 10

BESTSELLING MUSICALS ON VIDEO IN THE UK

	Film	Year film released
1	Dirty Dancing	1987
2	The Blues Brothers	1980
3	The Sound of Music	1965
4	Grease	1978
5	Mary Poppins	1964
6	The King and I	1956
7	South Pacific	1958
8	The Wizard of Oz	1939
9	Annie	1982
10	Saturday Night Fever	1977

Musicals (*Dirty Dancing* excepted) have never been important to the video rental business in the UK, but with the establishment of the low-price sales market, they have recently achieved consistent success, owing much to the "repeatability factor" of their high song content.

TOP 10

MOST-RENTED VIETNAM VIDEOS OF ALL TIME IN THE UK

1	Good Morning, Vietnam
2	Rambo: First Blood 2
3	Full Metal Jacket
4	Platoon
5	Born on the Fourth of July
6	The Deer Hunter
7	Hamburger Hill
8	Bat 21
9	Uncommon Valour
10	Casualties of War

Perhaps the oddest aspect of this list is that only the top film actually contains the word "Vietnam" in its title – an apparent taboo that would also apply if the list were extended to a Top 20 (with the marginal exception of the video of the Australian mini-series, *Nam*).

TOP 10

MOST-RENTED SCIENCE-FICTION VIDEOS OF ALL TIME IN THE UK

1	Robocop
2	Back to the Future
3	E.T. The Extra-Terrestrial
4	Aliens
5	Terminator 2: Judgement Day
6	Total Recall
7	The Terminator
8	Return of the Jedi
9	Universal Soldier
10	Inner Space

Since *E.T.* was viewed by so many people on illegal pirate videos in the years before its release, it should top this list. However, along with other lists, the rankings are based on legal rentals only.

TOP 10

BESTSELLING MUSIC VIDEOS OF ALL TIME IN THE UK

	Video	Artist(s)
1	The Three Tenors Concert	Pavarotti, Domingo, Carreras
2	Queen's Greatest Flix	Queen
3	The Immaculate Collection	Madonna
4	The Videos	Kylie Minogue
5	Making Michael Jackson's "Thriller"	Michael Jackson
6	Rattle and Hum	U2
7	Hangin' Tough Live	New Kids on the Block
8	Greatest Flix 2	Queen
9	Pavarotti in Hyde Park	Luciano Pavarotti
10	The Legend Continues	Michael Jackson

Traditionally considered a preserve of pop music, the music video field is proving to have far wider commercial horizons, being an excellent medium for presenting the more spectacular stagings of classical music. Hence the new No. 1, featuring the world's three greatest tenors at their 7 July 1990 World Cup concert in the Baths of Caracalla, Rome.

TOP 10

BESTSELLING MUSIC VIDEOS OF ALL TIME IN THE US

	Video	Artist(s)
1	Hangin' Tough Live	New Kids on the Block
2	Hangin' Tough	New Kids on the Block
3	Step by Step	New Kids on the Block
4	Moonwalker	Michael Jackson
5=	Garth Brooks	Garth Brooks
5=	This is Garth Brooks	Garth Brooks
7=	Justify My Love	Madonna
7=	The Three Tenors Concert	Pavarotti, Domingo, Carreras
9	Video Anthology 1978–1988	Bruce Springsteen
10	Hammer Time	MC Hammer

The Recording Industry Association of America's sales certifications for music videos began only in 1986, and it is likely that *Making Michael Jackson's "Thriller"* (1984) is the only earlier video that would appear here. Nos. 1, 2, and 3 in this list have all sold more than 1,000,000 copies each, while No. 4, *Moonwalker*, has sold 800,000 units. As sales of music videos in the US began a dramatic decline in 1992, only country superstar Garth Brooks currently seems able to shift more than 300,000 units.

THE COMMERCIAL WORLD

TOP 10

BRITISH COMPANIES WITH THE MOST EMPLOYEES

	Company	Employees
1	Post Office	201,937
2	British Telecom	183,100
3	Unilever	150,000
4	British Rail	137,770
5	BTR	135,333
6	ICI	117,500
7	British Aerospace	108,500
8	Lonrho	106,161
9	BP	105,750
10	GEC	104,995

TOP 10

OCCUPATIONS IN THE UK IN 1901

	Occupation	Men	Women	Total
1	Farmers and gardeners	2,110,000	152,000	2,262,000
2	Domestic servants	144,000	2,056,000	2,200,000
3	Carriers*	1,471,000	27,000	1,498,000
4	Textile operatives	595,000	867,000	1,462,000
5	Clothing trade	493,000	904,000	1,397,000
6	Metal workers	1,118,000	57,000	1,175,000
7	Builders, carpenters, etc.	1,130,000	2,000	1,132,000
8	Miners and quarry workers	937,000	6,000	943,000
9	Food trade	671,000	196,000	867,000
10	Professional (clergymen, teachers, lawyers, etc.)	383,000	351,000	734,000
	Total (including occupations not in Top 10)	*12,951,000*	*5,310,000*	*18,261,000*

* *"Conveyance of men, goods and messages"; includes 321,000 railway workers.*

The 1901 Census, which listed types of occupation for all aged 10 and over, also enumerated 632,000 men and 81,000 women as "commercial" (clerks, etc.), 253,000 in local and national government, 203,000 men in the army and navy, 70,000 street traders, and 61,000 fishermen.

THE WORLD OF WORK

T O P 1 0

MOST DANGEROUS JOBS IN THE UK

1	Asbestos worker
2	Crews of boats, ships, railway trains, and aircraft
3	Demolition contractor
4	Diver
5	Fireman
6	Miner
7	Oil/gas-rig worker
8	Steeplejack
9	Tunneller
10	Steel erector

Life assurance companies carefully base their premiums on actuarial statistics that take into account the likelihood of people in each job being involved in an accident that injures or kills them at work, or as a result of their contact with dangerous substances such as asbestos dust. This does not mean that assurance companies will not provide cover for such professions, but the riskier the job, the higher the premium.

MIXING OIL AND WATER
Divers are used to carry out maintenance and repair work on offshore oil rigs.

T O P 1 0

COUNTRIES WITH MOST WORKERS

	Country	Economically active population
1	China	584,569,000
2	India	314,904,000
3	USA	128,458,000
4	Indonesia	75,508,000
5	Russia	73,809,000
6	Japan	65,780,000
7	Brazil	64,468,000

	Country	Economically active population
8	Bangladesh	50,744,000
9	Germany	39,405,000
10	Pakistan	33,829,000
	UK	*28,295,000*

Excluding unpaid groups, such as students, housewives, and retired people.

T O P 1 0

COUNTRIES IN THE EC WORKING THE LONGEST HOURS

	Country	Average hours per week
1	UK	43.7
2	Portugal	41.9
3	Spain	40.7
4	Ireland	40.4
5	Greece	40.1
6=	Germany	39.9
6=	Luxembourg	39.9
8	France	39.6
9=	Denmark	39.0
9=	Netherlands	39.0

These are average working weeks for full-time employees. The two other EC countries are Italy (38.6) and Belgium (38.0).

T O P 1 0

COUNTRIES IN THE EC WITH MOST BANK HOLIDAYS

	Country	Annual bank holidays
1=	Germany	14
1=	Spain	14
3=	Greece	12
3=	Portugal	12
5	France	11
6=	Belgium	10
6=	Italy	10
6=	Luxembourg	10
9	Denmark	9
10=	Ireland	8
10=	Netherlands	8
10=	UK	8

T O P 1 0

SELF-EMPLOYMENT TRADES

1	Car repair
2	Building
3	Public houses
4	Road haulage
5	Hotels
6	Electrical/engineering
7	Accountancy
8	Printing
9	Farming/floristry
10	Carpentry

Based on a 1994 survey of members of the Federation of Small Businesses.

COMPANIES AND PRODUCTS

TOP 10

BANKS WITH THE MOST BRANCHES IN THE UK

	Bank	Branches
1	National Westminster Bank	2,541
2	Barclays Bank	2,281
3	Lloyds Bank	1,884
4	Midland Bank	1,716
5	TSB	1,369
6	Abbey National	680
7	Royal Bank of Scotland	633
8	Bank of Scotland	490
9	Clydesdale	330
10	Northern Ireland Banks	323

Girobank operates through Post Offices, and can thus claim to have a total of 21,211 branches.

TOP 10

EXPORT MARKETS FOR GOODS FROM THE UK

	Country	Total value of exports (£)
1	Germany	15,212,600,000
2	USA	12,228,700,000
3	France	11,484,700,000
4	Netherlands	8,503,200,000
5	Italy	6,146,900,000
6	Ireland	5,738,900,000
7	Belgium and Luxembourg	5,715,100,000
8	Spain	4,405,300,000
9	Sweden	2,439,000,000
10	Japan	2,231,500,000

The union of West and East Germany has created a combined market that in 1990 lay at the head of the list of UK export markets, which had long been led by the US. In the previous year, sales to the US were £12,098,500,000 and those to West Germany £11,110,600,000. Other countries importing more than £1,000,000,000-worth of goods from the UK include Denmark, Saudi Arabia, and Singapore.

TOP 10

BRITISH COMPANIES

	Company	Annual sales (£)*
1	British Petroleum (petroleum products, oil and gas exploration)	43,314,000,000
2	BAT Industries (tobacco, financial services, paper and pulp, retailing)	18,695,000,000
3	British Telecom (telecommunications)	13,242,000,000
4	ICI (chemicals, plastics, paints)	12,061,000,000
5	British Gas (gas supply)	10,254,000,000
6	British Aerospace (aerospace, vehicles)	9,977,000,000
7	BTR (construction)	8,841,000,000
8	Hanson (multi industry: tobacco, aircraft, construction, electrical)	8,798,000,000
9	J. Sainsbury (supermarkets and other domestic retail)	8,604,100,000
10	Sumimoto Corporation (commodities)	8,198,000,000

* *Based on sales in latest year for which figures are available; excluding banks and insurance companies.*

TOP 10

GOODS EXPORTED FROM THE UK

	Product	Total value of exports (£)
1	Road vehicles	8,893,600,000
2	Petroleum and petroleum products	6,660,600,000
3	Office machines, computers, etc	6,616,600,000
4	Electrical machinery	6,354,500,000
5	Power generating machinery	5,536,600,000
6	Transport equipment	4,834,900,000
7	Industrial machinery	4,579,500,000
8	Specialized machinery	4,048,100,000
9	Organic chemicals	3,699,200,000
10	Professional and scientific instruments	3,077,200,000
	Total (including goods not in Top 10)	108,507,500,000

In 1992 the UK exported machinery and vehicles totalling £44,420,100,000, manufactured goods worth £15,482,300,000, and chemicals totalling £14,976,300,000. Food exports amounted to £5,289,500,000 and beverage exports to £2,447,700,000. Overall, in the period since 1982, the total value of exports has almost doubled, from that year's total of £55,557,800,000. Some sectors of manufacturing industry have shown even greater increases: sales of telecommunications equipment, for example, along with animal foodstuffs and chemicals, have grown approximately four-fold, and paper, footwear, and road vehicles have undergone a three-fold growth. Among products that have experienced export decline over the same period are furs, petroleum, and coal. A comparison of exports with those of earlier periods in history shows that 100 years ago, when cotton goods were the UK's principal export, the country's exports per inhabitant (today amounting to £1,877) were just £7, and 200 years ago exports per inhabitant were barely £2.

T O P   1 0

GOODS IMPORTED TO THE UK

	Product	Total value of imports (£)
1	Road vehicles	12,118,500,000
2	Office machines, computers, etc	8,360,900,000
3	Electrical machinery	7,738,200,000
4	Petroleum and petroleum products	5,326,600,000
5	Clothing	4,477,900,000
6	Textile yarn, fabrics, etc	3,940,500,000
7	Paper, pulp, and paper products	3,801,300,000
8	Telecommunications and sound recording equipment	3,555,700,000
9	Transport equipment	3,406,300,000
10	Specialized machinery	3,206,900,000
	Total (including goods not in Top 10)	*125,866,800,000*

Machinery of all kinds and vehicles comprise the largest category of imports, with a total value of £47,317,000,000 in 1992.

SUN INSURANCE FIREMARK
In the 18th century, when insurance companies ran their own fire brigades, company plaques identified which houses were insured with them.

T O P   1 0

OLDEST-ESTABLISHED BRITISH INSURANCE COMPANIES

	Company	Established
1	Sun	1710
2	Union Assurance	1714
3	Westminster Fire	1717
4=	London Assurance	1720
4=	Royal Exchange	1720
6	Equitable Life	1762
7	Phoenix	1782
8	Norwich Union	1797
9	Essex & Suffolk	1802
10=	Law Union & Rock	1806
10=	London Life	1806

T O P   1 0

COUNTRIES THAT REGISTER THE MOST PATENTS

	Country	Patents
1	USA	97,443
2	Japan	92,100
3	Germany	46,520
4	France	38,215
5	UK	37,827
6	Italy	27,228
7	Netherlands	20,346
8	Sweden	18,672
9	Switzerland	18,642
10	Canada	18,332

A patent is an exclusive licence to manufacture and exploit a unique product or process for a fixed period. The figures refer to the number of patents actually granted during 1992 – which in most instances represents only a fraction of the patents applied for: a total of 384,456 applications were registered in Japan, for example, but the process of obtaining a patent can be tortuous, and many are refused after investigations show that the product is too similar to one that has already been patented. This international list is based on data from the World Intellectual Property Organization.

T O P   1 0

SOURCES OF IMPORTS TO THE UK

	Country	Total value of imports (£)
1	Germany	19,034,300,000
2	USA	13,714,000,000
3	France	12,223,400,000
4	Netherlands	9,907,800,000
5	Japan	7,442,200,000
6	Italy	6,765,700,000
7	Belgium and Luxembourg	5,741,100,000
8	Ireland	5,070,000,000
9	Switzerland	3,918,900,000
10	Norway	3,885,700,000

T O P   1 0

LARGEST PRIVATIZED BRITISH COMPANIES

	Company	Date privatized	Market value (£)*
1	British Telecommunications	3 Dec 1984	27,368,000,000
2	British Petroleum	20 Dec 1954	13,449,000,000
3	British Gas	8 Dec 1986	12,565,000,000
4	Cable & Wireless	28 Oct 1981	5,611,400,000
5	British Airports Authority	28 Jul 1987	2,669,700,000
6	National Power	12 Mar 1991	2,486,000,000
7	British Airways	11 Feb 1987	2,159,000,000
8	Enterprise Oil	27 Jun 1984	2,106,900,000
9	TSB Group	8 Oct 1986	1,791,900,000
10	PowerGen	12 Mar 1991	1,609,000,000

* *1993.*

SHOPPING LISTS

TOP 10

COMMONEST SHOPS IN GREAT BRITAIN

	Type of shop	Outlets
1	Confectionery, tobacco, and newsagents' shops	51,702
2	Women's and children's clothes shops	27,301
3	Small grocery shops	21,406
4	Electrical, gas, and music goods shops	19,216
5	Butchers and poulterers	16,637
6	Furniture shops	15,240
7	Greengrocers and fruiterers	13,885
8	Dairymen	13,415
9	Hardware, china, and fancy goods	13,234
10	Chemists	13,060

TOP 10

DEPARTMENT STORE GROUPS IN THE UK

	Group	Annual sales (£)*
1	John Lewis Partnership	1,033,676,000#
2	House of Fraser (Harrods)	1,000,067,000
3	Burton Group (Debenhams/ At Home)	854,400,000
4	Allders	286,600,000
5	Sears (Selfridges)	200,002,000
6	Fenwick	166,917,000
7	London & Edinburgh Trust (Owen Owen/ Lewis's)	152,457,000
8	Bentalls	72,434,000
9	James Beattie	74,611,000
10	Liberty	54,832,000

* Based on latest available accounts, generally 1992–93, excluding VAT.

Based on The Retail Rankings *(1994) published by* The Corporate Intelligence Group Ltd.

TOP 10

RETAILERS IN THE UK

	Retailer	Sales (£)* 1991–92	1992–93
1	J. Sainsbury	7,665,500,000	8,604,100,000
2	Tesco	7,097,400,000	7,581,500,000
3	Marks & Spencer	4,774,537,000	5,021,500,000
4	Argyll Group	4,729,200,000	5,196,300,000
5	Asda Group	4,526,300,000	4,601,700,000
6	Kingfisher	3,301,600,000	3,454,700,000
7	The Boots Company	3,037,400,000	3,266,800,000
8	Isosceles	3,024,200,000	2,867,000,000
9	Kwik Save Group	2,318,995,000	2,651,200,000
10	John Lewis Partnership	2,066,700,000	2,130,400,000

* Excluding VAT.

Based on The Retail Rankings *(1994) published by* The Corporate Intelligence Group Ltd.

TOP 10

SUPERMARKET GROUPS* IN THE UK

	Retailer	Sales (£)# 1991–92	1992–93
1	J. Sainsbury**	6,944,000,000	7,743,700,000
2	Tesco	7,097,000,000	7,571,500,000
3	Argyll Group (Safeway, etc.)	4,729,000,000	5,196,300,000
4	Asda Group	4,308,000,000	4,396,300,000
5	Isosceles (Gateway, etc.)	3,024,000,000	2,867,000,000
6	Kwik Save	2,273,000,000	2,593,400,000
7	William Morrison	1,118,000,000	1,316,700,000
8	JLP (Waitrose)	1,067,000,000	1,096,700,000
9	Iceland (including Bejam)	889,000,000	1,037,300,000
10	William Low	420,000,000	447,000,000

* Excluding Co-ops and "mixed goods" retailers, such as Marks & Spencer, which achieved £2,350,000,000-worth of food sales in 1992–93.
\# Excluding VAT.
** Excluding Savacentre (£395,000,000 in 1992–93).

Based on The Retail Rankings *(1994) published by* The Corporate Intelligence Group Ltd.

T O P 1 0

SHOPPING STREETS

	Street	Location
1	The Ginza	Tokyo, Japan
2	Pedder Street/ Chater Street	Hong Kong
3	East 57th Street	New York, USA
4	5th Avenue	New York, USA
5	Madison Avenue	New York, USA
6	Kaufinger Strasse	Munich, Germany
7	Hohe Strasse	Cologne, Germany
8	Kurfürstendamm	Berlin, Germany
9	Königsallee	Dusseldorf, Germany
10	Königstrasse	Stuttgart, Germany

Based on prime retail rents at end of 1992.

T O P 1 0

RETAILERS WITH THE MOST OUTLETS IN THE UK

	Retailer	Outlets*
1	Sears (including Selfridges, Dolcis, Freeman Hardy & Willis, etc.)	3,044
2	The Boots Company (including Halfords, Fads, etc.)	2,238
3	Burton Group (including Top Shop, Dorothy Perkins, Debenhams, Principles, etc.)	2,301
4	Kingfisher (including B & Q, Woolworths, Superdrug, etc.)	2,108
5	Gallaher (including Dollond & Aitchison, Forbuoys, NSS, etc.)	1,725
6	Whitbread (including Wine Rack, Peter Dominic, Thresher, etc.)	1,596
7	Allied Lyons (including Augustus Barnett, etc.)	1,516
8	Lloyds Chemist (including Holland & Barrett, etc.)	1,431
9	Thorn EMI (including HMV, DER, Rumbelows, Radio Rentals, etc.)	1,301
10	Signet Group (formerly Ratners; including H. Samuel, Ernest Jones, etc.)	1,096

* *Based on* The Retail Rankings *(1992).*

T O P 1 0

GROCERY BRANDS IN THE UK

	Brand/product	Manufacturer	Annual sales (£)*
1	Coca-Cola (soft drink)	Coca-Cola	246,900,000

Coca-Cola, invented by Dr John S. Pemberton of Atlanta, Georgia, first went on sale there on 8 May 1886. The name was registered in the US in 1893 and the drink was first sold in London in 1900. Pemberton, who died in 1888, and his son sold all their rights to what is today regarded as the most widely known and powerful brand name in the world.

2	Ariel (washing powder)	Procter & Gamble	237,500,000

Ariel, a revolutionary new product combining soap, synthetic detergents, and enzymes, was introduced nationally in January 1969 followed by Ariel Automatic in October 1981, Ariel Ultra in October 1989, and various other Ariel products.

3	Persil (washing powder)	Lever Brothers	234,300,000

Persil, the first-ever household detergent, originally went on the market in Germany on 6 June 1907. Its name may derive either from the parsley trademark of a French inventor ("persil" is French for parsley), or from two ingredients, perborate and silicate, used by Professor Hermann Geissler and Dr Hermann Bauer, the German inventors of dry soap powder.

4	Nescafé (instant coffee)	Nestlé	193,700,000

Nescafé was the original instant coffee, first sold in 1938 by the Swiss firm, Nestlé.

5	Andrex (toilet paper)	Scott	179,900,000

The name Andrex comes from the location of the factory where it was first made in 1945 (or relaunched – its 1942 launch was thwarted by wartime rationing): St Andrews Road, Walthamstow, London. About 16,898,112 km/10,500,000 miles of Andrex are produced every year – equivalent to more than 40 times the distance from the Earth to the Moon.

6	Walkers Crisps	PepsiCo	142,800,000

Walkers Crisps, a newcomer to this Top 10, is the bestselling brand of a product that has been around for 140 years. There is much dispute about how potato crisps began, but it is probable that they were adapted from a French recipe for what in Britain were once known as "game chips" (because they were eaten with pheasant and other game fowl). In the US, it is claimed that "potato chips" were devised by George Crum, an American Indian working as a chef at Moon Lake Lodge at the New York spa resort of Saratoga Springs. Although popular, they remained a specialized dish on both sides of the Atlantic and did not take off as a commercially available snack until the invention of the mechanical potato-peeler in the 1920s. Walkers Crisps were first made in 1949 by Walkers Pork Butchery of Leicester, in order to diversify as a response to post-war meat shortages. Today the product has a dominant share of the UK crisp market, which has total sales of 30,000,000 bags of crisps a day (equivalent to 347 bags per second of every day) weighing 900 tonnes, or more than twice the weight of a jumbo jet.

7	Whiskas (catfood)	Pedigree Petfoods	139,000,000

Whiskas is now the bestselling petfood brand in the world.

8	Silver Spoon (sugar)	British Sugar	137,400,000

Silver Spoon claims 55 per cent of the white granulated sugar market – a total of 300,000 tonnes a year.

9	Pampers (disposable nappies)	Procter & Gamble	134,800,000

Procter & Gamble launched disposable nappies in the USA in 1961 and their Pampers brand now counts for some 50 per cent of the total market – virtually worldwide.

10	Flora (margarine)	Van den Berghs & Jurgens (Unilever)	129,300,000

More than 60,000 tonnes of Flora, which was launched in 1964, are sold every year – equivalent to the weight of 4,800 double-decker buses.

* *Through grocery outlets only; total brand sales may be higher.*

DUTY FREE

DUTY-FREE PRODUCTS

	Product	Sales (US$)
1	Cigarettes	1,960,000,000
2	Women's fragrances	1,760,000,000
3	Scotch whisky	1,310,000,000
4	Women's cosmetics and toiletries	1,300,000,000
5	Cognac	1,200,000,000
6	Men's fragrances and toiletries	840,000,000
7	Accessories	720,000,000
8	Leather goods (handbags, belts, etc)	715,000,000
9	Confectionery	710,000,000
10	Jewellery and pearls	520,000,000

In 1992 total world duty-free sales were estimated to have reached $16,000,000,000, of which the Top 10 comprise $11,035,000,000, or 69 per cent.

DUTY-FREE FAVOURITES
Cigarettes top the duty-free product sales, ahead of perfumes and other women's fragrances, which have sales of over one and three quarter billion dollars annually.

DUTY-FREE FERRY OPERATORS IN THE WORLD

	Ferry operator/country	Annual sales (US$)
1	DSB Ferries (Denmark)	185,000,000
2	Viking Line Ferries (Finland)	180,000,000
3	Stena Line (Sweden)	135,000,000*
4	Stena Sealink Ferries (UK)	125,000,000*
5	P & O European Ferries (UK)	110,000,000
6	Silja Line (Finland)	100,000,000
7	Puttgarden-Rödby (Germany)	86,000,000
8	Sweferry/Scandlines (Sweden/Denmark)	85,000,000
9	Scandinavian Seaways (Denmark)	71,200,000
10	Color Line (Norway)	70,500,000

* Estimated.

TIME TO BROWSE
Ranking fourth in the world list of duty-free ferry operators, Stena Sealink Ferries are the second largest UK outlet for duty-free goods, ahead of London Gatwick Airport and beaten only by London Heathrow.

DUTY-FREE SHOPS IN THE WORLD

	Shop location	Annual sales (US$)
1	Honolulu Airport	427,000,000
2	Hong Kong Airport	400,000,000
3	London Heathrow Airport	348,000,000
4	Amsterdam Schiphol Airport	262,000,000
5	Paris Charles de Gaulle Airport	257,000,000
6	Tokyo Narita Airport	241,000,000
7	Frankfurt Airport	220,000,000
8	Singapore Changi Airport	200,000,000
9	DSB Ferries (Denmark)	185,000,000
10	Viking Line Ferries (Finland)	180,000,000

Despite the international recession, total global duty-free sales in 1992 increased to $16,000,000,000, of which the Top 10 accounted for about 17 per cent. Honolulu is not only the world's top duty-free shop in terms of total annual sales, but also one of the highest in average sales per passenger ($106.94, compared with Heathrow's average of $17.91).

IN-FLIGHT SHOPPING
International airlines, such as British Airways, figure prominently as duty-free outlets.

T O P 1 0
DUTY-FREE SHOPS IN THE UK

	Shop location	Annual sales (US$)
1	London Heathrow Airport	348,000,000
2	Sealink Ferries	125,000,000 *
3	London Gatwick Airport	121,000,000
4	P & O European Ferries	110,000,000
5	British Airways	64,350,000
6	Manchester Ringway Airport	48,300,000
7	Britannia Airways (charter airline)	42,000,000
8	Sally Line (ferry operator)	33,700,000
9	Monarch Airlines (charter airline)	22,000,000
10	Dan-Air (charter airline)	20,700,000

* Estimated.

T O P 1 0
DUTY-FREE AIRPORTS IN THE WORLD

	Shop location	Annual sales (US$)
1	Honolulu Airport	427,000,000
2	Hong Kong Airport	400,000,000
3	London Heathrow Airport	348,000,000
4	Amsterdam Schiphol Airport	262,000,000
5	Paris Charles de Gaulle Airport	257,000,000
6	Tokyo Narita Airport	241,000,000
7	Frankfurt Airport	220,000,000
8	Singapore Changi Airport	200,000,000
9	Copenhagen Airport	152,000,000
10	Osaka International Airport	146,000,000

T O P 1 0
DUTY-FREE AIRLINES IN THE WORLD

	Airline/country	Annual sales (US$)
1	Japan Air Lines (Japan)	80,000,000
2	Korean Air (Korea)	75,000,000 *
3	British Airways (UK)	64,350,000
4	Scanair (Scandinavia)	59,300,000 *
5	Lufthansa (Germany)	54,000,000
6	Conair (Denmark)	48,000,000 *
7	Sterling Airways (Denmark)	42,500,000
8	Britannia Airways (UK)	42,000,000
9	Alitalia (Italy)	40,000,000 *
10	Swissair (Switzerland)	39,500,000 *

* Estimated.

T O P 1 0
DUTY-FREE COUNTRIES IN THE WORLD

	Country	Total annual duty- and tax-free sales (US$)		Country	Total annual duty- and tax-free sales (US$)
1	UK	1,130,000,000	6	France	510,000,000
2	USA	885,000,000	7	Sweden	495,000,000
3	Denmark	630,000,000	8	Finland	450,000,000
4	Germany	620,000,000	9	Hong Kong	420,000,000
5	Japan	540,000,000	10	Netherlands	330,000,000

DID YOU KNOW

THE BIRTH OF DUTY-FREE

Duty free sales began in 1951 at Shannon Airport in Ireland, where transatlantic flights stopped to refuel on their way to New York. Dr Brendan O'Regan is credited with the idea of selling goods to people waiting in the transit lounge (technically not part of Irish soil, and so exempt from local taxes). By the end of the 1950s, airport shops had opened in Amsterdam, Brussels, London Heathrow, and Frankfurt.

MAIL AND TELEPHONES

TOP 10

OLDEST PILLAR BOXES IN DAILY USE IN THE UK

	Location	Date
1	Union Street, St Peter Port, Guernsey	1853
2	Barnes Cross, Bishops Caundle, Dorset	1853
3=	Mount Pleasant/College Road, Framlingham, Suffolk	1856
3=	Double Street, Framlingham, Suffolk	1856
3=	Market Place, Banbury, Oxfordshire	1856
3=	Mudeford Green, Christchurch, Dorset	1856
3=	Cornwallis/Victoria Road, Milford-on-Sea, Hampshire	1856
3=	Eastgate, Warwick	1856
3=	Westgate, Warwick	1856
3=	High Street, Eton, Berkshire	1856

The Penny Post was introduced in 1840, and the public soon pressed for roadside posting boxes, which already existed in Belgium and France. In 1851, Anthony Trollope (the famous author of *Barchester Towers*, who at that time was a Post Office Surveyor's Clerk) suggested their use in St Helier, Jersey. Four were set up there on 23 November 1852. No trace of them survives, though it is known that they were painted red. In 1853 one was erected in St Peter Port, Guernsey – the oldest still in use in the UK.

TOP 10

SENDERS OF DIRECT MAIL IN THE UK

	Sender	% of total volume
1	Mail order companies	17.4
2	Insurance companies	10.1
3	Banks and Girobank	9.1
4	Charities	8.2
5	Retailers	7.7
6	Travel agencies	6.0
7	Manufacturers	5.8
8	Credit card companies	5.3
9	Book clubs	4.4
10	Gas and electricity companies	2.9

The average household receives 6.6 items of direct mail every four weeks, whereas the average manager receives 14 items per week at work. In addition to these categories, entertainment, travel, and other sources of direct mail comprise an "Others" category totalling 23.3 per cent.

TOP 10

EUROPEAN COUNTRIES RECEIVING THE MOST DIRECT MAIL

	Country	Average no. of items per head per annum
1	Switzerland	107
2	Belgium	85
3	Germany	64
4	France	63
5	Netherlands	62
6=	Denmark	50
6=	Norway	50
8	Sweden	48
9	Finland	46
10	UK	39

TOP 10

MOST POPULAR TYPES OF GREETINGS CARD IN THE UK

	Occasion	Annual sales (£)
1	Birthday	360,500,000
2	Christmas	256,400,000
3	Anniversary	42,700,000
4	Mother's Day	35,100,000
5	Valentine	26,500,000
6	Father's Day	18,400,000
7	Easter	18,000,000
8	Get well	15,300,000
9	New baby	14,800,000
10	Wedding	12,200,000

More than 2,500,000,000 cards are sent in the UK every year – approximately 27 cards for every member of the population. Over 65 per cent are sent at Christmas, but Christmas cards cost, on average, much less than other greetings cards so their earnings do not reflect their predominance. A further £11,100,000 is spent on sympathy cards.

TOP 10

MOST POPULAR BRITISH COMMEMORATIVE STAMPS

	Issue	Date
1	Nature Conservation	May 1986
2	British Butterflies	May 1981
3	RSPCA	Jan 1990
4	Flowers	Mar 1979
5	Shire Horses	Jul 1978
6	Birds	Jan 1980
7	Dogs	Feb 1979
8	Birds/RSPB Centenary	Jan 1989
9	Queen Mother's 80th Birthday	Aug 1980
10	Wedding of Prince Charles and Lady Diana Spencer	Jul 1981

TOP 10
COUNTRIES SENDING AND RECEIVING THE MOST MAIL

	Country	Items of mail handled p.a.
1	USA	164,639,561,000
2	Japan	22,723,628,000
3	Russia	21,923,325,000
4	France	21,867,860,000
5	Germany (former West)	17,051,746,000
6	UK	16,412,000,000
7	India	14,626,630,000
8	Ukraine	13,466,000,000
9	Canada	9,004,547,000
10	Italy	8,995,333,000

TOP 10
COUNTRIES WITH THE MOST PUBLIC TELEPHONES

	Country	Telephones
1	USA	1,761,407
2	Japan	830,000
3	Italy	406,532
4	Republic of Korea	271,927
5	Brazil	263,643
6	Germany	200,000
7	France	190,497
8	Canada	172,049
9	India	145,577
10	Mexico	125,073
	UK	*110,000*

TOP 10
COUNTRIES THAT MAKE THE MOST INTERNATIONAL PHONE CALLS

	Country	Calls per head p.a.	Total calls
1	USA	6.5	1,651,913,000
2	Germany	12.6	1,011,600,000
3	UK	8.3	480,000,000 *
4	Italy	6.9	396,000,000
5	Netherlands	22	334,000,000
6	Switzerland	44.3	304,940,000
7	Canada	11.1	302,500,000 *
8	Japan	2.3	290,000,000
9	Belgium	24.7	243,906,000
10	Hong Kong	40.6	241,023,000

* Estimated.

TOP 10
COUNTRIES SENDING AND RECEIVING THE MOST MAIL 100 YEARS AGO

	Country	Items of mail handled p.a.
1	USA	7,028,000,000
2	Germany	2,488,000,000
3	UK	2,363,000,000
4	France	1,523,000,000
5	Austria	960,000,000
6	Italy	476,000,000
7	Russia	326,000,000
8	Australia	294,000,000
9	Belgium	290,000,000
10	India	274,000,000

Statistics for worldwide mail 100 years ago indicate the extent to which postal services were then developed, and the high numbers of letters and other items per head of certain populations: the USA leading the world with 110 per capita, followed by Australia with 82 items, reflecting the importance of long-distance internal mail, and the traffic between immigrants and their homelands.

TOP 10
COUNTRIES WITH THE MOST TELEPHONES

	Country	Telephones
1	USA	143,325,389
2	Japan	58,520,000
3	Germany	35,420,843
4	France	29,521,000
5	UK	26,880,000
6	Italy	23,708,388
7	Russia	22,778,601
8	Canada	16,227,000
9	Republic of Korea	15,865,381
10	Spain	13,792,156

It is estimated that there are some 574,860,000 telephone lines in use in the world, of which 234,083,000 are in Europe, 193,053,000 in North and South America, 127,290,000 in Asia, 10,336,000 in Oceania, and 10,098,000 in Africa. It is remarkable that, given its population, the whole of China has only 11,469,100 telephones – fewer than half the total for Italy.

TOP 10
COUNTRIES WITH THE MOST TELEPHONES/100 PEOPLE

	Country	Telephones per 100 inhabitants
1	Sweden	68.43
2	Switzerland	60.83
3	Canada	59.24
4	Denmark	58.30
5	USA	56.12
6	Luxembourg	55.07
7	Finland	54.57
8	Iceland	54.28
9	Norway	53.00
10	France	51.52
	UK	*46.75*

Contrasting with the Top 10 countries, where the ratio is around two people per telephone or better, there are many countries in the world with fewer than one telephone per 100 inhabitants. Most of Central and West Africa possesses fewer than one telephone for every 200 people.

FUEL AND POWER

COAL CONSUMERS
IN THE WORLD

	Country	Consumption 1991 (tonnes)
1	China	1,058,208,000
2	USA	806,483,000
3	Germany	469,095,000
4	Russia	395,000,000
5	India	227,921,000
6	Poland	168,783,000
7	South Africa	133,527,000
8	Japan	117,938,000
9	UK	108,247,000
10	Australia	98,881,000

COAL PRODUCERS
IN THE WORLD

	Country	Annual production (tonnes)
1	China	1,087,406,000
2	USA	901,877,000
3	Germany	458,102,000
4	Russia	353,000,000
5	India	224,500,000
6	Australia	214,030,000
7	Poland	209,782,000
8	South Africa	176,174,000
9	Ukraine	135,600,000
10	Kazakhstan	130,315,000
	UK	96,144,000

BURNING RUBBER

In 1993, as an alternative to power stations using conventional fuels such as coal or oil, plants were opened near St Louis, Missouri, and in Wolverhampton, UK, to burn used tyres. With similar targets (7,500,000 and 8,000,000 tyres respectively), the plants are designed to produce greater energy efficiency but with reduced sulphur emissions, and, even allowing for the cost of transporting the tyres, will save money. The British plant is expected to burn 23 per cent of the country's waste tyres in its first year of operation and provide electricity to 25,000 homes.

COUNTRIES WITH THE
GREATEST COAL RESERVES
IN THE WORLD

	Country	Reserves (tonnes)
1	Former USSR	265,582,000,000
2	USA	240,561,000,000
3	China	114,500,000,000
4	Australia	90,940,000,000
5	Germany	80,069,000,000
6	India	62,548,000,000
7	South Africa	55,333,000,000
8	Poland	41,200,000,000
9	Indonesia	32,063,000,000
10	Kazakhstan	25,000,000,000
	UK	3,800,000,000

ELECTRICITY-PRODUCING
COUNTRIES

	Country	Production (kw/hr)
1	USA	3,079,085,000,000
2	Russia	1,068,000,000,000
3	Japan	888,086,000,000
4	China	677,550,000,000
5	Germany	573,752,000,000
6	Canada	507,913,000,000
7	France	454,702,000,000
8	UK	322,133,000,000
9	India	309,370,000,000
10	Ukraine	279,000,000,000

ENERGY CONSUMERS
IN THE WORLD

	Country	Annual consumption coal equivalent (tonnes)
1	USA	2,481,686,000
2	Former USSR	1,931,301,000
3	China	922,183,000
4	Japan	512,110,000
5	Germany	457,300,000
6	UK	286,525,000
7	Canada	271,975,000
8	India	264,920,000
9	France	222,741,000
10	Italy	209,851,000

STANDARD ELECTRIC LIGHT BULB
The incandescent light bulb has a tungsten filament that glows yellow-white when electricity is passed through it. This type of bulb is very inefficient, converting only eight per cent of the electric energy to light.

COUNTRIES PRODUCING THE MOST ELECTRICITY FROM NUCLEAR SOURCES

	Country	Nuclear power stations in operation	Nuclear power as % of total power use	Output (megawatt-hours)
1	USA	109	22.3	98,729
2	France	55	72.9	57,688
3	Japan	44	27.7	34,238
4	Germany	21	30.1	22,559
5	Russia	28	11.8	18,893
6	Canada	21	15.2	14,874
7	Ukraine	15	25.0	13,020
8	UK	37	23.2	12,066
9	Sweden	12	43.2	10,002
10	South Korea	9	53.2	7,220
	World total	*412*		*323,497*

COUNTRIES CONSUMING THE MOST OIL

	Country	Consumption 1991 (barrels)
1	USA	4,921,000,000
2	Russia	3,700,000,000
3	Japan	1,432,000,000
4	China	905,000,000
5	Germany	667,000,000
6	UK	591,000,000
7	France	555,000,000
8	Saudi Arabia	534,000,000
9	Italy	533,000,000
10	Canada	486,000,000

PETROL STATIONS IN THE UK*

	Brand	Outlets
1	Esso	2,248
2	Shell	2,234
3	BP	1,569
4	Texaco	1,358
5	Burmah	1,134
6	Jet	1,125
7	Mobil	813
8	UK	750
9	Elf	721
10	Q8	656

* Including shared sites on motorways, etc.

COUNTRIES WITH THE LARGEST CRUDE OIL RESERVES

	Country	Reserves (barrels)*
1	Saudi Arabia	258,600,000,000
2	Russia	156,700,000,000
3=	Iraq	99,840,000,000
3=	Iran	99,840,000,000
5	Kuwait	92,428,000,000
6	United Arab Emirates	64,747,000,000
7	Venezuela	63,330,000,000
8	Mexico	51,225,000,000
9	Libya	38,190,000,000
10	China	29,600,000,000
	USA	*22,845,000,000*
	UK	*4,554,000,000*

* A barrel contains 42 US gallons/ 34.97 UK gallons.

CRUDE OIL PRODUCERS IN THE WORLD

	Country	Production (barrels per annum)
1	Saudi Arabia	2,975,000,000
2	USA	2,617,000,000
3	Russia	2,911,000,000
4	Iran	1,220,000,000
5	China	1,061,000,000
6	Mexico	1,009,000,000
7	Venezuela	865,000,000
8	United Arab Emirates	837,000,000
9	Norway	800,000,000
10	Canada	501,000,000

Despite its huge output, the US produces barely half the 4,921,000,000 barrels of oil it consumes every year – an energy consumption that is equivalent to 19 barrels per capita. The average US citizen thus uses one barrel of oil every 19 days. This compares with the UK's consumption of 591,000,000 barrels per annum – ten per capita, or one barrel every 36 days.

SAVING THE PLANET

TOP 10
CARBON DIOXIDE EMITTERS IN THE WORLD

	Country	CO$_2$ emissions (tonnes of carbon) per capita	total
1	USA	5.3301	1,345,969,180
2	Former USSR	3.3579	977,396,410
3	China	0.6035	694,153,740
4	Japan	2.4013	297,801,560
5	Germany	3.3131	264,637,260
6	India	0.2226	192,017,500
7	UK	2.7266	157,520,800
8	Canada	4.1518	112,070,740
9	Italy	1.9022	109,856,540
10	France	1.7924	102,104,730

The Carbon Dioxide Information Analysis Center at Oak Ridge, Tennessee, calculates CO$_2$ emissions from fossil fuel burning, cement manufacturing, and gas flaring. Their findings show that increasing industrialization in many countries has resulted in huge increases in carbon dioxide.

TOP 10
DEFORESTING COUNTRIES IN THE WORLD

	Country	Average annual forest loss in 1980s (sq km)
1	Brazil	36,500
2	India	15,000
3	Indonesia	9,200
4	Colombia	8,900
5	Mexico	6,150
6	Zaïre	5,800
7	Congo	5,260
8	Ivory Coast	5,100
9	Sudan	5,040
10	Nigeria	4,000

The loss of Brazilian forest at an annual average of 36,500 sq km means that over the decade of the 1980s the total loss was equivalent to the entire area of Germany, or one-and-a-half times the area of the UK.

TOP 10
RUBBISH PRODUCERS IN THE WORLD

	Country	Domestic waste per head per annum kg	lb
1	USA	864	1,905
2	Canada	625	1,378
3	Finland	504	1,111
4	Norway	473	1,043
5	Denmark	469	1,034
6	Luxembourg	466	1,027
7	Netherlands	465	1,025
8	Switzerland	424	935
9	Japan	394	869
10	UK	357	787

TOP 10
PERSONAL ENVIRONMENTAL IMPROVEMENT ACTIVITIES

	Activity	% already undertaking
1	Use of ozone-friendly aerosols	64
2	Picking up other people's litter	52
3	Avoiding use of pesticides in the garden	42
4	Taking bottles to a bottle bank	40
5=	Cutting down on the use of electricity	38
5=	Collecting old newspapers for recycling	38
7	Using alternative transport to the car	28
8=	Using recycled paper	25
8=	Making compost out of kitchen waste	25
10	Using unleaded petrol	22

This list is based on the results of the 1989 Department of the Environment Survey of Public Attitudes to the Environment conducted in England and Wales, which investigated what environment-improving activities people already undertake.

TOP 10
ENVIRONMENTAL CONCERNS

	Environmental problem	Total % worried
1	Chemicals put into rivers and the sea	91
2	Sewage contamination of beaches and bathing water	89
3	Oil spills at sea and oil on beaches	86
4	Destruction of the ozone layer	83
5	Loss of wildlife and habitats, destruction of species	82
6	Radioactive waste	81
7	Insecticides, fertilizers, and chemical sprays	80
8	Destruction of tropical forests	76
9	Acid rain	75
10=	Traffic exhaust fumes	74
10=	Litter and rubbish	74

A Department of the Environment Survey of Public Attitudes to the Environment last conducted in England and Wales in 1989 asked individuals how worried they were about environmental problems. Interviewees reported whether they were "very worried" or "quite worried", and the list combines the two degrees of concern.

TOP 10
LEAST POLLUTED CITIES IN THE WORLD*

1	Craiova, Poland
2	Melbourne, Australia
3	Auckland, New Zealand
4	Cali, Colombia
5	Tel Aviv, Israel
6	Bucharest, Romania
7	Vancouver, Canada
8	Toronto, Canada
9	Bangkok, Thailand
10	Chicago, USA

Based on levels of atmospheric sulphur dioxide.

TOP 10
COMMONEST TYPES OF LITTER

	1989	1993
1	Cigarette ends	Cigarette ends
2	Sweet wrappers	Sweet wrappers
3	Matchsticks	Matchsticks
4	Bits of paper	Chewing gum
5	Tickets and stickers	Glass fragments
6	Other litter (all materials)	Plastic fragments
7	Ring pulls	Bits of paper
8	Cigarette wrapping	Other plastic items
9	Other paper items	Other wood (lollipop sticks, etc)
10	Plastic fragments	Other litter (all materials)

A survey conducted by the Tidy Britain Group, which counted the number of items in each category in typical samplings of litter deposited on the UK's streets, parks, and other areas in 1989, was repeated in 1993. The latest survey, which examined some 12,218 individual sites, concluded that, overall, litter levels were 13 per cent down over the four-year period, with fast-food containers showing a striking 75 per cent reduction. However, the proportions of cigarette ends and chewing gum have increased and now respectively constitute 40 and 5.6 per cent of litter. The redesign of ring-pull cans, so that the pull is non-removable, has dramatically reduced that component in the litter mountain.

WASTE NOT WANT NOT
These paper logs are made by soaking and compressing old newspapers.

TOP 10
MOST POLLUTED CITIES IN THE WORLD*

1 Milan, Italy
2 Shengyang, China
3 Tehran, Iran
4 Seoul, South Korea
5 Rio de Janeiro, Brazil
6 São Paulo, Brazil
7 Xian, China
8 Paris, France
9 Peking, China
10 Madrid, Spain

* Based on levels of atmospheric sulphur dioxide.

Assessments made by the World Health Authority in the 1980s lacked information from Soviet bloc countries, where pollution levels may be even higher. Many countries have since taken steps to improve matters.

TOP 10
SULPHUR DIOXIDE EMITTERS IN THE WORLD

	Country	Annual SO_2 emissions (kg per head)
1	Canada	143
2	USA	83
3	UK	65
4	Spain	55
5	Finland	49
6	Ireland	47
7	Belgium	43
8	Denmark	38
9	Italy	35
10	Luxembourg	27

Sulphur dioxide, the principal cause of acid rain, is produced by fuel combustion in factories and power stations. During the 1980s, emissions by all countries declined.

TOP 10
USERS OF UNLEADED PETROL IN EUROPE

	Country	Consumption 1990 (tonnes) total petrol	total unleaded	Unleaded as % of market
1	West Germany	26,500,000	20,160,000	76
2	Denmark	1,560,000	910,000	58
3	Sweden	4,150,000	2,210,000	53
4	Austria	2,530,000	1,310,000	52
5	Switzerland	3,690,000	1,880,000	51
6	Netherlands	3,440,000	1,680,000	49
7	Finland	1,960,000	950,000	48
8	Norway	1,780,000	640,000	36
9	East Germany	3,900,000	1,350,000	35
10	UK	24,320,000	8,260,000	34

Based on data supplied by the UK Petroleum Industry Association.

The move towards environmentally less damaging unleaded petrol in Europe has proceeded apace: in 1988 the total European consumption was 17,180,000 tonnes, and by 1990 it was 43,700,000 tonnes. The unification of Germany has meant that East Germany has had to revolutionize its petrol supply to bring it in line with West Germany. This task has been undertaken with great speed: in 1989 East Germany had virtually no unleaded petrol; by 1990 unleaded accounted for 35 per cent.

INDUSTRIAL AND OTHER ACCIDENTS

TOP 10

WORST EXPLOSIONS IN THE WORLD
(*Excluding mining disasters, and terrorist and military bombs*)

	Location/incident	Date	Killed
1	Lanchow, China (arsenal)	26 October 1935	2,000
2	Halifax, Nova Scotia (ammunition ship *Mont Blanc*)	6 December 1917	1,635
3	Memphis, USA (*Sultana* boiler explosion)	27 April 1865	1,547
4	Bombay, India (ammunition ship *Fort Stikine*)	14 April 1944	1,376
5	Cali, Colombia (ammunition trucks)	7 August 1956	1,200
6	Salang Tunnel, Afghanistan (petrol tanker collision)	2 November 1982	over 1,100
7	Chelyabinsk, USSR (liquid gas beside railway)	3 June 1989	up to 800
8	Texas City, Texas, USA (ammonium nitrate on *Grandcamp* freighter)	16 April 1947	752
9	Oppau, Germany (chemical plant)	21 September 1921	561
10	San José, Cubatao, Brazil (oil pipeline)	25 February 1984	508

All these "best estimate" figures should be treated with caution, since, as with fires and shipwrecks, body counts are notoriously unreliable.

TOP 10

WORST MINING DISASTERS IN THE WORLD

	Location	Date	Killed
1	Hinkeiko, China	26 April 1942	1,549
2	Courrières, France	10 March 1906	1,060
3	Omuta, Japan	9 November 1963	447
4	Senghenydd, UK	14 October 1913	439
5	Coalbrook, South Africa	21 January 1960	437
6	Wankie, Rhodesia	6 June 1972	427
7	Dharbad, India	28 May 1965	375
8	Chasnala, India	27 December 1975	372
9	Monongah, USA	6 December 1907	362
10	Barnsley, UK	12 December 1866	361 *

* Including 27 killed the following day while searching for survivors.

A mining disaster at the Fushun mines, Manchuria, on 12 February 1931 may have resulted in up to 3,000 deaths, but information was suppressed by the Chinese government. Soviet security was also responsible for obscuring details of an explosion at the East German Johanngeorgendstadt uranium mine on 29 November 1949, when as many as 3,700 may have died.

TOP 10

COMMONEST CAUSES OF INJURY AT WORK IN THE UK

	Cause	Fatalities	Injuries*
1	Injured while handling, lifting, or carrying	–	48,519
2	Slip, trip, or fall on same level	4	27,845
3	Struck by moving (including flying or falling) object	32	19,310
4	Fall from height	56	11,003
5	Struck by something fixed or stationary	1	8,720
6	Contact with moving machinery or material being machined	21	6,190
7	Exposure to, or contact with, a harmful substance	6	3,673
8	Struck by moving vehicle	41	3,304
9	Injured by an animal	2	714
10	Contact with electricity	23	591
	Total (including causes not in Top 10)	*219*	*138,267*

* *Resulting in work absence of more than three days, employees only (excluding self-employed), 1992–93.*

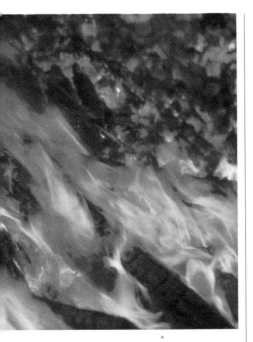

TOP 10

WORST FIRES IN THE WORLD*

	Location/incident	Date	Killed
1	Kwanto, Japan (following earthquake)	1 September 1923	60,000
2	Cairo (city fire)	1824	4,000
3	London Bridge	July 1212	3,000 #
4	Peshtigo, Wisconsin, USA (forest)	8 October 1871	2,682
5	Santiago, Chile (church of La Compañía)	8 December 1863	2,500
6	Chungking, China (docks)	2 September 1949	1,700
7	Constantinople, Turkey (city fire)	5 June 1870	900
8	Cloquet, Minnesota, USA (forest)	12 October 1918	800
9	Hinckley, Minnesota, USA (forest)	1 September 1894	480
10	Hoboken, New Jersey, USA (docks)	30 June 1900	326

* Excluding sports and entertainment venues, mining disasters, and the results of military action.
 # Burned, crushed, and drowned in ensuing panic.

TOP 10

COMMONEST TYPES OF ACCIDENT IN THE HOME

	Accident	No.*
1	Falls	1,004,000
2	Cutting/piercing	333,000
3	Being struck by a static object	186,000
4	Struck by a moving object	179,000
5	Foreign body	138,000
6	Burning	96,000
7	Jamming/pinching	85,000
8	Animal/insect bite	76,000
9	Poisoning	54,000
10	Over-exertion	25,000

* Per year.

Falls, the leading category, includes everything from tripping over (233,800 cases), and falling on or down stairs (197,800), to falling off ladders (23,200) or buildings (8,400). Official statistics also list 176,500 accidents of unknown cause and 79,100 as "other". Figures cover only non-fatal accidents within homes and gardens (and hence exclude traffic accidents, accidents at work, etc.) and do not include self-inflicted injury, suspected suicide attempts, or attack by other people.

TOP 10

COMMONEST TYPES OF FATAL ACCIDENT IN THE HOME

	Accident	No. per year		Accident	No. per year
1	Unspecified falls	1,451	6	Fall between two levels	116
2	Poisoning/inhalation	528	7	Fall on same level	88
3	Fall from stairs	525	8	Suffocating/choking	79
4	Uncontrolled fire	431	9	Fall from building	63
5	Foreign body	256	10	Drowning	57

TOP 10

WORST INDUSTRIAL DISASTERS

(Excluding mining disasters, and marine and other transport disasters)

	Location/incident	Date	Killed
1	Bhopal, India (methyl isocyanate gas escape at Union Carbide plant)	3 Dec 1984	over 2,500
2	Oppau, Germany (chemical plant explosion)	21 Sep 1921	561
3	Brussels, Belgium (fire in L'Innovation department store)	22 May 1967	322
4	Guadalajara, Mexico (explosions after gas leak into sewers)	22 Apr 1992	230
5	São Paulo, Brazil (fire in Joelma bank and office building)	1 Feb 1974	227
6	North Sea (Piper Alpha oil rig explosion and fire)	6 Jul 1988	173
7	New York City (fire in Triangle Shirtwaist Factory)	25 Mar 1911	145
8	Eddystone, Pennsylvania (munitions plant explosion)	10 Apr 1917	133
9	Cleveland, Ohio (explosion of liquid gas tanks at East Ohio Gas Co)	20 Oct 1944	131
10	Caracas, Venezuela (fuel tank fire)	19–21 Dec 1982	129

CHARITIES

T O P 1 0

FUND-RAISING CHARITIES IN THE UK

	Charity	Voluntary income (£)
1	Save the Children Fund	70,399,000
2	National Trust	65,207,000
3	Royal National Lifeboat Institution	55,791,000
4	Oxfam	53,254,000
5	Imperial Cancer Research Fund	44,118,000
6	Cancer Research Campaign	40,945,000
7	Barnardos	34,510,000
8	RSPCA	32,981,000
9	Salvation Army	31,407,000
10	Help the Aged	29,039,000

At the end of 1992 there were 170,357 registered charities in England and Wales alone, but the Top 10 remains similar from year to year. The order of the Top 10 is for voluntary income only. Most charities also receive income from other sources, such as rents and interest on investments – Save the Children Fund's total income from all sources totalled £140,799,000 in 1992.

FOR THOSE IN PERIL
Founded in 1824 by Sir William Hillary (originally under the title of the National Institute for the Preservation of Life from Shipwreck), the RNLI has saved an average of 500 lives a year since its inception.

T O P 1 0

CHILDREN'S CHARITIES* IN THE UK

	Charity	Voluntary income (£)		Charity	Voluntary income (£)
1	Save the Children Fund	70,399,000	7	Christian Children's Fund of Great Britain	2,780,000
2	Barnardos	34,510,000	8	Malcolm Sargent Cancer Fund for Children	2,562,000
3	National Society for the Prevention of Cruelty to Children	27,939,000	9	Masonic Trust for Girls and Boys	2,140,000
4	National Children's Home	10,802,000	10	Royal Scottish Society for the Prevention of Cruelty to Children	1,814,000
5	Variety Club Children's Charity	5,918,000			
6	Plan International (UK)	3,050,000			

* Excluding charities that aid both children and adults.

SAVE THE CHILDREN
The Princess Royal is the president of this international organization, which operates in more than 20 countries. Founded with the aim of promoting child health and welfare, Save the Children Fund has just celebrated its 75th anniversary.

T O P 1 0

ANIMAL CHARITIES IN THE UK

	Charity	Voluntary income (£)
1	Royal Society for the Prevention of Cruelty to Animals	32,981,000
2	Royal Society for the Protection of Birds	21,883,000
3	People's Dispensary for Sick Animals	16,064,000
4	World Wide Fund for Nature	15,029,000
5	Donkey Sanctuary	5,226,000
6	Blue Cross Animals' Hospital	4,150,000
7	National Canine Defence League	3,993,000
8	Dogs' Home Battersea	3,816,000
9	Cats Protection League	3,528,000
10	Animal Health Trust	2,791,000

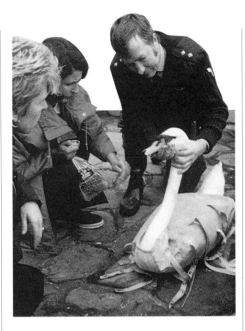

STICKING YOUR NECK OUT
Here, an injured swan is being prepared for transportation.

T O P 1 0

BRITISH COMPANIES DONATING TO CHARITY, 1992–93

	Company	Donations (£)
1	British Telecom	14,498,000
2	British Petroleum	11,000,000
3	National Westminster Bank	10,202,000
4	Barclays Bank	7,520,000
5	Abbey National	6,020,000
6	Marks & Spencer	5,800,000
7	Shell UK	5,523,000
8	Unilever	5,000,000
9	Lloyds Bank	4,972,000
10	TSB Group	4,460,000

T O P 1 0

BROADCAST APPEALS IN THE UK IN 1992–93

	Appeal	Amount raised (£)
1	Children in Need Appeal (BBC TV)	16,322,000 *
2	Comic Relief	16,000,000 *
3	Blue Peter Appeal (BBC TV)	1,337,000
4	Help a London Child Appeal (Capital Radio)	477,000
5	KLFM Appeal for Disabled (Hereward FM/CN FM)	140,000
6	Christmas Appeal (GWR FM)	116,000
7	Jailbreak (Radio Wyvern)	103,000
8	Snowball Trust (Mercia Sound)	102,000
9	Snowball Appeal	100,000
10	Victoria House Appeal (BBC GMR)	70,000

* Income continuing.

T O P 1 0

GRANT-MAKING TRUSTS IN THE UK, 1992

	Trust	Grants (£)		Trust	Grants (£)
1	Wellcome Trust	92,300,000	7	Henry Smith (Estates Charities)	11,687,000
2	Tudor Trust	20,234,000	8	Leverhulme Trust	10,549,000
3	Royal Society	17,383,000	9	City Parochial Foundation	8,887,000
4	British Academy	16,350,000	10	Baring Foundation	7,936,000
5	Wolfson Foundation	14,913,000			
6	Gatsby Charitable Foundation	13,701,000			

DID YOU KNOW

THE BIG BUSINESS OF GIVING

In the past ten years, the biggest single change among the UK's Top 10 charities has been the appearance in first position of Band Aid, followed by its equally rapid disappearance: in 1985 the charity, formed to raise income for Ethiopian famine relief, received £56,500,000, but by 1987 was in 179th place and was later discontinued. Despite the recession of recent years, most charities – especially the larger ones – have maintained or increased their overall income, with the greatest total increase among medical and health charities (in 1992 up by £32,300,000 over the previous year). In 1991–92, the Top 500 fund-raising charities in the UK received a total income of £3,056,900,000 – equivalent to the entire gross domestic product of countries such as Jordan, and greater than the GDPs of many developing countries. Of this, £1,586,800,000 came from voluntary sources, which include legacies, "planned giving" (deeds of covenant), broadcast appeals, and revenue from charity shops. (Oxfam's shops, for instance, raised £18,900,000 in 1991–92.) The balance comes from non-voluntary sources, which encompass retail trading, fees, grants, funds from the EC, and investments.

THE WORLD'S RICHEST

TOP 10

HIGHEST-EARNING ENTERTAINERS IN THE WORLD*

MONEY TALKS
Oprah Winfrey has transformed her daytime talk show into a multi-million dollar production company.

	Entertainer	Profession	1992–93 income ($)
1	Oprah Winfrey	TV host/producer	98,000,000
2	Steven Spielberg	Film producer/director	72,000,000
3	Charles M. Schulz	"Peanuts" cartoonist	48,000,000
4	David Copperfield	Illusionist	46,000,000
5	Siegfried & Roy	Illusionists	32,000,000
6	Tom Clancy	Novelist	31,000,000
7	Stephen King	Novelist/screenwriter	28,000,000
8	Xuxa	TV host/pop singer	27,000,000
9	John Grisham	Novelist	25,000,000
10=	Michael Crichton	Novelist	24,000,000
10=	Andrew Lloyd Webber	Composer	24,000,000

* Other than actors and pop stars. Used by permission of Forbes Magazine.

As in the previous year of this survey, Oprah Winfrey maintained her place at the top of the pile. Also firmly established in the list are illusionists David Copperfield and Siegfried & Roy, while the increasing presence of novelists reflects the success of blockbuster movies based on their work – such as Michael Crichton's *Jurassic Park*. If newcomer Xuxa is excluded as a candidate as a result of her dual career as a pop singer, British theatrical producer Cameron Mackintosh ($22,000,000) would join this showbiz elite.

TOP 10

HIGHEST-EARNING POP STARS IN THE WORLD

	Artist(s)	1992–93 income ($)		Artist(s)	1992–93 income ($)
1	Guns N' Roses	53,000,000	6	Julio Iglesias	40,000,000
2	Prince	49,000,000	7	Madonna	37,000,000
3=	Garth Brooks	47,000,000	8=	Eric Clapton	33,000,000
3=	U2	47,000,000	8=	Grateful Dead	33,000,000
5	Michael Jackson	42,000,000	10	Billy Ray Cyrus	29,000,000

Used by permission of Forbes Magazine.

Forbes Magazine's survey of leading entertainers' income covers a two-year period in order to iron out fluctuations, especially those caused by successful tours. Even so, such is the current importance of global tours that when groups such as the Rolling Stones, Aerosmith, and ZZ Top stop touring, they can find their incomes decline so dramatically that they depart from the reckoning altogether. Pink Floyd's international tour in the 1988–89 financial period, for example, netted a total of

$135,000,000, and the group themselves earned $56,000,000, despite which they have since vacated the Top 10. Michael Jackson's income peaked at $125,000,000 in the same period, but has been declining ever since. Hovering just outside the Top 10 are Neil Diamond, Paul McCartney, and Jimmy Buffet, while some former entrants – most notably erstwhile inhabitants of this list's top slot, New Kids on the Block – have now disbanded, and will never be seen in it again.

TOP 10

COUNTRIES WITH THE MOST DOLLAR BILLIONAIRES*

	Country	Billionaires
1	USA	108
2	Germany	46
3	Japan	35
4=	France	9
4=	Hong Kong	9
4=	Switzerland	9
7	Canada	7
8=	Italy	6
8=	Taiwan	6
8=	UK	6

* People with a net worth of $1,000,000,000 or more.

Based on data published in Forbes Magazine.

TOP 10

RICHEST PEOPLE OUTSIDE THE US
(Excluding royalty)

	Name	Country	Business	Assets ($ Millions)
1	Yoshiaki Tsutsumi	Japan	Property	9,000 *
2	Family of late Taikichiro Mori	Japan	Property	7,500
3=	Haniel family	Germany	Food wholesaling	6,200
3=	Erivan Haub	Germany	Supermarkets	6,200
5=	Hans and Gad Rausing	Sweden	Packaging	6,000
5=	Shin Kyuk-ho	Korea	Sweets, retailing	6,000
7	Theo and Karl Albrecht	Germany	Supermarkets	5,700
8	Kenneth Thomson	Canada	Publishing	5,400
9	Emilio Azcarraga Milmo	Mexico	TV, bullrings	5,100
10	Henkel family	Germany	Consumer products	4,900

* *Some sources suggest a figure as high as $22,500,000,000.*

Based on data published in Forbes Magazine.

TOP 10

RICHEST PEOPLE IN THE US

	Name	Profession/source	Assets ($ Millions)
1	Warren Edward Buffett	Textiles, etc	8,325
2	William Henry Gates III	Computer software	6,160
3	John Werner Kluge	Media and cellular telephone	5,900
4	Sumner Murray Redstone	Cinemas	5,600
5	Walton family (five members share $23,000,000,000)	Shops	4,600
6	(Keith) Rupert Murdoch	Publishing, TV and cinema	4,000
7	Ted Arison	Cruise liners	3,650
8	Ronald Owen Perelman	Varied businesses	3,600
9	Samuel Irving Newhouse Jr and Donald Edward Newhouse ($7,000,000,000 shared)	Publishing	3,500
10	Kirk Kerkorian	Film and other industries	3,100

Close runners-up in the more-than-two-billion dollars league include former Presidential candidate Henry Ross Perot ($2,400,000,000), the Mars (of Mars Bar fame) family (four members sharing $9,600,000,000), and broadcasting magnate (and husband of Jane Fonda) Ted Turner ($2,200,000,000). Paul G. Allen ($2,900,000,000), co-founder of Microsoft (with Bill Gates), and David Packard ($2,750,000,000) of computer giant Hewlett-Packard are two representatives of the new technology billionaire class.

Used by permission of Forbes Magazine.

TOP 10

HIGHEST-EARNING ACTORS IN THE WORLD (1992-93)

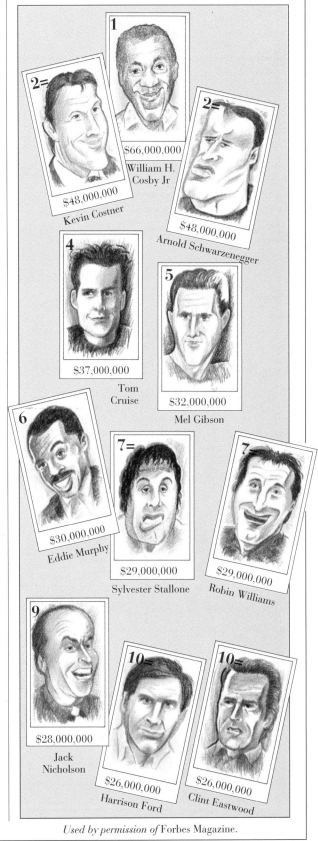

1 William H. Cosby Jr $66,000,000

2= Kevin Costner $48,000,000

2= Arnold Schwarzenegger $48,000,000

4 Tom Cruise $37,000,000

5 Mel Gibson $32,000,000

6 Eddie Murphy $30,000,000

7= Sylvester Stallone $29,000,000

7= Robin Williams $29,000,000

9 Jack Nicholson $28,000,000

10= Harrison Ford $26,000,000

10= Clint Eastwood $26,000,000

Used by permission of Forbes Magazine.

RICHEST IN THE UK

PAUL RAYMOND
Having built up a publishing, retailing, and entertainment empire worth one-and-a-half billion, Paul Raymond is estimated by Business Age to own as much as 65 per cent of London's Soho district.

T O P 1 0

RICHEST MEN IN THE UK

(All richest in the UK list are published by courtesy of Business Age)

	Name	Profession/source	Assets (£)
1	Paul Raymond	Publishing/property	1,500,000,000
2	David Sainsbury	Retailing	1,425,000,000
3	Viscount Rothermere	Newspaper publisher	1,300,000,000
4	Sir Evelyn Rothschild	Merchant banker	1,100,000,000
5	Duke of Westminster	Landowner	750,000,000
6	Lord Jacob Rothschild	Banking/investment	725,000,000
7	Sir James Goldsmith	Financier	700,000,000
8	Garfield Weston	Food manufacturing	600,000,000
9	Viscount Cowdray	Publishing/banking	475,000,000
10	Stephen Rubin	Footwear/clothing	450,000,000

T O P 1 0

RICHEST BRITISH ARISTOCRATS

(Excluding those listed elsewhere)

	Name	Assets (£)
1	Duke of Devonshire	255,000,000
2	Duke of Buccleuch	169,000,000
3	Duke of Atholl	145,000,000
4	Duke of Northumberland	130,000,000
5	Marquess of Tavistock	122,000,000
6	Viscount Petersham	110,000,000
7	Lady Virginia Stanhope	105,000,000
8	Marquess of Cholmondeley	98,000,000
9=	Baroness Willoughby de Erersby	97,000,000
9=	Viscount Portman	97,000,000

MONOPOLY MONEY
The Duke of Westminster owns some 120 hectares (300 acres) of prime site property, held by his family since the 17th century, in London's Mayfair – the most expensive on the Monopoly board! Declining property values have ousted him from his position as the UK's wealthiest man.

T O P 1 0

RICHEST BRITISH PUBLISHERS

	Name	Publishing interests	Assets (£)
1	Viscount Rothermere	Daily Mail	1,300,000,000
2	Viscount Cowdray	Penguin Books	475,000,000
3	Paul Hamlyn	Reed International	245,000,000
4	David Sullivan	Sunday/Daily Sport	173,000,000
5	Felix Dennis	Computer magazines	154,000,000
6	John Madejski	Autotrader	142,000,000
7	Peter Kindersley	Dorling Kindersley	80,000,000
8	Robert Iliffe	Regional newspapers	75,000,000
9	Earl of Stockton	Macmillan	60,000,000
10	Michael Heseltine	Haymarket	47,750,000

T O P 1 0

OLDEST RICHEST IN THE UK

	Name	Profession/source	Assets (£)	Age (years)
1=	Sir Owen Aisher	Industrialist	29,000,000	94
1=	HM The Queen Mother	Royal	26,000,000	94
3=	Barbara Cartland	Author	40,000,000	93
3=	Princess Alice, Duchess of Gloucester	Royal	26,500,000	93
5	Lord Home	Landowner	35,000,000	91
6	Sir Julian Hodge	Banker	35,000,000	90
7	Catherine Cookson	Author	30,000,000	88
8=	Lord Margadale	Landowner	45,000,000	87
8=	Phyllis Somers	Aviation	29,000,000	87
8=	Doris Thompson	Leisure	28,000,000	87

T O P 1 0

BRITISH ENTERTAINMENT FORTUNES

(Other than pop stars)

	Name	Profession	Assets (£)
1	Cameron Mackintosh	Theatrical producer	278,000,000
2	Sir Andrew Lloyd Webber	Theatrical producer	240,000,000
3	Michael Winner	Film director	47,500,000
4	Bernie Taupin	Songwriter	43,500,000
5	Peter Waterman	Songwriter	32,500,000
6	Tim Rice	Songwriter	32,000,000
7	Julie Andrews	Singer/actress	30,000,000
8	Michael Caine	Actor	28,000,000
9	Sean Connery	Actor	26,750,000
10	John Cleese	Actor	26,500,000

T O P 1 0

RICHEST WOMEN IN THE UK

	Name	Profession/source	Assets (£)
1	Chryss Goulandris	Shipping heiress	280,000,000
2	Lady Brigid Ness	Guinness heiress	250,000,000
3	Donatella Moores	Littlewoods heiress	235,000,000
4	Viscountess Boyd	Guinness heiress	225,000,000
5	Patricia Martin	Littlewoods heiress	184,000,000
6	Lady Grantchester	Littlewoods heiress	168,000,000
7	HM The Queen	Royal	150,000,000
8	Lady Elizabeth Nugent	Guinness heiress	141,000,000
9	Lady Virginia Stanhope	Heiress, landowner	105,000,000
10	Christina Foyle	Bookseller	102,000,000

T O P 1 0

RICHEST BRITISH POP STARS

	Name	Assets (£)		Name	Assets (£)
1	Paul McCartney	420,000,000	6	Mick Jagger	69,000,000
2	Tom Jones	252,000,000	7	Mark Knopfler	57,000,000
3	Phil Collins	118,000,000	8	Sting (Gordon Sumner)	52,000,000
4	Engelbert Humperdinck	95,000,000	9	Keith Richards	50,000,000
5	Elton John	80,000,000	10	Rod Stewart	39,000,000

PAUL McCARTNEY

T O P 1 0

YOUNGEST RICHEST IN THE UK

	Name	Profession/source	Assets (£)	Age (years)
1	Sean Lennon	Son of John Lennon	47,500,000	19
2	Serena Stanhope	Heiress	30,000,000	24
3	Jonathan Harmsworth	Publishing heir	33,000,000	26
4	Nicola Foulston	Business	24,000,000	27
5=	Sir Euan Anstruther-Gough-Calthorpe	Landowner	55,000,000	28
5=	Baron Inverforth	Shipping	35,000,000	28
5=	Portia Kennaway	Littlewoods heiress	45,000,000	28
8=	Earl Spencer	Landowner	88,000,000	30
8=	Louise White	Littlewoods heiress	45,000,000	30
8=	Earl of Yarborough	Landowner	65,000,000	30

T O P 1 0

RICHEST BRITISH AUTHORS

	Name	Assets (£)
1	Barbara Cartland	40,000,000
2	Barbara Taylor Bradford	35,500,000
3	Dick Francis	35,250,000
4	Jackie Collins	31,500,000
5	Catherine Cookson	30,500,000
6	Harry Patterson (Jack Higgins)	29,500,000
7=	Terry Pratchett	26,500,000
7=	Jeffrey Archer	26,500,000
9	Ken Follett	24,250,000
10	Wilbur Smith	16,000,000

THE WORLD OF WEALTH

TOP 10

COINS AND NOTES IN CIRCULATION IN THE UK

	Unit	Units in circulation	Value in circulation (£)
1	£10	574,300,000	5,743,000,000
2	£20	264,400,000	5,288,000,000
3	£50	50,300,000	2,515,000,000
4	£5	323,200,000	1,616,000,000
5	£1 coin	1,007,000,000	1,007,000,000
6	50p	604,000,000	302,000,000
7	20p	1,370,000,000	274,000,000
8	10p (old)*	1,470,000,000	147,000,000
9	5p (new)	2,440,000,000	122,000,000
10	2p	3,600,000,000	72,000,000

No longer legal tender.

Notes in circulation on 23 December 1992 (which included a total of £1,350,000,000 "other notes", such as the high value notes used internally by the Bank of England) totalled £18,558,402,353 – the equivalent of a pile of £5 notes 294 km/183 miles high. Surprising though it may seem, although they were last issued on 31 December 1984 and ceased to be legal tender on 11 March 1988, the value of £1 notes still in circulation (£59,000,000) is greater than that of 1p coins (5,800,000,000 units worth £58,000,000).

TOP 10

COUNTRIES WITH MOST CURRENCY IN CIRCULATION 100 YEARS AGO

	Country	Total currency in circulation (US $)
1	USA	2,142,000,000
2	France	2,104,000,000
3	India	960,000,000
4	Germany	900,000,000
5	UK	845,000,000
6	Russia	720,000,000
7	China	700,000,000
8	Italy	510,000,000
9	Austria	460,000,000
10	Spain	390,000,000

It is interesting to consider that, as a result of inflation during the past century, there are now individuals in these countries who, on paper at least, own more than the entire country's money supply in the 1890s. There is today in excess of $1,000,000,000,000 in circulation in the US.

TOP 10

COUNTRIES IN WHICH IT IS EASIEST TO BE A MILLIONAIRE

	Country	Currency unit	Value of 1,000,000 units in £
1	Zaïre	Zaïre	0.11
2	Poland	Zloty	33.69
3	Turkey	Lira	56.87
4	Vietnam	Dông	62.25
5	Guinea-Bissau	Peso	132.54
6	Croatia	Dinar	148.95
7	Mozambique	Metical	162.20
8	Cambodia	Riel	184.08
9	Somalia	Shilling	254.37
10	Indonesia	Rupiah	314.27

Runaway inflation in many countries has reduced the value of their currencies to such an extent as to make them virtually worthless. With an exchange rate running at 8,943,300 Zaïre to the pound Sterling, total assets of just 11p will qualify one as a Zaïrese millionaire.

TOP 10

POOREST COUNTRIES IN THE WORLD

	Country	GDP per capita (US $)
1	Mozambique	72
2	Tanzania	96
3	Somalia	100
4	Ethiopia	116
5	Uganda	164
6	Bhutan	177
7	Nepal	178
8	Afghanistan	195
9=	Cambodia	199
9=	Myanmar (Burma)	199

TOP 10

COUNTRIES WITH THE HIGHEST INFLATION

	Country	Annual inflation rate (%)
1	Zaïre	4,129.2
2	Brazil	2,146.3
3	Romania	255.2
4	Zambia	187.2
5	Turkey	66.1
6	Uruguay	54.1
7	Peru	48.6
8	Kenya	45.8
9	Ecuador	45.0
10	Venezuela	38.1

These figures are for 1993 and indicate the rise in consumer prices over the previous year, as calculated by the International Monetary Fund (except for Zaïre, where the latest available figure is for 1992 on 1991). Certain countries have markedly improved their rate. Peru's is down from an annual rate of 3,399 per cent in 1989.

T O P 1 0

GOLD PRODUCERS IN THE WORLD

	Country	Annual production (tonnes)
1	South Africa	619.5
2	USA	336.0
3	Australia	247.2
4	Former USSR	244.0
5	Canada	150.9
6	China	127.0
7	Brazil	74.7
8	Papua New Guinea	61.8
9	Indonesia	46.3
10	Ghana	41.4
	World total	2,216.5

As reported by Gold Fields Mineral Services Ltd's *Gold 1994*, after experiencing a temporary decline, world-dominating gold producer South Africa saw its output up again in both 1992 and 1993. Australia's output has increased dramatically over recent years: the country's record annual production had stood at 119 tonnes since 1903, but in 1988 it rocketed to 152 tonnes, and in 1992 for the first time overtook that of the former Soviet Union.

T O P 1 0

RICHEST COUNTRIES IN THE WORLD

	Country	GDP per capita (US $)
1	Switzerland	33,515
2	Luxembourg	30,950
3	Japan	26,919
4	Bermuda	26,600
5	Sweden	25,487
6	Finland	24,396
7	Norway	24,151
8	Denmark	23,676
9	USA	22,560
10	Iceland	22,362

T O P 1 0

LARGEST POLISHED GEM DIAMONDS IN THE WORLD

	Diamond/(last known whereabouts or owner)	Carats
1	"Unnamed Brown" (De Beers)	545.67
2	Great Star of Africa/Cullinan I (British Crown Jewels)	530.20
3	Incomparable/Zale (auctioned in New York, 1988)	407.48
4	Second Star of Africa/Cullinan II (British Crown Jewels)	317.40
5	Centenary (De Beers)	273.85
6	Jubilee (Paul-Louis Weiller)	245.35
7	De Beers (sold in Geneva, 1982)	234.50
8	Red Cross (sold in Geneva, 1973)	205.07
9	Black Star of Africa (unknown)	202.00
10	Anon (unknown)	200.87

The highest price paid for a polished diamond sold at auction is $12,760,000 paid by Robert Mouwad for an 11-sided pear-shaped 101.84-carat diamond now known as the *Mouwad Splendour*, at Sotheby's, Geneva, on 14 November 1990. The $880,000 paid at Christie's, New York, on 28 April 1987 for a 0.95 purplish-red stone is equivalent to a record $926,315.79 per carat. *The Incomparable*, No. 3 in the list, holds the world record for the highest failed bid – $13,200,000, when offered at auction at Christie's, New York, on 19 October 1988, which was insufficient to reach the reserve price set by its vendors.

T O P 1 0

LARGEST UNCUT DIAMONDS IN THE WORLD

	Diamond	Carats
1	Cullinan	3,106.00

The largest diamond ever found, it was cut into 105 separate gems, the most important of which are now among the British Crown Jewels.

2	Braganza	1,680.00

All trace of this enormous stone has been lost.

3	Excelsior	995.20

The native worker who found this diamond (in 1893 – in a shovelful of gravel at the South African Jagersfontein Mine) hid it and took it directly to the mine manager, who rewarded him with a horse, a saddle, and £500.

4	Star of Sierra Leone	968.80

Found in Sierra Leone on St Valentine's Day, 1972, the uncut diamond weighed 225 g/8 oz and measured 6.5 x 4 cm/2½ x 1½ in.

5	Zale Corporation "Golden Giant"	890.00

Its origin is so shrouded in mystery that it is not even known from which country it came.

6	Great Mogul	787.50

When found in 1650 in the Gani Mine, India, this diamond was presented to Shah Jehan, the builder of the Taj Mahal.

7	Woyie River	770.00

Found in 1945 beside the river in Sierra Leone.

8	Presidente Vargas	726.60

Discovered in the Antonio River, Brazil, in 1938, it was named after the then President.

9	Jonker	726.00

In 1934 Jacobus Jonker, a previously unsuccessful diamond prospector, found this massive diamond after it had been exposed by a heavy storm.

10	Reitz	650.80

Like the *Excelsior*, the *Reitz* was found in the Jagersfontein Mine in South Africa, in 1895.

The weight of diamonds is measured in carats (the word derives from the carob bean, which grows on the Ceratonia siliqua tree and which is remarkable for its consistent weight of 0.2 of a gram). There are approximately 142 carats to the ounce. Fewer than 1,000 rough diamonds weighing more than 100 carats have been recorded.

SWEET TEETH

SWEET-CONSUMING NATIONS IN THE WORLD

	Country	chocolate	Annual consumption (kg per head) other sweets	total
1	Netherlands	8.21	5.68	13.89
2	Denmark	6.91	6.39	13.30
3	Switzerland	10.03	2.90	12.93
4	UK	7.42	5.17	12.59
5	Belgium/Luxembourg	7.63	4.86	12.49
6	Ireland	6.65	5.78	12.43
7	Norway	7.89	4.37	12.26
8	Germany	6.57	5.68	12.25
9	Sweden	5.55	5.25	10.80
10	Austria	7.32	2.85	10.17
	USA	4.66	3.44	8.10

BESTSELLING SWEETS IN THE UK

	Product	Manufacturer
1	Fruit Pastilles	Rowntree
2	Extra Strong Mints	Trebor
3	Polo	Rowntree
4	Orbit Gum	Wrigley
5	Softmints	Trebor
6	Opal Fruits	Mars
7	Tunes	Mars
8	Wrigley's Extra	Wrigley
9	Original Wine Gums	Maynard
10	Liquorice Allsorts	Bassett

The total UK non-chocolate sweet market is estimated to have been worth some £1,247,000,000 in 1993 – equivalent to more than £21.00 per head.

COCOA-CONSUMING NATIONS IN THE WORLD

	Country	Total cocoa consumption (tonnes)
1	USA	593,300
2	Germany	264,200
3	UK	180,400
4	France	159,800
5	Japan	110,800
6	Brazil	81,200
7	Italy	73,200
8	Spain	60,000
9	Belgium/Luxembourg	57,300
10	Canada	49,300

Cocoa is the principal ingredient of chocolate, and its consumption is therefore closely linked to the production of chocolate in each consuming country. Like coffee, the consumption of chocolate occurs mainly in the West and in more affluent countries. Since some of the Top 10 consuming nations also have large populations, the figures for cocoa consumption per head present a somewhat different picture, dominated by those countries with a long-established tradition of manufacturing high-quality chocolate products:

COCOA-CONSUMING NATIONS IN THE WORLD (PER HEAD)

	Country	Consumption per head kg	lb	oz
1	Belgium/Luxembourg	5.500	16	12
2	Switzerland	4.821	10	10
3	Iceland	4.100	9	1
4	Germany	3.279	7	4
5	Austria	3.267	7	3
6	UK	3.118	6	14
7	Norway	2.914	6	7
8	France	2.785	6	2
9=	Denmark	2.488	5	8
9=	Italy	2.488	5	8

T O P 1 0

CADBURY'S CHOCOLATE PRODUCTS

1 Dairy Milk
2 Roses
3 Creme Eggs
4 Crunchie
5 Fruit & Nut
6 Caramel
7 Milk Tray
8 Whole Nut
9 Flake
10 Time Out

Despite the retail recession of recent years, sales of chocolate products have actually increased. (There is evidence that the market was similarly little affected by the Great Depression of the 1930s, and it seems clear that consumers regard chocolate as a treat to be enjoyed however adverse their financial circumstances.) In 1993 total UK chocolate sales exceeded £3,000,000,000 for the first time – equivalent to more than £1.00 per person per week. Sales of Cadbury's top product, Dairy Milk, are worth more than £100,000,000 per annum.

T O P 1 0

OLDEST-ESTABLISHED BRITISH CHOCOLATE PRODUCTS

	Product	Year introduced
1	Fry's Chocolate Cream	1866
2	Cadbury's Dairy Milk	1905
3	Cadbury's Bournville	1908
4	Fry's Turkish Delight	1914
5	Cadbury's Milk Tray	1915
6	Cadbury's Flake	1920
7	Cadbury's Fruit & Nut	1921
8	Terry's 1767 Bitter Bar	1922
9	Cadbury's Brazil Nut	1925
10	Cadbury's Crunchie	1929

T O P 1 0

ICE CREAM PRODUCTS IN THE UK

1 Wall's Cornetto
2 Wall's Magnum
3 Wall's Feast
4 Wall's Sparkles
5 Wall's Calippo
6 Wall's Strawberry Split
7 Wall's Chunky
8 Wall's Max the Lion
9 Wall's Mini Milk
10 Mars Bar

The ice cream market grew by a remarkable 62 per cent in the five years from 1986 to 1991 (when it was worth approximately £763,000,000). All but one of the Top 10 products (known in the jargon of the trade as "wrapped impulse ice cream brands") are manufactured by Wall's.

T O P 1 0

BESTSELLING HÄAGEN-DAZS ICE CREAM FLAVOURS

1 Vanilla
2 Pralines and Cream
3 Cookies and Cream
4 Belgian Chocolate
5 Strawberry
6 Vanilla Chocolate Fudge
7 Choc Choc Chip
8 Cookie Dough Dynamo
9 Caramel Cone Explosion
10 Macadamia Nut Brittle

When Reuben Mattus created a range of high quality ice creams in 1961, he chose a meaningless but Danish-sounding name to emphasize the rich, creamy nature of his product. His three flavours (vanilla, chocolate, and coffee) were sold through New York delicatessens. Today Häagen-Dazs shops across the US and Europe offer as many as 20 different flavours.

T O P 1 0

ICE CREAM CONSUMERS IN EUROPE

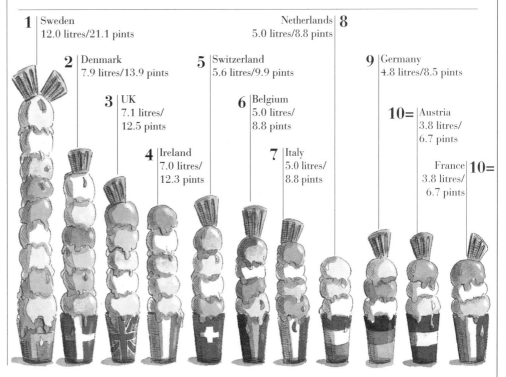

1 Sweden 12.0 litres/21.1 pints
2 Denmark 7.9 litres/13.9 pints
3 UK 7.1 litres/12.5 pints
4 Ireland 7.0 litres/12.3 pints
5 Switzerland 5.6 litres/9.9 pints
6 Belgium 5.0 litres/8.8 pints
7 Italy 5.0 litres/8.8 pints
8 Netherlands 5.0 litres/8.8 pints
9 Germany 4.8 litres/8.5 pints
10= Austria 3.8 litres/6.7 pints
10= France 3.8 litres/6.7 pints

FOOD – WORLD

CALORIE-CONSUMING NATIONS IN THE WORLD

	Country	Average daily per capita consumption
1	Ireland	3,952
2	Belgium/Luxembourg	3,925
3	Greece	3,775
4	Former East Germany	3,710
5	Bulgaria	3,695
6	USA	3,642
7	Denmark	3,639
8	Hungary	3,608
9	France	3,593
10	Former Czechoslovakia	3,574
	UK	*3,270*
	World average	*2,697*

A Calorie is a unit of heat (defined as the amount of heat needed to raise one kilogram of water 1° Centigrade in temperature). Calories are used by nutritionists as a means of expressing the energy-producing value of foods. The Calorie requirement of the average man is 2,700 and of a woman 2,500. Inactive people need less, while those engaged in heavy labour might have to consume much more, perhaps even double this amount of energy. Calories that are not consumed as energy turn to fat – which is why Calorie-counting is one of the key aspects of most diets. The high Calorie intake of certain countries, measured over the period 1988–90, reflects the high proportion of starchy foods, such as potatoes, bread, and pasta, in the national diet. In many Western countries the high figures simply reflect over-eating – especially since these figures are averages that include men, women, and children, suggesting that large numbers in each country are greatly exceeding them. While weight-watchers of the West guzzle their way through 30 per cent more than they need, every country in Europe (except Sweden) consuming more than 3,000 Calories per head, the Calorie consumption in Bangladesh and some of the poorest African nations falls below 2,000: in the Congo it is 1,760 – less than half that of the nations in the world Top 10.

MEAT-EATING NATIONS IN THE WORLD

	Country	Consumption per head per annum		
		kg	lb	oz
1	USA	116.9	257	11
2	Australia	104.0	229	5
3	New Zealand	100.8	222	3
4	Canada	98.6	217	6
5	Hong Kong	98.0	216	2
6	Hungary	97.5	215	0
7	France	96.6	213	0
8	Argentina	92.0	202	13
9	Austria	90.3	199	2
10=	Germany	90.2	198	14
10=	Spain	90.2	198	14
	UK	*71.8*	*158*	*0*

Figures compiled by the Meat and Livestock Commission show a huge range of meat consumption around the world, from the nations featured in the Top 10 to very poor countries such as India. Meat-eating reflects factors such as wealth; in general, the richer the country, the more meat is eaten (although in recent years concern about healthy eating in many Western countries has resulted in a deliberate decline in consumption). Availability is another significant factor – New Zealand's consumption of lamb is one of the world's highest, at 38.1 kg/84 lb per head. Culture also plays a role – as a result of dietary prohibitions very little pork is eaten in the Middle East, and the Japanese eat only 41.5 kg/91 lb of meat, but larger quantities of fish than many other nations.

CONSUMERS OF KELLOGG'S CORN FLAKES*

1	Ireland
2	UK
3	Australia
4	Denmark
5	Sweden
6	Norway
7	Canada
8	USA
9	Mexico
10	Venezuela

* Based on per capita consumption.

In 1894 the brothers Will Keith and Dr John Harvey Kellogg were running their "Sanatorium", a health resort in Battle Creek, Michigan. Attempting to devise healthy food products for their patients, they experimented with wheat dough that they boiled and passed through rollers. By accident, they discovered that if the dough was left overnight it came out as flakes, and that when these were baked they turned into a tasty cereal. The Kellogg brothers started making their new product on a small scale, providing cereal by mail order to former patients. In 1898 they replaced wheat with corn, thereby creating the Corn Flakes we know today. Will Keith left the Sanatorium in 1906 and set up a business manufacturing Corn Flakes with his distinctive signature on the packet. Corn Flakes were first exported to England in 1922 along with All Bran and, in 1928, Rice Krispies, and remain Kellogg's bestselling product. The company's corn mill in Seaforth, Liverpool, is Europe's largest and processes 1,000 tons of grain a day. The Kellogg Company, which in 1994 celebrated the centenary of the invention of Corn Flakes, achieves annual sales in 130 countries that are worth in excess of £4,000,000,000. The business is today regarded as such a dominant force worldwide that the importance of the Kellogg brand is rated second in the world, after Coca-Cola.

T O P 1 0

HEINZ PRODUCTS IN THE WORLD

1 Ketchup

2 Baby food

3 Tuna

4 Frozen potatoes

5 Soup

6 Weight Watchers' frozen entrées and desserts

7 Cat food

8 Sauces and pastes

9 Baked beans

10 Dog food

Henry John Heinz, the founder of the gigantic food processing and canning empire that bears his name, was born in Pittsburgh, Pennsylvania in 1844, of German immigrant parents. In 1869 he formed a partnership with a family friend, L.C. Noble, selling horseradish in clear glass jars (previously green glass disguised the dishonest practice of packing the horseradish out with turnip), beginning the Heinz reputation for quality and integrity. Their products were also sold on their lack of artificial flavourings and colourings long before these factors were thought desirable. Heinz & Noble steadily added other lines, including pickles. In 1876, with his brother John and cousin Frederick, H.J. formed the firm of F. & J. Heinz. One of their first products was ketchup – a staple product in every American household, but one previously made on a domestic scale, a task that involved the whole family stirring a cauldron over an open fire for an entire day.

The business was sufficiently well-established by 1886 for the Heinz family to visit Europe, and H.J. sold the first Heinz products in Britain to Fortnum & Mason, the upmarket Piccadilly emporium, astonishing them by his audacity at entering the store through the front door, rather than the tradesman's entrance. The first branch office in London was opened in 1895, by which time the company had become H.J. Heinz & Co.

Why "57 Varieties"? In 1896, travelling on the New York Third Avenue railway, H.J. saw a sign advertising "21 Styles" of shoe, "It set me to thinking", he later recalled. "I said to myself, 'We do not have styles of products, but we do have varieties of products'. Counting how many we had, I counted well beyond 57, but '57' kept coming back into my mind . . . 58 Varieties or 59 Varieties did not appeal to me at all – just '57 Varieties'." Henry went straight to his printers where he designed the first "Heinz 57" advertisement.

T O P 1 0

CONSUMERS OF HEINZ BAKED BEANS IN THE WORLD

	Consumer	Sales (cans per annum)*
1	UK	550,000,000
2	Sweden	2,460,000
3	West Africa	1,780,000
4	Bahrain	770,000
5	Dubai, UAE	580,000

	Consumer	Sales (cans per annum)*
6	Singapore	520,000
7	NAAFI, Germany	430,000
8	Spain	420,000
9	Greece	300,000
10	Kuwait	190,000

* *Based on 450g/1 lb can.*

These figures are not a mistake: the United Kingdom really does munch its way through 550,000,000 cans of Heinz baked beans a year – equivalent to 10 cans for every inhabitant, and 224 times as many as the next most important international market, Sweden (where the annual consumption is just 0.28 cans per head).

Of all their "57 Varieties", baked beans are Heinz's most famous product. They were originally test-marketed in the North of England in 1901, and imported from the US up until 1928 when they were first canned in the UK. The slogan "Beanz Meanz Heinz" was invented in 1967 over a drink in the Victoria pub in Mornington Terrace by Young and Rubicam advertising agency executive Maurice Drake.

In 1995 H. J. Heinz will celebrate the centenary of baked bean production and of opening the company's first London office.

T O P 1 0

SUGAR-CONSUMING NATIONS IN THE WORLD

	Country	Consumption per head per annum	
		kg	lb
1	Cuba	89.2	196.7
2	Swaziland	67.1	147.9
3	Singapore	65.3	144.0
4	Israel	59.9	132.1
5	Costa Rica	59.2	130.5
6	Iceland	58.6	129.2
7	Netherlands	57.9	127.7
8	Fiji	56.2	123.9
9	Austria	55.1	121.5
10	Hungary	54.1	119.3
	UK	*43.4*	*95.7*

Each citizen of Cuba, the world's leaders in the sweet-tooth stakes, would appear to consume a quantity equal to the familiar 1 kg/2.2 lb bag of sugar every four days.

FOOD – UK

FAST FOOD CHAINS IN THE UK

	Chain	Outlets	Sales (£) p.a.
1	McDonalds	446	512,900,000
2	Beefeater	281	210,750,000
3	KFC (Kentucky Fried Chicken)	288	152,000,000
4	Pizza Hut	287	150,388,000
5	Little Chef	366	128,100,000
6	Burger King	183	100,650,000
7	Brewers Fayre	140	70,000,000
8	Big Steak Pubs	132	66,000,000
9	Country Kitchen	26	60,100,000
10	Harvester	79	59,250,000

The UK's leading fast food chains are ranked by sales. The competitors of McDonalds, which serves 1,000,000 customers a day, have a long way to catch up – especially in the light of the company's declared intention of increasing its outlets to more than 1,000 over the next 10 years. If the parameters are extended to include takeaway sandwich chains, such as Baker's Oven and Greggs, they would appear in 6th and 8th places respectively. Wimpy, one of the oldest-established fast food chains (founded in the US in the 1930s, it opened its first restaurant in London in 1954), falls just outside the Top 10.

BESTSELLING BIRDS EYE FROZEN FOODS

	Product	Sales (£) p.a.
1	MenuMaster prepared meals	116,600,000
2	Captain's Table Fish Fingers	60,200,000
3	Country Club peas	49,100,000
4	Steakhouse Original Burgers	36,700,000
5	Captain's Table Fish in Sauce	27,600,000
6	Fish Cuisine	25,000,000
7	Potato Waffles	19,800,000
8	Country Club Cuisine	19,300,000
9	Homebake pies	17,900,000
10	Healthy Options meals	16,400,000

Although these figures are for retail sales in 1993, current figures for quantities are confidential. However, when this list was compiled in 1989 it was revealed that UK annual consumption of Birds Eye peas was 27,519 tonnes (equivalent to the weight of over 72 fully laden jumbo jets or 2,200 London buses) and that of fish fingers 13,000 tonnes (1,040 buses).

THE 10 MOST-ADVERTISED FOOD PRODUCTS IN THE UK*

	Product	Annual advertising expenditure (£)
1	Ready-to-eat cereals	82,718,000
2	Frozen ready-to-eat meals	33,358,000
3	Tea	32,482,000
4	Sauces, pickles, and salad cream	29,110,000
5	Instant coffee	26,548,000
6	Potato crisps and snacks	22,971,000
7	Ice creams and lollies	19,942,000
8	Margarine and low-fat spreads	19,436,000
9	Cheese	17,030,000
10	Milk and milk products	15,870,000

* Excluding confectionery, soft drinks, and alcohol.

In addition to those items in the Top 10, sums in excess of £10,000,000 were spent on advertising three further food categories: yoghurt, stock and stock cubes, and cooking sauces, as well as ranges of foods. In 1992 total expenditure on all products, ranging from cereals down to those where spending is measured in thousands rather than millions, such as frozen fruit (£2,000), was £481,970,000, or £8.35 per head.

FOOD AND DRINK ITEMS CONSUMED IN THE UK BY VALUE

	Product	Sales (£) p.a.
1	Beer	13,267,000,000
2	Meat	9,958,000,000
3	Wine, cider, and perry	6,032,000,000
4	Milk, cheese, and eggs	6,017,000,000
5	Spirits	5,313,000,000
6	Confectionery	4,081,000,000
7	Vegetables	3,852,000,000
8	Soft drinks	3,503,000,000
9	Fruit	2,911,000,000
10	Cereals	2,481,000,000

In 1992 UK consumers spent £45,264,000,000 (an average of £783 per head) on food and a further £24,612,000,000 (£426 per head) on alcohol. Perhaps surprisingly, bread is ranked in 13th place, with sales of £2,007,000,000, with potatoes in 11th and cakes and biscuits in 12th place.

TOP 10

FOOD AND DRINK ITEMS CONSUMED IN THE UK BY WEIGHT

(*Excluding beer and other alcoholic drinks*)

	Product	Average consumption per head per week (1992)	
		g	oz
1	Milk and cream	2,288	80.70
2	Vegetables (other than potatoes)	1,174	41.42
3	Meat	951	33.53
4	Potatoes	901	31.78
5	Bread	755	26.62
6	Fruit and nuts	670	23.62
7	Biscuits, cakes, cereals, etc.	411	14.50
8	Butter, oils, and fats	245	8.64
9	Fruit juices	222	7.83
10	Sugar and honey	201	7.10

The National Food Survey, on which this list is partly based, revealed that a number of changes in British eating habits had taken place during the 1980s, in line with increasing awareness of "healthy diets". Most notable was a move from whole milk to other types, such as semi-skimmed, and a more than 50 per cent reduction in the amount of butter and sugar consumed. Among other categories not represented in the Top 10 are fish (141 g/4.99 oz per week), eggs (an average of 2.08), and cheese (114 g/4.01 oz). Apples are the most-eaten fruit (187 g/6.59 oz) and poultry the most consumed meat (231 g/8.16 oz).

TOP 10

FRUITS AND VEGETABLES CONSUMED IN THE UK

	Product	Average consumption per head per annum		
		kg	lb	oz
1	Potatoes*	49.9	110	0
2	Apples	10.0	22	1
3	Bananas	6.8	15	0
4	Beans (canned)	6.4	14	2
5	Carrots	5.9	13	0
6	Tomatoes	5.0	11	0
7	Onions, shallots, and leeks	4.5	9	15
8	Cabbages	4.1	9	0
9=	Cauliflowers	3.9	8	9
9=	Oranges	3.9	8	9

* *Fresh only; excluding potato products.*

TOP 10

EXPORTERS OF FOOD AND DRINK TO THE UK

	Exporter	Value 1992 (£)
1	France	1,863,101,000
2	Netherlands	1,735,711,000
3	Ireland	1,426,324,000
4	Germany	982,946,000
5	Denmark	898,429,000
6	Italy	656,979,000
7	USA	559,245,000
8	Belgium/Luxembourg	547,587,000
9	Spain	543,455,000
10	New Zealand	323,908,000

TOP 10

FOOD AND DRINK PRODUCTS EXPORTED FROM THE UK

	Product	Value 1992 (£)
1	Alcoholic drinks	2,383,000,000
2	Cereal products (biscuits, etc)	534,000,000
3	Unmilled wheat	440,000,000
4	Chocolate products	282,000,000
5	Beef	266,000,000
6	Fresh fish	220,000,000
7	Concentrated or sweetened milk and cream	218,000,000
8	Sheep and goat meat	217,000,000
9	Unmilled barley	177,000,000
10	Shellfish	167,000,000

TOP 10

IMPORTERS OF FOOD AND DRINK FROM THE UK

	Importer	Value 1992 (£)
1	France	1,154,226,000
2	Ireland	790,635,000
3	Netherlands	615,385,000
4	Germany	571,208,000
5	Spain	539,155,000
6	USA	505,429,000
7	Italy	414,331,000
8	Belgium/Luxembourg	313,615,000
9	Japan	257,654,000
10	Canada	135,094,000

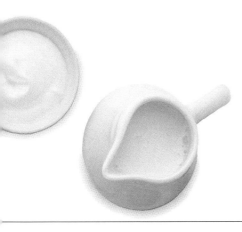

ALCOHOL

T O P 1 0

BEER-DRINKING NATIONS IN THE WORLD

	Country	Annual consumption per head litres	pints
1	Germany	142.7	251.1
2	Former Czechoslovakia	135.0	237.6
3	Denmark	125.9	221.6
4	Austria	123.7	217.7
5	Ireland	123.0	216.5
6	Luxembourg	116.1	204.3
7	Belgium	111.3	195.9
8	New Zealand	109.5	192.7
9	Hungary	107.0	188.3
10	UK	106.2	186.9

Despite its position as the world's leading producer of beer, the US is ranked only 13th in terms of consumption (87.4 litres/153.8 pints per head).

T O P 1 0

CHAMPAGNE IMPORTERS IN THE WORLD

	Country	Bottles imported
1	Germany	15,190,026
2	UK	14,649,105
3	USA	10,847,429
4	Switzerland	7,269,607
5	Belgium	6,265,211
6	Italy	6,025,848
7	Netherlands	1,907,693
8	Japan	1,015,069
9	Australia	918,282
10	Spain	873,282

A telling measure of the recession in recent years has been champagne consumption. In 1991 most imports of champagne declined – that of the UK by 34 per cent on the 1990 figure, relegating it from the first place it had held for many years. In 1993, though, world champagne exports increased by seven per cent – a sign of hope?

T O P 1 0

LARGEST BREWERIES IN THE WORLD

	Brewery	Country	Annual sales litres	pints
1	Anheuser-Busch, Inc	USA	10,430,000,000	18,354,223,790
2	Heineken NV	Netherlands	5,350,000,000	11,174,431,550
3	Miller Brewing Co	USA	5,260,000,000	11,016,053,780
4	Kirin Brewery Co Ltd	Japan	3,240,000,000	5,701,599,720
5	Foster's Brewing Group	Australia	3,050,000,000	5,367,246,650
6	Companhia Cervejaria Brahma	Brazil	2,530,000,000	4,452,175,090
7	Groupe BSN	France	2,500,000,000	4,399,382,500
8	Coors Brewing Co	USA	2,370,000,000	4,170,614,610
9	South Africa Breweries Ltd	South Africa	2,270,000,000	3,994,639,310
10	Companhia Antartica Paulista	Brazil	2,000,000,000	3,519,506,000
11	Guinness plc	Eire	1,900,000,000	3,343,530,700
19	Bass plc	UK	1,460,000,000	2,569,239,380

T O P 1 0

COMMONEST PUB NAMES IN THE UK

1	*The Red Lion*
2	*The Crown*
3	*The Royal Oak*
4	*The White Hart*
5	*The King's Head*
6	*The Bull*
7	*The Coach and Horses*
8	*The George*
9	*The Plough*
10	*The Swan*

DID YOU KNOW

NAME YOUR POISON

There are perhaps more than 25,000 different public house names, past and present, in the UK. "The Red Lion", with over 600, is the commonest, and probably derives from the lion featured on the coat of arms of John of Gaunt, Duke of Lancaster.

TOP 10

BRITISH PUBS WITH THE LONGEST NAMES

	Pub	Letters
1	*Bertie Belcher's Brighton Brewery Company at the Hedgehog and Hogshead – It's Really in Hove, Actually* Hove, East Sussex	83

This name is one of the most recent of many – some more absurd than others – deliberately contrived to appear at the top of lists such as this. ("... Hove, Actually" is a phrase much used by residents who object to being regarded as inhabitants of adjacent Brighton.)

	Pub	Letters
2	*Henry J. Bean's But His Friends, Some of Whom Live Down This Way, All Call Him Hank Bar And Grill* Fulham Road, London SW6	74
3	*The Old Thirteenth Cheshire Astley Volunteer Rifleman Corps Inn* Astley Street, Stalybridge, Manchester	55

In order to maintain its pre-eminence, it was renamed from its former 39-letter version, "The Thirteenth Mounted Cheshire Rifleman Inn", and was the longest pub name until Henry J. Bean et al came on the scene.

	Pub	Letters
4	*The Fellows, Moreton and Clayton Brewhouse Company* Canal Street, Nottingham	43
5	*The Ferret and Firkin in the Balloon up the Creek* Lots Road, London SW10	40
6=	*The London Chatham and Dover Railway Tavern* Cabul Road, London SW11	37
6=	*The Footballers and Cricketers Public Arms* Linlithgow, Lothian	37
8	*The Argyll and Sutherland Highlander Inn* Eastham, Cheshire	35
9=	*The Shoulder of Mutton and Cucumbers Inn* Yapton, West Sussex	34
9=	*The Green Man and Black's Head Royal Hotel* Ashbourne, Derbyshire	34

The 24-letter *I am the Only Running Footman*, Charles Street, London W1, was for many years London's longest-named pub. The shortest-named public house in the UK was the now defunct *X* at Westcott, Devon.

TOP 10

MOST EXPENSIVE BOTTLES OF WINE EVER SOLD AT AUCTION

	Wine	Price (£)
1	Château Lafite 1787 Christie's, London, 5 December 1985	105,000

The highest price ever paid for a bottle of red wine resulted from the bottle having been initialled by the third US President, Thomas Jefferson. It was purchased by Christopher Forbes and is now on display in the Forbes Magazine Galleries, New York.

	Wine	Price (£)
2	Château d'Yquem 1784 Christie's, London, 4 December 1986	39,600

The highest price ever paid for a bottle of white wine.

	Wine	Price (£)
3	Château Lafite Rothschild 1832 (double magnum) International Wine Auctions, London, 9 April 1988	24,000
4	Château Lafite 1806 Sotheby's, Geneva, 13 November 1988	21,700
5	Château Lafite 1811 (tappit-hen – equivalent to three bottles) Christie's, London, 23 June 1988	20,000

	Wine	Price (£)
6	Château Margaux 1784 (half-bottle) Christie's, at Vin Expo, Bordeaux, France, 26 June 1987	18,000

The highest price ever paid for a half-bottle.

	Wine	Price (£)
7	Château d'Yquem 1811 Christie's, London, 1 December 1988	15,000
8	Château Lafite Rothschild 1806 Sold at a Heublein Auction, San Francisco, 24 May 1979	14,000
9	Château Lafite 1822 Sold at a Heublein Auction, San Francisco, 28 May 1980	13,400
10	Château Lafite Rothschild 1811 International Wine Auctions, London, 26 June 1985	12,000

On 25 April 1989, No. 6 (also initialled by Thomas Jefferson), now with an asking price of £304,878, was smashed by a waiter's tray at a tasting in the Four Seasons restaurant, New York. A little of the wine was salvaged, but was declared virtually undrinkable.

TOP 10

WINE-DRINKING NATIONS IN THE WORLD

	Country	Litres per head per annum	Equiv. 75 cl bottles
1	France	66.8	89.1
2	Portugal	62.0	82.7
3	Luxembourg	60.3	80.4
4	Italy	56.8	75.7
5	Argentina	52.4	69.9
6	Switzerland	48.7	64.9
7	Spain	34.3	45.7
8	Austria	33.7	44.9
9	Greece	32.4	43.2
10	Hungary	30.0	40.0
	UK	*11.5*	*15.5*
	USA	*7.7*	*10.3*

TOP 10

WINE-PRODUCING COUNTRIES IN THE WORLD

	Country	Annual production (tonnes)
1	France	6,522,000
2	Italy	6,380,000
3	Spain	3,472,000
4	Former USSR	1,800,000
5	USA	1,545,000
6	Germany	1,340,000
7	Argentina	1,150,000
8	South Africa	930,000
9	Romania	750,000
10	Portugal	724,000
	World total	*28,825,000*

SOFT SELL

T O P 1 0

HOT DRINKS IN THE UK

	Drink	Type	Annual sales (£)*
1	Nescafé	Instant coffee	193,700,000
2	PG Tips	Tea	123,200,000
3	Tetley	Tea	120,000,000
4	Gold Blend	Instant coffee	50,000,000
5	Typhoo	Tea	45,000,000
6=	Maxwell House	Instant coffee	40,000,000
6=	Kenco	Instant coffee	40,000,000
8	Horlicks	Malt drink	35,000,000
9	Co-op 99	Tea	25,000,000
10	Options	Various	20,000,000

* Estimated; through grocery outlets only.

T O P 1 0

TEA-DRINKING NATIONS

	Country	Annual consumption per head		
		kg	lb oz	cups*
1	Ireland	3.00	6 10	1,320
2	UK	2.56	5 9	1,126
3	Turkey	2.25	4 15	990
4	Qatar	2.02	4 7	889
5	Hong Kong	1.96	4 5	862
6	Iran	1.69	3 12	744
7	Syria	1.54	3 6	678
8	New Zealand	1.51	3 5	664
9	Tunisia	1.46	3 4	642
10	Egypt	1.38	3 1	607
	USA	0.33	12	145

* Based on 440 cups per kg/2 lb 3 oz.

Despite the British passion for tea, during recent years the UK's consumption has lagged behind that of Ireland. Qatar's tea consumption has also dropped from its former world record of 3.97 kg/8 lb 12 oz (1,747 cups) per head. At the other end of the scale, Thailand's figure of 0.01 kg/ 0.4 oz (4 cups) is one of the lowest.

T O P 1 0

COFFEE-DRINKING NATIONS

	Country	Annual consumption per head			
		kg	lb	oz	cups*
1	Finland	12.26	27	0	1,839
2	Sweden	11.29	24	14	1,694
3	Denmark	11.13	24	9	1,670
4	Norway	10.29	22	11	1,544
5	Netherlands	10.08	22	4	1,512
6	Austria	9.23	20	6	1,385
7	Switzerland	8.65	19	1	1,298
8	Germany	8.04	17	12	1,206
9	Belgium/Luxembourg	5.88	12	15	882
10	France	5.87	12	15	881
	USA	4.24	9	6	836
	UK	2.61	5	12	392

* Based on 150 cups per kg/2 lb 3 oz.

The total coffee consumption of many countries declined during the 1980s. That of Belgium and Luxembourg, for example, went down by almost 70 per cent, from 7.17 kg/15 lb 13 oz (1,076 cups) in 1986 to 2.27 kg/5 lb 0 oz (341 cups) in 1990, but has recently risen again. That of both Finland and Sweden has remained high, however – the average Finn drinks more than five cups of coffee a day compared with just over one for the UK. Ireland's consumption is the EC's lowest at 1.54 kg/3 lb 6 oz (231 cups), but, as the comparative table shows, the country more than compensates with its pre-eminence in tea-drinking.

T O P 1 0

SOFT DRINK CONSUMERS IN THE WORLD

	Country	Consumption per head p.a.	
		litres	pints
1	Switzerland	105.0	184.8
2	Barbados	81.4	143.2
3	Bahamas	75.0	132.0
4	USA	74.7	131.5
5	Australia	73.9	130.0
6	Germany	72.0	126.7
7	Canada	69.3	122.0
8=	Belgium	65.0	114.4
8=	Japan	65.0	114.4
10	Singapore	61.4	108.1
	UK	39.0	68.6

T O P 1 0

COCA-COLA CONSUMERS IN THE WORLD

1	Iceland
2	USA
3	Mexico
4	Australia
5	Norway
6	Germany
7	Canada
8	Spain
9	Argentina
10	Japan
59	UK

This ranking is based on consumption per capita in these countries – although the actual volumes are secret. The figures for many small countries are distorted by the influx of large numbers of tourists.

T O P 1 0

CONSUMERS OF PERRIER WATER

1	France
2	USA
3	UK
4	Belgium/Luxembourg
5	Canada
6	Germany
7	Middle East*
8	Hong Kong
9	Switzerland
10	Greece

* Various countries.

In 1903 St John Harmsworth, a wealthy Englishman on a tour of France, visited Vergèze, a spa town near Nîmes. Its spring, Les Bouillens (which was believed to have been discovered by the Carthaginian soldier Hannibal in *c*.218 BC), was notable for the occurrence of carbon dioxide which is released from the surrounding rock, permeating through the water and making it "naturally sparkling". Harmsworth recognized the potential for selling the spa water and proceeded to buy the spring, naming it after its former owner, Dr Louis Perrier, a local doctor, and bottling it in distinctive green bottles – said to have been modelled on the Indian clubs with which he exercised. The company was sold back to the French in 1948 (and in 1992 the firm was bought by the Swiss company Nestlé). Perrier water has maintained a reputation as a popular beverage in sophisticated circles. In 1960 in *For Your Eyes Only* Ian Fleming even has James Bond drink it – "He always stipulated Perrier. . . ". In the late 1970s a combination of increased health consciousness and ingenious advertising and marketing enabled Perrier to broaden its appeal and to achieve its world dominance of the burgeoning mineral water business. Perrier is now drunk in 145 countries around the world, and its name has become virtually synonymous with mineral water. In the UK a decade ago, the total mineral water market was worth about £12,000,000 a year, of which Perrier's share was under 500,000 bottles. This rose during the 1980s to a peak of some 100,000,000 bottles a year. It has since declined, but the total consumption of Perrier in the UK remains equivalent to more than one bottle for every person in the country.

T O P 1 0

BRANDS OF BOTTLED MINERAL WATER IN THE UK

	Brand	Type	% of market
1	Evian	Still	11
2	Perrier	Sparkling	9
3	Buxton Spring	Still/sparkling	7
4=	Highland Spring	Still/sparkling	6
4=	Volvic	Still	6
6=	Strathmore	Still/sparkling	5
6=	Sainsbury's Caledonian Spring	Still/sparkling	5
8	Chiltern Hills	Still/sparkling	4
9=	Ballygowan	Still/sparkling	3
9=	Tesco's Mountain Spring	Still/sparkling	3

It is estimated that the total value of the UK market for bottled mineral water rose from £130,000,000 in 1988 to £345,000,000 in 1992, and it is predicted to double by 1997. The UK currently drinks 435,000,000 litres/765,492,555 pints a year, or 7.56 litres/13.30 pints per head. Consumption does not begin to rival that of Italy, however, which drinks the most per head of any country – 101.50 litres/178.61 pints a year.

T O P 1 0

CARBONATED DRINKS IN THE UK

	Drink	Annual sales (£)		Drink	Annual sales (£)
1	Coca-Cola	400,000,000	**6**	Irn Bru	45,000,000
2	Pepsi Cola	140,000,000	**7**	Lilt	40,000,000
3	Lucozade	85,000,000	**8**	7-Up	30,000,000
4	Tango	70,000,000	**9**	Suncharm	25,000,000
5	Schweppes mixers	50,000,000	**10**	Sunkist	20,000,000

Coca-Cola is not only the UK's bestselling fizzy drink, but also the top-selling brand. The sales figures are based on estimates of total purchases through grocers, sweet shops, filling stations, off-licences, and other outlets, so are greater than for grocery-only sales listed elsewhere. In some cases actual sales may be even higher, but such is the rivalry between the various manufacturers that they are a closely guarded trade secret.

The oldest manufacturer of carbonated drinks in the world is Schweppes. German-born Jean Jacob Schweppe (1740–1821) moved to Geneva where he worked as a jeweller. An amateur scientist, he became interested in the manufacture of artificial mineral waters (which had been pioneered in England in 1741 by Dr William Brownrigg of Whitehaven). He moved to London in 1792 and in his Drury Lane factory began producing his own brand of soda water, forming Schweppe & Co (later Schweppes Ltd). By the 1870s the company was also making ginger ale and "Indian Tonic Water" by adding quinine to sweetened soda water, after the style of the British in India who drank it as an antidote to malaria, thus beginning the fashion for gin and tonic. The Schweppes company merged with Cadbury Brothers Ltd in 1969, forming Cadbury Schweppes.

Schweppes' advertising has always been memorable, from its "Schweppervescence" campaign launched in 1946, and the advertisements in the 1950s and 1960s featuring Benny Hill, to the long-running series with actor William Franklyn, using just the "Schhh" sound of the name. It is among the factors accounting for the enduring appeal of the company's products.

TRANSPORT & TOURISM

TOP 10

MOST EXPENSIVE CARS EVER SOLD AT AUCTION

	Car/auction	Price (£)
1	1962 Ferrari 250 Gran Turismo Berlinetta Competition GTO Sotheby's, Monte Carlo, 1990	6,410,000
2	1931 Bugatti Royale Type 41 Chassis "41.141" Christie's, London, 1987	5,575,000
3	1929 Bugatti Royale Chassis "41.150" William F. Harrah Collection Sale, Reno, USA, 1986	4,300,000
4	1962 Ferrari 250 GTO The Auction, Las Vegas, USA, 1991	3,230,000
5	1960 Ferrari Dino 196SP Christie's, Monaco, 1990	2,574,591
6	1957 Aston-Martin DBR2 Christie's, Monaco, 1989	2,178,000
7	1934 Alfa Romeo Tipo B Monoposto Christie's, Monaco, 1989	1,971,000
8	1934 Mercedes-Benz 500K Special Roadster Sotheby's, Monaco, 1989	1,956,237
9	John Lennon's 1965 Rolls-Royce Phantom V Sotheby's, New York, 1985	1,768,462
10	Alfa Romeo Tipo 8C Corto 2300 Spyder Christie's, Monaco, 1989	1,763,000

Among the costliest cars sold privately are two purchased in 1989: the only surviving 1967 original ex-factory team Ferrari 330P4 sports prototype, bought by a Swiss collector for £5,800,000, and another 1962 Ferrari 250 GTO, one of only 36 made, bought by a Japanese collector for over £8,500,000.

TOP 10

EXPORT MARKETS FOR ROLLS-ROYCE MOTOR CARS

1	USA
2	Japan
3	Germany
4	Hong Kong
5	France
6	Singapore
7	Switzerland
8	Saudi Arabia
9	United Arab Emirates
10	Belgium

1909 ROLLS-ROYCE 40/50 "SILVER GHOST"
Since its first cars appeared at the beginning of the 20th century, the Rolls-Royce company has had a reputation for excellence. Because of the high-quality craftsmanship, and the cars' relative rarity, Rolls-Royces are favoured by rich and powerful people worldwide.

THE PROGRESSION OF HOLDERS OF THE LAND SPEED RECORD, 1900–90
(As at the first year of each decade, 1900–90)

Year	Driver	Country	Vehicle	Date	km/h	mph
1900	Camille Jenatzy	Belgium	*Le Jamais Contente*	29 Apr 1899	105.879	65.790
1910	Barney Oldfield	USA	*Blitzen*	16 Mar 1910	211.267	131.275
1920	Tommy Milton	USA	*Duesenberg*	27 Apr 1920	251.106	156.030
1930	Henry Segrave	UK	*Golden Arrow*	11 Mar 1929	372.476	231.446
1940	John Cobb	UK	*Railton*	23 Aug 1939	595.039	369.740
1950	John Cobb	UK	*Railton-Mobil Special*	16 Sep 1947	634.396	394.196
1960	John Cobb	UK	*Railton-Mobil Special*	16 Sep 1947	634.396	394.196
1970	Gary Gabelich	USA	*The Blue Flame*	23 Oct 1970	1,014.511	630.388
1980	Gary Gabelich	USA	*The Blue Flame*	23 Oct 1970	1,014.511	630.388
1990	Richard Noble	UK	*Thrust 2*	4 Oct 1983	1,019.468	633.468

T O P   1 0

BESTSELLING ROLLS-ROYCE AND BENTLEY CARS

	Model	Years manufactured
1	Silver Shadow I (short wheel-base)	1965–76
2	Silver Shadow II	1977–81
3	Silver Spirit	1980–91
4	Silver Spur	1980–92
5	Silver Ghost (British)	1907–25
6	Bentley VI	1946–52
7	Bentley Turbo R	1985–93
8	Rolls-Royce 20/25 HP	1929-36
9	Rolls-Royce Corniche Convertible	1971–87
10	Bentley S1 (short wheel-base)	1955–59

The term "bestselling" used in the context of Rolls-Royce and Bentley is substantially different from that applied to mass-market cars. To put it into perspective, the US giant General Motors produces about 100,000 cars every two weeks, which is more than the entire output of Rolls-Royce since the company started in 1904. About 16,717 of the number one bestselling Silver Shadow were sold in its 11 years of production, while the Silver Ghost, in production for nearly 20 years, sold a total of 6,173 of the British model (fewer than General Motors produces in a single day), with a further 1,703 made under licence in the US in the five years from 1921.

MOTOR VEHICLES

T O P 1 0

COUNTRIES PRODUCING THE MOST MOTOR VEHICLES

	Country	Cars	Commercial vehicles	Total
1	Japan	9,378,694	3,120,590	12,499,284
2	USA	5,663,284	4,038,218	9,701,502
3	Germany	4,863,721	330,221	5,193,942
4	France	3,329,490	438,310	3,767,800
5	Spain	1,790,615	331,272	2,121,887
6	Canada	1,024,739	943,758	1,968,497
7	South Korea	1,306,752	422,944	1,729,696
8	Italy	1,476,627	209,860	1,686,487
9	UK	1,291,880	248,453	1,540,333
10	Former USSR	930,000	600,000	1,530,000
	World total	*34,764,844*	*12,612,490*	*47,377,334*

T O P 1 0

MOTOR VEHICLE MANUFACTURERS IN THE WORLD

	Production company	Country	Cars	Commercial vehicles	Total
1	General Motors	USA	4,968,659	1,666,076	6,634,735
2	Ford Motor Company	USA	3,452,039	1,686,321	5,138,360
3	Toyota	Japan	3,597,179	914,040	4,511,219
4	Volkswagen	Germany	2,921,481	166,952	3,088,433
5	Nissan	Japan	2,333,276	692,483	3,025,759
6	PSA (Peugeot-Citroën)	France	2,257,454	209,773	2,467,227
7	Renault	France	1,705,821	298,416	2,004,237
8	Honda	Japan	1,765,403	143,361	1,908,764
9	Fiat	Italy	1,636,838	261,717	1,898,555
10	Chrysler	USA	660,200	1,014,089	1,674,289
	World total		*34,655,650*	*11,840,781*	*46,496,431*

Figures are for 1991 production, amalgamating worldwide production in all companies owned by the manufacturers, as compiled by the American Automobile Manufacturers Association. Two other Japanese companies, Mazda and Mitsubishi, actually produced more cars than Chrysler (1,250,714 and 1,103,606 respectively – the only other companies in the world to produce more than 1,000,000), but Chrysler's disproportionate commercial vehicle production provides the US company with a place in the Top 10. In this year, the output of the Rover Group, the only British-owned company in the world Top 40, with a total of 419,907 vehicles, meant that it was placed 22nd in the world league – a fall of three places. Japanese companies produced 15,381,180 vehicles, North American manufacturers 13,381,180, and western European companies 11,912,416. In response to the world economic recession, most companies produced fewer vehicles in 1991 than in 1990 – a drop of almost 2,000,000 in total.

T O P 1 0

CAR MODELS IN THE UK

	Make/model	Total sales (1993)
1	Ford Escort	122,002
2	Ford Fiesta	110,449
3	Vauxhall Astra	108,204
4	Vauxhall Cavalier	104,104
5	Ford Mondeo	88,660
6	Rover 200	77,745
7	Rover Metro	57,068
8	Peugeot 405	52,184
9	Vauxhall Corso	51,608
10	Renault Clio	45,269

Total sales of new cars in 1993 were 1,778,426, an increase of 11.6 per cent on the previous year (1,593,601), but well short of 1989's all-time record of 2,300,944. The cars in the Top 10 remained much the same, but with adjustments in the order, the Ford Escort maintaining its No. 1 position and the Fiesta regaining second place, and with certain replacement models (the Mondeo taking the place of the Sierra, and the Corso taking over from the Nova). The Renault Clio, a newcomer to the list in 1992, further increased its sales, perhaps benefiting from the ongoing "Papa!" "Nicole!" TV advertising campaign. Although Fords, Vauxhalls (some of whose models are made overseas), and Rovers dominate the Top 10, imported cars are hard on their heels in the rest of the Top 20. In 1993 the total sales of imported cars accounted for 55.4 per cent of the total market, with 8.1 per cent of the total originating in Japan.

VEHICLE-OWNING COUNTRIES IN THE WORLD

	Country	Cars	Commercial vehicles	Total
1	USA	142,955,623	45,416,312	188,371,935
2	Japan	37,076,015	22,838,608	59,914,623
3	Germany	37,609,165	3,093,621	40,702,786
4	Italy	28,200,000	2,521,000	30,721,000
5	France	23,810,000	5,020,000	28,830,000
6	UK	22,744,142	3,685,141	26,429,283
7	Former USSR	17,000,000	7,500,000	24,500,000
8	Canada	13,061,084	3,744,012	16,805,096
9	Spain	12,537,099	2,615,033	15,152,132
10	Brazil	12,283,914	921,011	13,204,925
	World	*456,032,819*	*139,273,829*	*595,306,648*

World motor vehicle ownership has increased more than fourfold from the 1960 total of 126,954,817. Of the world total, some 224,435,987 are in Europe, 219,498,039 in North America, 100,063,770 in Asia, 25,154,275 in South America, 14,321,597 in Africa, and 11,832,980 in Oceania. The ratio of people to vehicles has escalated from 23 in 1960 to 8.8 today. In car-conscious and affluent countries the ratio is much higher: 1.3 people per vehicle in the US and 2.1 in the UK. San Marino, uniquely, claims the equivalent of one vehicle per person. The biggest disparities naturally occur in the least developed economies, with 905 people per vehicle in Ethiopia, 897 in Bangladesh, 190 in India, and 188 in China.

MAKES OF CAR IN THE UK

	Manufacturer/country	UK-built	Total sales
1	Ford (UK/Germany/Belgium/Spain/USA)	238,638	381,671
2	GM-Vauxhall (UK/Germany/Belgium/Finland/Spain/USA)	196,792	303,926
3	Rover (UK)	238,003	238,003
4	Peugeot-Talbot (UK/France/Spain)	42,426	142,714
5	Renault (France)	0	93,213
6	Nissan (UK/Japan/Spain)	55,254	89,209
7	Audi-Volkswagen (Germany/Belgium/Spain)	0	84,024
8	Citroën (France/Spain)	0	80,826
9	Toyota (UK/Japan/USA)	0	52,190
10	Volvo (Sweden/Netherlands/Belgium)	0	43,740

Toyota entered the Top 10 for the first time in 1991 and, with the addition of British-made cars, consolidated its position in 1993. In the same year, American-made Hondas were imported into the UK for the first time, and the company (UK/Japan/USA) was, with 30,902 registrations, one of only four outside the Top 10 – all foreign-owned – achieving 1993 sales of more than 20,000 cars. The other three were Fiat (Italy/Portugal – 42,841 cars), BMW (Germany – 40,921), and Mercedes-Benz (Germany/Austria – 21,186).

CAR MANUFACTURERS IN THE UK

	Company	Total car production (1993)
1	Rover Group (Austin Rover and Land Rover)	406,804
2	Ford	271,793
3	Nissan	246,281
4	Vauxhall	232,569
5	Peugeot	72,902
6	IBC (Fronteras)	41,327
7	Toyota	37,314
8	Honda	32,139
9	Jaguar Daimler	29,567
10	Carbodies ("black cab" taxis)	1,530

In 1993 Ford re-established its position at No. 2. Honda, which arrived in the UK-produced Top 10 in 1992 with 1,000 vehicles, rapidly increased its output.

ROADS AND PUBLIC TRANSPORT

COUNTRIES DRIVING ON THE LEFT

	Country	Total vehicles registered
1	Japan	57,914,623
2	UK	26,429,283
3	Australia	9,649,500
4	South Africa	5,324,749
5	India	4,667,749
6	Indonesia	3,001,508
7	Thailand	2,727,509
8	Malaysia	2,400,000
9	New Zealand	1,867,649
10	Nigeria	1,400,000

While more countries drive on the right than on the left, there are 42 countries in the world that drive on the left, including the UK and most members of the British Commonwealth. The last country in Europe to change over from driving on the left to the right was Sweden, on 3 September 1967. At the time, it was estimated to have cost £42,000,000 to do so. There are innumerable explanations for keeping to the left, one being that it is common practice, especially among sword-wearing riders, to mount a horse from the left, and it is then simplest to remain on the left. Similarly, riding on the left facilitates right-handed sword defence against approaching riders. This does not explain, however, why other nations perversely drive on the right.

DID YOU KNOW

SWEDEN CHANGES SIDES

On 3 September 1967 Sweden, the last country in mainland Europe to drive on the left, switched sides. The operation, involving over 2,000,000 vehicles, 169.770 km/ 105,490 miles of roads, and all of the road signs, took four years' planning and a massive publicity campaign. At 1.00 am every vehicle on the road in Sweden stopped and moved gingerly to the opposite side, starting off again at 6.00 am — on the right.

LONGEST MOTORWAYS IN THE UK

	Motorway	Route	km	miles
1	M6	Rugby – Carlisle	368.7	229.1
2	M1	London – Leeds	301.9	187.6
3	M4	London – Port Abraham	292.1	181.5
4	M5	Birmingham – Exeter	265.5	165.0
5	M25	Circles London	194.7	121.0
6	M62	Liverpool – Humberside	173.3	107.7
7	M40	Birmingham – London	86.0	53.4
8=	M3	London – Winchester	82.1	51.0
8=	M11	London – Cambridge	82.1	51.0
10	M8	Edinburgh – Glasgow Airport	78.4	48.7

The first motorway in the UK was the Preston bypass section of the M6 (between junctions 29 and 32), which opened on 5 Dec 1958. The first section of the M1 opened on 2 Nov 1959.

T O P 1 0
COUNTRIES WITH THE LONGEST ROAD NETWORKS

	Country	km	miles
1	US	6,365,590	3,955,394
2	India	1,970,000	1,224,101
3	France	1,551,400	963,995
4	Brazil	1,448,000	899,745
5	Japan	1,111,974	690,949
6	China	1,029,000	630,391
7	Canada	884,272	549,461
8	Russia	879,100	546,247
9	Australia	837,872	520,629
10	Germany	466,305	289,748

T O P 1 0
BRITISH COUNTIES WITH THE LONGEST ROAD NETWORKS

	County	km	miles
1	Devon	14,150	8,792
2	Strathclyde	13,196	8,200
3	Greater London	13,195	8,199
4	North Yorkshire	9,425	5,856
5	Norfolk	9,067	5,634
6	Kent	8,823	5,482
7	Lincolnshire	8,699	5,405
8	Hampshire	8,671	5,388
9	Dyfed	8,127	5,050
10	Grampian	7,704	4,787

T O P 1 0
LONGEST ROADS IN THE UK

	Road	km	miles
1	A1*	655	407
2=	A6	465	289
2=	A9	465	289
4	A38	451	280
5	A30	440	273
6	A40	434	270
7	A5	400	249
8	M6	393	244
9	A39	344	214
10	A41	326	203

Including A1(M).

T O P 1 0
COMMONEST TYPES OF LOST PROPERTY ON LONDON TRANSPORT

	Type	Number of items found						
		1986–87	1987–88	1988–89	1989–90	1990–91	1991–92	1992–93
1	Books, cheque books, and credit cards	19,013	19,329	19,148	20,006	20,270	20,436	20,187
2	"Value items" (handbags, purses, wallets, etc.)	21,940	19,868	18,628	18,397	18,634	17,342	18,270
3	Clothing	16,497	15,211	14,954	15,088	14,624	13,704	14,328
4	Umbrellas	21,080	23,250	17,129	13,889	10,828	10,917	13,634
5	Cases and bags	9,222	9,317	9,155	9,272	9,034	8,513	8,056
6	Keys	9,923	9,265	8,793	8,595	8,348	7,559	7,694
7	Spectacles	5,975	5,754	5,756	5,985	5,944	5,362	5,683
8	Cameras, electronic articles, and jewellery	5,550	5,304	5,493	5,352	5,732	5,298	5,394
9	Gloves (pairs)	5,625	4,402	3,770	3,428	3,446	3,268	3,188
10	Gloves (odd)	844	701	576	577	606	520	540
	Total items in Top 10:	*115,669*	*112,401*	*103,402*	*100,589*	*97,466*	*92,919*	*96,974*

As we have noted in previous editions, there is an inexplicable consistency in the numbers of most categories of articles handed in to London Transport's Lost Property Office in Baker Street from year to year. Why do an average of about 100 individuals leave their spectacles on London's buses and tube trains every week? Why did the numbers losing their umbrellas halve and then begin to increase again? Books remain in the No. 1 position (oddly, cheque books and credit cards are now included with them) but changes in fashion have meant that hats, once one of the commonest lost items, no longer even warrant a separate category, while electronic calculators, radios, tape recorders,

and cameras are now lost in large numbers. Among the stranger items that have been lost in recent years are a skeleton, a box of glass eyes, breast implants, artificial legs and hands, a Yamaha outboard motor, a complete double bed, a theatrical coffin, a hundredweight sack of currants and sultanas, a stuffed gorilla, and an urn containing human ashes.

ON THE RIGHT TRACK

TOP 10

LONGEST RAIL PLATFORMS IN THE WORLD

	Station	Platform length m	ft
1	State Street Center Subway, Chicago, Illinois, USA	1,067	3,500
2	Khargpur, India	833	2,733
3	Perth, Australia	762	2,500
4	Sonepur, India	736	2,415
5	Bournemouth, England	720	2,362
6	Bulawayo, Zimbabwe	702	2,302
7	New Lucknow, India	686	2,250
8	Bezwada, India	640	2,100
9	Gloucester, England	624	2,047
10	Jhansi, India	617	2,025

TOP 10

LONGEST RAIL PLATFORMS IN THE UK

	Station	Platform length m	ft
1	Bournemouth	720	2,362
2	Gloucester	624	2,047
3	Colchester	604	1,920
4	York*	535	1,755
5	Perth	517	1,696
6	Crewe	510	1,672
7	Cambridge	503	1,650
8	Edinburgh Waverley	486	1,596
9	York*	475	1,558
10=	Manchester Victoria	457	1,500
10=	London Victoria	457	1,500

Different platforms at the same station.

TOP 10

LONGEST RAIL NETWORKS IN THE WORLD

	Country	Total rail length km	miles
1	USA	270,312	167,964
2	Canada	93,544	58,126
3	Russia	87,180	54,171
4	India	61,950	38,494
5	China	54,000	33,544
6	Germany	45,468	28,253
7	Australia	40,478	25,152
8	France	34,568	21,480
9	Argentina	34,172	21,233
10	Brazil	28,828	17,913

US rail mileage grew fast in the 19th century, but has declined steadily since 1916.

TOP 10

THE FIRST 10 COUNTRIES WITH RAILWAYS

	Country	First railway established
1	UK	1825
2	USA	1834
3=	Belgium	1835
3=	Germany	1835
5=	Canada	1836
5=	Russia	1836
7=	Austria	1837
7=	France	1837
9=	Italy	1839
9=	Netherlands	1839

Although there were earlier, horse-drawn railways, the UK had the first steam service.

TOP 10

FIRST BRITISH TRAINS TO ACHIEVE 100 MPH

	Train	Railway	Speed km/h	mph	Date
1	*City of Truro*	GWR	164.6	102.3	9 May 1904
2	*Flying Scotsman*	LNER	160.9	100.0	30 Nov 1934
3	*Papyrus*	LNER	173.8	108.0	5 Mar 1935
4	*Silver Link*	LNER	181.1	112.5	27 Sep 1935
5	*Silver Fox*	LNER	181.9	113.0	27 Aug 1936
6	*Coronation Scot*	LMS	181.1	112.5	29 Jun 1937
7	*Dominion of Canada*	LNER	176.2	109.5	30 Jun 1937
8	*Commonwealth of Australia*	LNER	170.6	106.0	Aug 1937
9	*Mallard*	LNER	202.8	126.0	3 Jul 1938
10	*Builth Castle*	GWR	160.9	100.0	31 Jul 1939

The first train in the world to exceed 160.9 km/h/100 mph was the *Empire State Express* on the run from Syracuse to Buffalo, USA, on 9 May 1893, when a maximum of 165.4 km/h/102.8 mph was recorded. There is some controversy over the *City of Truro*'s early claim of 164.6 km/h/102.3 mph (said to have been attained descending Wellington's Bank on the Plymouth to Bristol line), although 160.9 km/h/100 mph seems probable and hence qualifies it as the first British train to exceed the magic 100 mph.

T O P 1 0

LONGEST UNDERGROUND RAILWAY NETWORKS IN THE WORLD

	City	Built	Stations	km	miles
1	Washington DC	1976–93	86	612	380
2	London	1863–1979	272	430	267
3	New York	1868–1968	461	370	230
4	Paris (Metro & RER)	1900–85	430	301	187
5	Moscow	1935–79	115	225	140
6	Tokyo	1927–80	192	218	135
7	Berlin	1902–80	134	167	104
8	Chicago	1892–1953	142	156	97
9	Copenhagen	1934	61	134	83
10	Mexico City	1969–82	57	125	78

The substantial extension of Washington DC's metro completed in 1993 has lifted it from 10th to top position in this list. Other underground systems are also in the process of major development, among them Seoul, Korea, which currently comprises 116 km/72 miles and is expanding by 33 km/21 miles, which will put it into the Top 10.

T O P 1 0

FASTEST RAIL JOURNEYS IN THE WORLD

	Journey	Train	Distance km	Speed (km/h)
1	Massy – St Pierre, France	TGV 8501	206.7	245.6
2	Hiroshima – Kokuru, Japan	27 *Nozomi*	192.0	230.4
3	Madrid – Ciudad Real, Spain	4 *AVE*	170.7	217.9
4	Hannover – Göttingen, Germany	23 *ICE*	99.4	192.4
5	Skövde – Alingsås, Sweden	*X2000 421*	99.2	175.1
6	Doncaster – Grantham, UK	*InterCity 225*	81.2	171.1
7	Rome – Florence, Italy	*Cristoforo Colombo*	261.9	163.7
8	Philadelphia – Wilmington, USA	*Metroliner*	50.6	159.8
9	Toronto – Dorval, Canada	*Metropolis*	520.9	145.4
10	St Petersburg – Moscow, Russia	*ER200*	649.9	130.4

This list comprises the fastest journey for each country; all have other similarly – occasionally equally – fast services.

TRAIN A GRANDE VITESSE
The current world rail speed record is held by the French TGV, which on 18 May 1990 clocked 515.0 km/h/320.0 mph.

FIRST UNDERGROUND LINES IN LONDON

	Line	Date first section opened
1	Metropolitan	10 Jan 1863
2	District	24 Dec 1868
3	Circle	6 Oct 1884
4	Waterloo/Bank (BR)	8 Aug 1898
5	Central	30 Jul 1900
6	Bakerloo	10 Mar 1906
7	Piccadilly	15 Dec 1906
8	Northern	22 Jun 1907
9	Victoria	7 Mar 1969
10	Jubilee	1 May 1979

London's Underground system has grown to its present 430 km/267 miles in stages, usually fanning out from the centre, with suburban extensions being built as London expanded into the surrounding countryside. Many sections of line have been closed and there are consequently many "ghost" lines and stations, such as the British Museum station which closed on 24 September 1933, the platforms of which can still be spotted by sharp-eyed travellers on the Central Line.

T O P 1 0

OLDEST UNDERGROUND RAILWAY SYSTEMS IN THE WORLD

	City	Construction commenced
1	London	1863
2	New York	1868
3	Chicago	1892
4=	Budapest	1896
4=	Glasgow	1896
6	Boston	1897
7	Paris	1900
8	Wuppertal	1901
9	Berlin	1902
10	Philadelphia	1907

LAND TRANSPORT DISASTERS

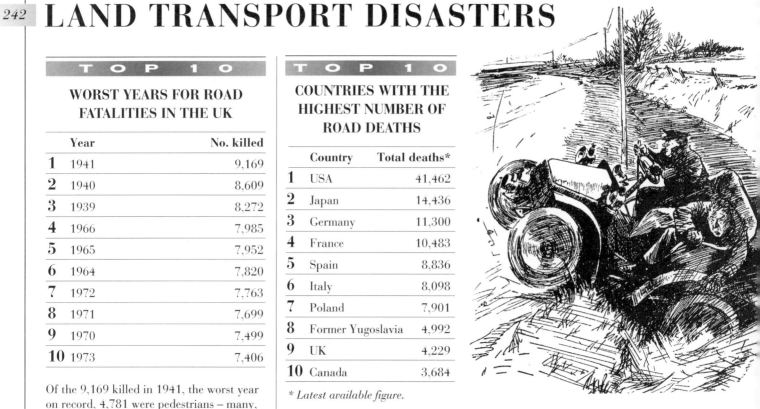

T O P 1 0

WORST YEARS FOR ROAD FATALITIES IN THE UK

	Year	No. killed
1	1941	9,169
2	1940	8,609
3	1939	8,272
4	1966	7,985
5	1965	7,952
6	1964	7,820
7	1972	7,763
8	1971	7,699
9	1970	7,499
10	1973	7,406

Of the 9,169 killed in 1941, the worst year on record, 4,781 were pedestrians – many, it may be surmised, run down during the wartime black-out. British road fatalities have steadily declined in recent years and, at 4,229 in 1992, are now back to the levels of the 1920s. In fact, a considerable improvement on those years is apparent when taking into account the population increase and relative numbers of road users: there were 1,700,000 vehicles on the road in 1926 compared with some 26,000,000 today, and the population in 1926 was less than 80 per cent of that in 1993.

T O P 1 0

YEARS WITH FEWEST ROAD FATALITIES IN THE UK SINCE 1926

	Year	No. killed
1	1992	4,229
2	1948	4,513
3	1952	4,706
4	1949	4,773
5	1947	4,881
6	1926	4,886
7	1954	5,010
8	1950	5,012
9	1988	5,052
10	1946	5,062

T O P 1 0

COUNTRIES WITH THE HIGHEST NUMBER OF ROAD DEATHS

	Country	Total deaths*
1	USA	41,462
2	Japan	14,436
3	Germany	11,300
4	France	10,483
5	Spain	8,836
6	Italy	8,098
7	Poland	7,901
8	Former Yugoslavia	4,992
9	UK	4,229
10	Canada	3,684

* Latest available figure.

T O P 1 0

WORST MOTOR VEHICLE AND ROAD DISASTERS IN THE WORLD

	Country/incident	Killed
1	Afghanistan, 3 November 1982	2,000+

Following a collision with a Soviet army truck, a petrol tanker exploded in the 2.7km/1.7 mile-long Salang Tunnel. Some authorities have put the death toll as high as 3,000.

2	Colombia, 7 August 1956	1,200

Seven army ammunition trucks exploded at night in the centre of Cali, destroying eight city blocks.

3	Thailand, 15 February 1990	150+

A dynamite truck exploded.

4	Nepal, 23 November 1974	148

Hindu pilgrims were killed when a suspension bridge over the River Mahahali collapsed.

5	Egypt, 9 August 1973	127

A bus drove into an irrigation canal.

6	Togo, 6 December 1965	125+

Two lorries collided with dancers during a festival at Sotouboua.

7	Spain, 11 July 1978	120+

A liquid gas tanker exploded in a camping site at San Carlos de la Rapita.

8	Gambia, 12 November 1992	c.100

A bus plunged into a river when its brakes failed.

9	Kenya, early December 1992	nearly 100

A bus carrying 112 skidded, hit a bridge, and plunged into a river.

10=	Lesotho, 16 December 1976	90

A bus fell into the Tsoaing River.

10=	India, 16 March 1988	90

In the state of Madhya Pradesh, the driver of a bus carrying a wedding party lost control and crashed while trying to change a tape cassette.

The worst-ever motor racing accident occurred on 13 June 1955 at Le Mans, France, when, in attempting to avoid other cars, French driver Pierre Levegh's Mercedes-Benz 300 SLR went out of control, hit a wall, and exploded in mid-air, showering wreckage into the crowd and killing a total of 82 (see also The 10 Worst Disasters at Sports Venues). The worst British road accident occurred on 27 May 1975 when a coach crashed near Grassington, North Yorkshire, killing 33.

WORST RAIL DISASTERS IN THE UK

Incident	Killed
1 22 May 1915, Quintinshill near Gretna Green	227

A troop train carrying 500 members of the 7th Royal Scots Regiment from Larbert to Liverpool collided head-on with a local passenger train. Barely a minute later, the Scottish express, drawn by two engines and weighing a total of 600 tonnes, ploughed into the wreckage. The 15 coaches of the troop train, 195 m/640 ft long, were so crushed that they ended up just 61 m/200 ft long. The gas-lit troop train then caught fire. Since their records were destroyed in the blaze, the actual number of soldiers killed was never established, but was probably 215, as well as two members of the train's crew, eight in the express, and two in the local train – a total of 227 killed and 246 injured. An enquiry established that the accident was caused by the negligence of the signalmen, George Meakin and James Tinsley, who were convicted of manslaughter and jailed.

2 8 October 1952, Harrow and Wealdstone Station	122

In patchy fog, Robert Jones, the relief driver of the Perth to Euston sleeping-car express, pulled by the City of Glasgow, failed to see a series of signal lights warning him of danger and at 8.19 a.m. collided with the waiting Watford to Euston train. Seconds later, the Euston to Liverpool and Manchester express (with two locomotives, Windward Islands and Princess Anne) hit the wreckage of the two trains. The casualties were 112 killed instantly, 10 who died later, and 349 injured.

3 4 December 1957, Lewisham, South London	90

A steam train and an electric train were in collision in fog, the disaster made worse by the collapse of a bridge on to the wreckage, leaving 90 dead and 109 seriously injured.

4 28 December 1879, Tay Bridge, Scotland	80

As the North British mail train passed over it during a storm, the bridge collapsed killing all 75 passengers and the crew of five. The bridge – the longest in the world at that time – had only been opened on 31 May the previous year, and Queen Victoria had crossed it in a train soon afterwards. The locomotive was salvaged from the bed of the Tay several months later. Surprisingly little damaged, it was repaired and continued in service until 1919.

5 12 June 1889, Armagh, Northern Ireland	78

A Sunday school excursion train with 940 passengers stalled on a hill. When 10 carriages were uncoupled, they ran backwards and collided with a passenger train, killing 78 (claims of 300 deaths have not been substantiated) and leaving 250 injured. Railway officials were charged with negligence.

6 5 November 1967, Hither Green, South London	49

The Hastings to Charing Cross train was derailed by a broken track. As well as those killed, 78 were injured, 27 of them very seriously.

7 28 February 1975, Moorgate Station, London	43

The Drayton Park to Moorgate tube ran into the wall at the end of the tunnel, killing 43 and injuring 74 in London Transport's worst rail disaster.

8 10 December 1937, Castlecary, Scotland	35

In heavy snow the Edinburgh to Glasgow train ran into a stationary Dundee to Glasgow train and rode over the top of it, killing 35 and leaving 179 injured.

9= 24 December 1874, Shipton near Oxford	34

The Paddington to Birkenhead train plunged over the embankment after a carriage wheel broke, killing 34 and badly injuring 65.

9= 12 December 1988, Clapham Junction, London	34

The 7.18 Basingstoke to Waterloo train, carrying 906 passengers, stopped at signals outside Clapham Junction; the 6.30 train from Bournemouth ran into its rear and an empty train from Waterloo hit the wreckage, leaving 33 dead (and one who died later) and 111 injured.

WORST RAIL DISASTERS IN THE WORLD

Incident	Killed
1 6 June 1981, Bagmati River, India	c.800

The carriages of a train plunged off a bridge near Mansi when the driver braked, apparently to avoid hitting a sacred cow. Although the official death toll was 268, many claim that the train was so overcrowded that the actual figure was in excess of 800.

2 3 June 1989, Chelyabinsk, Russia	up to 800

Two passenger trains on the Trans-Siberian railway, laden with holiday-makers were destroyed by exploding liquid gas from a nearby pipeline.

3 18 January 1915, Guadalajara, Mexico	600+

A train derailed on a steep incline, but details of the disaster were suppressed.

4 12 December 1917, Modane, France	573

A troop-carrying train was derailed. It has been claimed that the train was overloaded – 1,000 may have died.

5 2 March 1944, Balvano, Italy	521

A heavily-laden train stalled in the Armi Tunnel, and many were asphyxiated.

6 3 January 1944, Torre, Spain	500+

A collision and fire in a tunnel.

7 3 April 1955, near Guadalajara, Mexico	c.300

A night express carrying hundreds of holiday-makers plunged into a ravine.

8 29 September 1957, Gambar, near Montgomery, Pakistan	250–300

A collision between an express and an oil train.

9 1 February 1970, near Buenos Aires, Argentina	236

A collision between an express and a standing commuter train.

10 23 December 1933, Pomponne near Lagny, France	230

A collision in fog between an express and two stationary trains.

WATER TRANSPORT

ROYAL LINER
The Queen Elizabeth II, *launched by HM the Queen in 1972, is still in service today.*

THE PROGRESSION OF THE WORLD'S LARGEST LINERS IN SERVICE

Ship	Gross tonnage	Years in service
Great Eastern	18,914	1858–88
Oceanic	17,274	1899–1914
Baltic	23,884	1904–33
Lusitania‡	31,550	1907–15
Mauretania	31,938	1907–35
Olympic	45,300	1911–35
Titanic‡	46,232	1912
Imperator/ Berengaria*	52,022	1913–38
Vaterland/ Leviathan*	54,282	1914–38
Bismarck/Majestic/ Caledonia*	56,621	1922–39
Normandie/ Lafayette*‡	79,301/83,102#	1935–42
Queen Mary	80,774/81,237#	1936–67
Queen Elizabeth	83,673/82,998#	1938–72
France/ Norway*	66,348/76,049#	1961–
Sovereign of the Seas	73,192	1987–

‡ *Sunk.*
* *Renamed.*
# *Tonnage altered during refitting.*

TOP 10

FIRST SHIPS LAUNCHED BY HM THE QUEEN

	Ship	Location	Date launched
1	HMY *Britannia*	Clydebank	16 Apr 1953
2	SS *Southern Cross*	Belfast	17 Aug 1954
3	SS *Empress of Britain*	Govan	22 Jun 1955
4	HMS *Dreadnought*	Barrow	21 Oct 1960
5	SS *British Admiral*	Barrow	17 Mar 1965
6	*Queen Elizabeth II*	Clydebank	20 Sep 1967
7	HMS *Sheffield**	Barrow	10 Jun 1971
8	*The Royal British Legion Jubilee#*	Henley-on-Thames	17 Jul 1972
9	HMS *Invincible*	Barrow	3 May 1977
10	HMS *Lancaster*	Scotstoun	24 May 1990

* *Sunk 10 May 1982 after being struck by an Exocet missile during the Falklands Conflict.*
# *Lifeboat.*

TOP 10

LARGEST PASSENGER LINERS IN THE WORLD

	Ship	Year	Country built in	Passenger capacity	Gross tonnage
1	*France/Norway* (renamed)	1961	France	2,565	76,049
2=	*Majesty of the Seas*	1992	France	2,766	73,937
2=	*Monarch of the Seas*	1991	France	2,764	73,937
4	*Sovereign of the Seas*	1987	France	2,600	73,192
5=	*Sensation*	1993	Finland	2,634	70,367
5=	*Ecstasy*	1991	Finland	2,634	70,367
5=	*Fantasy*	1990	Finland	2,634	70,367
8=	*Crown Princess*	1990	Italy	1,590	69,845
8=	*Regal Princess*	1991	Italy	1,900	69,845
10	*QEII*	1969	Scotland	1,877	69,053

In 1997 the 77,000-tonne *Sun Princess*, currently being built at the Fincantieri shipyard in Monfalcone, Italy, will be joined by another of about 100,000 tonnes – and hence the world's largest liner. It will be 285m/935 ft long and have a passenger capacity of 2,600.

TOP 10
LARGEST OIL TANKERS IN THE WORLD

	Ship	Year built	Country	Deadweight tonnage
1	*Jahre Viking*	1979	Japan	564,650
2	*Kapetan Giannis*	1977	Japan	516,895
3	*Kapetan Michalis*	1977	Japan	516,423
4	*Nissei Maru*	1975	Japan	484,276
5	*Stena King*	1978	Taiwan	457,927
6	*Stena Queen*	1977	Taiwan	457,841
7	*Kapetan Panagiotis*	1977	Japan	457,062
8	*Kapetan Giorgis*	1976	Japan	456,368
9	*Sea Empress*	1976	Japan	423,677
10	*Mira Star*	1975	Japan	423,642

The 485.45-m/1,504-ft *Jahre Viking* (formerly called *Happy Giant* and *Seawise*) is the longest vessel ever built. It was extensively damaged during the Iran-Iraq War, but was salvaged, refitted, and relaunched in 1991.

TOP 10
OLDEST NAVIGABLE CANALS IN THE UK

	Canal	Date navigable
1	Fossdyke	*c.*AD120
2	Exeter	1751
3	Bridgewater	1767
4=	Birmingham	1772
4=	Staffordshire and Worcestershire	1772
6=	Chesterfield	1777
6=	Trent and Mersey	1777
8	Erewash	1779
9=	Coventry	1790
9=	Oxford	1790

TOP 10
LONGEST CANALS IN THE UK

	Canal	Length km	miles
1	Grand Union (main line)	220.5	137
2	Leeds and Liverpool	204.4	127
3	Trent and Mersey	149.7	93
4	Kennet and Avon	139.2	86.5
5	Oxford	123.9	77
6	Shropshire Union	107.0	66.5
7	Caledonian	96.6	60
8	Staffordshire and Worcestershire	74.2	46.1
9	Llangollen	74.0	46
10	Lancaster	68.4	42.5

STRAIGHT AND NARROW
This boat's characteristic long, narrow hull and flat bottom is tailored to life on sheltered canal waters.

TOP 10
SHIPPING COUNTRIES IN THE WORLD

	Country	No. of ships	Total GRT*
1	Panama	5,564	57,618,623
2	Liberia	1,611	53,918,534
3	Greece	1,929	29,134,435
4	Japan	9,950	24,247,525
5	Cyprus	1,591	22,842,009
6	Bahamas	1,121	21,224,164
7	Norway	785	19,383,417
8	Russia	5,335	16,813,761
9	China	2,501	14,944,999
10	Malta	1,037	14,163,357

* GRT or Gross Registered Tonnage is not the actual weight of a ship but its cubic capacity (1 ton = 100 cubic feet). The list includes only ships of more than 100 GRT.

Liberia held the record for many years, but has recently been overtaken by Panama. The USA is in 11th place with 5,646 ships totalling 14,086,825 GRT, and the UK lies in 26th place with 1,532 ships/4,116,868 GRT. The world total now comprises 80,655 vessels/457,914,808 GRT.

TOP 10
COUNTRIES WITH THE LONGEST INLAND WATERWAY NETWORKS*

	Country	km	miles
1	China	138,600	86,122
2	Former USSR	113,500	70,526
3	Brazil	50,000	31,069
4	USA#	41,009	25,482
5	Indonesia	21,579	13,409
6	Vietnam	17,702	11,000
7	India	16,180	10,054
8	Zaïre	15,000	9,321
9	France	14,932	9,278
10	Colombia	14,300	8,886

* Canals and navigable rivers.
 # Excluding Great Lakes.

MARINE DISASTERS

SPANISH ARMADA
Driven north by the English fleet under Drake, the remaining Spanish ships met a fierce storm.

THE PRINCESS ALICE

One of the worst boat accidents in British history was the sinking of the 250-tonne paddle-steamer *Princess Alice*, on the evening of Tuesday 3 September 1878. While returning from a day trip to Sheerness, with about 750 holidaymakers on board (mostly women and children), she was on the River Thames near Woolwich when she was struck on the starboard side by the 890-tonne collier *Bywell Castle*, which sliced her virtually in two. The *Princess Alice* sank almost immediately. The speed of the sinking and the vessel's lack of lifeboats meant that few survived: many of the women on board drowned when their voluminous crinolines became waterlogged. About 640 bodies were recovered and buried in mass graves. An appeal was launched to aid the relatives of the survivors.

One curious consequence – if she was to be believed – was that a Swedish-born woman called Elizabeth Stride was widowed and lost both her children in the tragedy. Her resultant poverty led her on to the streets, and 10 years later she became the third victim of Jack the Ripper.

TOP 10

WORST PRE-20TH-CENTURY MARINE DISASTERS

	Incident	Killed
1	Spanish Armada – Military conflict and storms combined to destroy the Spanish fleet in the English Channel and elsewhere off the British coast, August to October 1588.	c.4,000
2=	British fleet – Eight ships sunk in storms off Egg Island, Labrador, Canada, 22 August 1711.	c.2,000
2=	*St George*, *Defence*, and *Hero* – British warships stranded off the Jutland coast, Denmark, 4 December 1811.	c.2,000
4	*Sultana* – A Mississippi River steamboat destroyed by a boiler explosion near Memphis, 27 April 1865 – the US's worst ever marine accident, although the official death toll may be an underestimate.	1,547
5	*Capitanas* – Twin Spanish treasure vessels sunk in a hurricane off the Florida coast, 31 July 1715.	c.1,000
6	*Royal George* – British warship wrecked off Spithead, 29 August 1782, the worst ever single shipwreck off the British coast.	c.900
7	*Princess Alice* – Pleasure steamer in collision with *Bywell Castle* on the Thames near Woolwich, 3 September 1878.	786
8	*Queen Charlotte* – British warship burnt in Leghorn harbour, 17 March 1800.	c.700
9=	*Ertogrul* – Turkish frigate wrecked off the Japanese coast, 19 September 1890.	587
9=	*Utopia* – British steamer collided with British warship *Amson* off Gibraltar, 17 March 1891.	576

TOP 10

WORST OIL TANKER SPILLS OF ALL TIME

	Tanker/location	Date	Spillage (tonnes approx.)
1	*Atlantic Empress* and *Aegean Captain*, Trinidad	19 Jul 1979	300,000
2	*Castillio de Bellver*, Cape Town, South Africa	6 Aug 1983	255,000
3	*Olympic Bravery*, Ushant, France	24 Jan 1976	250,000
4	*Showa-Maru*, Malacca, Malaya	7 Jun 1975	237,000
5	*Amoco Cadiz*, Finistère, France	16 Mar 1978	223,000
6	*Odyssey*, Atlantic, off Canada	10 Nov 1988	140,000
7	*Torrey Canyon*, Scilly Isles, UK	18 Mar 1967	120,000
8	*Sea Star*, Gulf of Oman	19 Dec 1972	115,000
9	*Irenes Serenada*, Pilos, Greece	23 Feb 1980	102,000
10	*Urquiola*, Corunna, Spain	12 May 1976	101,000

It is estimated that an average of 2,000,000 tonnes is spilled into the world's seas every year. All these accidents were caused by collision, grounding, fire, or explosion. Military action has caused worse tanker oil spills: during the Gulf War tankers sunk in the Persian Gulf spilled more than 1,000,000 tonnes of oil. The *Exxon Valdez* grounding in Alaska on 24th March 1989 spilled about 35,000 tonnes, but resulted in major ecological damage.

WORST MARINE DISASTERS
OF THE 20TH CENTURY

Incident	Approx no. killed
1 *Wilhelm Gustloff* The German liner, laden with refugees, was torpedoed off Danzig by a Soviet submarine, *S-13*, 30 January 1945. The precise death toll remains uncertain, but is in the range 5,348 to 7,700.	up to 7,700
2 Unknown vessel An unidentified Chinese troopship carrying Nationalist soldiers from Manchuria sank off Yingkow, November 1947.	6,000+
3 *Cap Arcona* A German ship carrying concentration camp survivors was bombed and sunk by British aircraft in Lübeck harbour, 3 May 1945.	4,650
4 *Lancastria* A British troop ship sunk off St Nazaire, 17 June 1940.	4,000+
5 *Yamato* A Japanese battleship sunk off Kyushu Island, 7 April 1945.	3,033
6 *Dona Paz* The ferry *Dona Paz* was struck by oil tanker MV *Victor* in the Tabias Strait, Philippines, 20 December 1987.	3,000+
7 *Kiangya* An overloaded steamship carrying refugees struck a Japanese mine off Woosung, China, 3 December 1948.	2,750+
8 *Thielbeck* A refugee ship sunk during the British bombardment of Lübeck harbour in the closing weeks of the Second World War, May 1945.	2,750
9 *Arisan Maru* A Japanese vessel carrying American prisoners-of-war was torpedoed by a US submarine in the South China Sea, 24 October 1944.	1,790+
10 *Mont Blanc* A French ammunition ship collided with Belgian steamer *Imo* and exploded, Halifax, Nova Scotia, 6 December 1917.	1,600

Due to a re-assessment of the death tolls in some of the Second World War marine disasters, the most famous of all, the sinking of the *Titanic* (the British liner that struck an iceberg in the North Atlantic on 15 April 1912 and went down with the loss of 1,517 lives), no longer ranks in the Top 10. However, the *Titanic* tragedy remains one of the worst ever peacetime disasters.

WORST SUBMARINE DISASTERS
(Excluding those as a result of military action)

Incident	Killed
1 *Le Surcouf* – A French submarine accidentally rammed by a US merchant ship, *Thomas Lykes*, in the Gulf of Mexico on 18 February 1942.	159
2 *Thresher* – A three-year-old US nuclear submarine, worth $45,000,000, sank in the North Atlantic, 350 km (220 miles) east of Boston on 10 April 1963.	129
3= *Thetis* – A British submarine sank on 1 June 1939 during trials in Liverpool Bay, with civilians on board. Her captain and two crew members escaped. *Thetis* was later salvaged and renamed *Thunderbolt*. On 13 March 1943 she was sunk by an Italian ship with the loss of 63 lives.	99
3= *Scorpion* – This US nuclear submarine was lost in the North Atlantic, 400 km (250 miles) south-west of the Azores, on 21 May 1968. The wreck was located on 31 October of that year.	99
5 *I-67* – A Japanese submarine that foundered in a storm off Bonin Island to the south of Japan in 1940.	89
6= *Ro-31* – A Japanese submarine lost off Kobe, Japan, on 21 August 1923 when a hatch was accidentally left open as she dived. There were only five survivors.	88
6= Unnamed Soviet November Class submarine – lost 110 km (70 miles) off Land's End on 12 April 1970.	88
8= *I-63* – This Japanese submarine sank on 2 February 1939 after a collision in the Bungo Suido (between Kyushu and Shikoku, Japan). Six crew members were saved.	81
8= *Dumlupinar* – A Turkish submarine lost in collision with a Swedish freighter on 4 April 1953, with five survivors.	81
10 HMS *Affray* – A British submarine lost on 17 April 1951 in Hard Deep, north of Alderney, Channel Islands.	75

THE FIRST TO FLY

FIRST MANNED BALLOON FLIGHTS*

1 21 November 1783

François Laurent, Marquis d'Arlandes, and Jean-François Pilâtre de Rozier took off from the Bois de Boulogne, Paris, in a hot-air balloon designed by Joseph and Etienne Montgolfier. This first-ever manned flight covered a distance of about 9 km/5 1/2 miles in 23 minutes, landing safely near Gentilly. (On 15 June 1785 de Rozier and his passenger were killed near Boulogne when their hydrogen balloon burst into flames during an attempted Channel crossing, making them the first air fatalities.)

2 1 December 1783

A crowd of 400,000 watched as Jacques Alexandre César Charles and Nicholas-Louis Robert made the first-ever flight in a hydrogen balloon. They took off from the Tuileries, Paris, and travelled about 43 km/27 miles north to Nesle in about two hours. Charles then took off again alone, thus becoming the first solo flier.

3 19 January 1784

La Flesselle, a 40-m-/131-ft-high Montgolfier hot-air balloon named after its sponsor, the local Governor, ascended from Lyons piloted by Pilâtre de Rozier with Joseph Montgolfier, Prince Charles de Ligne, and the Comtes de La Porte d'Anglefort, de Dampierre, and de Laurencin – and the first aerial stowaway, a man called Fontaine, who leaped in as it was taking off.

4 25 February 1784

Chevalier Paolo Andreani and the brothers Augustino and Carlo Giuseppi Gerli (the builders of the balloon) made the first-ever flight outside France, at Moncuco near Milan, Italy.

5 2 March 1784

Jean-Pierre François Blanchard made his first flight in a hydrogen balloon from the Champ de Mars, Paris, after experimental hops during the preceding months.

6 14 April 1784

A Mr Rousseau and an unnamed 10-year-old drummer boy flew from Navan to Ratoath in Ireland, the first ascent in the British Isles.

7 25 April 1784

Guyton de Morveau, a French chemist, and L'Abbé Bertrand flew at Dijon.

8 8 May 1784

Bremond and Maret flew at Marseilles.

9 12 May 1784

Brun ascended at Chambéry.

10 15 May 1784

Adorne and an unnamed passenger took off but crash-landed near Strasbourg.

* The first 10 flights of the ballooning pioneers all took place within a year. Several of the balloonists listed also made subsequent flights, but in each instance only their first flights are included.

Joseph and Etienne Montgolfier conducted the first *unmanned* hot-air balloon test in the French town of Annonay on 5 June 1783 . They were then invited to demonstrate it to Louis XVI at Versailles. On 19 September 1783 it took off with the first-ever airborne passengers – a sheep, a rooster, and a duck.

After the first 10 manned flights, the pace of ballooning accelerated rapidly. On 4 June 1784 a Monsieur Fleurant took as his passenger in a flight at Lyons a Mme Elisabeth Thiblé, an opera singer, who was thus the first woman to fly (the Marchioness de Montalembert and other aristocratic ladies had ascended on 20 May 1784, but in a tethered balloon). On 27 August, James Tytler (known as "Balloon Tytler"), a doctor and newspaper editor, took off from Comely Gardens, Edinburgh, achieving an altitude of 107 m/350 ft in a 0.8-km/1/2-mile hop in a home-made balloon – the first (and until Smeath in 1837, the only) hot-air balloon flight in the UK. On 15 September, watched by a crowd of 200,000, Vincenzo Lunardi ascended from the Artillery Company Ground, Moorfields, London, flying to Standon near Ware in Hertfordshire, the first balloon flight in England. (An attempt the previous month by a Dr Moret ended with the balloon catching fire and the crowd rioting.) Lunardi went on to make further flights in Edinburgh and Glasgow. On 4 October 1784 James Sadler flew a Montgolfier balloon at Oxford, thereby becoming the first English pilot.

FIRST PEOPLE TO FLY IN HEAVIER-THAN-AIR AIRCRAFT

1 Orville Wright (1871–1948), US

On 17 December 1903 at Kitty Hawk, North Carolina, Wright made the first-ever manned flight in his Wright Flyer I. It lasted 12 seconds and covered a distance of 37 m/120 ft.

2 Wilbur Wright (1867–1912), US

On the same day, Orville's brother made his first flight in the Wright Flyer I (59 sec).

3 Alberto Santos-Dumont (1873–1932), Brazilian

At Bagatelle, Bois de Boulogne, Paris, Santos-Dumont made a 60-m/193-ft hop on 23 October 1906 in his clumsy No. 14-bis.

4 Charles Voisin (1882–1912), French

Voisin made a short 6-second hop of 60 m/197 ft at Bagatelle on 30 March 1907 in a plane built by himself and his brother Gabriel to the commission of Léon Delagrange.

5 Henri Farman (1874–1958), British, later French

Farman first flew on 7 October 1907, and by 26 October had achieved 771 m/2,530 ft.

6 Léon Delagrange (1873–1910), French

On 5 November 1907 at Issy-les-Moulineaux, France, Delagrange flew his Voisin-Delagrange I (see 4) for 40 seconds.

7 Robert Esnault-Pelterie (1881–1957), French

On 16 November 1907 at Buc, France, he first flew his REP 1 (55 sec; 600 m/1,969 ft).

8 Charles W. Furnas (1880–1941), US

On 14 May 1908 at Kitty Hawk, Wilbur Wright took Furnas, his mechanic, for a spin in the Wright Flyer III (29 sec; 600 m/1,968 ft). Furnas was thus the first passenger in the US.

9 Louis Blériot (1872–1936), French

After some earlier short hops, on 29 June 1908 at Issy, France, Blériot flew his Blériot VIII; on 25 July 1909 he became the first to fly across the English Channel.

10 Glenn Hammond Curtiss (1878–1930), US

On 4 July 1908 at Hammondsport, New York, Curtiss flew an AEA June Bug (1 min 42.5 sec; 1,551 m/5,090 ft), the first "official" flight in the US watched by a large crowd.

T O P 1 0

FIRST FLIGHTS OF MORE THAN ONE HOUR

	Pilot	Location	Duration			Date
			hr	min	sec	
1	Orville Wright	Fort Meyer, USA	1	2	15.0	9 Sep 1908
2	Orville Wright	Fort Meyer, USA	1	5	52.0	10 Sep 1908
3	Orville Wright	Fort Meyer, USA	1	10	0.0	11 Sep 1908
4	Orville Wright	Fort Meyer, USA	1	15	20.0	12 Sep 1908
5	Wilbur Wright	Auvours, France	1	31	25.8	21 Sep 1908
6	Wilbur Wright	Auvours, France	1	7	24.8	28 Sep 1908
7	Wilbur Wright*	Auvours, France	1	4	26.0	6 Oct 1908
8	Wilbur Wright	Auvours, France	1	9	45.4	10 Oct 1908
9	Wilbur Wright	Auvours, France	1	54	53.4	18 Dec 1908
10	Wilbur Wright	Auvours, France	2	20	23.2	31 Dec 1908

First-ever flight of more than one hour with a passenger (M.A. Fordyce).

The first pilot other than one of the Wright Brothers to remain airborne for longer than an hour was Paul Tissandier, who on 20 May 1909 flew for 1 hr 2 min 13 sec at Pont-Lond, near Pau, France. He was followed by Hubert Latham, an Anglo-French aviator, who on 5 June 1909, at Châlons, France, flew an *Antoinette IV* for 1 hr 7 min 37 sec, and by Henry Farman (20 July 1909, at Châlons), with a flight of 1 hr 23 min 3.2 sec duration, Roger Sommer (who broke Wilbur Wright's record on 7 August 1909 with a flight of 2 hr 27 min 15 sec), and Louis Paulhan. The first flight lasting over an hour in the UK was by Samuel Franklin Cody (an American, but later a naturalized British citizen, and the first person in the UK to fly), in London on 8 September 1909; the flight lasted 1 hr 3 min 0 sec.

T O P 1 0

FIRST TRANSATLANTIC FLIGHTS

1 16–27 May 1919*
Trepassy Harbor,
Newfoundland to Lisbon, Portugal
US Navy/Curtiss flying boat *NC-4*

Lt-Cdr Albert Cushing Read and a crew of five (Elmer Fowler Stone, Walter Hinton, James Lawrence Breese, Herbert Charles Rodd, and Eugene Saylor Rhoads) crossed the Atlantic in a series of hops, refuelling at sea.

2 14–15 June 1919
St John's, Newfoundland to Galway, Ireland
Twin Rolls-Royce-engined converted Vickers Vimy bomber

British pilot Capt John Alcock and Navigator Lt Arthur Whitten Brown achieved the first non-stop flight, ditching in Derrygimla bog after their epic 16 hr 28 min journey.

3 2–6 July 1919
East Fortune, Scotland to Roosevelt Field, New York
British *R-34* airship

Major George Herbert Scott and a crew of 30 (including the first-ever transatlantic air stowaway, William Ballantyne) made the first east–west crossing. It was the first airship to do so and, when it returned to Pulham, England on 13 July, the first to complete a double crossing.

4 30 March–5 June 1922
Lisbon, Portugal to Recife, Brazil
Fairey IIID seaplane *Santa Cruz*

Portuguese pilots Admiral Gago Coutinho and Commander Sacadura Cabral were the first to fly the South Atlantic in stages, though they replaced one damaged plane with another.

5 2–31 August 1924
Orkneys, Scotland to Labrador, Canada
Two Douglas seaplanes, *Chicago* and *New Orleans*

Lt Lowell H. Smith and Leslie P. Arnold in one biplane and Erik Nelson and John Harding in another set out and crossed the North Atlantic together in a series of hops via Iceland and Greenland.

6 12–15 October 1924
Friedrichshafen, Germany to Lakehurst, New Jersey
Los Angeles, a renamed German-built ZR 3 airship

Piloted by its inventor, Dr Hugo Eckener, with 31 passengers and crew.

7 22 January–10 February 1926
Huelva, Spain to Recife, Brazil
Plus Ultra, a Dornier Wal twin-engined flying boat

The Spanish crew– General Franco's brother Ramón with Julio Ruiz De Alda, Ensign Beran, and mechanic Pablo Rada – crossed in stages.

8 8–24 February 1927
Cagliari, Sardinia to Recife, Brazil
Santa Maria, a Savoia-Marchetti S.55 flying boat

Francesco Marquis de Pinedo, Capt Carlo del Prete, and Lt Vitale Zacchetti crossed in stages as part of a goodwill trip to South America from Fascist Italy.

9 16–17 March 1927
Lisbon, Portugal to Natal, Brazil
Dornier Wal flying boat

Portuguese flyers Sarmento de Beires and Jorge de Castilho took the route via Casablanca.

10 28 April–14 May 1927
Genoa, Italy to Natal, Brazil
Savoia-Marchetti flying boat

A Brazilian crew of João De Barros, João Negrão, Newton Braga, and Vasco Cinquini set out on 17 October 1926, flying in stages via the Canaries and Cape Verde Islands.

* *All dates refer to the actual Atlantic legs of the journeys; some started earlier and ended beyond their first transatlantic landfalls.*

AIRPORTS AND AIRLINES

TOP 10

BUSIEST AIRPORTS IN THE WORLD

	Airport	City/country	Terminal passengers per annum*
1	Chicago O'Hare	Chicago, US	64,441,087
2	DFW International	Dallas/Fort Worth, US	51,943,567
3	LA International	Los Angeles, US	46,964,555
4	London Heathrow	London, UK	44,964,000
5	Tokyo-Haneda International	Tokyo, Japan	42,638,852
6	Hartsfield Atlanta International	Atlanta, US	42,032,988
7	San Francisco International	San Francisco, US	31,789,021
8	Stapleton International	Denver, US	30,877,180
9	Frankfurt	Frankfurt, Germany	30,183,000
10	J.F. Kennedy International	New York, US	27,760,912

* *International and domestic flights.*

CHICAGO O'HARE
Like the other six US airports in the world's ten busiest, O'Hare handles mainly domestic passengers. Only JFK sees enough international flights to put it in the international Top Ten.

TOP 10

BUSIEST AIRPORTS IN EUROPE

	Airport	City/country	Passengers per annum
1	London Heathrow	London, UK	44,964,000
2	Frankfurt	Frankfurt, Germany	30,183,000
3	Orly	Paris, France	25,009,000
4	Charles de Gaulle	Paris, France	24,770,000
5	London Gatwick	London, UK	19,842,000
6	Fiumicino	Rome, Italy	19,334,000
7	Schiphol	Amsterdam, Netherlands	18,714,000
8	Madrid	Madrid, Spain	18,097,000
9	Arlanda	Stockholm, Sweden	12,880,000
10	Copenhagen	Copenhagen, Denmark	12,685,000

TOP 10

BUSIEST INTERNATIONAL AIRPORTS IN THE WORLD

	Airport	International passengers per annum
1	London Heathrow London, UK	38,246,000
2	Frankfurt Frankfurt, Germany	23,814,000
3	Charles de Gaulle Paris, France	22,444,000
4	Hong Kong	22,060,000
5	Tokyo/Narita, Japan	19,022,000
6	London Gatwick Gatwick, UK	18,688,000
7	Schiphol Amsterdam, Netherlands	18,607,000
8	Singapore International	17,087,000
9	J.F. Kennedy International New York, US	15,110,000
10	Zurich Zurich, Switzerland	12,008,000

TOP 10

BUSIEST AIRPORTS IN THE UK

	Airport	Passengers per annum
1	London Heathrow	44,964,400
2	London Gatwick	19,842,400
3	Manchester	11,693,300
4	Glasgow	4,670,300
5	Birmingham	3,651,600
6	Edinburgh	2,539,200
7	London Stansted	2,332,400
8	Belfast Aldergrove	2,241,300
9	Aberdeen	2,146,500
10	Luton	1,943,100

Four other British airports handled more than 1,000,000 passengers in 1992: Newcastle-upon-Tyne (1,941,600), Jersey (1,595,800), East Midlands (1,250,500), and Bristol (1,025,900).

CONCORDE
The only supersonic passenger aircraft, Concorde flies at twice the speed of sound.

T O P 1 0

ROUTES OF PASSENGERS USING LONDON HEATHROW

	Origin/destination	Passengers (1992/93)
1	Paris (Charles de Gaulle), France	2,843,000
2	Dublin, Ireland	1,677,000
3	New York (JFK), US	1,615,000
4	Amsterdam, Netherlands	1,603,000
5	Edinburgh, UK	1,319,000
6	Glasgow, UK	1,297,000
7	Belfast, UK	1,182,000
8	Frankfurt, Germany	1,045,000
9	Los Angeles, US	996,000
10	Tokyo (Narita), Japan	955,000

T O P 1 0

AIRLINES IN THE WORLD

	Airline/country	Aircraft in service	Passenger-km flown per annum*
1	Aeroflot (Russia)	103	137,198,200,000
2	American Airlines (US)	552	123,924,492,000
3	United Airlines (US)	462	122,219,206,000
4	Delta Airlines (US)	444	94,918,792,000
5	British Airways (UK)	228	66,794,988,000
6	Continental Airlines (US)	386	63,042,012,000
7	Northwest Airlines (US)	321	57,212,200,000
8	USAir (US)	454	57,211,439,000
9	TWA (US)	206	55,596,484,000
10	JAL (Japan)	98	55,195,157,000

* Total distance travelled by aircraft of these airlines multiplied by number of passengers carried.

T O P 1 0

AIRLINES USING LONDON HEATHROW

	Airline	Passengers per annum
1	British Airways (UK)	20,868,800
2	British Midland (UK)	3,573,300
3	Aer Lingus (Ireland)	1,770,100
4	Lufthansa (Germany)	1,630,400
5	United Airlines (USA)	1,519,70
6	Air France (France)	1,395,100
7	American Airlines (US)	1,061,100
8	SAS (Denmark/Norway/Sweden)	1,057,200
9	Alitalia (Italy)	881,400
10	Swissair (Switzerland)	812,300

British Airways is also the leading airline at Gatwick Airport (3,198,800 passengers in 1992/93), as well as at Glasgow, Edinburgh, and Aberdeen.

LONDON HEATHROW
With nearly 45 million passengers annually, of whom 85 per cent are on international flights, Heathrow tops several lists.

T O P 1 0

AIRLINE-USING COUNTRIES

	Country	Passenger-km flown per annum*
1	US	735,189,000,000
2	Russia	240,802,000,000
3	UK	104,999,000,000
4	Japan	100,501,000,000
5	France	52,912,000,000
6	Canada	47,115,000,000
7	Germany	42,397,000,000
8	Australia	40,797,000,000
9	Singapore	31,600,000,000
10	Netherlands	29,036,000,000

* Total distance travelled by aircraft of national airlines multiplied by number of passengers carried.

AIR DISASTERS

DOWN IN FLAMES
The Hindenberg *was the ultimate in luxury air travel, but the explosion of the airship, which contained 200,000 cubic metres (7,000,000 cubic feet) of hydrogen gas, put an end to plans to expand the use of lighter-than-air craft.*

T O P   1 0

FIRST AIRCRAFT FATALITIES

	Name	Nationality	Location	Date
1	Lt Thomas Etholen Selfridge	American	Fort Myer, USA	17 Sep 1908
2	Eugène Lefèbvre	French	Juvisy, France	7 Sep 1909
3	Captain Ferdinand Ferber	French	Boulogne, France	22 Sep 1909
4	Antonio Fernandez	Spanish	Nice, France	6 Dec 1909
5	Aindan de Zoseley	Hungarian	Budapest, Hungary	2 Jan 1910
6	Léon Delagrange	French	Croix d'Hins, France	4 Jan 1910
7	Hubert Leblon	French	San Sebastián, Spain	2 Apr 1910
8	Hauvette-Michelin	French	Lyons, France	13 May 1910
9	Thaddeus Robl	German	Stettin, Germany	18 Jun 1910
10	Charles Louis Wachter	French	Rheims, France	3 Jul 1910

Following the Wright Brothers' first flights in 1903, the first four years of powered flying remained surprisingly accident-free. Although there had been many fatalities in the early years of ballooning and among pioneer parachutists, it was not until 1908 that anyone was killed in an aeroplane. On 17 September at Fort Myer, Virginia, Orville Wright was demonstrating his Type A *Flyer* to the US Army. On board was a passenger, 26-year-old Lieutenant Thomas Etholen Selfridge of the Army Signal Corps. At a height of just 23 m/ 75 feet, one of the propellers struck a wire, sending the plane out of control. It crash-landed, injuring Wright and killing Lt Selfridge, who thus became powered flying's first victim.

T O P   1 0

WORST AIRSHIP DISASTERS IN THE WORLD

	Incident	No. killed
1	3 April 1933, off the Atlantic coast of the US	73

US Navy airship Akron *crashed into the sea in a storm, leaving only three survivors in the world's worst airship tragedy.*

	Incident	No. killed
2	21 December 1923, over the Mediterranean	52

French airship Dixmude, *assumed to have been struck by lightning, broke up and crashed into the sea; wreckage, believed to be from the airship, was found off Sicily 10 years later.*

	Incident	No. killed
3	5 October 1930, near Beauvais, France	50

British airship R101 crashed into a hillside leaving 48 dead, with two dying later, and six saved.

	Incident	No. killed
4	24 August 1921, off the coast near Hull, UK	44

Airship R38, sold by the British Government to the USA and renamed USN ZR-2, broke in two on a training and test flight.

	Incident	No. killed
5	6 May 1937, Lakehurst, New Jersey, USA	36

German Zeppelin Hindenburg caught fire when mooring.

	Incident	No. killed
6	21 February 1922, Hampton Roads, Virginia, USA	34

Roma, an Italian airship bought by the US Army, crashed killing all but 11 men on board.

	Incident	No. killed
7	17 October 1913, Berlin, Germany	28

German airship LZ18 crashed after engine failure during a test flight at Berlin-Johannisthal.

	Incident	No. killed
8	30 March 1917, Baltic Sea	23

German airship SL9 was struck by lightning on a flight from Seerappen to Seddin, and crashed into the sea.

	Incident	No. killed
9	3 September 1915, mouth of the River Elbe, Germany	19

German airship L10 was struck by lightning and plunged into the sea.

	Incident	No. killed
10=	9 September 1913, off Heligoland	14

German navy airship L1 crashed into the sea, leaving six survivors out of the 20 on board.

	Incident	No. killed
10=	3 September 1925, Caldwell, Ohio	14

US dirigible Shenandoah, the first airship built in the US and the first to use safe helium instead of inflammable hydrogen, broke up in a storm, scattering sections over many miles of the Ohio countryside.

T O P 1 0

WORST AIR DISASTERS IN THE WORLD

Incident	Killed
1 27 March 1977, Tenerife, Canary Islands	583

Two Boeing 747s (Pan Am and KLM, carrying 364 passengers and 16 crew and 230 passengers and 11 crew respectively) collided and caught fire on the runway of Los Rodeos airport after the pilots received incorrect control-tower instructions.

2 12 August 1985, Mt Ogura, Japan	520

A JAL Boeing 747 on an internal flight from Tokyo to Osaka crashed, killing all but four on board in the worst-ever disaster involving a single aircraft.

3 3 March 1974, Paris, France	346

A Turkish Airlines DC-10 crashed at Ermenonville, north of Paris, immediately after take-off for London, with many English rugby supporters among the dead.

4 23 June 1985, off the Irish coast	329

An Air India Boeing 747 on a flight from Vancouver to Delhi exploded in mid-air, perhaps as a result of a terrorist bomb.

5 19 August 1980, Riyadh, Saudi Arabia	301

A Saudia (Saudi Arabian) Airlines Lockheed Tristar caught fire during an emergency landing.

6 3 July 1988, off the Iranian coast	290

An Iran Air A300 airbus was shot down in error by a missile fired by the USS Vincennes.

7 25 May 1979, Chicago, USA	279

The worst air disaster in the US occurred when an engine fell off a DC-10 as it took off from Chicago O'Hare airport and the plane plunged out of control, killing all 277 on board and two on the ground.

8 21 December 1988, Lockerbie, Scotland	270

Pan Am Flight 103 from London Heathrow to New York exploded in mid-air as a result of a terrorist bomb, killing 243 passengers, 16 crew, and 11 on the ground in the UK's worst-ever air disaster.

9 1 September 1983, Sakhalin Island, off the Siberian coast	269

A Korean Air Lines Boeing 747 that had strayed into Soviet airspace was shot down by a Soviet fighter.

10 26 April 1994, Nagoya airport, Japan	62

A China Airlines Airbus A300-600R, on a flight from Taipai, Taiwan, stalled and crashed while landing at Nagoya airport, Japan.

Three further air disasters have resulted in the deaths of more than 250 people: on 11 July 1991 a DC-8 carrying Muslim pilgrims from Mecca to Nigeria crashed on take-off, killing 261; on 28 November 1979 an Air New Zealand DC-10 crashed near Mount Erebus, Antarctica, while on a sightseeing trip, killing 257 passengers and crew; and on 12 December 1985 an Arrow Air DC-8 crashed on take-off at Gander, Newfoundland, killing all 256 on board, including 248 members of the 101st US Airborne Division.

T O P 1 0

WORST AIR DISASTERS IN THE UK

Incident	Killed
1 21 December 1988, Lockerbie, Scotland	270

(see World List, No. 8)

2 18 June 1972, Staines, Middlesex	118

A BEA Trident crashed after take-off.

3 12 March 1950, Siginstone, Glamorgan	81

An Avro Tudor V carrying Welsh rugby fans from Belfast inexplicably crashed while attempting to land at Llandow; three survived, one dying later. It was the worst air crash in the world up to this date.

4 23 August 1944, Freckelton, Lancashire	76

A US Air Force B-24 crashed onto a school.

5 4 June 1967, Stockport, Cheshire	72

A British Midland Argonaut airliner carrying holidaymakers returning from Majorca crashed, en route to Manchester airport, killing all but 12 on board.

6 24 August 1921, off the coast near Hull	62

Airship R38, sold by the British Government to the US, broke in two on a training and test flight.

7 22 August 1985, Manchester	55

A British Airtours Boeing 737 caught fire on the ground.

8 5 January 1969, near Gatwick Airport	50

An Ariana Afghan Airlines Boeing 727 crash-landed; the deaths include two on the ground.

9 8 January 1989, M1 Motorway	47

A British Midland Boeing 737-400 attempting to land without engine power crashed on the M1 Motorway embankment near East Midlands Airport.

10= 15 November 1957, Isle of Wight	45

Following an engine fire, an Aquila Airlines Solent flying boat struck a cliff.

10= 6 November 1986, off Sumburgh, Shetland Islands	45

A Boeing 234 Chinook helicopter ferrying oil rig workers ditched in the sea making it the worst-ever civilian helicopter accident.

A number of major air crashes involving British aircraft have occurred overseas. One of the earliest was that of British airship *R101* (*see* The 10 Worst Airship Disasters in the World). The Imperial Airways Argosy biplane *City of Liverpool* crashed near Dixmude in Belgium on 28 March 1933, killing all 12 passengers and three crew (one passenger fell out before the crash, and sabotage or attempted hijacking was suspected, as the aircraft was carrying silver bullion). On 4 March 1962 a chartered Caledonian DC-7C crashed near Douala, Cameroon, with the loss of 111 lives; at the time, this was the worst disaster involving a British airliner and the worst in Africa. In the crash of a Dan-Air Boeing 727 at Santa Cruz de Tenerife, Canary Islands, on 25 April 1980, all 146 on board perished.

UK TOURISM

TOP 10
TOURIST ATTRACTIONS CHARGING ADMISSION

	Attraction	1992 visits	1993 visits
1	Alton Towers, Staffordshire	2,501,379	2,618,365
2	Madame Tussaud's, London	2,263,994	2,449,627
3	Tower of London	2,235,199	2,332,468
4	St Paul's Cathedral, London	1,400,000 *	1,900,000
5	Natural History Museum, London	1,700,000	1,700,000
6	Chessington World of Adventures	1,170,000	1,495,000
7	Thorpe Park, Surrey	1,026,000	1,327,000
8	Science Museum, London	1,212,504	1,277,417
9	Tower World, Blackpool	1,300,000	1,250,000
10	Drayton Manor Park, Staffordshire	950,000	1,060,000

* Estimated.

TOP 10
TOURIST ATTRACTIONS IN SCOTLAND*

	Attraction	1993 visits
1	Edinburgh Castle	986,305
2	Glasgow Museum and Art Gallery	874,688
3	Royal Botanic Gardens, Edinburgh**	662,459
4	Edinburgh Zoo	496,084
5	Museum of Transport, Glasgow**	492,978
6	Royal Museum of Scotland, Edinburgh**	460,249
7	The Burrell Collection, Glasgow**	425,380
8	New Lanark Village**	400,000 #
9	National Gallery of Scotland, Edinburgh	358,235
10	Culzean Castle and Country Park, Maybole	353,204

* Excluding country parks and leisure centres.
# Estimated.
**Free.

EDINBURGH CASTLE
The castle, built on cliffs of basalt, dominates the skyline of the city.

TOP 10
TOURIST ATTRACTIONS IN WALES*

	Attraction	1993 visits
1	Ocean Beach Amusement Park, Rhyl	700,000 #
2	James Pringle Weavers, Llanfair	447,695
3	Erias Park, Colwyn Bay	400,000 #
4	Barry Island Log Flume	380,357
5	Pembrey Country Park	377,256
6	Welsh Folk Museum, St Fagans	349,164
7	Oakwood Leisure Park, Nr Narberth	314,353
8	Portmeirion, Penrhyndeudraeth	266,619
9	National Museum of Wales, Cardiff	255,601
10	Swallow Falls, Betwys-y-Coed	245,941

* Excluding leisure centres.
# Estimated.

TOP 10
MOST VISITED NATIONAL TRUST PROPERTIES

	Property	1993 visits
1	Fountains Abbey and Studley Royal, North Yorkshire	285,823
2	Stourhead Garden, Wiltshire	251,820
3	Wakehurst Place, West Sussex	229,250
4	Polesden Lacey House and Garden, Surrey	204,873
5	St Michael's Mount, Cornwall	191,673
6	Sissinghurst Garden, Kent	175,513
7	Bodiam Castle, East Sussex	172,435
8	Chartwell, Kent	170,256
9	Bodnant Castle, Gwynedd	168,398
10	Corfe Castle, Dorset	154,501

Over 10,000,000 people a year visit properties administered by the National Trust in England, Wales and Northern Ireland (the National Trust for Scotland is a separate organization).

TOP 10
HISTORIC HOUSES AND MONUMENTS

	Property	1993 visits
1	Tower of London	2,332,468
2	Edinburgh Castle	1,049,693
3	Roman Baths and Pump Room, Bath	898,142
4	Windsor Castle, State Apartments	813,059
5	Warwick Castle	751,026
6	Stonehenge, Wiltshire	668,607
7	Shakespeare's Birthplace, Stratford-on-Avon	606,697
8	Hampton Court Palace	576,664
9	Leeds Castle, Kent	533,000
10	Beaulieu, Hampshire	481,223

TOP 10
MUSEUMS AND GALLERIES

Museum/gallery	1993 visits
1 British Museum, London*	5,823,427
2 National Gallery, London*	3,882,371
3 Tate Gallery, London*	1,760,091
4 Natural History Museum, London	1,700,000
5 Science Museum, London	1,277,417
6 Victoria and Albert Museum, London	1,072,092
7 Royal Academy, London	922,135
8 National Museum of Photography, Bradford*	853,784
9 Glasgow Art Gallery and Museum*	796,380
10 Jorvik Viking Centre, York	752,586

Free admission.

TOP 10
GARDENS

Garden	1993 visits
1 Hampton Court Gardens	1,100,000*
2 Tropical World, Roundhay Park, Leeds‡	1,095,961
3 Kew Gardens	940,035
4 Royal Botanical Gardens, Edinburgh‡	787,107
5 Wisley Gardens, Surrey	672,446
6 Botanic Gardens, Belfast‡	500,000*
7 Botanic Gardens, Glasgow‡	350,000*
8 Sir Thomas and Lady Dixon Park, Belfast‡	300,000*
9 Walsall Arboretum Illuminations	290,990
10 University of Oxford Botanic Gardens‡	257,313*

Estimated.
‡ Free admission.

TOP 10
WILDLIFE ATTRACTIONS

Attraction	1993 visits
1 London Zoo	863,352
2 Chester Zoo	814,883
3 Sea Life Centre, Blackpool	592,000
4 Edinburgh Zoo	515,823
5 Whipsnade Wild Animal Park, Bedfordshire	406,912
6 Twycross Zoo, Atherstone	399,337
7 Knowsley Safari Park, Prescot	390,000
8 Bristol Zoo	352,000
9 Cotswold Wildlife Park, Burford	330,693
10 Birmingham Nature Centre*	317,684

Free admission.

TOP 10
LEISURE PARKS AND PIERS

Leisure park/pier	1993 visits
1 Blackpool Pleasure Beach‡	6,750,000*
2 Palace Pier, Brighton‡	3,500,000*
3 Alton Towers, Staffordshire	2,618,365
4 Pleasure Beach, Great Yarmouth‡	2,400,000*
5 Pleasureland, Southport‡	2,000,000*
6 Chessington World of Adventures	1,495,000*
7 Thorpe Park, Surrey	1,327,000
8 Frontierland, Morecambe‡	1,300,000*
9 Blackpool Tower	1,250,000
10 Hornsea Pottery, Hornsea‡	1,200,000*

Estimated.
‡ Free admission.

TOP 10
MOST VISITED NEWLY OPENED* TOURIST ATTRACTIONS

Attraction/opened	1993 visits
1 Granada Studios Tour, Manchester (1988)	700,000
2 Pleasure Island, Liverpool (1992)	680,000
3 Sea Life Centre, Blackpool (1990)	595,000
4 Rock Circus, London (1989)	554,483
5 Metroland, Gateshead (1988)	450,000
6 Cadbury World, Bournville (1990)	416,000
7 Museum of the Moving Image, London (1988)	374,692
8 Eurotunnel Exhibition Centre, Folkestone (1988)	295,000
9 Sea Life Centre, Scarborough (1991)	293,000
10 Eureka! The Museum for Children, Halifax (1992)	250,000

Charging admission, opened 1988–92.

WORLD TOURISM

TOP 10

COUNTRIES WITH MOST TOURISTS

	Country	Annual arrivals/departures
1	France	58,500,000
2	USA	45,500,000
3	Spain	36,054,000
4	Italy	26,974,000
5	Hungary	22,500,000
6	Austria	19,474,000
7	UK	17,855,000
8	Mexico	17,587,000
9	Germany	15,950,000
10	Canada	15,400,000

Spain has been dislodged from its former No. 1 position in this list, while, as a result of the recent military conflict in the Balkans, former Yugoslavia, a country which once featured prominently in the Top 10 (in 2nd place a decade ago), had by 1992 plummeted to 62nd place with just 700,000 intrepid tourists.

TOP 10

CRUISE SHIP VISITS

	Country	Annual arrivals
1	Bahamas	2,020,000
2	Mexico	1,629,000
3	US Virgin Islands	1,215,000
4	Puerto Rico	891,000
5	Spain	826,000
6	St Martin	502,000
7	Jamaica	490,000
8	Korea	481,000
9	Cayman Islands	475,000
10	Martinique	417,000

The cruise vessel business is the most rapidly growing sector of the travel industry, with a compound annual growth rate of almost 10 per cent over the past 12 years. In 1992 a total of 130 ships served the US and Canadian market alone, sailing particularly from Miami and other ports in Florida, and serving some 3,500,000 passengers.

THE LOUVRE
The Musée du Louvre – home to the Mona Lisa *– contains one of the world's most important art collections. It was originally constructed in 1190 as a fortress to protect Paris from Viking raids, and was first opened to the public in 1793, following the Revolution.*

TOP 10

DESTINATIONS OF JAPANESE TOURISTS

	Country	Trips (%)
1	USA	28.0
2	Korea	12.2
3	Hong Kong	10.6
4	Singapore	7.5
5	Taiwan	6.9
6=	Germany	5.6
6=	Italy	5.6
8	China	5.4
9	Guam	4.9
10	Thailand	4.7

In recent years tourism by Japanese nationals has become one of the most important contributors to the international travel industry. Japanese subjects are especially welcomed by the retail trade as the highest spending per head of any travellers. Almost 12,000,000, some 10 per cent of the entire population, went abroad in 1992, and it is predicted that, by the year 2005 their expenditure and that of Germany, another major overseas spending nation, will together exceed that of the current world leader, the United States.

EIFFEL TOWER
When the Eiffel Tower was erected for the Universal Exhibition of 1889, it was meant to be a temporary addition to the Paris skyline. In fact, it outraged many Parisians who felt it was an eyesore. The world's tallest building until New York's Empire State Building was completed in 1931, the Eiffel Tower has become the symbol of Paris.

TOP 10

OVERSEAS DESTINATIONS MOST FEARED BY THE BRITISH

	Country	% fearing
1	Bosnia	86
2	Iraq	80
3	Iran	67
4	Libya	61
5	El Salvador	46

	Country	% fearing
6	Nicaragua	40
7	Colombia	35
8	Russia	33
9	Egypt	32
10	Bolivia	30

This list is based on a survey conducted among British holidaymakers by the Home and Overseas Insurance Company, which insures one in three British holiday makers. The survey also reported that, following reports of robbery and violence in Florida and other US resorts, 21 per cent included the United States among their "most feared". Most European countries, other than Russia, are considered 99–100 per cent safe. This compares with just 16 per cent who said they feared travelling in Peru, a country which is included on the US State Department's "no go" list, and 14 per cent who believed that China and India were unsafe. Of Western European countries, Britons placed Germany at the head of their list – although their fear of visiting the country may be allied more to their concerns about the rate of exchange between the Deutsche Mark and Sterling than to any perceived danger.

TOP 10 — TOURIST EARNERS

	Country	Annual receipts ($)
1	USA	53,861,000,000
2	France	25,000,000,000
3	Spain	22,181,000,000
4	Italy	21,577,000,000
5	UK	13,683,000,000
6	Austria	13,250,000,000
7	Germany	10,982,000,000
8	Switzerland	7,650,000,000
9	Hong Kong	6,037,000,000
10	Mexico	5,997,000,000

TOP 10 — TOURIST SPENDERS

	Tourist country of origin	Annual expenditure ($)
1	USA	39,872,000,000
2	Germany	37,309,000,000
3	Japan	26,837,000,000
4	UK	19,831,000,000
5	Italy	16,617,000,000
6	France	13,910,000,000
7	Canada	11,265,000,000
8	Netherlands	9,330,000,000
9	Taiwan	7,098,000,000
10	Austria	6,895,000,000

TOP 10 — TOURIST ATTRACTIONS IN FRANCE

	Attraction	Annual visitors
1	Euro Disney	11,000,000
2	Pompidou Centre, Paris (art and culture centre)	8,262,513
3	Eiffel Tower, Paris	5,757,357
4	Parc de La Villette, Paris (City of Science)	5,300,000
5	Musée du Louvre, Paris	4,900,000
6	Versailles Palace	4,211,000
7	Musée d'Orsay, Paris	3,000,000
8	Les Invalides, Paris (museums, Napoleon's tomb)	1,212,271
9	Parc Astérix (theme park)	1,100,000
10	Chenonceaux Château, Loire Valley	850,000

France's newest Top 10 tourist attraction, Euro Disney, created in the French countryside at a cost of $4,000,000,000, opened to the public on 12 April 1992. Despite attaining its annual target of 11,000,000 visitors it has been beset with financial problems, losing more than $930,000,000 in 1993.

TOP 10 — TRAVEL SHOPPERS

	Country of origin	Average spend per head ($)*
1	Japan	389.83
2	Korea	360.00
3	Australia	340.91
4	Qatar	312.50
5	South Africa	300.00
6	Norway	260.00
7	Kuwait	250.00
8	New Zealand	237.50
9	Israel	216.67
10	Oman	200.00
	USA	190.48

* Shopping during travel overseas, including duty-free purchases.

Shopping by international travellers was reckoned to be worth $50,000,000,000 in 1992. The US was the greatest beneficiary, with earnings of some $5,600,000,000, followed by France ($3,350,000,000) and the UK ($3,250,000,000). The country receiving the highest average spend per traveller was the United Arab Emirates, with an estimated $848.38.

SPORTS & GAMES

T O P 1 0

LONGEST-STANDING CURRENT OLYMPIC RECORDS

	Event	Winning time/distance	Competitor/ nationality	Date when record was set
1	Men's long jump	8.90 m	Bob Beamon (USA)	18 Oct 1968
2	Men's javelin	94.58 m	Miklos Nemeth (Hun)	25 Jul 1976
3	Women's shot	22.41 m	Ilona Slupianck (GDR)	24 Jul 1980
4	Women's 800 metres	1 min 53.43 sec	Nadezhda Olizarenko (USSR)	27 Jul 1980
5	Women's 4 x 100 metres relay	41.60 sec	GDR	1 Aug 1980
6	Men's 1500 metres	3 min 32.53 sec	Sebastian Coe (UK)	1 Aug 1980
7	Women's marathon	2 hr 24 min 52 sec	Joan Benoit (USA)	5 Aug 1984
8	Men's 800 metres	1 min 43.00 sec	Joaquim Cruz (Bra)	6 Aug 1984
9	Decathlon	8,847 points	Daley Thompson (UK)	9 Aug 1984
10	Men's 5000 metres	13 min 05.59 sec	Said Aouita (Mor)	11 Aug 1984

Bob Beamon's record-breaking jump in 1968 is regarded as one of the greatest achievements in athletics. He was aided by Mexico City's rarefied atmosphere, but to add a staggering 55.25 cm/21¾ ins to the old record, and win the competition by 72.39 cm/28½ ins, was no mean feat. Beamon's jump of 8.90 m/29 ft 2½ ins was the first beyond both 28 and 29 feet (8.53 and 8.84 m). The next 8.53 m/28 ft jump in the Olympics was not until 1980, 12 years later. The "unbeatable" world record was finally broken during the 1991 World Championships in Tokyo, by American Mike Powell.

Roger Bannister (UK)
Oxford, England
6 May 1954
3:59.4

John Landy (Aus)
Turku, Finland
21 Jun 1954
3:58.0

Derek
Ibbotson (
London,
England
19 Jul 195
3:57.2

FASTEST MEN ON EARTH

	Athlete/nationality	Venue	Date	Time (sec)
1	Leroy Burrell (USA)	Lausanne	6 Jul 1994	9.85
2	Carl Lewis (USA)	Tokyo	25 Aug 1991	9.86
3	Leroy Burrell (USA)	Tokyo	25 Aug 1991	9.88
4=	Dennis Mitchell (USA)	Tokyo	25 Aug 1991	9.91
4=	Davidson Ezinwa (Nig)	Azusa	11 Apr 1992	9.91
6	Linford Christie (UK)	Tokyo	25 Aug 1991	9.92
7=	Calvin Smith (USA)	Colorado Springs	3 Jul 1983	9.93
7=	Mike Marsh (USA)	Walnut	18 Apr 1992	9.93
9=	Jim Hines (USA)	Mexico City	14 Oct 1968	9.95
9=	Frankie Fredericks (Nam)	Tokyo	25 Aug 1991	9.95

The fastest-ever 100 metres, with wind assistance, was at Indianapolis on 16 July 1988, when Carl Lewis was timed at 9.78 seconds, but he had the benefit of winds measuring 5.2 metres/17 feet per second.

LONGEST LONG JUMPS

	Athlete/nationality	Location	Date	Distance (m)
1	Mike Powell (USA)	Tokyo	30 Aug 1991	8.95
2	Bob Beamon (USA)	Mexico City	18 Oct 1968	8.90
3	Robert Emmiyan (USSR)	Tsakhadzor	22 May 1987	8.86
4=	Carl Lewis (USA)	Indianapolis	19 Jun 1983	8.79
4=	Carl Lewis (USA)	New York*	27 Jan 1984	8.79
6=	Carl Lewis (USA)	Indianapolis	24 Jul 1982	8.76
6=	Carl Lewis (USA)	Indianapolis	18 Jul 1988	8.76
8	Carl Lewis (USA)	Indianapolis	16 Aug 1987	8.75
9	Larry Myricks (USA)	Indianapolis	18 Jul 1988	8.74
10	Carl Lewis (USA)	Seoul	26 Sep 1988	8.72

* *Indoors.*

THE PROGRESSION OF THE WORLD MILE RECORD SINCE THE FIRST SUB-FOUR-MINUTE MILE

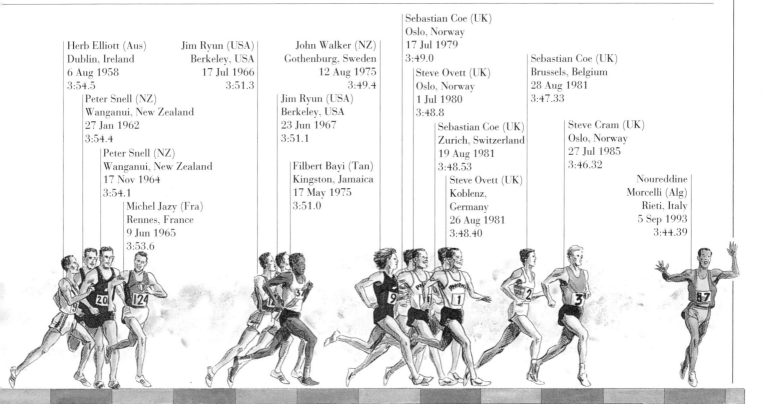

Herb Elliott (Aus)
Dublin, Ireland
6 Aug 1958
3:54.5

Peter Snell (NZ)
Wanganui, New Zealand
27 Jan 1962
3:54.4

Peter Snell (NZ)
Wanganui, New Zealand
17 Nov 1964
3:54.1

Michel Jazy (Fra)
Rennes, France
9 Jun 1965
3:53.6

Jim Ryun (USA)
Berkeley, USA
17 Jul 1966
3:51.3

Jim Ryun (USA)
Berkeley, USA
23 Jun 1967
3:51.1

Filbert Bayi (Tan)
Kingston, Jamaica
17 May 1975
3:51.0

John Walker (NZ)
Gothenburg, Sweden
12 Aug 1975
3:49.4

Sebastian Coe (UK)
Oslo, Norway
17 Jul 1979
3:49.0

Steve Ovett (UK)
Oslo, Norway
1 Jul 1980
3:48.8

Sebastian Coe (UK)
Zurich, Switzerland
19 Aug 1981
3:48.53

Steve Ovett (UK)
Koblenz, Germany
26 Aug 1981
3:48.40

Sebastian Coe (UK)
Brussels, Belgium
28 Aug 1981
3:47.33

Steve Cram (UK)
Oslo, Norway
27 Jul 1985
3:46.32

Noureddine Morcelli (Alg)
Rieti, Italy
5 Sep 1993
3:44.39

TEST CRICKET

HIGHEST INDIVIDUAL TEST INNINGS

	Batsman	Match/venue	Year	Runs
1	Brian Lara	West Indies v England (Antigua)	1994	375
2	Gary Sobers	West Indies v Pakistan (Kingston)	1957–58	365*
3	Len Hutton	England v Australia (The Oval)	1938	364
4	Hanif Mohammad	Pakistan v West Indies (Bridgetown)	1957–58	337
5	Walter Hammond	England v New Zealand (Auckland)	1932–33	336*
6	Don Bradman	Australia v England (Leeds)	1930	334
7	Graham Gooch	England v India (Lord's)	1990	333
8	Andrew Sandham	England v West Indies (Kingston)	1929–30	325
9	Bobby Simpson	Australia v England (Manchester)	1964	311
10	John Edrich	England v New Zealand (Leeds)	1965	310*

* Not out.

Brian Lara's remarkable performance put an end to Gary Sobers' record, which stood for 35 years. Sobers' next best score was 226 against England at Bridgetown in 1959–60. Apart from his 365 not out, it was his only other Test double century. Sobers' record-breaking score came in his 17th Test, which was the 3rd Test of the series against Pakistan. Prior to his 365, his highest Test innings had been 80 in the previous Test at Port-of-Spain just three weeks earlier.

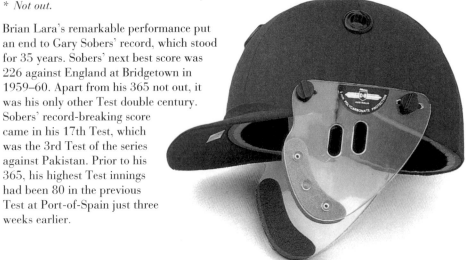

HIGHEST TEAM TOTALS IN TEST CRICKET

	Match	Venue	Year	Score
1	England (v Australia)	The Oval	1938	903–7 dec
2	England (v West Indies)	Kingston	1929–30	849
3	West Indies (v Pakistan)	Kingston	1957–58	790–3 dec
4	Australia (v West Indies)	Kingston	1954–55	758–8 dec
5	Australia (v England)	Lord's	1930	729–6 dec
6	Pakistan (v England)	The Oval	1987	708
7	Australia (v England)	The Oval	1934	701
8	Pakistan (v India)	Lahore	1989–90	699–5 dec
9	Australia (v England)	The Oval	1930	695
10	West Indies (v England)	The Oval	1976	687–8 dec

YOUNGEST TEST CRICKETERS

	Player/country/debut	Age yrs	days
1	Mushtaq Mohammad (Pakistan) 26 Mar 1959	15	124
2	Aaqib Javed (Pakistan) 10 Feb 1989	16	189
3	Sachin Tendulkar (India) 15 Nov 1989	16	205
4	Aftab Baloch (Pakistan) 8 Nov 1969	16	221
5	Nasim-ul-Ghani (Pakistan) 17 Jan 1958	16	248
6	Khalid Hassan (Pakistan) 1 Jul 1954	16	352
7	Laxman Sivaramakrishnan (India) 28 Apr 1983	17	118
8	Derek Sealy (West Indies) 11 Jan 1930	17	122
9	Sanjeeva Weerasinghe (Sri Lanka) 6 Sep 1985	17	189
10	Maninder Singh (India) 23 Dec 1982	17	193

FIRST GROUNDS TO BE USED FOR TEST CRICKET

	Ground	First used
1	Melbourne Cricket Ground	15 Mar 1877
2	Kennington Oval, London	6 Sep 1880
3	Sydney Cricket Ground	17 Feb 1882
4	Old Trafford, Manchester	11 Jul 1884
5	Lord's, London	21 Jul 1884
6	Adelaide Oval	12 Dec 1884
7	St George's Park, Port Elizabeth	12 Mar 1889
8	Newlands, Cape Town	25 Mar 1889
9	Old Wanderers Ground, Johannesburg	2 Mar 1896
10	Trent Bridge, Nottingham	1 Jun 1899

TOP 10

OLDEST TEST CRICKETERS

	Player/country	Last Test	Age yrs	days
1	Wilf Rhodes (England)	12 Apr 1930	52	165
2	Herbert Ironmonger (Australia)	28 Feb 1933	50	327
3	W.G. Grace (England)	3 Jun 1899	50	320
4	George Gunn (England)	12 Apr 1930	50	303
5	James Southerton (England)	4 Apr 1877	49	139
6	Miran Bux (Pakistan)	16 Feb 1955	47	302
7	Jack Hobbs (England)	22 Aug 1930	47	249
8	Frank Woolley (England)	22 Aug 1934	47	87
9	Donald Blackie (Australia)	8 Feb 1929	46	309
10	Dave Nourse (South Africa)	19 Aug 1924	46	206

TOP 10

TEST RUN-MAKERS

(As at the end of the 1993 season)

	Batsman/country	Years	Runs
1	Allan Border (Aus)	1978–93	10,695
2	Sunil Gavaskar (India)	1971–87	10,122
3	Javed Miandad (Pakistan)	1976–93	8,689
4	Viv Richards (West Indies)	1974–91	8,540
5	Graham Gooch (Eng)	1975–93	8,293
6	David Gower (Eng)	1978–92	8,231
7	Geoff Boycott (Eng)	1964–82	8,114
8	Gary Sobers (West Indies)	1954–74	8,032
9	Colin Cowdrey (Eng)	1954–75	7,624
10	Gordon Greenidge (West Indies)	1974–91	7,558

TOP 10

FIRST TEST CENTURIES SCORED BY ENGLAND BATSMEN

	Batsman	Venue	Score	Date
1	W.G. Grace	The Oval	152	6–8 Sep 1880
2	George Ulyett	Melbourne	149	10–14 Mar 1882
3	Allan Steel	Sydney	135 not out	17–21 Feb 1883
4	Allan Steel	Lord's	148	21–23 Jul 1884
5	Walter Read	The Oval	117	11–13 Aug 1884
6	William Barnes	Adelaide	134	12–16 Dec 1884
7	John Briggs	Melbourne	121	1–5 Jan 1885
8	Arthur Shrewsbury	Melbourne	105 not out	21–25 Mar 1885
9	Arthur Shrewsbury	Lord's	164	19–21 Jul 1886
10	W.G. Grace	The Oval	170	12–14 Aug 1886

All 10 centuries were scored against Australia. W.G. Grace's two centuries were the only ones he scored in Test cricket.

TOP 10

LOWEST COMPLETED INNINGS IN TEST CRICKET

	Match	Venue	Year	Total
1	New Zealand (*v* England)	Auckland	1954–55	26
2=	South Africa (*v* England)	Port Elizabeth	1895–96	30
2=	South Africa (*v* England)	Birmingham	1924	30
4	South Africa (*v* England)	Cape Town	1898–99	35
5=	Australia (*v* England)	Birmingham	1902	36
5=	South Africa (*v* Australia)	Melbourne	1931–32	36
7=	Australia (*v* England)	Sydney	1887–88	42
7=	New Zealand (*v* Australia)	Wellington	1945–46	42
7=	India* (*v* England)	Lord's	1974	42
10	South Africa (*v* England)	Cape Town	1888–89	43

* *India batted one man short.*

England's lowest total is 45, when dismissed by Australia at Sydney in 1886–87.

FOOTBALL – THE TOP TEAMS

262

T O P 1 0
COUNTRIES IN THE WORLD CUP*

	Country	Win	R/u	3rd	4th	Total
1	Germany/West Germany	3	3	2	1	26
2	Brazil	3	1	2	1	20
3	Italy	3	1	1	1	18
4	Argentina	2	2	-	-	14
5	Uruguay	2	-	-	2	10
6=	Czechoslovakia	-	2	-	-	6
6=	Holland	-	2	-	-	6
6=	Hungary	-	2	-	-	6
6=	Sweden	-	1	1	1	6
10=	England	1	-	-	1	5
10=	France	-	-	2	1	5

* Based on 4 points for winning the tournament, 3 points for runner-up, 2 points for 3rd place, and 1 point for 4th. Up to 1993 only.

T O P 1 0
TEAMS IN THE THREE MAJOR EUROPEAN CLUB COMPETITIONS

	Club/country	EC	ECWC	UEFA*	Total
1	Real Madrid (Spain)	6	0	2	8
2=	AC Milan (Italy)	5	2	0	7
2=	Barcelona (Spain)	1	3	3	7
4	Liverpool (England)	4	0	2	6
5	Juventus (Italy)	1	2	2	5
6=	Ajax Amsterdam (Holland)	3	1	0	4
6=	Bayern Munich (Germany)	3	1	0	4
6=	Inter Milan (Italy)	2	0	2	4
9=	Anderlecht (Belgium)	0	2	1	3
9=	Tottenham Hotspur (England)	0	1	2	3
9=	Valencia (Spain)	0	1	2	3

* EC = European Champions' Cup; ECWC = European Cup-winners' Cup; UEFA = UEFA/Fairs Cup.

T O P 1 0
OLDEST FOOTBALL LEAGUE CLUBS

	Club	Year formed
1	Notts County	1862
2	Stoke City	1863
3	Nottingham Forest	1865
4	Chesterfield	1866
5	Sheffield Wednesday	1867
6	Reading	1871
7	Wrexham	1873
8=	Aston Villa	1874
8=	Bolton Wanderers	1874
10=	Birmingham City	1875
10=	Blackburn Rovers	1875

Scotland's oldest club is Queen's Park, formed in 1867. It remains the only amateur team in League soccer in England or Scotland.

IAN RUSH
A firm favourite with Liverpool fans since his bargain £300,000 transfer from Chester in 1980, Ian Rush has gone on to become the club's all-time top scorer.

T O P 1 0
EUROPEAN CLUBS WITH THE MOST DOMESTIC LEAGUE TITLES*

	Club/country	Titles
1	Glasgow Rangers (Scotland)	42
2	Linfield (Northern Ireland)	41
3	Benfica (Portugal)	30
4	Rapid Vienna (Austria)	29
5	CFKA Sredets (Bulgaria)	27
6=	Olympiakos (Greece)	25
6=	Real Madrid (Spain)	25
6=	Floriana (Malta)	25
9=	Ferencvaros (Hungary)	24
9=	Ajax Amsterdam (Holland)	24

* To end of 1993–94 season.

The top English club is Liverpool with 18 League titles. Glasgow Rangers has won six consecutive League titles. Aberdeen has finished runners-up to them in five of the last six seasons. Rangers won its first title in the Scottish League's first season (1890–91) and has won at least one title every decade since then.

TEAM STRIP
The introduction of sponsorship and advertising to football has changed the look of today's game.

TOP 10
CLUBS WITH THE MOST BRITISH TITLES

	Team	League titles	FA Cup	League Cup	Total
1	Glasgow Rangers	44	26	19	89
2	Glasgow Celtic	35	29	9	73
3	Liverpool	18	4	4	26
4=	Arsenal	10	6	2	18
4=	Aston Villa	7	7	4	18
4=	Manchester United	9	8	1	18
7	Aberdeen	4	7	4	15
8=	Everton	9	4	-	13
8=	Heart of Midlothian	4	5	4	13
10	Tottenham Hotspur	2	8	2	12

TOP 10
HIGHEST-SCORING FOOTBALL LEAGUE GAMES

	Match	Division	Season	Score	Goals
1	Tranmere Rovers *v* Oldham Athletic	3N	1935–36	13–4	17
2=	Aston Villa *v* Accrington	1	1891–92	12–2	14
2=	Manchester City *v* Lincoln City	2	1894–95	11–3	14
2=	Tottenham Hotspur *v* Everton	1	1958–59	10–4	14
5=	Stockport County *v* Halifax Town	3N	1933–34	13–0	13
5=	Newcastle United *v* Newport County	2	1946–47	13–0	13
5=	Barrow *v* Gateshead	3N	1933–34	12–1	13
5=	Sheffield United *v* Cardiff City	1	1925–26	11–2	13
5=	Oldham Athletic *v* Chester	3N	1951–52	11–2	13
5=	Hull City *v* Wolverhampton Wanderers	2	1919–20	10–3	13
5=	Middlesbrough *v* Sheffield United	1	1933–34	10–3	13
5=	Stoke City *v* West Bromwich Albion	1	1936–37	10–3	13
5=	Bristol City *v* Gillingham	3S	1926–27	9–4	13
5=	Gillingham *v* Exeter City	3S	1950–51	9–4	13
5=	Derby County *v* Blackburn Rovers	1	1890–91	8–5	13
5=	Burton Swifts *v* Walsall Town Swifts	2	1893–94	8–5	13
5=	Stockport County *v* Chester	3N	1932–33	8–5	13
5=	Charlton Athletic *v* Huddersfield Town	2	1957–58	7–6	13

Gillingham has figured in the only two League games to finish 9–4 and has been on both ends of the scoreline.

TOP 10
SCORING TEAMS IN FA CUP FINALS

	Team	Finals	Goals
1	Manchester United	11	28
2	Tottenham Hotspur	9	23
3	Blackburn Rovers	8	18
4=	Everton	11	15
4=	Liverpool	10	15
6=	Arsenal	12	14
6=	Newcastle United	11	14
6=	Sheffield United	6	14
9=	Sheffield Wednesday	6	13
9=	West Bromwich Albion	10	13

Twenty-seven of Manchester United's 28 goals have been at Wembley, the most by one team at the "home" of the Cup Final. Tottenham is second with 17 Wembley goals. Bury, with 10 goals in two Cup Final appearances, has the best average of five goals per game.

TOP 10
TEAMS THAT HAVE KNOCKED OUT THE FA CUP HOLDERS THE FOLLOWING SEASON

	Team	Defeats*
1=	Bolton Wanderers	7
2=	Liverpool	6
2=	Manchester United	6
4=	Nottingham Forest	4
4=	Tottenham Hotspur	4
6=	Aston Villa	3
6=	Chelsea	3
6=	Everton	3
6=	Preston North End	3
6=	Sheffield United	3
6=	Sunderland	3
6=	West Bromwich Albion	3
6=	West Ham United	3

* *Of Cup holders during following season.*

GOLF – THE MAJORS

T O P   1 0

PLAYERS TO WIN THE MOST MAJORS IN A CAREER

	Player/ nationality	British Open	US Open	Masters	PGA	Total
1	Jack Nicklaus (USA)	3	4	6	5	18
2	Walter Hagen (USA)	4	2	0	5	11
3=	Ben Hogan (USA)	1	4	2	2	9
3=	Gary Player (SA)	3	1	3	2	9
5	Tom Watson (USA)	5	1	2	0	8
6=	Harry Vardon (UK)	6	1	0	0	7
6=	Gene Sarazen (USA)	1	2	1	3	7
6=	Bobby Jones (USA)	3	4	0	0	7
6=	Sam Snead (USA)	1	0	3	3	7
6=	Arnold Palmer (USA)	2	1	4	0	7

The four Majors are the British Open, US Open, US Masters, and US PGA. The oldest is the British Open, first played at Prestwick in 1860 and won by Willie Park. The first US Open was at the Newport Club, Rhode Island, in 1895 and won by Horace Rawlins, playing over his home course. The US PGA Championship, probably the least prestigious of the four Majors, was first held at the Siwanoy Club, New York. Jim Barnes beat Jock Hutchison by one hole in the match-play final. It did not become a stroke-play event until 1958. The youngest of the four Majors is the Masters, played over the beautiful Augusta National course in Georgia. Entry is by invitation only and the first winner was Horton Smith. The Masters, and the Augusta course, were the idea of Robert Tyre "Bobby" Jones, the greatest amateur player the world of golf has ever seen. No man has won all four Majors in one year.

T O P   1 0

LOWEST WINNING TOTALS IN THE US OPEN

	Player	Year	Venue	Score
1=	Jack Nicklaus (USA)	1980	Baltusrol	272
1=	Lee Janzen (USA)	1993	Baltusrol	272
3	David Graham (Aus)	1981	Merion	273
4=	Jack Nicklaus (USA)	1967	Baltusrol	275
4=	Lee Trevino (USA)	1968	Oak Hill	275
6=	Ben Hogan (USA)	1948	Riviera	276
6=	Fuzzy Zoeller (USA)	1984	Winged Foot	276
8=	Jerry Pate (USA)	1976	Atlanta	277
8=	Scott Simpson (USA)	1987	Olympic Club	277
10=	Ken Venturi (USA)	1964	Congressional	278
10=	Billy Casper (USA)	1966	Olympic Club	278
10=	Hubert Green (USA)	1977	Southern Hills	278
10=	Curtis Strange (USA)	1988	Brookline	278
10=	Curtis Strange (USA)	1989	Oak Hill	278

T O P   1 0

MOST SUCCESSFUL BRITONS IN MAJORS

	Player	Titles
1	Harry Vardon	7
2=	James Braid	5
2=	John Henry Taylor	5
4=	Tom Morris Sr	4
4=	Tom Morris Jr	4
4=	Willie Park Sr	4
4=	Nick Faldo	4
8=	Willie Anderson	3
8=	Robert Ferguson	3
8=	Henry Cotton	3

All except Vardon (US Open 1900) and Faldo (US Masters 1989 and 1990) won their Majors on British soil.

T O P   1 0

LOWEST WINNING SCORES IN THE US MASTERS

	Player	Year	Score
1=	Jack Nicklaus	1965	271
1=	Raymond Floyd	1976	271
3	Ben Hogan	1953	274
4=	Severiano Ballesteros (Spa)	1980	275
4=	Fred Couples	1992	275
6=	Arnold Palmer	1964	276
6=	Jack Nicklaus	1975	276
6=	Tom Watson	1977	276
9=	Bob Goalby	1968	277
9=	Gary Player (SA)	1978	277
9=	Ben Crenshaw	1984	277
9=	Ian Woosnam (UK)	1991	277
9=	Bernhard Langer (Ger)	1993	277

All players from the US unless otherwise stated.

The Masters is the only Major played on the same course each year, at Augusta, Georgia.

PROGRESSION OF LOWEST FOUR-ROUND TOTALS IN THE BRITISH OPEN

Golfer	Venue	Year	Total
Harold Hilton	Muirfield	1892	305
Harry Vardon	Prestwick	1903	300
Jackie White	Sandwich	1904	296
James Braid	Prestwick	1908	291
Bobby Jones	St Andrews	1927	285
Gene Sarazen	Prince's	1932	283
Bobby Locke	Troon	1950	279
Peter Thomson	Royal Lytham	1958	278
Arnold Palmer	Troon	1962	276
Tom Watson	Turnberry	1977	268
Greg Norman	Sandwich	1993	267

TOP 10

MOST FREQUENTLY USED COURSES FOR THE BRITISH OPEN

	Course	First used	Last used	Times used
1=	Prestwick	1860	1925	24
1=	St Andrews	1873	1990	24
3	Muirfield	1892	1992	14
4	Royal St George's, Sandwich	1894	1993	12
5	Hoylake	1897	1967	10
6	Royal Lytham	1926	1988	8
7	Royal Birkdale	1954	1991	7
8=	Musselburgh	1874	1889	6
8=	Royal Troon	1923	1989	6
10	Carnoustie	1931	1975	5

The only other courses to have staged the Open are Turnberry (three times), Deal (twice), Prince's, Sandwich (once), and Royal Portrush (once) – the only Irish course to play host to Britain's only Major. The Carnoustie course in 1968 was the longest ever used for the Open, measuring 6,592 m/7,252 yd.

TOP 10

LOWEST FOUR-ROUND TOTALS IN THE BRITISH OPEN

The first time the Open Championship was played over four rounds of 18 holes was at Muirfield in 1892 when the amateur Harold H. Hilton won with scores of 78, 81, 72, and 74 for a total of 305. Since then the record has kept falling. At Turnberry in 1977 Tom Watson and Jack Nicklaus decimated British Open records with Watson winning by one stroke with a championship record 268. It remained unbeaten for 16 years until Australia's Greg Norman became the first champion to shoot four rounds under 70 when he won with a 267 at Royal St George's, Sandwich in 1993.

TOM WATSON
With more than $6,000,000 in career earnings, five British Open wins, and success in the US Open and Masters, Tom Watson can rightly be labelled one of the most feared opponents faced by today's players.

	Player/nationality	Venue	Year	Total
1	Greg Norman (Aus)	Sandwich	1993	267
2	Tom Watson (USA)	Turnberry	1977	268
3=	Jack Nicklaus (USA)	Turnberry	1977	269
3=	Nick Faldo (UK)	Sandwich	1993	269
5=	Nick Faldo (UK)	St Andrews	1990	270
5=	Bernhard Langer (Ger)	Sandwich	1993	270
7	Tom Watson (USA)	Muirfield	1980	271
8=	Ian Baker-Finch (Aus)	Royal Birkdale	1991	272
8=	Nick Faldo (UK)	Muirfield	1992	272
8=	Corey Pavin (USA)	Sandwich	1993	272
8=	Peter Senior (Aus)	Sandwich	1993	272

The lowest individual round is 63, which has been achieved by seven golfers: Mark Hayes (USA), Turnberry 1977; Isao Aoki (Jap), Muirfield 1980; Greg Norman (Aus), Turnberry 1986; Paul Broadhurst (UK), St Andrews 1990; Jodie Mudd (USA), Royal Birkdale 1991; Nick Faldo (UK), Sandwich 1993; and Payne Stewart (USA), Sandwich 1993. Hubert Green (1980), Tom Watson (1980), Craig Stadler (1983), Christy O'Connor Jr (1985), Seve Ballesteros (1986), Rodger Davis (1987), Ian Baker-Finch (1990 and 1991), Fred Couples (1991), Nick Faldo (1992), Raymond Floyd (1992), Steve Pate (1992), Wayne Grady (1993), and Greg Norman (1993) have all recorded rounds of 64. A further 23 men have registered rounds of 65; the first to do so was Henry Cotton at Sandwich in 1934. Experts regard Cotton's second round 65 as one of the finest in the inter-war era of Championship golf. He had already opened with a 67, and thus became the first man to shoot two sub-70 rounds in the Open. His 65 lowered the Open record of 67 set by Walter Hagen at Muirfield in 1929. Cotton went on to become the first British winner of the Open for 11 years when he beat South Africa's Sid Brews by five strokes with a then record total of 283, which was not surpassed until 1977.

HORSE RACING – THE ENGLISH CLASSICS

EPSOM DERBY WINNING JOCKEYS

	Jockey	Years	Winners
1	Lester Piggott	1954–83	9
2=	Jem Robinson	1817–36	6
2=	Steve Donoghue	1915–25	6
4=	John Arnull	1784–99	5
4=	Bill Clift	1793–1819	5
4=	Frank Buckle	1792–1823	5
4=	Fred Archer	1877–86	5
8=	Sam Arnull	1780–98	4
8=	Tom Goodison	1809–22	4
8=	Bill Scott	1832–43	4
8=	Jack Watts	1887–96	4
8=	Charlie Smirke	1934–58	4
8=	Willy Carson	1979–94	4

Rae Johnstone and Pat Eddery have each ridden three winners.

OWNERS OF EPSOM DERBY WINNERS

	Owner	Years	Winners
1=	3rd Earl of Egremont	1782–1826	5
1=	HH Aga Khan III	1930–52	5
3=	John Bowes	1835–53	4
3=	Sir Joseph Hawley	1851–68	4
3=	1st Duke of Westminster	1880–99	4
3=	Sir Victor Sassoon	1953–60	4
7=	1st Earl of Grosvenor	1790–94	3
7=	5th Duke of Bedford	1789–97	3
7=	Sir Frank Standish	1795–99	3
7=	3rd Duke of Grafton	1802–10	3
7=	Sir Charles Bunbury	1780–1813	3
7=	5th Earl of Jersey	1825–36	3
7=	5th Earl of Rosebery	1894–1905	3
7=	HM King Edward VII*	1896–1909	3
7=	17th Earl of Derby	1924–42	3
7=	HH Aga Khan IV	1981–88	3

* First two winners as the Prince of Wales.

TRAINERS OF EPSOM DERBY WINNERS

	Trainer	Years	Winners
1=	Robert Robson	1793–1823	7
1=	John Porter	1868–99	7
1=	Fred Darling	1922–41	7
4=	Frank Neale	1782–1804	6
4=	Mat Dawson	1860–95	6
4=	Vincent O'Brien	1962–82	6
7=	Richard Prince	1795–1819	5
7=	Dixon Boyce	1805–28	5
7=	James Edwards	1811–36	5
7=	John Scott	1835–53	5

The Derby is named after the 12th Earl of Derby, who owned the winner of the eighth race in 1787. But the race could well have been named after Sir Charles Bunbury, owner of three Derby winners. The two men were good friends and when the establishment of such a race was first discussed, they tossed a coin to decide which it should be named after. If Sir Charles had won the toss, we would have had the Epsom Bunbury each year – not to mention the Kentucky Bunbury, Soap Box Bunbury, and so on. Some small compensation for Sir Charles's not having the race named after him was that he owned Diomed, the first winner of the Derby in 1780.

JOCKEYS IN THE OAKS

	Jockey	Years	Wins
1	Frank Buckle	1797–1823	9
2=	Frank Butler	1843–52	6
2=	Lester Piggott	1957–84	6
4=	Sam Chifney Jr	1807–25	5
4=	John Day	1828–40	5
4=	George Fordham	1859–81	5
7=	Sam Chifney Sr	1782–90	4
7=	Dennis Fitzpatrick	1787–1800	4
7=	Tom Cannon	1869–84	4
7=	Fred Archer	1875–85	4
7=	Jack Watts	1883–93	4
7=	Joe Childs	1912–21	4
7=	Harry Wragg	1938–46	4
7=	Willie Carson	1978–90	4

JOCKEYS IN THE ST LEGER

	Jockey	Years	Wins
1	Bill Scott	1821–46	9
2=	John Jackson	1791–1822	8
2=	Lester Piggott	1960–84	8
4=	Ben Smith	1803–24	6
4=	Fred Archer	1877–86	6
6=	John Mangle	1780–92	5
6=	Tom Challoner	1861–75	5
6=	Jack Watts	1883–96	5
6=	Gordon Richards	1930–44	5
10=	Bob Johnson	1812–20	4
10=	Joe Childs	1918–26	4
10=	Charlie Smirke	1934–54	4
10=	Joe Mercer	1965–81	4

DERBY DYNASTY
Several descendants of the 12th Earl of Derby (pictured here with his second wife) have also shown a keen interest in horse racing. The 17th Earl's entries won the Derby in 1924, 1933, and 1942.

JOCKEYS IN ENGLISH CLASSICS

	Jockey	Years	1,000 Guineas	2,000 Guineas	Derby	Oaks	St Leger	Wins
1	Lester Piggott	1954–92	2	5	9	6	8	30
2	Frank Buckle	1792–1827	6	5	5	9	2	27
3	Jem Robinson	1817–48	5	9	6	2	2	24
4	Fred Archer	1874–86	2	4	5	4	6	21
5=	Bill Scott	1821–46	0	3	4	3	9	19
5=	Jack Watts	1883–97	4	2	4	4	5	19
7	Willie Carson	1972–94	1	5	4	4	3	17
8=	John Day	1826–41	5	4	0	5	2	16
8=	George Fordham	1859–83	7	3	1	5	0	16
10	Joe Childs	1912–33	2	2	3	4	4	15

The first of Piggott's record 30 winners was Never Say Die in the 1954 Derby. Piggott was only 19 years of age at the time. His 30th and last to date was in the 1992 2,000 Guineas.

TRAINERS OF ENGLISH CLASSIC WINNERS

	Trainer	Years	1,000 Guineas	2,000 Guineas	Derby	Oaks	St Leger	Total
1	John Scott	1827–63	4	7	5	8	16	40
2	Robert Robson	1793–1827	9	6	7	12	0	34
3	Mat Dawson	1853–95	6	5	6	5	6	28
4	John Porter	1868–1900	2	5	7	3	6	23
5	Alec Taylor	1905–27	1	4	3	8	5	21
6=	Fred Darling	1916–47	2	5	7	2	3	19
6=	Noel Murless	1948–73	6	2	3	5	3	19
8	Dixon Boyce	1805–29	3	5	5	4	0	17
9	Vincent O'Brien	1957–84	1	4	6	2	3	16
10=	Frank Butters	1927–48	1	1	2	6	5	15
10=	Dick Hern	1962–89	1	2	3	3	6	15

JOCKEYS IN THE 1,000 GUINEAS

	Jockey	Years	Wins
1	George Fordham	1859–83	7
2	Frank Buckle	1818–27	6
3=	Jem Robinson	1824–44	5
3=	John Day	1826–40	5
5=	Jack Watts	1886–97	4
5=	Fred Rickaby Jr	1913–17	4
5=	Charlie Elliott	1924–44	4
8=	Bill Arnull	1817–32	3
8=	Nat Flatman	1835–57	3
8=	Tom Cannon	1866–84	3
8=	Charlie Wood	1880–87	3
8=	Dick Perryman	1926–41	3
8=	Harry Wragg	1934–45	3
8=	Rae Johnstone	1935–50	3
8=	Gordon Richards	1942–51	3
8=	Walter Swinburn	1989–93	3

JOCKEYS IN THE 2,000 GUINEAS

	Jockey	Years	Wins
1	Jem Robinson	1825–48	9
2	John Osborne	1857–88	6
3=	Frank Buckle	1810–27	5
3=	Charlie Elliott	1923–49	5
3=	Lester Piggott	1957–92	5
3=	Willie Carson	1972–91	5
7=	John Day	1826–41	4
7=	Fred Archer	1874–85	4
7=	Tom Cannon	1878–89	4
7=	Herbert Jones	1900–09	4

LAWN TENNIS

T O P 1 0

WINNERS OF MEN'S
GRAND SLAM SINGLES TITLES

	Player/nationality	A	F	W	US	Total
1	Roy Emerson (Aus)	6	2	2	2	12
2=	Bjorn Borg (Swe)	0	6	5	0	11
2=	Rod Laver (Aus)	3	2	4	2	11
4=	Jimmy Connors (USA)	1	0	2	5	8
4=	Ivan Lendl (Cze)	2	3	0	3	8
4=	Fred Perry (GB)	1	1	3	3	8
4=	Ken Rosewall (Aus)	4	2	0	2	8
8=	René Lacoste (Fra)	0	3	2	2	7
8=	William Larned (USA)	0	0	0	7	7
8=	John McEnroe (USA)	0	0	3	4	7
8=	John Newcombe (Aus)	2	0	3	2	7
8=	William Renshaw (GB)	0	0	7	0	7
8=	Richard Sears (USA)	0	0	0	7	7
8=	Mats Wilander (Swe)	3	3	0	1	7

A = *Australian Open*; F = *French Open*; W = *Wimbledon*;
US = *US Open.*

T O P 1 0

WINNERS OF WOMEN'S
GRAND SLAM SINGLES TITLES

	Player/nationality	A	F	W	US	Total
1	Margaret Court (*née* Smith) (Aus)	11	5	3	5	24
2	Helen Wills-Moody (USA)	0	4	8	7	19
3=	Chris Evert-Lloyd (USA)	2	7	3	6	18
3=	Martina Navratilova (Cze/USA)	3	2	9	4	18
5	Steffi Graf (Ger)	4	3	5	3	15
6	Billie Jean King (*née* Moffitt) (USA)	1	1	6	4	12
7	Maureen Connolly (USA)	1	2	3	3	9
8=	Suzanne Lenglen (Fra)	0	2	6	0	8
8=	Molla Mallory (*née* Bjurstedt) (USA)	0	0	0	8	8
8=	Monica Seles (Yug)	3	3	0	2	8

A = *Australian Open*; F = *French Open*; W = *Wimbledon*;
US = *US Open.*

T O P 1 0

PLAYERS WITH THE MOST WIMBLEDON TITLES

	Player/nationality	Years	Singles	Doubles	Mixed	Total
1	Billie Jean King (*née* Moffitt) (USA)	1961–79	6	10	4	20
2	Elizabeth Ryan (USA)	1914–34	0	12	7	19
3	Martina Navratilova (Cze/USA)	1976–93	9	7	2	18
4	Suzanne Lenglen (Fra)	1919–25	6	6	3	15
5	William Renshaw (GB)	1880–89	7	7	0	14
6=	Louise Brough (USA)	1946–55	4	5	4	13
6=	Lawrence Doherty (GB)	1897–1905	5	8	0	13
8=	Helen Wills-Moody (USA)	1927–38	8	3	1	12
8=	Reginald Doherty (GB)	1897–1905	4	8	0	12
10=	Margaret Court (*née* Smith) (Aus)	1953–75	3	2	5	10
10=	Doris Hart (USA)	1947–55	1	4	5	10

Billie Jean King's first and last Wimbledon titles were both in the ladies' doubles. The first, in 1961, as Billie Jean Moffitt, was with Karen Hantze when they beat Jan Lehane and Margaret Smith 6-3, 6-4. When Billie Jean won her record-breaking 20th title in 1979 she partnered Martina Navratilova to victory over Betty Stove and Wendy Turnbull. Two of the foremost male player William Renshaw's titles were in the doubles in 1880 and 1881, then known as the Oxford University Doubles Championship, but which are now regarded as having full Wimbledon championship status. William and his twin brother Ernest won 22 titles between them. The Doherty brothers' dominance of world tennis began with Reginald, known as "Big Do", winning the 1897 Wimbledon singles title. For the next eight years Reginald and Lawrence reigned supreme, winning a total of 25 titles.

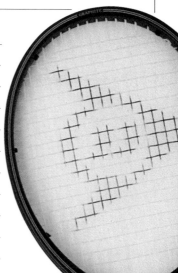

TOP 10

PLAYERS WITH MOST US SINGLES TITLES

	Player/nationality	Years	Titles
1	Molla Mallory (née Bjurstedt)	1915–26	8
2=	Richard Sears	1881–87	7
2=	William Larned	1901–11	7
2=	Bill Tilden	1920–29	7
2=	Helen Wills-Moody	1923–31	7
2=	Margaret Court (Aus)*	1962–70	7
7	Chris Evert-Lloyd	1975–82	6
8	Jimmy Connors	1974–83	5
9=	Robert Wrenn	1893–97	4
9=	Elisabeth Moore	1896–1905	4
9=	Hazel Wightman (née Hotchkiss)	1909–19	4
9=	Helen Jacobs	1932–35	4
9=	Alice Marble	1936–40	4
9=	Pauline Betz	1942–46	4
9=	Maria Bueno (Bra)	1959–66	4
9=	Billie Jean King	1967–74	4
9=	John McEnroe	1979–84	4
9=	Martina Navratilova	1983–87	4

* Includes two wins in Amateur Championships of 1968 and 1969 which were held alongside the Open Championship.

All players are from the US unless otherwise stated.

TOP 10

GRAND SLAM TITLES BY BRITONS SINCE THE SECOND WORLD WAR

Name	Singles	Mixed Doubles	Doubles	Total
1= Ann Jones (née Haydon)	3	3	2	8
1= Virginia Wade	3	5	-	8
3 Angela Mortimer	3	1	-	4
4= Shirley Bloomer	1	1	1	3
4= John Lloyd	-	-	3	3
6= Christine Truman	1	1	-	2
6= Roger Taylor	-	2	-	2
6= Angela Buxton	-	2	-	2
6= Jeremy Bates	-	-	2	2
6= Jo Durie	-	-	2	2

TOP 10

PLAYERS WITH MOST FRENCH CHAMPIONSHIP SINGLES TITLES

	Player/nationality	Years	Titles
1	Chris Evert-Lloyd (USA)	1974-86	7
2	Bjorn Borg (Swe)	1974-81	6
3	Margaret Court (née Smith) (Aus)	1962-73	5
4=	Henri Cochet (Fra)	1926-32	4
4=	Helen Wills-Moody (USA)	1928-32	4
6=	René Lacoste (Fra)	1925-29	3
6=	Hilde Sperling (Ger)	1935-37	3
6=	Yvon Petra (Fra)	1943-45	3
6=	Ivan Lendl (Cze)	1984-87	3
6=	Mats Wilander (Swe)	1982-88	3
6=	Monica Seles (Yug)	1990-92	3
6=	Steffi Graf (Ger)	1987-93	3

The French Championship was inaugurated in 1891 but was a "closed" tournament for French Nationals only until 1925 when it went open to players from other countries. The list is of winners since that year. Prior to 1925, Max Decugis won 8 titles.

MARTINA NAVRATILOVA
Her tally of nine championship titles put her at the top of the Wimbledon singles list.

TOP 10

PLAYERS WITH MOST AUSTRALIAN CHAMPIONSHIP SINGLES TITLES

	Player/nationality	Years	Titles
1	Margaret Court (née Smith)	1960–73	11
2=	Nancy Bolton (née Wynne)	1937–51	6
2=	Roy Emerson	1961–67	6
4	Daphne Akhurst	1925–30	5
5=	Pat Wood*	1914–23	4
5=	Jack Crawford	1931–35	4
5=	Ken Rosewall	1953–72	4
5=	Evonne Cawley (née Goolagong)	1974–77	4
5=	Steffi Graf (Ger)	1988–94	4
10=	Joan Hartigan	1933–36	3
10=	Adrian Quist	1936–48	3
10=	Rod Laver	1960–69	3
10=	Martina Navratilova (USA)	1981–85	3
10=	Mats Wilander (Swe)	1983–88	3
10=	Monica Seles (Yug)	1991–93	3

* Men's singles.

All players are from Australia unless otherwise stated.

MOTOR RACING

DRIVERS WITH THE MOST WORLD TITLES

Driver/nationality	Titles
1 Juan Manuel Fangio (Arg)	5
2 Alain Prost (Fra)	4
3= Jack Brabham (Aus)	3
3= Niki Lauda (Aut)	3
3= Nelson Piquet (Bra)	3
3= Jackie Stewart (UK)	3
7= Alberto Ascari (Ita)	2
7= Jim Clark (UK)	2
7= Graham Hill (UK)	2
7= Emerson Fittipaldi (Bra)	2
7= Ayrton Senna (Bra)	2

DRIVERS WITH THE MOST WINS IN A SEASON

Driver/nationality	Year	Wins
1 Nigel Mansell (UK)	1992	9
2 Ayrton Senna (Bra)	1988	8
3= Jim Clark (UK)	1963	7
3= Alain Prost (Fra)	1984	7 *
3= Alain Prost (Fra)	1988	7 *
3= Alain Prost (Fra)	1993	7
3= Ayrton Senna (Bra)	1991	7
8= Alberto Ascari (Ita)	1952	6
8= Juan Manuel Fangio (Arg)	1954	6
8= Jim Clark (UK)	1965	6
8= Jackie Stewart (UK)	1969	6
8= Jackie Stewart (UK)	1971	6
8= James Hunt (UK)	1976	6
8= Mario Andretti (USA)	1978	6
8= Nigel Mansell (UK)	1987	6 *
8= Ayrton Senna (Bra)	1990	6

* Did not win world title that year.

In 1988 the Marlboro-McLaren pair of Ayrton Senna and Alain Prost completely dominated the Grand Prix scene by winning 15 of the 16 rounds between them.

THE 10 DRIVERS WITH THE MOST BRITISH GRAND PRIX WINS

Driver/nationality/years	Wins
1= Jim Clark (UK) 1962–65, 1967	5
1= Alain Prost (Fra) 1983, 1985, 1989–90, 1993	5
3 Nigel Mansell (UK) 1986, 1987, 1991–92	4
4= Jack Brabham (Aus) 1959–60, 1966	3
4= Niki Lauda (Aut) 1976, 1982, 1984	3
6= José Froilan Gonzalez (Arg) 1951, 1954	2
6= Alberto Ascari (Ita) 1952–53	2
6= Stirling Moss (UK) 1955, 1957	2
6= Jackie Stewart (UK) 1969, 1971	2
6= Emerson Fittipaldi (Bra) 1972, 1975	2

The British Grand Prix at Silverstone on 13 May 1950 was the first race in the newly instituted World Drivers' Championship and it has remained a round in the championship every year since then.

MANUFACTURERS WITH THE MOST WORLD TITLES

Manufacturer	Titles
1 Ferrari	8
2 Lotus	7
3= McLaren	6
3= Williams	6
5= Brabham	2
5= Cooper	2
7= BRM	1
7= Matra	1
7= Tyrrell	1
7= Vanwall	1

TRACK RECORD
Driver Alain Prost of France wins the San Marino Grand Prix in 1993.

MANUFACTURERS WITH THE MOST GRAND PRIX* WINS

	Manufacturer	Years	Wins
1	McLaren	1968–91	104
2	Ferrari	1951–90	103
3	Lotus	1960–87	79
4	Williams	1979–93	71
5	Brabham	1964–85	35
6	Tyrrell	1971–83	23
7	BRM	1959–72	17
8	Cooper	1958–67	16
9	Renault	1979–83	15
10	Alfa Romeo	1950–51	10

* Up to and including the Canadian Grand Prix, 2 June 1991.

On 8 July 1990 Frenchman Alain Prost won his home Grand Prix at the Paul Ricard circuit at La Castellet, thereby creating motor racing history as Ferrari became the first manufacturer to win 100 Grand Prix. Ferrari's first win was at Silverstone in 1951, when the Argentinian José Froilan Gonzalez won the British Grand Prix. To date, a total of 30 different men have driven Ferraris to Grand Prix success, including the Britons John Surtees (4 wins), Mike Hawthorn (3), Peter Collins (3), Nigel Mansell (3), and Tony Brooks (2).

TOP 10

YOUNGEST WORLD CHAMPIONS OF ALL TIME

	Driver/nationality	Year	Age* yrs	mths
1	Emerson Fittipaldi (Bra)	1972	25	10
2	Niki Lauda (Aut)	1975	26	7
3	Jim Clark (UK)	1963	27	7
4	Jochen Rindt (Aut)	1970	28	6
5	Ayrton Senna (Bra)	1988	28	7
6=	James Hunt (UK)	1976	29	2
6=	Nelson Piquet (Bra)	1981	29	2
8	Mike Hawthorn (UK)	1958	29	6
9	Jody Scheckter (SA)	1979	29	8
10=	John Surtees (UK)	1964	30	8
10=	Alain Prost (Fra)	1985	30	8

* If a driver would have appeared on the list twice, only his youngest age is considered.

Whilst Jochen Rindt clinched the world title in October 1970, 28 years and 6 months after his birth, he had, in fact, lost his life a month earlier while practising for the Italian Grand Prix at Monza, and is the only man to win the World Championship posthumously.

TOP 10

OLDEST WORLD CHAMPIONS OF ALL TIME

	Driver/nationality	Year	Age* yrs	mths
1	Juan Manuel Fangio (Arg)	1957	46	2
2	Giuseppe Farina (Ita)	1950	43	11
3	Jack Brabham (Aus)	1966	40	6
4	Graham Hill (UK)	1968	39	9
5	Mario Andretti (USA)	1978	38	8
6	Alain Prost (Fra)	1993	38	7
7	Nigel Mansell (UK)	1992	37	11
8	Niki Lauda (Aut)	1984	35	8
9	Nelson Piquet (Bra)	1987	35	3
10	Alberto Ascari (Ita)	1953	35	1

* If a driver would have appeared on the list twice, only his oldest age is considered.

BUILT FOR SPEED
Like the competition, this Williams 1990 Formula One racing car has a low, streamlined body, an open cockpit, and huge slick tyres for extra grip.

TOP 10

DRIVERS WITH THE MOST GRAND PRIX WINS IN A CAREER

	Driver(nationality)	Years	Wins
1	Alain Prost (Fra)	1981–93	51
2	Ayrton Senna (Bra)	1985–93	41
3	Nigel Mansell (UK)	1985–92	30
4	Jackie Stewart (UK)	1965–73	27
5=	Jim Clark (UK)	1962–68	25
5=	Niki Lauda (Aut)	1974–85	25
7	Juan Manuel Fangio (Arg)	1950–57	24
8	Nelson Piquet (Bra)	1980–91	23
9	Stirling Moss (UK)	1955–61	16
10=	Graham Hill (UK)	1962–69	14
10=	Jack Brabham (Aus)	1959–70	14
10=	Emerson Fittipaldi (Bra)	1970–75	14

TOP 10

MOST GRAND PRIX WINS BY BRITISH DRIVERS

	Driver	Years	Wins
1	Nigel Mansell	1985–92	30
2	Jackie Stewart	1965–73	27
3	Jim Clark	1962–68	25
4	Stirling Moss	1955–61	16
5	Graham Hill	1962–69	14
6	James Hunt	1975–77	10
7=	Tony Brooks	1957–59	6
7=	John Surtees	1963–67	6
9	John Watson	1976–83	5
10=	Mike Hawthorn	1953–58	3
10=	Peter Collins	1956–58	3
10=	Damon Hill	1993–	3

RUGBY

HIGHEST WINNING SCORES IN BRITISH RUGBY LEAGUE HISTORY

	Match (winners first)	Date	Competition	Score
1	Huddersfield v Swinton Park Rangers	28 Feb 1914	Challenge Cup	119–2
2	Wigan v Flimby and Fothergill	15 Feb 1925	Challenge Cup	116–0
3	St Helens v Carlisle	14 Sep 1986	Lancashire Cup	112–0
4	St Helens v Trafford Borough	15 Sep 1991	Lancashire Cup	104–12
5	Leeds v Coventry	12 Apr 1913	League	102–0
6	Hull Kingston Rovers v Nottingham City	19 Aug 1990	Yorkshire Cup	100–6
7	Doncaster v Highfield	20 Mar 1994	Division 2	96–0
8	Castleford v Huddersfield	18 Sep 1988	Yorkshire Cup	94–12
9=	Rochdale Hornets v Runcorn Highfield	5 Nov 1989	Division 2	92–0
9=	Leigh v Keighley	30 Apr 1986	Division 2	92–2
9=	Wigan v Runcorn Highfield	13 Nov 1988	John Player Trophy	92–2
9=	Australians v Bramley	9 Nov 1921	Tour Match	92–7
9=	Hull Kingston Rovers v Whitehaven	18 Mar 1990	Division 2	92–10

The highest score in the First Division is Leeds' 90–0 victory over Barrow on 11 February 1990.

RUGBY LEAGUE TEAMS

	Club	Titles
1	Wigan	60
2	Leeds	34
3	St Helens	28
4=	Huddersfield	26
4=	Widnes	26
6	Bradford Northern	23
7	Warrington	22
8	Oldham	21
9	Wakefield Trinity	18
10=	Hull	17
10=	Hull Kingston Rovers	17

This list, for games up to the end of the 1993–94 season, is based on the number of wins in the major competitions: Challenge Cup, Regal/John Player Trophy, Division 1 and 2 Premierships, Championship play-off (1906–73), Divisions 1 and 2 (since 1973), and the Lancashire/Yorkshire Cup.

WINNERS OF THE CHALLENGE CUP

	Club	Years	Wins
1	Wigan	1924–94	15
2	Leeds	1910–78	10
3	Widnes	1930–84	7
4	Huddersfield	1913–53	6
5=	Wakefield Trinity	1909–63	5
5=	Warrington	1905–74	5
5=	St Helens	1956–76	5
5=	Halifax	1903–87	5
9=	Bradford Northern	1906–49	4
9=	Castleford	1935–86	4

CLUBS WITH THE MOST FIRST DIVISION WINS SINCE 1973–74*

	Club	Seasons	Wins
1	St Helens	21	383
2	Widnes	21	379
3	Wigan	20	366
4	Leeds	21	347
5	Warrington	21	333
6	Bradford Northern	20	325
7	Castleford	21	320
8	Hull Kingston Rovers	19	295
9	Hull	16	251
10	Featherstone Rovers	18	234

* To end of 1993–94 season.

The two-division system was re-introduced in 1973–74. Since then a total of 30 clubs have appeared in the top division, with Castleford, Leeds, St Helens, Warrington, and Widnes being the only ones to the end of 1993–94 to maintain a continuous presence. During that period, the only clubs to spend every season in the Second Division or Third Division were Batley, Doncaster, and Highfield (formerly Huyton and Runcorn Highfield). Carlisle had just one season in the First Division and their 2 wins is the smallest total of all 30 clubs to have appeared in Division 1.

SCORING TEAMS IN CHALLENGE CUP FINALS

	Team	Points*
1	Wigan	376
2	Leeds	229
3	Widnes	158
4	St Helens	139
5	Huddersfield	130
6	Warrington	129
7	Hull	128
8	Wakefield Trinity	118
9	Halifax	110
10	Featherstone Rovers	83

T O P 1 0
WINNERS OF THE COUNTY CHAMPIONSHIP

	County	Titles			County	Titles
1	Lancashire	16		8	Kent	3
2	Gloucestershire	15		9=	Cheshire	2
3	Yorkshire	12		9=	Cornwall	2
4	Warwickshire	9		9=	East Midlands	2
5=	Durham	8		9=	Hampshire	2
5=	Middlesex	8		9=	Midlands	2
7	Devon	7		9=	Northumberland	2
				9=	Surrey	2

T O P 1 0
BRITISH LIONS TEST WINS

	Opponents	Venue	Test/year	Score
1	Australia	Brisbane	2nd Test 1966	31–0
2	South Africa	Pretoria	2nd Test 1974	28–9
3	South Africa	Port Elizabeth	3rd Test 1974	26–9
4=	Australia	Sydney	2nd Test 1950	24–3
4=	Australia	Sydney	2nd Test 1959	24–3
6	South Africa	Johannesburg	1st Test 1955	23–22
7	South Africa	Port Elizabeth	3rd Test 1938	21–16
8	New Zealand	Wellington	2nd Test 1993	20–7
9	Australia	Brisbane	2nd Test 1989	19–12
10	Australia	Sydney	3rd Test 1989	19–18

T O P 1 0
CLUBS WITH MOST APPEARANCES IN THE JOHN PLAYER/PILKINGTON CUP FINAL

	Club	Wins	Finals
1=	Bath	8	8
1=	Leicester	4	8
3=	Bristol	1	4
3=	Harlequins	2	4
3=	Gloucester	3	4
6=	Moseley	1	3
6=	Gosforth	2	3
8=	Rosslyn Park	0	2
8=	Wasps	0	2
8=	Coventry	2	2

T O P 1 0
POINTS-SCORERS IN AN INTERNATIONAL CHAMPIONSHIP SEASON

	Player	Country	Year	Points
1	Simon Hodgkinson	England	1991	60
2	Jean-Patrick Lescarboura	France	1984	54
3=	Ollie Campbell	Ireland	1983	52
3=	Gavin Hastings	Scotland	1986	52
3=	Paul Thorburn	Wales	1986	52
6	Peter Dods	Scotland	1984	50
7	Michael Kiernan	Ireland	1985	47
8=	Ollie Campbell	Ireland	1980	46
8=	Ollie Campbell	Ireland	1982	46
8=	Didier Camberabero	France	1991	46

T O P 1 0
WINS IN THE INTERNATIONAL CHAMPIONSHIP

	Match (winners first)	Venue	Year	Score
1	Wales v France	Swansea	1910	49–14
2	France v Ireland	Paris	1992	44–12
3	England v France	Paris	1914	39–13
4	England v France	Twickenham	1911	37–0
5	France v England	Paris	1972	37–12
6	Scotland v Ireland	Murrayfield	1989	37–21
7	France v Wales	Paris	1991	36–3
8	England v Ireland	Dublin	1938	36–14
9=	Wales v France	Swansea	1931	35–3
9=	England v Ireland	Twickenham	1988	35–3

274

SNOOKER

T O P 1 0

RANKED BRITISH PLAYERS 1994–95

	Player/nationality	World ranking
1	Stephen Hendry (Sco)	1
2	Steve Davis (Eng)	2
3	Jimmy White (Eng)	4
4	John Parrott (Eng)	5
5	Alan McManus (Sco)	6
6	Darren Morgan (Wal)	8
7	Ronnie O'Sullivan (Eng)	9
8	Peter Ebdon (Eng)	10
9	Nigel Bond (Eng)	11
10	Joe Swail (N. Ireland)	12

T O P 1 0

MONEY-WINNERS 1993–94

	Player	Winnings (£)
1	Stephen Hendry (Sco)	380,271.54
2	Steve Davis (Eng)	225,233.75
3	Alan McManus (Sco)	241,071.77
4	Jimmy White (Eng)	183,057.63
5	Ronnie O'Sullivan (Eng)	170,000.67
6	James Wattana (Thai)	162,370.67
7	John Parrott (Eng)	127,145.67
8	Peter Ebdon (Eng)	117,639.03
9	Ken Doherty (Ire)	106,619.03
10	Darren Morgan (Wal)	105,525.00

A comparison between this list and that of prizewinners 10 seasons ago shows that Davis, who won £115,555 in 1983–84, has almost doubled his former figure – although inflation over this period means that in real terms he has scarcely increased his income from this source. Comparing the 10th place in the 1983-84 season (Kirk Stevens, who earned £24,700) with the current No. 10 is perhaps a more revealing indication of the influx of cash into the game. The fortunes of certain players have been in decline, however: Alex Higgins was 7th top earner in 1983-84 with £33,319, but in today's list appears in 42nd place with £14,860.

T O P 1 0

RANKED NON-BRITISH PLAYERS, 1994–95

	Player/nationality	World ranking		Player/nationality	World ranking
1	James Wattana (Thai)	3	6	Fergal O'Brien (Ire)	42
2	Ken Doherty (Ire)	7	7	Cliff Thorburn (Can)	54
3	Tony Drago (Malta)	16	8	Jim Wuch (Can)	56
4	Dene O'Kane (NZ)	20	9	Silvano Francisco (SA)	57
5	Alain Robidoux (Can)	32	10	Eddie Charlton (Aus)	60

T O P 1 0

THE FIRST OFFICIALLY RATIFIED MAXIMUM BREAKS

	Player/nationality	Venue	Date
1	Joe Davis (Eng)	Leicester Square Hall, London	22 Jan 1955
2	Rex Williams (Eng)	Prince's Hotel, Newlands, South Africa	22 Dec 1965
3	Steve Davis (Eng)	Civic Centre, Oldham	11 Jan 1982
4	Cliff Thorburn (Can)	Crucible Theatre, Sheffield	23 Apr 1983
5	Kirk Stevens (Can)	Wembley Conference Centre, London	28 Jan 1984
6	Willie Thorne (Eng)	Guildhall, Preston	17 Nov 1987
7	Tony Meo (Eng)	Winding Wheel Centre, Chesterfield	20 Feb 1988
8	Alain Robidoux (Can)	Norbreck Castle Hotel, Blackpool	24 Sep 1988
9	John Rea (Sco)	Marco's Leisure Centre, Glasgow	18 Feb 1989
10	Cliff Thorburn (Can)	Hawth Theatre, Crawley	8 Mar 1989

Steve Davis's maximum was the first to be recognized in tournament play; the 147 achieved by both Joe Davis and Rex Williams were in exhibition matches.

T O P 1 0

MEN TO BEAT STEVE DAVIS IN THE WORLD PROFESSIONAL SNOOKER CHAMPIONSHIP AT THE CRUCIBLE THEATRE

	Opponent/nationality	Score	Round	Year
1	Dennis Taylor (NI)	11–13	1	1979
2	Alex Higgins (NI)	9–13	Quarter-final	1980
3	Tony Knowles (Eng)	1–10	1	1982
4	Dennis Taylor (NI)	17–18	Final	1985
5	Joe Johnson (Eng)	12–18	Final	1986
6	Jimmy White (Eng)	14–16	Semi-final	1990
7	John Parrott (Eng)	10–16	Semi-final	1991
8	Peter Ebdon (Eng)	4–10	1	1992
9	Alan McManus (Sco)	11–13	2	1993
10	Stephen Hendry (Sco)	9–16	Semi-Final	1994

TOP 10

HIGHEST BREAKS IN THE WORLD PROFESSIONAL CHAMPIONSHIP

(At the Crucible Theatre, Sheffield)

	Match	Year	Break
1=	Cliff Thorburn *v* Terry Griffiths	1983	147
1=	Jimmy White *v* Tony Drago	1992	147
3	Doug Mountjoy *v* Ray Reardon	1981	145
4	Steve Davis *v* Peter Ebdon	1993	144
5=	Willie Thorne *v* Alex Higgins	1982	143
5=	Bill Werbeniuk *v* Joe Johnson	1985	143
7	Bill Werbeniuk *v* John Virgo	1979	142
8	Stephen Hendry *v* Terry Griffiths	1989	141
9=	Steve James *v* Rex Williams	1988	140
9=	John Parrott *v* Cliff Thorburn	1990	140
9=	Jimmy White *v* Neal Foulds	1991	140

The highest break in the pre-Crucible days was 142 made by Rex Williams in his challenge match against John Pulman in 1965.

TOP 10

RANKED PLAYERS (1991–92, 1981–82)

1991–92		1981–82	(1991–92 ranking)
Stephen Hendry (Sco)	1	Ray Reardon (Wal)	126
Steve Davis (Eng)	2	Alex Higgins (NI)	120
Jimmy White (Eng)	3	Cliff Thorburn (Can)	36
John Parrott (Eng)	4	Steve Davis (Eng)	2
Gary Wilkinson (Eng)	5	Eddie Charlton (Aus)	27
Neal Foulds (Eng)	6	Kirk Stevens (Can)	58
Steve James (Eng)	7	Doug Mountjoy (Wal)	10
Mike Hallett (Eng)	8	David Taylor (Eng)	74
Dennis Taylor (NI)	9	Bill Werbeniuk (Can)	146
Doug Mountjoy (Wal)	10	Jimmy White (Eng)	3

In compiling the 1991–92 rankings, performances in eight tournaments over the previous two years were considered, but in 1981–82 only performances in the previous three years' World Championships were taken into account.

TOP 10

PLAYERS WITH THE MOST WORLD TITLES

	Player	Titles
1	Joe Davis	15
2	John Pulman	7
3=	Ray Reardon	6
3=	Steve Davis	6
5=	Fred Davis	3
5=	John Spencer	3
5=	Stephen Hendry	3
8=	Walter Donaldson	2
8=	Alex Higgins	2
8=	Horace Lindrum (Aus)	1
8=	Cliff Thorburn (Can)	1
8=	Dennis Taylor	1
8=	Terry Griffiths	1
8=	Joe Johnson	1
8=	John Parrott	1

All players are British unless otherwise stated.

TOP 10

WINNERS OF RANKING TOURNAMENTS

	Player/nationality	Wins
1	Steve Davis (Eng)	27
2	Stephen Hendry (Sco)	17
3	Jimmy White (Eng)	9
4	John Parrott (Eng)	7
5	Ray Reardon (Wal)	5
6=	Tony Knowles (Eng)	2
6=	Doug Mountjoy (Wales)	2
6=	Dennis Taylor (NI)	2
6=	Cliff Thorburn (Can)	2
6=	Ronnie O'Sullivan (Eng)	2
6=	James Wattana (Tha)	2

Ranking tournaments are those which carry points towards the annual ranking system which is re-calculated after the World Championship each year.

PROGRESSION OF OFFICIALLY RATIFIED SNOOKER RECORD BREAKS

Player	Year	Break
Tom Newman	1919	89
Joe Davis	1925	96
Joe Davis	1928	100
Joe Davis	1930	105
Joe Davis	1933	109
Joe Davis	1933	114
Horace Lindrum (Aus)	1936*	131
Sidney Smith	1936*	133
Joe Davis	1937	135
Joe Davis	1938	137
Joe Davis	1938	138
Joe Davis	1947	140
Joe Davis	1949	141
George Chenier (Can)	1950	144
Joe Davis	1954	146
Joe Davis	1955	147

All players are British unless otherwise stated.
* Records set on the same day.

WATER SPORTS

T O P 1 0

FASTEST WINNING TIMES IN THE BOAT RACE

	Winner	Year	Distance (lengths)	Time min	sec
1	Oxford	1984	3¾	16	45
2	Oxford	1976	6½	16	58
3	Oxford	1991	4¼	16	59
4	Cambridge	1993	3½	17	0
5	Oxford	1985	4¾	17	11
6	Oxford	1990	2¼	17	15
7=	Oxford	1974	5½	17	35
7=	Oxford	1988	5½	17	35
9	Oxford	1992	1½	17	48
10	Cambridge	1948	5	17	50

D I D   Y O U   K N O W

COLOSSAL CATCHES

Far exceeding all British freshwater rod-caught records, on 27 March 1933 a 176-kg/388-lb sturgeon that measured 2.79 m/9 ft 2 in was gaffed in the River Towy, and on 1 June 1937 another sturgeon weighing a remarkable 230 kg/507 lb was netted in the River Severn. Details remain scanty about an alleged 209-kg/460-lb monster caught in the River Esk in 1810.

T O P 1 0

LARGEST SPECIES OF FRESHWATER FISH CAUGHT IN THE UK

	Species	Angler/location/year	Weight kg	g	lb	oz
1	Salmon	Miss G.W. Ballantine, River Tay, Scotland, 1922	29	29	64	0
2	Carp	C. Yates, Redmire Pool, Hertfordshire, 1980	23	358	51	8
3	Pike	Michael G. Linton, Ardleigh Reservoir, Colchester, Essex, 1987	20	353	44	14
4	Catfish	R.J. Bray, Wilstone Reservoir, Tring, Hertfordshire, 1970	19	730	43	8
5	Rainbow trout	J. Moore, Pennine Trout Fishery, 1989	10	965	24	3
6	Sea trout	Samuel Burgoyne, River Leven, Scotland, 1989	10	205	22	8
7	Brown trout	J. Gardner, Delver Springs Trout Fishery, 1991	9	178	20	4
8	Zander	R.N. Meadows, Cambridge Stillwater, 1988	8	390	18	8
9	Common bream	Anthony Bromley, private fishery, Staffordshire, 1986	7	427	16	6
10	Grass carp	J.P. Buckley, Horton Fishery, Berkshire, 1990	7	285	16	1

T O P 1 0

LARGEST SPECIES OF SALTWATER FISH CAUGHT IN THE UK

	Species	Angler/location/date	Weight kg	g	lb	oz
1	Tunny	L. Mitchell Henry, Whitby, Yorks, 1933	385	989	851	0
2	Mako shark	Mrs J.M. Yallop, off Eddystone Light, Cornwall, 1971	226	786	500	0
3	Porbeagle shark	J. Potier, off Padstow, Cornwall, 1976	210	910	465	0
4	Thresher shark	S. Mills, off Portsmouth, Hants, 1982	146	504	323	0
5	Halibut	C. Booth, Dunnet Head, off Scrabster, Highland, 1979	106	136	234	0
6	Common skate	R. Banks, off Tobermory, Mull, 1986	102	961	227	0
7	Blue shark	N. Sutcliffe, Looe, Cornwall, 1959	98	878	218	0
8	Opah	A.R. Blewett, Mounts Bay, Penzance, Cornwall, 1973	58	57	128	0
9	Conger	N. Ball, off Dartmouth, Devon, 1992	51	30	112	8
10	Sunfish	T.F. Sisson, off Saundersfoot, Dyfed, 1976	48	986	108	0

Based on National Anglers' Council data.

All fish in both freshwater and saltwater lists were rod-caught.

TOP 10

MOST SUCCESSFUL OLYMPICS SWIMMING COUNTRIES

	Country	gold	silver	bronze	Total
1	USA	215	164	134	513
3	E. Germany	40	34	25	99
5	USSR (CIS)	24	32	37	93
7	Hungary	26	22	17	65
9	Japan	15	18	17	50
2	Australia	39	34	41	114
4	Germany/ W. Germany	22	31	42	95
6	UK	18	22	29	69
8	Sweden	13	20	21	54
10	Canada	10	15	17	42

Mark Spitz of the US holds the record for winning the most gold medals at one Games – seven in 1972 – which is the most by any competitor in any sport.

* Including those awarded for diving and water polo.

TOP 10

OLYMPIC SWIMMING GOLD MEDAL WINNERS

	Swimmer/nationality	Years	Gold medals*
1	Mark Spitz (USA)	1968–72	9
2=	Matt Biondi (USA)	1984–92	8
2=	Kristin Otto (GDR)	1988	6
4=	Charles Daniels (USA)	1904–08	5
4=	Johnny Weissmuller (USA)	1924–28	5
4=	Don Schollander (USA)	1964–68	5
7=	Henry Taylor (UK)	1906–08	4
7=	Pat McCormick (USA)	1952–56	4
7=	Murray Rose (Aus)	1956–60	4
7=	Dawn Fraser (Aus)	1956–64	4
7=	Roland Matthes (GDR)	1968–72	4
7=	Kornelia Ender (GDR)	1976	4
7=	John Naber (USA)	1976	4
7=	Vladimir Salnikov (USSR)	1980–88	4
7=	Greg Louganis (USA)	1984–88	4

* Including those awarded for diving.

TOP 10

MEN'S WORLD WATER-SKIING TITLE WINNERS

	Skier/nationality	Overall	Slalom	Tricks	Jump	Total
1	Patrice Martin (Fra)	3	0	4	0	7
2	Sammy Duval (USA)	4	0	0	2	6
3=	Alfredo Mendoza (USA)	2	1	0	2	5
3=	Mike Suyderhoud (USA)	2	1	0	2	5
3=	Bob La Point (USA)	0	4	1	0	5
6=	George Athans (Can)	2	1	0	0	3
6=	Guy de Clercq (Bel)	1	0	0	2	3
6=	Wayne Grimditch (USA)	0	0	2	1	3
6=	Mike Hazelwood (UK)	1	0	0	2	3
6=	Ricky McCormick (USA)	0	0	1	2	3
6=	Billy Spencer (USA)	1	1	1	0	3

SPORTING MISCELLANY

TOP 10

HIGHEST-EARNING SPORTSMEN IN THE WORLD IN 1993

	Name	Sport	Income (US $)		
			Salary/ winnings	Other*	Total
1	Michael Jordan	Basketball	4,000,000	32,000,000	36,000,000
2	Riddick Bowe	Boxing	23,000,000	2,000,000	25,000,000
3	Ayrton Senna	Motor racing	14,000,000	4,500,000	18,500,000
4	Alain Prost	Motor racing	12,000,000	4,000,000	16,000,000
5	George Foreman	Boxing	12,500,000	3,300,000	15,800,000
6	Shaquille O'Neal	Basketball	3,300,000	11,900,000	15,200,000
7	Lennox Lewis	Boxing	14,000,000	1,000,000	15,000,000
8	Cecil Fielder	Baseball	12,400,000	300,000	12,700,000
9	Jim Courier	Tennis	3,600,000	9,000,000	12,600,000
10	Joe Montana	American football	5,000,000	6,500,000	11,500,000

* *From sponsorship and royalty income from endorsed sporting products.
Used by permission of Forbes Magazine.*

Some $32,000,000 of list-leader Michael Jordan's "other income" is reckoned to come from his sponsorship deal with sports footwear manufacturer Nike. Boxing is the sport perhaps most affected by the peaks and troughs of success and failure, its volatile rewards exemplified by the fates of boxers such as Razor Ruddock (7th in 1991, but unplaced in the Top 40 in 1992 and 1993), George Foreman (who plunged from 4th highest earner in 1991 to 19th in 1992, but bounced back at No. 5 in 1992), and Evander Holyfield (No. 2 in 1992, No. 12 in 1993). Several other sports stars found themselves outside the Top 10 in 1993, but nevertheless earned total incomes in excess of $7,000,000. Among them were motor racing drivers Emerson Fittipaldi, Nigel Mansell, and Gerhard Berger; and golfers Arnold Palmer, Jack Nicklaus, and Greg Norman.

TOP 10

MOST WATCHED SPORTS EVENTS ON BRITISH TELEVISION IN 1993

	Event/programme	Sport	Channel	Viewers
1	Grand National	Horse racing	BBC	16,500,000
2	Chris Eubank v Nigel Benn	Boxing	ITV	16,400,000
3	Holland v England	Soccer	ITV	14,100,000
4	Frank Bruno v Carl Williams	Boxing	BBC	13,900,000
5	Arsenal v Sheffield Wednesday*	Soccer	BBC	13,400,000
6	England v San Marino	Soccer	BBC	11,800,000

	Event/programme	Sport	Channel	Viewers
7	Men's 100 Metres Final (World Athletics Championships)	Athletics	BBC	11,500,000
8	Grandstand: Final Score (Grand National Day)	General	BBC	11,300,000
9	Arsenal v Sheffield Wednesday#	Soccer	BBC	10,900,000
10	Linford Christie v Carl Lewis	Athletics	ITV	10,700,000

* *FA Cup Final replay.*   # *FA Cup Final.*

TOP 10

INDIVIDUAL OLYMPIC GOLD MEDAL WINNERS

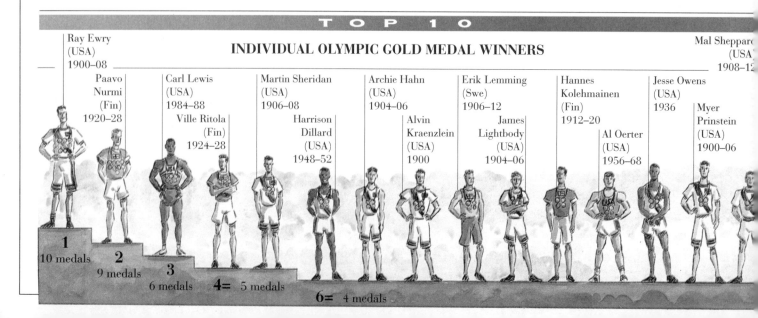

Ray Ewry (USA) 1900–08

Paavo Nurmi (Fin) 1920–28

Carl Lewis (USA) 1984–88

Ville Ritola (Fin) 1924–28

Martin Sheridan (USA) 1906–08

Harrison Dillard (USA) 1948–52

Archie Hahn (USA) 1904–06

Alvin Kraenzlein (USA) 1900

Erik Lemming (Swe) 1906–12

James Lightbody (USA) 1904–06

Hannes Kolehmainen (Fin) 1912–20

Al Oerter (USA) 1956–68

Jesse Owens (USA) 1936

Myer Prinstein (USA) 1900–06

Mal Sheppard (USA) 1908–12

1 10 medals   **2** 9 medals   **3** 6 medals   **4=** 5 medals   **6=** 4 medals

TOP 10

HIGHEST-EARNING FILMS WITH SPORTING THEMES

	Film	Sport
1	*Rocky IV* (1985)	Boxing
2	*Rocky III* (1982)	Boxing
3	*Rocky* (1976)	Boxing
4	*A League of Their Own* (1992)	Baseball
5	*Rocky II* (1979)	Boxing
6=	*Days of Thunder* (1990)	Stock car racing
6=	*White Men Can't Jump* (1992)	Basketball
8	*Chariots of Fire* (1973)	Athletics
9	*Field of Dreams* (1989)	Baseball
10	*The Main Event* (1979)	Boxing

The boxing ring dominates Hollywood's most successful sports-based epics, which are led by superstar Sylvester Stallone's *Rocky* series. Baseball is a popular follow-up, both in the films represented in the Top 10 and in others just outside, including *The Natural* (1984), *Bull Durham* (1988), and *Major League* (1989). Stock car racing, women's baseball, and basketball are all unique as the sporting themes of successful films.

TOP 10

WORST DISASTERS AT SPORTS VENUES

(20th century only)

	Location/disaster	Date	No. killed
1	Hong Kong Jockey Club (stand collapse and fire)	26 Feb 1918	604
2	Lenin Stadium, Moscow, Russia (crush in football stadium)	20 Oct 1982	340
3	Lima, Peru (football stadium riot)	24 May 1964	320
4	Sinceljo, Colombia (bullring stand collapse)	20 Jan 1980	222
5	Hillsborough, Sheffield, UK (crush in football stadium)	15 Apr 1989	96
6	Le Mans, France (racing car crash)	11 Jun 1955	82
7	Katmandu, Nepal (stampede in football stadium)	12 Mar 1988	80
8	Buenos Aires, Argentina (riot in football stadium)	23 May 1968	73
9	Ibrox Park, Glasgow, Scotland (barrier collapse in football stadium)	2 Jan 1971	66
10	Bradford Stadium, UK (fire in football stadium)	11 May 1985	56

Before the Ibrox Park disaster, the worst accident at a British stadium was caused by the collapse of a stand at Burnden Park, Bolton, on 9 March 1946, which left 33 dead and 400 injured. Such tragedies are not an exclusively modern phenomenon: during the reign of Roman Emperor Antoninus Pius (AD 138–161), a stand at the Circus Maximus collapsed during a gladiatorial spectacle and 1,162 spectators were killed.

TOP 10

BESTSELLING SINGLES BY SPORTS TEAMS IN THE UK

	Single	Team
1	*Back Home*	England 1970 World Cup Squad
2	*World In Motion*	England with New Order (1990)
3	*Come On You Reds*	Manchester United FC (1994)
4	*This Time We'll Get It Right*	England 1982 World Cup Squad
5	*Anfield Rap (Red Machine In Full Effect)*	Liverpool FC (1988)
6	*We Have A Dream*	Scotland 1982 World Cup Squad
7	*Ole Ola (Muhler Brasileira)*	Rod Stewart with Scotland 1978 World Cup Squad
8	*Ossie's Dream (Spurs Are On Their Way To Wembley)*	Tottenham Hotspur FC (1981)
9	*Blue Is The Colour*	Chelsea FC (1972)
10	*Snooker Loopy*	Matchroom Mob with Chas & Dave (1986)

All these singles made the UK Top 10, and the first two were chart-topping hits. Some of the sportsmen (none of the records feature women) received professional help from the likes of New Order and Rod Stewart, while Chas & Dave, who bolstered the only non-football entry (by the Matchroom Mob of snooker professionals), also had an uncredited appearance on the Spurs single at No. 7.

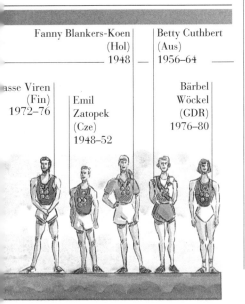

Fanny Blankers-Koen (Hol) 1948 — Betty Cuthbert (Aus) 1956–64 —

asse Viren (Fin) 1972–76 — Emil Zatopek (Cze) 1948–52 — Bärbel Wöckel (GDR) 1976–80

TOYS & GAMES

BESTSELLING TOYS OF 1993 IN THE UK

(Excluding computer and board games)

	Toy	Manufacturer
1	Barbie	Mattel
2	Thunderbirds	Matchbox
3	Captain Scarlet	Vivid Imaginations
4	Polly Pocket	Bluebird
5	WWF wrestlers	Hasbro
6	Tomy train sets	Tomy
7	Action Man	Kenner
8	Sylvanian Families	Tomy
9	Jurassic Park dinosaurs	Kenner
10	Little Mermaid	Tyco

HAMLEYS' TOYS AND GAMES IN 1993

1	Sega Computer Games – MegaDrive/Game Gear
2	Squiggle Wiggle Writer
3	Self-tying shoelaces
4	Nintendo Computer Games – Super NES/Game Boy with Tetris
5	Changeable colouring pens
6	Rapidough (boxed game)
7	Tomy Carg-G (remote-controlled car)
8	Barbie – Hollywood Hair/TeenTalk
9	Air Art Blitzer (airbrush and felt-tip pens)
10	Lego castle range

Hamleys of Regent Street, London, the world's oldest-established and largest toy shop, stocks more than 35,000 different toys and games on seven floors. In the run-up to Christmas, over 200,000 customers a week visit the store. In addition to the Top 10, Hamleys' Christmas 1993 season featured a wide range of merchandise associated with the recently-released Disney film, *Aladdin*, and with the revived TV series, *Captain Scarlet*.

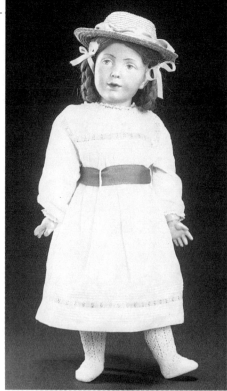

ALL DOLLED UP
Fetching £188,500 in 1994, this realistic Kämmer and Reinhardt bisque doll is the most expensive toy ever auctioned in the UK.

W.H. SMITH'S GAMES IN 1993

1	Pictionary		6	Monopoly
2	Trivial Pursuit		7	Boggle
3	Atmosfear		8	Pass the Pigs
4	Taboo		9	Outburst
5	Scrabble		10	Balderdash

MOST LANDED-ON SQUARES IN MONOPOLY®

1	Trafalgar Square
2	Go
3	Fenchurch Street Station
4	Free Parking
5	Marlborough Street
6	Vine Street
7	King's Cross Station
8	Bow Street
9	Water Works
10	Marylebone Station

Monopoly® is a registered trademark of Parker Brothers division of Tonka Corporation, USA, under licence to Waddington Games Ltd.

MOST EXPENSIVE TOYS EVER SOLD AT AUCTION IN THE UK

	Toy/sale	Price (£)
1	Kämmer and Reinhardt doll Sotheby's, London, 8 February 1994	188,500
2	Titania's Palace, a doll's house with 2,000 items of furniture, Christie's, London, 10 January 1978	135,000
3	Kämmer and Reinhardt bisque character doll, German, c.1909, Sotheby's, London, 16 February 1989	90,200
4	Hornby 00-gauge train set (the largest ever sold at auction), Christie's, London, 27 November 1992	80,178
5	William and Mary wooden doll, English, c.1690, Sotheby's, London, 24 March 1987	67,000
6	Russian carousel (tinplate ferris wheel), c.1904 Sotheby's, London, 10 February 1993	62,500
7	Dual-plush Steiff Teddy bear, c.1920 (the record price for a Teddy bear) Sotheby's, London, 19 September 1989	55,000
8	"Eliot", a blue Steiff bear, 1908 Christie's, London, 6 December 1993	49,500
9=	Tinplate carousel by Märklin, c.1910, Sotheby's, London, 23 January 1992	47,300
9=	Set of Märklin horse-drawn fire appliances, c.1902, Sotheby's, London, 23 January 1992	47,300

Models by the German tinplate maker Märklin, regarded by collectors as the Rolls-Royce of toys, similarly feature among the record prices of auction houses outside the UK, where high prices have also been attained. The most expensive tinplate toy ever sold, however, is a model of a fire hose-reel made by American manufacturer George Brown & Co, c.1875, which was auctioned at Christie's New York, in 1991 for $231,000/£128,330.

TOP 10

MOST EXPENSIVE TEDDY BEARS SOLD AT AUCTION IN THE UK

	Bear/sale	Price (£)*
1	"Happy", dual-plush Steiff Teddy bear, 1926 Sotheby's, London, 19 September 1989	55,000

Although Happy's value was originally estimated at £700–£900, competitive bidding pushed the price up to the world record, when the bear was bought by collector Paul Volpp.

	Bear/sale	Price (£)*
2	"Eliot", a blue Steiff bear, 1908 Christie's, London, 6 December 1993	49,500

Eliot was produced as a sample for Harrods, but was never manufactured commercially.

	Bear/sale	Price (£)*
3	Black Steiff Teddy bear, c.1912, Sotheby's, London, 18 May 1990	24,200
4	"Alfonzo", a red Steiff Teddy bear, c.1906–09 Christie's, London, 18 May 1989	12,100

This bear was once owned by Princess Xenia of Russia.

	Bear/sale	Price (£)*
5	Rod-jointed Steiff apricot plush Teddy bear, c.1904 Sotheby's, London, 9 May 1991	11,770
6	Black Steiff Teddy bear, c.1912, Phillips, London, 19 October 1990	8,800
7	Apricot-coloured Steiff Teddy bear, c.1904, Sotheby's, London, 31 January 1990	7,700
8=	White plush Steiff Teddy bear, c.1904, Sotheby's, London, 31 January 1990	6,050
8=	White plush Steiff Teddy bear, c.1905, Sotheby's, London, 18 May 1990	6,050
10	White plush Steiff Teddy bear, c.1920, Sotheby's, London, 22 January 1991	4,620

Prices include buyer's premium.

It is said that, while on a hunting trip, US President Theodore ("Teddy") Roosevelt refused to shoot a young bear. This became the subject of a famous cartoon by Clifford K. Berryman, published in the *Washington Post* on 16 November 1902. Immediately afterwards, Morris Michtom, a New York shopkeeper (and later founder of the Ideal Toy and Novelty Company) made stuffed bears and – with Roosevelt's permission – began advertising them as "Teddy's Bears". At about the same time, Margarete Steiff, a German toymaker, began making her first toy bears, exporting them to the US to meet the demand "Teddy Bears" had created. In 1903 Steiff's factory produced 12,000 bears; by 1907 the figure had risen to 974,000. Steiff bears, recognizable by their distinctive ear tags, are still made and are sold internationally, but it is the early examples that are most prized among collectors, with the result that all the Top 10 are Steiffs.

GRIN AND BEAR IT
Arctophily, or Teddy bear collecting, is an increasingly serious hobby.

TOP 10

BESTSELLING COMPUTER GAMES IN THE UK, 1992

	Game*	Manufacturer
1	*Sonic the Hedgehog 2*	Sega
2	*Sonic the Hedgehog*	Sega
3	*Super Mario Land 2*	Nintendo
4	*Super Kick Off*	Various
5	*Donald Duck*	Sega
6	*Mickey Mouse*	Various
7	*Tazmania*	Sega
8	*Desert Strike*	Electronic Arts
9	*Super Mario Land*	Nintendo
10	*European Club Soccer*	Virgin

* *Console games.*

TOP 10

BESTSELLING COMPUTER GAMES IN THE UK, 1993

	Game	Manufacturer
1	*Mortal Kombat*	Various
2	*Sonic the Hedgehog 2*	Sega
3	*Lemmings*	Various
4	*Super Kick Off*	Various
5	*FIFA International Soccer*	Electronic Arts
6	*Ecco*	Sega
7	*Super Mario Kart*	Nintendo
8	*Jurassic Park*	Various
9	*PGA Golf Tour 2*	Electronic Arts
10	*Jungle Strike*	Electronic Arts

INDEX

ACKNOWLEDGMENTS

I would like to thank Caroline Ash for her continuing assistance in compiling *The Top 10 of Everything*, and the following individuals and organizations who kindly supplied the information to enable me to prepare many of the lists:

John Amos, Richard Braddish, Steve Butler, Terry Charman, David Chesterman, Robert Clark, Ludo Craddock, Luke Crampton, Paul Dickson, Christopher Forbes, Monika Half, Richard Halstead, Max Hanna, Peter Harland, William Hartston, Duncan Hislop, Robert Lamb, Barry Lazell, Dr Benjamin Lucas, Hugh Meller, Allen Meredith, Allan Mitchell, Dr Jacqueline Mitton, Giles Moon, Ian Morrison, Sir Tim Rice, Adrian Room, Tom Rubython, Rocky Stockman MBE, James Taylor, Carey Wallace, Tony Waltham, David Way, Steve Yeates

Academy of Motion Picture Arts and Sciences, AGB Group, Airport Operators Council International, American Forestry Association, *Animal World*, *Annual Abstract of Statistics*, Art Sales Index, Arts Council, Associated Examining Board, Association of British Investigators, Association of Comics Enthusiasts, Audit Bureau of Circulations Ltd, Automobile Association, Backnumbers, Banking Information Service, Bank of England, BBC Enterprises, BBC Publicity, BBC Written Archives, Bellows Karaoke/Peter Frailish, Bird's Eye Frozen Foods UK, Bonhams, Bookwatch Ltd, Brewers Society, British Airports Authority, British Allergy Foundation, British Astronomical Society, British Bankers' Association, British Broadcasting Corporation, British Cave Research Association, British Interplanetary Society, British Library, British Museum, British Rail, British Rate & Data, British Tourist Authority, British Trust for Ornithology, British Waterways Board, *Business Age*, Cadbury Schweppes Group, Cameron Mackintosh Ltd, Carbon Dioxide Information Analysis Center/Greg Marland/Tom Boden, Central Statistical Office, Champagne Bureau, Channel Four Television, Channel Swimming Association, Charities Aid Foundation, Christie's East, Christie's London, Christie's South Kensington, Civil Aviation Authority, Classic FM, Coca-Cola Great Britain and Ireland, Corporate Intelligence Group Ltd, Countryside Commission, Countryside Council for Wales, *Criminal Statistics England & Wales*, *Daily Mail*, *Daily Telegraph*, Dateline, De Beers, Department of Health, Department of Trade and Industry, Department of Transport, Diamond Information Centre, Direct Mail Information Service, English Heritage, Euromonitor, European Leisure Software Publishers Association, Federation of Small Businesses, Feste Catalogue Index Database/Alan Somerset, Food and Agriculture Organization of the United Nations, Food From Britain, *Forbes Magazine*, Forestry Commission, Fresh Fruits and Vegetable Information Bureau, Gallup, General Accident Fire and Life Assurance Corporation plc, Generation AB, Geological Museum, Gold Fields Mineral Services Ltd, Governing Council of the Cat Fancy, Häagen-Dazs UK, Hamleys of Regent Street Ltd, Health and Safety Executive, H.J. Heinz Co Ltd, Home and Overseas Insurance Company, Home Office, Infoplan, International Cocoa Organization, International Coffee Organization, International Tea Committee, International Union of Geological Sciences Commission, *International Water Power and Dam Construction Handbook*, International Wine Auctions, ITV Network Centre, Kellogg Company of Great Britain, Kennel Club, Keynote Publications, Letterbox Study Group, Lloyds Register of Shipping, London Regional Transport, London Theatre Record, London Transport Lost Property, MARC Europe, *Marketing*, MEAL, Meat and Livestock Commission, Meteorological Office, MORI, Motor Vehicle Manufacturers Association of the United States Inc, MRIB, Museum of the Moving Image, NASA, National Alliance of Women's Organisations, National Anglers' Council, National Blood Transfusion Service, National Canine Defence League, National Grid Company plc, National Maritime Museum, National Pier Society, National Theatre, National Trust, Nature Conservancy Council for England, A.C. Nielsen Co Ltd, Nielsen Media Research, Nobel Foundation, NTL, Nuclear Engineering International, Office of Population Censuses and Surveys, Open University, Ordnance Survey, Organization for Economic Development and Cooperation, Oxford University Press, Penguin Books Ltd, *Petroleum Review*, Phillips West Two, Phobics Society, Post Office, HM Prison Service, Produktschap voor Gedistilleerde Dranken, Proprietary Association of Great Britain, Public Lending Right, Pullman Power Products Corporation, *Railway Gazette International*, RAJAR/RSL, Really Useful Group, Registrar General, Relate, *The Retail Rankings*, Rolls-Royce Motor Cars, Royal Academy, Royal Aeronautical Society, Royal College of General Practitioners, Royal Institute of British Architects, Royal Mint, Royal Opera House, Royal Society for the Prevention of Cruelty to Animals, Royal Society for the Protection of Birds, Science Museum, Scottish Natural Heritage, Scottish Office, Scottish Tourist Board, Scout Association, *Screen Digest*, Shakespeare Birthplace Trust, Siemens AG, W.H. Smith & Son Ltd, Society of Motor Vehicle Manufacturers and Traders Ltd, Sotheby's London, Sotheby's New York, Southern Examining Group, *Spaceflight*, *Statistical Abstract of the United States*, Tate Gallery, Taylors of Loughborough, Technomic Consultants, Theatre Museum, D.C. Thomson & Co Ltd, Tidy Britain Group, *The Times*, *The Times 1000*, Trebor Bassett, Tree Register of the British Isles, Trinity House Lighthouse Service, TUC, *UBS Phillips & Drew Global Pharmaceutical Review*, UK Petroleum Industry Association, *Uniform Crime Statistics*, Unilever/Wall's, United Nations, University of Westminster, University Statistical Record, US Bureau of the Census, *Variety*, Victoria & Albert Museum, Water Services Association, Welsh Tourist Office, Woolworths, World Association of Girl Guides and Girl Scouts, World Health Organization, World Intellectual Property Organization, *World of Travel Shopping*

PICTURE CREDITS

t = top; c = centre; b = bottom; l = left; r = right
The J Allan Cash Photolibrary: 102l
Bassano & Vandyk Portrait Studios: 63tr; 64br
British Library: 68 tr;122 bl
British Museum: 222b
Bruce Coleman/Johnny Johnson: 26cl
Channel Four Television: 193br
Christie's Images: 156tl
Mary Evans Picture Library: 2bl; 8br; 62bl; 162bl; 164c; 246tl; 252tl; 266bc
Ronald Grant Archive: 1br; 166br; 167tr; 168br; 170bl; 187bl; 188tl; 188tr; 189c; 189cl
Greenpeace/Hodson: 200tr
Robert Harding Picture Library: 16bl; 20bl; 113bc; 136tc
The Hulton Deutsch Collection: 3br; 60tl; 61r; 71tr; 86tr; 81tl; 155tl
Image Bank: 15br; 159tr; 237tr; /Walter Bibikow: 214; /Gary Cralle: 116t; /Steve Dunwell: 250cl; /Romilly Lockyer: 251bc; /Colin Bell: 254bl

Impact/Marc Henley: 97tc
The Imperial War Museum: 84br; 85cr
ITV: 192cl
Kobal Collection: front cover cl; 168br; 171cr; 172br
La Belle Aurore Picture Library: 112tr
Magnum Photos Ltd./Elliot Erwin: 68tl; /Burt Glinn: 70bl; /George Rodger: 87b; /Danny Lyon: 80bl; /Mike Nichols: 238tl; /Stuart Franklin: 253b
Memorial Museum of Cosmonautics, Moscow: 14bc; 15tr
Museo Archeologico di Napoli: 25b
Musee d'Orsay, Paris: 132c
NASA: 10cb; 10tl
National Maritime Museum: Title page; 64tl; 65b; 88r; 244bl; 247br
National Motor Museum, Beaulieu: 234br; 235b
The National Trust: 254tr
The Open University: 115br
Rex Features Ltd.: front cover tr; 3tr; 24tl; 58tl; 76cl; 82bc; 114cl; 126tr; 127br; 138cl; 142br; 143tr; 144l; 148tl; 152bl; 153tr; 153bc; 174bc; 178bc; 179tr; 182tr; 182bl; 183br; 184cl; 184c; 184br; 185br; 187br; 190tr; 191tr; 195tc; 218tl; 220tr; 220bl; 243; 244tr
Riverside Press: 77br
Royal Artillery Historical Trust, London: 83br
Royal Geographical Society: 65cr
Royal Lifeboat Association: 216tc
Royal Marines Museum, Portsmouth: 48tc
RSPCA Picture Library: 217tc
Save the Children Fund: 216bc
The Science Museum: 9cr; 249c
Science Photo Library: /Maptec International: 8trb; /NASA: 23tr; /Tony Buxton: 26tr
Sotheby's: 135tc; 157b; 158; 280tc
Sporting Pictures (UK) Ltd.: front cover br; 258tl; 258tra; 258trb; 262c; 265tr; 269bl; 270tr; 275tr; 280tc
Stena Sealink: 207bl
Tony Stone Images: 110tr; 206tr; /Val Corbett: 105bl
Syndicate International: 141t
Transport and General Workers' Union: 56tr
World Scout Bureau: 57bc

ADDITIONAL PHOTOGRAPHY

Geoff Brightling, John Bulman, Jane Burton, Martin Cameron, Peter Chadwick, Andy Crawford, Brian Deff, Philip Dowell, Mike Dunning, David Exton, Neil Fletcher, Philip Gatwood, Steve Gorton, Bob Guthany, Chas Hawson, Steven Hayward, J. Heseltine, Ed Ironside, Colin Keates, Roland Kemp, Dave King, Cyril Lauscher, Andrew McRobb, Cameron MacKintosh, Roy Moller, Steven Oliver, Brian Pitkin, Laurence Pordes, Tim Ridley, Dave Rudkin, Philippe Sebert, Rodney Shackill, Karl Shone, Chris Stevens, James Stevenson, Clive Streeter, Kim Taylor, Mathew Ward, Richard Ward, Dan Wright, Jerry Young

ILLUSTRATIONS

Paul Collicutt, Janos Marffy, Richard Ward, Dan Wright

DORLING KINDERSLEY WOULD LIKE TO THANK:

Heather McCarry, Katie John, Ellen Woodward, Charyn Jones, Peter Jones, Andrea Horth, Dingus Hussey, Josephine Buchanan, Lynne Brown

PICTURE RESEARCH

Valya Alexandra

INDEX

Patricia Coward